Exemplary Economists, Volume I

Exemplary Economists

Volume I: North America

Edited by

Roger E. Backhouse

Professor of the History and Philosophy of Economics
University of Birmingham, UK

Roger Middleton

Reader in the History of Political Economy
University of Bristol, UK

Edward Elgar
Cheltenham, UK • Northampton, MA, US

Published by
Edward Elgar Publishing Limited
Glensanda House
Montpellier Parade
Cheltenham
Glos GL50 1UA
UK

Edward Elgar Publishing, Inc.
136 West Street
Suite 202
Northampton
Massachusetts 01060
USA

A catalogue record for this book
is available from the British Library

ISBN 1 85898 959 0 (Volume I)
      1 85898 960 4 (Volume II)
      1 84064 405 2 (2-volume set)

Printed and bound in Great Britain by Biddles Ltd, www.biddles.co.uk

Contents

Acknowledgements

The editors wish to thank the economists whose autobiographical essays are presented here for permission to include them and for their co-operation in revising them for publication. They also wish to thank the publishers, in particular Edward Elgar and Dymphna Evans, for their support.

Roger Backhouse undertook part of the work towards this project whilst holding a British Academy Research Readership and wishes to thank the British Academy for its support.

Introducing exemplary economists

Roger E. Backhouse and Roger Middleton

0.1   INTRODUCTION

These two volumes make more accessible the autobiographies of thirty-six eminent economists. With three exceptions, they are based on autobiographical introductions to volumes in the series *Economists of the Twentieth Century*. The exceptions are Jack Wiseman, whose volume of essays was not in the series but the introduction to which was sent out to potential contributors to the series as a model that they might follow, and the two founding editors of the series, Mark Blaug and Mark Perlman. The essays have been extensively edited and some have been revised substantially by their authors, Mark Perlman going so far as to write a completely new essay.

These essays are valuable for several reasons. At the most basic level they provide substance to people who would otherwise remain, for most economists, no more than names attached to publications. They will satisfy those such as Wiseman (II, p. 29) who writes, 'I can recall how as a student I used to speculate about the personalities behind the names in my reading lists; if there are others like me, they may enjoy my story.' As *auto*biographies, they also constitute, subject to well-known provisos concerning the reliability of memory and what people choose to reveal about their own lives (Walker 1983; Breit 1987), primary source material for studies of the economics profession and of the organisations (universities, government departments and international organisations) and episodes to which these economists contributed. They complement existing volumes of autobiographies such as Szenberg (1992) and Breit and Spencer (1995) on Nobel laureates, the ones written for the *Banca Nazionale del Lavoro* that have been reprinted in Kregel (1988; 1989),[1] the ones commissioned by

---

[1] Ones not included in Kregel's volumes include Boulding (1989), Brus (1993), Cairncross (1992), Chenery (1992), Georgescu-Roegen (1993), Goodhart (1997), Hahn (1994), Harcourt (1995), Klein (1991), Maddison (1994), Patinkin (1995), Reddaway (1995), Revell (1998), Rothschild (1991), and Scitovsky (1991).

Heertje (1993; 1995; 1997; 1999) and the interviews contained in Tribe (1997), Snowdon and Vane (1999) and Ibanez (1999).

Economists' biographies are also relevant to the history of economic thought. The interpretation of economists' writings depends on their context and autobiographies, especially ones in which economists reflect on the circumstances in which their work was undertaken, provide an important part of this context. The evolution of economic ideas is the result of choices made by individuals and autobiographies provide insights into why those choices were made. Autobiographical essays also reveal, in a way that economists' research output does not, the networks within which economists worked and the role of these networks in influencing their ideas.

Selecting autobiographies in the way that is done here means that the process is far from being a random one. It is biased towards economists writing a sufficiently high proportion of their output in English to produce a volume of English-language essays. The economists selected are eminent in that they are leading figures within the fields within which they are working, known to everyone working in those fields and familiar names to many economists working in other fields. However, they do not represent the ostensible pinnacle of the profession in that they do not include Nobel Prize winners. The economists included are all still alive, with the exception of Wiseman, Maddala and Grilliches, the last two of whom died after the project started. There may also be bias resulting from the selection of those contributors to the series who chose to write autobiographical introductions and to exclude those who chose not to do so. A wide variety of fields within economics are represented: microeconomics, macroeconomics, international economics, public finance, monetary economics, econometrics, economic history, the history of economic thought and many others.

0.2   CAREER PATTERNS

If conclusions are to be drawn from these essays concerning the evolution of the economics profession, it is important to note that the economists included here are all representative of a particular generation. They were born between 1912 and 1945. For those born at the beginning of this period, the war meant a spell either in the armed forces or in war-related work. This group included Beckerman, Dorfman, Giersch, Greenhut, Perlman, Richardson and Wiseman. Dorfman worked on economics during the war, first for the Office of Price Administration and later for the US Air Force. For the others, their wartime experiences either made them late-comers into academic work or meant they came to it with greater experience. The exception was Black, whose academic career advanced more rapidly, in neutral Ireland, when he had to cover for a Professor who left to help with the war effort in Britain. There was also a significant group, generally slightly younger, who were either forced or induced to migrate as a result of the war. This included Corden (Germany to Australia), Mayer (Austria to the US), Blaug (The Netherlands to Britain and then the US) and Quandt (Hungary to the US). Polak moved with the League of Nations from Europe to the US. Amemiya and Tsuru were not forced to move in the same way, but the war was crucial to their final locations. A further major influence common to this generation of economists was the experience of the depression of the 1930s. Brittan, Giersch, Greenhut, Laidler and Lipsey all talk explicitly about this and it was clearly in the background to the work of others as a reason that brought them into economics. Lindbeck does not talk explicitly of the depression, but refers to the poverty he saw during his childhood. To quote Greenhut (I, p. 52):

> I rather imagine most economists of ages 65–80 today [born 1915–30], regardless of family wealth during the 1930s, were motivated to study our science because of the real economic crises that prevailed back then.

In a similar vein, Negishi writes of the background to his entry into economics being the postwar devastation experienced by Japan.

For economists born later in the period, in contrast, there was no comparable experience. There was a higher proportion that went straight into an academic career and stayed there. However, a large number spent years in government or international organisations. Polak spent his entire career as an international official, from 1937 onwards. Mayer worked in the Tax Division of the US Treasury and in the Office of Price Stabilization. Lipsey worked in the Canadian civil service, Lindbeck in the Swedish Treasury, Beckerman in the OEEC and OECD, Eltis with the National Economic Development Office, Kenen with the Bank of England. Usher worked with the UN, Blaug, Thirlwall and Lal with several international organisations. Brittan did not hold an academic post, instead making his career in financial journalism, but had a brief spell in a government department. On top of this, very many economists combined active involvement in policy making or the provision of economic advice with an academic career. Interestingly, only two economists in this group spent a significant part of their careers in business. Corden started his careeer with a spell in newspaper management and Richardson spent several years as Chief Executive at Oxford University Press. (He had also worked in the Foreign Office.) It is therefore noticeable how wide is the variety of experiences that this group of economists went through. There is no homogeneity in career patterns.

Some of the heterogeneity in career patterns can be explained in terms of differences in national traditions. Most noticeable is the contrast between Britain and the United States in attitudes towards graduate education. For North American economists, the necessity for graduate training at the level of the PhD was taken for granted. Of the thirteen economists born in North America, all obtained a PhD. In contrast, half the economists born in Britain failed to get a PhD. Richardson (II, p. 133) writes that obtaining a Fellowship obviated the need for a PhD. Eltis (II, p. 303), an émigré whose entire career was in Britain, makes exactly the same comment (he eventually obtained a PhD, at the age of 57). Wiseman (II, p. 43) reports that publications were more important than a PhD for obtaining tenure at LSE in the late 1940s. Even where British students did take a PhD, they were left substantially to their own devices (e.g. Lipsey's experience at LSE in 1953; I, p. 116). This is something that changed in the 1980s when Britain moved towards the North American model (see Backhouse 1997). Economists born in continental Europe are predominantly those who were forced to emigrate, mostly to the US, at an early age and they conform to the US pattern. The exception is Eltis. With the exception of those forced to emigrate, those Europeans who were born and made their careers outside Britain (Black, Giersch, Polak and Lindbeck) all obtained PhDs in their native country. Of the Indians, two went to the US and obtained PhDs; one went to Oxford and did not. The high proportion of Japanese economists who obtained US PhDs is simply the result of the selection criteria for the volumes.

The choices facing economists were also influenced by the state of the job market when they were starting their careers. This has varied enormously. Dorfman (I, p. 28) writes of the early postwar years in the US as a time when opportunities were enormous:

> I could not have embarked on the profession of professor of economics at a more propitious time. Graduate study in universities was a boom industry fed by demand accumulated during the war years and accentuated by the GI Bill of Rights. In particular, interest in applying mathematics in the social sciences, especially economics, was at an unprecedented level, possibly because of spectacular wartime successes in applying mathematics outside its traditional fields. And, closest to my personal interests, the hottest areas for applying mathematics in economics were linear programming and its close relative, game theory. I couldn't have planned my debut as a professor of economics better if I had the power to do so.

A few years later, when the postwar boom was over, it was more difficult to get a job. According to Mayer (I, p. 99):

> The postwar enrolment boom had come to an end, leaving many schools with larger faculties than they required. The outbreak of the Korean war, with the

resulting resumption of the draft, did not help. And, unlike now, economics was then not a good field for academic jobs. In addition, the academic employment market was badly organized. Jobs were not advertised; when they had vacancies, department chairs would notify a few graduate schools as well as their friends. If your professors were not plugged into this network, did not want to play this game, or did not push you, that was that.

With the expansion of higher education in the 1960s, in many countries including both the US and Britain, the number of openings increased again. By the 1980s, however, the job market had turned again and positions were much harder to find (see Laidler, I, pp. 303, 319).

In other countries, the structure of academia made for a different environment. Tsuru (II, p. 11) explains that obtaining a job in 1940 was so difficult that he chose to stay in the US once he had finished graduate work. His explanation is the 'guild-like cliquism' in university faculties typically staffed by 'an in-bred hierarchy usually headed by a commanding "master of the guild"'.

Many of the essays attest to the enormous role of chance in career development. Lipsey (II, p. 116) made the significant decision to go to LSE instead of Chicago on the grounds that Chicago had not yet dropped its French-language requirement. Greenhut (I, p. 54) did go to Chicago only to comment on the high opportunity cost imposed by this. Usher (I, p. 285) became an economist by accident because of a chance exposure to left-wing political views at a summer camp, after which he decided to study social science. Beckerman (II, p. 201) emphasises the role of luck in his career. His study of Anglo-Danish trade, supervised by Stone, came about as an excuse to visit a Danish girlfriend and it was a chance meeting that resulted in his going to the OECD rather than the Treasury. Desai (II, p. 357), at that time ignorant of maths and statistics, was assigned to work with Klein on the grounds that he was supposed to know something about commodity agreements and it was taken as a stylised fact that all Indians were good statisticians. Mueller (I, pp. 367, 368, 388, 389) emphasises the repeated role of chance in his career. He was put off one college by the thought of spending his leisure time drinking beer and watching 'skin flicks'. He failed to study nuclear engineering because the letter offering him a scholarship at Columbia never arrived and he transferred an NSF scholarship from MIT to Princeton in ignorance of MIT's higher ranking.

0.3   NETWORKS AND INFLUENCES

Even a sample of thirty six economists is too small to undertake a serious analysis of the networks within which economists learn and use their skills. This is especially true for countries outside Britain and the US. However, a few tentative conclusions can be drawn. The first is the range of institutions through which people could end up doing top-level research: The American University, Berkeley, Columbia, Harvard, Johns Hopkins, Princeton, Texas A&M, UCLA, and Yale. As one would expect, the largest numbers are associated with Chicago (Barzel, Laidler, Maddalla and Usher), Columbia (Blaug, Mayer and Perlman), Harvard (Kenen, Lazonick, Quandt and Tsuru) and Princeton (Ashenfelter, Black, Mueller and Quandt). Names that crop up most frequently among influential teachers include Milton Friedman, George Stigler (then at Columbia), Fritz Machlup, Wassily Leontief and Joseph Schumpeter. In Britain, the range of institutions is much smaller: LSE was clearly dominant (Corden, Kenen, Laidler, Lipsey and Wiseman) followed by Cambridge (Beckerman, Brittan and Eltis). The most influential economists for this generation of British economists were clearly Lionel Robbins and later Harry Johnson at LSE, Joan Robinson at Cambridge and John Hicks at Oxford.

Virtually all economists in this sample spent significant periods outside the country in which they were based, to such an extent that dividing them along geographical lines is to a great extent arbitrary. If any generalisation is to be made it is that the economists included were almost all internationally mobile at some stage of their careers. Those forced to migrate because of the rise of the Nazi Party and the Second World War have already been mentioned. Others undertook graduate work (several Europeans received Rockefeller Fellowships for study in the US) abroad whilst many others worked a year or more in a country other than the one where they spent most of their career. Even Brittan, whose only formal training was at Cambridge, took a course from Milton Friedman, there on a year's sabbatical. Desai attended a lecture course by Alvin Hansen whilst still in India. These autobiographies describe an essentially international profession. This international dimension extends to the reading lists on which these economists were trained. Few of the autobiographies discuss the syllabuses or reading on which their training was based, but amongst those books most frequently mentioned are Marshall's *Principles* (1920), Hansen's *Guide to Keynes* (1953), Hicks's *Value and Capital* (1939), Chamberlin's *Theory of Monopolistic Competition* (1933), Patinkin's *Money, Interest and Prices* (1956) and Samuelson's *Foundations* (1947). Two points are perhaps of particular interest. The first is that Marshall's book, despite its age, was still being used by Barzel, Laidler and

Lipsey, and that Desai recounts his resistance to his teacher's attempts to engender enthusiasm for the book. The second is that, though this was the period of Keynesian hegemony, few of these authors recount being caught up in the excitement over Keynes's *General Theory* (1936) (Tsuru, as a member of the Harvard class that included Samuelson, is an exception). Lipsey (I, p. 113) writes that he graduated (at the University of British Columbia in 1951) 'innocent of Keynesian economics'. Perhaps this is because most of them entered the profession after the war rather than just before it. However, when people do mention the *General Theory*, it is often to say that it was a difficult book and that Hansen's *Guide to Keynes* was much easier to understand.

The essays point to the very different types of training provided in different institutions and in different countries. LSE and Cambridge adopted a very *laissez-faire* attitude to doctoral work (as was possible in a system based solely on the production of a thesis, and no examinations).

Underlying all this are differences in the academic culture. Columbia, for a long time the largest producer of PhDs, was still dominated by institutionalists and failed to provide rigorous technical training, though, as Greenhut recounts, the theoretical element in the program was strengthened in 1948 with the arrival of Stigler and Vickrey. Mayer (an undergraduate at City University New York) points out that its failure to offer an intermediate micro course was normal in the 1940s. Kenen recalls the opposition to theory that still prevailed at Columbia when he was there in the early 1950s. Dorfman describes the Berkeley department at the same period as being split beween institutionalists, who had typically joined it during the depression, and a younger, more theoretically-inclined generation. In contrast, LSE in the 1960s provided a more rigorous training but still offered an environment in which people could move in a variety of directions. Thus Lazonick, who took a Masters there, argued that LSE trained him in neoclassical economics but allowed him to turn against the mainstream. This attitude is also reflected by Desai, on the LSE staff since 1967, who writes that though employed as an econometrician he could work on other areas and and adopt an unorthodox approach. The ethos of LSE is summed up by Wiseman: it is a broad church, transcending individual schools of thought.

Some economists write of the freedom they were allowed in writing their PhD thesis, whether at Cambridge (Beckerman, choosing a topic that was far too difficult), Lipsey (at LSE) and Sato (Johns Hopkins). At Chicago, on the other hand, the writing process was, as Barzel (I, p. 226) put it, 'socialized' through the system of workshops. The impact that Chicago could have on graduate students is described in several essays. Barzel (I, p. 225) writes:

> The intellectual atmosphere at Chicago [in the late 1950s] was electrifying; the economics faculty was free of deadwood and did virtually no consulting. Small

talk occurred, of course, but it occupied only a small fraction of our time, the rest of which was relentlessly overtaken by economics.

Usher (I, p. 287), who joined the department in 1956, described the place in similar terms:

> It was a heady time to be a student of economics. You can often judge the tone of a place by its afternoon tea time or coffee hour. At Chicago in those days, the faculty and graduate students assembled every day in the faculty lounge to discuss, to analyse and to argue. There was, as I remember, no respite and little gossip. Economics was too important.

Chicago was seen as a place where 'the frontiers of knowledge were being pushed back in a big way': Friedman was taking on Keynes and monetarism was about to challenge the wisdom of central banks. This was also Laidler's experience: 'At Chicago, economics was treated as a relevant and socially useful discipline, not a compendium of intellectual games to be played for the fun of it' (I, p. 300). The market was King but this belief was not achieved by brainwashing. Laidler recalls being urged by Harry Johnson to get to know the entire literature, not just what was being done at Chicago, and being exposed to a variety of visitors who held contrary views. He points out that Friedman awarded him a fellowship in his final year even though he still proclaimed himself a socialist.

However, although Chicago took economics seriously, Laidler (I, p. 335) argues that its strength was that (unlike Berkeley in the mid 1960s) it was not *too* earnest:

> What had attracted me to economics at the LSE, and had continued to do so at Chicago, were working atmospheres in which people not only thought that what they were doing was important, but in which they were evidently enjoying themselves as well. The Essex department in the late 1960s was another such place, not surprisingly perhaps, since it was the creation of Chris Archibald and Dick Lipsey [both from LSE].

These reactions can be compared with the contrast Beckerman (II, p. 183) offers a similar comparison of his experience on moving from Oxford to London in 1969. His experience of University College London was that even when they took breaks, everyone continued to talk 'shop'. This was something that would have been impossible in the environment of Balliol College, where very few of the fellows would have been in the same discipline. He valued the interdisciplinary contacts that were absent in London. Perlman, generalising from his experience at Pittsburg, goes beyond regarding such contacts as valuable, seeing them as an integral part of the way universities functioned. From the 1960s, however, he suggests that it was undermined by a combination of two developments: the increasing prominence of natural science and professional schools; and the ideological divisions that began to surface at the time of the Vietnam War. Laidler (I, p. 319), too, sees universities as having become a less attractive environment in which to work but traces it to two trends that originated in the 1980s. One is that because of demographic trends, rising numbers of young academics were trying to establish themselves in a system that, because the number of jobs was no longer growing, had become far more competitive. As a result they became more aggressive and harder to live with. The other was the 'professionalisation' of university administration and the trend towards seeing academic staff as 'human resources' whose task was not education and research so much as to 'service clients'. This is not, he suggests, what his generation thought a university was for.

Given the range of people who influenced this group of economists, it is impossible to discuss them all. One, however, appears in so many autobiographies that his role merits being picked out: Harry Johnson. Brittan describes him, then at Cambridge, as the supervisor from whom he derived most benefit. Eltis (II, p. 305), also at Cambridge, describes how Johnson would talk for half an hour only to say 'but you don't need all that for a First'. His inflence on Beckerman was more direct in that his lectures persuaded him to do a thesis on international trade. At LSE, Johnson provided the stimulus that Lipsey needed to publish his early work on trade theory and he encouraged Corden's work on protection. Corden says that, though Johnson could be a tough critic, there was one occasion when he immediately sent an article on which Corden had sat apprehensively for six months, to Machlup for publication. Corden argues that every young economist needs an advocate, and his was Johnson, whose citation of his articles gave them the publicity they needed. Other mentions of Johnson are symptomatic of the dominant role Johnson played in British economics in the 1960s.[2] When Corden was interviewed for a Readership at Oxford, Johnson was the external. Laidler discusses Johnson's role in the Money Study Group and British monetarism, whilst Lal became involved in the Trade Policy Research Centre, of which Johnson was one of the founders. He is also mentioned by Laidler in his role on the committee of the British Association for the Advancement of Science, and by Lipsey in his role as an associate editor (effectively running the journal) of the *Review of Economic Studies*. On top of this, Johnson was a significant figure at Chicago. He taught Laidler during a year when Friedman was on sabbatical and was influential in persuading Laidler to accept positions at Manchester and later Western Ontario. Hamada describes how last minute work he did on a paper Johnson

---

[2] This is also discussed briefly in Backhouse (1997); see also Middleton (1998, esp. pp. 21–6).

had invited him to present at Chicago led to the publication of his most widely known paper. Lindbeck, who had no direct institutional contact, says that he was inspired by Johnson's work. Even Lazonick, who reacted against Johnson's neoclassical economics whilst at LSE suggests that having been a student of Johnson's helped him get a particular job in Geneva (where Johnson also taught). He mention's Johnson's reputation as the most published economist in history.[3]

A lesson from the other teachers whom these essays pick out as having been influential is that to be influential does not mean being a 'good teacher' in the conventional sense of the term. Barzel (I, p. 223) writes of Abba Lerner that he 'was probably the laziest teacher I had'. Preparation would comprise nothing more than asking a student to discuss a chapter of his book, *The Economics of Control* (1944). However, he would then ask questions and direct the discussion so as to weed out the student's mistakes and reveal the power of equating at the margin. 'Lerner's brilliance more than compensated for his slipshod presentation.' Five of the essays mention George Stigler's influence as a teacher and it is noticeable that the three who were supervised or examined by him have harsh words to offer on his methods. Blaug writes that 'he had a reputation for destroying students ... when Stigler said that something you had written was nonsense, he produced so many crushing reasons to back up his judgement that you could not but be grateful that he had condescended to criticise you'. Perlman first met Stigler as his external examiner, convinced that he had come to the examination 'loaded for bear', having tried to convince the other examiners to fail him. After the examination Perlman (I, p. 82) asked Stigler, 'What do I have to do to get by you – memorize your goddamned book?' only to get the reply, 'That will be good for starters, but you ought to do more.'

0.4   THE STATE OF ECONOMICS

The careers of these economics cover the period when the prestige of the neoclassical synthesis of Keynesian economics and general equilibrium theory was at its height. In Blaug's words (II, p. 212):

> The discipline of economics was never so confident as it was in the late 1950s and early 1960s: we *knew* that general equilibrium theory was the last word in theoretical elegance, that input–output analysis and linear programming would soon make it not just elegant but operational, and that 'the neo-classical synthesis' had successfully joined Keynesian macroeconomics to Walrasian microeconomics.

[3] Longawa (1984).

It is also true that virtually all the economists in this collection would endorse a broadly 'neoclassical' view of economics. Several (for example, Beckerman, Blaug, Brittan, Lal and Usher) recount a shift away from 'socialism' towards greater confidence in free markets and greater scepticism about what government could achieve. Mayer describes himself as having become more conservative. Greenhut moved from liberal Keynesianism to supply-side Keynesianism. If we count Wiseman's subjectivism as just within this category, the only exceptions are Perlman (still strongly influenced by Wisconsin-style institutionalism), Richardson (who came to question the concept of perfect competition), Lazonick (an economic historian who, as such stands apart from the others) and Tsuru (a Marxist). However, despite this broad consensus, it would be hard to deny that they represent a wide variety of approaches to, and perspectives on, economics. It is possible to do little more than make conjectures about the reasons.

One possibility is that economic theory, even with the neoclassical synthesis, was far from unified. Formal modelling techniques were not pervasive, especially in applied fields, in the way they have since become. Another is that the extensive experience of these economists outside academia meant that they kept in touch with the realities facing policy makers. Perhaps this impression arises because the economists in this sample include a high proportion of 'applied' economists. Whilst one might argue that this causes bias in that theorists are more important in the profession than the sample suggests, it serves as a corrective to the perspective that arises through focusing on key theoretical developments. Most economists undertake applied economics.

These two points are related in that, whilst there may have been consensus over the broad theoretical framework, there was less consensus over the precise ways in which applied economics was to be undertaken. In part this is because methods were to a great extent dictated by the problems being tackled and, given that these were largely set by experiences outside academia rather than by an agenda 'internal' to the profession, this necessitated non-standard methods. Thus Kenen used predominantly geometric theoretical models to draw conclusions about trade policy, Mayer, Laidler and Ashenfelter used a combination of econometric and institutional analysis, whilst Usher engaged in field work that went behind the generalisations of national accounting statistics.

The period during which these economists worked saw the rise to prominence of mathematical methods in economics. It is thus not surprising we can find among them a very wide range of attitudes towards mathematics (even though virtually everyone had to learn mathematics at some point). One pole is represented by Dorfman (I, p. 30):

My principal concern during my years at Berkeley, 1950–5, was to convey both to my students and to the economics profession the remarkable strides in the use of mathematics in economics that emerged from World War II. My missionary zeal in this cause was expressed in both teaching and writing, and continued for several years after I transferred to Harvard.

Others for whom the ability to use mathematics in developing economic theory was a highly attractive aspect of economics include Sato and Negishi. At the other extreme are several economists who, despite having made significant contributions to economics, confess to being mathematically weak. These include Kenen (who says he would not do well in graduate school today) and Laidler (who says he was never able to rise above being a mediocre technician). Others confess to acquiring their mathematics later than would be expected today. Thus Desai learned mathematics whilst working on his PhD with Klein, whilst Lipsey confesses that he learned to differentiate x^2 whilst a graduate student at LSE (one of his undergraduate teachers had advised him that it would be a waste of time to study mathematics).

Contrasting views are expressed on the effect that the increased use of mathematics has had on the subject. Dorfman says that, though he has become aware of the high cost imposed by the time taken to learn mathematics as well as economics, the attitude that underlay his early missionary zeal has not changed. In contrast, Beckerman (II, p. 193) notes that, in economics, 'second-rate mathematicians can make a decent living churning out mathematical answers to trivial and irrelevant questions'. In the same vein, Blaug (II, p. 221) denounces the sterile formalism of modern economics, including general equilibrium theory, under the spell of which he had fallen in the 1960s.

0.5 CONCLUSIONS

One of the main points to emerge from these autobiographies is the sheer variety of motives for entering economics, career patterns, attitudes towards the main trends in the discipline and views about how economics should be undertaken. They show that to be a good economist, one needs to know more than can be learned from standard textbooks but that this can be acquired in many ways. An interesting question, beyond the scope of this chapter, is how far lessons drawn from this group of economists are unique to the historical period in which they lived. This had three major characteristics. First, events in Europe in the interwar period together with the Second World War caused upheaval for many of these economists. They had no opportunity to pursue 'standard' career patterns. Second, the economics profession was, like much of academia, expanding rapidly and thereby changing its character in many countries. Third, this was a period when the content of economics stabilised, in a transition that has been described as 'From prewar pluralism to postwar neoclassicism'.[4] The experience of the generation whose careers began in the 1960s and 1970s will have been different in all three respects. Whilst it would be interesting to speculate on the effects this may have had, or be having, on the discipline, to do so would be going beyond the scope of this volume.

REFERENCES

Backhouse, R.E. (1997) 'The changing character of British economics', in A.W. Coats (ed.) (1997) *The post-1945 internationalization of economics*. Durham, NC: Duke University Press, pp. 31–60.

Backhouse, R.E. (1999) 'Economics in mid-Atlantic: British economics, 1945–95', in A.W. Coats (ed.) (1999) *The development of economics in western Europe since 1945*. London: Routledge, pp. 20–41.

Boulding, K.E. (1989) 'A bibliographical autobiography', *Banca Nazionale del Lavoro Quarterly Review*, 42 (4), pp. 365–93.

Breit, W. (1987) 'Biography and the making of economic worlds', *Southern Economic Journal*, 53 (4), pp. 823–33.

Breit, W. and Spencer, R. (eds) (1995) *Lives of the laureates: thirteen Nobel economists*, 3rd edn. Cambridge, MA: MIT Press.

Brus, W. (1993) 'The bane of reforming the socialist economic system', *Banca Nazionale del Lavoro Quarterly Review*, 46 (4), pp. 363–405.

Cairncross, A.K. (1992) 'From theory to policy making: economics as a profession', *Banca Nazionale del Lavoro Quarterly Review*, 45 (1), pp. 3–20.

Chamberlin, E.H. (1933) *The theory of monopolistic competition: a re-orientation of the theory of value*. Cambridge, MA: Harvard University Press.

Chenery, H. (1992) 'From engineering to economics', *Banca Nazionale del Lavoro Quarterly Review*, 45 (4), pp. 369–405.

Georgescu-Roegen, N. (1993) 'An emigrant from a developing country: autobiographical notes – II', *Banca Nazionale del Lavoro Quarterly Review*, 46 (1), pp. 3–30.

Goodhart, C.A.E. (1997) 'Whither now?', *Banca Nazionale del Lavoro Quarterly Review*, 50 (4), pp. 385–430.

Hahn, F.H. (1994) 'An intellectual retrospect', *Banca Nazionale del Lavoro Quarterly Review*, 47 (3), pp. 245–58.

Hansen, A.H. (1953) *A guide to Keynes*. New York: McGraw-Hill.

---

[4] This is the title of Morgan and Rutherford (1998). They use the phrase to refer to economics in the US but it is still usable in this broader context.

Harcourt, G.C. (1995) 'Recollections and reflections of an Australian patriot and a Cambridge economist', *Banca Nazionale del Lavoro Quarterly Review*, 48 (3), pp. 225–54.

Heertje, A. (ed.) (1993) *The makers of modern economics*, Vol. I. Brighton: Harvester Wheatsheaf.

Heertje, A. (ed.) (1995) *The makers of modern economics*, Vol. II. Aldershot: Edward Elgar.

Heertje, A. (ed.) (1997) *The makers of modern economics*, Vol. III. Cheltenham: Edward Elgar.

Heertje, A. (ed.) (1999) *The makers of modern economics*, Vol. IV. Cheltenham: Edward Elgar.

Hicks, J.R. (1939) *Value and capital: an inquiry into some fundamental principles of economic theory*. Oxford: Clarendon Press.

Ibanez, C.U. (1999) *The Current State of Macroeconomics: Leading Thinkers in Conversation*. London: Macmillan.

Johnson, H.G. (1968) 'A catarrh of economists?: from Keynes to Postan', *Encounter*, 30 (5, May), pp. 50–4.

Johnson, H.G. (1977) 'Cambridge as an academic environment in the early 1930s: a reconstruction from the late 1940s', in D. Patinkin and J.C. Leith (eds) (1977) *Keynes, Cambridge and the General theory*. London: Macmillan, pp. 98–114.

Keynes, J.M. (1936) *The general theory of employment, interest and money. Collected writings of John Maynard Keynes*, Vol. VII (1973). London: Macmillan.

Klein, L.R. (1991) 'Econometric contributions of the Cowles commission, 1944–47: a retrospective view', *Banca Nazionale del Lavoro Quarterly Review*, 44 (2), pp. 101–17.

Kregel, J.A. (ed.) (1988) *Recollections of eminent economists*, Vol. 1. London: Macmillan.

Kregel, J.A. (ed.) (1989) *Recollections of eminent economists*, Vol. 2. London: Macmillan.

Lerner, A.P. (1944) *The economics of control: principles of welfare economics*. London: Macmillan.

Longawa, V.M. (1984) 'Harry G. Johnson: a bibliography', *Journal of Political Economy*, 92 (4), pp. 659–711.

Maddison, A. (1994) 'Confessions of a Chiffrephile', *Banca Nazionale del Lavoro Quarterly Review*, 47 (2), pp. 123–65.

Marshall, A. (1920) *Principles of economics*. 8th edn. London: Macmillan.

Middleton, R. (1998) *Charlatans or saviours? Economists and the British economy from Marshall to Meade*. Cheltenham and Northampton, MA: Edward Elgar.

Morgan, M. and Rutherford, M. (1998) *From interwar pluralism to postwar neoclassicism*. Supplement to *History of Political Economy*, volume 30. Durham, NC: Duke University Press.

Patinkin, D. (1956) *Money, interest and prices: an integration of monetary and value theory*. New York: Harper & Row.

Patinkin, D. (1995) 'The training of an economist', *Banca Nazionale del Lavoro Quarterly Review*, 48 (4), pp. 351–95.

Reddaway, W.B. (1995) 'Recollections of a lucky economist', *Banca Nazionale del Lavoro Quarterly Review*, 48 (1), pp. 3–16.

Revell, J. (1998) 'Recollections of a late entrant', *Banca Nazionale del Lavoro Quarterly Review*, 51 (3), pp. 231–45.

Rothschild, K.W. (1991) 'Glimpses of a non-linear biography', *Banca Nazionale del Lavoro Quarterly Review*, 44 (1), pp. 3–13.

Samuelson, P.A. (1947) *Foundations of economic analysis*. Cambridge, MA: Harvard University Press.

Scitovsky, T. (1991) 'Hindsight economics', *Banca Nazionale del Lavoro Quarterly Review*, 44 (3), pp. 251–70.

Snowdon, B. and Vane, H. (1999) *Conversations with Leading Economists: Interpreting Modern Macroeconomics*. Cheltenham: Edward Elgar.

Szenberg, M. (ed.) (1992) *Eminent economists: their life philosophies*. Cambridge: Cambridge University Press.

Tribe, K. (1997) *Economic Careers: Economics and Economists in Britain, 1930–1970*. London and New York: Routledge.

Walker, D.A. (1983) 'Biography and the study of the history of economic thought', *Research in the History of Economic Thought and Methodology*, 1, pp. 41–59.

1. Jacques J. Polak (b. 1914)[1]

© *International Monetary Fund*

1.1   STUDYING ECONOMICS, 1932–7

After finishing the Gymnasium Erasmianum in Rotterdam, I enrolled in the study of economics for an old-fashioned reason: to join the family business. Not the business of importing and wholesaling textiles that my great-great-grandfather had started with his five sons in 1808; that firm had been liquidated in 1911, three years before I was born, mostly on account of a lack of interest in business by the younger generation of partners. Perfect foresight would have led to the same decision: with the rise of the Dutch textile industry, the import of standard textiles was bound to lose ground. But after 1911 my father had studied, in the Netherlands and in England, to become a certified public accountant and had built up a respectable CPA practice. It seemed natural that I should join the firm, and prepare for it via the academic route: only recently, the study of accountancy in the Netherlands had been given an academic cachet as the newly established departments of economics in Rotterdam and Amsterdam offered it as a subject of post-graduate study.

---

[1]   Polak (1994b), as revised by the author. I have two volumes of selected essays in the series (Polak 1994a) and have been the recipient of a festschrift (Frenkel and Goldstein 1991) which contains an essay (Frenkel *et al.* 1991) exploring the major themes in my writings.

The choice of Amsterdam over Rotterdam was easy: Amsterdam offered the benefit of studying away from home, as well as the full academic fare that Rotterdam's 'higher business school' lacked. I received my MA in economics in 1936 and then started to divide my time between taking the required courses in accountancy and exploring a subject for a doctoral dissertation. It did not take me long to discover that accountancy as a science (at least in the way it was taught at the time in Amsterdam) had little appeal for me, whereas further work in economics offered a tempting variety of challenges. My thesis supervisor (Professor Herman Frijda) suggested that I take a look at Richard Kahn's now famous article on the multiplier (Kahn 1931). This hint proved fortuitous in a number of respects.

To begin with, Kahn's subject was of immediate relevance to the economic problem of the time – the unemployment of the depression years. His paper, and the abundant literature to which it pointed, proved to be an excellent starting point for a dissertation with a strong policy orientation (Polak 1937). Second, the subject of the dissertation forced me to become acquainted with the writings of many contemporary English and American economists to which I had not paid sufficient attention in my earlier studies. A further advantage was that Kahn and others of his generation (Meade, Harrod, Lerner) allowed me an easier entry into Keynesian economics than was possible from the master himself; *The general theory* seemed to reveal a needlessly difficult struggle with material that the younger generation handled with greater ease and elegance. Third, having had the benefit in Amsterdam of Professor Jan Tinbergen's lectures on econometrics, it was obvious to me that his dynamic models of the whole economy of a country (those for the Netherlands and the US had just appeared) were a quantum jump ahead of the rudimentary models of Kahn, and thus a superior source for calculations of the employment effects of particular policy measures.

1.2   THE LEAGUE OF NATIONS, 1937–43

The contacts I had had with Tinbergen in my attempts to use his models in my dissertation produced, out of the blue, an offer to become his assistant at the League of Nations in Geneva where he was engaged in econometric testing of business cycle theories. Even though my thesis had not yet been finished, I jumped at the opportunity and started working in Geneva in October 1937. Nearly three months into the job, I managed to get a little over a week's leave – which had to suffice to travel to Amsterdam, defend my thesis and get my degree, get married, have a honeymoon in Paris and report back for work in Geneva.

It would be an understatement to describe my job in the League as Tinbergen's assistant as ideal for a beginning economist. For some obscure reason, I was given a little table to work at in Tinbergen's room, at right angles to his desk; I looked straight south into the park of the Palais des Nations, the lake, and on clear days the majesty of Mont Blanc. Sharing an office with Tinbergen, I had the opportunity to absorb his method of work as if by osmosis. I learned more mathematics and even, I believe, more economics in that office than during my entire studies. The kind of work done in Geneva was at the very front line of economics and econometrics. Hardly a week passed that we did not chance upon new and unexpected linkages – new statistical approximations, new variables that deserved a place in the model. Subjects suitable for journal papers were as easy to find as coloured eggs on Easter morning. It was impossible to use them all, even for a fast writer like Tinbergen. Any subject that would take too much of his time to write up – and he was good at estimating the time in advance – was passed over. More than eight or ten hours? Forget it!

One subject on which Tinbergen encouraged me to write for publication in the United States was the consumption function in his US model. This also provided me with a first opportunity to publish in English. This paper (Polak 1939a) gives a glimpse into the kitchen of Tinbergen's model-building technique with its pragmatic mixture of theory, common sense and inferences drawn from the data. In a final section of this paper I also seized the opportunity to branch out on my own by drawing some inferences on the multiplier, joining the lively debate on that subject that was then in progress. Eight years later, I returned to that issue at greater length, with particular reference to the foreign trade multiplier, where I took exception to the common practice of treating a partially endogenous variable (in this case the trade balance) as the multiplicand in multiplier exercises (Polak 1947a). This provoked a sharp 'Comment' from Haberler (1947), which led to the rare happy ending of a joint 'Restatement', all three pieces appearing in the same issue of the *American Economic Review* (Haberler and Polak 1947).

After Tinbergen's return to the Netherlands in late 1938, the business cycle work continued for some months under Tjalling Koopmans. But with the outbreak of war in Europe – which had a devastating effect on the morale of the staff of an organization designed to avoid war – the focus of the League's economic work changed to studies of the immediate post-World War I and interwar periods, in a search for lessons applicable to the period following this war. By mid-1940, when half of France had been overrun and German troops were at the Swiss border a few miles north of the Palais, a radical decision was made to save the best of the economic work of the League for the benefit of its remaining membership – and for the United States. The League accepted an offer, which had the support of the US

Government, to bring a key group of economic and financial officials from Geneva to the Institute for Advanced Studies in Princeton, NJ for the duration of the war.[2] The group that made the trip included the Director of the Department, Alexander Loveday, and about ten senior officials and their families. I was not 'senior' either by rank or age, but with my wife and my young son I became part of the group that travelled by bus through the utter confusion of Vichy France and the desolation of Franco Spain to Barcelona, by train from there to Lisbon and finally by boat to New York. We started life in the United States on 20 September 1940.

Much serious economic work was done in Princeton, both by the staff and by a number of League committees that continued to meet, as far as circumstances permitted. In many respects the documents produced in Princeton (of which Nurkse's *International currency experience: lessons of the interwar period* (1944) is probably the best known) anticipated and indeed helped to structure allied attitudes on international monetary cooperation (as later embodied in the IMF) and on full employment policies as pursued in the early years of the Economic and Social Council of the UN. I prepared a number of reports on food relief, balance of payments assistance and business cycles during the early post-World War I years. In connection with these and other studies I also wrote two papers drawing more general inferences on the debt and inflation problems of that period. The first of these (Polak 1943a) attempted to find an answer to the following question: why was it that the European countries which had financed their reconstruction after World War I in part by relying on foreign capital ended up with horrendous payments problems in the 1930s? Did they spend the money on the wrong things? Were their overall policies on saving and investment misguided? Is foreign borrowing inherently dangerous? Or does the danger lie in the fact that lenders may simply stop lending?[3] The second paper (Polak 1943b) constructed a model to explain the interlinked processes of inflation (including hyperinflation) that had occurred in a number of European countries in the early 1920s.

Our salaries in Princeton were low even by contemporary standards.

---

[2] One of the persons who warmly welcomed us in Princeton was Arthur Sweetser, who was then an economist associated with the Institute. I had once met Mr. Sweetser casually in Geneva and learned that he was then a staff member of the League secretariat. Curious where in the League a national of a non-member might be employed, I searched the telephone book which provided a departmental acronym after each name. The book did give his affiliation, namely 'BMS'. That did not ring any bell, so I went to the front of the book, where I received the answer to my query: 'BMS' was identified as 'Bureau de Monsieur Sweetser'.

[3] When asked to authorize a translation of this paper for a Mexican journal, I realized that the analysis would be equally relevant, prospectively, to developing countries relying heavily on imported capital.

What had seemed generous in Swiss francs in Geneva proved much less so converted into dollars at American prices. The League's finances were (or at least that was what we were told) precarious, making raises difficult. My wife's attempt to improve the family income by a job at the Princeton Listening Center, monitoring and translating German broadcasts, came to an abrupt end when Washington ruled that this could not be done by a foreigner. I was very pleased, therefore, when I was offered a moonlighting job, at a stipend of $100 a month, to provide the Netherlands Indies with a figure for its national income. The commission that represented the Netherlands Indies (which by that time were occupied by the Japanese) in the US had realized that every self-respecting country should have a national income (neither GNP nor GDP was yet in fashion). The Princeton University library proved equal to the task: it had annual statistical volumes that contained good data on agricultural output, foreign trade and government finance. These sources, plus a bit of legerdemain (such as interpolation by correlation) allowed me to overperform on my assignment, producing data for nineteen years instead of one, plus a breakdown by groups of the population (Polak 1943c). That breakdown proved to be the study's undoing, at least as far as its publication was concerned. The commission members decided that it would be less damaging for the reputation of the Netherlands Indies to lack a national income than to be known as a country where the average income of 'Europeans' (a term of art that included Japanese and Americans) was about fifty times as high as that of the average Indonesian (less so, of course, in real terms). As a result, it limited my first edition to twenty mimeographed copies.

1.3 THE NETHERLANDS EMBASSY AND UNRRA, 1943–6

The work of the Princeton group continued until the remaining League staff was merged into the United Nations Organization in 1946. I left, however, in 1943 to take a position at the Netherlands Embassy in Washington. Not familiar with diplomatic usage, I reported for duty at 9 o'clock on 7 April 1943. I learned that my new boss was not expected till 10, and in the meantime I was given the day's *New York Times*. It contained the text of the Keynes and White Plans for what was ultimately to become the International Monetary Fund. By the time my boss showed up, I had read the plans and could tell him that that was precisely what I was qualified to work on in the Embassy.

Much of the work by the Netherlands authorities on the novel monetary proposals was done at the seat of the wartime government in London, under the guidance of Willem Beyen, a brilliant economist who headed the Netherlands delegation in Bretton Woods, and later, as foreign minister, was one of the architects of the European Economic Community. But the embassy also had its input, taking part in discussions with American experts at the Treasury and the Federal Reserve, and in the preliminary international conferences on the plans held in Washington in June 1943 and in Atlantic City a year later. This experience earned me a place in the Netherlands delegation to the Bretton Woods conference in July 1944, an event – I would almost be inclined to write a 'happening' – on which many of the participants later looked back as the most exciting professional experience in their lives.

By contrast, most of the work in the Embassy, which involved a good deal of reporting on the US economy, was much less stimulating. Only one professional undertaking deserves to be recorded, if only because it gave me an unusual experience relevant to my future job in the IMF. Unlikely as it may seem, the embassy had a role to play in the setting of an exchange rate. The US and UK authorities needed 'invasion rates': exchange rates at which the troops liberating Belgium and the Netherlands would exchange dollars or pounds for Belgian francs and guilders. The Netherlands and Belgian governments in exile in London had, in their October 1943 monetary agreement to regulate payments between the two countries after the war, fixed an exchange rate between their two currencies of 16.52 Belgian francs to one guilder. That rate equalled the prewar gold parity which appeared to remain appropriate given the similar impact of the war on the two countries. That one equation, of course, did not help to find a rate against allied currencies. But there was a second equation: the Belgian franc was set at par with the colonial franc for the Belgian Congo (later Zaire). And that was a real currency with a meaningful exchange rate against the dollar, for the Congo was the source of uranium for the US. Accordingly, in a rare instance of the tail wagging the dog next door, the *prima facie* choice for the invasion rate for the Netherlands guilder against the US dollar would have to be 16.52 times the rate for the Congo franc, or about 37.7 US cents. The Ministry of Finance in London had judged this rate to be acceptable on economic grounds; our task in Washington was to make this case to the American authorities. Fortunately, the statistics we had on price developments in the occupied Netherlands showed this to be a defensible choice and the Netherlands embassy submitted a lengthy statistical and analytical note to that effect to the US Treasury. What persuaded the Americans (in particular Harry White) to accept the rates proposed by the Belgians and the Dutch was not my note, but the proper answer by the Belgian negotiator to a question by

White inspired, one must assume, by the theory of purchasing power parity.[4] In 1946, the rate for the Netherlands guilder as determined by this process became the initial par value that the Netherlands declared to the IMF and it survived until the general devaluation of European currencies in September 1949.

The less than two years that I spent at the Embassy constituted only a short interruption in a lifelong career as an international official. In the autumn of 1944 I joined UNRRA (the United Nations Relief and Rehabilitation Administration), whose birth at a conference in Atlantic City I had attended a year earlier as a member of the Netherlands delegation. UNRRA had been created by the United Nations (this was before the United Nations Organization existed, when 'United Nations' was still used as a plural noun) to bring relief and rehabilitation supplies to European and Asian countries ravaged by war and to assist with the refugee problem the world over. It was an unusual organization in that the Soviet Union was an effective member: UNRRA had field missions in two Soviet republics (the Ukraine and Byelorussia) and Russian nationals performed senior staff functions on a fully integrated basis – all this reflecting the wartime collaboration of the Western powers with the Soviet Union. My main task as Economic Adviser to the Director General (first Herbert Lehman, previously Governor of the State of New York, and then Fiorello Laguardia, ex-Mayor of New York City) was to prepare a report on the progress made in the countries that UNRRA was assisting, with the idea that this report (Polak 1946) would lay the groundwork for a second round of contributions to fund the organization's work beyond 1946. But at a conference in Geneva in August 1946 that idea was shot down by the US government, which had lost interest in an organization built on close cooperation between the West and the USSR. UNRRA thus became an early victim of the Cold War, leaving a hole in the postwar structure that was filled, in a somewhat different way, by the Marshall Plan a year later.

1.4   JOINING THE STAFF OF THE IMF, 1947

Although it took a year or two to wind up UNRRA's worldwide activities, I had liquidated my small section by the end of 1946 and was looking for a new job. I had been offered a chair in macroeconomics at my alma mater,

---

4 'What is the price charged in a cloak room in Belgium?', White asked Ansiaux (who later became the governor of the National Bank of Belgium). 'One franc', Ansiaux pulled out of the air. White thought this over and concluded: 'Your rate is right' (Polak 1994c, p. 192).

Amsterdam University, but I preferred to stay in the US to work in an international organization. In the last months of 1946 I did some comparison shopping in this narrow market.

Three new entities were recruiting economists at the time: the United Nations Secretariat, the World Bank and the IMF. The UN had already attracted a number of prominent economists (for example, Michal Kalecki) and its mandate, especially in the area of full employment policies, was highly attractive. But the heavy hand of politics over economics, of writing committee reports over doing original research, was already clearly visible. I was particularly discouraged to note that the top man in the economic section was not a well-known economist but a (French) career civil servant. The World Bank was also in the market for economists as well as the possessors of other useful skills, but the first director of its economics department did not give one the impression that economics, or economists, would be expected to play a dominant role in the functioning of the Bank.

Against these two alternative places of employment, the advantages of the Fund were overwhelming. It was already evident that its task – to put into effect the structure for a better international monetary system agreed at Bretton Woods – exercised a tremendous appeal to young economists the world over. Its first Managing Director (Camille Gutt, of Belgium) had shown himself as an imaginative finance minister in 1944 when, upon liberation of the country, he combined devaluation of the Belgian franc with a strong stabilization policy. The Research Department constituted the heart of the Fund and accounted for the great majority of the professional staff. Its director, Edward M. Bernstein, had come to the US Treasury during the war from a distinguished academic career and had shown himself a master of the most intricate economic and technical aspects of the Fund charter at Bretton Woods. The Fund was thus my obvious choice – but by December 1946 almost all its senior posts had already been filled. Subject to approval by the Managing Director, Bernstein offered me the only division chief place that was still open – head of the Statistics Division – with the promise that this could become the locus for any econometric work in the department. He suggested that I come to Mr Gutt's Christmas eggnog party for the whole staff (which at that time could still be held in his office) to get the word.

At the party I had a pleasant conversation with Mr Gutt, who knew me from the wartime discussions on the Congo franc and from the close Belgian–Dutch cooperation at Bretton Woods. But approval for a position in the Fund turned out to be much more than a formality. Appointment of a division chief required consultation with the Executive Board and, Mr Gutt told me, he felt he could not approach the Board so soon after having submitted a number of earlier appointments. But in a few months, things would be easier. In the meantime, if I wanted to come and work in the Fund on any subject that interested me, he felt confident he would be able to appoint me later, retroactive to 1 January 1947. It was a curious sort of job offer, but I took the gamble.

It worked out extremely well. In my spare time in Geneva I had constructed a mini-model of the world economy (Polak 1939b). The model was reasonably successful in explaining each country's income as a function of world income and the country's effective exchange rate. I believed that the Fund would need a more elaborate and realistic model of this general nature as background for shaping its views on member-country policies in a world setting. I had a general idea how such a model should be constructed and I welcomed the opportunity to do a few months of concentrated work on it. In the new version, the extreme reliance on the reduced form would be abandoned by introducing at least three behaviour equations for each of the 25 countries covered. Abstracting from special factors recognized in individual equations, the structure of the new model was as follows: world exports determine the exports of country i; exports of i determine its income via a 'marginal propensity to spend'; income determines imports, and world exports equal the sum of all countries' imports.[5] By the time my appointment came through – with retroactive pay, as promised – the construction of the model was well in hand. But with my new job, I found I had less time available for research work; it took about two more years before a full draft of the paper was circulated in the Fund, and another four years before the Chicago University Press published the study as a book (Polak 1953). As far as I can recall, the idea of the Fund publishing a book of this nature did not occur to anyone at the time. Over time, modelling of the world economy became the work of at least a division of the Research Department, with the product incorporated in the World Economic Outlook and in the successive versions of MINIMOD and MULTIMOD.

My employment on the staff of the Fund lasted exactly one-third of a century, from January 1947 to the end of April 1980. In 1958, I succeeded Bernstein as Director of Research and in 1966 I was also appointed as The Economic Counsellor. After my retirement from the staff, the Netherlands authorities asked me to become a Director on the Executive Board of the Fund, to succeed Onno Ruding, effective 1 January 1981. I accepted that

---

[5] In the same year that this model was published, and with some last-minute mutual foreknowledge, Neisser and Modigliani (1953) published a far more extensive and refined study, but along the same statistical lines, explaining the imports and exports of a number of countries and groups of countries. The main difference in principle between their study and mine was that they did not close the circuit by linking each country's imports (via its income) to its exports, rejecting as 'an unacceptable oversimplification' the idea of considering at least the endogenous component of investment as a function of income. Consequently, they deprived themselves of the chance to produce an integrated world system.

offer and, for a period of nearly six years, represented on the board a 'constituency' of five member countries: the Netherlands, Yugoslavia, Romania, Israel and Cyprus.

During my long association with the Fund (which in some sense continues to this day thanks to an office I occupy in the Fund building), I performed a wide variety of interconnected functions: research, the direction of research, administration and, increasingly over time, policy work. I may mention here briefly two major policy areas that took a large part of my time. First, the development of the Fund's financial policies, which included periodic quota exercises; tranche policies and conditionality; the negotiation and activation of the General Arrangements to Borrow; the design and application of the Compensatory Financing Facility in favour of countries suffering export shortfalls, and of the Oil Facility introduced to mitigate the effects of the 1973 oil shock; the 1976–80 gold sales – to mention only some of the most prominent issues related to the Fund as a financial institution. And, second, relations with individual member countries, of which the Article VIII consultations with the United States and the negotiation of a stand-by arrangement with the United Kingdom in 1965 were probably the most interesting and demanding.

Four other major policy areas deserve a more detailed discussion, mainly because they involved a considerable application of economics. These areas are: exchange rates, the monetary approach to the balance of payments, international liquidity and the international monetary system. By way of background of my work in these four areas, I shall first try to describe the unique place that economic research occupied, and to some extent still occupies, in the Fund.

1.5   RESEARCH IN THE FUND

The first decade of the Fund represented in some respects a let-down from the high hopes held at Bretton Woods. The institution spent an inordinate amount of time on legal issues, such as the definition of multiple rates or whether members could sell gold at premium prices. Convertibility – after a disastrous try by the UK in 1947 – remained limited to the currencies of North and Central America. Even after the fundamental issues of the conditionality and the temporary nature of the use of Fund resources had been settled by 1952, transactions remained limited to a few a year. Indeed, the Fund had so little business that the interest income on its outstanding loans proved insufficient to cover its modest administrative budget. During the period of the Marshall Plan (1948–52) the Fund ceased lending to the countries of Western Europe; in fact, throughout the 1950s it was primarily the Governing Board of the European Payments Union, rather than the Executive Board of the Fund, that exercised surveillance over the financial policies of these countries.

These discouraging developments led to the resignation of a number of staff members in the Research Department, including some of Bernstein's close associates. But on the whole, staff members who had a strong interest in economics stayed and additional ones joined them, thus giving the department the critical mass necessary both to attract successive classes of graduates in the profession and to provide an in-house capacity for critical appraisal of ideas developed by members of its staff. Indeed, the mutual exchange of ideas among economists was so little constrained as to leave no clear record of who thought up what and when. One example of this is cited below in the context of the monetary approach to the balance of payments; Bernstein (1991) gives another, related to the absorption theory.

The professional challenges and opportunities that the economists in the Research Department faced were indeed exceptional. The early postwar years posed again, often in a new light, many of the problems that had occupied the profession in the interwar period. There was the dominant US economy whose productivity threatened (some feared) to create a permanent dollar shortage, perhaps intensified every few years by sharp cyclical downturns. The Bretton Woods exchange-rate regime was in need of definition and testing, starting with the criteria for acceptance of initial par values. In connection with later changes of par values, it would be necessary to make the concept of 'fundamental disequilibrium' operational. The roles of domestic fiscal and monetary policies required clarification. All the questions of international liquidity with which the League of Nations had struggled throughout the interwar period still remained unanswered: the supply of gold; the role of reserve currencies (aggravated by the growth of sterling balances); the control of capital movements. What contribution could the financial resources of the Fund make to these problems? And, most generally, what were the features of the international monetary system that the Fund should seek to encourage, and what would be the role of the Fund itself in that system?

The Fund's work with individual countries also opened up a wide range of challenging problems. The young economists who joined the staff at that time were of course interested in 'inflation', but for them that term meant the kind of inflation then experienced by the US or UK. Their work in the Fund confronted them with inflations of a far more virulent type, such as those that raged in Chile or China. It has been said that the place for a young physician to get quick experience with the world's most dreaded diseases is a hospital in a major harbour city. The wards of the Fund were similarly filled with pathological cases – and at that time, before the wide dissemination of data and the ready availability of travel funds, few economists outside the international organizations had an opportunity to study them.

It helped that, in the face of these conditions crying out for innovative economic work, the Fund in general and the Research Department in particular were definitely research friendly. The decision to start a scientific publication – *IMF Staff Papers*, first issue in February 1950 – reflected this attitude and in turn worked as a magnet to attract promising economists to the Fund.[6] The initiative for this journal had, incidentally, come from outside the Fund. When Bernstein wrote his umpteenth letter to Professor Dennis Robertson in Cambridge University asking his opinion on yet another of his students that the Fund considered hiring, Robertson answered with two letters. One contained warm support for the applicant (T.C. Chang who, after a brief career in the Fund[7] and many years on the staff of the UN, rejoined the Fund as the first Executive Director for the People's Republic of China); the other warned Bernstein against enticing too many of the current generation of bright economists to sink into, what he called, 'an anonymous international bureaucracy'. Against this risk he recommended that the Fund start a journal in which staff could publish non-confidential work under their own names.

Staff members were encouraged not only to publish, but also to teach. I took advantage of this possibility when I responded enthusiastically to an invitation from Fritz Machlup to give a graduate seminar on international economics at The Johns Hopkins University in Baltimore (1949–50). During the next five years I taught evening classes at George Washington University. That was before classrooms were air conditioned, and during the hot evening hours of summer school, the hardest task of the teacher often seemed to be keeping students from dozing off. The solution I found was to restrict my summer teaching to a small seminar; with many of the student Bank or Fund staff members, I conducted the seminar sessions in my air-conditioned office in the Fund. (It was also the time before Fund and Bank buildings were protected by security passes.)

It would not be inaccurate to say that in these early days of the Research Department – perhaps during its first two decades – a considerable amount of its research could be described as being at the cutting edge of international economics. That became very obvious to us whenever we invited some

---

[6] I recall asking a young Dutch economist (Wim Duisenberg, now the President of the European Central Bank), how he had made up his mind to apply to the Fund rather than the World Bank for his first job after graduation. His answer: 'the Fund has *Staff Papers*'.

[7] Chang was my main collaborator on the world model on Polak (1953). He himself had anticipated many of the ideas that entered into that model in a series of journal papers in the 1940s and in a book published in 1951 (Chang 1951) and deservedly republished in 1985.

world-famous university professor to lecture to our staff seminar. On these occasions, we found ourselves often surprised (indeed, sometimes shocked) to find that what the great professor offered as the new findings of academe had been common knowledge among us for years. In subsequent decades, the quality of research in the Fund has been maintained and its scope extended. But with the enormous growth of economic and financial research in the universities and research institutes, the Fund no longer commands that special comparative advantage of the earlier period.

1.6   EXCHANGE RATES

Over its entire history, the IMF has been at the very centre of thought and action – research and policy making – about exchange rates. I have given a full account of these activities in the fifty-years commemorative issue of *IMF Staff Papers* (Polak 1995).[8] Here I shall only mention the particular activities with respect to exchange rates for which I was most directly responsible.

One of the issues concerning exchange rates that preoccupied us in the early years was whether, even if the elasticities met the Marshall-Lerner conditions, currency devaluation could be relied upon to correct a payments imbalance. In Chang and Polak (1950) we investigated empirically the first effect of exchange rate changes: to what extent, and depending on what circumstances, were these changes effective, in lowering the price level, in foreign currency, of the devaluing country? Two other papers addressed the problem of systemic stability that arise if countries successively respond to imbalances in their payments by exchange rate changes that produce new imbalances for other countries (Polak 1947b; Polak and Liu 1954). The second of these papers was prepared jointly with T-C Liu in a rather unusual assignment of tasks: I asked the questions and Liu mastered the mathematics that could provide the answers. Finally, and explicitly provoked by the Fund's consideration of Mexico's abandonment of its par value in 1948 in a setting of excessive demand, Polak (1948) adumbrates the absorption theory of the balance of payments by focusing on the proposition that 'if devaluation is to cure a payments deficit, it must either increase production with consumption and investment constant, or decrease consumption and investment with output constant, or achieve some combination of the two'.[9]

Returning from my first home leave in September 1949, I just missed out on the excitement (eight Board meetings in three days) caused by the

---

[8] Some additional aspects are covered in another paper in the same issue (Blejer *et al.* 1995).

[9] The citation is from Polak (1952). Polak (1948) was not published until 1991.

devaluation of sterling, quickly followed by that of many other currencies, at the time of the Fund's Annual Meeting. Although these devaluations did not come as a surprise – the Fund's 1948 Annual Report had plainly suggested the emerging need for them a year earlier – I was still chagrined to learn about the actual fact from 'the market': the sudden closing of the perfume shop on the Ile de France because it did not know what dollar prices to charge. I tried to make up for what I had missed by starting a rather ambitious programme of studies to measure the effects of these devaluations, of which Polak (1951) was the major product.

Once it became evident that the 1949 devaluations had established, at least for the time being, a viable system of exchange rates among the industrial countries, the interest in exchange rate questions temporarily declined. By the mid-1960s, however, the presumption of a viable set of rates had worn thin, but the main industrial countries, under US leadership, sought to minimize the use of, and the reference to, parity changes. In the first report by the Deputies of the G-10, then chaired by Robert Roosa, exchange rate changes were kept out of a list of six policy instruments available to bring about balance of payments adjustment, receiving only a backhanded mention by way of a reference to 'the IMF obligation to maintain stable exchange parities which are subject to change only in cases of fundamental disequilibrium' (Group of Ten 1964, para. 6).

My colleagues and I in the Research Department did not believe, however, that exchange rate questions could in this manner be abolished by fiat, and we became involved in highly confidential calculations about individual currencies and almost equally sensitive explorations concerning the par value system. The staff made extensive calculations in anticipation of the devaluation of sterling in 1967, which permitted that operation to proceed 'unusually smoothly', as noted by De Vries (1985). It made similar calculations in connection with a devaluation of the French franc that was semi-publicly debated at the infamous November 1968 Bonn conference but which did not take place until August 1969; and then again in preparation of a possible new set of parities, when it had become clear, in the summer of 1971, that the US was no longer in a position to continue to defend the parity of the dollar; this exercise continued until the Smithsonian agreement of December 1971. This was a period not only of considerable excitement – including, as I learnt much later, the possibility (but no more than that) of being kissed by Paul Volcker[10] – but primarily of professional satisfaction:

---

[10] The occasion was a Paris meeting of the G-10 deputies in which 'a number of Europeans turn[ed] to the IMF representative ... in effect asking him to tell me the American calculations were way off base. He replied that he did not know that [an improvement in the current account of] $13 billion was required, but the IMF's calculations suggested that the number was a big one. I could have kissed him' (Volcker and Gyohten 1992, pp. 81–2).

we believed that we had developed a tolerably satisfactory method to calculate equilibrium exchange rates.[11] We have had to become a good deal more modest since, primarily because the dramatic increase in capital mobility over the last twenty years has made it much more difficult to come up with a plausible value for one of the crucial components of such calculations – 'normal capital movements'.[12]

The currency crises of the late 1960s also led to an extensive reappraisal in the Fund of the systemic properties of the par value regime. The reappraisal included the lengthy 'informal' discussions that the Executive Board held during 1969 on improving the exchange rate mechanism, the drafting of the Directors' 1970 report, *The role of exchange rates in the adjustment of international payments*, and, after August 1971, all the work on the reform of the system which lasted through most of the 1970s.

1.7 THE MONETARY APPROACH TO THE BALANCE OF PAYMENTS

Over the past forty years, the monetary approach to the balance of payments has been an important research topic in the Fund (Polak 1998). Perhaps even more important, it has become, and remained, a standard element of the Fund's financial relations with its members, forming the basis for its financial programming, which in turn underlies the administration of its conditionality. Some exploration of its origins may therefore be of interest.

In combining income flows and money stocks in one model, my initial paper on this subject (Polak 1957b), had both Keynesian and monetary roots. The Keynesian antecedents of the 'monetary approach' obviously go back, via the discussion on the foreign trade multiplier (Polak 1947a), to my doctoral dissertation (Polak 1937). But the monetary antecedents also go back to the 1930s. In a comment on Kahn's (1931) multiplier paper, John Maurice Clark (1935, pp. 34–7) suggested that the effects of a public works

---

[11] The Fund's history characterizes the Research Department's feelings at its 'triumph' of the realignment at the Smithsonian as 'euphoric' (De Vries 1985, vol. I, p. 126). Perhaps so, but the appraisal of the methodology that I gave only a few weeks after the Smithsonian (and before its flaws had become evident) does not exactly exude euphoria. After an enumeration of weaknesses of the approach used in arriving at the Smithsonian rates, it concludes by noting that this approach 'can at this stage yield at best only rather vaguely defined equilibrium zones' (Polak 1972).

[12] Frenkel *et al.* (1991, p. 18) have correctly pointed out that the difficulty of defining sustainable capital flows also qualifies the validity of attempts, which I have tended to favour, to estimate the need for payments adjustment on a decentralized, country-by-country basis.

policy might also be derived by an alternative approach, via the volume of money and the income velocity of circulation. While the Kahn method leads to a geometrically declining series of effects, Clark postulates that the results of the monetary approach would continue as a straight line into infinity. He does not see a contradiction in this, but rather stresses the need to study the factors that may, at every step of the continuing process, affect the validity of the assumptions of each approach.

The literature of the 1930s had thus left unresolved the issue of how to merge these two theoretical strands, to which I had wanted to return at some point. The actual time to do this – the early part of the 1950s – was very much determined by the problems and the opportunities that I encountered in the IMF. The problems concerned the apparent inability of many in the staff to integrate questions of demand management, money and the balance of payments, and more particularly to establish clear numerical relations between financial measures that the Fund encouraged and the balance of payments objectives that countries were intended to achieve. The opportunities were provided by the monetary statistics that, from the very start, the Fund had been collecting and had encouraged member countries to compile. From its first printed issue in 1948, *International Financial Statistics* published these data in the form of a 'monetary survey', showing foreign and domestic assets of the consolidated banking system as the main counterpart to the money supply. This presentation was in line with the work by Robert Triffin (who was one of the early staff members of the Research Department) on 'money of foreign and domestic origin'. It helped direct attention to the definitional linkages between the balance of payments and the monetary survey. But it failed to bring out the endogenous character of the money supply by overlooking the endogenous explanation of imports. This constitutes the missing link between the two approaches discussed by Clark. In an open economy, the presence of an import leak (a leak of both income and of money) means that a given injection of money will produce a finite, not an infinite, income effect.

It took a long gestation period for these intellectual and operational strands to converge into a presentable paper. The first results of the model found their way into a paper that Bernstein presented to the Executive Board of the Fund in April 1950. That paper addressed the question of how major coffee exporters could avoid dissipating their increased foreign exchange receipts resulting from the large rise in the coffee price in 1949–50. The paper included an analysis (in non-mathematical and qualitative terms) of the equilibrium effects of a increase in exports and found that it would lead to a temporary trade surplus and a finite increase in reserves that would cease after cash balances had been saved in the amount required to finance the higher level of money income (IMF 1950). More than forty years later,

Bernstein recalls (which I had forgotten) that that part of his presentation had been based on a series of equations connecting the balance of payments and the money supply that I had provided him with at the time (Bernstein 1991, p. 62).

It proved difficult, however, to complete the model in a dynamic form and to distinguish clearly the postulated causal mechanism from the ever-present identities of the monetary survey. During this period I also pursued a number of side roads (Polak and White 1955; Polak 1957a). An essential assumption of the former paper was that the velocity of circulation was not constant but depended on the rate of interest. Indeed, this paper contains rather elaborate attempts to measure both the elasticity of demand and the elasticity of supply for money in the US. I had previously attempted to measure these elasticities (Tinbergen 1939, pp. 80–8) and assumed that, to get more up-to-date coefficients, I would simply have to get myself invited for lunch by the research people at the Federal Reserve Board (at that time, the Federal Reserve anyway had the best cafeteria in town). But they proved flabbergasted by the request and Bill White, my co-author, and I had to do the work of estimating the coefficients ourselves.

The development of the monetary approach benefited greatly from contributions by many colleagues in the Research Department. Inspiration also came from outside the Fund. I followed closely, through frequent discussions and a rather extensive correspondence, the (in many respects parallel) monetary analysis that Dr M.W. Holtrop, the President of the Netherlands Bank, had developed independently since 1951 (Holtrop 1957a; b). I learned much from some central bankers, such as Don Rodrigo Gomez of the Bank of Mexico, who had absorbed the monetary approach to the balance of payments, not as some interesting theoretical construct, but as the painfully obvious lesson of central banking in countries with a simple financial structure (Gomez 1964, p. 31). I also asked my colleagues in the area departments for opportunities to join staff missions to countries where the model might usefully be put to a practical test; this led to instructive trips to Colombia, Nicaragua and Iceland in the mid-1950s.

1.8 INTERNATIONAL LIQUIDITY

Questions concerning the adequacy of international liquidity occupied the staff of the Research Department from the early years of the Fund, but the greatest activity on this subject occurred between 1963, when the Deputies of the Group of Ten were first instructed to study this problem, and the 1969 Annual Meeting when the Governors voted for the first allocation of SDRs

(Special Drawing Rights). What went on during this six-year period was as interesting for its intellectual as for its political content.

Conceptually, there were no precedents for a new money, issued by an international organization, that would have both sufficient inherent value to be willingly held by central banks and the ensured usability necessary to serve as a means of payment among them. The difficulties in the design of such a money were in part technical, in part psychological and, as it became increasingly clear, in large measure political. The technical problems, such as the measurement of the need for reserves, keys for the distribution of newly created reserves, maintenance of value, backing, and designation, were mostly solved by a small group of Fund economists (Marcus Fleming, Rudolph Rhomberg and myself) and lawyers (Joseph Gold and George Nicoletopoulos). At the level of psychology, the design had to contend with the natural allergy of high officials of central banks and treasuries to an activity that amounted to the creation of money *ex nihilo*. Much effort thus had to be invested in the design of various safeguards to ensure that the new system could not become an engine of inflation.

But beyond these intellectual and psychological difficulties, the process that finally culminated in the design of the SDR was held up time and again by a series of political roadblocks. In the beginning, the US and the UK were concerned about the competition that a new international reserve asset would represent to the two main reserve currencies. France continued to push for an enhanced role for gold and for an end to the 'exorbitant privilege', as General de Gaulle called it, enjoyed by the reserve centres. Collectively, the Group of Ten tried for a long time to set themselves apart from the other members of the IMF by insisting that the benefits of the newly created reserves should accrue only to themselves ('liquidity creation of the Ten, by the Ten, for the Ten', as the Fund's Managing Director, Pierre-Paul Schweitzer, characterized it), with at best a separate window dispensing comparable amounts of credit to the rest of the Fund membership. They did not abandon that position until stung by a warning that 'separate but equal' treatment would prove unacceptable in the Fund, just as the US Supreme Court had found it unconstitutional with respect to American education a few years earlier. I cited that expression at a Washington meeting of the G-10 deputies, spurred on (I recall) by the locale of the meeting, the building of the Federal Reserve Board on the Washington avenue named after the constitution. To my disappointment, nobody at the meeting seemed moved by the challenge. There was a stronger reaction when I reported about the meeting in the same terms to the Executive Board of the Fund. And when Mr. Schweitzer used the same expression in a public speech a few days later, the chairman of the deputies, Otmar Emminger, called a press conference in the Bundesbank to deny any discriminatory intentions on the part of the deputies.

Despite (or perhaps because of) the sometimes frantic activity that the liquidity project provoked, including frequent commuting between Washington and Paris, all my papers on this topic except the first one were written after 1970. By that time, and thanks in part to a major conference on the subject held in the Fund,[13] we had acquired a better understanding of the character of the new reserve asset and were anxious to disseminate these new insights (Polak 1970; 1971), as well as their implications for the pre-existing credit activities of the Fund (Polak 1979).

The laborious labours of the 1960s to design the SDR scheme had been motivated by fear of a developing general shortage of international liquidity. Although a general shortage of reserves ceased to be a problem since the early 1970s, it was a real problem in the 1960s and governments deserve credit for seeking a solution to it, although it may fairly be said that they might, at the same time, have tried harder to come to grips with the even more difficult political problems of balance of payments adjustment. Surely, governments should not be blamed for not anticipating the events that made the liquidity problem disappear so soon after a solution to it had been found, agreed and on a modest scale implemented. It should be recalled that in the late 1960s capital markets were not yet free or deep enough to enable governments to meet their reserve needs by borrowing. A few small countries could, but larger countries could not. It took the petro-dollar deposits of the 1970s, themselves the after-effects of the first oil shock, to get the commercial banks into the sovereign lending business on a massive scale; it was that fundamental change in the international monetary system which removed most of the case for regular SDR allocations. The impasse onto which this systemic change plunged the SDR is analysed in Polak (1988).

1.9   THE INTERNATIONAL MONETARY SYSTEM

The most general questions that arose during my stay in the Fund were those relating to the international monetary system and the role of the Fund within that system. I was first invited to speak on this broad subject at the 1961 meeting of the Netherlands Economic Society (Vereniging voor de Staathuishoudkunde; Polak 1962). The questions I was asked to address ranged over the compatibility of national policy targets, the respective roles of consultative procedures and 'rules', and the tasks in this connection of

---

[13] See IMF (1970). One of the crucial aspects of the SDR that was clarified at this conference (which took place after the first decision to allocate SDRs had been taken!) was the role of the rate of interest on the SDR in determining its character – a subject that had been largely overlooked until then.

international organizations such as the OECD and the IMF. One of the points I stressed was the limited validity in practice of the traditional distinction, introduced by Tinbergen, between targets and instruments, as governments find that the use of some of the latter (exchange rates, but also interest rates) may entail considerable costs. On some issues – at the time, exchange rates – coordination through an international institution is found to be practicable; on others, such as full employment, coordination had already proved essentially futile, in spite of strong commitments under the UN Charter. I further pursued a number of these and related questions on later occasions where I developed a certain preference for 'rules' over 'coordination' (Polak 1981; 1991a). While in pure theory coordination can, admittedly, yield on each occasion a result that is superior to that produced by a rule, the practical outcome of a system without rules may be that the parties often fail to agree on any solution; by contrast, a rule-based regime makes it likely (in view of the recognized cost attached to breaking the rule) that something at least reasonably appropriate will be done in response to a particular situation.

After the United States closed the gold window on 15 August 1971 interest in the system changed from analysis to reform. Six weeks later, at the 1971 Annual Meeting of the Fund, the Board of Governors asked the Executive Directors to submit a report on 'the measures ... necessary or desirable for the improvement or reform of the international monetary system'. The scope of the report was defined broadly, including reserve currencies, gold, SDRs, convertibility, exchange rates and destabilizing capital movements. After wrestling with these subjects for a few months, the Board asked 'the staff' to come up with an 'artist's sketch' of the main features of a reformed system. Given the controversial nature of virtually every aspect of reform, it would have been hopeless to attempt to prepare an agreed staff paper that still had any substantive content. Accordingly, I decided, drawing heavily on ideas worked on by others in the Research Department, to write an essentially personal paper, which I entitled 'Reform of the international monetary system: a sketch of its scope and contents' (Polak 1972). Starting from this sketch, the Executive Directors agreed in August 1972 on a report to the Board of Governors (IMF 1972).

After my retirement from the Fund staff, I discussed on a number of occasions in the last fifteen years this changing role of the IMF in the international monetary system. At a conference at Bretton Woods organized as a 'Forty Years After' celebration, I presented a paper that focused among other matters on the Fund's intrinsic problem of finding the right balance between adjustment and financing (Polak 1984). Over the years, the attitude of the institution with respect to this problem has shifted, and this shift has been accompanied by a gradual change in the role played by the conditionality attached to the use of Fund credit (Polak 1991b). In Polak

(1989) I paid particular attention to the effects that developments in the world economy, in particular the great increase in international capital movements and the spread of floating exchange rates, have had on the Fund. These effects include the fact that nowadays only the developing countries and the transition economies require the Fund's credit, which in turn has limited the effectiveness of its surveillance over the industrial countries.

SELECTED WORKS

(1937) 'Publieke werken als vorm van conjunctuurpolitiek' ['Public works as a form of business cycle policy'], Ph.D. dissertation, The Hague: Nijhoff.

(1939a) 'Fluctuations in United States consumption, 1919–1932', *Review of Economic Statistics*, 21 (1), pp. 1–12.*

(1939b) 'International propagation of business cycles', *Review of Economic Studies*, 6 (2), pp. 79–99.*

(1943a) 'Balance of payments problems of countries reconstructing with the help of foreign loans', *Quarterly Journal of Economics*, 57 (2), pp. 208–40.* Rep. and trans. in J.J. Polak (1948) 'La balanza de pagos y las inversiones financiadas can préstamos exteriores', *El Trimestre Economico*, 15 (3/4), pp. 158–69.

(1943b) 'European exchange depreciation in the early twenties', *Econometrica*, 11 (2), pp. 151–62.*

(1943c) *The national income of the Netherlands Indies, 1921–1939.* New York: Netherlands and Netherlands Indies Council of the Institute of Pacific Relations, mimeo. Rep. in P. Creutzberg (ed.) (1979) *Changing economy in Indonesia.* Vol. 5: *National income.* The Hague: Nijhoff.

(1946) *Economic recovery in the countries assisted by UNRRA.* Washington, DC: United Nations Relief and Rehabilitation Administration.

(1947a) 'The foreign trade multiplier', *American Economic Review*, 37 (5), pp. 889–97.*

(1947b) 'Exchange depreciation and international monetary stability', *Review of Economic Statistics*, 29 (3), pp. 173–82.*

(1947) (with G. Haberler) 'A restatement', *American Economic Review*, 37 (5), pp. 906–7.*

(1948) 'Depreciation to meet a situation of overinvestment', unpublished paper. Rep. in J.A. Frenkel and M. Goldstein (eds) (1991) **q.v.**, pp. 46–57.*

(1950) (with T.C. Chang) 'Effect of exchange depreciation on a country's export price level', *IMF Staff Papers*, 1 (1), pp. 49–70.*

(1951) 'Contribution of the September 1949 devaluations to the solution of Europe's dollar problem', *IMF Staff Papers*, 2 (1), pp. 1–32.*

(1952) 'International trade theory: discussion', *American Economic Review*, 42 (2, Papers & Proceedings), pp. 179–81.

(1953) *An international economic system.* Chicago: University of Chicago Press.

(1954) (with T-C Liu) 'Stability of the exchange rate mechanism in a multi-country system', *Econometrica*, 22 (3), pp. 360–89.*

(1955) (with W.H. White) 'The effects of income expansion on the quantity of money', *IMF Staff Papers*, 4 (3), pp. 398–433.*

(1957a) 'The capacity of the banking system to finance development', *Memoria*, Reunión de Técnicos de los Bancos Centrales del Continente Americano, Fifth (Bogotà), 2, pp. 171–81.*

(1957b) 'Monetary analysis of income formation and payments problems', *IMF Staff Papers*, 6 (1), pp. 1–50.*

(1962) 'International coordination of economic policy', *IMF Staff Papers*, 9 (2), pp. 149–79.*

(1970) 'Money: national and international', in OECD (1970) *Essays in honour of Thorkil Kristensen*. Paris: OECD, pp. 171–86. Rep. in IMF (1970) **q.v.**, pp. 510–20.*

(1971) *Some reflections on the nature of Special Drawing Rights*. IMF pamphlet series no. 16. Washington, DC: IMF.

(1972) 'Reform of the international monetary system: a sketch of its scope and content', paper submitted to the Executive Board of the IMF, 7 March. Printed in M.G. De Vries (1985) **q.v.**, vol. III, pp. 3–15.*

(1979) *Thoughts on an International Monetary Fund based fully on the SDR*. IMF pamphlet series no. 28. Washington, DC: IMF, pp. 1–26.*

(1981) 'Preface', in Group of Thirty (1981) *Coordination of national economic policies*. Occasional paper no. 7. New York: Group of Thirty, pp. 1–21.*

(1984) 'The role of the Fund', in Federal Reserve Bank of Boston (1984) *The international monetary system: forty years after Bretton Woods*. Boston: Federal Reserve Bank of Boston, pp. 245–66.*

(1988) 'The impasse concerning the role of the SDR', in W. Eizenga, E.F. Limburg and J.J. Polak (eds) (1988) *The quest for national and global economic stability*. Dordrecht: Kluwer, pp. 175–89.*

(1989) 'Strengthening the role of the IMF in the international monetary system', in C. Gwin and R.E. Feinberg (eds) (1989) *The International Monetary Fund in a multipolar world: pulling together*. New Brunswick, NJ: Transaction Books, pp. 45–68.*

(1991a) 'International policy coordination and the functioning of the international monetary system: a search for realism', in H.J. Blommestein (ed.) (1991) *The reality of international economic policy coordination*. Amsterdam: North Holland, pp. 151–71.*

(1991b) *The changing nature of IMF conditionality*. Essays in international finance no. 184. Princeton, NJ: Princeton University Press.

(1994a) *Economic theory and financial policy: selected essays*, 2 vols. Aldershot: Edward Elgar.

(1994b) 'Introduction', in J.J. Polak (1994a) **q.v.**, pp. xiii–xxx.

(1994c) 'Financial relations between the Netherlands and Belgium', in A. Bakker *et al.* (eds) (1994) *Monetary stability through international cooperation: essays in honour of André Szász*. Dordrecht: Kluwer, pp. 183–200.

(1995) 'Fifty years of exchange rate research and policy at the International Monetary Fund', *IMF Staff Papers*, 42 (4), pp. 734–61.

(1998) 'The IMF model at forty', *Journal of Economic Modeling*, 15 (Special Issue, Empirical models and policy-making), pp. 395–410.

BIBLIOGRAPHY

Bernstein, E.M. (1991) 'The early years of the International Monetary Fund', in J.A. Frenkel and M. Goldstein (eds) (1991) **q.v.**, pp. 58–63.

Blejer, M.I., Khan, M.S. and Masson, P.R. (1995) 'Early contributions of *Staff Papers* to international economics', *IMF Staff Papers*, 42 (4), pp. 707–33.

Chang, T.C. (1951) *Cyclical movements in the balance of payments.* Cambridge: Cambridge University Press.

Clark, J.M. (1935) *Economics of planning public works.* Washington, DC: National Planning Board, Federal Emergency Administration of Public Works.

De Vries, M.G. (1985) *The International Monetary Fund, 1972–1978.* Washington, DC: IMF.

Frenkel, J.A. and Goldstein, M. (eds) (1991) *International financial policy: essays in honor of Jacques J. Polak.* Washington, DC: IMF.

Frenkel, J.A., Goldstein, M. and Khan, M.S. (1991) 'Major themes in the writings of Jacques J. Polak', in J.A. Frenkel and M. Goldstein (eds) (1991) **q.v.**, pp. 3–37.

Gomez, R. (1964) 'Economic growth and monetary stability', Washington, D.C., The Per Jacobsson Foundation.

Group of Ten (1964) *Ministerial Statement of the Group of Ten*, Annex prepared by Deputies, Paris, August.

Haberler, G. (1947) 'Comment', *American Economic Review*, 37 (5), pp. 898–906.

Holtrop, M.W. (1957a) 'Method of monetary analysis used by the Netherlands Bank', *IMF Staff Papers*, 5 (3), pp. 303–16.

Holtrop, M.W. (1957b) 'Ueber die Bedeutung Monetaerer Erscheinungen', *Weltwirtschaftliches Archiv*, 79 (2), pp. 242–66.

IMF (1950) 'The price of coffee and monetary policy', Staff Memorandum no. 464, mimeo, 24 April; published in Spanish as E.M. Bernstein (1950) 'El precio del cafe y la politica monetariar, *El Trimestre Economico*, 17 (3), pp. 416–38.

IMF (1970) *International reserves: needs and availability.* Washington, DC: IMF.

IMF (1972) *Reform of the international monetary system.* Washington, DC: IMF.

Kahn, R.F. (1931) 'The relation of home investment to unemployment', *Economic Journal*, 41 (2), pp. 173–98.

Neisser, H. and Modigliani, F. (1953) *National income and international trade: a quantitative analysis.* Urbana: Studies of the Institute of World Affairs.

Nurkse, R. (1944) *International currency experience: lessons of the interwar period.* Geneva: League of Nations.

Tinbergen, J. (1939) *Business cycles in the United States of America, 1919–1932,* Geneva: League of Nations.

Volcker, P.A. and Gyohten, T. (1992) *Changing fortunes.* New York: Times Books.

2. Robert Dorfman (b. 1916)[1]

2.1 ONTOGENY OF AN ECONOMIST

My central concern during most of my career has been social decisions: how to reach them and how to judge them. This may seem to be a strange preoccupation for an economist until you pause to consider that social decision-making and welfare economics have such extensive overlaps that they cannot be disentangled. That central concern, though, does not imply that social decisions have been the explicit topic of most of my research and writing. On the contrary. Social decision-making is much too broad and inclusive a topic to be tackled bluntly and in its entirety. Instead, I have approached it piecemeal and somewhat deviously. But social deciding, by which I mean taking decisions that affect two or more people and take all their interests into account, has been lurking in the background and motivating nearly all my work. Obviously this circuitous approach to my central topic needs some explaining, so I shall provide it, beginning at the beginning.

---

[1] Dorfman (1997b), as revised by the editors. I have one volume of selected essays in the series (Dorfman 1997a).

2.2 EDUCATION AND EARLY CAREER, 1933–50

When I was an undergraduate in Columbia University in the 1930s, my field of concentration was mathematical statistics under the tutelage of Harold Hotelling, the leading theoretical statistician in the country at that time. When I graduated, in the midst of the Great Depression, there were practically no jobs for recent graduates with so little training, so I stayed on at Columbia for an MA degree in economics. (In those ancient days, few, if any, American universities offered advanced degrees in statistics; Columbia was not one.)

With this modest credential in my CV, and with Hotelling's help, I tried my hand at a number of statistical jobs that proved unsatisfactory for various reasons. Finally, I answered a 'help wanted' ad. placed by a commercial night school that gave cram courses for people preparing for Federal civil service examinations. They needed someone to teach the material for the Junior Statistician exam. I fitted that description and so, every Wednesday night for the following two months, I expounded the basic facts about means, medians, bar charts, and so on to about 50 hopeful students. I don't know how the students made out, but when the course was over I felt highly prepared for the examination, so why shouldn't I take it myself? I did, and I earned the second highest score in New York State. About a month later, I was offered a position in the Bureau of Labor Statistics (BLS) in Washington. The salary, though not munificent, was about 50 per cent higher than my current earnings at the time. I accepted, and worked at the BLS for about two years, receiving several promotions while there.

Meanwhile, the Depression had ended and the United States was moving rapidly towards a wartime footing. In particular the Office of Price Administration (OPA) had been established, was growing rapidly, and needed economic statisticians. They offered me an impressive-sounding job as a section chief in the Research Division. I accepted, and worked there for the next two years. While working for the OPA, I wrote a short note on a subject entirely unrelated to price administration. It was accepted by the *Annals of Mathematical Statistics*, and was fairly influential (Dorfman 1943).

The summer of 1943 found me still at the OPA, concerned with repressing retail price inflation. World War II was being waged in full violence on three continents. I was eager to find a role more directly related to the fighting, but was strongly averse to trusting my fate to the punch-card machines that, in those days, assigned recruits to the wide variety of tasks that constitute modern warfare. (My brother, for example, fought his war as the mess sergeant in an infantry officers' mess.) I felt that I could make war most effectively at a task that utilized my training and experience in statistics. Just then the new field of operations research, recently invented by the Royal Air

Force, was being introduced in the American armed forces. I heard of it, applied, was accepted, and was shipped off, after two or three weeks of preparation, to be an operations analyst with the Thirteenth Air Force in the South Pacific. My speciality was bombing tactics, though I had never actually seen a bomb or been aboard a military aircraft of any kind.

I remained in the South Pacific for a bit more than a year, analysing and comparing the results of a variety of bombing tactics used in that theatre. I was then transferred to Air Force Headquarters in the Pentagon. This seemingly routine move changed the direction of my career. In the Pentagon, I met George Dantzig, a young statistician who was also working in Air Force Headquarters. Though his work was entirely unrelated to mine, we had many interests in common and became friendly.

When the atomic bombs were dropped on Hiroshima and Nagasaki, bringing World War II to an abrupt end, I was still in the Pentagon. I had no connection with the Manhattan District project or any of its work. Nevertheless, I was asked to participate in planning and conducting the mammoth experiment of exploding two atomic bombs in Bikini Atoll to observe and measure their effects under controlled conditions. After the experiment it was time for me to reconvert to a less warlike occupation.

To this end, I applied for admission to the Ph.D. programme in economics in the University of California at Berkeley, and was admitted. I chose economics because my work in the BLS and OPA gave me a head start in that field, and because economics seemed to embrace the critical social problems then confronting the country and the world. I chose Berkeley because I had visited San Francisco several times during the war and was charmed, and because I had been greatly impressed by several people I had met, mostly statisticians, connected with that campus. Admittedly, these were not good reasons for choosing a lifetime career, but it worked out well enough.

I spent two years in Berkeley studying economics, then was lured back to the Air Force by the prospect of earning a living wage. When I returned, I found my old friend Dantzig there, in a state of great excitement and frantic activity. In the interim, he had been engaged in an important and challenging project that bears some description.

Basically, his task was to develop an improved system for planning and budgeting the Air Force's long-run procurement and training programmes. At that time, the amount of paperwork and calculation needed to develop a long-run programme, complete with budgetary implications, for a large military organization was truly daunting. A small army of officers was required to labour with pencils and paper for most of a year to calculate the details of a plan, its implications and its costs. By the time they had constructed a plan in which the numerous details of purchasing, construction, training, and so on were reasonably consistent with each other, the assumptions and data used at the beginning would be out of date.

Dantzig's project was motivated by the thought that the time and manpower required to elaborate a plan could be reduced greatly if the mass of considerations that the staff officers had to take into account could be expressed as a set of equations solvable by punch-card machines. Using punch-card machines for more than routine bookkeeping was novel at the time. The proposed approach to military planning had never been taken before, and many of the experienced staff officers regarded it as impracticable. That is why the job was turned over to a mathematical statistician.

Dantzig struggled with this ill-defined task for more than a year. At first he groped almost blindly, but gradually pieces of a solution fell into place. He built upon Leontief's input-output economic model, which had to be generalized substantially, tried numerous devices for solving the resulting equations, became acquainted with the first electronic computers and saw that they, rather than punch-card machines, were needed to perform the requisite calculations. Finally, in the summer of 1947, the pieces fitted together. In that September he solved the first pitifully small linear programming problem, using a mechanical desk calculator. Later that fall, the 'diet problem', consisting of finding the least expensive combination of 77 foods that met the Bureau of Home Economics' daily requirements for nine nutrients, was solved by his method, again using desk calculators. Since then Dantzig had been subjecting his discovery to a series of increasingly demanding tests. It performed beautifully every time, and he was becoming more and more confident that it could do the job specified by the Air Force. He reported all this to me in a state of high excitement.

By then, I had learned enough economics to appreciate the importance of this discovery, not only for business and economic planning, but for economic theory. In fact, I put it to work almost immediately, and used a mild generalization of Dantzig's findings as a basis for my doctoral dissertation (Dorfman 1950). Along with Tjalling Koopmans and one or two others, I thus became one of the first economists to learn of linear programming and its implications for economics.

I remained in the Pentagon for about a year, during which time Dantzig and I had many excited discussions about linear programming and its potential impact on economics. Then the doctoral dissertation that I had submitted was accepted and I was qualified to be invited back to Berkeley as an assistant professor.

2.3   MATHEMATICAL ECONOMIST

I could not have embarked on the profession of professor of economics at a more propitious time. Graduate study in universities was a boom industry fed by demand accumulated during the war years and accentuated by the GI Bill of Rights. In particular, interest in applying mathematics in the social sciences, especially economics, was at an unprecedented level, possibly because of spectacular wartime successes in applying mathematics outside its traditional fields. And, closest to my personal interests, the hottest areas for applying mathematics in economics were linear programming and its close relative, game theory. I couldn't have planned my debut as a professor of economics better if I had the power to do so. Naturally, my principal responsibility when I joined the Berkeley faculty was to introduce instruction in mathematical methods in economics.

Here, perhaps, is the place to record some of my personal reservations. I did offer instruction in mathematical economics in Berkeley for five years, and then moved with my courses to Harvard. But I was always disturbed by the need to reduce the amount of instruction in the social science side of economics to make way for the mathematics. I remain ambivalent about the costs and benefits of the change, though I don't doubt that it was an inevitable part of the 'mathematization' that our culture has been experiencing since World War II. I shall return later to these worries.

1950 was a wonderful time to embark on a career of university teaching and research, and especially wonderful at the University of California, Berkeley. The Depression and the war were safely behind us. We appeared to be on the way to solving many of the world's most urgent problems. The Marshall Plan was reinvigorating Europe. The Agency for International Development (then called The International Cooperation Administration) was achieving some spectacular results by introducing the 'green revolution' in the so-called 'third world'. Here in the US, the postwar depression that many economists anticipated failed to appear. Instead, the transition from a wartime to a peacetime economy went smoothly and prosperously.

The universities enjoyed a boom during the 1950s and early 1960s, fed largely by the GI Bill of Rights and a variety of Federal research grants. In California, the university acquired a dynamic president in Clark Kerr, who busily set about realizing his vision of a truly state-wide university with university-scale campuses spanning California from Sacramento to San Diego. Everything seemed on its way to becoming bigger and better.

There were, however, some blemishes in this latter-day Eden, just as in the original one. In Washington, there were Rep. Martin Dies, Sen. Joe McCarthy and their epigones, who were threatening everyone who believed in free speech, faculty members and Federal government workers especially. Locally, there was the chronic academic ailment of splits of departments into more-or-less hostile factions. Members of any of these factions were (and, I suspect, are) not only unfriendly towards members of opposing factions, but worse, contemptuous of them on the grounds that they were unfeeling, or ignorant, or both.

The economics department at Berkeley was split into two factions along doctrinal and generational lines, which coincided. It is pretty accurate to call them the institutional and theoretical factions. The institutional faction had joined the department, typically, during the deepest years of the Great Depression. They were strongly motivated by sympathy with the sufferings of workers, the unemployed, the tenant farmers and the propertyless in general, under a callous capitalist regime. Probably the only name that might still be remembered is Dorothea Lange, the classic photographer of impoverished and dispossessed farmers, who was wife of a member of the institutional wing.

The theoretical faction was younger. Its members were recruited mostly during the heyday of the New Deal, after the publication of Keynes's *General theory* and during or immediately after World War II. They believed that the free markets that flourished under capitalism were the essential force of a productive economic system, that they understood that force and that they knew how to correct the socially disruptive side-effects that it engendered. The reader should have no trouble conjecturing to which faction I belonged.

The split in the department not only breached collegiality, but generated both open and covert conflicts over every proposal to change an academic requirement or, most important, every proposed tenure appointment or promotion. Some time after I joined the department, I found out that the proposal to invite me had created a lively brouhaha, and that the then chairman, an institutionalist, had tried to avert the appointment by 'losing' some essential documents. That sort of unpleasantness seems to be an inevitable part of the cost of faculty self-government. A physicist once told me that physics advances funeral by funeral.

In spite of these blemishes, teaching at Berkeley, with its alert students, stimulating colleagues and amenities of the Berkeley-San Francisco environment, was an enjoyable privilege. It ended for me after five years, when I was invited to join the faculty at Harvard. Once again, a member of the institutionalist faction was chairman of the Berkeley department. I was at loggerheads with him for reasons, doubtless adequate, but now long since forgotten. I reported the invitation to the chairman, in the hope of obtaining some sort of concession. Instead, he simply congratulated me and wished me Godspeed. So ended my sojourn at Berkeley.

As my list of publications reflects, my principal concern during my years at Berkeley, 1950–5, was to convey both to my students and to the economics profession the remarkable strides in the use of mathematics in economics that emerged from World War II. My missionary zeal in this cause was expressed in both teaching and writing, and continued for several years after I transferred to Harvard. In this regard, I must recount one episode from those years, because it perhaps has a moral.

My doctoral dissertation concerned the applicability of linear programming to the behaviour of monopolistic and quasi-monopolistic firms (Dorfman 1950). It was not entirely successful because the profit that such firms are presumed to maximize is not a linear function of their production and marketing choices. At best it can be represented as a quadratic function. How to apply the programming approach to problems involving nonlinear functions was then still unsolved. It was clearly an important problem for economics, since nearly all economic maximization problems turn out to have nonlinear objective functions.

So I teamed up with Edward Barankin, a professor in the mathematics department, to solve this problem. We struggled with it for several years, producing Barankin and Dorfman (1958), with several interesting theorems but no practicable solution. Whereupon a student of George Dantzig's, Philip Wolfe, using our theorems and his own good sense, produced the definitive solution (Wolfe 1959). It is clear now how this happened. Both Wolfe and ourselves were strongly influenced by the iterative approach embodied in Dantzig's simplex method for solving linear problems. But we followed Dantzig almost slavishly by first finding a starting solution that satisfied the constraints of the problem and then seeking an iterative procedure that produced a succession of approximate solutions, each yielding a greater value of the objective (for example, the profit) than any before and never violating any of the constraints. Wolfe's strategy, on the other hand, was to find an iterative procedure that began by violating some constraints and continued by finding a succession of approximate solutions in which the extent of constraint violations was steadily reduced while the value attained by the objective function never fell (and often rose). This apparently simple shift in strategy was the key that unlocked the problem. We never even considered the possibility of iterating while some of the constraints were still violated. Moral: The greatest obstacle to solving a scientific problem is often self-imposed blinkers.

As I said, while at Berkeley I zealously expounded the virtues of using any expedient mathematics to tackle problems in economics. I expressed my beliefs in a brief note, 'A catechism: mathematics in social science' (Dorfman 1954b), and acted on them in four expository papers (Dorfman 1953; 1954a; 1960; 1969b).

My opinions have not changed but, as I indicated a few pages ago, I have become uncomfortably aware of the cost of mathematizing economics. The only solution I can see is for economics, like physics, engineering, medicine and law, to expect students to equip themselves with the necessary knowledge of mathematics and statistics before enrolling for graduate study in economics. This, too, is unpleasant. It is likely to squeeze out valuable preparation in philosophy, history and social sciences during the student's undergraduate years. But it has become essential.

2.4   FLEDGLING POLITICAL ECONOMIST

I began to act on my concern with public decision-making shortly after I moved to Harvard, where applied economics enjoyed more attention and prestige than it received at Berkeley. During my second year at Harvard, I joined a seminar organized by Gordon M. Fair, a distinguished and dignified professor of sanitary engineering (accordingly known, behind his back, as 'Flush Gordon'), and Arthur Maass, a young political scientist, to study the design and operation of complex water supply systems. The seminar met for seven or eight years. It pioneered in applying mathematical model-building and digital simulations on large main-frame computers to the analysis of complex systems of rivers, reservoirs, multipurpose dams and hydro-electric power plants. The major accomplishment was *Design of water resource systems* (Maass *et al.* 1962), which remained the leading treatise on analysis of large-scale water resource systems for more than a decade. A few years later, the seminar published *Models for managing regional water quality* (Dorfman *et al.* 1972), but it was not as original or influential as *Design.*

Around this time, I published two papers dealing with public decisions on a more theoretical plane (Dorfman 1969a; 1971). Both express my long-standing conviction that it is not profitable to conceive of public decisions as the results of coherent maximization processes. Rather, I believe, public decisions should be regarded as outputs of pulls, pushes, trades and compromises among amorphous and rather ill-defined groups in the body politic all trying to influence public decisions in directions favourable to their interests and aspirations. Voting and elections are best understood as formalized procedures in the chiefly informal processes by which the groups that compose the body politic deal with each other and with the government decision-making apparatus. This is a theme that will appear repeatedly in my intellectual itinerary from here on. To be sure, it is alien territory for an economist, but necessary for him or her to explore if economics is to comprehend the important decisions that governments make. It would be helpful to consider the paper entitled, 'Incidence of the benefits and costs of environmental programs' (Dorfman 1977a) along with the aforementioned, although it was published somewhat later, since it is essentially a continuation of the same concerns.

When I wrote 'General equilibrium with public goods' (Dorfman 1969a), the welfare properties of perfectly competitive economies were well established, but there were no comparable theories for economies in which nonmarket goods or public goods were important. 'General equilibrium with public goods' was written to fill the gap. It studies the characteristics of equilibrium in a closed economy divided into two broad sectors: a private sector and a public or government sector. The private sector is just an Arrow-Debreu perfectly competitive economy. The government sector purchases inputs from the private sector and uses them to produce public goods and services which it donates to the private sector. It finances these activities by taxes on the private sector.

The chief contribution and difficulties of the paper concern the properties of the public sector equilibrium. This is by no means unexplored territory. On the contrary, it bulks large in the literature of political science and is the subject of more previous papers in economics than I can list. The problem is that there have been too many explorers returning with maps that contradict each other. The view of governmental decisions that seems most helpful to me is derived from Bentley's (1908) scheme of interest groups' manoeuvring and compromising to form (and sometimes to desert) coalitions large enough to have the policies they advocate adopted or the ones they oppose rejected.

The first half of the paper is devoted mostly to setting forth my view of this complex process. The remainder works out the prices and quantities in an equilibrium of such a two-sector (public and private) system, if an equilibrium is reached.

I think the exposition is unnecessarily difficult, partly because the notation is over-elaborate and partly because the approach is formal and mathematical rather than intuitive. Approached intuitively, the study of the equilibrium of a two-sector economy breaks up into three relatively straightforward sub-problems: the equilibrium of the public sector, that of the private sector, and the interaction between the two. All take the equilibrium vector of prices of private goods as the point of departure.

In equilibrium, the public sector produces the quantities of public goods that the interest groups have agreed on, as discussed above, by using the least costly vector of private goods inputs possible, so that the cost of producing the agreed-on vector of public goods, measured by the equilibrium price vector for private goods, will be minimized. The result will be a point on the government's transformation frontier at which the marginal rate of transformation of any two public goods produced will equal the ratio of their costs of production, in accordance with the government's production function.

The equilibrium of the private sector is determined similarly. Each interest group consists of similar and similarly situated households who choose input vectors (with outputs, as of labour, counted as negative inputs) on the highest indifference surfaces they can reach without violating their budget constraints. At the points so chosen, the marginal rates of substitution between the members of each pair of private goods consumed equals the slope of the budget constraint, that is, the ratio of the prices of the goods.

The third and final sub-problem is to determine the scale of economic activity so that the sum of the input vectors to all the sectors, the government sector and all the interest groups, is a point on the outer boundary of the community's feasible production set. Careful equation counting will show that, at least for production sets that are convex with constant returns to scale, the numbers of disposable variables and constraining equations just balance, as required for unique solvability of such a system of conditions. The first two sub-problems are standard problems in nonlinear programming. The third sub-problem concerns a single scaling parameter which can be found by trial and error.

But we should not let ourselves be misled by reaching a tidy result that confirms our hopes and expectations. The whole argument depends on the ability of the jockeying by interest groups to reach conclusions consistent with the public's considered preferences. I'm not sure that such confidence in the process has ever been well founded. Certainly, the writers of the US Constitution did not evince much faith in the wisdom of the public. That is why they provided for indirect election of the president and senators. For this reason also, restrictions on the privilege of voting used to be quite prevalent. Not only was the female half of the population disenfranchised, but some states used to have property qualifications for voters, and I remember from my childhood in New York when prospective voters had to pass literacy tests. In recent years, the introduction of expensive modern merchandizing methods into political campaigns has created further reasons to doubt the likelihood that contests among interest groups can guide governments to compromises that reconcile the different interests optimally. All in all, I now regard 'General equilibrium with public goods' as an exercise in optimism.

The 'Incidence of benefits and costs' paper (Dorfman 1977a) consists of two loosely connected parts. The first concentrates attention on the distributional implications of governmental programmes, including provision of public goods, taking as its example the American programmes for reducing polluting emissions into the air and public waters. It found that the effects of those programmes on families with different incomes differed dramatically. The costs of those programmes to families in the lowest income strata were substantially greater than the amounts those families would have paid voluntarily for the benefits they received from them. But those programmes provided substantial consumer surpluses to families in the highest strata, while families in the intermediate strata received benefits that they regarded as worth just about their share of the costs.

That finding called attention to the concept that I called 'exactions', which was already implicit in the 'General equilibrium' paper. A governmental programme imposed an 'exaction' on a family to the extent that that family's share of the costs exceeded the amount that it would pay voluntarily to have the programme. Moreover, there is an asymmetry between imposing an exaction and providing a citizens' surplus. Citizens tend to resent bearing exactions, but to regard surpluses as more or less due to them. Thus, even aside from ethical considerations, it is politically unwise to impose exactions on any more citizens than necessary, and it is often possible to adjust the financing of public programmes so as to minimize the amount of exactions entailed.

The 'General equilibrium' paper assumed, unrealistically, that exactions were altogether forbidden; the 'Incidence' paper weakened that restriction to saying only that experienced politicians could and would adjust programmes so as to reduce the level of exactions, even at the cost of increasing the total costs of the programmes. One should therefore not take it for granted that the goal of public decisions is to achieve the intended results at minimum possible social cost.

The third member of this triad on the economic theory of public decisions, 'Social decisions without social preferences' (Dorfman 1971), attempted to apply the formation of n-person game theory to the interest-group depiction of public decisions. I think it was basically inconclusive because the most successful aspects of game theory depend on the role of side-payments in forming and cementing coalitions. But the use of side-payments presupposes some form of transferable utility, which most instances of interest-group politics lack.

There is a second theme in my professional work that, like the second theme in the sonata form, underlies and interacts with the main theme. It is capital theory, which I like to view as the theory of time, since capital is merely wealth that yields its services over substantial periods of time. The connection with the main theme is that the effects of most important public decisions extend over substantial lengths of time.

In my case, the second theme was announced actually before the main theme. When I was a graduate student, capital theory was covered in the basic microeconomics course. (This is usually no longer the case, to the intellectual impoverishment of the students.) I was fascinated by it, particularly by the Austrian school exemplified by Böhm-Bawerk, who disposed of as sharp an intellect as anyone who ever practised economics. Böhm-Bawerk presents difficulties, however, especially to anyone who, like me, has a mathematical turn of mind. In order to follow his chain of reasoning, I translated it into mathematics (a method of reading, I learned much later, that Alfred Marshall often used), thereby discovering a significant flaw in the logic. I did not see how to correct the error at that time. I published my exposition some dozen years later in, 'A graphical exposition of Böhm-Bawerk's interest theory' (Dorfman 1959), with Böhm-Bawerk's mistake uncorrected and some of my own errors added to it. Some years after publishing 'A graphical exposition', I discovered an elegant and revealing way to correct Böhm-Bawerk's error, and taught it in my course in the history of economics. I have yet to publish the correction because interest in capital theory had waned so completely by then that I didn't and don't know of any journal that would be likely to publish it. My own interest in capital theory has not waned, and capital-theoretic papers, for instance Dorfman (1981b; 1995), have continued to dribble out.

Along the way, I published several disconnected theoretical papers. Two of them, 'Optimal advertising and optimal quality' (Dorfman and Steiner 1954) and 'A formula for the Gini coefficient' (Dorfman 1979), were merely transcripts, with some refinements, of sessions of the microeconomics course that I was giving at the time.

2.5   RESOURCE AND ENVIRONMENTAL ECONOMIST

Occasionally, I closed my books and looked at 'the real world', and practically all of those applications dealt with resource or environmental problems. For the most part, they did not result in journal articles. The work on *Design of water resource systems* (Maass *et al.* 1962) is a case in point. But three papers dealing with practical problems in natural resource or environmental economics represent this phase of my work.

The earliest of these papers was 'Forty years of cost-benefit analysis' (Dorfman 1978). Almost twenty additional years of experience with benefit-cost analysis have accumulated since then. It might be supposed that later developments, including the recent 'Why benefit-cost analysis is widely disregarded and what to do about it' (Dorfman 1996), have superseded the 1978 paper, but that is not entirely so. The 'Forty years' paper includes a careful examination of the logical underpinnings of benefit-cost analysis, which is generally lacking in the extensive literature on the method, including my own subsequent papers. In consequence, benefit-cost analysis is frequently misapplied, the results are misinterpreted and unjustified conclusions are drawn. The first 40 years of experience with benefit-cost analysis exhibited these defects in application; the subsequent 20 years have confirmed them.

The most recent of the papers in the group is 'Why benefit-cost analysis is widely disregarded and what to do about it', just mentioned. The one-sentence answer it gives to the rhetorical question is, 'Because it doesn't answer the right questions'. For one thing, benefit-cost analysis carefully evades the critical question of who enjoys the benefits and who sustains the costs. In a democracy made up of diverse groups pursuing divergent interests, that question is of dominating concern to decision-makers. The paper calls attention to this and several other grave shortcomings in the way benefit-cost analysis is practised and used.

'The lessons of pesticide regulation' (Dorfman 1982) is a digest of what I learned as chair of a National Research Council committee charged with investigating why the enforcement of the Federal Insecticide, Fungicide, and Rodenticide Act (FIFRA) had been at a virtual standstill for the 30 years since the Act was passed. The investigation turned into a case study in the daily nitty-gritty of trying to implement many of the regulations that Congress promulgates so blithely. Working on the study was a sobering experience for me. I hope that this digest of it conveys at least a faint whiff of the stresses and frustrations encountered in trying to comply with far-reaching, and apparently reasonable, governmental mandates. Although all the evidence and examples mentioned in the paper related to the implementation of FIFRA, they exemplify problems encountered throughout the Environmental Protection Agency (EPA) and beyond.

The earlier paper, 'Transition costs of changing regulations' (Dorfman 1981a), pursues a similar theme. By and large, benefit-cost analyses compare the costs and benefits generated when the economy has attained equilibrium in response to alternative governmental policies. But the authors of those analyses, including myself, are well aware that the economy is rarely in equilibrium and that the economy's responses to being out of equilibrium are always costly. This paper assumes, for the sake of the argument, that new policies or regulations are imposed on an economy already in equilibrium, and considers the costs of moving to an equilibrium consistent with the changed state of affairs. These adjustment costs should be added to the costs included in conventional benefit-cost analyses.

'An economist's view of natural resource and environmental problems' (Dorfman 1985a) is a rapid survey of the economic issues that arise in formulating policies for managing the country's natural resources and protecting its environment. It does not take a stand on any concrete issue, but is content with pointing out the main questions of principle that have to be faced. 'Food for a developing world' (Dorfman and Falcon 1987), written with Walter P. Falcon of Stanford's Food Research Institute, is quite different. It was written for an interdisciplinary conference on 'Resources and World Development' at a time when there was considerable concern about the ability of the planet to meet the requirements and depredations of a population that might well grow to 12 billion or so in the next 50 years. Several scientists made estimates of the size of the population that the planet could feed, taking account of the amount of arable land available, the average amount of solar energy received per arable hectare, the efficiency of plants at converting solar energy into biomass, and related considerations. A typical estimate, made by Roger Revelle (1975), director of the Harvard Center for Population Studies, found that the planet could provide subsistence diets (about 2000 calories per day for adults) for 76 billion people, plus or minus a few billion. At a more varied and adequate diet of, say, 3000 calories per day, about 50 billion people could be supported. Revelle, like most of the other scientists, was aware that actual dietary requirements depend on more than simple physiological calculations but did not venture into this more complicated terrain.

Falcon and I, being social scientists, took a more empirical approach. We were impressed by the persistently paradoxical behaviour of markets for farm products in most countries. On the one hand, when the paper was written as well as today, about half of the world's population suffered from chronic undernourishment and occasional famines, while farmers were glutting their markets with so much produce that farm prices would fall to less than the costs of production but for drastic governmental interferences. Millions lived on the verge of starvation while farmers could produce more food than people could buy!

Thus the physical limits to agriculture could not explain the worldwide under-nutrition. The paper presents several charts and tables to drive home the point that the world could produce plenty of food for its population when the paper was written, and still can, while about half the world's population doesn't earn enough to buy the food they need.

Since most of the undernourished people are farmers and peasants, increasing their productivity (despite the apparent glut) will provide the income they need to buy the food they need and simultaneously provide the food. This analysis leads to four major recommendations: (1) improve both the physical infrastructure in agricultural areas (for example, farm-to-market roads) and the organizational support for farming (such as agricultural extension service and farm credit facilities); (2) promote modernized technology (for example, high-yield varieties, chemical pesticides); (3) permit market prices that encourage rather than inhibit agriculture, particularly by terminating forced requisitions of agricultural products at administrative prices; and (4) follow macroeconomic policies that promote exports and hinder inflation. We concede that the transition to the farm economy that these four recommendations would create would impose painful sacrifices on some people, but we see no other way to foster a farm economy that can attract and support an adequate work force and provide a significant market for urban products.

Like our predecessors, we refrain from guessing how large a population the world can support at a comfortable standard of living. We rest content with the finding that physical productivity does not set the limit; the distribution of income does. Undernutrition and its attendant evils are economic problems, not agronomic ones.

'Protecting the global environment' (Dorfman 1991) is another of the papers that oversteps the boundaries within which an economist speaks with some authority. It was inspired by a major achievement in the effort to protect the global environment, the 'Montreal Protocol' for limiting the production and use of chemicals that deplete the protective ozone layer in the upper atmosphere. The ozone layer shields all terrestrial life from excessive exposure to ultraviolet solar radiation. In 1974, two scientists discovered that a family of industrial chemicals, the chlorofluorocarbons or CFCs, once released into the atmosphere, rise to the protective layer and destroy much of the ozone through chemical reactions. By then, the ozone layer had been noticeably thinned in several places. What then happened is instructive. The scientific findings were never called into question. The chemicals involved are not essential to important industries in any nations, though manufacturing and distributing them is profitable to several companies, notably Dupont in the United States and ICI in England. Nevertheless, it took 14 years of persistent effort by scientists and environmental advocates to persuade some 45 countries to agree to regulate the manufacture and use of CFCs about half as stringently as the scientists estimated was needed to arrest the erosion of the ozone layer. The resultant Montreal Protocol, of which we are so proud, appears to have retarded the destruction of the protective layer but has by no means halted it. Accordingly, the Protocol had to be renegotiated after about five years.

'On optimal congestion' (Dorfman 1984a) is included in this group, although congestion is not a resource or environmental problem strictly speaking, because it is formally similar to environmental problems. Congestion arises, as do many environmental malfunctions, in situations where each individual makes choices he or she judges to be in his or her own best interest, without much incentive to take into account the effects of such actions on other users of the same facilities. In the case of congestible facilities (highways, public libraries, public beaches, and so on) these interpersonal effects give rise to a peculiar type of demand curve in which the total usage of the facility enters each user's demand function.

This type of demand function has been dubbed 'a ccdd' (constant crowding demand function) because it consists of a family of ordinary demand curves, each of which tells how much of a commodity consumers will demand at each price in some range, always on the apparently contradictory assumption that the level of market demand remains unchanged. The apparent self-contradiction lies in the implicit question: How much of a commodity will consumers demand if the price is p and each consumer believes that the total demand will be Q? Except for the one price, p, at which the total demand actually is Q, the consumers' beliefs will be falsified, the expectation will be revised and a new ccdd curve will become effective. Equilibrium will not be attained until the price and expectations are such that the expectations will be confirmed.

The paper works through the algebra of this sort of self-fulfilment and comes to a surprising conclusion. Ever since the days of the classic Pigou-Knight controversy over socially optimal toll road charges, economists have believed that the optimal toll would be the one that maximized the toll-operators' net profit. Not so in general. Things would work out that neatly only in a special group of cases to which the Pigou-Knight roads, Garrett Hardin's commons and Scott Gordon's fishery all belong.

2.6   SOCIAL DECISIONS

My continuing concern with public decisions is most explicit in the group of papers, dated from 1970 to 1985, that can be identified as dealing with 'social decisions'. In some of them, I ventured far from an economist's legitimate turf into the areas of sociology and political theory. For those infractions, I apologize to the authorized practitioners, but feel no remorse. An economist cannot get on with his or her own task if he or she ignores the spillovers into the domains of neighbouring disciplines.

'Social decisions without social preferences' and 'Incidence of the benefits and costs' have already been discussed. 'The functions of the city' (Dorfman 1970) reverts to my thesis that a modern community consists of a number of diverse groups with divergent interests, beliefs and values, who must somehow adjust to living in close proximity and sharing opportunities and resources. This paper argues that these groups fulfil a deep-seated, ineradicable human need, and that one of a city's principal tasks is to maintain reasonably harmonious working relationships among the groups that comprise it.

The argument smacks of Wilson's 'sociobiology' (1975), and there is more than a faint hint of it in Adam Smith's *Theory of moral sentiments*

(1759). For nearly all of the million or two years that humans have inhabited the Earth, the species consisted of fairly small hunting-gathering tribes, clans, bands, and so on, each deriving its sustenance from a limited turf that it guarded jealously from the incursions of neighbouring tribes, while invading neighbouring territory when circumstances permitted. The survival of any tribe and its members depended heavily on the dedication of its members to protecting its territory and each other. Macaulay expressed the essential spirit eloquently:

> And how can a man die better
> Than facing fearful odds
> For the ashes of his fathers
> And the temples of his gods?

Thus was bred into us the virtues of loyalty and patriotism, and the need to be a respected member of a tightly knit group of individuals distinguished in some manner from all other members of the species. Other social animals acquire similarly the need and ability to identify, even unto death, with some close-knit group of kith or kin.

The age of the primitive clan ended only 10,000 or 20,000 years ago with the discovery and spread of settled agriculture, but the need to affiliate with a group of loyal allies remained and evolved, somewhat sublimated, into loyalty to medieval barons, to patriotism to the modern state, to the clannishness of ethnic groups in modern American cities, and so on. The paper describes how this vestigial human tendency affects the economics and social structures of modern cities, particularly in the United States.

'The technical basis for decision making' (Dorfman 1974) was a hard paper to write, and may be almost as hard to read. The problem with writing it was that it describes work very much in progress and, therefore, far from well digested and organized. A description from the perspective of 20 years may therefore be helpful.

The paper was written to set the stage for a 'Resources for the Future' conference on how decisions about the use of common property resources should be analysed, a topic dear to my heart and about which I had (and have) strong opinions. The result was a paper with a strong didactic flavour and, I'm afraid, a somewhat patronizing style.

The first four pages are devoted to the dull but often necessary task of clarifying terminology. The bulk of the paper is a conscientious survey of a variety of methods for sorting out and ranking alternative policies and projects, ranging from benefit-cost analysis to applying game-theoretic models, with numerous way-stations. The basic logic and also the shortcomings of all the methods are pointed out. Finally, the last five pages describe and cautiously advocate an analytic approach that is immune to the objections raised against the others.

The recommended approach is one developed by the Environmental Systems Program at Harvard. We called it 'Paretian Environmental Analysis', despite the unfortunate acronym. It faced frankly the problem that has come up so many times in my narrative, of making judgements that would be binding on population groups with conflicting interests. The basic idea is to think of a matrix with a row for each alternative considered and a column for each population group concerned. Each cell in the matrix contains a ranking or rating of the alternative corresponding to its row judged from the point of view of the group designated by its column. If it should happen when any pair of alternatives is compared that the rating of one of them is higher than that of the other in every column, then the alternative with the lower ratings is 'dominated' and can be dropped from further consideration. More sensitive measures of rating than comparative ranks and some methods for comparing the political significances of political groups are required to proceed beyond merely eliminating dominated choices, but such measures are often more practical in practice than in theory.

As far as I know, this approach has been carried through only once, but the result was spectacular. The application concerned a project known as the Cross-Florida Barge Canal. The canal would cross the Florida Peninsula from Jacksonville on the Atlantic coast to near Yankeetown on the Gulf of Mexico, slicing some 700 miles off the barge journey between Atlantic ports and Gulf ports in Louisiana, Texas, and so on. This canal had been debated for generations. Construction was even started in the 1930s, but abandoned during World War II. Jacksonville businessmen, the barge canal companies and the US Corps of Engineers favoured the canal; sportsmen, environmentalists, some farmers, and others opposed it. In the 1970s Congress authorized a fresh study which was carried out under the supervision of the Corps of Engineers according to the principles of PEA analysis, somewhat impeded by legal requirements and limited financing. The results were surprisingly clear cut. The groups that historically had opposed the canal continued to do so, as expected. But no group, not even the barge operators, expressed more than mild support for building it. Apparently, shipping freight by barge is so cheap that even the large saving in mileage per shipment is not enough to offset the construction and disruption costs of building and operating the canal. When even the shippers were shown to recognize how modest the saving would be, support for the canal project vanished. It has not been heard from since.

A single success cannot establish the primacy of PEA as a method for resolving political conflicts of interest, though it may establish a presumption of usefulness. The Environmental Systems Program ran out of steam and money years ago, but further trials of the approach seem to be worthwhile.

The motive for my paper on environmental quality indexes (Dorfman 1977b) was entirely different. Since as far back as I remember, people have been proposing measures of overall environmental quality intended to be useful for comparing the quality of the environments in different localities, for following trends in environmental quality, and the like. None of them has gained wide acceptance. I could not help noticing that, whereas the public was concerned about the effects of environmental conditions on human health and welfare, none of the proposed indexes measured those effects; the indexes are simply averages of selected environmental descriptors, such as the coliform count in public waters or the concentration of sulphur dioxide in the atmosphere, without considering the descriptors' importance to human well-being. I therefore proposed an index that went directly to the effects of the environment on humans. Though my proposal was received with the same apathy as the others, I am including it in this collection because I believe that it has considerable merit.

The 'social index' measures the effects of environmental conditions on human activities and welfare from the outset. Since the paper explains its construction in some detail, here I need mention only that it has three components: economic effects, health effects and effects on amenities. The economic effects are measured by comparing the actual value of economic output in the relevant region with what that value would be under pristine conditions. The health effects are similarly measured by comparing actual mortality and morbidity indicators with what they would be under pristine conditions. The amenity effects are fussier. Essentially they are measured by the amount the communities concerned would be willing to pay to have various natural, historical and aesthetic amenities improved to defined standards.

The advantage of the social index is that it measures the conditions that are of direct concern to people and government officials. Its drawback, a serious one, is that it is a good deal more demanding, and therefore expensive, than merely describing physical and ecological conditions as the other indexes do. Still, that expensive step is necessary to make an environmental indicator suitable for establishing priorities for environmental protection and improvement.

Rogers (1996) has suggested a compromise that might be useful. It is to measure environmental quality by the cost of bringing the environmental conditions included in a conventional index up to a target standard. This would be substantially cheaper and easier than the type of measure that I suggest, and, though not quite what is needed, could serve as a helpful guide to environmental policy.

My paper on ethics, economics and the environment (Dorfman 1985b) is my only excursion into applied philosophy. I was lured into it by observing the contortions forced upon the EPA by contradictions in the laws that Congress instructed it to enforce. It didn't take much study to perceive that Congress did not invent the contradictions; it inherited them from the philosophers, who had been struggling with them since the eighteenth century at least.

The contradictions in question reflect the views of two broad schools of ethical philosophy. One, traceable back to Aristotle, is based on the concepts of natural rights and duties. In the trade, these theories are called deontological. The other school, that perhaps emerged as recently as the Enlightenment, holds that the moral value of any act or policy depends only on its consequences. It is therefore called consequentialist. Bentham is a leading exponent.

The practical problem is that these two schools of thought are often contradictory. Further, not only are both deeply embedded in American laws and traditions, as my paper emphasizes, but, I have come to realize, many people (including myself) subscribe to both of them. Clearly, this circumstance is bound to lead to the kind of confusions that afflict Congress and the EPA.

After the essay was published, I was delighted to learn that some redoubtable philosophers, including Alasdair MacIntyre (1981) and Amartya Sen (1987) were bothered enough by this same contradiction to treat it at length. Neither, however, considered its legislative implications, as I did. Nor do I find in either of them a satisfying way to resolve the contradictions, or to deny them. We must, I conclude, live with inconsistency.

2.7 HISTORIAN OF ECONOMICS

It is recorded that Billy Rose once held the title of World's Fastest Typist, but was a professional typist for only a short time. In fact, for almost his entire career he did not type even his own correspondence. Why? He soon discovered that his comparative advantage lay in promoting musical extravaganzas. Billy Rose is a dramatic example, but perhaps is a poor place to start a discussion of comparative advantage. 'Comparative advantage' is very likely the most democratic of all economic concepts. Everybody has some, although few have Billy Rose's problem of having to ignore one remarkable talent to free time for exercising a different one.

This brings me to my point: professors of economics emeritus often have a comparative advantage in pursuing the history of economics. In the first place, we have longer memories than our younger colleagues. We have experienced how much economics (and, indeed, the world) has changed in just a few decades. We have seen fashions come and go and still bring us no closer to equilibrium (though perhaps an excessive amount of economics is devoted to analysing equilibrium). We are acutely aware that change is what matters; equilibrium stasis is evanescent. Our memories even include some episodes in which economics changed particularly swiftly. We may know first-hand how those changes came about, what forces promoted or resisted them, what and how lasting their consequences were. I, for one, don't have to read about the confusion into which Keynes's *General Theory* (1936) plunged the profession. Economists born, say, ten years after me will never grasp it; from the perspective of 60 years the impassioned controversies it generated are much too boring, and even silly, to read about.

My memory is scarred also by other significant changes – though none as important as the introduction of Keynesianism and the daunting obstacles that had to be surmounted to bring them about. All of which gives us professors emeritus much more than a verbal appreciation of the stresses and tensions of change and of the accompanying threats to practising economists as their stock of knowledge becomes obsolete.

We emeriti also lose the ability to internalize the new developments that constitute change. (By 'new' I mean since we passed our final exams.) I, for one, despite considerable effort, am still not entirely at home with rational expectations or the capital asset pricing model, let alone alternative economics. In short, the area on which our competence is focused recedes inexorably into the past. So it is that many of us turn to thinking and writing about economic history, where our comparative advantage lies ever more emphatically.

I highlight six of my papers in this field. I watched three of the developments discussed in them as they occurred and was a minor participant in one. The other three took place long before even my ancient times.

Wassily Leontief's major contribution was input-output analysis, developed in the 1930s and brought to fruition in the 1950s. It still provides the basic framework for most analyses of relationships among sectors of the economy, a position that appears unlikely to be challenged in the visible future. I wrote Dorfman (1973) at the behest of the Royal Swedish Academy of Sciences and, sure enough, he received the award.

Gerard Debreu's selection as a Nobel Laureate culminated efforts beginning with those of Leon Walras, more than a century ago, and continued by Abraham Wald, Kenneth Arrow and Debreu himself, to formulate mathematically the structure of economic equilibrium. Dorfman (1983) was written in honour of Debreu's award because it is intended to clear up some misunderstandings (not shared by Debreu) about the nature of his accomplishment. Debreu did *not* confirm Adam Smith's insight that a competitive economy would perform perfectly efficiently without any government intervention. He, along with Kenneth Arrow, *did* establish certain conditions, 'sufficient conditions', under which a competitive economy would be perfectly efficient. But those conditions are so restrictive that no real economy comes close to satisfying them or could conceivably do so. The practical value of Debreu's theorems is that they greatly clarify the conditions in which a real economy can be expected to perform well, even if not perfectly, and the nature of policies that can improve the performance of real economies. The Arrow-Debreu conditions have been somewhat refined and relaxed in the 40-odd years since they were discovered, but basically remain unchallenged.

The story of linear programming (Dorfman 1984b) illustrates how scientific progress stumbles forward. Robert Remak formulated the conditions for economic equilibrium as a system of linear inequalities as early as 1929, but no one had the faintest idea of how to solve them. In 1939, L.V. Kantorovich proposed a method for solving very small (three or four) variable systems. His method rapidly became burdensome for larger systems and, absent the electronic computers still a dozen years in the future, utterly impracticable. Tjalling Koopmans solved a very important special case during World War II. But the first really general and truly implementable solution was Dantzig's 'simplex method', discovered in 1947. Dantzig had the enormous advantage over his predecessors that he did his work when the electronic computer was already in sight (but not yet operational) and he knew in broad outline what it would be able to do.

Almost immediately after the simplex method was announced, linear programming was accepted enthusiastically as the primary method for optimizing complex programmes in both private industry and governmental economic planning. Its use spread quickly all over the world. Some refinements were discovered and adopted, and several alternative methods have been discovered, but none have supplanted it after 50 years of use. Studying and applying linear programming have become a large sub-profession. Linear programming now is not quite as important as it was ten or 20 years ago because fantastic decreases in the cost of computing have made optimization of nonlinear programming problems feasible, and preferable in applications where nonlinearity is too marked to be ignored.

In addition to its usefulness in government and industrial planning, linear programming has led to important advances in economic theory, largely in the form of Tjalling Koopmans's generalization called 'activity analysis'. This aspect is based on the duality theorems developed largely by John von Neumann, A.W. Tucker and Dantzig himself. These theorems show more vividly than can be seen without them that finding the prices that induce an economy or firm to function efficiently and finding the quantities of commodities that an economy or firm can produce when functioning efficiently are essentially the same problem; neither can be solved without solving the other, at least implicitly. One important implication, for example, is that charging interest for the use of capital is not an artefact of capitalistic methods of production, but is necessary in all production, no matter what the institutional arrangements, if resources are not to be wasted. The old Soviet economy, where charging interest was heretical, was a sad demonstration of the cost of ignoring these theorems.

Professor I. Bernard Cohen of the Harvard Department of the History of Science was responsible for urging me to write out the story of the birth of linear programming, and offered many valuable suggestions while it was in progress.

Of all the papers in my Edward Elgar collection (Dorfman 1997a), 'Thünen at two hundred' (Dorfman 1986) is the one I most enjoyed writing. It is a comment on a paper with the same title by Paul Samuelson. Samuelson, following the precedent of Joseph Schumpeter and several other redoubtable economists, charged Thünen with a mistake in the calculations he used to derive his famous formula for the 'natural wage'. My paper points out that it was the critics who made the mistake. Their mistake was to take it for granted that Thünen's formula was intended to maximize the concept that they would have maximized if they had been in Thünen's shoes. But Thünen, writing at the very beginning of the development of the theory of production, had a very different image of entrepreneurial goals, and maximized his own concept correctly rather than the one that later generations would prefer. Samuelson conceded. Moral: When reading a work in economics written 100 or more years ago, beware the pitfall of imputing to the author the same implicit images of the economy and of economic actors and motivations that you have. Many of the concepts and ideas familiar to first-year students now had not been invented then.

Robert Malthus and David Ricardo (Dorfman 1989) were the oddest couple in the history of economics. One was a member of the country gentry and the inner circles of the English Establishment, but didn't have much money. The other was an outsider, a member of the London Jewish financial community, and very wealthy. Despite these different backgrounds, they were dear friends and worked intimately together while they argued vehemently with each other in private and in print. Ricardo once said of Malthus, 'I could not love you more if you agreed in opinion with me'. In short, they exhibited a degree of fair-mindedness, civility and tolerance that few people can attain. I wrote this essay because I felt that more economists should be aware that so much decency, humaneness and open-mindedness could exist among members of our profession.

Böhm-Bawerk and Fisher are another interesting contrasting pair. They were not friends; in fact, I'm not sure they ever met, though it seems probable. They are associated because they independently, and not quite simultaneously, undertook the same problem and reached conclusions that are the same in essence though different in most details. The interesting aspect of their relationship is how the characteristics of their separate milieus are reflected in their solutions to their common problem.

The question that seized them both was the legitimacy of charging and paying interest for the use of capital. Each of them found in his own way that interest payments are legitimate and, indeed, inevitable in all but the most primitive modes of production. In fact, they both arrived at the same principles for determining the rate of interest.

But their arguments were quite different. Böhm-Bawerk conceived of an economy that consisted of two classes of people: those who owned property and those who owned only their bare hands, just as in the late nineteenth-century central European society with which he was familiar. It was perfectly fair for property-owners who placed their property at the disposal of workers to claim a share of the output, equivalent to the increased product that using the property (or capital) made possible. Dorfman (1959) provides additional details about Böhm-Bawerk's position.

Fisher, however, observing the one-class society of nineteenth-century Connecticut and imbibing its scale of values, argued that interest would arise when people who could use profitably more capital than they owned borrowed it from people who had more than they could, or would, use profitably. All that was needed for interest to arise was for capital to be scarce and for people's opportunities to use it to vary. The result was much the same as Böhm-Bawerk's in spite of the radical difference in social images and causations.

The differences between these theories may have some bearing on today's controversies over 'relativism', the doctrine, I gather, that 'truth' is not universal but is related to the culture and circumstances in which it is believed. The contrast between Böhm-Bawerk's and Fisher's theories is somewhat more subtle. The conclusions of the two theories are essentially the same in the two cultures from which they arose, and may very well be the same in any other culture in which the same question could be posed. But the justifications for the conclusions are saturated with the differences between the two. Relativism may relate less to substantive assertions than to their interpretations in differing cultural contexts.

SELECTED WORKS

(1943) 'The detection of defective members of large populations', *Annals of Mathematic Statistics*, 14 (4), pp. 436–40.*

(1950) 'Behavior of firms in imperfect competition', unpublished Ph.D. dissertation, University of California, Berkeley.

(1953) 'Mathematical or "linear" programming: a nonmathematical exposition', *American Economic Review*, 43 (5, pt. I), pp. 797–825.*

(1954a) 'The nature and significance of input-output', *Review of Economics and Statistics*, 36 (2), pp. 121–33.*

(1954b) 'A catechism: mathematics in social science', *Review of Economics and Statistics*, 36 (4), pp. 374–7.*

(1954) (with P.O. Steiner) 'Optimal advertising and optimal quality', *American Economic Review*, 44 (5), pp. 826–36.*

(1959) 'A graphical exposition of Böhm-Bawerk's interest theory', *Review of Economic Studies*, 26 (2), pp. 153–9.*

(1960) 'Operations research', *American Economic Review*, 50 (4), pp. 575–86, 602–7, 613–23.*

(1969a) 'General equilibrium with public goods', in J. Margolis and H. Guitton (eds) (1969) *Public economics: an analysis of public production and consumption and their relations to the private sector*. London: Macmillan, pp. 247–75.*

(1969b) 'An economic interpretation of optimal control theory', *American Economic Review*, 59 (5), pp. 817–31.*

(1970) 'The functions of the city', in A.H. Pascal (ed.) (1970) *Thinking about cities: new perspectives on urban problems*. Belmont, CA: Dickenson, pp. 32–40.*

(1971) 'Social decisions without social preferences', in M. Kaser and R. Portes (eds) (1971) *Planning and market relations*. London: Macmillan, pp. 117–29.*

(1972) (Ed. with H.D. Jacoby and H.A. Thomas) *Models for managing regional water quality*, Cambridge, MA: Harvard University Press.

(1973) 'Wassily Leontief's contribution to economics', *Swedish Journal of Economics*, 75 (3), pp. 430–49.*

(1974) 'The technical basis for decision making', in E.T. Haefele (ed.) (1974) *The governance of common property resources*. Baltimore: Johns Hopkins University Press, pp. 5–25.*

(1977a) 'Incidence of the benefits and costs of environmental programs', *American Economic Review*, 67 (1), pp. 333–40.*

(1977b) 'Towards a social index of environmental quality', in B. Balassa and R. Nelson (eds) (1977) *Economic progress, private values and public policy: essays in honor of William Fellner*. Amsterdam: North-Holland, pp. 121–35.*

(1978) 'Forty years of cost-benefit analysis', in J.R.N. Stone and W. Peterson (eds) (1978) *Econometric contributions to public policy*. London: Macmillan, pp. 268–84.*

(1979) 'A formula for the Gini coefficient', *Review of Economics and Statistics*, 61 (1), pp. 146–9.*

(1981a) 'Transaction costs of changing regulations', in A.R. Ferguson (ed.) (1981) *Attacking regulatory problems*. Cambridge, MA: Ballinger, pp. 39–54.*

(1981b) 'The meaning of internal rates of return', *Journal of Finance*, 36 (5), pp. 1011–21.*

(1982) 'The lessons of pesticide regulation', in W.A Magat (ed.) (1982) *Reform of environmental regulation*. Cambridge, MA: Ballinger, pp. 13–29.*

(1983) 'A Nobel quest for the invisible hand', *New York Times*, 23 October, section 3, (Money and Business), p. 15.*

(1984a) 'On optimal congestion', *Journal of Environmental Economics and Management*, 11 (2), pp. 91–106.*

(1984b) 'The discovery of linear programming', *Annals of the History of Computing*, 6 (3), pp. 283–95.*

(1985a) 'An economist's view of natural resources and environmental problems', in R. Repetto (ed.) (1985) *The global possible: resources, development and the new century*. New Haven: Yale University Press, pp. 67–95.*

(1985b) 'Ethics, economics and the environment', in S. Asefa (ed.) (1985) *Economic decision making: private and public decisions*. Ames: Iowa State University Press, pp. 65–79.*

(1986) 'Comment: P.A. Samuelson, "Thünen at two hundred"', *Journal of Economic Literature*, 24 (4), pp. 1773–6.*

(1987) (with W.P. Falcon) 'Food for a developing world', in D.J. McLaren and B.J. Skinner (eds) (1987) *Resources and world development*, part B: *Water and land*. Chichester: John Wiley, pp. 767–85.*

(1989) 'Thomas Robert Malthus and David Ricardo', *Journal of Economic Perspectives*, 3 (3), pp. 153–64.*

(1991) 'Protecting the global environment: an immodest proposal', *World Development*, 19 (1), pp. 103–10.*

(1995) 'Austrian and American capital theories: a contrast of cultures', *Journal of the History of Economic Thought*, 17 (1), pp. 21–34.*

(1996) 'Why benefit-cost analysis is widely disregarded and what to do about it', *Interfaces*, 16 (5), pp. 1–6.*

(1997a) *Economic theory and public decisions: selected essays*. Cheltenham: Edward Elgar.

(1997b) 'Introduction', in R. Dorfman (1997a) **q.v.**, pp. xiii–xxxiii.

BIBLIOGRAPHY

Barankin, E.W. and Dorfman, R. (1958) 'On quadratic programming', *University of California Publications in Statistics*, 2, pp. 285–318.

Bentley, A.F. (1908) *The process of government: a study of social pressures*. Chicago: University of Chicago Press.

Keynes, J.M. (1936) *The general theory of employment, interest and money*. London: Macmillan.

Maass, A. *et al.* (1962) *Design of water-resource systems: new techniques for relating economic objectives, engineering analysis and governmental planning*. Cambridge, MA: Harvard University Press.

Macintyre, A. (1981) *After virtue*. Notre Dame: University of Notre Dame Press.

Revelle, R. (1975) 'Will the earth's land and water resources be sufficient for future populations?' in *The population debate: dimensions and perspectives*, Papers of the World Population Conference, Bucharest, 1974, II. New York: United Nations, pp. 3–14.

Rogers, P. *et al.* (1996) 'Measuring sustainable development in Asia: environmental quality indices', Division of Engineering and Applied Science, Harvard University, Cambridge, MA.

Sen, A.K. (1987) *On ethics and economics*. Oxford: Basil Blackwell.

Smith, A. (1759) *The theory of moral sentiments*. Indianapolis: Liberty Classics, 1976. Orig: London: Longman.

Wilson, E.O. (1975) *Sociobiology: the new synthesis*. Cambridge, MA: Harvard University Press.

Wolfe, P. (1959) 'The simplex method for quadratic programming', *Econometrica*, 57 (3), pp. 382–98.

3. Melvin L. Greenhut (b. 1921)[1]

3.1   EARLY LIFE

I will profess to having been essentially a product of the Depression years, during which time my father worked as a part-time policeman, a window washer, and probably at many other tasks I was sheltered from knowing about. This bleak history, combined with my mother's work in a factory and their insistence that I acquire at least a high school education (which neither of them had), played on my mind throughout my young life. It was probably the fact of being poor, never owning a bicycle nor even a baseball glove, i.e., until my father learned I played a game in right field using a friend's catcher's mit, which surely served as the sources of a personal drive I have had. Most importantly, my father and mother were inspirational to me. Their stick-to-it policy of work, work, work, and take care of yourself, stands in stark contrast to the 'perhaps excessive and unending' welfare gratuities of today. I can easily add at this point the fact of inspiration derived later on in

---

[1]   Greenhut (1995b; c), as revised by the editors. I have two volumes of selected essays in the series, the first my collected papers in locational economics (Greenhut 1995a) and the second my papers in spatial microeconomics (Greenhut 1995c). I have also been honoured by a festschrift (Ohta and Thisse 1993).

life from my Father- and Mother-in-law, Evan and Huldah Griffith, each of whom lived by the same take care of yourself ethic.

Throughout the Depression years, I wondered why an army of unemployed – as large in number as the combined American Army, Navy, Marine Corps, and Coast Guard of World War II – had to exist. What was wrong with economists? What did they know? What did they do? I rather imagine most economists of ages 65–80 today, regardless of family wealth during the 1930s, were motivated to study our science because of the real economic crises that prevailed back then.

3.2   A SKETCH OF MY CAREER

But enough of these personal reflections about the dark ages. Allow me to insert below a few statements by Hiroshi Ohta that were based on information my son, John, had provided him for a book he was coediting with Jacques Thisse (Ohta and Thisse 1993, pp. 2, 3). Because this book was brought to my attention only after its publication, I have corrected a slight error and added minor updating to Professor Ohta's remarks to reflect a change in my University position which had taken place but which had not been publicized at that time. After the insertion, I shall sketch in personalized form what some of my years as an academician were like, as well as a few immediately preceding ones. After these sketches are complete, I shall provide a brief summary of the articles included in my Edward Elgar selected essays (Greenhut 1995a; b):

> For readers who are not completely familiar with Mel Greenhut's career, we take a moment to provide the following brief sketch. Mel received his Ph.D. degree from Washington University in 1951. His first professorial position was at Auburn. He was side-tracked into administration as Associate Dean at the University of Richmond, during which time he consulted extensively with AT&T . . . and research companies located in Washington, DC. He was consulting editor to *Industrial Development*, and also served on the National Economic Policy Committee of the US Chamber of Commerce and the executive committee of the Southern Economic Association. He was on the board of editors of the Association's journal and a professor at Florida State University for many years. Since 1966, he has been at Texas A&M University, initially as Professor and Department Head, and from 1969 up to the present as Distinguished Professor of Economics; in 1986 he also became the George and Gladys Abell Professor of Liberal Arts, and in 1992 the title of emeritus was added. For many years, Mel Greenhut served as Adjunct Distinguished Professor at the University of Oklahoma and at the University of Karlsrühe, in Germany. He has lectured extensively throughout Europe and the Orient, besides the United States. Summer visiting appointments included Michigan State University and the Universities of

Cape Town and Pittsburgh.

His publications consist (at present count) of a dozen books, and articles numbering in the three digits. His latest interests include work in fuzzy mathematics. He is a contributor to *The New Palgrave* and to the latest *Encyclopedia of Economics*, under publication by McGraw-Hill. He was listed in the initial 1981 *Who's Who in Economics* and the editions that have followed.

On a personal side, he is married to Elmara Griffith Greenhut, has four children – Peggy Chase, Pam Blaylock, John Greenhut, and Pat Thomsen – and ten grandchildren. He served actively and in the US Army reserve, obtaining the rank of major. He has been listed in *Who's Who in the United States* for more than 30 years.

'Drop everything else.' This is one of the colonel-like orders Professor Greenhut would give to his students. But they knew that he was a decisive and conscientious teacher who cares. He cares about any fuzzy idea a student may bring forth. The caring teacher would then say, 'Sounds great!' The decisive colonel would hasten to add, 'Let's work out a paper. Drop everything else.' The conscientious teacher would then sweat on working *for* and *with* the student repeatedly for improvement of the output. Upon completion of the work, Mel would finally say, 'Well done. Have a day off this weekend. Well, make it a half.'

In many ways, the second leg of my professional career (in spatial microeconomics) started with Hiroshi Ohta. But well before Hiroshi Ohta, I had visualized my field of specialization in the form of the old and new location economics, indeed much as Hisao Nishioka described in Ohta and Thisse (1993, pp. xvii–xx). This Professor Nishioka, formerly a President of the Aoyama Gakuin University in Tokyo, knew as well as I did my views on location economics. This gentleman had translated my *Plant location* (Greenhut 1956) book into Japanese besides also other writings of mine. I had become interested initially in location economics because a new head (Werner Hochwald) took over the economics department at Washington University; I believe it was in 1948. He quickly advised me that because a senior professor who I virtually idolized, Orval Bennett, was retiring in a year or so, and because I was moving to Auburn University (then called the Alabama Polytechnic Institute), I had *better* select a different dissertation subject than the antitrust laws (Professor Bennett's field of specialization). Professor Hochwald recommended industrial location and the southern economy. I decided – absolutely no!

One thing any military experience can teach is the reality that if you are unwilling to go it all by yourself, you should take the order and swallow your pride (or desire, is it?) until you can say to hell with everyone and everything. Until then, do it the Army, Navy way, as the pilots who were then all in the Army or Navy Air Force had often been told. So although I had happily volunteered three times for certain duties during my days in the Army – probably the only thing that looked special on my Army records – and regardless of whether the good Lord negated my fantasies on each occasion in order to protect me and/or my comrades in the army, I knew that in my new world as a graduate student I could simply say no to Dr Hochwald. So I forthrighteously and independently 'volunteered' to write on industrial location in Alabama. Because back then the Ph.D. was dragged out by professors even more mercilessly than today, I later on left out of the dissertation the main cogs of my thinking at that time, my 1952 papers on location theory (Greenhut 1952a; b); in effect, I left my dissertation (Greenhut 1951a) essentially restricted to a rehashing of early-accepted location theory along with some data on the location of industry. My conformist decision, and by this stage of my life I had a wife and three very young offspring to support (so I really had to conform), allowed me to convert my dissertation a few years later to a better manuscript, a book entitled *Plant location in theory and practice* (1956).

To my way of thinking, the main contributions in the book were to convert the von Thünen-Weber school of thought via Lösch into a new location economics. This belief was highlighted by the papers I wrote in the early 1950s and 1960s that are reprinted in Greenhut (1995a, pt. II). Permit me to recognize that the good Lord had sent a young German to study at Auburn in addition to the many other blessings He had given me. Since the Lutheran Church in Auburn, for which I had the honour to serve as a trustee, was sponsoring this student, I had the good fortune to be with him often. In what I can call a partial – but unfair to him – exchange, this young student helped me with my attempts to read German while I helped him in his studies in the principles of economics course at Auburn. (For those unfamiliar with the Ph.D. requirements of yesteryears, reading skills in two foreign languages were required, and German was my second choice.) The book that *we* worked with, not yet translated into English (nor for that matter until many years later), was August Lösch's *Die räumliche Ordnung der Wirtschaft* (1939). Talk about good luck, good fortune, or *God*-given breaks in life, I had them!

My late 1940s, my 1950s, and early 1960s were dotted with diverse academic positions, including an associate deanship that subsequently led to an offer of a full deanship which I most fortunately rejected. During this period, I worked essentially in the field of what I would call the old and the new location economics, including their applications. This emphasis took place in partial conjunction with some writings, actually a couple of books on macroeconomics. My side interest in macroeconomics probably reflected the Depression years effect on me to become a do-gooder economist.

If good luck, or frankly more to the way I truly feel, the great fortune of having had *God* protecting me was ever in doubt in my mind, this possibility had been dispelled in very late 1950, a half-year or so before my dissertation was completed and the Ph.D. awarded me. As many reservists feared during the Korean War, I received a military service recall (and this clearly, by coincidence) to the division that I had been with about six and a half years previously, the 87th (Acorn) Division. But the recall notice (including about 80 other Alabamans) had been misdelivered to each of us. Without this particular knowledge of misdelivery, when I learned about being recalled from my tearful wife at *the front door of our home in Auburn*, I was truly shaken. Because I hated goodbyes, my wife was convinced that I had deliberately failed to tell her I was going back on active duty. She expected me suddenly to be packed up and announce I had been recalled to service as I walked out of the front door to a waiting taxi.

If you are familiar with Special Orders of the Military, you can appreciate the fact that my wife misread the orders. The order I had received was a cancellation order, a cancellation involving about 80 men who had never shown up for duty at the posts they were assigned to. Indeed, though I was familiar with the cryptic language of Special Orders, I will admit that I was so nervous and upset about the order she had shoved at me, along with my sudden thoughts of having to leave my family and in all possibility never getting my dissertation completed nor approved nor the Ph.D. awarded, that I missed for at least 30 minutes the fact that what we had received was a cancellation. Having once quivered at the door of a military plane fearing possible bail out orders, I have ever since that day in Auburn wondered which of these two events gave me the shakier knees. When a couple of years later, towards the end of the Korean War, our military establishment offered reservists with some (unrecalled) combined number of years of active and reserve service the option to go standby, I jumped at going standby. This status meant no future reserve duty pay nor in-line active training service that would lead to promotions in the reserve, but among other benefits the opportunity to still feel patriotic by remaining in the reserve. Most vitally, the great advantage of standby status was the fact that only Congress in a declaration of war could henceforth immediately claim my services in place of the very happy, pleasant, and safe days I was having as an academician. Of course, when I say 'safe days as an academician', I am recalling that back then students were not as violent as we somehow or other have permitted them to be today.

A few final words about *God*-provided grace and good fortune are warranted before I can turn my attention to certain events in the 1960s which serve as direct background to my work. First, back in the servile days when I was still a graduate student, I was fascinated by the underlying theoretical framework of the writings of von Thünen, Weber and followers. This fascination led me to construct my two 1952 articles in the *Southern Economic Journal* (Greenhut 1952a; b). Why that journal? Well, the editor was Gus Schwenning, a delightful individual of German ancestry. He knew and virtually worshipped the writings of August Lösch much as I, the latter condition to be readily apparent to readers of the first volume of my selected essays. More germane to present statements about good fortune, if ever anyone meets a journal editor more interested in the author's subject than I did in meeting Professor Schwenning, I would like to hear of it. Our joint fascination with the German writers on location economics, combined with my early contacts and discussions with Professor Schwenning, had led me to the philosophical interests about thought frameworks which led me to my specialization in the economics of space.

3.3   PHILOSOPHICAL FRAMEWORKS

I began both volumes of my Edward Elgar selected essays with a few papers on the subject of philosophical frameworks. In particular, the roots to my location economics are developed in a number of early papers which deal respectively with economics as a science and an art (Greenhut 1960b), and whether realistic assumptions are important (Greenhut 1966c; 1968). In a generalized sense, they enquire into the concept of economic space and how that dimension impacts on economic theory. Certainly the last theme moves us towards what I call the field of spatial microeconomics, as it contends that via the spatial requirement of oligopolistic markets and hence behavioural uncertainty, the conception of a zero-profit general equilibrium cannot hold. As one would accordingly anticipate, my papers on space and economic value contend that for many objectives, such as regulating utilities, the simplistic unrealistic models that have so often been heralded by writers of the Chicago School (e.g. Milton Friedman) are insufficient. Greater postulated realism provides more far-reaching advances than too simplistic a set of assumptions. Indeed, if the missing parts in a model significantly change the consequences of the theory, and if the more complete model yields results actually conforming closer to observed reality than the less complete one, the need for more inclusive and realistic models is obvious (see also Machlup 1952). To say the least, space (the cost of distance) reshapes the preference scheme of people.

As is manifest throughout these early location papers (also Greenhut 1959a), although I consider realism of models to be a secondary objective *per se*, it is especially vital to any normative theory. This is so because normative theory, and for that matter dynamic theories, especially those which seek to provide microscopic details of future states will be difficult to provide, and certainly very costly to apply. These theories cannot be readily confirmed by testing their consequences, so the most realistic assumptions which can be grasped and controlled must be used. This requirement of realism, and hence use of verifiable assumptions, serves in place of testing the deductions in the theory. These papers recognize inexorably that location economics is a field of study which (presumably) seeks to explain the spatial ordering of production based on a spatial ordering of consumption. The existence of costly distances generates oligopoly markets.

I had felt for many years that the standard neo-classical spaceless microeconomics must be subsumed within an analytical framework that included distances. My spatial economics papers call for greater realism, such as I had believed was needed for the old location economics. In particular, they provide a general theory of maximum profits which fits a spaceless as well as the spatial microeconomic world (Greenhut 1962). To buttress my belief that classical spaceless microeconomics is both inadequate as well as irrelevant *per se*, Greenhut (1958) returns to the subject of realism in tracing the mathematical properties and restrictions which then applied to the theory of business management. It is further in order for me to propose at this point that all of us in academia are pompous, perhaps because if we lacked strong belief in our own way of thinking and in our subject matter specialization, we could not teach nor write with the conviction that is necessary for self-fulfilment. If I were writing that same paper today, I would now – in conformance with the preceding statement – have to include my own beliefs of the inadequacy of the crisp number mathematics which we apply in the form of the calculus *vis-à-vis* the more realistic logic of (and need to use) fuzzy math: a theme I return to later.

More to the point of my philosophical frameworks, it follows naturally from my theory of what maximum profits portend *and* my belief that more realistic mathematics is needed to explain how most entrepreneurs resolve their decision problems that further words of philosophical order were required, as in Greenhut (1966a). Finally, because all of us who have been attracted to the science of economics have some 'do gooder' in our make-up, I chose as a fundamental closing point to these early writings my paper on normative microeconomic theory (Greenhut 1967). How things ought to be is a captivating subject which involves complex postulational roots to support any meaningful normative theory.

These papers all help frame the overall philosophical basis which led me to probe further into the field of economic space, and especially into what I call spatial microeconomics. This extension of my early thoughts on the subject of industrial location opens up a new thought system which, in my opinion, includes as a sub-part the spaceless microeconomics that many of our Veblenesque economists of today insist on maintaining. Why not move closer to the real world, I keep wondering? Perhaps my later papers (reprinted in Greenhut 1995b, pts II–III) will convince a few readers of the applicability and inclusiveness of spatial microeconomics.

3.4   LOCATION ECONOMICS: OLD AND NEW

Within location economics I initially focused attention on the analytical frameworks and theories of von Thünen and Weber (for example, Greenhut 1952a). The microeconomic theory basis for their models lies in the theory of pure competition. Indeed, rather surprisingly perhaps, the phenomenon of space in the old location economics, or shall I say, in the economics that supposedly included the realism of costly distance, had no philosophical impact on classical and neoclassical economic theory. It failed in this regard because the von Thünen-Weber least cost location school of thought was simply a sub-discipline, a specialized applied enquiry *derived from* the prevailing general economic theory of the times. But later writings are shown to depart from the old location models. Specifically, the new location economics centres on the inclusions which Lösch and E.M. Hoover had essentially pioneered: the study of market areas, shapes and sizes. That subject matter and theoretical results depend in part on the price policies of firms.

Even more fundamentally perhaps, the literature on location interdependence (which reflected the interests in imperfect competition economics of H. Hotelling, A. Smithies, and others) served in turn to lead us still further from the old to the new economics. This cross-over is evidenced in my early articles which endeavoured to formulate a general integrated theory of plant location (Greenhut 1955). The fact that price policies determine market area sizes and shapes and relate to the spatial interdependence of firms signifies that more than cost of production and distribution is involved in plant locations: viz., the distribution of demands. Moreover, the shape of the demand function affects the marginal revenue intersection with marginal costs in determining what is indeed the optimal (*real* least cost) location.

The subjects of market areas and spatial interdependence require references to and indeed evaluation of discriminatory pricing and its impacts. For this reason I co-authored a paper with Professor Ohta on Joan Robinson's theory of discrimination in *spaceless* markets (Greenhut and Ohta 1976). The effect of spatial price discrimination on market areas, both in size and shape, is particularly intrinsic to the extensions that followed the writings of August Lösch and Ed Hoover.

In understanding the evolution of my work I admit to some back-sliding from earlier positions. I must admit that among the numerous surveys I conducted I often interviewed entrepreneurs who *insisted* that they sought psychic income not profit maximization. Early in my career, I therefore proposed a maximum satisfaction alternative to maximum profits, typically concluding with either the contention that the maximum profit 'economic-man' was sufficiently inclusive of all important decisions made in the business world, and hence sufficed for the purposes of our science, or that they were equivalent. Such equivalence would apply because the effective working lifetime and total income earned by a person requires sufficient psychic pleasures in order for a factor to continue in production and the firm to be viable. Indeed, in more recent years, following the second idea just noted, I have gone so far in my thoughts, as evidenced in Greenhut (1970a), as to include the economic decision of every rational person as being a profit-maximizing decision. Oddly enough, in rereading my papers for the purpose of this Introduction, I ran across a quotation I had long forgotten that I had included in my first published paper (Greenhut 1951b). I am not certain that George Stigler meant what I now assert I personally believe, namely, to paraphrase Stigler: psychic income winners actually have lower costs of production than others, ceteris paribus, and hence will prove to be viable in the market-place.

I do not believe I 'back-slided' or 'changed gears as it were', but if I did, I will also admit I was once a liberal Keynesian and am now a converted supply-side Keynesian. Lest some readers challenge the last possibility, please write to me: I have a book on that subject (Greenhut and Stewart 1983) which alas did not sell too well, but which I do believe converts the original demand-side Keynesian theory to a demand, supply-side Keynesian theory.

I have undertaken a number of empirical studies formulated to reject (or support, as it were) my theoretical papers in location economics (reprinted in Greenhut 1995a, pt. III). These are based on my maximum profit theory of location and with substantial emphasis given as to how meaningful surveys could be conducted. It is noted that many surveys conducted by research companies and development Commissions were designed to encourage development of the state or region in question. Spurious semantics are employed in the surveys, all of which tend to prove whatever was wanted by the employing institution. My very first work (Greenhut 1951b) compared and described the location motives of entrepreneurs. Next I proposed 'An empirical model and a survey' (Greenhut 1959b) for conducting studies of why firms are located in certain areas. My paper, 'Size of markets vs. transport costs' (Greenhut 1960a) stresses the double meaning which undefined terms can provide. These papers, as noted above, establish the foundations for objective studies of why industry has moved to certain states, regions, etc.

Related to the reasons why managers located plants where they did is the question of the fundamental advantages certain places have, an advantage set commonly described by location theorists as the area's economic base (Greenhut 1966b). There are two approaches here to regional economic development theory: the one is based on the opinion that the location theorists who followed Weber, Lösch and Hoover were theoretical economists more so than practitioners; the other is that the many writers in recent years who stress what is referred to as regional science have been more of the applied type of scholars. They have formulated economic base theory besides the use of programming, gravity models, and factor analysis among other tools, as they directed their attention to regional economic development.

It will be seen that several of my papers proceed to discuss different regional developments, city growth, and public facility locations vis-à-vis private company locations (for example, Greenhut and Mai 1980). To 'round-out' the study of applied location economics. I have also written on plant expansions and multiplant site selections (Greenhut *et al.* 1974; Greenhut and Hwang 1978) and on the important influence on locations of regulated carriers *and* the way firms conceive of their optimal spatial price patterns (Greenhut *et al.* 1986), where the latter is based in part on market types and customer distributions. These papers lead directly to my work in spatial microeconomics.

I have been developing interest in applying game theory to location economics. Actually, this tendency represents a take-off from the theory of locational interdependence. Readers interested in considering locational interdependence theory chronologically and *in greater detail* than that provided in the initial papers of Greenhut (1995a, pt. II) are recommended my *Plant location in theory and practice* (1956, ch. VI). For present purposes, it may suffice for us to consider the manager of a duopoly firm which is planning a location somewhere along a line market extending over the interval (0, 1). We postulate homogenous consumers being evenly distributed along the line with each of them possessing a demand curve given by $p = b - aq$. For simplicity, cost of production is zero.

Now the manager of 'our' firm might select a quartile location i in expectation that the rival firm's manager would locate optimally at the opposite quartile j, while next adopting the equilibrium profit-maximizing price. That location j, to repeat, is at the opposite quartile to the one i is considering. Each firm's manager has been making noises in favour of symmetrical locations, where by making noises I mean hiring a real estate agent to procure a purchase *option* for a selected piece of real estate where a plant could be constructed. The rival's location at j would likely lead to that firm adopting the mill price $b/2$. And of course the manager of firm i has no reason to locate differentially (or competitively) against the rival firm; so our firm i's manager is inclined to exercise the option for quartile site i, at which location the required price decision would also be mill price $b/2$.[2] Significantly, these prices are set by each firm in the second stage of the game, with the game solved because $\pi_i\,(P^*_i, P^*_j) \geq \pi_j\,(P^*_i, P^*_j)$.

However, consider the following alternative scenario. In contrast to the aforementioned expectations, if doubt exists as to the rival's conjecture that firm j should be located at the other quartile, and instead that it is likely to be located closer to the centre of the market, our firm i would also be likely to be moved closer to the centre of the line market. Then in the second stage, prices would be less than $b/2$. Such lower prices must arise if the firms are to be able to sell to buyers located at their peripheral market points $(0, 1)$. Extension of the location price game beyond two firms is, of course, part of the literature on locational interdependence. In game theory terms, that problem involves an n person game.

It is important to recognize that the price decision is of the Bertrand-type subject to a capacity constraint, where in location price games the rival's capacity constraints are themselves given by the locations that are selected. Under these constraints, the Bertrand price does not sink to the $P = MC$ level in instances of a dispersed industry. Effectually then, as in the paper 'Games, capitalism and general location theory' (Greenhut 1957) or my joint paper on Bertrand and Cournot (Greenhut, Lee and Mansur 1991), we have, in substance, game theory evaluations of location price decisions.

It is in a sense unfortunately the case that the oligopolistic industrial distributions which typically prevail in free enterprise systems run the gauntlet from (a) several different sized firms located at a production centre, say X, to (b) a few (often small) rival firms distributed variously over areas which are neither connected by a single line or even necessarily by just a few lines, up to (c) other production centres located at diverse distances and directions from the production centre X. This panorama suggests that game theory *per se* cannot approach in scope nor analytical depth the broader framework of thought provided by Lösch, Hoover and followers. Instead, in this writer's view, it is more along the line of the papers in Greenhut (1995a, pt. II) plus a fuzzy math game theory approach, and an appendix my son inspired, which Ohta and I included in our book, *Theory of spatial prices and market areas* (1975) that the needed generalized framework is likely to be found.

---

[2] George Norman in reading this Introduction pointed out to me that the standard $b/2$ solution fails to consider the competition between firms 'for consumers at the centre of the market'. Using *Mathematica* output, his intuition was proven with the final optimal price involving a complicated expression (too lengthy to warrant specification here) which approaches the old $b/2$ solution.

3.5   TEXAS A&M

During the late 1960s, I had the exciting challenge to develop a top-quality department of economics at Texas A&M. I leaped at the opportunity partly because of my frustration with the growth of our department of economics at Florida State University (FSU). Two top quality economists, Jim Buchanan and Charles Ferguson, had expressed interest in relocating at FSU in the middle 1960s, in Jim's case to return to FSU. However, between our faculty, its head, and the Dean of the College, their joining us fell through the cracks.

Alas, I had long wanted to be in an economics department which had many research-leading economists. This appetite had been whetted by a summer visiting professorship and possible permanent stay that I had at Michigan State, as well as opportunities to go to Berkeley and College Park, among other exciting places. I had turned down these overtures because of my wife's *strong* desire to remain in the southern part of the United States. So, when Texas A&M invited me to give a few lectures and subsequently offered me a veritable *carte blanche* to build a top quality department, I had little reason not to move.

The President at that time of Texas A&M University was Earl Rudder, a general in the US Army Reserve, a graduate of A&M, and a former Light Colonel who had led the charge of our forces in scaling the heights at Pointe du Hoc. He was also a close friend of Larry Fouraker, then Dean of the Harvard Business School. Rather interestingly, Larry, an A&M graduate, had been on the faculty at Penn State and had been responsible many years prior to the 1960s in having his department enquire as to whether I would be interested in moving from Auburn, Alabama to College Park, Pennsylvania. Larry, by the way, has long been interested in multinational corporate oligopolies, and my own writings from the early days had heralded the importance of oligopolistic markets. Mr. Rudder, who dearly loved A&M, as do most of its former students, was a close friend of Governor Connally. The University was then a male-only institution, half of whom were in the Corps of Cadets with the other 3000 having interests outside of the military in their minds for the years following graduation. Earl Rudder wanted another University of Texas type for his A&M. But during his early days as President of A&M, he had learned to his deep regret that, beyond the military accomplishments of its graduates plus the rather selective albeit limited research accomplishments of its faculty, the University had not achieved the status among the elites of academia that he wanted.[3] Need I say that Larry

---

[3]   Interestingly, George Patton is said to have stated, 'Give me an Army of West Point graduates and I will win a battle; give me an Army of Texas A&M Aggies and I will win a

Fouraker recommended me to Earl Rudder.

I received a blank cheque from Earl Rudder to develop a top-quality department which would offer the Ph.D. degree. The blank cheque included ten secretaries for ten faculty members when I first moved there in 1966,[4] plus first class airline passage for me anytime I felt there was advantage in my travelling to DC or elsewhere. Within three years, we had converted a faculty of four Ph.D.s and seven with masters degrees only to a faculty of about 24 Ph.D.s and three or so without. Our seven MA student candidates had become some unremembered number, several times the original; and we had up to 40 Ph.D. candidates walking our corridors by 1969.

Professors Ferguson, Basmann, Furubotn, Saving and many other very well-known men today were part of our new faculty, including, for example, Bob Ekelund, Horst Siebert, Phil Gramm, Ray Battalio, John Kagel, Chuck Maurice, Phil Rahbany, Steve Pejovich, Rufus Waters, Bert Bowden plus others. Oskar Morgenstern was a regular visiting adjunct professor with us for a few years and Herman Hartley, J.N.K. Rao, Ron Hocking, and Rudy Freund of the TAMU Institute of Statistics provided teaching and related support to our department. Our other faculty, including Al Chalk, its former head, and Irv Linger, a long-time faculty member, carried diverse administrative responsibilities and heavier teaching loads than those who were specifically mentioned above. They were primarily responsible for trying to maintain the teaching excellence that had characterized the department prior to my joining it. This, by the way, was the hardest, and in some respects the impossible, target for a publish-perish group interested chiefly in working with graduate students.

Among our Ph.D. students was Hiroshi Ohta. My good friend Hisao Nishioka, who had had the courtesy of visiting me and my family in Tallahassee years earlier with his wife and daughter, had recommended Hiroshi, his brightest student, to me. Hiroshi, the nephew of a World War II Kamikaze crewman, was as challenging to me as a student as had been Professor Nishioka when he was translating (and questioning me regularly about) my *Plant location* book. After a few years at A&M of rounding out my own prior efforts to advance the integration of location interdependence and market area theory with, may I call it, the old location theory, Hiroshi joined me in seeking to integrate location economics with general microeconomic theory. Manifestly, for one who lived in Texas, spatial distances had their impacts on production and consumption. Also quite clear

---

war.' That there were more officers in the Army from Texas A&M than from the Point may help buttress this claim.

4 My severest constraint up until my move to A&M was in not having sufficient secretarial support to counterbalance my poor handwriting and writing skills and hence the multiple rewriting attempts I found necessary for improving the prose of my papers.

to our way of thinking, space must be integrated with time in order for any truly meaningful advanced theory of microeconomics to arise.

3.6   SPATIAL MICROECONOMICS

My spatial microeconomics papers stem chiefly from interactions I had with graduate students at Texas A&M, with my son, John, now a Finance Professor at Arizona State University West, and with George Norman. These papers start with one I wrote many many years ago with Bill Pfouts, a paper that probed into the pricing policies of the *spatial* monopolist (Greenhut and Pfouts 1957). This early jump start, as it were, on a topic that has continued to fascinate me over the years led among other papers to my first paper with my son (Greenhut and Greenhut 1975). In that paper, we probed theoretically into the different price schedules and location effects that competitive firms at alternative production centres would have over both their local and their distant markets. As one might expect, that paper next required evaluation of how firms actually do price in free enterprise countries. Included among those that were studied are the US, then West Germany, and Japan (Greenhut *et al.* 1980; Greenhut 1981a; Greenhut, Hwang and Shwiff 1984).

One extension of different pricing policies is to compare the *output* effects of monopoly and competitive f.o.b. pricing with spatially discriminatory pricing. These particular roots of space microeconomics are themselves just part of the panoply of differences that is brought about by conceiving of a microeconomics which includes the spatial dimension. My papers along these lines also relate to a paper entitled 'Impacts of distance on microeconomic theory' (Greenhut 1978) which brings into focus the full spatial picture I had visualized during the late 1970s.

Perhaps the most general and pervasive impact of the spatial phenomenon is that it points to the oligopoly market type as the *only* realistic market entity. It follows that whether or not oligopolistic markets can be revealed as having deterministic solutions in the short- and long-run becomes critical subject matter. This is especially the case for those of us who believe that greater realism is needed in economic theory. Two of my papers (1970b; 1978) which followed my conception of a deterministic theory of oligopoly met with particular criticism, *and I continue to* claim that the subject of economic space has no greater requirement than appreciating the impacts on it of different demand functions (Greenhut *et al.* 1975).[5] These impacts are

5   See my responses in Greenhut (1974; 1981b) and, in general, in Greenhut *et al.* (1987, app. A).

not only central to spatial economics *per se*, but provide insights into the long-run determinacy of oligopoly markets. Indeed this analysis also points to the legal and other applied spin-offs from the theory of spatial microeconomics (Greenhut and Greenhut 1977; Greenhut with Soper, Norman and Benson 1991).

My first applied paper in spatial microeconomics discusses errors we economists are subject to, especially if we ignore space as a dimension to be included with time (Greenhut, Greenhut and Ohta 1984). But space is much more than just a needed dimension. My very recent papers with John Greenhut demonstrate alternative uses for the spatial framework of thought; i.e., uses beyond those stressed in a general paper (Greenhut and Greenhut 1992a). For example, the portfolio theory and CAPM model of the recent Nobel Laureates in finance economics, namely Markowitz and Sharpe, can be evaluated and extended under the spatial framework (Greenhut and Greenhut 1992b). Indeed a basic reason for being more realistic in economic theory is that the theory of pure competition and its simple monopoly alternative offer restricted applications of economic theory. Whatever the specific uses, especially those which would involve trial lawyers, requires that we be cognizant of interest group impacts; moreover, we must be able to distinguish between non-predatory and predatory pricing, both within a nation and between nations. The spatial framework provides a helpful vista. In fact, as one focuses on the international scene, the impact of taxes becomes clearer when viewed from the perspective of spatial micro theory. Furthermore, they are central to the policies legislators have practised in the past and may practise in the future (Greenhut and Norman 1988).

What merger constraints, among other legislative enactments, are really desirable from the consumer welfare standpoint is also clarified in my opinion when constructed on the foundations of spatial microeconomics rather than the classical spaceless microeconomics. I have written several papers along these lines, including analysis of the base-point pricing system (Greenhut, Benson and Norman 1990a; b). Applications of spatial microeconomics are next shown to reflect the relation between free entry conditions and the legalized trademark support of product differentiation. Most vitally, conceiving of differentiated products along a line is but a simple carry-over from the line focus of location economics. That spatial microeconomics even answers such classic problems as why and how the fees of MD's have been found to increase with an increase in their supply *ceteris paribus*, in complete denial of elementary demand–supply economics, is also explained (Greenhut *et al.* 1985). Finally, I have also considered selected aspects of airline deregulation against the backlight of spatial microeconomics (Greenhut, Greenhut and Norman 1991).

It should be evident from my previous sketch of my papers that the same type of observation Mark Blaug (1986) entered about the classical English economists being reformers who addressed themselves to the economic policy issues of their day also applies to spatial price theorists. Most important to many of us in this field of study is the need to determine whether overall efficiency characterizes the economic landscape. A by-product of this need is well evident in my papers dealing with mergers, delivered pricing systems, and general antitrust policy (for example Greenhut and Ohta 1972; 1979a; b).

3.7   GAME THEORY AND FUZZY MATH

While mathematics has been used as extensively in the field of spatial microeconomics as it is in all of present-day economic literature, one future difference may stem from our natural emphasis on oligopolistic industries, which industries point directly to the importance of game theory and fuzzy math. I will accordingly later propose that the uncertain action-reaction decisions of oligopolists involves fuzzy numbers, not crisp ones. I further predict that fuzzy math must (and will) become a vital topic in the future. But first, let us turn to some thoughts about game theory, *viz.* locational interdependence.

Present-day location theory, unlike that of von Thünen, Weber and their followers, has focused to no small extent on the locational interdependence of firms. The writers who were interested in locational interdependence, including H. Hotelling, A. Smithies, M. Copeland, A. Lerner, H.W. Singer, and E.H. Chamberlin, among many others, stressed duopoly-oligopoly markets pursuant to their central interest in imperfect competition economics. This school of thought also had roots in game theory, and as noted in my writings on location theory proved to be integrateable with the classic location economics of von Thünen and Weber. In substance, the writers on locational interdependency, and more recently present-day location, price (quantity) game theory, considered all feasible location alternatives while, in effect, selecting the best prices (quantities) for each location. In substance, price became the proper sub-game.

Consider in the game theory context a perfect information game, which means that the players (firms) know the history of the game, i.e., they know all of the past moves of the game. Any of the players can, accordingly, reconstruct the game, starting from any point in the game. This corresponds to assuming that two chess players have such perfect recall that if, because of an earthquake, the chess board were to fall to the ground, either of the players can reconstruct the game and arrive at the positions that existed prior to the quake. The perfect information game requires each player to know meticulously the history of competition in his/her market. Simply put, the past is an open, well documented book.

A multi-stage game commits the participants to playing the game in stages (sub-games). If the payoffs (profits) are distributed to the players at the end of the last stage, then rational players must commit themselves to playing all of the sub-games. A common application of multi-stage games to the space economy was the two-stage game. Here, the firms determine all of their feasible locations in the first stage, and then confirm their profit maximizing location via the equilibrium price (output) that is next derived. In substance, they determine their profit maximizing prices (outputs) given all potential profit maximizing (optimal) locations (capacities). One can recognize that the full game is solved recursively, i.e., the last stage, when solved, proves the feasibility of the location that was expected to be the best in the first stage.

It is manifest that the relevant sets of strategies are virtually infinite in each game. Locations are practically countless and so are the prices. Nevertheless, the theory of games points to a Nash equilibrium provided the strategies are finite. In order to invoke Nash's theory, economists close the location (capacity) and price (output) spaces by making them bounded and convex. Thus the location is set at a point in a closed interval (or over the circumference of a circle) while the price is bounded by a reservation value from above and by 0 from below. We have in reverse order $0 < p <$ reservation price, with output greater than or equal to zero, and restricted by the length of the interval (or the circumference of the location circle). To repeat, the location is synonymous with capacity. With sufficient abstractions, including explicit capacity constraints, a location, price equilibrium pair could be obtained for each firm. Most significantly, the theory of games does not tell us *per se* which equilibrium results when there are many equilibria, nor does it tell us how to play the game.

At an opposite end of the same spectrum as game theory stands a new sub-field of mathematics, fuzzy sets, a field that a former student of mine, Dr Yusuf Mansur, and I found impelling. Where game theory requires multiple abstractions, fuzzy sets can model and process *generalizations* as its special form of abstracting. For example, taste cannot typically be specified precisely, but it can be identified as slightly differentiated among all buyers; *or* elasticities of demand and supply cannot be precisely numbered, but they can be approximated as being more elastic for a certain good than another; *or* products which cannot be said to be identical or to differ from one to another on a scale of one to ten can be defined as just being similar; *and* market boundaries which cannot be said to be 1.427 miles in all directions from St Louis can be defined as being at varying distances within the market space of a St Louis firm. All of these statements, along with the locations of competitors, relate to fuzzy sets. For further example, the locations of rivals can be distinguished by the semantic that they are proximate to our production centre ABC, or that they are somewhat distant from ABC, or that their location is very distant from ABC, etc. In other words, we can model vague or incomplete knowledge via fuzzy sets to replicate empirical phenomena. And this is the way you and I actually consider most real-life alternatives, especially those involving our own actions and reactions to the actions and reactions of others. One must in contrast severely violate reality in employing crisp number game theory.

Perhaps a still more precise statement of the use of fuzzy mathematics in spatial economics requires inclusion here. Consider a firm that competes with five other firms in a large market, each member firm of which produces products similar to those of the others. Not all of the firms need be full competitors; rather, each firm may compete with the representative firm at a different level of interdependence. Their market sizes may be estimated subjectively by approximations, and the similarity of their products may be designated to varying extents, such as very similar, basically similar, not too similar, etc. May we say that the heterogeneous economic space which characterizes their competition can be described realistically. In fact, it can be described in a manner consistent with human cognitive processes and devoid of totally unrealistic abstraction, such as assuming (explicitly or implicitly) that all buyers and/or all sellers are located at a single point in space, as in the theory of perfect competition.

May I sum up my thoughts about game theory, spatial microeconomics, and fuzzy math as follows: The classic spaceless economy solutions of oligopoly that are so well known from the writings of Cournot, Bertrand, Stackelberg, Chamberlin, Robinson, and countless others can be easily extended to the spatial economy.[6] In similar manner, game theory can be applied to location economics. Most vitally, any microeconomics inclusion of costs of distances brings oligopoly firms into focus and these interdependent sellers run smack into fuzzy concepts. The fuzzy number reality of their economic decision making process colours the game that one would ascribe to these sellers. By what are called alpha cuts, along with the use of selected fuzzy-math principles, much is nevertheless salvageable. The only basic problem that remains lies in the fact that applications of fuzzy numbers signify that a band of solutions obtain rather than a single crisp number result. Of course, this condition places significant limits on the information which game theory can provide, as must next be emphasized.

---

[6] For example, I included a direct spatial take-off of Cournot in Greenhut (1970b, pp. 111–13). This spatial take-off was done under the sub-heading 'Introducing economic space into Cournot's model: buyers distributed over space.'

In the long run a precise microeconomic solution obtains given a world of fuzzy (oligopolistic behavioural uncertainty) relationships. The long-run precision I claim will hold is proposed in several papers (Greenhut 1978; 1981b and Greenhut and Ohta 1979a; b). Correspondingly, it is only in reflection of a precisely determined long-run optimal space economy solution that any definitive game can arise; this is so because the characteristic function and other game parameters can be prespecified only for that point in time as a spin-off from the unique equilibrium which that microeconomic theory will provide. It follows that a deterministic (unique-equilibrium) game theory derivation can stem only from a microeconomic theory of the long run, for it is in that period alone that crisp numbers do obtain. In this respect, game theory is therefore a sub-discipline within the general confines of spatial microeconomics (see Greenhut *et al.* 1994).

This writer thus proposes that a uniquely determinate crisp number Nash equilibrium game can obtain only in the long run of the space economy. In the short run, subjectively altered crisp numbers prevail or, more precisely, fuzzy numbers apply. Moreover, with respect to the more recent game theory which recognizes the existence of multiple oligopolistic equilibria alternatives *and* the use of subjectively weighted probabilities, the need to employ and advance fuzzy mathematics is quite evident. In sum, it is my belief that fuzzy mathematics will soon rise to the forefront in economics, including the present-day game theory which has been centring its attention more and more on the behaviourally uncertain actions and reactions of oligopolists (see Greenhut *et al.* 1995).

3.8 CONCLUSIONS

As mentioned at this chapter's outset, I was motivated to become an economist by the depression of the 1930s. In college in the late 1930s, and in graduate school in the late 1940s, the emphasis of my teachers was on trying to prove (perhaps just to themselves) that capitalism is the natural system, and as such is efficient and good. But the main line of thinking about economic systems then and for decades after World War II centred on proving market efficiency on the basis of perfect competition. But spatial realities generate oligopoly markets. As an advocate of spatial microeconomics, the question arises how can one demonstrate the efficiency of free enterprise economies without appeal to perfect (or let us say pure) competition. My 1971 book and some later ones, along with single-authored articles and papers written chiefly with my son John, George Norman and Hiroshi Ohta, have centred on such proof. Economists who still believe a main purpose should be to prove or disprove the viability of a free enterprise system (one that remains capitalistic in a classical sense distinct from one that is excessively regulated and subject to undue welfare interferences) can find many places in the writings just referred to with respect to which they could agree or disagree. Clearly, I hope our discipline will return to greater emphasis on its political economy roots, doing this via spatial price theory. Perhaps most importantly, such economic policies as those involving antitrust laws and the bureaucratic evaluations of these laws would reappear in a noticeably different light (as in Greenhut and Greenhut 1995). I trust that some readers of this chapter will consider carefully this contention.

As I point towards the conclusion, I would like to make certain 'political-type' and personal remarks. I should note initially that I have never kept a personal diary. So the challenge given me by Edward and Sandy Elgar to include autobiographical materials has stirred up thoughts about academic politics which, in time, would probably have been forgotten. Specifically, about ten years after I had received my Ph.D., I was busily engaged in side-line consulting work with the Amerad Research Co., and with an executive committee of AT&T, and with other organizations. I was offered the President-Elect position of the Southern Economic Association, but turned it down then because I was just too busy. A decade and a half later, I was again honoured that way by the association, but rejected it again. This time I wanted the Dean of the Liberal Arts College at Texas A&M to provide me with an *extra* secretary who would handle all of my added needs. He told the department head (Bob Tollison, I think it was then) that Mel will take the honour without my having to give him *extra* secretarial support; he already 'consumes' too much help. I surprised him. The honour of being president of an economics association was not a personal goal. Over the last 20 plus years, I have in fact tried my best to stay outside of the glad-handing fraternity. We academicians, to my way of thinking, often act too much like politicians, and that is such a low form of behaviour that I have preferred to limit my days of attendance at conventions. This has bothered my son, John, who has frequently criticized me for this, while often telling me about meeting someone who said, 'I know of your Dad but never met him, never ever saw him, what is he like?' I guess the final answer might be I am a recluse, except I do enjoy tennis, I used to be an avid golfer, and I find going to good parties and dances among the best events of life.

SELECTED WORKS

(1951a) 'Some factors influencing industrial location, with special reference to the small independent manufacturing firms in Alabama', unpublished Ph.D. dissertation, Washington University.

(1951b) 'Observations of motives to industrial location', *Southern Economic Journal*, 18 (2), pp. 225–8.*

(1952a) 'Integrating the leading theories of plant location', *Southern Economic Journal*, 18 (4), pp. 526–38.

(1952b) 'The size and shape of the market area of a firm, *Southern Economic Journal*, 19 (1), pp. 37–50.

(1955) 'A general theory of plant location', *Metroeconomica*, 7 (1), pp. 59–72.*

(1956) *Plant location in theory and practice*. Chapel Hill, NC: University of North Carolina Press, rep. (1982). Westport, CT: Greenwood Press.

(1957) 'Games, capitalism and general location theory', *Manchester School*, 25 (1), pp. 61–88.*

(1957) (with R.W. Pfouts) 'The pricing policies of a spatial monopolist', *Metroeconomica*, 9 (3), pp. 153–66.

(1958) 'Mathematics, realism and management science', *Management Science*, 4 (3), pp. 314–20.*

(1959a) 'Space and economic theory', *Papers and Proceedings*, Regional Science Association, pp. 267–80.*

(1959b) 'An empirical model and a survey: new plant locations in Florida', *Review of Economics and Statistics*, 41 (4), pp. 433–8.*

(1960a) 'Size of markets vs. transport costs in industrial location surveys and theory', *Journal of Industrial Economics*, 8 (2), pp. 172–84.*

(1960b) 'Science, art and norms in economics', *Journal of Philosophy and Phenomenological Research*, 21 (2), pp. 159–72.*

(1962) 'A general theory of maximum profits', *Southern Economic Journal*, 28 (3), pp. 278–85.*

(1966a) 'The decision process and entrepreneurial returns', *Manchester School*, 34 (3), pp. 247–67.*

(1966b) 'Needed: a return to the classics in regional economic development theory', *Kyklos*, 19 (3), pp. 461–79.*

(1966c) 'On the question of realism in economic theory and the regulation of public utilities', *Land Economics*, 42 (3), pp. 260–67.*

(1967) 'Hypotheses in science and an evaluation of normative microeconomic theory', *South African Journal of Economics*, 35 (2), pp. 134–44.*

(1968) 'On realism and unrealism in economic theory: a rejoinder', *Land Economics*, 44 (1), pp. 135–9.*

(1970a) *A theory of the firm in economic space*. New York: Appleton-Century-Crofts, rep. (1992). London: Gregg Revivals.

(1970b) 'The theory of the spatial and nonspatial firm', *Weltwirischaftliches Archiv*, 105 (1), pp. 87–113.

(1972) (with H. Ohta) 'Monopoly output under alternative spatial pricing techniques', *American Economic Review*, 62 (4), pp. 705–13.*

(1974) 'Mr Gripsrud and a theory of oligopoly', *Weltwirischaftliches Archiv*, 110 (3), pp. 518–24.

(1974) (with M.J. Hwang and H. Ohta) 'Price discrimination by regulated motor carriers: comment', *American Economic Review*, 64 (4), pp. 780–84.

(1975) (with J.G. Greenhut) 'Spatial price discrimination, competition and locational effects', *Economica*, n.s. 42 (4), pp. 153–66.*

(1975) (with M.J. Hwang and H. Ohta) 'Observations on the shape and relevance of the spatial demand function', *Econometrica*, 43 (4), pp. 669–82.

(1975) (with H. Ohta) *Theory of spatial prices and market areas*. Durham, NC: Duke University Press.

(1976) (with H. Ohta) 'Joan Robinson's criterion for deciding whether market discrimination reduces output', *Economic Journal*, 86 (1), pp. 96–7.*

(1977) (with J.G. Greenhut) 'Nonlinearity of delivered price schedules and predatory pricing', *Econometrica*, 45 (8), pp. 1871–5.

(1978) 'Impacts of distance on microeconomic theory', *Manchester School*, 46 (1), pp. 17–40.*

(1978) (with M.J. Hwang) 'Balancing multisite-multiplant operations over economic space', *Academia Economic Papers*, 6 (2), pp. 93–111.

(1979a) (with H. Ohta) 'Output effects of spatial price discrimination under conditions of monopoly and competition', *Southern Economic Journal*, 46 (1), pp. 71–84.*

(1979b) (with H. Ohta) 'Vertical integration of successive oligopolists', *American Economic Review*, 69 (1), pp. 137–41.

(1980) (with J.G. Greenhut and S-Y Li) 'Spatial pricing patterns in the United States', *Quarterly Journal of Economics*, 94 (2), pp. 329–50.*

(1980) (with C.C. Mai) 'Towards a general theory of public and private facility location', *Annals of Regional Science*, 14 (2), pp. 1–11.*

(1981a) 'Spatial pricing in the United States, West Germany and Japan', *Economica*, n.s. 48 (1), pp. 79–86.*

(1981b) 'Mr Dorward and impacts of distance on microeconomic theory', *Manchester School*, 49 (3), pp. 259–65.*

(1983) (with C. Stewart) *From basic economics to supply-side economics*. Lanham, MD: University Press of America.

(1984) (with J.G. Greenhut and H. Ohta) 'Theoretical error, economic space, price theory and data', *Aoyama Journal of International Politics, Economics and Business*, 1 (1), pp. 181–97.*

(1984) (with M. Hwang and S. Shwiff) 'Differences in spatial pricing in the United States: a statistical analysis and case study', *Annals of Regional Science*, 18 (3), pp. 49–66.*

(1985) (with C. Hung, G. Norman and C. Smithson) 'An anomaly in the service industry: the effect of entry on fees', *Economic Journal*, 95 (1), pp. 169–77.

(1986) (with C.C. Mai and G. Norman) 'Impacts on optimum location of different pricing strategies, market structures and customer distribution over space', *Journal of Regional Science and Urban Economics*, 16 (3), pp. 329–51.

(1987) (with G. Norman and C. Hung) *The economics of imperfect competition*. New York: Cambridge University Press.

(1988) (with G. Norman) 'Spatial pricing with a general cost function: the effects of taxes on imports', *International Economic Review*, 27 (3), pp. 761–76.

(1990a) (with B.L. Benson and G. Norman) 'On the basing-point system', *American Economic Review*, 80 (3), pp. 584–8.*

(1990b) (with B.L. Benson and G. Norman) 'On the basing-point system: reply', *American Economic Review*, 80 (4), pp. 963–7.*

(1991) (with J.G. Greenhut and G. Norman) 'Financial-economic aspects of airline deregulation', *International Journal of Transport Economics*, 18 (1), pp. 3–30.*

(1991) (with C.S. Lee and Y. Mansur) 'Spatial discrimination: Bertrand vs. Cournot: comment', *Journal of Regional Science and Urban Economics*, 21 (1), pp. 127–34.*

(1991) (with J.B. Soper, G. Norman and B.L. Benson) 'Basing point pricing and production concentration', *Economic Journal*, 101 (3), pp. 539–56.

(1992a) (with J.G. Greenhut) 'Alternative uses of spatial microeconomics', *Annals of Regional Science*, 26 (3), pp. 257–67.*

(1992b) (with J.G. Greenhut) 'Industrial structures components of finance theory's CAPM', *Review of Industrial Organization*, 7 (2), pp. 361–73.*

(1994) (with Y. Mansur and C. Temponi) 'Fuzzy set underpinnings of oligopoly markets', Proceedings of the December 1994 International Joint Conference of NAFIPS, TIFC, ISC and the NASA Joint Technology Workshop on neural networks and fuzzy logic.

(1995a) *Location economics: theoretical underpinnings and applications.* Cheltenham: Edward Elgar.

(1995b) 'Introduction', in M.L. Greenhut (1995a) **q.v.**, pp. xii–xxiii.

(1995c) *Spatial microeconomics: theoretical underpinnings and applications.* Cheltenham: Edward Elgar.

(1995d) 'Introduction', in M.L. Greenhut (1995c) **q.v.**, pp. xiv–xxv.

(1995) (with J.G. Greenhut) 'Using modern price theory, not Herfindahl-Hirschman for antitrust principles and policy', *Journal of Forensic Economics*, 10 (3), pp. 247–59.

(1995) (with J.G. Greenhut and Y. Mansur) 'Oligopoly and behavioral uncertainty: an application of fuzzy set theory', *Review of Industrial Organization*, 10 (3), pp. 269–88.

BIBLIOGRAPHY

Blaug, M. (1986) *Economic history and the history of economics.* Brighton: Harvester.

Lösch, A. (1939) *Die räumliche Ordnung der Wirtschaft*, 2nd edn. (1954) trans. as *The economics of location.* New Haven, CT: Yale University Press.

Machlup, F. (1952) *The economics of sellers' competition: model analysis of sellers conduct.* Baltimore, MD: Johns Hopkins Press.

Ohta, H. and Thisse, J. (1993) *Does economic space matter?: essays in honor of Melvin L. Greenhut.* London: Macmillan.

4. Mark Perlman
(b. 1923)[1]

4.1 INTRODUCTION

Some say that while you can take the boy out of the country, it is much harder to take the country out of the boy. This essay starts as an attempt to identify my 'country' elements in order to explain the peculiar kind of communitarianism that underlies much of my thinking. Because I have already gathered the pertinent details of my education and subsequent career in 'What makes my mind tick' (Perlman 1995) it is redundant to rework that material. Moreover, that essay with about two dozen others are analyzed by Kurt Dopfer (1998) in order to identify an idiosyncratic research method, which he termed 'the participant-observer.' His essay is even something of a psychoanalysis, about which I can only say that he 'has my number.'

How do I peg myself? I judge most things from the standpoint of an empiric. But mine is an episodic, rather than the more usual quantitative empiricism. While many empirics are not oriented to social problems, some

---

[1] This is a new essay for this volume. Another – not in this series – of selected essays (Perlman 1996) contains a reprint of an earlier autobiographical essay (Perlman 1995) which deals with the idiosyncratic aspects of my education, my career failures and successes, and my views on teaching, research, and the editing of journals and books (of which I have done more than the normal share).

are. And that was for many years my propensity.

4.2 WAYS OF VIEWING THE WORLD

From my standpoint the usual American *Weltanschauungen* seem to fall into four categories:

- Essential individualism, of which the best examples include such fellow Pittsburghers as Andrew Carnegie and George Westinghouse. They were exemplar industrial entrepreneurs, individualistic and highly competitive.[2] Bill Gates is probably the exemplar a century later. These men, by nature optimistic, seem to fear little and are willing to take chance into their own hands.
- Anti-monopoly individualism, where the biggest pigs are prevented from getting their trotters into the trough. This is more than simple rugged individualism with a wing clipped. It is the kind of thing that the Anti-Trust Division of the Justice Department is supposed to pursue. People of this ilk have fears of being squeezed out, and they look to the government to protect their otherwise natural opportunity. Theirs is a qualified optimism.
- University faculties, labor unions, industrial organizations, and other forms of non-state communitarianism comprise a third view. At its best it is an effort to preserve order while desirable changes are taking place; at its worst, this form of communitarianism falls prey to a doctrine of vested interests. Its practitioners can be wise men ('in all things moderation') or they can be Mafia-like buccaneers. Optimally, it strives for a dynamic (evolutionary) bargaining system where various factions interact peacefully. It is best envisioned in James Madison's *Tenth Federalist Paper*, where he notes that eliminating factions makes the cure worse than the disease. This approach is based on some pessimism – that life will be full of surprises, so it is best to have group safety-nets to ease the adjustment.
- Socialism, be it of a Christian or Kibbutz-like brotherhood, a Lange-Lerner social efficiency model, or the traditional Leninist 'Executive Committee of the Proletariat', is the fourth approach. What this view offers is a belief that the political state should bear the full responsibility for social and economic justice. Often, but not always, while preferring

[2] They were true entrepreneurs, later replaced by managers – Carnegie immediately, Westinghouse eventually. The managers lacked entrepreneurial imagination.

equity to economic growth they hope to offer both; more frequently they seem to lose both. Socialists, by and large, think of themselves as optimists – always confident that a proper education can bring out the best in everyone's individual character, but in practice they chose levelling, not the progress associated with optimism.

My own views approximate the third approach, and I came to it through the influence of the Wisconsin Progressive culture. Progressivism, a proper noun, was a program attributed to Robert Marion LaFollette (1855–1925), its political voice. But it was more truly the product of the Departments of Economics and History at the University of Wisconsin, a bare mile from the capitol. The intellectual leaders were Charles McCarthy (1873–1921),[3] a Frederick Jackson Turner Ph.D. in History, and John Rogers Commons (1862–1945), a Professor of Economics. The career of each man is fascinating, but we must leave this subject, providing only bibliographical references (Fitzpatrick 1944; Commons 1934).

Together McCarthy and Commons fashioned much of the Progressive legislation originally found in Wisconsin's tripartite approach to industrial safety, public utility regulation, and vocational schooling (combining labor, management, and 'public' ways of balancing industrial interests). In the 1930s this Wisconsin tradition was grafted onto a similar but more state-oriented New York tradition, and together they made up Roosevelt's New Deal program.

When I was a boy in my father's home I heard his colleagues discuss the New Deal legislation. I was too young to remember any talk on farm legislation, most of which came out of Cornell, and virtually all of which was initially held to be unconstitutional. But I do recall the discussions about labor legislation, particularly the Wagner and the Social Security Acts in 1935 (cf. Witte 1962). At the time the Wisconsin Department of Economics' view was that what was good in the Wagner Act was not new, and what was new they worried about. Edwin E. Witte, John R. Commons's student, who had succeeded Charles McCarthy at the Wisconsin Legislative Reference Bureau but was by this time a member of the Department, believed that the essential piece of legislation had been the earlier Norris-LaGuardia Act, which made it almost impossible for employers to get injunctive orders in the name of property protection (cf. Witte 1932). Thus, in theory, after 1933 employers were supposed to bargain in good faith with their employees' unions, as mandated by section 7a of the 1933 National Industrial Recovery

---

[3] Charles McCarthy is not to be confused with Joseph McCarthy (1908–1957), who not only defeated the last 'Progressive' (Robert Marion LaFollette, Jr.) but in the 1950s came to epitomize bullying populism.

Act, but in practice it was another story. That law was declared unconstitutional (for other reasons), and Senator Robert Wagner (Democrat, New York) proposed the 1935 National Labor Relations Act, creating a mechanism to force employers to comply. What bothered Witte and others in the Commons's group was that they thought this mechanism would make unions too reliant upon outside, governmental assistance.[4] On balance I think that their fears were understandable, and likely somewhat justified. What they did not imagine was that the mechanism might turn anti-union, as indeed it has done at some times.

To put the matter in a more basic form, the Commons group had a nineteenth century view that societies were free only in the sense that they permitted groups to form freely. In a real sense John Dewey's classic *The public and its problems* (1927) summarizes the philosophical expression of their view.

The Wisconsin Progressives and the New York State Liberal Reform group[5] also differed somewhat on the matter of social welfare legislation. Wisconsin had had about four years of experience with unemployment insurance, and the Wisconsin types in Washington prevailed on the matter of retaining unemployment legislation on the State level, except that the funds were to be handled nationally in order to keep the state systems honest.

The differences I recall within the Wisconsin group related to the desirability of the 1938 Wages and Hours Law. Carl Rauschenbusch, the son of the famous Christian socialist Unitarian minister in Rochester, New York, was the author of the Wisconsin Unemployment Compensation Act. His wife, Elizabeth Brandeis, the daughter of Louis Dembitz Brandeis, was a lecturer in the Department; earlier she had been identified with the losing side of the 1923 *Adkins v. Children's Hospital* case, where the Supreme Court had ruled against minimum wage/maximum hours legislation. The 1938 Wages and Hours bill was opposed by the American Federation of Labor on the grounds that its membership did not need federal intervention. This left the members of the Wisconsin group in something of a dilemma. And it left me there, too. On the one hand it was clear that low-paid workers, particularly in the Southern textiles factories, seemed too fearful of local pressures to join effective unions, and they needed federal intervention if their plight was to be improved. On the other hand, 'Put not your trust in Princes' (Psalms, 183.3). No one took seriously the professional economics truism that wages were set

---

[4] Commons had written of Industrial Government, which he contrasted with Government in Industry.

[5] Francis Perkins, Franklin Roosevelt's Secretary of Labor, became the titular head of this group, but I.M. Rubinow and Isador Lubin developed the ideas and programs.

by fair market forces, particularly in dynamic situations.[6]

The dilemma centred on State Welfarism. During World War II when I had plenty of time to study (I was at that point an interpreter with Italian service troops),[7] my father suggested that I do some systematic reading and not inconsiderable essay writing. The first assigned book report was on William Beveridge's *Full employment in a free society* (1944), which I read with growing enthusiasm. Beveridge's reasoning was attractive, and I then was assigned Friedrich Hayek's *The road to serfdom* (1944), which I read with mounting fury. They were followed by a writing assignment on Karl Polanyi's attack on the universality of the experience of Britain's first industrial revolution and of its free market system found in his *The great transformation* (1944), and other books as well. In the end I wrote eight essays, by which time I described myself as a convinced 'Swedish Middle-Way Social Democrat.'

Shortly afterwards, my military service was over, and I returned to the University in Madison. I also returned to two hour evening intellectual discussions with my father, whose health having deteriorated, tended to go to bed immediately after the evening meal. I was then reading Abba Lerner's *The economics of control* (1944)[8] and Barbara Wootton's *Freedom under planning* (1945), both of which seemed to make eminent sense to me. They did not to my father, who asked me just who was going to 'bell the union cat.' How did Miss Wootton, for example, expect to get unions, that had never trusted intellectuals, to accept a wages policy? My father further noted that while unions had ever to be aware of their social responsibilities, they were unlikely to let any academic intellectual define them. Worse than that, he destroyed my admiration for Hobson's underconsumption theories, by pointing out that I should study Pigou carefully and note that business downturns and upturns were coordinated more with changes in

---

[6] I recall being told in the late 1940s that India proved this proposition. In Calcutta textile workers earned poorly, but in Bombay the reverse was the case. The Bombay industry was flourishing (with the help of considerable capital substitution).

[7] There were Italian prisoners, largely taken by the British in Africa in 1941 and later in 1943, who agreed after the Italian surrender to work as quartermaster labor in American Army camps.

[8] When I returned to the University I reorganized the economics graduate student society. I took the lead in inviting the speakers, mostly from Chicago. The first was Frank Knight; I think that the fourth was Abba Lerner. Their trips to Madison were paid for directly by the student members; my bonus was that I spent the day with each of them and, of course, personally questioned them and learned a great deal. The bills were minimal; Frank Knight even insisted that he took public transportation to the Northwestern Railroad Station in Chicago and that he took a sandwich from home to eat on the train. It was an era when academics knew about scrimping and appreciated student interest that was strong enough to invite them to speak at the students' collective expense. Jacob Marshak, the third invitee, stayed at my parents' home.

businessmen's expectations than they were with consumer demand. It was a cold dose of what I then called his 'recidivist anti-Keynesianism.'[9] Again, he pushed back, and told me that while he greatly admired Keynes's leadership abilities, he had great doubts about the governmental manipulation inherent in the 1936 *General theory*.[10] Thus I was led back to my roots, and since that time I have maintained the scepticism learned at my father's bedside.

During my first year at Columbia University (1948–9) I took Robert R. MacIver's course on political theory. Among the assigned readings was his *The web of government* (1947), which I read very carefully only to discover that my conversations with my father and John Gaus[11] had come pretty much to similar conclusions, except that MacIver's lectures linked the idea of voluntarism more solidly to its development as both a positive and a negative reaction to Hobbes's Social Contract. Juxtaposing Hobbes's with Rousseau's Social Contract, MacIver described with obvious enthusiasm Madison's *Tenth Federalist Paper*, which earlier at Wisconsin I had discovered as the quintessential perception of my idea of appropriate self-defined group decision-making. There were many MacIver disciples at Columbia, but for me his 'stuff', although not old-hat, had been discovered before.

When I wrote my dissertation in Australia, published as *Judges in industry* (1954), my views regarding groups' self-organization and organic development had become sufficiently firm to build on them. I contrasted two separate approaches to judicial intervention into labor negotiations. The one was 'administrative', with the judges insinuating into their decisions their own knowledge and social value systems. The other was 'institutional', where the judges minimized their own insinuations. Using this matrix I then explained why arbitration was successful in the pastoral and machine tools

---

[9] Keynes and he had met twice – in 1931 when Keynes participated in a summer program at the University of Chicago (somewhere I heard of that group as the 'soft-boiled egg-heads, but I could never find the source), and in Cambridge in the late winter of 1938–9. They admired each other but they differed in methodology. Keynes was an abstractionist, and my father was an episodic empiric.

[10] At the time I was taking a course on Business Cycles with Paul T. Ellsworth, a missionary in the Keynesian ranks. I tried to raise my father's reservations about Keynesianism in class; I got nowhere. Worse, I antagonized Ellsworth and was rewarded with a B+, as I recall the only B I got that year. Later when I went to Columbia and joined Arthur Frank Burns's seminar, these same points were received favorably. My last conversation with Ellsworth (as I recall it) was in the summer of 1948, when he asked me what I thought of Columbia. I told him that I had become a Mitchell-Burns enthusiast. He received the news without enthusiasm.

[11] I returned home from the Army in April of 1946, a good two months before the summer semester began. My father kindly interceded, and two of his friends offered to give me personal tutorials to fill in the time. One was John A. Gaus, the eminent political scientist, who not only oriented me to John Dewey, but after giving me a stern scolding delivered over a lunch, forced me to read carefully. I recall subsequently outlining *The public and its problems* in 27 single-spaced typewritten pages. Gaus had made his point.

industries and why it was unsuccessful in the stevedoring and coal-mining industries. Of course most of the Australian union leaders with whom I met and talked, particularly Albert Monk, the President of the Australian Council of Trade Unions, were either Fabian or Marxian socialists, and they thought my personal judgements lacked empathy, as well as being jejune (Monk said I was trying to 'teach my grandmother to suck eggs').[12] My third book, *The machinists: a new study in American trade unionism* (1961) was a further effort explaining the advantages and the limitations of self-developing institutions.[13]

By the early 1970s, influenced by Fritz Machlup and Herbert Giersch, I began reading Hayek again (Hayek 1952; 1960; 1973), and I was amazed at 'how much he had learned since 1944.'[14] But I could never become a true Hayekian because I could not accept the nineteenth-century liberalism of John Stuart Mill. I suppose that I should blush when I say that I really do not believe in unlimited freedom of speech nor in unlimited freedom of contract. Speech that is meant to be hurtful may be too dangerous to the intended victims to be tolerated; I believe that as in Britain the simple test for libel should not be untruthfulness but the desire to defame. Indeed, to quote the maxim, 'the greater the truth, the greater the libel.'

Freedom of contract as an abstraction also sounds good; but the history of civilization is the collective attempt to keep the strong from exploiting the poor, a condition which freedom of contract easily permits. Both of these views are anathema to Milton Friedman, another person from whom I have learned much.[15] Instead, I prefer the Adam Smith of *The theory of moral sentiments* (1759), with its emphasis on empathy (his phrase was sympathy)

---

[12] Mr. Justice [Alfred] Foster (of the Arbitration Court) was a Marxian socialist, yet he found my views so interesting that he invited his mentor, Mr. Justice John [Vincent] Barry of the Supreme Court of Victoria to join us for a sandwich lunch in his chambers. Out of that contact came one of the greatest friendships of my life. Barry and I corresponded every week until his death in 1969. I recall spending the afternoon after the sandwich lunch arguing that private monopolies had their virtues – there was the Schumpeter angle about monopolies being able to invest profits in research and development, and furthermore private monopolies could be effectively sanctioned by the courts. Barry was unconvinced.

[13] The Machinist membership was forever rejecting their officers' pleas to admit blacks. I discovered in their confidential files (opened to me for my research) that eventually the officers went to the National Labor Relations Board and asked that the union be ordered to do so. All of this was done in 1948; I suspect by the time the Lyndon Johnson Civil Rights legislation got through a reluctant Congress, such an effort might not have been necessary.

[14] My colleague, Charles R. McCann, has also bent my mind; he helped me write a 1998 essay on Commons and Hayek wherein I pointed out that they had come to much the same conclusion except that Commons was a Hegelian and Hayek was a Kantian.

[15] Friedman had an ill-fated year at Wisconsin in 1940–1, during which Rose and he were social friends of my parents. In 1967 he proposed that I create the *Journal of Economic Literature*. His recollection of that year and my parents, as well as his satisfaction with the *Journal* are recorded in their memoirs (Friedman and Friedman 1998, pp. 91–104, 235–36).

and the role of the 'detached observer [in every good man's mind]', to his overly-simple, perfectly-in-control-of-passions, and thoroughly informed *homo economicus*, found in the earlier Books (but not the last) of his *The wealth of nations* (1776). While on this subject let me say a little more on economic theory.

4.3 ECONOMIC THEORY AND THEORISTS

My first course was at Wisconsin with James Earley, whose training in good part was at the London School of Economics at the time that both Hayek and Robbins were in control. Earley's course, as I survey my notes, was excellent; what it lacked was the teacher's missionary conviction.

When I had decided to leave Wisconsin I went to the University of Chicago to see if that place was right for me. There I had a disastrous luncheon interview with Paul Douglas[16] and a very pleasant hour interlude with Milton Friedman. Friedman was interested in (and apparently approved of) the reading assignments in Earley's course, but Douglas's personal hostility precluded my applying for admission to Chicago.

Instead, thinking that I would learn theory from Jacob Viner, I took a one year Instructor's assignment at Princeton. Unfortunately Viner was not teaching theory (but I sat in on the other courses he taught); theory was taught by Friederich Lutz, whose lecture hours conflicted with the courses for which I was a preceptor.

The following year (September 1948) I went to Columbia. It was the autumn that the theory offerings there were broadened. George Stigler came

---

[16] Paul Douglas, formulator of the Cobb-Douglas function, was a man of many intellectual and other adventures. In the 1920s he was if not a dues-paying Communist a thorough admirer of Lenin and Stalin. He was also something of an activist. Later he became a reform-minded City Councilman in Chicago. Although well into middle age, early in World War II he enlisted as a Marine. He came out of the War a major, but with a painfully-wounded arm and vehement anti-communist sentiments. At our lunch at the Quandrangle Club he first asked if I were ready to fight the Russians. I replied (as I recall), 'God, No; I've wasted enough time in the Army.' He then asked what I had done in the Army; had I seen action? I replied that I had been a high-grade sergeant, but had not been in battle. To this he grunted, 'You're of those Jewish intellectuals who talk but don't fight. Are you a communist like your father?'

I replied aggressively, 'Look who is calling whom a communist. Professor Douglas, when you reviewed his *A theory of the labor movement* (S. Perlman 1928) in the late 1920s, you attacked him because he wasn't and you were.'

Douglas was elected to the United States Senate in 1948. Afterwards he became something of an academic icon. I assume that that luncheon was typical only of a period when he was deranged due to physical pain. However, he had periods of similar instability while serving in the Senate.

from Brown to teach price theory; Bill Vickrey taught a mathematically-oriented price theory course. And John Maurice Clark gave a sweeping course on the history of economic theory. I took Clark's course, one of the most interestingly interpretive experiences I have ever had – even though Clark was reputed to be just about the dullest lecturer around. I expected that he would be the theorist at my orals examination. About 24 hours before that examination I was told that the new department chairman, James Waterhouse Angell, had changed the practice; no longer would the candidate choose his theory examiner.[17] So that is how I first met George Stigler. Whether he came 'loaded for bear' or I only thought so, the record is that he could not persuade the others to fail me, and he gave me a 'conditional pass' – with the right to reexamine me at the defence of my dissertation. I was told to talk to him immediately after the examination. I recall distinctly saying, 'What do I have to do to get by you – memorize your goddamned book?' His reply was pure Stigler, 'That will be good for starters, but you ought to do more.' Thirteen months later I had, and he did. We turned into friends; indeed, he recommended to Milton Friedman that I be asked to found the *Journal of Economic Literature*.

But the real story is that I found the determinism of price theory not Euclidianly-interesting, but philosophically-boring. In the autumn of 1946 at Wisconsin, Earley had assigned an essay on Frank Knight's concept of competition. My paper, as I have recently looked it over, had two points – first, that every good and every service conceptually competed with every other, and that the concept of differentiated markets was not explained. Second, I was attracted by his idea of uncertainty. It was the first theme which had led me to John Maurice Clark, who as a quondam colleague of Knight had much the same inquisitiveness, but Clark's was without bitterness or dogmatism.[18]

---

[17] The results were sufficiently disastrous that Angell went back to the old system. When, a year later, my wife Naomi took her orals, Clark was the examiner. He found her hovering over a detective story as she waited. Sensing her fears, he told her not to worry – he, too, had been so frightened before his Columbia orals that when the committee chairman asked him his name he replied, 'John *Bates* Clark.'

[18] When I was at Princeton I chanced upon a conversation with Frank A. Fetter, by then something of an octogenarian. Fetter was full of praise for Commons (with whom he had traveled across the country checking empirically the Pittsburgh Plus pricing system in the steel industry) but was personally bitter at John Bates's son, John Maurice. He called him a 'turncoat and a betrayer of his father's principles.' Rather than putting me off, that intrigued me all the more.

Clark was wonderful to me. I wrote a paper for him, and he told me that while it covered everything, it lacked any sign of originality, hence the B+. Yet he wrote a strong letter on my behalf for a Social Science Research Council Fellowship. He always called me by my first name (he, too, knowing something about being a son in the same field as a famous

I suppose that it was Fritz Machlup who put the 'theory business' into better perspective. Not only did he point out to me that there was no long-run price theory (something that I really should have emphasized), but in his course on methodology it became clear that I was too much of an empiricist to have sufficient sympathy with any but the most elementary abstractions. And that, I decided, was where my deep-seated troubles began.

Yet, when I became chairman at Pitt the first person I invited as a Visiting Professor was George Shackle, whose idea of uncertainty I came to realize was infinitely better than the von Thünen-Knight variant. Shackle was among the best writers of prose in the profession, and I admired him greatly for that as well. The breadth of his knowledge and the patience with which he expostulated overwhelmed me. I felt honored to become his friend as well as his student; he even dedicated a book to me, characteristically entitled *An economic querist* (Shackle 1973).

Thus the stages of my thinking. To begin, I was trained by my father and the Wisconsin group as an empiric, oriented to episodic rather than quantitative empiricism. That body of knowledge was tested when I fancied myself a Social Democrat. My father then had me 'run the obstacle course', returning me to the peculiar type of Progressive thinking which Commons had fostered. Nonetheless I continued to wonder about economic theory. At first the National Bureau of Economic Research's quantitative empiricism learned from Arthur Frank Burns, served as the answer to macroeconomic questions; later Simon Kuznets considerably broadened the macroeconomic interests I had. What dazzled me about Kuznets was his broad erudition and how much he worried about whether his data series were relevant. A propos of micro theory, I was ground down somewhat while going through the Stigler 'elementary mill', but it was Machlup who eventually made clear to me what I was looking for. In the end, it was likely Shackle who showed me how answers might be found. My early feeling for episodic empiricism surfaced in my doctoral dissertation and in my third and fourth books (Perlman 1954; 1961; 1962).

father), and I recall with warmth Carter Goodrich's look of amazement when he heard Clark do it.

4.4   MY YEARS AT THE UNIVERSITY OF PITTSBURGH

Demographic Economics

After I came to Pitt I worked initially with Edgar M. Hoover on two empirical studies in demographic economics. The first was funded by the Planned Parenthood Federation; it wanted us to demonstrate that reductions of fertility would encourage business growth. We found, instead, that reductions of fertility in developed countries would lead to age imbalances affecting the labor force, and quite likely would not have the outcome desired by the Federation. The Federation then suggested that we not publish our findings. The second study was a contract with the US Administration for International Development to consider what a reduction in fertility would do to release capital for private investment.[19]

My initial teaching assignments at Pitt were in labor economics, American economic history and the history of economic thought. During the first year I proposed to Hoover that he teach demographic economics so that I could learn it; and starting with the third year (by which time I had become Chairman) I co-taught it with him. By that time Professor Julius Rubin had joined the History Department, and although I thought that I should continue to teach in economic history, it seemed to me to be less important than the other areas where I was teaching. Accordingly my reading of new material in American history tapered off. But I continued my investments in demographic economics and the history of economic thought.

Methodology

I have already alluded to Kurt Dopfer's (1998) study of my methodology. Earlier I remarked that I was formally introduced to the topic when I sat in on a course Fritz Machlup gave at Hopkins. Later while I was editing the *Journal of Economic Literature* and a series for the Cambridge University Press, I had the inspiration to ask Mark Blaug to present his thoughts on the subject. The resulting book (Blaug 1980) turned out to be the best seller in a series that sold magnificently. Deirdre McCloskey, of 'the rhetoric of economics fame', mentioned in the first article she prepared on the subject that even earlier I had noted that economists were more likely advocates than

---

[19] Our study showed that if a strong anti-natality policy were implemented, Pakistan could develop free of international capital movements within a decade and a half. The Pakistanis were encouraged by our findings and used it to show why immediate increased expenditures on arms could be afforded.

scientists (McCloskey 1983). But the fact is that although I admire Blaug tremendously and I have the greatest regard for McCloskey's views, mine differ somewhat in that they are eclectic. I fear that I eschew making up my mind. What Dopfer concludes is that in an age of growing intellectual specialization I have tried to bring to each topic every explanatory insight that I could find. I look into everything I can find to explain what was T. R. Malthus's frame of reference before the first edition of *An essay on population* (1798) and what caused it to change afterwards. What was happening that Ricardo sought to make Smith's economics into an abstraction? Why did the introduction of mathematics into economic analysis remain so long on the level of simple algebra and the calculus? And so forth.

Dopfer calls this approach 'the participant observer', I suppose as differentiated in some way from Smith's 'detached observer'. Part of the interest in Dopfer's lengthy review is his explanation of why I developed that approach. Well after I had done so, I became acquainted in depth with Isaiah Berlin's essays, and I realized that he stated years before what I was doing, and he put it far better than I could.

The History of Economic Thought

Over the years my course in the history of economic thought, given originally only to Ph.D. students, was opened to honours undergraduates, who, for the most part, were prepared to do more reading than the graduate students claimed that they had time for. More and more the emphasis in the course design shifted to the typical Jewish question, 'By what authority does one believe what one believes?'[20] What emerged, of course, was that there were all sorts of authorities underlying most people's thinking processes. Hobbes's use of 'conjectural history' (*histoire raissoné*) is one example. Locke's faith in the direct man-God relationship is another. But currently in academia the two most frequently cited authorities are Francis Bacon's 'Scientific Method' (systematic investigation and iterative efforts to form a stable generalization) and René Descartes's mathematical model-building (employing logic to build abstract statements of causal relationships). My first efforts at focusing on this approach were in my 1985 presidential address to the History of Economics Society, where I contrasted the 'magisterial' approaches of Wesley Clair Mitchell, Joseph A. Schumpeter, and Karl Pribram in interpreting the history of economic thought (Perlman 1986, pp. 9–28; 1996, pp. 63–86). The most recent effort, on a far more general plane, is in the

---

[20] Characteristic of typical Christian questions are St. Augustine's concern with the contradictions in Free Will and Divine Omniscience or Martin Luther's juxtaposition of Faith and Good Deeds.

book that I and my quondam student and more recent research partner, have published (Perlman and McCann 1998).

University Genossenschaften

I will come back to this aspect of my career later, but at this point I want to return to a topic mentioned earlier, the nature of university communities and the varieties of its governance.

At times I have been at universities with long histories of self-realized communities. Among them I would include Wisconsin, Princeton, Hopkins, and Harvard. Participation in those communities (that is, when I was there) required a catholic interest; specialization occurred, yet faculty members were supposed to be literate – if not about fine arts and classical music, at least about recent biographies and novels.

Until the late 1960s entertaining at dinner was a general practice. When I arrived at the Hopkins, I recall G. Heberton Evans mentioning to a new young faculty member that during the course of the academic year he would likely be invited to each full professor's home. As he was unmarried he would not be expected to reciprocate, but bringing candy, flowers, or wine might be a good idea. He would be asked if he wished to bring a companion, and he should do so only if the relationship seemed to be very serious.

As the dinners tended to be slightly argumentative and full of intellectual joking, they were more like waltzes than minuets. But we enjoyed them, because it was an effort to extend the community spirit. Of course if a person did not fit in there was no easier place to realize it than to be excluded from invitations. And many newcomers found that they did not fit in. This sense of community, called *Genossenschaft* by Otto von Gierke, was wonderful when it was extended.[21] When it was not, unless one had become thick-skinned or had no place to go, it was a sign that the time had come to move on. By the time that I became an Assistant Professor the social prejudice against non-WASPs was quickly disappearing, and I recall few embarrassments on that score.

The obverse side of the social side of faculty *Genossenschaft* was a sense of faculty importance, that could lead to institutional self-government. Before getting to that point, let me mention that American universities are virtually all technically governed by boards of trustees or regents or as in the case of Harvard a small number of Senior Fellows. They are the ones who make the rules as well as the appointments. From the standpoint of modern American law they are not required to consult with the faculty, unless the faculty has

---

[21] My own experiences with *Genossenschaft* at the New York State School of Industrial Relations and at Johns Hopkins are discussed in Perlman (1995).

unionized, as there are laws forcing them to negotiate in good faith only with unions.

At universities with a long sense of the importance of faculty *Genossenschaft*, a kind of *stare decisis* reigned, and the trustees as well as their administrators felt a real need to explain their decisions if not to everyone, certainly to the important professors. The professors, themselves, maintained a kind of Guelph separatism and in that display of independence they usually gained respect from the administrators. By way of contrast, at most schools where there is no such sense of the importance of the faculty-defined community, there tends to be a strong Ghibelline force, making the deans and their 'superiors' rather independent of even the well-known professors.

All of the foregoing seemed to change in the social turmoil of the late 1960s and early 1970s. The same thing had happened during World War I when some leading academics at Columbia, like Charles A. Beard, were fired for disloyalty, and such eminent scholars as Wesley Clair Mitchell left in protest. But that episode was a blip; in a decade it had been largely forgotten. But the angst within university communities over the Vietnam War, over the character of Richard Nixon, and over the capture of the Democrat Party by its academic intellectuals led to irreconcilable faculty divisions. My own belief is that these divisions would normally have healed, but the makeup of the faculties had changed. The humanities and social sciences no longer dominated; rather the natural scientists and the professional school faculties became the dominant force, and they eschewed the tradition of a common culture, necessary to friendly dinner parties.[22]

My wife, Naomi, and I tried for years to maintain the old pattern, but it was a vain effort. People seemed to enjoy the food, but we found that the conversations were getting ever more stilted.[23] We wondered whether the change was because we were no longer members of the prevailing *Genossenschaft* – I had been a hard-liner during the 1960s, both on the subject of Vietnam and about such critical issues as Affirmative Action.

What has replaced the old friendly arguments has been ideological division. Professionally thwarted in my early years by prevailing selection systems based on other than merit,[24] I was also skeptical of Affirmative

---

[22] Of course later there were other factors, most important of which is that faculty wives developed careers of their own and dinner entertainment became too expensive in time and in cost to remain in vogue.

[23] Whether this was true only of Pitt is a good question, but I am told by friends at Harvard and Hopkins that the atmosphere there has also changed. Some say, however, that is not the case at Chicago.

[24] For the most part I was not consciously aware of any decisions involving my own appointments except for an offer I received in 1950 from the then chairman of the

Action programs. But then again, at the time I was hiring skilled women and blacks; indeed while I was chairman I recommended the tenured appointment of three women (Marina von Neumann Whitman, Janet Chapman and Barbara Warne Newell) as well as two black professorial scholars (John Iton and Huntley Manhertz), a record never again approached.[25]

Thus it was that as early as 1970 I was becoming something of a loner in the Pitt community. Several men whom I had brought to Pitt became enraged at the way that I had been running the department, and the new dean (with whom I had been very friendly) probably felt that I was a 'maker of waves' – for men like him something not to be tolerated – and took away the basis of my leadership role within the department. As I was at that precise time head-over-heels involved in creating the *Journal of Economic Literature*, I immediately resigned my chairmanship.[26] And with the exception of one or two later forays I made no efforts to rejoin what I had thought was the *Genossenschaft*. The likely fact was that I was 'out-of-the-loop' also because there was not much of a loop left. The government of universities became increasingly the product of efficiency-administrators, usually persons with little remaining interest in their own personal scholarship and with virtually no interest in concentrating on the internal problems of attracting students' attention towards becoming part of a broad-based local intellectual community.

So I found myself concentrating on my view about authority systems in economics, rather than such systems in universities. I volunteered to give up my editorship of the *Journal of Economic Literature* in the very late 1970s – I felt strongly that the power to choose which books were to be reviewed was too great to leave in the hands of any person for as long as 10 years. Shortly afterwards I became the General Editor of the Joseph A. Schumpeter Society, and in time Professor Horst Hanusch (its Secretary-General) and I founded the *Journal of Evolutionary Economics*.

I must confess that I am not a Schumpeterian, although I have written much about him (Perlman 1994; 1997). By the time he came to America, Schumpeter was eschewing policy questions. While the obvious reason is that he had been badly burned when he entered politics in Austria, I think that

University of California, Los Angeles economics department. He offered me a place very reluctantly, explaining that my salary was going largely to be met by the Industrial Relations Section. But he wanted me to know that no Jew had ever been happy at UCLA's Economics Department. I went to Hawaii instead.

[25] More difficult in a way was my hiring of a German – he told me later that I mentioned this to him in his first interview, and then he knew for sure that he had the job.

[26] Earlier I had been appointed University Professor – a 'rank' indicating acknowledged significant contributions in more than one discipline; in my case it was economics, history, and public health.

between his jealousy of Maynard Keynes and his contempt for the American institutionalists, whom he considered country-bumpkins, whatever alliances he could have made he chose not to try. But I have enjoyed working within the Schumpeterian group, for it has offered the sense of *Genossenschaft* that I lost at Pitt.

A Winter's Tale

My seventieth birthday was in December 1993, and I was retired under the old law. The fact is that I was glad to step down. Too much had changed. I feel like the Revolutionary War veteran in Oliver Wendell Holmes's *The last leaf.* Like him I appear quaint. While most professors wear sweaters and blue jeans, I wear a suit and a bow tie. I don't shop in malls. I talk about books and book reviews, and even though I live in what was until recently called, 'the City of Champions', I have only the weakest interest in the fortunes of the Pirates, the Penguins, and the Steelers. New models of automobiles come out, and I remain in the dark about them. And although I am moderately computer-literate, the fact is that I still mail most letters, and many are lengthy, through the post office.

I miss the old sense of university *Genossenschaft* with its capacity for enjoyable, cultured, and witty faculty conversations over lunch or dinner and for its conviction that it ought to be the running the place, including the students. I miss the sense of community concern for working out local and national social and economic problems.

In my own discipline of economics I regret the shift in emphasis from problems of the economy to fascination with sets of integrated coherent models that have little, if anything, to do with public policy. Those who aspire to careers in economics have become monotonously ideological about 'free markets' as the solution for even moral questions. Even worse, those in the other social sciences who are not economists want to become like the model-building economists, sterile as their thinking often is.

Yet one could not have feared the outcome of World War II as all of us in the 1930s and early 1940s did and be a disappointed man. The gates of academe were opened to Jews in a way that I had never anticipated. The changes in salary structures for professors since 1958 have been so unimaginably generous that I can only feel lucky beyond belief. The opportunities given to me to found journals, to lecture all over the world, and to teach able, hard-working, and grateful students have exceeded any dreams that I may have had. Most of all, the numerous times that I have met great teachers and learned from them was not possible in earlier epochs when transportation was slow and costly.

As a small boy I wondered whether I would live to the year 2001. I suppose that I shall, but while it will represent a world that in undeniable respects is so much more, it is also something less.

SELECTED WORKS

(1954) *Judges in industry: a study in labour arbitration in Australia*. Melbourne: Melbourne University Press.

(1961) *The machinists: a new study in American trade unionism*. Cambridge, MA: Harvard University Press.

(1962) *Democracy in the International Association of Machinists*. New York: Wiley.

(1986) 'Perceptions of our discipline: three magisterial treatments of the evolution of economic thought', *Bulletin of the History of Economics Society*, (Winter), pp. 9–28. Rep. in M. Perlman (1996) **q.v.**, pp. 63–86.

(1994) 'Introduction', in J.A. Schumpeter (1954) *History of economic analysis*, new edn. London: Routledge, pp. v–xxx.

(1995) 'What makes my mind tick', *American Economist*, 39 (2), pp. 6–27. Rep. in M. Perlman (1996) **q.v.**, pp. 1–32.

(1996) *The character of economic thought, economic characters and economic institutions: selected essays*. Ann Arbor, MI: University of Michigan Press.

(1997) 'Introduction' in J.A. Schumpeter (1952) *Ten great economists from Marx to Keynes*, new edn. London: Routledge, pp. vii–xli.

(1998) 'Hayek, the purposes of the economic market and the institutionalist tradition', in S.F. Frowen (ed.) *Hayek, the economist and social philosopher: a critical retrospect*. London: Macmillan, pp. 221–35.

(1998) (with C.R. McCann) *The pillars of economic understanding: ideas and traditions*. Ann Arbor, MI: University of Michigan Press.

BIBLIOGRAPHY

Beveridge, W.H. (1944) *Full employment in a free society*. London: George Allen & Unwin.

Blaug, M. (1980) *The methodology of economics or how economists explain*. Cambridge: Cambridge University Press.

Commons, J.R. (1934) *Myself*. New York: Macmillan.

Dewey, J. (1927) *The public and its problems*. New York: H. Holt.

Dopfer, K. (1998) 'The participant observer in the formation of economic thought: summa oeconomiae Perlmanensis', *Journal of Evolutionary Economics*, 8 (2), pp. 139–56.

Fitzpatrick, E.A. (1944) *McCarthy of Wisconsin*. New York: Columbia University Press.

Friedman, R.D. and Friedman, M. (1998) *Two lucky people: memoirs*. Chicago: University of Chicago Press.

Hayek, F.A. von (1944) *The road to serfdom*. Chicago: University of Chicago Press.

Hayek, F.A. von (1952) *The counter-revolution of science: studies on the abuse of reason*. Glencoe, IL: Free Press.

Hayek, F.A. von (1960) *The constitution of liberty*. Chicago: University of Chicago Press.

Hayek, F.A. von (1973) *Economic freedom and representative government*. London: Institute of Economic Affairs.

Keynes, J.M. (1936) *The general theory of employment, interest and money*. New York: Macmillan.

Lerner, A.P. (1944) *The economics of control: principles of welfare economics*. New York: Macmillan.

MacIver, R.M. (1947) *The web of government*. New York: Macmillan.

Malthus, T.R. (1798) *An essay on the principle of population*. Works of Thomas Robert Malthus, Vol. I (1986), eds E.A. Wrigley and D. Souden. London: William Pickering.

McCloskey, D.N. (1983) 'The rhetoric of economics', *Journal of Economic Literature*, 21 (2), pp. 481–517.

Perlman, S. (1928) *A theory of the labor movement*. New York: Macmillan.

Polanyi, K. (1944) *The great transformation.* New York: Farrar & Rinehart.

Shackle, G.L.S. (1973) *An economic querist*. Cambridge: Cambridge University Press.

Smith, A. (1759) *The theory of moral sentiments*. Glasgow edition of the works and correspondence of Adam Smith, Vol. I (1976), eds. D.D. Raphael and A.L. Macfie. Oxford: Oxford University Press.

Smith, A. (1776) *An inquiry into the nature and causes of the wealth of nations*, 2 vols. *Glasgow edition of the works and correspondence of Adam Smith*, Vol. II (1976), ed. W.B. Todd. Oxford: Oxford University Press.

Witte, E.E. (1932) *The government in labor disputes*. New York: McGraw-Hill.

Witte, E.E. (1962) *The development of the Social Security Act: a memorandum on the history of the Committee on Economic Security and Drafting and legislative history of the Social Security Act*. With a foreword by Frances Perkins. Madison: University of Wisconsin Press.

Wootton, B. (1945) *Freedom under planning*. Chapel Hill: University of North Carolina Press.

5. Thomas Mayer (b. 1927)[1]

5.1   ECONOMIC SCIENCE AND THE ECONOMIST

Economics is a science, a domain of facts, reason and mathematics and thus entirely independent of the background of the scientist. Hence, there is no reason to bother with the personal background of an economist and with his or her 'presuppositions', whatever these are.[2] Are we not right to keep our personality so carefully out of our work that many consider it a *faux pas* even to use the first person singular in our papers?

Though many do claim to write with the disembodied Voice of Science, this claim is pretentious nonsense. As Patinkin (1972, p. 142) put it:

> I will begin to believe in economics as a science when out of Yale there comes an empirical Ph.D. thesis demonstrating the supremacy of monetary policy in some historical episode and out of Chicago, one demonstrating the supremacy of fiscal policy.

Since Patinkin wrote this, Yale may have become more willing to accept the

---

[1] Mayer (1990b), as revised by the author. I have two volumes of selected essays in the series (Meyer 1990a; 1995).

[2] For criticisms of this position, see Breit (1987).

importance of monetary policy, but the principle still holds. What theories we adhere to depends to a considerable extent on our pre-scientific (one might almost say metaphysical) presuppositions, which in turn depend in part on our personal experiences.

Brunner and Meckling (1977, pp. 71–3) have contrasted the economic perception of man as a 'resourceful, evaluating, maximizing' entity with the sociological conception of man as a 'conformist and conventional' creature, who is 'not an evaluator, any more than ants, bees and termites are evaluators'. One's view on many issues in economics is likely to depend upon which of these perceptions of man one holds. But surely, one's choice between them is not determined so much by regression coefficients and t statistics, as by one's preconceptions, and hence one's personal experience. Those who have found that their planning has paid off are more likely to accept the economic interpretation of man, and hence oppose government planning, than are those who have felt helpless in their personal lives.

In pointing to the influence of an economist's personal background I do not denigrate economics as a science or justify subjectivism. The progress of science is not nullified by scientists' preconceptions on which even the most austere physical sciences rely. In Lakatos' picture of scientific research programmes there is a core (akin to ideology) that is usually treated as outside empirical testing, and a protective belt of testable hypotheses derived from this metaphysical core. It is in the protective belt that the scientific action takes place. What I have called preconceptions are part of the metaphysical core, and scientists as a group will adhere to or abandon this core depending upon what happens in the protective belt. The progress of science depends no more upon each scientist being rational and objective in choosing his or her metaphysical core, than the validity of neoclassical economics depends upon each economic agent being rational. If my preconceptions, regardless of why I uphold them, induce me to formulate hypotheses that survive the scientific competition of the protective belt, then these hypotheses are scientific, even though my adherence to the metaphysical core that generated them may be the result of being dropped on my head as a child. All this should be quite obvious, but the adherents to the Voice-of-Science taboos act as though any personal references would cause economics to be stripped of its mantle of scientific validity.

Although a cataloguing of the preconceptions that lurk behind a set of hypotheses obviously cannot determine the validity of these hypotheses, it is still useful because it can clarify them. Thus it can demonstrate a link that explains why a particular person accepts, or rejects, all of them. More generally, preconceptions function as hidden assumptions, and hence should be brought out into the open.

Consider, for example, Harrod's (1951) masterly analysis of the preconceptions of Keynesian policy recommendations, of what he called 'the presuppositions of Harvey Road'.[3] These induced Keynes to believe that governments, or at least British governments, are enlightened enough to be trusted with the tools of fiscal policy. By bringing these preconceptions into the open, and by explaining what in Keynes' background induced him to adhere to them, Harrod enables us to understand Keynes' thinking more clearly. Moreover, he allows us to evaluate Keynes' views better because we can decide whether or not we agree with these presuppositions. Someone who is not aware of them may well feel uneasy about Keynesian policy, but not know why.

5.2   MY BACKGROUND

In Vienna, around the time I was born, in 1927, a popular joke was: 'Things are so bad that it would be better not to have been born at all. But who has such luck? One in ten thousand.' The economy had received a massive shock from the break-up of the Hapsburg empire after World War I, a shock that generated massive unemployment among white-collar workers in particular. Then came the Great Depression. One of my graphic childhood memories, dating from about 1936, is looking into the eyes of an unemployed man who tried to get passers-by to enter an exhibit made by unemployed people. Somehow it dawned on me that not only was he hungry today, but that he had been hungry the previous day, and expected to be hungry the next day too. The way in which the scourge of unemployment had marked the Viennese was brought home to me many years later in New York when I told my mother that I had decided to look for a better job. She replied: 'It is almost sinful to look for a job when you already have one.'

Soon the threat of Hitler added political danger to depressed conditions. In my parents' circle of middle-class Jews, the response to this threat was denial – 'Oh the West would never allow Hitler to annex Austria'. (After the Anschluss my father said that if it comes to war Germany will collapse like a house of cards.) But they knew they were whistling in the dark. In case they ever forgot, an illegal, but active, local Nazi party was there to remind them of it.

With no other job being available my father worked as a sales agent, conscientiously, but not successfully. He was deeply interested in languages and in science, particularly in natural history, lacked any interest in business, and was modest and shy. He was thus utterly miscast as a sales

---

[3]   Harvey Road was the address of Keynes' parents.

representative. My mother helped out by doing occasional work as a typist at home. She was a warm person with numerous friends. I was an only child, born late in my parents' life, and rather spoilt.

This early environment seems to have significantly affected my subsequent thinking. Although my father had never attended university he had great respect for education. My mother, in accordance with the Viennese custom of her time, had only a limited formal education, but had absorbed quite a bit from her environment. On both sides of my family everyone traditionally published something, even if only cooking recipes. It is therefore not surprising that I became an academic. However, in my early years I was not a good student, except in those few subjects I was interested in, such as biology and Latin. At ten I barely passed the entrance exam for an academic high school (Gymnasium).

Another thing I absorbed from my parents, both social democrats, was concern for the welfare of the poor. I refrain from calling it a 'social conscience' which mainly seems to be a fervent belief that *other* people should be made to help the poor. People like to buy their feeling of moral worth, as they do other things, in the cheapest market, and having the 'right' political opinions allows one to bask in a feeling of moral worth at no cost. But concern about other people has not kept me on the left of the political spectrum because of a deep pessimism, which I will discuss later. I do not know all the origins of this, but some of it I probably absorbed in my childhood from the pessimism I saw around me.

A further attitude I absorbed as a child is a feeling that life is serious; that you get nothing for nothing. I was not brought up in the belief that seems so prevalent today, that one has a right to success and fortune as a natural reward for having allowed oneself to be born. And clearly, seeing around me economic misery and political crimes, such as the assassination of Chancellor Dollfuss by the Nazis, spurred an interest in economics and politics. Political decisions could, and did, affect one's life.

For some unknown reason I also developed the attitude of a loner and outsider, someone who was reluctant to play with other children. This has stuck with me all my life and has prevented me from joining wholeheartedly any school of economics.

In March 1938 Hitler marched into Austria. In September 1938 I marched out. It was clear to my parents that we would have to emigrate, but that was easier said than done. The problem was not so much being permitted to leave, which would not become a serious problem until much later, but being allowed to enter another country. Getting a visa became the focus of one's life. Britain had a provision for accepting refugee children, and hence I could get a visa for Britain. At the last moment a hitch developed! I could not get a transit visa to pass through Belgium – this was before flying became the normal way to travel. I left without it and fortunately was not stopped at the Belgian frontier.

My parents could leave only later, and separately. In November my father was arrested. He was then given the choice of staying imprisoned or leaving the country within 48 hours. Under these conditions he too could get a visa to Britain, but my mother would have to stay behind. My father rightly chose to go without her since he could do more to get her a visa in England than he could in Vienna. And she did get one just a few days before war broke out. But the British consulate in Vienna having already packed up, my mother could not pick up her visa. In March 1938 my parents had applied for a visa to the United States, and in November 1941 their quota number came up. My mother left for New York on the last boat before Pearl Harbor closed that escape route. My father and I could not join her until April 1944.

In England I attended three schools. In the first, near Brighton, where I spent about six months, I was taught only English, of which I knew very little when I left Vienna. The teaching consisted of lectures on English grammar – in English – a catch-22 situation. But eventually I did learn English from the other children. Then, in 1939 I was sent to a very poor school in London in which I learned little.

Fortunately in 1942 my father, who had been interned as an 'enemy alien' was released and was able to take care of me. (Prior to his internment he had no work permit. But now during the war this regulation was waived.) He sent me to an excellent school called Bunce-Court that had been evacuated from Germany to England in the 1930s and was located in Shropshire for the duration of the war. It was a remarkable place. It gave not only a first-rate classroom education but provided what so few schools do, a highly intellectual atmosphere. Students were interested in, and indeed excited by, what they were learning. Moreover, our intellectual interests were not confined to classroom learning, but encompassed politics, literature and art. Given the impact that political events had on our lives, it is hardly surprising that we were highly politicized. At least one other economist, Lucien Foldes of the LSE, emerged from this intellectual pressure cooker.

This school had an immense effect on me. What would have become of me had I not moved there? In the previous school, our normal activity had been on the level of playing with toy soldiers, and here it was discussing postwar reconstruction. I took to this atmosphere with great delight. I was in my element. Most of the students were socialist, and I developed a socialist ardour that outdid that of most others. My life centred on political arguments.

It was at that school that I encountered economics, though this subject was not taught. I realized that I would need to know some economics to substantiate my political opinions, so I read a short 'principles' text which I found unexciting. But I decided to read another, asking a friend who was going to the local library to bring me one. He brought the *General theory*. I was hooked. Of course I understood none of it. But mystery makes for fascination. I decided to stay with economics until I understood that book. Eventually I did, but by that time it was too late; I was an economist.

It was fortunate that none of my teachers had much interest in economics, at least in technical economics. Thus, having nobody to steer me to the unchallenging, and hence mostly rather dull books that are appropriate for a beginner, I read widely, from Marx and Engels to Adam Smith, with a heavy dose of Fabian pamphlets. Trying to learn a subject such as economics entirely on one's own is in many ways inferior to formal training. But it can also be extremely beneficial. It allows one to explore the most interesting parts, and forces one to think for oneself. It therefore helps greatly in making the transition from being a reader of economics to being a 'producer' of economics, a transition that many graduate students find so difficult when the time comes to write a dissertation. (It is a terrible indictment of our graduate training that so many students have to ask their teachers: 'What should I write about?' In my ideal university students would not take any classes for the first semester (or term). They would just be given a library card and told that at the end of the semester they will be examined in the subject or sub-discipline of their choice.)

In April 1944 my father and I left England to join my mother in New York. Although I have lived happily in the United States since then, I retain fond memories of England and usually spend a few days in London whenever a conference gives me an excuse to go to Europe.

I experienced culture shock in the United States. Here was a capitalist system that seemed radically different from the one I had known. It was dynamic and growth-oriented. The capitalist class was proud to welcome able recruits from the working class. My views slowly changed from socialist to liberal, and ultimately to fairly conservative. In part, this was probably the result of studying economics – a typical reaction, as George Stigler (1959) has shown. But learning economics can better explain my shift from socialism to liberalism than my subsequent move to conservatism, since many of my teachers were liberals.

5.3   UNDERGRADUATE EDUCATION

After working as a stock clerk for a few months, I enrolled at Queens College, one of the (then) free municipal colleges operated by the City of New York. After completing a semester, having reached 18, I entered the army. The war ended when I was still in basic training, and I spent the remainder of my short service working as a clerk in separation centres. In September 1946 I was back at Queens College, now with the benefit of the G.I. bill which gave me a modest stipend for almost three years. By taking extra courses I was able to get my B.A. in two years plus the semester I had taken before entering the army, so that I had a year left on the G.I. bill for graduate work.

Queens College, which then was rather selective, provided a good education, because it was much more demanding than colleges are nowadays. We were expected to show our gratitude for receiving a free education by working hard. For example, in the senior year there were comprehensive exams covering material studied in the freshman and sophomore years, as well as a comprehensive exam in the major. The prevailing philosophy at Queens College stressed a rounded education, and we were loaded down with numerous required courses, some of them quite poor. Not being allowed to specialize 'excessively', I felt that I had much too little freedom of choice.

It is probably very different now, but at that time the economics department at Queens did not offer a good education, both because it was too easy-going and because of its anti-theoretical bent. No intermediate micro-theory course was offered. (The absence of an intermediate macro-theory course was standard at the time.) With the 'Principles' course lasting just one semester students could carry on with virtually no economic theory. To learn some theory I had to take a graduate course at the New School for Social Research. I did, however, have one fortunate experience in my undergraduate economics training. One of my professors, William Withers, invited me to write a paper with him on the optimal savings rate. He then went away for the semester break, leaving me on my own. I found Frank Ramsey's (1928) classic paper which I could not understand, and that was that. But this invitation reinforced my convictions that economics can be written as well as read. All the same, I was eager to finish college and get to graduate school, where I thought the real action was.

5.4   GRADUATE EDUCATION

I then entered Columbia University, expecting to get an M.A. and then work for some time to accumulate the funds needed to go on to a Ph.D. At that time, 1948, graduate students faced a quite different situation than they do now. If I remember correctly, among the 200 or so graduate economics students at Columbia there was only one teaching assistant; about half a dozen students taught an evening course (which paid a salary just equal to the tuition); about three held fellowships that provided a stipend in excess of tuition, and a handful had tuition scholarships. I was lucky to get a fellowship for the second year, as well as a job teaching an evening course, so I was able to complete all my class work and reach the all-but-dissertation stage in 1950.

The teachers who influenced me the most were Albert Hart and George Stigler, particularly the former. They provided a sense of excitement about and commitment to economics that were lacking in some of my other classes. I remember in particular Hart's course on stabilization policy. He would come into class and talk about a book or paper he had just read, then he would wait for a student to raise some issue and respond to that. Hardly a well-prepared performance that would win plaudits from the educational establishment, but extraordinarily exciting and helpful for students who could learn the basics of the subject on their own. James W. Angell was just the opposite, a rather stodgy but extremely methodical teacher, whose lectures could be understood at various levels of sophistication, depending on the students' preparation.

I wrote my M.A. thesis with William Vickrey, a delightful person as well as a first rate economist, whom I did not appreciate enough because of my lack of mathematics. The thesis, which dealt with the effect of a wage cut on employment, was subsequently published in the *Economic Journal* (Mayer 1951).

After my second year, having completed everything except the dissertation, it was time to take a job. This was then standard practice in economics. Finding a job turned out to be difficult. The postwar enrolment boom had come to an end, leaving many schools with larger faculties than they required. The outbreak of the Korean war, with the resulting resumption of the draft, did not help. And, unlike now, economics was then not a good field for academic jobs. In addition, the academic employment market was badly organized. Jobs were not advertised; when they had vacancies, department chairs would notify a few graduate schools as well as their friends. If your professors were not plugged into this network, did not want to play this game, or did not push you, that was that. Eventually, however, through the good offices of Albert Hart, I got a job at the tax research division of the Treasury.

Although this was a good job in one of the more prestigious government agencies, I did not like it, nor did I perform well. It emphasized persuasive writing, since much of the work involved trying to influence congressional decisions on taxes. Not only did I write badly, but being still a callow youth, I was more oriented to making obscure theoretical points than to setting out the more pedestrian arguments that actually persuade people. Moreover, like most jobs that give you the potential for influencing policy, you also had to let policy influence you. In many cases you knew what conclusions your memos were supposed to reach. This I did not like. However, I did have the good fortune to work some of the time for Joseph Pechman, from whom I learned much. He invited me to co-author a paper criticizing Colin Clark's (1945) hypothesis that taxes cannot in the long run exceed 25 percent of income (Pechman and Mayer 1952).

After about fifteen months I switched to the Office of Price Stabilization. That turned out to be a bad move. In the Division of Research and Statistics, where I was located, there was little to do. Since it would not have been appropriate to leave right away, I stuck it out for a few months until Congress had enough sense to abolish price controls. I then went to work on the input-output project, mainly on deriving lead times for investment in various industries. This experience was the impetus behind my subsequent work on the lag of monetary policy. The input-output project was divided among various government agencies, my part being located in the Bureau of Mines. This was the only one of my three government posts that I enjoyed. There was useful work to be done, the research was entirely objective and, unlike the Treasury job, it did not stress writing.

All in all, I was at that time not cut out for a government job. I do not derive any enjoyment from one of the great benefits of government work, the feeling of having influence. I have never hankered after power, probably because I lack sufficient conviction that I am right. And I do not readily adjust my views to conform with those of my superiors. I am much happier in academia where I can say what I want. If it has no effect on anything, that does not really bother me.

In any case, I had never intended to stay in Washington permanently, planning to leave as soon as I finished my dissertation when I hoped to be more marketable in academia. (At that time many academics lacked a Ph.D., so having one gave you a competitive edge.) I had worked on my dissertation nights and weekends, and in 1953 finally had it done. That was just in time, because in that year the input-output project was wound up, and I had to look for another job. Having the degree made a big difference, though the dissertation was a failure. It dealt with the demographic aspects of the stagnation thesis, a topic that had lost all relevance by 1953, so it was never published (Mayer 1953).

5.5   ACADEMIC CAREER

I found a one-year visiting assistant professorship at West Virginia University. I loved it. It was so wonderful being back in academic life that I did not even mind exchanging the cultural opportunities of Washington for those of Morgantown, West Virginia. The next year, 1954, I moved to the finance department at Notre Dame University. Although I enjoyed many things about it, I felt uncomfortable being, not in the economics but in the finance department, where there were few courses I could teach. Nor was there much contact between the two departments. Moreover, at that time the finance department did not offer graduate work, so there was little emphasis on research, and teaching loads were high. When I hear some of my young colleagues complain about their teaching loads I tell them that I wrote the major part of my most labour-intensive, and perhaps best, paper (on the lag of monetary policy, Mayer 1958) while teaching 12 hours per week.

I was therefore happy when, in 1956, I was offered an assistant professorship at Michigan State University. It was a remarkable place. At that time, at least in economics, the US academic landscape was very different from what it is now. A handful of research universities accounted for most of the papers published in the better journals, and most other schools had little use for research. I suspect that having publications on one's CV helped a candidate for an assistant professorship in one quarter of the schools, hurt in another quarter, and made no difference in the rest. Unlike now, there did not exist a substantial number of economics departments trying get into the big time.

Michigan State was one of the first to attempt this transition. Since most schools did not compete for researchers, and since Michigan State paid higher salaries than most others, it was able to attract a remarkably hardworking and ambitious group of young economists. At that time the journals did not carry papers that rated schools, so to raise morale, I once had my research assistant rank departments by their contributions to major journals. Helped by being an unusually large department, Michigan State came in among the very top, ahead of both Berkeley and Stanford. It was indeed an extraordinarily exciting atmosphere where one could get much stimulus and help from numerous colleagues. I benefited particularly from Paul Strassmann's assistance. As mentioned previously, my writing was very bad. I had not had any difficulty in English classes, when I wrote on topics that did not matter to me. But when writing economics and presenting my own ideas I froze up, qualifying everything into an unqualified mess. Paul forced me to drop this awful habit and to improve my writing.[4]

I loved the hardworking, striving atmosphere of Michigan State, but there were three drawbacks. One was that, despite our high productivity, economists in the better universities still looked down their noses at us. The second was that there was a great deal of turmoil and animosity, perhaps in

---

4 There now exists an excellent book for anyone suffering from such problems, Becker (1986).

part the result of having so many ambitious people in the department. The third, and the one I felt the most, was that East Lansing, where Michigan State is located, was not a pleasant environment, particularly for a bachelor. I felt that it was a great place for working, but not for anything else. (I have never liked small towns that are not near large cities.)

Accordingly, when I was invited to spend the 1960–1 academic year at Berkeley I jumped at the opportunity. But, alas, Hyman Minsky, whom I was replacing for the year, came back. Despite its stimulating professional atmosphere, I could not face returning to Michigan State. Fortunately I was offered a professorship (I had since been promoted to professor at Michigan State) at the Davis campus of the University of California. This campus, located about 60 miles from Berkeley, was in the process of expanding from a specialized agricultural school into a general campus. I accepted, even though it meant moving to a department with only four other economists, one that was just about to start M.A. courses and would not have a Ph.D. programme for some time. But that seemed minor compared to the fact that when I had audited a philosophy of science course given by Karl Popper, I had met a young lady who was to become my wife. In any case, it was clear that the Davis economics department would expand greatly, both in size and in quality, as in fact it did. However, I continue to live in Berkeley, in part because I cannot stand the hot weather of the Sacramento Valley, and in part because Davis, like East Lansing, is a small town. The commute was a nuisance, though a manageable one, but I did miss the opportunity of seeing more of my colleagues, particularly as the department grew both in quantity and in quality.

Although I have written a few papers on microeconomic topics, such as on the distribution of ability and earnings (Mayer 1960), and on financial institutions, such as on a proposal to set FDIC insurance premiums on the basis of risk (Mayer 1965), most of my work has been in applied macroeconomics and monetary economics, particularly monetary policy. My first substantial paper (Mayer 1958) in this area was an early attempt to measure the lag of monetary policy. The most elaborate and time-consuming one was a book on the permanent income theory and life-cycle hypothesis (Mayer 1972) in which I tried to synthesize the existing empirical evidence on these theories, as well as present new tests. With great bad luck, this appeared just before Robert Hall's fundamental reformulation of consumption-function theory. Besides, to reconcile all the existing evidence I had to use a theory with ill-defined parameters, something that offended the growing taste for precision. But perhaps the book's criticism of the proportionality hypothesis (i.e. the hypothesis that the savings ratio is independent of the level of permanent income) did contribute to the modern deemphasis of that part of the original permanent income theory.

I had much better luck with an essay on monetarism (Mayer 1975a; b) which, together with comments on this essay by a number of prominent economists, was published as a book, *The structure of monetarism* (1978).

By the 1990s, in response to the new methodology of macroeconomics that the new classical revolution brought forth, I became much more interested in methodology and published a critique, *Truth versus precision in economics* (Mayer 1993). Since then, although I have continued to do some work in monetary economics, such as trying to explain the Fed's policy in the 1965–79 inflation (Mayer 1999), I have worked mostly on methodology. Unlike many methodologists I have concentrated on the day-to-day methodological problems that practising economists face, rather than on the deeper epistemological problems, problems that overtax my very limited knowledge of philosophy.

At the end of 1992 when I was almost 65 my university faced a budget crunch and offered very generous early retirement benefits. (These came out of a different budget.) Since I was almost 65 I took advantage of this offer rather than continue teaching as I had initially intended until 68. However, I have continued to do research, mainly on methodology, though I am now working considerably fewer hours than before. Sooner or later I will have to stop, but work is a hard habit to break.

Like most economists of my generation I did not receive as a student the mathematical training that is now standard. But unlike many I never made a serious effort to remedy this deficiency, for two reasons. First, I lack mathematical aptitude, and second I believe in division of labour. When everyone else is using a shovel you do very well indeed if you have a bulldozer. But if everyone else is using a bulldozer, you can do quite well with a shovel.

5.6 PRECONCEPTIONS, BIASES AND BELIEFS

One preconception that conditions my thinking both on economic theory and policy is a pervasive pessimism (which, fortunately, I do not carry forward into my personal life). At least partly as a result of this pessimism I do not hanker after The Truth. I do not deny that it is out there somewhere, but I doubt that we can grasp it at this stage in the development of economics. Hence, I prefer theories that present little truths to those that claim to have solved the whole grand maximization problem in one elegant formulation. Moreover, even when we think that we have grasped a little truth, such as the correct theory of the consumption function, we should be sceptical and remember how often what seems obviously true to one generation is shown to be an error by the next.

My pessimism also makes me sceptical of many liberal prescriptions. I agree that a private enterprise economy suffers from excessive unemployment and inflation, and from misallocations resulting from consumer ignorance, externalities and monopoly power. Many economists seem to jump from this to the conclusion that government intervention is desirable. But that seems to me a leap of faith, based at least in part on an unwarranted 'can-do' spirit, and on a belief that somehow human misery can be reduced if we just apply enough goodwill and common sense. I cannot make this leap of faith. There is something to Senator Moynihan's dictum: 'No good deed goes unpunished.' This does not mean that we should eschew all government intervention, but it does mean that the mere recognition that a situation is bad does not imply that we should try to eliminate it. That is an obvious point, but one often ignored in the urge to demonstrate one's goodness and also one's ability to overcome a popular, but often naively rationalized, anti-government attitude.

My methodological prejudices are, to a considerable extent, those of a logical empiricist. I too have read and enjoyed Kuhn, and realize that logical empiricism is no longer a feasible position. But I do wish it were. In a field like economics, where the observable facts provide so little discipline, the attitude that anything goes, as long as the relevant scientists accept it, is a dangerous prescription. Apart from this I greatly prefer research that explains puzzling observations to that which polishes and makes more rigorous some previously-known result. Didn't someone (Einstein?) once say: 'Elegance is for tailors'? If I believe that a certain hypothesis has a 99 percent probability of being true, I am not all that interested in a paper that raises this probability to 99.99 percent. Time is short; there are too many other hypotheses to think about, and besides, I am impatient. This impatience also makes me dissatisfied with the high degree of roundaboutness in the structure of production of economics. I am less interested in papers that teach me something about an economic model than in those that teach me something about the economy *per se.*

In addition, I hold the Marshallian view that economics comprises 'the study of mankind in the ordinary business of life' (Marshall [1890] 1947, p. 11) rather than the Robbinsian view that it is the application of the tools for maximizing utility (Robbins 1932). Hence, we should pay attention to how the government makes economic decisions, even if these decisions cannot be explained entirely, or even largely, by the tools of economic analysis. In doing so one usually cannot achieve the degree of precision that is obtainable in dealing with problems to which the tools of economic analysis are more applicable. But a vague analysis is preferable to what is so often done when giving policy advice: ignoring a relevant aspect of the problem entirely, or else resorting to mere assertion.

Finally, as already mentioned, I am an outsider. Even if I agree with a certain school on many issues, I do not feel any great urge to agree with it on all issues or to be a loyal member of it.

As I will discuss shortly, given these characteristics it is not surprising that eventually I became attracted to monetarism. But as a graduate student, like nearly all my colleagues, I was strongly Keynesian. *The general theory* was the text to be read and reread. When assigned some book in a macro course I would first look at the index to see how often Keynes was cited. That told me how seriously to take it. Yet I was also sceptical of Keynesian orthodoxy. For example, at that time Keynesians made a great fuss about speculative liquidity preference. Unlike others I was bothered by the lack of data on the proportion of the money supply that was held in speculative balances. Perhaps it was trivial. Arguments by assertion and group-think seemed to play too large a role in the then prevailing Keynesian orthodoxy.

When Milton Friedman's *Studies in the quantity theory of money* (1956) appeared, I was excited by it and assigned it as a text in a graduate course that summer. (Only to have one student complain that I should have used a more up-to-date textbook!) Here was a new approach, or at least new to anyone who, like me, had not been privy to the Chicago oral tradition. It might be wrong, but was certainly worth exploring. Some major developments of Keynesian economics, such as the life-cycle hypothesis, were still to come, but its main structure was already well established, offering little opportunity for new work. By contrast, the research programme of the quantity theory offered dazzling prospects to both potential supporters and critics. My first publication on it (De Prano and Mayer 1965) was mainly critical. But as Chicago economists piled up more and more evidence on the importance of money, and as they (and Brunner and Meltzer) provided impressive evidence on the damage that Fed policy had done, I moved closer to monetarism. Yet I never came close enough for monetarists to consider me one of their own. I did serve for some time on the Shadow Open Market Committee, set up by Brunner and Meltzer to pressure the Fed into adopting monetarist policies. But I continually argued for a more moderate policy than the Committee wanted, so it is not surprising that after some time I was purged for left-wing deviationism.

I do call myself a moderate monetarist, but that is an arbitrary label, which I adopt in part because monetarists are in a minority. If it were the dominant school I would probably call myself a moderate Keynesian.

It was surely not just the objective evidence, but also my preconceptions and biases and my background that drew me to monetarism. I would have found it more difficult to break with the Keynesian tradition had I done my graduate work at Keynesian Harvard and come under the personal influence of Alvin Hansen, rather than at more middle-of-the-road Columbia, where I was influenced by the partially-Chicagoan Albert Hart. Similarly, had I taught at the Keynesian University of Michigan instead of at the more intellectually diversified Michigan State, peer pressure would have made it harder for me to break with Keynesian theory. Not impossible perhaps, since I am by inclination an outsider, but certainly harder. Being an outsider, as well as being sceptical of any claims to have discovered The Truth, also made it easier for me to abandon the dominant tradition.

Perhaps more important is that I share many of the methodological presuppositions of Friedman, and hence feel strongly sympathetic to his work, not only on money, but also on other topics. I was unaware of this source of attraction until reading, a few months ago, Hirsch and De Marchi's (1990) superb book on Friedman's methodology. They show that Friedman focuses on hypotheses that throw light on specific problems rather than seeking grand over-arching generalizations, and that he relies on an interplay of theory and empirical tests. These are characteristics I have always found strongly appealing. Friedman's pragmatism and insistence on economics as a discipline that addressed practical issues also struck chords, particularly in the late 1950s and the 1960s when so much of Keynesian analysis consisted of proliferating growth models. In addition, Friedman's work is imbued with a Marshallian spirit, and this too I like. These characteristics are also found in the work of Brunner and Meltzer, and if I have focused on Friedman's methodology it is because of the availability of Hirsch's and De Marchi's work on that subject.[5]

The monetarists' doubts about the efficacy of stabilization policy appeals to me both because of my sense of pessimism and my doubts about how much we really know about the economy. This may seem strange because the monetarists' pessimism about the ability to pursue stabilizing policy is matched by their optimism about the inherent stability of a market economy. But monetarists spend much more time expounding why stabilization policy will not work than in documenting that the private sector is stable. Hence, in reading their work one gets the impression of pessimism. I do not, however, believe that they have demonstrated the superiority of rules over discretion. I am too much of a sceptic to think that this issue is settled. But I do value their work as a counter to Keynesian smugness and self-congratulation. Since writing this passage I have criticized both sides of the debate, the monetarists for claiming too much strength for their case, and the Keynesians for blithely ignoring the considerable strength that it does have (Mayer 1998). In any

---

[5] The best-known characteristic of Friedman's methodology, his rejection of tests by assumptions, has always struck me as a somewhat too radical statement of what is a sound heuristic position.

case, with the prevailing instability of velocity, and with the development of rules for central bank response, such as the Taylor rule, the traditional debate about monetary policy rules is now badly dated.

While I share some of the monetarists' doubts about government intervention as an effective tool to improve the economy, I am not as eager as most of them are to cut government expenditure. The government is not efficient enough to cut out unnecessary items while leaving necessary ones. And I am more favourably disposed to moderate income redistribution than are some monetarists: I do like Friedman's idea for a negative income tax.

SELECTED WORKS

(1951) 'The effects of a wage change upon prices, profits and employment', *Economic Journal*, 61 (3), pp. 518–30.

(1952) (with J. Pechman) 'Mr Colin Clark on the limits of taxation', *Review of Economics and Statistics*, 34 (3), pp. 232–42.

(1953) 'The population growth argument of the stagnation thesis', unpublished Ph.D. dissertation, Columbia University.

(1958) 'The inflexibility of monetary policy', *Review of Economics and Statistics*, 40 (4), pp. 358–74.

(1960) 'The distribution of ability and earnings', *Review of Economics and Statistics*, 42 (2), pp. 189–95.

(1965) (with M. De Prano) 'Tests of the relative importance of autonomous expenditures and money', *American Economic Review*, 46 (4), pp. 729–52.

(1972) *Permanent income, wealth and consumption: a critique of the permanent income theory, the life-cycle hypothesis and related theories.* Berkeley: University of California Press.

(1975a) 'The structure of monetarism, pt. I', *Kredit und Kapital*, 8 (1), pp. 191–218. Rep. in T. Mayer (ed.) (1978) **q.v.**, pp. 1–25.

(1975b) 'The structure of monetarism, pt. II', *Kredit und Kapital*, 8 (2), pp. 293–316. Rep. in T. Mayer (ed.) (1978) **q.v.**, pp. 26–46.

(1978) (Ed.) *The structure of monetarism.* New York: W.W. Norton.

(1990a) *Monetarism and macroeconomic policy.* Aldershot: Edward Elgar.

(1990b) 'Getting older, but not much wiser', in T. Mayer (1990a) **q.v.**, pp. 1–16.

(1993) *Truth versus precision in economics.* Aldershot: Edward Elgar.

(1995) *Doing economic research: essays on the applied methodology of economics.* Aldershot: Edward Elgar.

(1998) 'Monetarists vs. Keynesians: a case study of a flawed debate', in R.E. Backhouse, D.M. Hausman, U. Mäki and A. Salanti (eds) (1998) *Economics and methodology: crossing boundaries.* London: Macmillan, pp. 254–302.

(1999) *Monetary policy and the great inflation in the United States: the Federal Reserve and the failure of macroeconomic policy, 1965–79.* Cheltenham: Edward Elgar.

BIBLIOGRAPHY

Becker, H. (1986) *Better writing for social scientists*. Chicago: University of Chicago Press.

Breit, W. (1987) 'Biography and the making of economic worlds', *Southern Economic Journal*, 53 (4), pp. 823–33.

Brunner, K. and Meckling, W.H. (1977) 'The perception of man and the conception of government', *Journal of Money, Credit and Banking*, 9 (1, pt. I), pp. 70–85.

Clark, C.G. (1945) 'Public finance and changes in the value of money', *Economic Journal*, 55 (4), pp. 371–89.

Friedman, M. (ed.) (1956) *Studies in the quantity theory of money*. Chicago: University of Chicago Press.

Harrod, R.F. (1951) *The life of John Maynard Keynes*. London: Macmillan.

Hirsch, A. De Marchi, N. (1990) *Milton Friedman: economics in theory and practice*. Hemel Hempstead: Harvester Wheatsheaf.

Marshall, A. (1890) *Principles of economics: an introductory volume.*, 8th edn. (1947). London: Macmillan.

Patinkin, D. (1972) 'Keynesian monetary theory and the Cambridge school', *Banca Nazionale del Lavoro Quarterly Review*, 25 (2), pp. 138–58.

Ramsey, F.P. (1928) 'A mathematical theory of saving', *Economic Journal*, 38 (4), pp. 543–59.

Robbins, L.C. (1932) *An essay on the nature and significance of economic science*. London: Macmillan.

Stigler, G.J. (1959) 'The politics of political economists', *Quarterly Journal of Economics*, 73 (4), pp. 522–32.

6. Richard G. Lipsey (b. 1928)[1]

All my life I wanted to know. Others wanted to be discoverers; I wanted to know what they had discovered. When I was ten, we were introduced at school to some elementary astronomy and that night I lay awake trying to get my mind around the idea of infinity. I resolved to become an astronomer when I grew up. (I meant cosmologist but didn't know the word at the time.) When I survey the great advances in that field during my lifetime, taking us to the very moment of the universe's creation, I often regret that I got seduced by this crazy subject, economics, that purported to have universal laws about the behaviour of people rather than stars.

In high school, although I was an indifferent scholar, I read and read and read: natural history, biology, geography, history, astronomy. (I followed H.G. Wells' *History of the world* in a great intellectual odyssey, discovering the beginnings of Western civilization in ancient Mesopotamia and following it up through the First World War.) Darwin was an early intellectual treat, as were adventures with Freud in late high school days – when I was reading the *Interpretation of dreams*, I became very adept at remembering my own.

---

[1] Lipsey (1997c), as revised by the editors. Further career details can be found in my interview with Keith Tribe (Lipsey 1997d). I have three volume of selected essays in the series, the first my collected papers in microeconomics, growth and political economy (Lipsey 1997a), the second my papers in macroeconomic theory and policy (Lipsey 1997b) and the third my joint papers with Curtis Eaton on the foundations of monopolistic competition and economic geography (Eaton and Lipsey 1997). I have also been honoured with a festschrift (Eaton and Harris 1997).

We used to play a game of 'what would you die for?' My answer was always the same: I would 'happily' die if for one short hour before my demise I could know the secret of the origin of the universe!

6.1 UNDERGRADUATE DAYS, 1946–50

My indifferent performance as a student carried on into first year university, where at Victoria College,[2] I continued to get most of my intellectual fodder from outside the classroom. Added to books, however, was another great stimulation. I entered the college in 1947 with the first wave of Second World War veterans. These men and women were five to 15 years older than we adolescents; they had seen the world and some of the horrors of war; many had suffered through the Great Depression, leaving school in the 1930s for lack of financial support. They set us high standards and they became our mirror onto the world. I became close friends with a veteran who was over ten years my senior, and who I found to be in love with me in a way that I did not know existed and could not reciprocate. From him, I learned at least as much as from my voracious reading.

In my second year, I enrolled in three courses that were to change my life: the history of western philosophy, introductory psychology and introductory economics (with a fine text book by John Ise which was really Alfred Marshall for those not yet ready to be turned loose on the master).[3]

Discovering the pagan origins of many Christian dogmas shook the belief in revealed, absolute, religious truth in which I had been raised; reading psychology gave me a more rationalist view of people than I had had before; learning about the complexities of the hidden hand shook my fussy, naive, do-gooding, liberalism (in the American sense of the term). Every day in that fateful autumn with ideas swirling in my head, I walked over the hill from my home in Oak Bay to the college (on the site of what was the old normal school and is now Camosun College). Each day, as I added new knowledge, the ferment swirled faster. Finally one morning in late November, half way to my destination, the whole fabric of my earlier beliefs fell away. I stopped in the middle of the road aghast. Suddenly I believed in nothing that I had inherited from my past; I found everything – factual beliefs, religious explanations, moral precepts – up for re-examination and to be put back in

---

[2] That small precursor of the University of Victoria was then a two-year, arts college extension of the University of British Columbia (BC).

[3] At the same time, a Canadian university course lasted an entire academic year and a student took five or six courses each year.

place only if they looked acceptable now. I had had what I subsequently found Descartes had called an intellectual house cleaning. In one short hour, everything, including the religion in which I had been raised and in which I strongly believed, fell away (and, in the case of religion, never to return). It was one of the great experiences of my life – at least on a par with the discovery of the full power of sex.

During that year, I transferred my main intellectual stimulus from outside to inside the classroom. Economics especially was a revelation. I found I could do it intuitively. I always seemed to know one step ahead of the lecturer just what assumption was needed to complete the argument. I ended up explaining the concepts to fellow classmates, many of whom were ten years my senior. I finished with a general equilibrium model in my mind, composed of demand and supply curves made of wire, and all interlocking so that a shock in one market had repercussions on all others, and an intervention that prevented the attainment of equilibrium in one market, set off smoke and sparks in the other markets. I subsequently found out that I had in my mind a rather dramatized, mechanical version of a Walrasian general equilibrium system.

Suddenly I went from being an indifferent B-level student to a straight A student. After some worry about specialization versus a general education, I decided to enrol in honours economics for my last two years which were taken at UBC in Vancouver. The courses continued to open many doors; I joined the economics club where we read papers to each other and debated openly with our professors in an intellectually challenging atmosphere.

In my third year, I took intermediate economic theory, taught by Professor Joseph Crumb and using Boulding's *Economic analysis* (1941) as a text. Already I was becoming frustrated with the number of theoretical exercises which seemed to end in no new insights into real-world behaviour. Then one of the great moments of intellectual excitement occurred when I read Boulding's exposition of Hotelling's model of duopolists locating on a line. Boulding was extravagant in the range of applications that he suggested for what he dubbed 'the principle of minimum differentiation'. This was mind boggling; this was what I had come to economics to find: theories that explained a wide range of real world observations. So in my third year I formed a major research programme: to find out more about the range of applications of Hotelling's model and to check out some of the more extravagant of Boulding's claims for it. It was decades before I returned to this programme in a long series of papers with Curtis Eaton that is included in our joint volume of collected works (Eaton and Lipsey 1997).

Sometime in my third year, I made an appointment to see Professor Crumb. I proposed that the economic theory I was studying seemed to have a mathematical form and, since I was learning 'verbal mathematics', wouldn't it be a good idea to learn some formal mathematics? 'No', he advised me, 'economics is based on the three pillars of history, accounting and statistical analysis; learn those as outside courses but do not waste time on mathematics'. The advice was right on some counts, but disastrously wrong on the key one. This was one of the very few influences at UBC that were unhelpful.

William Merrit taught a wonderful honours seminar where we read everything in sight: Sombart, MacKinder, bits of Pareto's *Mind and society* (1935), Mahan's *The influence of seapower on history* (1895), James Burnam, Thorstein Veblen, H.L. Mencken and countless others in a mélange of ideas about understanding human behaviour in social and economic settings. I read Hayek's *The road to serfdom* (1944) and was profoundly impressed. The most important book for me, however, was Schumpeter's *The theory of economic development* (1911). It gave me a model of the circular flow of income and output, taking place in real time and disturbed by dramatic innovations which made static welfare maximization more or less irrelevant and perfect competition the wrong norm. At times in the future, this vision became clouded over but it never fully left me and it gave me what I often described as 'an effective inoculation against the excesses of Hicksian comparative statics'. Without clearly realizing it, I had formed another research programme: to evaluate Schumpeter's criticisms of neoclassical, static-equilibrium, maximizing economics.

Professor Robert Clark taught me the history of economic thought and I read Smith, Ricardo, Mill and bits of Marx with great interest. Most influential of all the books I read in that course was Lionel Robbins' *An essay on the nature and significance of economic science* (1932). Coming to economics as a renegade scientist, I was always interested in methodology: how could anyone really establish natural laws about something so complex as human behaviour? Robbins said many wise things from which I profited greatly, but when I came to his chapter on economic statistics, I balked. There I read for the first time the methodology of the Austrian school, which was, as I later learned from Mark Blaug, also the methodology of many of the classical economists. According to this methodology, which is Euclidean in conception, investigators first make assumptions that are intuitively self-evident, then apply the rules of logic to deduce propositions that may not be self-evident. In economics, the trick was to establish assumptions that really were self-evident, standing the test of introspection. Since the assumptions are obviously correct, the deductions must also be correct, no matter how unobvious they may be. If the facts appear to disagree with the deductions of theories, then the facts must be wrong; the deductions cannot be wrong – providing only that they are logically correct deductions – since they are based on assumptions that we know to be correct through introspection. In short, facts are used to illustrate theories but not to test them.

I read and reread the chapter. 'This cannot be right', I said to myself, 'facts based on careful empirical observation must play a more important part in the development of our understanding of the economy than as mere illustrations to be cast aside whenever they disagree with the prevailing theory.' These concerns shaped another of my research programmes: to find out what was wrong with the methodology of Robbins (1932) which, as far as I knew, was the prevailing methodology of all economists.

I wrote my honours graduating essay under Robert Clark, doing a major empirical study of the relation between land and building values in commercial property in Vancouver. This involved getting real estate assessments of the value of land and improvements for several thousand properties, visiting each individually to see if the building also included living quarters, and testing for the factors that caused the ratio of improvement values to land values to vary throughout the city. This was a major task worth at least an MA. (I subsequently found that an MA had been given at the Wharton School for a similar study.) Completing all my field work delayed my graduation for a year until 1951. The study gave me an abiding respect for how important it was to get reliable data, and for how easily observations could upset ideas which seemed intuitively plausible at the outset of any study.

I graduated with straight As in all my economics courses, with one exception. In Money and Banking I could never understand the relation between stocks and flows in the quantity theory of money that we were taught, and a grade of B+ was the result. (Unknown to me at the time, this failure established another research programme in my mind.)

I finished my fourth year at UBC in 1950 and left (with an honours essay still to be completed a year later) still innocent of Keynesian economics. Students who took one of the options that I missed, international trade, talked knowingly about multipliers which to me were a mystery.[4]

---

[4] In private correspondence, Colin Harbury has offered the following observations '... as an LSE undergraduate 1947–50 I did not end up innocent of Keynes but, arguably worse, had to struggle to try to understand the cryptic series of papers in the *EJ* between Robertson and JMK which it seemed at the time were not fully appreciated by my teachers! I was, however, luckier than you on grasping the stock/flow distinction because I had the great advantage of watching James Meade operate the Phillips water machine and reading the *Economica* articles on it.'

6.2   THE CIVIL SERVICE, 1950–1

During my third year, I became engaged to a girl who was five years my senior and a veteran with overseas experience. Anticipating the continuing obligations of marriage, I had applied for jobs as an economist with several provincial governments. During the period of the final examinations, my engagement broke up. After completing the exams, I travelled to Toronto in the company of one of my professors, Bill Merrit, as a first step to seeing the world. At the time, the first Toronto subway was being built and I intended to get a construction job on it when my money ran out. I was aiming at graduate school but only after a year or two gaining experience outside of the ivory tower.

In one of those quirks of fate that have so often influenced my life, I got a telephone call in Toronto offering me a job with the BC provincial government in what was then the Bureau of Economics and Statistics of the Department of Trade and Industry. Had I not been planning to marry, I never would have applied for the job and now that I was off to see the world, there was even less reason to take a civil service job. But I was flattered at being picked from apparently a large field of applicants so, mumbling about being caught by respectability and responsibility (I was deep into George Bernard Shaw at the time), I took the train to Victoria and reported to the Bureau in September.

I worked there for a year and then was given a leave of absence to do a two-year MA programme at Toronto. I returned to work at the Bureau after each of my academic years in Toronto, working mid-May to mid-September, getting the statutory raises and full annual holidays (with pay). My period there was not without interest and I learned many useful lessons – not the least important of which was that there are ivory towers outside of academia and that government research often means providing reasons to justify decisions already taken on political grounds. My final job before leaving the Bureau was to help a senior economist write a paper advising on the extension of the government-owned railroad into the interior of the province and on into the Peace River district of Alberta. It rapidly became apparent that this would be a big money loser. But advice to this effect was unwelcome, while Chamber of Commerce material on why the railroad would build an empire was what we were being asked to provide. Rather than write what I didn't believe, I asked to be relieved from the job and departed the government a few weeks later a sadder and wiser person.

6.3   MA YEARS, 1951–3

Two years as an MA student at the University of Toronto, where I went on the strong urging of Bill Merrit, taught me much. We had an excellent course in microeconomic theory, and I was introduced to the mysteries of Keynesian economics. But Toronto was most famous for its economic history and I got all of it that I could. I was particularly privileged to take Harold Innis's course on empire and communications given in the last year of his life. I will always remember his last lecture which he, and some of us, knew was his farewell to the academic world.

I shared an office with a left wing political science student, Ted Goldberg, who later went on to become a senior negotiator with the Union of Automobile Workers and even later, to return to the University of Toronto as head of the Department of Hospital Administration. Ted, his wife, Grace and I became life-long friends. I remember being profoundly influenced by an argument we had on the future of socialism. I said that planned economies would stand or fall on their ability to allocate resources efficiently. Ted poured scorn on the idea 'as if, with all the important issues facing society today, efficiency of resource allocation mattered much, let alone enough to determine the success or failure of the great socialist experiment'. I was impressed by his argument and it took decades before I saw how wrong he was.

At Toronto, I continued to maintain my A results on all economics courses. In retrospect, the biggest missed opportunity was the course which Bill Hood (fresh from Hood and Koopmans (1953, pp. 112–99) on the identification problem) taught in mathematical economics. Several of us wanted him to take us through Hicks's appendix to *Value and capital* (1939) and teach us the required mathematics of which I was totally innocent. Unfortunately, on a vote, this plan lost to the majority who wanted to learn about the latest fad, linear programming. So I lost an opportunity to learn at least some relevant mathematics.

Between my first and second years at Toronto I had married and begun a tumultuous seven-year relation which finally ended in 1959.[5] Partly because my wife looked fondly on earlier years in England during her first marriage, and partly because we students still looked to England as the intellectual leader in economics, I asked my professors about study in the UK. On advice from Professor Nat Wolf, I applied to, and was accepted at, Wadham

---

[5]   I will not say more about my first marriage except to note that the name of my first wife will convey to many that the word 'tumultuous' is not an over-dramatization: she was the Assia Gutman (whom I met as Pam Steele) whose association with Sylvia Plath and Ted Hughes was later to achieve international notoriety.

College, Oxford, as a research student. As an insurance policy, I had also applied to Chicago and the London School of Economics (LSE). When I was offered a prestigious Frank Knight scholarship, I decided, after much soul searching, to accept Chicago and say no to Wadham. (LSE had also offered me a place but did not require an early decision.) Shortly before hearing of my success at Chicago, I saw a small notice advertising the Sir Arthur Sims Fellowship to study in the UK. Since it was open to anyone in the social sciences and humanities, I thought it a long shot but applied in any case. I was interviewed in Ottawa and, rather to my surprise, was offered the fellowship a few days after I had accepted the Chicago scholarship. Much agonizing produced no obvious reasons for deciding between the LSE and Chicago. Finally, I made the decision to go to the LSE because they had dropped French as a Ph.D. requirement while Chicago still maintained the old language-competence requirement. Being a total dunce at foreign languages, and having taken seven years to get through five years of required French in high school and college, I opted for the easy route: avoid any more foreign language requirements. So I made one of the most momentous decisions of my life, to go to the UK rather than the US, on the basis of avoiding a minor language requirement – and once again made, for the wrong reasons, what in retrospect turned out to be the right decision!

6.4   PH.D. AT LSE, 1953–5

The LSE in the fall of 1953 was an exciting place. Students from all over the world crammed into the graduate common room. I wondered if I was up to the challenge intellectually. When asked about my prospective research on the fellowship application form, I had chosen, rather by default, an empirical study of the changing pattern of Canadian trade with the US and the UK. The LSE at the time followed a fully *laissez-faire* policy with respect to research students. I was assigned to Helen Makower in international trade and on our first interview, she told me to go to whatever lectures attracted me, read as I wished, and come back when I had something written to show her.

I attended James Meade's seminar on international trade, and Lionel Robbins's great Wednesday afternoon general economics seminar in which the whole of economics was grist for our mill. Outside of that, I spent my first term playing bridge and chess. I had played some duplicate with my father who went on to become a life master and I wanted to learn the ACOL system used by the championship-winning British bridge players. I was innocent of chess but soon learned the rudiments and then dug myself into several books. Euwe's *Judgement and planning in chess* was particularly valuable. In between the two regular seminars, chess and bridge, I had time to attend maybe six or eight lectures in the whole term. I tried Professor Meade's lectures in which he was expounding what was later published as *Trade and welfare* (Meade 1955). My fellow graduate student, Max Corden, attended religiously, but one dose of apples and blankets was too much for me and I stupidly gave up the opportunity to hear it all from the master. I also listened to Lionel Robbins lecture once or twice on the history of economic analysis.

In that first term, I dropped in on one lecture by my supervisor, Helen Makower, on advanced economic analysis given to the undergraduate economics specialists. By chance, she happened to be expounding Viner's new book on customs unions (Viner 1950). I listened to her exposition of trade creation and trade diversion and said to myself, 'this is all supply side, which no doubt is important, but there must also be a demand component'. I went home in a fit of intellectual excitement and scratched out numerical examples which got me nowhere and then went to indifference curves. About 2 a.m., after finishing a bottle of sherry, I had the outlines of what eventually became my article 'Trade diversion and welfare' (Lipsey 1957). This was the first time I had ever done a piece of economic analysis on my own. I showed it to my supervisor who wasn't quite sure what to make of it. Nonetheless, I decided to do my thesis on customs union theory (not then knowing that Professor Meade was working on the same problems) but I put my article aside until I could fit it into a wider analysis – and could persuade my supervisor that it was interesting. Sometime later, when I met Harry Johnson for the first time, I told him about my proof that a country could gain from joining a purely trade diverting customs union with no trade creation. He was excited.

Work on my thesis was hampered by my lack of technique. I had been taught only two techniques for analysing problems in international trade. The first was numerical examples. I had read Frank Graham's *The theory of international values* (1948) in which he solves by pencil and paper calculations ten-country, ten-commodity numerical models! The second was geometry which was the dominant tool of analysis and which was well expounded in Meade's *A geometry of international trade* (1952), and at which Harry Johnson was a master.

But customs unions problems as I saw them required three countries and three commodities. I could no longer avoid the conclusion that I had been discouraged from reaching as an undergraduate: mathematics was indispensable for analysing many economic problems. So, like many economists before me, I set out to read Allen's *Mathematical analysis for economists* (1938) and as a Ph.D. student at the LSE I began to teach myself how to differentiate x^2!

Early in my second year at the LSE, I accepted an unlikely job. The movement that was to end in the European Economic Community was just getting up to full steam and it held, as part of its evolution, a meeting in London called the Council of Westminster with delegations from most of the European states and those countries with close relations to them. The Canadian government wanted to be represented, but not thinking it worthwhile to send a delegation from Canada, they cast around for Canadians already in the UK to become delegates. They settled on three of us. My old teacher Robert Clark, who was spending a sabbatical year at Manchester, Harry Johnson, already famous as an *enfant terrible* among UK economists, and myself, a research student on a prestigious fellowship at the LSE. I knew some trade theory but little about trade policy and nothing about diplomacy or the formation of the EEC, so this was pretty heady stuff.

We were briefed by the Canadian High Commissioner in London and this was when I met Harry Johnson for the first time. Spaak, Monet and several other great Europeans attended the conference. Urged on by Bob Clark, I even made an intervention arguing that to make permanent exceptions from the free trade obligations for former colonies on the grounds that they were LDCs was dangerous. I argued that the rules should, sooner or later, apply with equal force to all. (A theme I returned to decades later with a lot more knowledge to back it up than I had then.) After my intervention, I met Bill Phillips for the first time. He was a New Zealand delegate on the same terms as we Canadians were. He greeted me with 'a little bit of religion got mixed up with the economics in your speech'. I was impressed, and depressed: I had not thought of the principle of equality in a customs union as being religious. It was a long time before I returned to this theme of trade policy. It was an even longer time before experience with the GATT exemptions granted to LDCs convinced me that I was right in my naive 1954 intervention. I now realize that Bill's accusation of religion was a characteristic put down that has to be endured by anyone who feels that free market principles are worth establishing generally.

One of my fellow students at the LSE was Jacques Parizeau, subsequently to gain fame as a Quebec separatist and leader of the Parti Quebecois. He had money and sophistication, whereas I was poor and provincial. Jacques took my wife and me to my first French meal and taught me a bit about French wine, and cheese-that-was-not-cheddar. Jacques used to visit our fourth floor garret in Goodge Street where my wife and I lived in poverty in one room with the lavatory three floors below which we shared with the employees of the ground floor shops. Since Assia was invariably unready when he arrived, he would wait at the working man's pub across the street. When we came to fetch him, we would find him, pint of beer in hand, dressed immaculately in a pinstriped suit with a bowler hat and furled umbrella reading *The Times*, and surrounded by beer drinking, Andy-Capp-style, British working men. We always welcomed Jacques's visits because not only did we enjoy his company, but he invariably brought bottles of beer with him. After he left, we would return the bottles to the pub and spend the refunded deposit money on the two staple items of our diet: potatoes and bacon pieces (the small scraps of bacon left over after all possible slices had been taken off a hunk of bacon which sold for sixpence a pound).

6.5   AN LSE STAFF MEMBER, 1955–64

After two years as a research student, I was asked by Helen Makower to apply for one of the three assistant lectureships that the LSE was advertising that year.[6] I was amazed, not thinking myself worthy of being considered for such an august appointment. My interview consisted of a long debate with the senior liberal professors. They asked sceptically how I could contend that reducing any tariff, by means of either a customs union, a GATT agreement or unilaterally, could possibly be anything but unambiguously beneficial?

After our interview, we were taken to lunch in the senior common room. I sat next to a junior staff member with whom I had played bridge, George Morton. I told him of a great discovery that I had just made: if a country has two imports subject to tariff, removing one tariff may not raise welfare; indeed there would generally be a non-zero rate that would be best to select for this variable tariff. George expressed disbelief, surprise and then great interest in that order. He invited me to his home and together we worked out the mathematical proof that appears in section VI of the 'The general theory of second best' (Lipsey and Lancaster 1956): given a tariff on one import, the second best optimum tariff on the second import is greater than zero but lower than the given tariff if the two imports are substitutes. This was the first mathematical proof that I had ever developed and I doubt that I could have done it without a great deal of help from George Morton.

In due course, Kelvin Lancaster, Hans Leisner and I were appointed to the LSE staff as assistant lecturers. The next three years were an intellectual feast, with a degree of freedom from administration and onerous teaching duties that I was never again to experience. Duties consisted of taking five

---

[6]   UK ranks then were Assistant Lecturer (non-tenured), Lecturer (tenured), Senior Lecturer (the top grade for those who did not have a distinguished research career) and Reader (the typical top grade for those with a distinguished research career). A Professor (who was said to hold a chair) was rare. In many smaller departments, there was only one professor who was also the head of department. LSE was unusual in having about ten professors of economics.

discussion classes per week which backed up the first year microeconomic lectures given by Ralph Turvey and the second year lectures on macroeconomics given by Kurt Klappholz. The format at the LSE was for each student to attend a weekly lecture given to the entire years' group of several hundred students, and one discussion class with 15–20 students. Assistant lecturers gave the discussion classes.

We all attended Lionel Robbins's great Wednesday afternoon seminar and we had time to read, talk and write. Kelvin Lancaster, Chris Archibald, Ed Mishan, Kurt Klappholz, Lucien Foldes, Maurice Peston, Bob Gould and many others were stimulating company. We all read everything that each other wrote, made detailed notes on, and had long discussions about each article. In a very real sense, everything that any of us published was a joint piece by all of us. Ed Mishan kept us up to date with developments elsewhere and we held discussion groups on the latest works such as Friedman's (1957) new book on the permanent income hypothesis.

During my first year on the staff, two sequences of events stand out. The first began one morning when I was in my room reading an article by Andrew Ozga on customs unions. Kelvin Lancaster came in for the usual morning gossip. I said to him in high excitement, 'You know these guys are all discovering the same theorem in all sorts of different guises.' Kelvin replied that ever since he had read Samuelson's *Foundations* (1947), he had wondered why people put such stress on fulfilling selected optimum conditions when all of them could never be fulfilled. I went to the common room for coffee and, as luck would have it, I bumped into Harry Johnson and explained our great insight to him. 'Publish immediately' was his advice. Kelvin worked out the general proof and I worked on my customs union example and the literature survey. Harry played an important part in arguing that if the article was to have the impact it deserved, we should do an exhaustive survey of the literature. He suggested several articles of which we were unaware and helped us write an article which had world-wide impact rather than going unnoticed as it might have done if less care had been spent on it.

The second sequence began when I ran into Harry Johnson in the senior common room and he reminded me of the point I had made to him about trade diversion and welfare some 12 months previously. He asked, 'Had I done anything about publishing it?' 'No', said I. 'Well' said Harry, 'I have had a similar article submitted to the *Review of Economic Studies* and I advise you to publish your idea quickly.' I wrote it up in a few days and submitted it to *Economica*, the LSE house journal. It was published about the same time as the *Review of Economic Studies* published the same point in an article by Hans Gehrels (1957). In my version, however, I had warned that my two-commodity geometrical demonstration could be misleading because customs unions raised three-commodity problems in which some, but not all, tariffs were removed (Lipsey 1957). Gehrels seemed to miss this point and concluded that the consumption effect invariably worked to raise welfare – so I had a second publication pointing out Gehrels's omission and making the second-best point in more detail. So once again accident played a key role in my professional life. If I had chosen any other lecture of Helen Makower's to attend in my first term as an LSE graduate student, the odds are that I would have remained innocent of customs unions long after I had chosen another thesis topic; and if I had not told Harry Johnson of my idea, I might never have published it.[7]

Harry also got me on the programme of the Association of University Teachers of Economics (AUTE) to talk about my thesis on customs unions a year or two later. I never thought to publish my talk but I met my LSE colleague Professor Frank Paish in the staff lavatory not long after and he said he thoroughly enjoyed my talk and that I really should write it up. So one of my most widely read articles, 'The theory of customs unions: a general survey' had a rather accidental birth (Lipsey 1960b).

Then in my second year on the staff, we all read Patinkin's *Money, interest and prices* (1956). Our first reaction was that it was a beautiful piece of work and Lionel decided to spend the year going through it in his seminar, chapter by chapter. Controversy quickly arose about just what the real balance effect amounted to. This was in many ways the most intense three months of my life. My marriage had reached its most hectic state and my mind was shifting back and forward between personal and professional matters. I often lay awake at nights with visions of stocks and flows swirling in my head. When I had some of my ideas more or less sorted out, I gave a paper on the real balance effect in Robbins's seminar. In it, I unconsciously followed Patinkin in only dealing with instantaneous (what Hicks called weekly) equilibrium. Andrew Ozga asked me what would happen if I let the model evolve for n

---

[7] I have several times been the subject of historical reconstructions that were wide of reality – so much so as to make me mistrust all such historical accounts written by third persons. One obvious error was in Harry Johnson's (1972) review of my thesis whose belated publication is explained in the text. According to Harry, I was a 'soldier' trained for 'active combat' and 'sent into battle by the [LSE] high command.' Anyone who knew the LSE at the time would know that my account of LSE's totally *laissez-faire* approach to supervision was the correct one rather than Harry's assumption that the LSE in the 1950s was like the Chicago he knew in the 1960s, in which Ph.D. students were directed to particular subjects by their supervisors. (Naturally I prefer Max Corden's 1972 review of my dissertation.) Two other reconstructions are Neil de Marchi's (1988) version of the days of the M²T seminar and Nancy Wulwick's (1987; 1989; 1994; 1996) interpretation of Phillip's and Lipsey's motives in writing the famous Phillips curves papers. Giving my side of these matters would require more than the space available in this far-reaching essay – although Mark Blaug has several times urged me to 'correct' de Marchi's version. Fortunately, Robert Leeson (1994; 1997) is doing his best to cope with the myths that Nancy Wulwick is trying to create.

periods and the penny dropped: Patinkin only analysed weekly equilibrium and that was why he needed such very restrictive assumptions to get quantity theory results. For example, any increase in the money supply had to be distributed to each agent in proportion to the amount of money he or she already held. It had seemed to us that if the quantity theory depended on such strong, unrealistic assumptions, it was not worth much. I worked out the results for full equilibrium (which became part 1 of my subsequent paper on monetary and value theory, Lipsey and Archibald 1958) and then joined forces with Chris to work on the question of the classical dichotomy (part 2 of our paper). Robert Clower later said that our paper got stocks and flows correctly sorted out for the first time in the history of monetary economics. We got the whole of the quantity theory and the real balance effect right in ten pages, which I still think were the most elegant ten pages I was ever involved in writing. Now, at last, I understood why the undergraduate course on the quantity theory of money had not made sense to me; it, the instructor, and I, were hopelessly confused about stocks and flows and temporary and full equilibrium.

At the end of my third year on the staff, I came up for tenure which came with promotion to full lecturer. I was urged to complete my thesis which I had put aside on being appointed to the staff in order to write articles on customs unions, monetary theory and second best. I spent a full year working out the various analyses in the second half of the work. Then I got ill and the decision to give me tenure came before my thesis was finished. When I finally defended it, James Meade, now moved to Cambridge, was my external examiner. After I had successfully completed that hurdle, Helen Makower asked me about publication. I replied, without a lot of consideration, that I thought the work too crude to publish. Nothing more was said until 12 years later when people were still working on problems I had studied and it was recommended that the thesis be included in the LSE dissertation series being published by Weidenfeld and Nicolson. So, it finally saw the light of day as Lipsey (1970), over 12 years after I had finished it. I am sorry that I did not publish it in 1958 since it contains many ideas still not fully exploited in the literature. Many of them were couched in a numerical example first used by Makower and Morton and closed by me with a balance of payments equilibrium condition. Once the general equilibrium condition was included, all sorts of surprising things happened. Many of these could have been investigated in more general terms than I had used but they have not been taken up (see Lipsey 1970, ch. 9).

The next year, our group of young economists read, in manuscript, Phillips's (1958) article on unemployment and wage rates. I was fascinated and brought it back to Bill after a weekend's study bestrewn with comments only to discover to my surprise that the article was already in page proof without, as far as I could tell, having been criticized and improved by comments from his LSE colleagues in the economics department. Bill, however, encouraged me to follow up on my comments and possibly turn them into an article. This I did and spent a year working out regressions (at least my research assistant, June Wickens, did so on a mechanical calculator at the rate of about two a day) and trying to understand the curve in terms of microeconomic theory. My attempt (Lipsey 1960a) has been judged defective by the profession but it did help to set the agenda of trying to understand such macro relations in terms of micro behavioural relations.

6.6 METHODOLOGY AND TEXTBOOKS

All through my first years on the staff, I continued to worry about methodology. The prevailing methodology was that described by Robbins (1932). That methodology has been so totally swept away that it is hard for today's economists to imagine a world in which the accepted method of criticizing a theory was to ask if its assumptions were 'reasonable'. Nonetheless, we all spent countless hours arguing about the reasonableness of the assumptions of various theories. As theories became more complex, grappling with more involved forms of behaviour, this method became less and less satisfactory. My dissatisfaction was shared by several of the other young Turks at the LSE and, in the mid-1950s, we began to meet to discuss methodology. From Agassi we learned about Popper and, at some point towards the end of our first year of discussions, the resolution to my undergraduate worries became apparent:

1. a theory has empirical content in so far as it rules out some states of the universe;
2. the more it rules out, the more content it has;
3. a theory that is consistent with all states of the universe has no empirical content;
4. a theory is tested by confronting its predictions with evidence to see if the states that it rules out actually occur.

About that time, I read Friedman's (1953) famous essay on positive economics. Although I agreed with much of it, I found its arguments much cruder than Popper's subtle reasoning, and in one of our meetings I registered fundamental disagreement with his position that only predictions should be tested. It seemed to me that everything empirical that is contained in a theory, assumptions and predictions, should be confronted with facts wherever possible.[8] For example, if a theory with an obviously incorrect factual assumption makes predictions that consistently pass test, we would like to know why. Possibly the incorrect assumption is not necessary for the predictions being tested (in which case it might as well be stripped away) or the theory may contain a second, offsetting, incorrect assumption. Surely then we will learn by identifying these.

No doubt we were naive in thinking it would be easy to test and to refute theories. But we did find an effective way around the methodological impasse created by the Euclidian-Austrian-Robbinsian methodology. Although many methodological positions have been advocated in post-Popperian methodology, few have advocated going back to that earlier methodology in which the only test of a theory was the intuitive plausibility of its assumptions, and the only use of facts was to illustrate theories. I believe that our efforts played some small part in making that methodology unacceptable.

After a year, we formalized our meetings into the LSE staff seminar on Methodology, measurement and testing in economics (the M^2T seminar). This was heady stuff. Just ten years after the young, first-generation university student in a small provincial Canadian university had read the book by the great Lionel Robbins and said 'There must be something wrong with its methodology', I was on Robbins's staff and helping to identify what we all came to believe was wrong and what had to be done about it.[9]

By 1960 we were pretty clear about our new methodology. (At least it was new for us, although people such as Terence Hutchinson had been on to it much earlier.) At that time, I conceived the idea of writing a first-year textbook that would convey the new methodology. The idea came to me in Easter 1960 while walking across a field in Hertfordshire and, in a rush of intellectual excitement, I began to write. The chapter on methodology came

---

[8] We should not worry that some assumptions are untestable, nor should we insist, dogmatically, that only testable statements should be admitted into theory. My only point is that everything in a theory that has empirical content, whether in its assumptions or its predictions, is a valid subject for testing because we want to know if anything we can say that has factual content is actually consistent with the known facts.

[9] Neil de Marchi (1988, p. 147) has me '... itching to get into combat against Robbins and other old-line liberals such as Plant and Paish'. To me this seems nonsense. I was a first-generation university student from a provincial corner of a provincial ex-colony. I was awed to be in this intellectual company. I was itching to figure out my methodological concerns and when I did, I wrote my text *An introduction to positive economics* (*IPE*) to proselytize them but I always had the highest respect for Lionel Robbins. When I went to Essex I sought to recreate the atmosphere of his Wednesday afternoon seminar. There is no doubt that I was then to the left of the old-line liberals, but I did not have a great interest in politics and was concerned mainly to understand and evaluate the basis for the claim that economics was, or could become, a genuine science.

pretty quickly as did most of the micro chapters.[10] After some indecision, I decided to call the book *An introduction to positive economics* (Lipsey 1963), and for years it was known as *IPE*, until it followed the fate of virtually all other successful textbooks and became known by its author's name, *Lipsey*.

In writing the book, I had at least two main objectives.[11] The first was to sell the new methodology; the second was to make microeconomics interesting and relevant. At the time, the prevailing US textbook was Samuelson. I had taught my first introductory course – a summer school session at UBC in 1956 – out of its third edition (Samuelson 1955). The macro was great, but the micro was not. When one had finished the macro, the micro came as an afterthought with the kind of attitude 'Well kiddies, the examiners will want you to know some of these curves so here they are, boring though they may be'. I had been raised a microeconomist and firmly felt that all macro relations had to be derived from micro foundations and I set out to make micro as interesting and as relevant as it had been under Marshall. To some extent I think I succeeded in the early editions of *IPE* with both of these objectives. Certainly, the Robbinsian methodology which dominated our discussions in 1955 was totally unused by 1970.[12]

In the first edition, I followed most of my colleagues in the M^2T seminar in being a naive falsificationist. But I was always uneasy with this position and had many arguments with colleagues who were more convinced than I. Finally, my experience with trying to test some of the theories of the 'Phillips loops', which, sadly, I never published, convinced me that there was no such thing as a categorical refutation of a theory. As a result, I moved to the position that neither refutation nor confirmation could ever be final because they were both subject to error and revision. The result was an alteration in the second edition of *IPE* that became famous and the subject of much debate.[13]

I had trouble with the macro part of the book because that was neither my

---

[10] In the preface to early editions to *IPE* I incorrectly asserted that the book grew out of my first-year lectures. (I am not sure why I told this fib, but it might have been because I thought it would help to sell the book.) The facts were the reverse. I volunteered to give the first year lectures in the revised degree introduced in 1961 because I was already well on with my book.

[11] Since there has been some controversy about my reasons for writing *IPE* and about what I thought was important in it, it is fortunate that I committed my views to print at the time (Lipsey 1964).

[12] Colin Harbury has pointed out in private correspondence that, compared with the average UK text in use at that time, Samuelson contained much empirical material. I agree, but still maintain that this was almost all on the macro side. In contrast, he neglected microeconomics in the way I describe.

[13] In Lipsey (1997a, ch. 24) I reproduce the relevant four pages from the 4th edition of *IPE* where I had finally settled on a form of words with which I was happy.

strong point nor my major interest. I had had to attend Kurt Klappholz's lectures on basic macro in order to learn enough to run the discussion classes on that part of economics during my early years on the staff. As I wrote the early macro chapters, I quickly ran into the prevailing theory that the national income identities could be used to restrict the universe of possible outcomes. (I remember a visiting US economist telling us that Keynes had 'discovered' some of the economy's most important identities which allowed us to deduce all sorts of things.) This, of course, worried a methodologist: if a definitional identity is consistent with all possible states of the universe, how can it be used to restrict possible outcomes, i.e., to give content to theories?

I had learned much of my macro from Swedish process analysis and from the Phillips water-flow model and so saw macroeconomics as describing behaviour in real time in disequilibrium situations (no Walrasian auctioneer). As a result, I tried to put down a circular flow model with the values of the flows of S, I and C as they would be given by recorders on a Phillips water-flow model of the circular flow of income taking place in real time. But I could not get the numbers and the identities to come out. This set me worrying about what was meant by the Keynesian identities and by the prevailing interpretation, found in virtually all of the textbooks of the time, that out of equilibrium actual S was made equal to actual I by unintended changes in inventories. But this seemed to imply that we could deduce an empirical prediction, inventories must be changing out of equilibrium, from a definitional identity. Furthermore, the prediction seemed to be contradicted by the evidence: inventories do not always rise when income is below potential and fall when income is above potential.

It took me a year to resolve this problem. When I had finished the macro part of *IPE* in mid-1962, I wrote up the results of my thoughts on identities in an article which *Economica* rejected and which I subsequently used for my contribution to the festschrift honouring Lionel Robbins's 70th birthday (Lipsey 1972). I was later sorry, since the article went largely unnoticed. I did, however, have two private satisfactions. First, I was right about identities when virtually all other economists were wrong.[14] Second, I saw my interpretation that $S = I$ must be understood as an equilibrium condition, while the accounting identity of $S \equiv I$ plays no part in the operation of the behavioural model, slowly adopted in the textbooks without anyone noticing the change.[15]

It took me several editions to get it exactly right in the textbook, and by

---

[14] Two others who got it right, and made some related criticisms of the use of identities in economics, were Kurt Klappholz and Ed Mishan (1962), both members of the M^2T seminar.

[15] In the old model, when ex ante S did not equal ex ante I, unintended investment occurred in the form of inventory accumulation so that the identity $S \equiv I$ could be fulfilled.

that time, the new interpretation of S = I as an equilibrium condition was accepted. I dropped the circular flow resolution with measured S not equal to measured I.[16] *IPE* began my career as a textbook writer. The book was an instant success. The first printing sold out in a few months and the first edition went through six reprints, each larger than the one before.

No sooner was the book in print than Peter Steiner and I set out to write what we thought would be an American adaptation, entitled *Economics*. It soon became clear, however, that *IPE* was too austere and too sophisticated for the typical first-year US undergraduate. (At the time some seven per cent of UK teenagers went on to university while the number was closer to 40 per cent in the US.) Slowly, over the editions, three-quarters of all the things that made *IPE* distinctive were eliminated from *Economics*. One of the important casualties was most of the questioning at the end of every part suggesting that the theory being taught might be wrong, or at least in need of serious amendment. This slowly gave way under enormous US market pressure to teach theory as something closer to (but not exactly) revealed truth, particularly in micro. It was a very painful process and, although a good but more orthodox book emerged, I felt at every stage that I was taking part in the dismemberment of my own baby. It was not my co-author's doing, it was the relentless pressure of the US market. Fortunately, the British book, *IPE*, remained my own and I did to it what I wanted, including keeping at the end of each part a full chapter on measurement, testing, criticism and, where appropriate, alternative theories.

My next textbook grew out of a course I invented at the LSE where any lecturer was allowed to advertise and teach his own course. After learning some maths, I became worried about the strongly anti-maths attitude in the core sub-department of LSE economics called Economics A&D.[17] People with a high degree of mathematical competence could be found in the statistics department and a few other places, but there were almost none in A&D. One exception was Bill Phillips, but he was not a part of our group and conversed mainly with the statisticians. So to help remedy the deficiency of mathematics in A&D, I invented a course in which I took the economics the students knew and taught them the maths that was implicit in it. Several staff

---

[16] In Lipsey (1997b, ch. 18) I reproduce the section, 'Equilibrium national income in a spendthrift economy', from the 5th edition of *IPE* (1979).

[17] The LSE first degree was three years. After a common Part I, students specialized in any of the many social sciences taught at the school. Those who chose economics could specialize in International Economics, Money and Banking or Economics Analytical and Descriptive (A&D), where most of the theorists and many of the applied economists were located. In the old degree, Part I took two years; in the new degree instituted in 1961, Part I was only one year. Until I left to go to Essex, I taught the basic micro-macro theory course in the new degree.

members attended, and when I went on leave to Berkeley in 1963–4, Chris Archibald took it over and worked it up into a much more coherent course. We then wrote it up into a book entitled *An introduction to a mathematical treatment of economics* (Lipsey and Archibald 1967). Its distinctiveness was that it was not just a maths cookbook. Rather it alternated a chapter of maths with a chapter that applied that maths to economies the readers already knew. The book was highly successful in the UK and went through three editions over 20 years. Its US version was not a success – although it did get a few highly enthusiastic users. I often wonder if the US version failed because the publishers insisted on promoting it just like any other mathematics cookbook.

In the early 1980s, I joined forces with Professor Colin Harbury of City University in London to rewrite a short book of his called *Descriptive economics*, which had already gone through six editions. We worked it into a longer applied book designed to complement *IPE* and entitled *An introduction to the UK economy* (Harbury and Lipsey 1983). In my earlier experience, UK students had often studied two books, a basic theory book such as *IPE* and an institutional-descriptive book which covered the structure of the UK economy. It has always seemed to me to be a shame that North American courses did not do the same. In North America, we typically turn out students who have been exposed to some quite complex economic theory but who know virtually nothing about the economy to which that theory is meant to apply.[18]

Two years later, Colin and I began to write a textbook called *First principles of economics* directed at the UK sixth form which is the UK equivalent of grades 12 and 13 (last year of high school and first year of university in many places). I was concerned about what seemed to me to be the low quality of textbooks available at that level and about the fact that, by introducing high school algebra into the macro part of the 6th edition of *IPE*, published in 1983, I had written it out of sixth form use.[19] Our job turned out to be much more difficult than we had anticipated and it occupied too much of my available time over three long years. In the end, it was only a modest success and, although I enjoyed and profited from my collaboration with Colin Harbury, it remains the one textbook I suspect I would not write if I

---

[18] In private correspondence, Colin Harbury has challenged this view saying that UK students typically studied only one book that mainly covered pure theory. Colin certainly has more experience than I, so possibly my sample was a biased one. In any case, what I advocate still seems a good idea to me, even if it only existed in a fictional UK Utopia of my imagination.

[19] Readers of the manuscript have suggested other reasons why the use of *IPE* declined in the early 1980s. Be those as they may, the sales of the first year of the 6th edition set a one-year record but then fell off significantly. This is consistent with my view that the elementary algebra that I introduced into the macroeconomics section of that edition does much to account for the book's rapid disappearance from use in the UK sixth form.

had it all to do over again (Lipsey and Harbury 1988).

This raises the more general question: would I become a textbook writer if I had my life as an economist to live over again? The big negative is the amount of time and the unrelenting demands of publication schedules. Over the 35 years since I first began to write *IPE* I have been the only author, or the equal co-author, of 30 editions of six distinct textbooks.[20] In most of them, we rewrote a third to half of the material each time. The way we worked was for all of us to be responsible for all the material, and on successive editions, to alternate the chapters on which each author did the first draft of the revisions. This meant, as my co-authors will attest, that having more than one author, increased rather than reduced the workload because there were more critics to suggest new additions and revisions of old material. Also, the publisher's schedules are unrelenting. Miss a deadline by weeks, and you miss selling for the whole teaching year. I estimate that something like half of my research time, and something like one third of the time I would have otherwise devoted to my personal life has gone into the textbooks. Had I not written all these, I would have written probably twice the number of articles in learned journals; I would have written a book with Curtis Eaton on the work that we did in the 1970s on the foundations of imperfect competition and spatial economics; and I would have written a book on methodology.

On the plus side are four considerations. First, *IPE* fulfilled my research programme of finding out what was wrong with the Robbinsian methodology which I had been taught. I think it did something – largely unnoticed by the profession – to end the old methodology in which the test of a theory was the reasonableness of its assumptions. Second, I think I did something to restore student interest in microeconomics, particularly in the UK and in the many foreign countries in which *IPE* has been sold. (*IPE* has been translated into 15 foreign languages and sold in a UK subsidized, English-language (the ELBS) version to the former British territories in Asia and Africa.) Travelling about the world, I meet my students everywhere and get immense satisfaction

---

[20] I did the full version of seven editions of *IPE* and half of the eighth (having brought in a co-author, Professor Alec Chrystal of City University, London for the 8th edition published in 1995); I shared equally in revisions of ten editions of *Economics* and took a small part in the 11th published in 1995 (and have now passed this book over fully to Paul Courant for the 12th and subsequent editions). I did all three editions of *An introduction to a mathematical treatment of economics* equally with Chris Archibald; I took over half responsibility for the Canadian edition of *Economics* with Doug Purvis from the third edition and did the eighth myself after Doug's untimely death, and I have now recruited a co-author, Chris Ragan of McGill University, to share the ninth with me and eventually to take over the whole of the Canadian edition; I did both editions of *First principles* equally with Colin Harbury and two of *An introduction to the UK economy*. This makes altogether 30 editions of major textbooks in which I was either the only author or an equal co-author.

from their personal testimonies. Once, while passing through a remote checkpoint in Kashmir, the official inspecting my passport looked up and said, 'You are not the man who wrote the book?' When I said, 'If you mean *Positive economics*, the answer is yes', he grasped my hand and said, 'Thank you'. That kind of satisfaction of meeting students for whom my books have been a real learning experience is massive compensation for learned articles not written. Third, all of the textbooks have helped to keep me the generalist that I wanted to be. I estimate that you need to know a minimum of three times as much as you write down in a chapter if you are to do it right. That means that, on every revision, you have to do an enormous amount of reading on all those areas in which you are not actively keeping up in the course of your own research. This is something which I know I would not have done if it were not for the relentless discipline of the textbooks. Finally, it would be less than honest not to mention money. I think I am one of the last writers of first-year textbooks not to have known that there was real money at the end of all the effort. I remember being in Lionel Robbins's office sometime after I had finished the micro half of the book. Lionel said he had heard that I was writing a textbook and did I know that John Hicks still made £500 a year on royalties from *Value and capital*. The floor opened up and nearly swallowed me: 'Five hundred pounds a year' said I. I went home with dreams of real money to spend – and fortunately not knowing that £500 was what the book would make for me in its first weeks not its first year.

6.7   PUBLIC POLICY AND THE *REVIEW OF ECONOMIC STUDIES*

In 1962, the conservative government under Harold Macmillan set up the National Economic Development Council (nicknamed Neddy) to investigate the conditions causing slow growth in the UK and advise on how the growth performance could be improved. Sir Donald MacDougall was appointed its director of economics under Sir Robert Shone. Donald asked me to join the staff. The LSE said I was needed for the first-year lectures so I merely spent all my spare time as a consultant. My co-worker and I botched a job of testing Frank Paish's views that operating the economy a little below potential was more conducive to growth than operating it a little above it.[21] When we finally got it right, a brief report appeared in the first Neddy report and a long paper that I wrote on it was never published (although I gave it at

---

[21] Sir Douglas tells this story in some detail in his memoirs (MacDougall 1987, p. 139).

many US universities during my sabbatical year in the US in 1963–4).[22]
Early in the 1960s, I had been invited to join the XYZ club which met over
dinner in the House of Commons and was meant to expose Labour politicians
and sympathetic academics to each other's thoughts. I greatly enjoyed these
dinners and, walking over Westminster Bridge from Neddy, where I was
helping to advise the Conservative government, to attend dinner with Labour
MPs, I was often struck with how far I had come from my beginnings in
Victoria.

One memorable dinner came a day or two after Labour's surprising
election victory in October 1964. We were given to believe that the new
prime minister, Harold Wilson, spent the weekend after the election deciding
on his policy with respect to the balance of payments, which was showing a
large deficit at the time. He decided against devaluing sterling and thereby
hampered his entire first administration with the overriding need to support
the overvalued pound. At dinner, a senior LSE colleague who was also a
member of the club gave a defence of Wilson's decision. I was appalled. I
was sure that devaluation at the outset of the term, which could in any case be
blamed on the outgoing Tories, was the right thing to do. It was an early
object lesson to me in the power of exchange rates to mesmerize politicians
and academics, leading them down counter-productive alleys. This
experience was much in my mind when I wrote 'The balance of payments
and the common market' (Lipsey 1967).

In the late 1950s, I was appointed to the board of the *Review of Economic
Studies* still edited by its first editor, Ursula Hicks, but run to a great extent
by its assistant editor Harry Johnson. After Harry had gone to Manchester,
the Hickses and the Kaldors had a falling out. One of them had written an
unfavourable review of a book written by another of them (I forget which).
Nicky Kaldor and I had become good friends and to get back at the Hickses,
Nicky hatched the plot of having me replace Ursula as the journal's editor.
He was correct in arguing that, although a good applied economist, she was
not in touch with the kind of theory her journal was then publishing so that
she really should be replaced. But his real motives were less honourable. His
plan was that the young economists on the board would lead a revolution and
install me as editor with Frank Hahn, John Black and John Parry Lewis as
assistant editors. The young board members met and agreed that a change
was in order but, disagreeing with Nicky's motivation, we decided to ask
both Nicky and Ursula to go. So the plot backfired, when on the appointed
day the revolutionaries called for a replacement for all senior editors and we

---

[22] If Nancy Wulwick's allegations that I was a card-carrying member of the Labour Party, or
even a prominent supporter, was correct, I would never have been asked, or agreed, to serve
on Neddy.

four youngsters were installed as the new team.

Not long after being installed, we began to get signals that all was not well with the administration. Letters asking about unfilled subscriptions, unanswered letters and uncashed cheques crossed our desk. After a few discrete enquiries, the person in Cambridge who had been handling the administrative side of the journal suddenly departed. We visited her office and there we found literally hundreds of unanswered letters, unopened telegrams and uncashed cheques. More than half the correspondence of the previous year had been unanswered. It took Frank Hahn and I many weeks to sort out the mess and write to the many confused, and often irate, subscribers.

6.8   NEW FRONTIERS AT ESSEX, 1964–70

Sometime in early 1963, I received a phone call from Albert Sloman wanting to talk to me about a new university.[23] I was very busy with Neddy and did not reply. He pursued me relentlessly until, more to get rid of him than to oblige him, I agreed to lunch at the French Club. Earlier, Chris Archibald, Bernard Corry and I had submitted a brief to the Robbins committee on higher education in which we argued that the proposed new universities were too small – a maximum enrolment of 3,000 was targeted for each. Sloman said he was stuck with this size, at least as the first phase, but intended to meet our concerns by concentrating on only a few departments so that each could reach optimal size, even though the whole university was still small. He also saw the university as a research institution which would give professional training to British students on the model of MIT rather than a dilettante's education on the model then prevailing in the Oxford PPE degree. I was swept away with the idea of a new frontier in which we would give the UK an educational institution suited to the professional needs of the last half of the 20th century. I came home from lunch and announced to my wife 'I am going to Essex!'.

I think I was the only person to leave a chair to go to a new university. (In 1961, I had been appointed an LSE Professor at the then early age of 33.) Most of the others who were appointed to the new universities as founding professors were bright young lecturers who were offered the carrot of early promotion to a chair.

I will never forget the day when the five founding professors, the vice chancellor and the registrar sat down in the Senate House of the University of London and the VC said, 'Well gentlemen, let us proceed to build a

---

[23] For Sloman's account in relation to economics at Essex, see Sloman (1997).

university'. For five years, I inhabited our new frontier. We all loved Albert Sloman and would have followed him to the ends of the earth.

I became Dean of the School of Social Studies, Chairman of the Department of Economics, and filled a host of other offices, such as chairman of the disciplinary and the catering committees (!) and member of the VC's unofficial inner advisory group which consisted of four or five key deans and department chairmen meeting once a week in the VC's room.

My experiences in those five years deserve an essay on their own. Suffice it to say that they were exhilarating, maddening, rewarding and frustrating in more or less equal amounts. At first, we had an idealized version of a Greek city state. Every person with tenure was a member of Senate and our debates were informed, constructive and witty. The staff was so small that we all lunched together in the local pub. Then as numbers increased, the scientists began lunching together, and the social scientists and arts people lunched as a second group. Then, as numbers rose further, the members of each discipline began lunching by themselves and the barriers that old universities attribute to some archaic practices and strive to break down asserted themselves quite naturally.

The student revolutions hit us hard and early. We mismanaged the disciplinary actions following a student breakup of a seminar given by a scientist from the government's chemical warfare research laboratory. From that time on, I was in the thick of many staff–student battles, student takeovers, strikes and who knows what else. Although the events poisoned many relationships, I was proud of the staff (both academic and support) and the graduate students in the economics department who acted as a moderating force and a liaison between staff and student leaders through our many battles.

Our greatest success at Essex was to help to establish postgraduate training in the social sciences as the norm for the UK and to build large, research-oriented departments within a small university. At the time, it was usual for a person to get a good bachelor's degree and then take employment as a professional economist in the academic, private or public sectors. It was apparent to the younger economists that this was no longer appropriate. More training was needed. When I was promoted to professor at the LSE, I had tried to get a taught MA instituted, but to my surprise, my colleagues voted it down with many arguments, including the assertion that teaching beyond the bachelor's degree was too American in outlook. So I went to Essex precisely because Sloman saw the need for professional graduate training which went hand in hand with large, research-oriented departments (not at all the UK norm at the time). We succeeded beyond our wildest dreams. It turned out that the students were more attuned to the needs of the times than their professors. What UK academics everywhere had rejected, the taught MA in the social sciences, was voted for by students with their feet. Graduate students came in large numbers to the University of Essex and within four years we were one of the largest graduate schools of social science in the UK. My memory says that we were second largest after the LSE but I cannot verify that. What is certain is that we had many students and the academic world is peppered with Essex economics graduates. Of our first graduating BA class of ten economists, at least four went on to become academic economists.

Then came a slap in the face. We were visited by the University Grants Committee which received the entire amalgamated university finance as a lump sum from the government every five years which it allocated among the universities. The committee was dominated by old-line professors who had rejected expansion of their universities, more professional graduate training and large research-oriented departments – all of the things that Essex stood for and was making work. They paid us back by criticizing us strongly in front of our lay council at the end of their visit and then determining that we got one of the lowest operating grants (my memory says it was the lowest but again I may be wrong on details) of all the 44 British universities. It was so low that we would not have been able to accept enough students (2,000) to fill the buildings that were already built. There was a question in Parliament and our grant was raised somewhat.[24]

This episode made me recall a conversation that I had with a well-connected LSE colleague before I left for Essex. He told me that the UK establishment did not want new universities to challenge the existing great ones. They wanted only second rate and obviously inferior copies. 'If you do succeed in what you are hoping to do in Essex, they will find a way of killing you' was his parting shot. Well, they did not kill us but they certainly found a way of wounding us. I said to myself, 'I have devoted five years to building a university for the late 20th century and the country does not seem to want it'. I went home and phoned some friends in Canada and quizzed them about the academic scene there. Prospects looked good so I decided to take a year's leave to visit Canada and sound things out.

This was not my only reason for leaving Essex. A second reason concerned my own professional career. After five years of intense work in the administration, I had done little reading in economics and was aware of falling behind a rapidly advancing frontier. I had to decide whether my future lay in administration or in remaining a professional economist. After much soul searching, I opted for the economist. It then became apparent that I must get out of all administration and that it would be very difficult to do so inside the university where I was so much a part of the fabric. With the best will in

---

[24] No doubt there were many other reasons for the UGC's rejection of Essex.

the world, the VC and I would find it difficult to keep me out of administration, especially in times of crisis.

Leaving Essex was like leaving one's first love. It was our creation and we loved it and were proud of it. I am still proud of what we accomplished and pleased that the School of Social Studies has gone on from strength to strength and currently rates among the top UK universities in the UGC's assessment of research accomplishments.

6.9   RETURN TO CANADA, 1970

Nonetheless, my decision to return to economics required leaving Essex, and the attitude of the UK establishment made it easier to leave the UK. Still, this was not an easy decision, as I had come to regard myself as British and I spoke of 'emigrating back home'. Furthermore, my second wife was English and all of my four children had been raised in England. For them, leaving England was in no sense of the term 'going home'.

After a year in 1969–70 as visiting professor at the University of British Columbia, I accepted the post of Sir Edward Peacock Professor at Queens University in Kingston, Ontario.

While visiting the University of British Columbia, I returned to my undergraduate interest in Hotelling's model. I also met Curtis Eaton and discovered that we were both working on the same model but from different perspectives. We decided to join forces and began a highly productive cooperation which lasted ten years and produced about a dozen papers on what we came to call 'address models of value theory'. Another research programme laid down when I was an undergraduate was now being fulfilled. These papers are published in the volume of our joint collected works (Eaton and Lipsey 1997).

At Queens, I began by teaching welfare economics and stabilization policy, which was applied macro. I quickly reinforced what I knew already, that I had fallen way behind the frontier. I sat up late into the night reading just ahead of my students and it was three years before I felt I was back near the frontier of macroeconomics (which, contrary to popular belief, had never been my major interest).

Ever since my early work on the Phillips curve, I had been interested in incomes policies. A piece that Michael Parkin and I published became quite influential, in spite of its flawed econometrics (Lipsey and Parkin 1970). In the autumn of 1975, I was visiting the UK when the news broke of the Trudeau government's resort to a wage control policy in Canada. I immediately fired off a telegram whose approximate wording was

'STRONGLY PROTEST THE INTRODUCTION OF WAGE-PRICE CONTROLS IN CANADA STOP THEIR DIRECT EFFECTS ARE DUBIOUS AND THEIR LONG-TERM EFFECTS ARE HARMFUL'.

When I returned to Canada, I was asked to go to Ottawa with a number of economists to advise the lawyers who were considering the possibility of a Canadian Labour Council (CLC)-financed court challenge. Since Canadian provinces have jurisdiction over labour matters, the Federal government needed to infringe on provincial powers to set up wage controls. The Feds found their justification in the 'Peace Order and Good Government (POGG) Clause' in the British North American Act which gives the Federal government almost unlimited powers in times of a national emergency. The issue was whether or not ten per cent inflation, which had persisted for a year or two and had not yet been attacked by any of the traditional tools of fiscal and monetary policy, constituted a 'national emergency'. This was a pretty weak case.

Shortly thereafter, I was asked if I would prepare the expert evidence to accompany the CLC's constitutional challenge. The Federal government then referred the case directly to the Supreme Court rather than fighting the challenge through the lower courts. They must have known that this tactic made it harder for experts to attack their case since the Supreme Court is supposed to rule only on matters of law, not fact.

The question arose whether or not expert evidence could be submitted at all. There was no precedent for it. Yet the case turned on the question of fact 'is there or is there not a national emergency?' We decided that I would prepare the evidence and the lawyers would submit it hoping that the Supreme Court would have to read it in order to decide whether or not it was admissible.

I had two weeks to do the job. The first week was spent planning and the second week in writing. I holed up in my office at Queens, chain smoking cigars, and working my very good secretary day and night. For the last 72 hours I never closed my eyes. It is the longest I have ever stayed awake. When I was done, I drove the nearly 200 page manuscript up to the Kingston bus station – there were no courier firms in those days – and put it on the bus to Ottawa where an employee of the law firm collected it and delivered it to the Supreme Court. On the way home, I saw flying saucers – a phenomenon I later learned was common with people suffering extreme sleep deprivation. Considering the haste with which it was written, I think it was a pretty good document. It was later translated into French and published in a French Canadian journal but its only English record is in the Supreme Court of Canada's papers.

The outcome was that the Supreme Court, for the first time in its history, took notice of expert evidence by explicitly responding to its arguments. In doing so, the justices split three ways. The minority said the government could do more or less anything under POGG, while the majority said a rare emergency was required for action under POGG. That majority, however, split into two groups, one of which said there *was* such a rare emergency while the other said there was not! The net result was in favour of the government's current actions by the judgment of the first two groups, but simultaneously, by the judgment of the second and the third, to find that the government must not use this power lightly, implying that next time the result might be different. That seemed a good result to me. We cannot have the Supreme Court routinely second guessing the government on matters of national emergency but the courts can say in effect 'Be careful, do not abuse this power (as you may well have done this time but we do not want to say so)'.

In 1979–80, I spent six months in the UK as visiting professor at City University and then a year at Yale as Irving Fisher Professor. I returned to Queens in the fall of 1980 and continued to teach graduate courses in macro theory and in stabilization policy. About this time, rational expectations and the new classical approach to macro theory, and soon real business cycle theory, began to become established. I sat up nights learning the new theories in order to teach them to my students and then add 'the hypothesis of rational expectations is a potentially fruitful one but I think the new-classical, market-clearing model is a dead-end line of enquiry; I think, however, that the profession will have to explore that alley all the way before the advocates accept that it has a dead end'. It seemed to me that I did not want to spend my own scarce time as part of that investigation so I decided to leave macroeconomics as a teaching field. By that time, I had, in any case, become increasingly interested in microeconomic policy. I had written several policy papers and was writing a regular monthly column in the *Financial Times*. First, I wrote the column alone but later I joined forces with my good friend and Queens professor, Douglas Purvis. Our efforts were honoured in 1982 when we received the National Business Writing Award 'for distinguished financial writing by Canadians who are not primarily journalists'.

While spending the summer of 1982 at our house in Ireland, I received a phone call from New York asking me to contribute a chapter on economic issues to a volume commissioned by the American Assembly entitled *Canada and the United States: enduring friendship, persistent stress*. This was a new version of a volume first published in the 1950s and widely used since then. I knew nothing about Canada–US trade relations and did not even know a countervailing from an anti-dumping duty and certainly had not heard of 'escape clause actions'. So, under normal circumstances, I would have said 'No'. However, in another one of those chances which have been so influential in my life, I had just learned of a serious personal tragedy and, to get the speaker off the line so that I could worry about my personal affairs, I said yes.

Over the next six months, I gave myself a crash course in trade policy and institutions. By the time I had finished my review of Canada–US trade policy and multilateralism under the GATT (having first learned more about the GATT than its name), I had become alarmed about the outlook for Canada (Lipsey 1985). Protectionist sentiment seemed to be growing everywhere, particularly in the US. As a small trading nation, Canada seemed particularly vulnerable. On the positive side, when I studied Canadian industry's adjustment to the large tariff cuts instituted by the Kennedy and Tokyo rounds of GATT negotiations, I concluded that the infant industry stage was over and large sections of Canadian industry could stand on their own feet. It was high time, it seemed to me, that we removed the rest of our still-comparatively-high tariffs letting those firms that could compete prosper and those who could not compete disappear.[25]

6.10   THE C.D. HOWE INSTITUTE, 1983–9

While I was working on the Canada-US manuscript, and becoming depressed with the state of academic macroeconomics, I was visited by Wendy Dobson, president of the prestigious C.D. Howe Institute, a sort of Canadian counterpart of Brookings and the Institute for International Economics combined. She had heard that I was unhappy with academia and offered me good terms to move to Toronto and become Senior Economic Advisor to the Institute. I agreed and began five fruitful years at the Institute. Wendy has told much of the story of my time at the Institute in her article in the festschrift in my honour (Eaton and Harris 1997).

Soon after moving to the Howe Institute, I finished my essay on Canada–US economic relations. I immediately suggested to Wendy that I write a book assessing Canada's trade options and testing my growing conviction that a free-trade agreement with the US was the best route to preserving and expanding the international trade that was Canada's life blood. I soon joined forces with Murray Smith who knew much more than I did about current trade policy and institutions. We thought we would be two small voices crying in the wilderness. By the time we were finished (Lipsey and Smith 1985), however, we were two early voices in a mounting chorus suggesting that the free-trade option be seriously considered – in spite of the Canadian

---

[25] My Edward Elgar selected essays (Lipsey 1997a; b) do not include my writings on trade policy which would in any case fill a volume on their own.

conventional wisdom that it was political suicide even to suggest free trade with the US.

Under Wendy's tutelage, I learned to master economic policy, not just its analysis but how to influence it. Wendy taught me that to have influence, one had to appreciate the constraints under which policy makers were acting and advocate feasible policies, not just first-best policies. She also taught me the futility of the typical academic, over-the-transom approach: publish an article advocating some policy then move on to another issue. When Murray Smith and I had finished our book on free trade, I thought we were done. But to Wendy that was just the beginning. She made dozens of appointments in Ottawa for us. We expounded our analysis to all the relevant politicians and civil servants. At first it was intimidating, but after a while it was exhilarating. I particularly remember a meeting at the Department of External Affairs when about a dozen senior mandarins marched into the room all holding copies of our book, well thumbed and full of markers. For two hours they proceeded to grill us in detail on its contents and suggestions. With Wendy's assistance, we helped to make it acceptable for Canada–US free trade to be taken seriously in Ottawa.

After our book came out, followed closely by the MacDonald commission report which made big news for its advocacy of free trade with the US, the government of Canada made the fateful decision to open negotiations. Fortunately, the opposition did not take the possibility seriously until too late. Once the government had made the decision to negotiate, there was little the mounting opposition could do to reverse the decision (see also Lipsey 1986). Nonetheless, the debate got hard and dirty. I made speeches all over the country; I wrote about a dozen pamphlets, and close to ten chapters in books; I appeared on numerous radio and TV talk shows and debates. One of the early debates was with Mel Hurtig, publisher and prominent opponent of free trade with the US. The televised debate was in the Grand Theatre in Kingston, Ontario, a town associated with the name of Sir John A. Macdonald, the father of Canadian Confederation and the architect of the 'National Policy of 1878' which first introduced high tariffs to protect Canadian manufacturing industry.

When the agreement was finally signed, the opposition-dominated Senate blocked the enabling legislation and an election was fought on the issue of free trade. I had just finished my second book on Canada–US free trade (Lipsey and York 1988). I took to debating platforms once again and, with a small band of engaged Canadian economists such as John Crispo, Murray Smith and Ron Wonnacott, we fought the detractors with the spoken and the printed word. From August to November, 1988 I never took a single full day off while I was in Toronto. I did get away from Canada from time to time but never while in Toronto was there a day free from the battle.

On election night, Robert York and I watched the returns in my Toronto apartment. I had bought a bottle of Dom Perignon and said that, before the night was over, it would either be thrown unopened down the rubbish shute or opened in celebration of a victory for free trade. By midnight, the bottle was open and a celebration well under way.

After the election, the let-down was enormous and in early December I suffered what used to be called a nervous breakdown. When I told my doctor how I had behaved over the last six months, he said I was lucky to be alive.[26]

I was involved in several other important policy issues while at C.D. Howe. We tried our best to make the newly elected Conservative government take the budget deficit seriously in 1984–5. We failed. Had they done so, the pain would have been over before they came up for re-election and the country would not have been in the fiscal shambles it was in ten years later. I also wrote an 'Inflation Monitor' that tracked the anti-inflation policies of the 1980s and I commissioned work on the Bank of Canada's policy of zero inflation. I knew this policy was going to cause one of the great disputes of the decade as soon as I heard the Governor announce it in a speech. As a result of my early commissioning of articles, we had a volume ready for distribution just as the debate broke out in earnest (Lipsey and York 1990).

6.11   THE CANADIAN INSTITUTE FOR ADVANCED RESEARCH AND RETURN TO BRITISH COLUMBIA SINCE 1989

In 1988, I was asked to become a member of the academic advisory board of the Canadian Institute for Advanced Research (CIAR). Led by a great Canadian, Fraser Mustard, the Institute was breaking new paths in encouraging advanced research. They had begun in the natural sciences, had branched out into population health and were now ready to get into economics with concern over economic growth. Fraser Mustard and I never agree on who seduced who but we were both willing partners in my becoming leader of the project entitled 'Economic Growth: Science and Technology and Institutional Change in a Global Economy'.

Fraser Mustard, when he read an earlier draft of this piece had the

[26] I also played a not insignificant part in Canada's decision to invite itself to the US-Mexican free trade talks and to turn a hub-and-spoke model of bilateral agreements for hemispheric trade liberalization into a NAFTA which embraced all contracting parties within one agreement. This was done while I was a member of the government's International Trade Advisory Committee (ITAC) and chairman of the working party overseeing the working of the US-Canada FTA, so the story must be told at a much later date.

following to offer:

> Ruth Macdonald [the wife of the former finance minister Donald Macdonald] was with the Institute and knew about our frustrations that there seemed to be little appreciation in Canada about the role of science and technology in economic growth. Ruth was a great friend of Wendy Dobson, President of the C.D. Howe Institute where Lipsey was acting as senior economic advisor, and in their discussions they suggested that the Institute should consider a program in economic growth and that Dick Lipsey should head it. Ruth and Wendy arranged for Dick and Fraser to have lunch with them at the University club. From Fraser's perspective ... he thought he was going to meet a fairly traditional economist. I [Fraser] was, of course, thrilled to find you [RGL] making the point that understanding technological change and economic growth was one of the largest if not the largest challenge facing economists. There was no doubt in my mind that you had to create the program.

So it appears that I am like the grown man who returns to the high school reunion to find that he was seduced by the school charmer when, at the time, he was fully convinced that he had seduced her.

Once I accepted the offer to lead the project, I needed a university base. Simon Fraser University made me, and the CIAR, offers we could not refuse. So in the summer of 1989, my wife and I went to British Columbia. For me it was a return to God's Country where I had been born; for Diana it was a move to the best climate and most exciting part of Canada. My daughter, Joanna, became the project's administrator and moved out to BC with her partner at the same time.

I led the programme for three years. (I should say that Fraser and I led it for he was very much a hands-on administrator, who took a strong interest in all of the projects he was funding.) Early in 1994, I passed the leadership over to Elhanan Helpman but I remain a Fellow of the Institute and a member of the Growth and Policy Project.

Rarely does a person get a chance to change fields so drastically in his 60s. For me, however, it was a golden opportunity to fulfil the last of my undergraduate research programmes: to understand and further develop the concepts that Schumpeter advocated and that so impressed me in my now-distant undergraduate days. Because I was launching myself into a field in which I was not well read, I embarked on two years of intensive reading into conventional macro growth theory and, more importantly, into the vast amount of empirical research on the innovative process and on the theories that are designed to have contact with that knowledge and that stem from the seminal work of Richard Nelson and Sidney Winter. It was also a chance to return to teaching, which I had given up in 1983. Since coming to SFU in 1990, I have given each year a course on 'Technological change and economic growth', emphasizing historical and theoretical understanding and the need to have a deep knowledge of technology in order to understand the processes driving economic growth. A selection of my early articles on this subject is included in Lipsey (1997a).

The great discovery for me after my return to this subject was the profound implications of accepting that technological change is endogenous to the economic system. As John Rae understood in the nineteenth century, much of classical and neo-classical economics is turned on its head when the implications of endogenous technological change are understood. I refer to the micro understanding of endogenous technological change that grew up in the 1950s and 1960s, decades before macro theorists discovered the concept. In 'Markets, technological change and economic growth' (Lipsey 1994), I take up the Schumpeterian theme of the irrelevance of perfect competition as a standard of efficiency and show how the stylized facts of endogenous technological change buttress the Schumpeterian position. In 'A structuralist view of economic growth' (Lipsey and Bekar 1995), I return to the grand themes of long-term growth: major changes in what we call 'enabling technologies' that cause occasional periods of deep structural adjustment, starting with the neolithic agricultural revolution and culminating in the ICT revolution that is today transforming our society with changes as deep as any in this millennium. My book on growth and change is scheduled for completion at the beginning of 2000 (Lipsey *et al.* 2000). In line with my original motivation, to know rather than to discover, it will be a synthesis of what is already known. I hope, however, that it will add new understanding to the process of long-term growth and change by drawing together knowledge developed in many different strands of empirical and theoretical research.

It is too early to say where all this current work will end, but the journey that has taken me to the Schumpeterian ideas about long-term growth has been a fulfilling one, and I would not have had it differently. Theoretical research, university administration, applied research, policy advocacy and broad historical analysis, coming in that order have been a varied and satisfying diet.

6.12   A POSTSCRIPT ON POLITICAL VIEWS

My political views have often been a subject of public speculation. I have never supported a political party. Many of my Mount Pèlerin Society friends find me a wishy-washy liberal (in the US sense of the word), while many of my social democratic friends regard me as a reactionary conservative. While an undergraduate and an MA student in Canada, I began as a follower of von

Hayek and von Mises but then, as I saw more of market failures and human suffering, I moved closer to the position of J.S. Mill in accepting the organizing power of the market economy but believing in a strong social policy to alleviate some of the harmful effects created by free markets.

While I lived in the UK, I termed myself a fellow traveller of the Labour Party, in sympathy with their social policies but not willing to join them because I could not accept their non-market economic policies. During that time, I was in any case more interested in economic theory and methodology than in politics. I also fell victim to an error that I have repeatedly warned against in my later writings. I was raised on the formal defence of the price system that perfect competition produced an optimum allocation of resources. When my early experiences in Europe showed me how far that defence was from any economic reality, I erroneously concluded that there was no adequate defence of the price system. Only much later did I come to appreciate the enormous power of the informal defence, particularly in the context of economic growth driven by endogenous technological change.

Throughout most of my life I found myself more at home with the humanity and sympathy of my social democratic companions than with the attitudes of my friends on the more extreme right. Over the years, however, I have slowly come to accept that good intentions often produce measures with unambiguously bad results. I have also come to believe that the big state is not the best defender of the rights of the less powerful. Instead, it too often becomes the tool of the powerful, operating through such power groupings as unions and special interest groups. I believe that, as the twentieth century was the century of the big government, the twenty-first century will become the century of smaller government and increasing private-sector initiatives, even in the social welfare sphere. I have also been forced to admit that my right wing friends were correct in claiming that many social welfare measures would end up adversely affecting the recipients as they responded rationally to the incentives we gave them. The result is dependent groups, and sometimes even dependent societies, as sections of the Canadian Atlantic provinces come close to being.

So I have ended up where I began, a follower of Hayek and a Gladstonian liberal (i.e., a liberal in the nineteenth-century European sense of the term). I have always accepted the value of the price system as a means of coordinating decentralized decisions on economic matters. Although I still believe that it should not be beyond human wit to alleviate some of the more socially undesirable results that the price system produces, I have also learned through bitter experience that this is much easier to say than to do. We must go on trying, but we must also realize that every social welfare experiment needs to be reversed as soon as it is clearly seen to have failed in its purpose.

SELECTED WORKS

(1956) (with K. Lancaster) 'The general theory of second best', *Review of Economic Studies*, 24 (1), pp. 11–32.

(1957) 'The theory of customs unions: trade diversion and welfare', *Economica*, n.s. 24 (1), pp. 40–6.*

(1958) (with G.C. Archibald) 'Monetary and value theory: a critique of Lange and Patinkin', *Review of Economic Studies*, 26 (1), pp. 1–22.*

(1960a) 'The relation between unemployment and the rate of change of money wage rates in the United Kingdom, 1862–1957: a further analysis', *Economica*, n.s. 27 (1), pp. 1–31.*

(1960b) 'The theory of customs unions: a general survey', *Economic Journal*, 70 (3), pp. 496–513.*

(1963) *An introduction to positive economics*. London: Weidenfeld & Nicolson.

(1964) 'Positive economics in relation to some current trends', *Journal of the Economics Association*, 5 (Spring), pp. 365–72.*

(1967) 'The balance of payments and the common market', *Journal of the Economics Association*, 7 (Autumn), pp. 5–17.*

(1967) (with G.C. Archibald) *An introduction to a mathematical treatment of economics*. London: Weidenfeld & Nicolson.

(1970) *The theory of customs unions: a general equilibrium analysis*. London: Weidenfeld & Nicolson.

(1970) (with J.M. Parkin) 'Incomes policy: a re-appraisal', *Economica*, n.s. 37 (2), pp. 115–38.*

(1972) 'The foundations of the theory of national income: an analysis of some fundamental errors', in B.A. Corry and M.H. Peston (eds) (1972) *Essays in honour of Lionel Robbins*. London: Weidenfeld & Nicolson, pp. 3–42.

(1985) 'Canada and the United States: the economic dimension', in C.F. Doran and J.H. Stigler (eds) (1985) *Canada and the United States: enduring friendship, persistent stress*. Englewood Cliffs, NJ: Prentice Hall, pp. 69–100.

(1985) (with M. Smith) *Taking the initiative: Canada's trade options in a turbulent world*. Toronto: C.D. Howe Institute.

(1986) 'Will there be a Canadian-American free trade association?', *The World Economy*, 9 (3), pp. 217–38.

(1987) (with M. Smith) *Global imbalances and US policy responses: a Canadian perspective*. Toronto: C.D. Howe Institute.

(1988) (with C.D. Harbury) *First principles of economics*. London: Weidenfeld & Nicolson.

(1988) (with R.C. York) *Evaluating the free trade deal: a guided tour through the Canada-US agreement*. Toronto: C.D. Howe Institute.

(1990) (Eds with R.C. York) *Zero inflation*. Toronto: C.D. Howe Institute.

(1994) 'Markets, technological change and economic growth', *Pakistan Development Review*, 33 (4, pt. I), pp. 327–52.*

(1995) (with C. Bekar) 'A structuralist view of technical change and economic growth', in T.J. Courchene (ed.) (1995) *Technology, information and public policy*. Kingston, Ontario: John Deutsche Institute, pp. 9–75.*

(1997a) *Selected essays*. Vol. I: *Microeconomics, growth and political economy*. Cheltenham: Edward Elgar.

(1997b) *Selected essays*. Vol. II: *Macroeconomic theory and policy*. Cheltenham: Edward Elgar.

(1997c) 'An intellectual autobiography', in R.G. Lipsey (1997a) **q.v.**, pp. ix–xxxvii.
(1997d) 'Richard Lipsey', in K. Tribe (ed.) (1997) *Economic careers: economics and economists in Britain, 1930–1970*. London: Routledge, pp. 206–24.
(1997) (with B.C. Eaton) *On the foundations of monopolistic competition and economic geography*. Cheltenham: Edward Elgar.
(2000) (with K. Carlaw and C. Bekar) *Time, technology and markets: explorations in economic growth and restructuring*, forthcoming.

BIBLIOGRAPHY

Allen, R.G.D. (1938) *Mathematical analysis for economists*. London: Macmillan.
Boulding, K.E. (1941) *Economic analysis*. New York: Harper & Row.
Corden, W.M. (1972) Review of Lipsey (1970), *Journal of International Economics*, 2 (1), pp. 89–91.
De Marchi, N.B. (1988) 'Popper and the LSE economists', in N.B. De Marchi (ed.) (1988) *The Popperian legacy in economics*. Cambridge: Cambridge University Press, pp. 139–66.
Dobson, W. (1997) 'Liberalizing and stabilizing the Canadian economy', in B.C. Eaton and R.G. Harris (eds) (1997) **q.v.**, pp. 186–97.
Eaton, B.C. and Harris, R.G. (eds) (1997) *Trade, technology and economics: essays in honour of Richard G. Lipsey*. Cheltenham: Edward Elgar.
Friedman, M. (1953) 'The methodology of positive economics', in M. Friedman (1953) *Essays in positive economics*. Chicago: University of Chicago Press, pp. 3–43.
Friedman, M. (1957) *A theory of the consumption function*. Princeton, NJ: NBER/ Princeton University Press.
Gehrels, H. (1957) 'Customs unions from a single country viewpoint', *Review of Economic Studies*, 24 (1), pp. 61–4.
Graham, F.D. (1948) *The theory of international values*. Princeton, NJ: Princeton University Press.
Harbury, C.D. and Lipsey, R.G. (1983) *An introduction to the UK economy: a companion to positive economics*. London: Pitman.
Hayek, F.A. von (1944) *The road to serfdom*. London: Routledge & Kegan Paul.
Hicks, J.R. (1939) *Value and capital: an inquiry into some fundamental principles of economic theory*. Oxford: Clarendon Press.
Hood, W.C. and Koopmans, T.C. (eds) (1953) *Studies in econometric method*. Cowles commission monograph no. 14. New York: John Wiley.
Johnson, H.G. (1972) Review of Lipsey (1970), *Economic Journal*, 82 (2), pp. 728–30.
Klappholz, K. and Mishan, E.J. (1962) 'Identities in economic models', *Economica*, n.s. 29 (2), pp. 117–28.
Leeson, R. (1994) 'Some misunderstandings concerning the contributions made by A.W.H. Phillips and R.G. Lipsey to the inflation-unemployment literature', *History of Economics Review*, 22 (Summer), pp. 70–82.
Leeson, R. (1997) 'The trade-off interpretation of Phillips' dynamic stabilisation exercise', *Economica*, n.s. 64 (2), pp. 155–73.

MacDougall, G.D.A. (1987) *Don and mandarin: memoirs of an economist.* London: John Murray.

Mahan, A.T. (1899) *The influence of seapower on history, 1600–1805*, 1st US edn. (1980). Englewood Cliffs, NJ: Prentice Hall.

Meade, J.E. (1952) *A geometry of international trade.* London: Allen & Unwin.

Meade, J.E. (1955) *The theory of international economic policy.* Vol. II: *Trade and welfare.* London: Oxford University Press.

Pareto, V. (1935) *Mind and society*, 4 vols. New York: Harcourt Brace.

Patinkin, D. (1956) *Money, interest and prices: an integration of monetary and value theory.* New York: Harper & Row.

Phillips, A.W.H. (1958) 'The relationship between unemployment and the rate of change of money wage rates in the United Kingdom, 1861–1957', *Economica*, n.s. 25 (4), pp. 283–99.

Robbins, L.C. (1932) *An essay on the nature and significance of economic science.* London: Macmillan.

Samuelson, P.A. (1947) *Foundations of economic analysis.* Cambridge, MA: Harvard University Press.

Samuelson, P.A. (1955) *Economics: an introductory analysis*, 3rd edn. London: McGraw-Hill.

Schumpeter, J.A. (1911) *The theory of economic development.* Cambridge, MA: Harvard University Press.

Sloman, A. (1997) 'Sir Albert Sloman', in K. Tribe (ed.) (1997) *Economic careers: economics and economists in Britain, 1930–1970.* London: Routledge, pp. 225–37.

Viner, J. (1950) *The customs union issue.* New York: Carnegie Endowment for International Peace.

Wulwick, N.J. (1987) 'The Phillips curve: which? whose? to do what? how?', *Southern Economic Journal*, 53 (4), pp. 834–57.

Wulwick, N.J. (1989) 'Phillips' approximate regression', *Oxford Economic Papers*, n.s. 41 (1), pp. 170–88.

Wulwick, N.J. (1994) 'Notes on reading a text: response', *History of Economics Review*, 22 (Summer), pp. 83–94.

Wulwick, N.J. (1996) 'Two econometric replications: the historic Phillips and Lipsey-Phillips curves', *History of Political Economy*, 28 (3), pp. 391–439.

7. Allan H. Meltzer (b. 1928)[1]

© *Stan Franzos*

7.1   INTRODUCTION

My career as a professional economist began in the winter of 1952 when I enrolled in graduate school at the University of California, Los Angeles. I had been out of school for more than three years in a pattern that became rather common later but, except for war veterans, was not usual at the time. Economics had been my undergraduate major. As with many students, lack of use had eroded much of what I once knew. Graduate school was for me very much a new start. I knew nothing about the UCLA faculty. I chose UCLA because of its proximity; I had moved to Los Angeles in 1948 and married in 1950. We lived not far from my wife's work, and I cannot recall that we ever considered moving or trying to revive earlier admissions to eastern graduate schools.

Luck was with me. One of my teachers was the frustrating but challenging Armen Alchian. Far more important for me was Karl Brunner, then a new

---

[1]   Meltzer (1995b), as revised by the editors. Further details of my life philosophy can be found in my *American Economist* essay (Meltzer 1990) and in Nicodano (1993) which was prepared for the Raffaele Mattioli lectures that I gave with Karl Brunner (Brunner and Meltzer 1993). I have one volume of collected writings in the series (Meltzer 1995a).

assistant professor. Brunner was Swiss with a doctorate from Zurich, but he had studied at the London School of Economics before the war and had learned a lot of modern economics as a Rockefeller Fellow at the Cowles commission, then resident at the University of Chicago. He had become interested in econometrics there and also in macroeconomics. Under the influence of Rudolph Carnap, then in the UCLA Philosophy Department, he had developed a strong interest in the philosophy of science, hypothesis testing, and methodology that lasted all of his life.

My stay at UCLA was a relatively brief one, lasting from February 1952 to June 1955. I believed firmly then, and more firmly now, that learning is something one does mainly alone. Teachers and colleagues can help by pointing out pitfalls, recommending reading material, and in other ways. But mastering a subject is impossible without personal effort. To me, a Ph.D. is a licence to learn and a certification that the holder has enough grasp of some discipline to proceed without close supervision.

Like many students, my choice of field was shaped by the chance that a particular professor developed his material in an appealing way. Karl Brunner awakened my interest in monetary theory by showing its relevance for many real world problems. One day during a reading course on business cycle theory, I told him that I wanted to apply for a grant to work on my thesis and that I had a long-standing desire to go to France. I wanted a topic that would give me reason to do so. After complaining that I was in too much of a hurry, he suggested that I work on the French money supply under wartime and postwar conditions.[2] I applied for and received support as a Fulbright Scholar and a fellow of the Social Science Research Council.

It is an understatement to say that I did not have a clear idea of how to go about writing a thesis. As an undergraduate and graduate student, I had been called upon to write very few term papers in economics and the very few that I had done had been in economic history as an undergraduate. My education had concentrated on learning not producing knowledge. Reading did not prove to be a very good method of learning how to do research or how to write a professional paper.

The thesis was an application to France, and an empirical test, of the ideas Karl Brunner had developed about the determinants of the money stock. My task was to learn about French monetary arrangements, formulate the structural equations and estimate them. That sounds easier today than it did then. Those born in the computer age can have no understanding about the effort required to calculate multiple regressions with three or four independent variables using an electric calculator. The time required was measured in hours or days, not micro-seconds. The possibility of error was

---

[2] The main part of the thesis was published as Meltzer (1959).

always present, so it was necessary to calculate a check on the computation as part of the estimation. Almost 40 years later, I can still recall the frustration when the checking procedure indicated an error and the relief when it did not.

I don't recall having very definite career plans. I expected to teach. At the time, teaching loads in even the best schools were three or four courses a semester, so teaching was a relatively more important activity than it later became. Since I had acquired a taste for research while working on my thesis, I hoped to get an appointment that would let me do both.

While I was still in France, the late Irving Kravis hired me, sight unseen, as a lecturer at the University of Pennsylvania beginning in fall 1956. The economics department was then in the Wharton School, but all the macroeconomics was taught by the finance department faculty. A gentle, kind finance colleague, Raymond Whittlesley, encouraged me. By mid-year, however, I decided that Penn was not the place for me. I wrote letters to several departments, offering my services, and was fortunate to be interviewed and hired by Lee Bach, the founding Dean of the Graduate School of Industrial Administration at Carnegie Institute of Technology, later Carnegie Mellon University. With some time off for good behaviour, I have remained there since fall 1957.

My interest in real world problems has never flagged. A major interest has been inflation and the determinants of the pace of economic activity. For many years, I concentrated on topics related to money, monetary theory and economic policy. Interest in policy issues and participation for many years in the Interlaken Seminar on Analysis and Ideology (that Karl Brunner started in the early 1970s) stimulated my concern for efforts to formalize the role of politics in economic policy. This led me to work on political economy. The work would not have made much progress without the collaboration of two friends, Scott Richard and Alex Cukierman. Most of this work has been collected in our book, *Political economy* (1991).

A considerable part of my work in monetary economics was joint work with Karl Brunner. Together we developed a model of the money supply in which the stock of money was determined jointly with portfolio decisions of the banking system and the public. This framework could readily be extended to include the role of other intermediaries. At first, we worked on the determination of money and credit, the latter defined as the stock of earning assets held by banks. We extended this to incorporate the demand for money and, later, output and the price level. The stock-flow model combining these assets, output and the price level gave a framework for analysing the effects of monetary and fiscal changes directly and through the effects of the resulting budget deficits and surpluses. A considerable part of this work has been collected in our *Monetary economics* (1989)

In my early years at Carnegie, I poked at several research topics before beginning work on the demand for money. I chose this topic after a visit by Karl Brunner, probably in 1961. He asked me to collaborate in writing a textbook on monetary economics. I suggested that we try to combine his new work on US money supply with empirical work on both demand and supply functions for money. We agreed to do new research that would be the basis for our textbook. My task was to work on the demand for money while he worked on supply. Later we would combine our efforts.

I had no idea that I had embarked on a lifetime collaboration, nor did Karl. I guessed it would take no more than five to seven years to complete the research and the textbook. In retrospect, the time was infinite; we never wrote the textbook. Aside from *Monetary economics*, the only effort we made to bring our work together was in the Raffaele Mattioli lectures that we gave jointly in Milan in 1987. This was in part retrospective. We had both moved on to other interests. But we tried also to develop some of our ideas about rational expectations and real business cycles and about why prices are sticky. The book containing these lectures was completed in 1988 but not published for another five years (Brunner and Meltzer 1993) long after Karl's death in April 1989. In the remainder of this chapter I present samples of the broad topics that have interested me at various times since 1960.

7.2   THE DEMAND FOR MONEY

The public's demand for money is a critical link between monetary policy actions and their effects on economic activity and prices. When I began work on this topic, there was still much discussion about whether money had any reliable effect on economic activity or prices. Conjectures about liquidity traps or unstable velocity changes were common.

'The demand for money: the evidence from the time series' (Meltzer 1963a) was my first undertaking for the joint project with Brunner. I used a long-term interest rate and several different measures of wealth, permanent and current income to test different specifications of the demand equation. Measures of wealth or permanent income dominated current income. I took the opportunity to test a central proposition in all economic analysis – first degree homogeneity of the demand for money in prices and the value of financial assets – and I estimated the equation over various sub-periods to test for consistency of results or, as I described it at the time, parameter stability.

One of my principal findings was a comparatively large (−0.5 to −0.8) and statistically important coefficient for the long-term interest rate. Earlier empirical work by Friedman (1959, p. 349) had dismissed the role of interest rates in the demand for money; he claimed to be unable 'to find any close connection between changes in velocity from cycle to cycle and any of a number of interest rates'. My findings reversed this conclusion. My work showed that cyclical variations in interest rates had an economically relevant effect. Friedman (1966) later responded to criticisms of his conclusion about interest rates by insisting that the numerical value of the interest elasticity of the demand for money is not a 'fundamental issue' as long as it is not infinite and by arguing that under some conditions the monetary and real sectors can be dichotomized. These arguments had no bearing on the cyclical effect of interest rates on velocity or on the effect of permanent changes in expected inflation. Other relative prices may modify the response, but the size of the interest elasticity remains important for monetary dynamics.

Standard work on the demand for money did not use long-term rates and wealth as constraints. Most research took a traditional, Keynesian approach using a short-term interest rate and current income. The estimated interest elasticity in these studies was often less than −0.1. For a time, it did not seem to make a substantial difference, but in the mid-1970s the variability of interest rates increased. The traditional Keynesian equations made large errors, in part reflecting the relatively small value of the estimated interest elasticity. The same problem returned in the early 1980s. Later Lucas (1988) showed that much of the alleged instability of the demand for money resulted from use of a Keynesian specification. His estimated interest and wealth elasticities supported my earlier findings by extending them to a much longer time period.

No single empirical study can bear much weight in economics. Robust findings are often more relevant than state-of-the-art econometrics for persuading economists to accept a conclusion. 'Predicting velocity: implications for theory and policy' (Brunner and Meltzer 1963) was written for the December 1962 meeting of the Allied Social Science Association. Our aim was to provide additional evidence on the demand for money by comparing alternative hypotheses. My earlier paper on the demand for money, based on time series data for 30 to 60 year periods, had been completed but was not yet published.

In 'Predicting velocity', Brunner and I used annual data for overlapping, moving ten-year periods to compare 17 different specifications of the demand for money found in the literature. The specifications included several Keynesian hypotheses that used an interest rate and current income, some following Milton Friedman that used permanent income but omitted any interest rate, and some that used measures of permanent income or wealth and an interest rate. To complete the comparison, Brunner and I introduced as our choice of a naive hypothesis an equation that would later be familiar as a random walk; current velocity depended only on its lagged value and an error term. We also compared narrow and broad monetary aggregates as the denominator of monetary velocity. To compare the alternatives, we computed means and variances of prediction errors using the parameters estimated for a particular ten-year sequence to predict the next year. This gave 39 predictions for each equation.

The random walk equations typically had lower means and variance than any of the equations using current income but higher means and variance than the equations with wealth or permanent income. This seemed a strong test of the two alternatives, although it had little effect on subsequent discussion.

The median value of the interest elasticity of M_1 velocity computed from 39 estimates of three different equations was between 0.30 and 0.36. Some of these equations included, and others excluded, measures of income or wealth. These estimates of the interest elasticity were lower than the estimates I had found for the period as a whole but substantially higher than the estimates from the Keynesian equations, used by the Federal Reserve and many others, based on traditional Keynesian specifications. The interest elasticities we estimated would have substantially reduced the errors reported for money demand equations in the 1970s and 1980s.

One of the conclusions of 'Predicting velocity' is mainly of interest for the history of economic ideas. At the time, the view still remained that money is irrelevant for the pace of economic activity. This view has been based on many different arguments. In the 1930s and the 1950s the existence of a liquidity trap or a near trap was used to argue that interest rates did not respond to changes in the quantity of money. Or, the response of interest rates was said to be small. Or, business investment was said to be insensitive to interest rates, so that, whether small or large, changes in interest rates had little effect on economic activity. Monetary policy was said to be impotent. Much later, when real business cycle theory became prominent, the argument shifted. Money was found or claimed to be always strictly neutral; changes in money affected prices but did not cause short-term changes in real values such as output or investment.

The evidence showed that monetary velocity, therefore the demand for money, was a stable function of a few variables. This is a necessary condition for the relevance of money.

To complement the empirical work on the aggregate demand for money, I studied money holdings by business firms as reported in survey data collected by the Federal Trade Commission (Meltzer 1963b). All of the data for the industries and years studied were consistent with the unit wealth or income elasticity I had estimated from time series data. There was no evidence of economies of scale in cash balances as suggested in an influential paper by Baumol.[3]

In 'Economies of scale in cash balances reconsidered' (Brunner and Meltzer 1967) we reconciled the Baumol result with the empirical evidence by showing that Baumol's hypothesis implied economies of scale only if firms that pay out money do not receive money during the period. This is, of course, inconsistent with aggregate analysis.

Once payments and receipts are considered together, the relation between a firm's cash balances and its transactions is a quadratic in sales or transactions. The relative size of the linear and quadratic terms depends on the relative size of fixed and marginal costs of receiving and withdrawing cash. A relatively small fixed cost makes the quadratic term insignificant. Empirical data suggest that this is the case.

7.3   MONEY SUPPLY AND OUTPUT

'Monetary theory and monetary history' (Meltzer 1965) is a review of Friedman and Schwartz's *Monetary history of the United States, 1867–1960* (1963). I praised the book as a classic from the time it appeared. It did not require great insight to see that the book was an outstanding work.

My review tried to bring out the authors' argument by writing down the theory that, I claimed, the authors used to interpret monetary history. I restated the theory of the money stock and used Friedman's earlier work to relate money to nominal income and the price level. The framework I developed helped me to show how the authors related money to temporary fluctuations in output and permanent changes in the price level. I criticized their failure to explain how the business cycle – transitory income in their framework – was related to money, and other variables. Now, thirty years later, after many attempts to develop explanations of economic fluctuations, I am less convinced about economists' ability to develop a verifiable explanation of cyclical fluctuations. Much of the profession has accepted the random walk hypothesis of changes in real output. This hypothesis is not very different from 'transitory income', the explanation of output fluctuations I attributed to Friedman and Schwartz.

A long chapter of Friedman and Schwartz's *Monetary history* discussed the Great Depression. The Federal Reserve's behaviour in the 1930s, and its consequences for money, output, prices and employment is puzzling. Why did the Federal Reserve do so little to prevent deflation? Friedman and

---

3   Baumol (1952); see also Tobin (1956) whose paper does not claim that there are economies of scale in cash balances, although it is usually cited along with Baumol's.

Schwartz emphasized the death of Benjamin Strong, President of the New York Federal Reserve Bank. This was unsatisfactory and unverifiable.

As part of our study of Federal Reserve policy and actions for the House Committee on Banking and Currency, Karl Brunner and I developed a model of Federal Reserve behaviour (Brunner and Meltzer 1964). The model, based on work by Federal Reserve economists W.W. Riefler and W.R. Burgess, directed attention to member bank borrowing and short-term interest rates as indicators of the current stance of monetary policy. Increases in borrowing indicated tightening in the money market – a tighter policy position – and reduced borrowing indicated less restraint or greater ease.

Our paper, 'What did we learn from the monetary experience of the United States in the Great Depression?' compared changes in member bank borrowing and short-term interest rates during business contractions in 1923–4, 1926–8 and 1929–31 (Brunner and Meltzer 1968). We showed that the Federal Reserve increased the monetary base much more in the first two contractions than in 1929–31. This was consistent with our hypothesis: short-term interest rates declined much more in 1929–31 than in the earlier contractions. When short-term rates rose, following Britain's departure from the gold standard and at other times, the Federal Reserve injected reserves. When interest fell, or remained unchanged, they took no action.

Our hypothesis is that the Federal Reserve misinterpreted the movements in interest rates and member bank borrowing as evidence of monetary 'ease'. The evidence suggests that the hypothesis is consistent with the decisions taken, and the different outcomes, in the three contractions.

I wrote 'Monetary and other explanations of the start of the Great Depression' (Meltzer 1976) in honour of Homer Jones's seventieth birthday. Jones had played an important role as an official of the St Louis Federal Reserve Bank in reviving monetary analysis within the Federal Reserve System.

I used the occasion to compare a monetary explanation of the start of the 1930s depression to the non-monetary explanations proposed by Peter Temin (1976). The main difficulty for the monetary explanation of the start of the depression is that the fall in the price level is much larger than predicted by any monetary explanation. Temin's explanation, however, relies on a fall in the demand for money; this implies that money was in excess supply. Temin argues that the fall in the demand for money is the counterpart of an autonomous reduction in spending. The paper argued that Temin's explanation was of doubtful validity and inconsistent with the data for the period and with the behaviour of the Federal Reserve.

Many countries experienced 'stagflation' in the 1970s; output fell while prices rose. My paper, 'Stagflation, persistent unemployment and the permanence of economic shocks', written with Karl Brunner and Alex

Cukierman (Meltzer *et al.* 1980), reconciles 'stagflation' with rational behaviour. In the model economy that we consider, markets always clear and people use all available information efficiently. These are introduced to isolate the particular information problem that we emphasized: people do not know which changes (shocks) will persist or how long they will persist. In this case, rational strategy is to adjust partially to any unforeseen change.

We used the model to analyse a large change in productivity, such as the oil price increases of the 1970s. The model implies that large changes of this kind increase unemployment and raise prices on impact. Unemployment persists because real wages do not fully respond to the shock until the permanence of the shock is recognized. Prices continue to rise during the adjustment.

The model suggests that the difficulties people face in distinguishing permanent and transitory changes can account for sluggish adjustment of wages and prices and for stagflation in a world with rational expectations. More generally, costs of acquiring information can explain persistence in the direction of adjustment of prices and output that are characteristic of business cycles. Brunner, Cukierman and I pursued this line of research in a subsequent paper (Meltzer *et al.* 1983). We were able to show that inventory cycles could result from permanent-transitory misperception.

'Stability under the gold standard in practice' (Meltzer and Robinson 1989) was one of several studies I did in the middle 1980s comparing the properties of different monetary systems. This paper, written for a conference in honour of Anna J. Schwartz, compares variability of prices and output under the classical gold standard, the Bretton Woods system of fixed but adjustable exchange rates, and the recent period of (largely) managed floating.

The myth of the gold standard, promoted by its advocates, presents that standard as stable and non-inflationary. Robinson and I examined this claim using a Kalman filter to forecast prices and output and to compute forecast errors. This is surely a more powerful method than was available at the time, but it separated anticipated from unanticipated values: the results for most countries showed much more variability under the gold standard than in the Bretton Woods or floating rate regimes. The gold standard had the lowest rate of inflation of the three regimes but, we argue, this is *ex post* observation based on actual instead of anticipated values. The relatively high variability of inflation from year to year may have given rise to very different perceptions about price stability at the time.

7.4   CREDIT AND MONEY

One of my earliest post-thesis research efforts was the relation of credit to money. This interest was whetted by claims that monetary changes had larger effects on small rather than on large firms. Complaints about the 'discriminatory' effect of monetary policy were common after the 1955–7 experience with rising interest rates.

'Mercantile credit, monetary policy and size of firms' (Meltzer 1960) investigated this issue by considering one of the many ways in which markets distribute the effects of policy over firms and households. The paper tests the hypothesis that large firms extend more credit to small firms when banks reduce lending. Small firms are typically net borrowers from large firms.

I found that the net amount of trade credit extended by large firms increased during the period studied. Large firms increased borrowing principally from the capital markets, giving them an advantage over small firms. By lending to small firms, they shared some of this advantage with their customers. I speculated that they did this to finance their sales. In a subsequent study for the Commission on Money and Credit, I examined the responses of a sample of individual firms that responded to a questionnaire to test this hypothesis.

Adjustment of trade credit is one of the many ways in which cyclical or short-term changes in monetary velocity can offset or augment the effect of changes in money on nominal output. The insights gained from my work on trade credit led me to consider the more general problem of changes in velocity and the demand for money. But it also encouraged me to work on the role of intermediation, a subject that became popular at about this time following publication of Gurley and Shaw's (1960) theory of intermediaries.

Some of these same issues returned in the 1990s. Ben Bernanke and others analysed the role of lending and borrowing relationships, and the Federal Reserve (and many others) blamed both the depth and persistence of the 1991 recession and the subsequent sluggish recovery on the slow growth of private credit at US banks. Bernanke (1983) argued that, in the Great Depression, the breakdown of credit relationships played an independent role.

In 'Money and credit in the monetary transmission process' (Brunner and Meltzer 1988), we agree with many of Bernanke's arguments. Several of his principal conclusions accord with our long-standing views on the relation of credit to money. We are sceptical, however, about his claim that lending arrangements have an independent effect on output and prices. In our analysis, changes in a bank's lending and securities purchases are an endogenous response to policy and other changes. The size of this response in a severe deflation, such as the Great Depression, increases as prices fall.

The reason is that a decline in prices that is expected to persist can impair lenders' equity.

The early 1990s saw a less pervasive and less damaging repetition. As belief spread that the rate of inflation had been reduced permanently, asset prices fell. The fall in asset prices impaired the solvency of financial intermediaries in many countries. Uncertainty about the future value of financial assets induced an increase in the demand for money and a fall in monetary velocity. In the Great Depression, these deflationary impulses, unleashed by the decline in money, were strengthened by the failure of the Federal Reserve to serve as lender of last resort. The milder disinflation of the 1990s was less costly, in part because it was milder. In most countries experiencing disinflation and falling asset prices, there was little doubt about the response of the lender of last resort.

The housing market has often been singled out as the market in which credit 'availability' is most important. Conjectures about credit availability and the alleged discriminatory effects of monetary restriction on housing gave impetus to public policies intended to offset these effects. Regulation Q controls on interest rates in the United States during the 1960s and 1970s and the many mortgage market interventions are examples.

Some of the cyclical behaviour of housing arises because housing is a durable asset. As such, purchases are postponed when households believe that interest rates are temporarily high and purchases increase when interest rates are low relative to recent norms. Partly for this reason, I was sceptical of claims that government mortgage market operations had much effect on the production or sale of housing.

There was a more basic reason for scepticism: mortgages are nominal assets; issuing more mortgages should not have any effect on a real asset, housing. A subsidy would have some effect on the timing of purchases if it were unanticipated. In fact, there was not much evidence showing that, the effects of durability aside, housing was subject to adverse treatment by banks and other intermediaries.

The people in the housing industry association believed firmly that they deserved special assistance. Knowing my general views, they asked me to study the issue, believing that if the data persuaded me, I could help to persuade others. I agreed on condition that the results would be mine to publish if I chose to do so. Needless to say, I did not persuade them, nor did my evidence.

One part of my study appeared in the *Journal of Finance* as 'Credit availability and economic decisions: some evidence from the mortgage and housing markets' (Meltzer 1974). Jack Guttentag was editor of the *Journal* at the time. To his credit he published a paper critical of views that he had often expressed.

During this century, the mortgage market has expanded much more than total assets or the housing stock. The duration of mortgages has increased, and many special programmes and innovations have made mortgage credit less expensive relative to other types of borrowing. The outstanding stock of mortgages increased relative to the value of housing and relative to total liabilities. Mortgage credit substituted for other liabilities, particularly loans to carry common stocks or consumer credit to purchase durables. Yet housing assets as a share of total assets remained unchanged. There was, in short, considerable evidence that government policy and market innovations had increased the stock of mortgage credit, but there was no evidence that these changes had affected housing relative to other assets.

The 'Credit availability' paper also examined some of the studies that often reached opposite conclusions. The studies did not support the availability doctrine. The most robust finding from these studies is that changes in the relative supply of mortgages, through mortgage market operations and other activities, have little effect on housing.

7.5   FINANCIAL REGULATION

My interests in banking and intermediation led me inevitably to the subject of financial regulation. I wrote a survey of bank regulation for an American Bankers' Association conference of university professors in 1966 (Meltzer 1967), and I served as the staff of the housing representative on President Nixon's study of financial structure in the early 1970s – the so-called Hunt Commission. I was an outsider in this area, so I lacked knowledge of details, but an outsider's distance from the professional consensus is sometimes useful. My bankers' association conference paper concluded that much banking regulation confused the consequences of individual bank failures with systemic failures. I criticized government deposit insurance as a mistake, based on policymakers' and Congressional misinterpretation of the reason for bank failures. It subsidized risk taking by insolvent banks. At the time, I favoured private deposit insurance and public disclosure of each bank's risk position. Research by others and observation eventually changed my opinion about the viability of a private insurance system.

By the time George Kaufman asked me to prepare a paper for a 1985 conference on financial structure, I was less certain about private deposit insurance. Thus my 'Financial failures and financial policies' (Meltzer 1986), does not repeat my earlier proposal. Much of my concern in that paper is with the regulators' mishandling of the foreign debt problem after the Mexican default in the summer of 1982. I was an early advocate of recognizing the losses, writing down the debt, and exchanging debt for equity. These solutions, a few years later, became part of the Treasury's plan for bringing the problem to an end. The delay was costly, however, to the US and even more to the debtors.

I wrote about the international debt problem for several different audiences. A piece in *Fortune* in November 1983 urged exchanges of debt for equity at the market value of the debt. Paul Volcker, then Chairman of the Board of the Governors of the Federal Reserve System, dismissed this approach in private conversation. He remained unwilling to recognize the losses that had already occurred.

From September 1988 to January 1989, I served as a full-time consultant and acting member of President Reagan's Council of Economic Advisers. My responsibilities included production of the *Economic Report of the President*. My efforts to include a section on the merits of debt-equity swaps at the market value of the debt was met by strong opposition from the Treasury Department to any statement beyond praise for the misguided policies that had sustained the problem for most of the decade. They could not object to statements of fact, so the Report noted that debt-equity exchanges 'accounted for $10 billion to $12 billion in debt reduction, or almost one-half of the total debt reduction accomplished since 1982' (Council of Economic Advisers 1989, p. 142). After much wrangling, the Report was able to do no more than recommend 'leaving negotiations between debtors and private creditors to determine changes in the value of outstanding debt and the associated debt service' (p. 144). Soon after, however, the Treasury changed its position and began the process that ended the international debt problem.

Finance has been a major area for development and enrichment of economic analysis in the past quarter century. As a professor in a management school, I followed these developments through seminars, appointments and promotions. An invitation to present a paper at an American Enterprise Institute conference on securities regulation gave me an opportunity to review part of this literature and explore its implications for regulation.

My paper 'On efficiency and regulation of the securities industry' (Meltzer 1969) develops what has become known as the capture hypothesis. The paper shows how the Securities and Exchange Commission promoted or protected monopolies in the securities industry. Competition from third markets leading to loss of market share by the New York Stock Exchange later eroded some of the monopoly rents and encouraged competition.

7.6 UNCERTAINTY

Along with much of the economics profession, my interest in uncertainty and costs of information increased over time. Discussions with Karl Brunner and Armen Alchian in the 1960s convinced me that, although money was part of wealth, the distinguishing characteristic of money was its service as medium of exchange. Brunner and I developed part of this analysis in the middle 1960s and, in Brunner and Meltzer (1971), used costs of acquiring information and uncertainty to explain the role of money as a medium of exchange.

Several examples of my later work on uncertainty include an application to business cycles and the explanation of 'stagflation' found in 'Stagflation, persistent unemployment and the permanence of economic shocks' (Meltzer *et al.* 1980). The uncertainty in that paper is whether disturbances to the economy are permanent or temporary.

Karl Brunner often commented on the number of people employed by the financial industry to explain Federal Reserve and budget policies to their clients. He believed that the large amount of talent employed in this way was evidence of the difficulty of learning about the current policy thrust by observing the main policy variables. Observation cannot separate persistent and transitory components of policy and other variables. Economists employed as 'Fed watchers' try to discern when permanent changes have been, or are about to be, made.

I wrote 'Rational expectations, risk, uncertainty and market responses' (Meltzer 1982) to develop some of these ideas. The simple generic model allowed persistent and transitory changes in levels and growth rates. In a celebrated paper, John Muth (1960) had earlier shown that expectations of this kind can be rational and had used the model to derive forecasts based on a distributed lag of past observations. My paper uses a model in which changes can be persistent or transitory and information is costly to acquire to discuss why some prices are set while others are variable. Elsewhere (Meltzer 1988), I used the distinction between persistent and transitory change as central to an understanding of Keynes' *General theory.*

Meltzer (1982) distinguishes between variations around a known mean (risk) and shifts in the mean value or mean rate of change (uncertainty). My 'Monetary reform in an uncertain environment' uses the distinction between risk and uncertainty to discuss types of monetary rules – fixed exchange rates, so-called free banking, and a rule for money growth (Meltzer 1983). The latter sets the growth rate of the monetary base equal to the difference between output growth and velocity growth. This rule maintains price stability, on average, in a world of uncertain changes in the demand for money, output, financial intermediation, and other variables and arrangements.

7.7   POLICY STUDIES

Economics for me is not just a set of abstractions or a branch of applied mathematics. Its value lies in the implications, or at times only suggestions, about how to improve the functioning of an economy. Thinking about uncertainty, observing and studying the conduct of policy and the outcomes of policy decisions has convinced me that economics has an important role in policymaking, but economists often exaggerate and overstate what they can achieve reliably.

In selecting the papers for the Edward Elgar selected essays that illustrated my macro policy writings I tried to choose some that presented my general views and the reasons that I hold them and some that gave a sense of the way in which the views were used. Testimony before Congress, newspaper columns, and papers at conferences and in professional journals offered a broad selection of topics. I chose three papers that present my views on the general policy problem and examples of policy recommendations developed with colleagues on the Shadow Open Market Committee.

At the end of the 1970s, inflation and unemployment had increased beyond anything that had been expected only a few years earlier. Journalists and some social scientists wrote about the failure of economics and the need for a new Keynes to show us the way to solve our problems. The editors of a public policy journal, *The Public Interest*, commissioned essays on 'The crisis in economics'.

My invited contribution to the volume, 'Monetarism and the crisis in economics' (Meltzer 1980) argued that there was no crisis. The problem was not a failure of economics. There had been exaggerated claims about economists' ability to make well-timed, discretionary changes in monetary or fiscal aggregates so as to maintain high employment without inflation. There was never any basis for these claims. The experience in many countries that based policies on economists' forecasts or on their ability to smooth fluctuations showed that economics is 'not the science that gives accurate quarterly projections of employment, prices, profits and other variables'.

I saw the failure as a failure of Keynesian demand management policies. There was never a strong empirical or theoretical foundation for these policies. Reliance on guideposts, price controls, interest rate controls, and other restrictions in the 1960s and 1970s had no firm foundation in economic analysis. The failure of these policies was no more a failure of economics than the inability to cure the common cold is a failure of biology.

A few years later, in 1986, I used my presidential address to the Western Economic Association to develop part of this theme and combine my conclusions about forecasting with my discussion of persistent and transitory disturbances. 'Limits of short-run stabilization policy' (Meltzer 1987) compares publicly reported forecasts of the rates of change of prices and output obtained using a variety of forecasting methods. The comparison showed that, on average, quarterly or annual forecast errors for real GNP growth and inflation are large relative to the average rate of change. The absolute size of forecast errors and their variability suggest that policies based on forecasts can increase rather than reduce instability

An alternative way to reduce fluctuations or variability is to change policy procedures. I compared variability in the United States and Japan before and after both countries changed to fluctuating rates and announced monetary targets. The data show a substantial reduction in the variability of Japanese prices and output.

The paper proposes two rules, an adaptive rule for domestic price stability based on the quantity equation and a rule for greater exchange rate stability. The latter requires the three major currencies – dollar, mark and yen – to adopt compatible rules for price stability. These rules provide public goods. Participating countries can achieve price stability and reduce exchange rate variability. Third countries that choose to fix their exchange rate to a major currency can import price stability.

One of the recurrent themes in policy discussion is the variability of real exchange rates in a flexible exchange rate regime. The appreciation of the dollar between the summer of 1980 and the winter of 1985 followed by its subsequent depreciation is often used as an example of the instability of real exchange rates.

My 'Real exchange rates: some evidence from the postwar years' is an empirical study of the trade weighted, real, dollar exchange rate from 1962 to 1991 (Meltzer 1993). I presented the paper at a conference honouring my fellow graduate student and long-time friend, A.B. Balbach, on his retirement as senior vice president of the Federal Reserve Bank of St Louis.

The empirical model separates the real exchange rate into a permanent component and a transitory component. The former is affected by perceived permanent values of policy and other variables. Transitory changes are treated as random and have no lasting effect on the real exchange rate.

Real money balances and, particularly in the 1980s, US real defence spending explain a large part of the variance of levels and changes of the real exchange rate. Although the effect of the budget deficit on the real exchange rate was widely discussed as a cause of exchange rate changes, I found no evidence of its effect.

The distinction between permanent and transitory changes explains much of the movement of the real exchange rate. Many exchange rate changes appear to be random, but the effect of perceived permanent changes in policy and other variables suggests that movements of real exchange rates are not well described as pure random walks.

7.8 POLICY PROPOSALS AND THE SHADOW OPEN MARKET COMMITTEE

Throughout my career, I have taken an active part in policy discussions by commenting on events and the proposals of others and by offering proposals for change. Much of this discussion takes place outside academic journals. The main sources include testimony before Congressional committees, signed articles in major newspapers or magazines, appearances on radio and television, comments in current news stories, statements by consultants to major agencies, and discussions or debates before business, political and other groups.

As a long-time participant in all of these forums, I have reservations about the value of most of them. Congressional and agency staff often select witnesses to present opinions their patrons want to hear. Or, like many journalists, they believe that truth is found by listening to extreme opinions on opposite sides of an issue. (Since 'monetarism' was considered a distinctly minority view, I was asked to participate frequently in the 1960s and 1970s.) Congressmen and administration executives are not likely to be swayed by discussions at hearings or consulting groups even if they are persuaded by argument or evidence.[4] Most committee members don't come unless television cameras (other than C-Span) are expected to be present.

Karl Brunner and I talked many times about the drift of policy and what might be done to encourage the public to demand improvements. After organizing ad hoc groups that issued statements opposing President Nixon's use of price controls and some other policies, we decided to develop a regular forum. We enlisted support from several academic and business economists and, in September 1973, started the Shadow Open Market Committee (SOMC).

Our name suggested our initial intent. We would function like a 'shadow'

---

[4] One experience is worth mentioning. Before a Congressional hearing in the 1970s, a well-known Congressman congratulated me on the correctness of my views about the inflationary outcomes of past policies. When the hearing opened, he read into the record a statement that was very critical of the policies I had favoured.

member of the House of Commons offering alternatives but unable to control policies. At the start there were 12 members as on the official Federal Open Market Committee. This proved cumbersome. As co-chairman (and later chairman) I assigned members to present parts of our statement at a press conference and answer questions. There was not enough for 12 people to do. Deaths and resignations, often for government service, reduced our membership to between six and eight where it has remained for many years. Two of the original members – Anna Schwartz and Robert Rasche – have stayed on the committee since its inception. Mickey Levy and Erich Heinemann have served for more than a decade. William Poole, Lee Hoskins and Charles Plosser joined in the 1980s.

The idea of the SOMC was that, as professionals, we would discuss and criticize policies and propose alternatives. We hoped in this way to accomplish several different objectives. We wanted to raise the quality of policy discussion. Instead of the popular treatment showing that economists differed, we would offer a statement about the reason for differences and the likely outcomes. Instead of criticizing policy outcomes with hindsight, we presented alternatives in advance. Instead of attempts to persuade policy officials or members of Congress, we hoped to use the media to inform the public and encourage them to demand changes.

Our initial concern was with monetary policy. Subsequently, we broadened our mandate to include other policies. One of my frustrations has been our inability to arouse much interest in trade policy. The late Jan Tumlir served as a member in the 1970s, but we were unable to get much attention focused on his presentations or our summaries of the problem of rising protection.

One problem we have often faced is how to measure our success or failure. There is no doubt that monetary policies in many countries changed in the 1980s. Less clear is how to assess our influence. I have long been convinced that economists can do little more than offer repeated warnings and propose alternatives based on analysis and evidence. When, or if, policymakers face a serious problem and decide to change course, the proposed alternative has a better chance of being adopted than some stop-gap measure proposed by the bureaucracy. In the 1980s, many countries adopted some type of monetary control to end inflation. None of the major countries used price controls or other ad hoc arrangements that had found favour at other times and in other places.

One mark of success is imitation. There are at this time a Shadow Securities and Exchange Commission and a Shadow Financial Regulatory Committee. In the past, there have been shadow committees on defence policy and budget policy and, to counter our positions, a Monetary Policy Forum. Some of these groups continued for only a few meetings. Among the groups that no longer exist, I should mention the Shadow European Economic Policy Committee that Karl and I organized with several European economists. After several annual meetings, in Paris or Brussels, we gave up the effort. The European countries did not have the same tradition of active criticism by academics or outsiders.

Preparation for a semi-annual SOMC meeting starts with telephone discussions with some of the members about the issues that we should consider. Several members prepare background papers, and I prepare the draft statement based on what the members have written in their background papers and my own views. At Sunday afternoon meetings in March and September, we discuss the background papers and the draft statement. A revised statement is then prepared. Erich Heinemann, a former working journalist, and Anna Schwartz, a skilled editor, do much of this work with me. We present the statement, copies of the background papers and a press release at a Monday press conference.

There are at this time more than 40 statements. I have selected a sample for my Edward Elgar collection (Meltzer 1995a, ch. 19). The first statement we issued, dated 14 September 1973, sets out four policy options for reducing inflation. We favoured a gradual approach because we believed that, at rates of inflation below 10 per cent, gradual reduction of inflation is both feasible and may be less costly. We have often claimed that zero expected inflation has long-term benefits, but the 1973 statement and those that followed always pointed out that ending inflation would be costly.

The economy was in recession when we met in March 1975. As usual, the Federal Reserve allowed money growth to fall during recession, as interest rates fell. At the March meeting we favoured increasing money growth, to the previous average rate. As they have done many times, the Federal Reserve blamed the decline in money growth on falling loan demand, not on their policy. This excuse was repeated, and generally accepted, in the early 1990s. In our 1975 statement, as in many others, we discussed the role of interest rates. We have not had any success in developing understanding that interest rates do not accurately measure monetary ease or restraint. Nominal and real interest rates can be low because the economy is weak or in recession.

The September 1975 statement recognizes that the 1975 recession was, in part, a one-time decline in output as a consequence of the oil shock. The SOMC was one of the first to make this distinction and to draw its implications for money growth. The statement is critical of the Congressional Budget Office and others who argued for increased money growth to offset the oil shock. We also comment on exchange rate policy and the financing of the budget deficit. At the time, we were more certain about the effects of government debt on interest rates than later evidence warranted.

In March 1977, inflation fell to about 5 per cent. The Carter administration began a stimulus programme and the Federal Reserve supported it with higher money growth. We warned about the effects – a spurt in output growth followed by higher inflation. By 1979 inflation was in the 8 per cent to 9 per cent range.

In October 1979, the Federal Reserve started an experiment that is often called a 'monetarist' experiment. The precise content of the change was not clear at first. By September 1980, we were convinced that the actual change was very different from what had been announced, and we were concerned about the increased variability and uncertainty that accompanied the policy change. We continued to urge changes in budget policy, particularly policies that would encourage investment.

Beryl Sprinkel challenged me to develop a programme to increase accountability and responsibility. By the time I presented a statement to the March 1981 meeting, Sprinkel had become Undersecretary of the Treasury. The statement proposed that the members of the Board of Governors offer their resignations if they failed to achieve the target they announced. Later, I had the opportunity to present this proposal to the Reserve Bank of New Zealand. The New Zealand government adopted a modified version.

By 1984, we had recognized that the connection between budget deficits and interest rates was far from close. The March 1984 statement concentrated on government spending and the composition of spending. We also were concerned about the growth of the monetary base in 1984. We were mistaken about the prospects for inflation.

Experience in the early and middle 1980s led me to think about adaptive rules and the adaptive rule later found its way into the SOMC statements, but we did not emphasize the rule until September 1993. That statement compares the rate of money growth required for zero inflation to the current rate of base money growth. The charts show why we were wrong to predict inflation in 1984 but right about recession in 1989 and 1990.

SELECTED WORKS

(1959) 'The behavior of the French money supply, 1938–54', *Journal of Political Economy*, 67 (3), pp. 275–96.

(1960) 'Mercantile credit, monetary policy and size of firms', *Review of Economics and Statistics*, 42 (4), pp. 429–37.*

(1963a) 'The demand for money: the evidence from the time series', *Journal of Political Economy*, 71 (3), pp. 219–46.*

(1963b) 'The demand for money: a cross-section study of business firms', *Quarterly Journal of Economics*, 77 (3), pp. 405–21.

(1963) (with K. Brunner) 'Predicting velocity: implications for theory and policy', *Journal of Finance*, 18 (2), pp. 319–54.*

(1964) (with K. Brunner) 'The Federal Reserve's attachment to the free reserve concept', US House of Representatives Committee on Banking and Currency Subcommittee on Domestic Finance, 88th Congress, 7 May. Rep. in K. Brunner and A.H. Meltzer (1989) **q.v.**, pp. 21–96.

(1965) 'Monetary theory and monetary history', *Schweizerische Zeitschrift für Volkswirtschaft und Statistik*, 101 (December), pp. 404–22.

(1967) 'Major issues in the regulation of financial institutions', *Journal of Political Economy*, 75 (4, pt II, Supplement), pp. 482–501.

(1967) (with K. Brunner) 'Economies of scale in cash balances reconsidered', *Quarterly Journal of Economics*, 81 (3), pp. 422–36.*

(1968) (with K. Brunner) 'What did we learn from the monetary experience of the United States in the great depression?', *Canadian Journal of Economics*, 1 (2), pp. 334–48.*

(1969) 'On efficiency and regulation of the securities industry', in H. Manne (ed.) (1969) *Economic policy in the regulation of corporate security*. Washington, DC: American Enterprise Institute, pp. 217–38.*

(1971) (with K. Brunner) 'The uses of money: money in the theory of an exchange economy', *American Economic Review*, 61 (5), pp. 784–805. Rep. in K. Brunner and A.H. Meltzer (1989) **q.v.**, pp. 230–58.

(1974) 'Credit availability and economic decisions: some evidence from the mortgage and housing markets', *Journal of Finance*, 29 (3), pp. 763–77.*

(1976) 'Monetary and other explanations of the start of the great depression', *Journal of Monetary Economics*, 2 (4), pp. 455–71.*

(1980) 'Monetarism and the crisis in economics', *The Public Interest*, (Special issue), pp. 35–45. Rep. in D. Bell and I. Kristol (eds) (1981) *The crisis in economic theory*. New York: Basic Books, pp. 35–45.*

(1980) (with K. Brunner and A. Cukierman) 'Stagflation, persistent unemployment and the permanence of economic shocks', *Journal of Monetary Economics*, 6 (4), pp. 467–92.*

(1982) 'Rational expectations, risk, uncertainty and market responses', in P.A. Wachtel (ed.) (1982) *Crisis in the economic and financial structure*. Lexington, MA: Lexington Books, pp. 3–22.*

(1983) 'Monetary reform in an uncertain environment', *Cato Journal*, 3 (1), pp. 93–112.*

(1983) (with K. Brunner and A. Cukierman) 'Money and economic activity, inventories and business cycles', *Journal of Monetary Economics*, 11 (3), pp. 281–319. Rep. in K. Brunner and A.H. Meltzer (1989) **q.v.**, pp. 193–229.

(1986) 'Financial failures and financial policies', in G. Kaufman and R. Kormendi (eds) (1986) *Deregulating financial services: public policy in flux*. Cambridge, MA: Ballinger, pp. 79–96.*

(1987) 'Limits of short-run stabilization policy', *Economic Inquiry*, 25 (1), pp. 1–14.*

(1988) *Keynes's monetary theory: a different interpretation*. Cambridge: Cambridge University Press.

(1988) (with K. Brunner) 'Money and credit in the monetary transmission process', *American Economic Review*, 78 (2, Papers & Proceedings), pp. 446–51.*

(1989) (with K. Brunner) *Monetary economics*. Oxford: Basil Blackwell.

(1989) (with S. Robinson) 'Stability under the gold standard in practice', in M.D. Bordo (ed.) (1989) *Money, history and international finance: essays in honor of Anna J. Schwartz*. Chicago: University of Chicago Press, pp. 163–202.*
(1990) 'My life philosophy', *American Economist*, 34 (Spring), pp. 22–32.
(1991) (with A. Cukierman and S.F. Richard) *Political economy*. New York: Oxford University Press.
(1993) 'Real exchange rates: some evidence from the postwar years', *Federal Reserve Bank of St. Louis Review*, 75 (2), pp. 103–17.*
(1993) (with K. Brunner) *Money and the economy: issues in monetary analysis*. Cambridge: Cambridge University Press.
(1995a) *Money, credit and policy*. Aldershot: Edward Elgar.
(1995b) 'Introduction', in A.H. Meltzer (1995a) **q.v.**, pp. xi–xxvii.

BIBLIOGRAPHY

Baumol, W.J. (1952) 'The transactions demand for cash: an inventory theoretic approach', *Quarterly Journal of Economics*, 66 (4), pp. 545–56.
Bernanke, B.S. (1983) 'Non-monetary effects of a financial crisis in the propagation of the great depression', *American Economic Review*, 73 (3), pp. 257–76.
Council of Economic Advisers (1989) *Economic report of the President*, January. Washington, DC: United States Government Printing Office.
Friedman, M. (1959) 'The demand for money: some theoretical and empirical results', *Journal of Political Economy*, 67 (4), pp. 327–51.
Friedman, M. (1966) 'Interest rates and the demand for money', *Journal of Law and Economics*, 9 (1), pp. 71–8. Rep. in M. Friedman (1969) *The optimum quantity of money and other essays*. Chicago: Aldine, pp. 141–55.
Friedman, M. and Schwartz, A.J. (1963) *A monetary history of the United States, 1867–1960*. Princeton, NJ: Princeton University Press.
Gurley, J.G. and Shaw, E.S. (1960) *Money in a theory of finance*. Washington, DC: Brookings Institution.
Lucas, R.E. (1988) 'Money demand in the United States: a quantitative review', *Carnegie Rochester Conference Series on Public Policy*, 29 (Autumn), pp. 137–68.
Muth, J.F. (1960) 'Optimal properties of exponentially weighted forecasts', *Journal of the American Statistical Association*, 55 (2), pp. 299–306.
Nicodano, G. (1993) 'Allan H. Meltzer', in K. Brunner and A.H. Meltzer (1993) **q.v.**, pp. 351–61.
Temin, P. (1976) *Did monetary forces cause the great depression?* New York: W.W. Norton.
Tobin, J. (1956) 'The interest elasticity of transactions demand for money', *Review of Economics and Statistics*, 38 (3), pp. 241–7.

8. Zvi Griliches (1930–1999)[1]

© *Diane Asséo Griliches*

8.1 INTRODUCTION

I started in agricultural economics, a field that took both data and econometrics seriously and used them to attack substantive problems. Econometrics was a tool, not an end in itself, and this became also my attitude to it. When I started, the field was quite primitive. The leading textbook was Ezekiel's *Methods of correlation analysis* (1941), but I had the luck of encountering two first-rate teachers at Berkeley: Ivan Lee, an Iowa State Ph.D. in statistics, and George Kuznets (Simon's brother), a Stanford Ph.D. in psychometrics. They were both following and teaching the emerging literature from the Cowles commission. Even though my mathematical background was almost nil, they turned me on to the field and when I was deciding where to continue my education I had little difficulty in choosing the University of Chicago.

Chicago had a strong agricultural economics group under the leadership of

---

[1] Griliches (1998b), as revised by the editors. Further details of my work can be found in Griliches (1988b), the introduction to the first volume of my selected writings which covered technology, education and productivity (Griliches 1988a). My second volume of selected essays, those on econometrics, were for this series (Griliches 1998a). There is a third volume of papers, on R&D and productivity (Griliches 1998c).

Theodore Schultz and D. Gale Johnson and it had the Cowles commission itself. Little did I know that, as I was arriving at Chicago, the Cowles commission was packing and leaving for Yale. Still, I was lucky in my teachers at Chicago. In econometrics I was taught by Marschak, Radner (who was teaching econometrics then), Martin Beckmann (linear programming) and Carl Christ. Two visiting teachers, Henri Theil and Trygve Haavelmo, had a great influence on my subsequent work. Theil introduced me to his work on aggregation and to his approach to specification analysis which became the central paradigm for my own teaching of econometrics in the years to come. Haavelmo, who did not teach econometrics on his visit but rather the theory of investment (a book that he was writing at the time), emphasized the importance of asking the right question and being sensitive to the possibility that the data were moved by forces other than those included in the model one might be considering at the moment.

I also learned much from fellow students. The world was much smaller and less competitive then. At Berkeley I studied together with Yair Mundlak and overlapped with Irma Adelman and Arnold Zellner. My Chicago class included Yehuda Grunfeld, Walter Oi and Meyer Burstein. Around me, participating in the Public Finance Workshop under the leadership of Arnold Harberger were Gregory Chow, Richard Muth, Marc Nerlove, Lester Telser and others. Gary Becker was still there and Martin J. Bailey, Jacob Mincer, Robert Mundell and John F. Muth were post-doctoral fellows (in different years). Dale Jorgenson visited there in 1962–3. It was one of the great Chicago eras.

After I started teaching at Chicago in 1957 and at Harvard in 1969, I continued to learn from my students and collaborators. And I was lucky in encountering very good ones and allowing myself to be influenced by them. An incomplete list would include at Chicago: Yoram Barzel, Eitan Berglas, Robert Evenson, Giora Hanoch, Yoav Kislev, Robert Lucas, G.S. Maddala, Neil Wallace and Finis Welch. At Harvard I gained a great deal from my association with Gary Chamberlain and Ariel Pakes and my many other students, especially Eli Berman, Charles Brown, Iain Cockburn, Judy Hellerstein, Adam Jaffe, Edward Lazear, David Neumark, Paul Ryan and Manuel Trajtenberg.

As my research interests expanded I also made friends outside the immediate departmental setting, including a number of visitors to both Harvard and the National Bureau of Economic Research, without whom much of my work would not have happened. A short but incomplete list would include Ernst Berndt, Yoram Ben-Porath, Franklin Fisher, Bronwyn Hall, Jerry Hausman, Alberto Holly, Dale Jorgenson, Tor Jacob Klette, Jacques Mairesse, Hashem Pesaran, Haim Regev, Vidar Ringstad and Sherwin Rosen. I am grateful to all of them and to others whose names I may have overlooked.

8.2   AGRICULTURAL ECONOMICS AND ECONOMETRICS

My first published paper, 'Specification bias in estimates of production functions' (Griliches 1957b), combined both my interest in econometrics and its application to a substantive question. It was stimulated by Schultz's question in class about the contradiction between farm accounting studies which indicated increasing returns to farm size and production function estimates which showed no such results. I was sitting at the same time in Theil's class and thought that the methodology that he was teaching could be applied to Schultz's question. Both the methodology and the question remained with me, leading to the book on economies of scale with Vidar Ringstad (1971) and continuing to date in my work with Tor Jacob Klette (Klette and Griliches 1996) and Jacques Mairesse.

In my Ph.D. thesis (Griliches 1957a, upon which Griliches 1957c was based) I had used logistic curves to analyze the diffusion of a new technology (hybrid corn). The goal of this work was to show that the process of diffusion of an important technological innovation was amenable to economic analysis. It was rather common, in formal economic analysis of the time, to put such events outside the scope of normal 'equilibrium' theory. Technological change was, and often still is, treated as an exogenous event, something to be taken as given from outside the economic system which needs to be explained by it. The paper indicates that such a dichotomy was not necessary.

The paper interprets the innovation process, that is, the supply of new technology in the form of specific hybrids adaptable to particular areas, and also the diffusion of technology, the speed with which it was being adopted, as being both under the influence of economic variables. It shows how observed differences in the timing of such processes across states and regions can be rationalized by measurable differences in economic incentives. Using the logistic growth curve to summarize the spread of hybrid corn in the various regions of the US, it focused on the estimates of its three main parameters (origin, slope and ceiling) in these regions as different aspects of the diffusion process to be explained by other economic variables.

A number of issues raised or implied in this paper have reverberated through the subsequent literature: Is the logistic the 'right' functional form for the study of diffusion processes? Do most new technologies diffuse in a similar pattern? What is the appropriate model to use in describing and observing diffusion processes? How important are considerations of information diffusion and uncertainty about the qualities of the technology as compared to considerations of size, access to funds, and personal characteristics of the actors in these events?

When I chose the logistic form to analyze diffusion behavior I did it both because the data in front of me looked as if the logistic would fit quite well and because one could give a reasonable theoretic interpretation to it, either as an information-spread phenomenon based on mathematical epidemic models, or as a learning under uncertainty process based on sequential sampling or Bayesian considerations. But I did not claim then, and in fact I do not believe it to be the case now, that the logistic function represents some underlying invariant 'law' of diffusion behavior. That is why I have been somewhat nonplussed by the various efforts to derive 'the' model of diffusion or to argue at length about particular modifications of the functional form, adding more parameters or changing to another growth curve family, such as the Gompertz. If I were to return to this topic today I would take a more 'dynamic' point of view and respecify the model so that the ceiling is itself a function of economic variables that change over time. I tried something like that in an appendix to my thesis, but the state of econometric technology at that time prevented me from pursuing it very far.

Diffusion research emphasizes the role of time (and information) in the transition from one technology of production or consumption to another. If all variables describing individuals and affecting them were observable, one might do without the notion of diffusion and discuss everything within an equilibrium framework. Since much of the interesting data are unobservable, time is brought in to proxy for a number of distinct forces: (1) the decline over time in the real cost of the new technology due to decreasing costs as the result of learning by doing and to cumulative improvements in the technology itself; (2) the fall in price charged for the new technology due to rising competitive pressures faced by its original developers and the growth in the overall market for it; (3) the dying-off of old durable equipment, slowly making room for the new; and, (4) the spread of information about the actual operating characteristics of the technology and the growth in the available evidence as to its workability and profitability. In the work on hybrid corn I focused on the fourth 'disequilibrium' interpretation, and emphasized the importance of differences in profitability both as a stimulus toward closing the disequilibrium gap and as the determinant of the time it takes to become aware of its existence. ('Disequilibrium' here means that additional change, diffusion, will happen even if prices and incomes do not change further, driven by changes in the information available to individual decision makers.) Alternatively (see, for example, David 1969), one can focus on reasons (1) or (3), in which case the existing size distribution of firms or the existing age distribution of the equipment to be replaced becomes one of the major determinants of the rate of 'diffusion' and explanation of how and why 'ceilings' shift over time. The relative importance of these forces varies from technology to technology, and the optimal mode of analysis is likely to be quite sensitive to that and to the kinds of data available to the analyst. In any case, all such approaches lay stress on the economic determinants of diffusion although they differ in the emphasis that they put on them.

In my original paper I emphasized differences in 'profitability' as the major determinant of the rate of diffusion, and claimed in a final footnote that all other possible determinants such as various personal variables suggested by sociologists could be given an economic interpretation. This led to some controversy in the pages of *Rural Sociology* (see Brandner and Strauss 1959 and Havens and Rogers 1961). One of my responses to such comments, 'Profitability versus interaction: another false dichotomy' (Griliches 1962), gives the flavor of this type of debate. If I were to rewrite my original paper today, I would still take the same position but add 'and vice-versa' at the end of that footnote. This view was reflected in the conclusions to my second rejoinder in this series with the following comment:

> In general I see little point in pitting one factor against another as *the* explanation of the rate of adoption. The world is just too complicated for such an approach to be fruitful. Thus I regret some of my previous 'all or none' remarks. . . . If one broadens my 'profitability' approach to allow for differences in the amount of information available to different individuals, differences in risk preferences, and similar variables, one can bring it as close to the 'sociological' approach as one would want to. The argument here is really not about different explanations of the same phenomenon, but about the usefulness of different languages in interpreting [it]. . . . While this is not a trivial issue, the same explanations can usually be stated in either language. Problems of terminology are ultimately of secondary importance. Terminology is a means not an end. (Griliches 1962, p. 330)

The central fact studied in my work on agriculture was the delay in adjustment to the introduction of a new technology and the slow diffusion of this technology across farmers, space and time. When I turned from hybrid corn to the analysis of other major changes that were happening in US agriculture, mechanization and the growth in fertilizer use, it was clear that I needed a different model, one with shifting 'ceilings', where these ceilings were themselves functions of economic ('profitability of use') variables. A suitable alternative approach to the study of such delays was developing at Chicago, inspired in part by Milton Friedman's (1957) distinction between permanent and transitory influences on behavior and Cagan's (1956) work on adaptive expectations in hyperinflations, and reflected in Nerlove's paper (1956; see also his 1958 thesis for Johns Hopkins University but written largely at Chicago) on the supply response of farmers. Marc Nerlove was a student at Chicago at about the same time, Phil Cagan had just finished his dissertation there, and Hans Theil, who was one of my teachers, had brought Koyck's (1954) model to Chicago. In this model the 'desired' level of use, which I identified with the 'ceiling' of my earlier model, is a function of the underlying, more permanent, economic variables, while actual use approaches this level only gradually, both because of uncertainty about its exact location and because of costs of adjustment and other inertia factors. I used this model rather successfully to analyze the rise in fertilizer use and the growth in the demand for tractors, showing that their spread could be explained as a response to falling real prices plus a reasonable lag in adjustment to such changes (see Griliches 1958a; 1959; 1960a). The switch to a 'demand' model was not thought by me as an abandonment of the diffusion model. It was rather an alternative approach to the same type of problem:

> Let this be clear. The author's argument is not that there was no learning involved in effecting these large increases in fertilizer consumption, only that the process should not be treated as exogenous. This learning process can be viewed largely as the result of changing relative prices and should be treated within the framework of economics and not outside of it. Any substantial change in relative prices will always involve some 'learning' on the part of the entrepreneurs. While things are stable there is no point in knowing anything more than the physical and economic facts in the neighborhood of the current equilibrium. Only when there are substantial changes in the relevant variables is there an incentive to get busy and learn 'new' things (Griliches 1958a, pp. 605–6; see also Atkinson and Stiglitz 1969 for a much later working out of similar ideas).

As I started using partial adjustment models in an alternative analysis of the spread of tractors and fertilizer use in agriculture (Griliches 1958a; 1960a), I became aware of the specification problems raised by the presence of lagged dependent variables in such models.

8.3   AGGREGATION AND THE FUNCTIONAL FORM

At the same time as I was writing my first papers, Yehuda Grunfeld was working on his thesis on investment behavior, using time series on a number of large US firms (Grunfeld 1960). It raised the question, what was the gain from using micro data instead of the then more readily available industry level aggregates? Using methodology partly borrowed from Theil we showed that in the context of incomplete and misspecified micro-models the gain from disaggregation could be illusory (Griliches and Grunfeld 1960). Grunfeld died in a tragic accident in 1960. In 1963–4 I visited Theil's institute in Rotterdam and pursued this topic further, in part as a memorial to Yehuda (Griliches and Wallace 1965). Our original paper, with its ambiguous message, was quite controversial and led to a small literature (Aigner and Goldfeld 1974; Edwards and Orcutt 1969; Barker and Pesaran 1990, among others). I myself did not heed this message and pursued the analysis of micro data for most of the rest of my professional life. Nevertheless, it came back to haunt me, as I came to realize again and again how much error, or rather irrelevant variation, there was in the micro data and how incomplete were our models as descriptions of actual individual behavior. This realization permeates many of my subsequent papers.

My paper on 'Cost allocation in railroad regulation' (Griliches 1972) started out as a consulting report and an analysis of alternative ways of dealing with heteroskedasticity but turned quickly into another example of specification analysis where the answer depends largely on the way the question is posed. The issue was economies of scale, but the methodology did not produce a unique answer to it. Since the resulting function was nonlinear, the answer depended on the level at which the scale elasticity was evaluated. It mattered whether the question was asked for the average railroad or the average ton-mile, since the railroads in the sample differed greatly in size.

8.4   MORE ECONOMETRICS: DISTRIBUTED LAGS, ERRORS IN VARIABLES AND PANEL DATA

The central problem with lagged adjustment models of the type I was using in the analysis of the demand for fertilizers and tractors is the difficulty of distinguishing the source of the apparent slowness in response: Are the actors slow because they face high adjustment costs? Are they slow because they are uncertain about the information available to them and are waiting for more evidence for a move? Or are they only apparently slow because the models leave out important forces affecting their behavior which change only slowly?

Pondering the latter question led me to write 'A note on serial correlation bias' (Griliches 1961a) which suggested a way of distinguishing between the first and last interpretation of what appeared to be rather low adjustment coefficients estimated by OLS. The simple idea was to nest the first in the third, by adding lagged x's to the equation, and testing the pure serial correlation interpretation. This suggestion became popular in the UK literature under the Comfac Test name and has been attributed to the late Denis Sargan. Denis had actually visited Chicago at about the time I was writing this. Neither of us, I think, thought of it as all that original. It was pretty obvious and clearly in the air at that time.

Working with distributed lag models one quickly wants to move beyond the simple geometric form introduced by both Cagan and Koyck. A number of efforts were made to generalize the available functional forms, most notably by Almon (1965) and Jorgenson (1966). What I did in my distributed lags survey paper (Griliches 1967a) was to connect both the functional form and identification issues in an applied context. I still believe that there is much useful material there, though the field has moved away from such models to the estimation of unconstrained VARs at one extreme and an emphasis on 'cointegration' at the other.

The increased availability of panel data has made possible the estimation of more general models but also faced us with new problems. Estimating distributed lag models requires a history of the relevant influences but, because of the shortness of such panels, much of the relevant history is 'pre-history' and is absent from the data. The paper written with Ariel Pakes assumes a relatively simple pattern for such 'pre-histories' which allows it to estimate the 'visible' part of the lag structure even in the absence of earlier data (Griliches and Pakes 1984). This topic is considered further in Griliches (1986b).

My move towards the analysis of micro data faced me with a new set of problems, primarily in the form of erroneous or missing data. I struggled with various aspects of such problems in a number of papers. The first in this series (Griliches and Ringstad 1970) uses a very simple model to show that there is a sense in which random errors in variables lead to even greater biases in nonlinear models than in linear ones. The second, my Oslo Schultz lecture (Griliches 1974), surveys the field more generally and discusses issues of specification associated with left-out 'unobservable' variables, such as 'ability', common to several equations or observations, and introduces the work on siblings which I had started with Gary Chamberlain. The next paper on brothers is joint with Chamberlain and represents one of my efforts to 'solve' the left-out 'ability bias' problem in the estimation of returns to education (Griliches and Chamberlain 1975). I had already started worrying about it earlier (Griliches 1970; Griliches and Mason 1972) and it also constitutes the main topic of my more applied papers assembled in Griliches (1998a, pt. IV.c).

Panel data suffer from a variety of missing data problems. Moreover, when one tries to 'solve' them by just using the 'good' and balanced portion of the data, one runs into serious sample selectivity problems. My paper, written jointly with Jerry Hausman and Bronwyn Hall (1978), represents an early attempt to grapple with such issues. It is still useful, I think, for its relatively simple introduction to Heckman's (1979) methodology, its generalization to a two-equation system, and the elementary exposition of the missing data problem. The latter topic is pursued further in Bound, Griliches and Hall (1986). Further results can be found in Clint Cummins (1989) and Little and Rubin (1987) and the literature cited therein. For more recent approaches to the sample selection problem see, for example, Olley and Pakes (1996) and Woolridge (1990).

Many of my papers discuss the consequences of various misspecifications for the interpretation of relatively simple modes of analysis, usually simple least squares, without presenting alternative estimation methodologies (except for a plea for better data and less ambitious questions). My paper with Hausman (Griliches and Hausman 1986) presents a rather ingenious solution to the random errors in variables problem in panel data, where past and future values of the same variables are available to be used as instruments This has had a significant impact on the literature and I am rather proud of it; see Biorn (1996) and Klette and Willassen (1993) for more recent discussion of this topic.

8.5   PRODUCTIVITY AND R&D

Most of the papers in Griliches (1988a) grew out of my interest in productivity measurement and attempts to do it 'right', or at least better than was being done at the time. The productivity literature of the time computed rather large unexplained 'residuals' in output growth and attributed them largely to 'technological change'. I was dissatisfied with this state of affairs. As an econometrician I found the spectacle of our economic models yielding large residuals uncomfortable, even when we fudged the issue by renaming the residual as technical change and then claimed credit for 'measuring' it. Also the link between such a residual and my earlier work on actual changes in techniques, e.g. hybrid corn, was tenuous and unclear. My own approach to this problem could be best described as a version of specification analysis, a topic which became the major concern in my work on econometric methodology. I wanted to examine both the specification of the model used to compute such 'residuals' and the ingredients, the data, used in their implementation. My first published paper in this area, 'Measuring inputs in agriculture' (Griliches 1960b), already sounds this note, though it is focused primarily on issues associated with the measurement of some of the most important inputs in agriculture: fertilizer, farm machinery and labor. All of the issues raised in this paper, especially the correct measurement of capital, the right price indexes for deflating output and input, and the role of education in affecting the quality of the labor force, continued to preoccupy me in the years to come.

It may be useful, at this point, to sketch out a more explicit statement of the productivity measurement problem. It provides a framework and a motivation for much of the research that was to come. A conventional measure of residual technical change (TFP) in an industry can be written as

$$\hat{t} = y - sk - (1-s)n$$

where y, k, and n are percentage rates of growth in output, capital and labor respectively; s is the share of capital in total factor payments, and the relevant notion of capital corresponds to an aggregate of actual machine hours weighted by their respective base period (equilibrium) rentals. This procedure assumes that all the variables are measured correctly, that all the relevant variables are included, and that factor prices represent adequately the marginal productivity of the respective inputs. The last assumption is equivalent to the assumption of competitive equilibrium and constant returns to scale. To analyze t, the 'unexplained' part of output growth, it is useful first to think in terms of a more general underlying production function:

$$y^* - f = \alpha(k^* - f) + \beta(n^* - f) + \gamma z + t$$

$$y = y^* + u$$

where the 'true' production function is defined in terms of correctly measured outputs and inputs (the starred magnitudes) and at the technologically more relevant plant or firm level. That is, f is the rate of growth of the number of plants (firms) in the industry and, implicitly, the production function is defined at the average plant level; α and β are the true elasticities of output with respect to capital and labor, while γ is the elasticity of output with respect to the z's, the inputs (or, rather, their rate of growth) which affect output but are not included in the standard accounting system. These could be services from the accumulated stock of past private research and development expenditures or services from the cumulated value of public (external) investments in research and extension in agriculture and other industries, or measurable disturbances such as weather or earthquakes. The measurement error in output is u. It differs from t in being more random and transitory while the forces behind t are thought to be more permanent and cumulative. The α, β, and γ coefficients need not be constants. If they are we have the Cobb-Douglas case. The whole framework can be complicated and generalized by adding square terms in rates of growth as approximations to a CES or translog type production function.

Defining two more shorthand terms: $s^* = \alpha/(\alpha + \beta) = \alpha/(1 + h)$ where s^* is the true relative share of capital, and $h = \alpha + \beta - 1$ is a measure of economies of scale with respect to the conventional inputs k and n; the production function can be rewritten in terms of the 'true' residual measure of technical change t, as

$$t = (y - u - f) - (1 + h)[s * k * + (1 - s*)n * - f]$$

Subtracting this from the conventional measure of residual technical change $\hat{t}$ we get an expression for the total 'error' in our usual measures of total factor productivity growth:

$$\hat{t} - t = s(k * - k) + (1 - s)(n * - n) + (s * - s)(k * - n*)$$
$$+ h[s * k * + (1 - s*)n * - f] + \gamma z + u$$

The various terms in this formula can be interpreted as follows. The first term is the effect of the rate of growth in the measurement error of conventional capital measures on the estimated 'residual'. The second term reflects errors in the measurement and definition of labor input. The third term reflects errors in assessing the relative contribution of labor and capital to output growth. It would be zero if factor shares were in fact proportional to their respective production function elasticities or if all inputs were growing at the same rate (then the relative weights do not matter). The fourth term is the economies of scale term. It would be zero if there were no underlying economies of scale in production ($h = 0$) or if the rate of growth in the number of new firms (plants) just equalled the growth in total (weighted) input. The fifth term (γz) reflects the contribution of left-out inputs (private or public), while the sixth term (u) represents the various remaining errors in the measurement of output.

This list of issues dominated my subsequent research activities, and provides a unifying framework for what at times appear to be rather disparate strands of work. My interest in the measurement of 'correct' prices started with difficulties in the measurement of fertilizer and machinery capital in agriculture and led me to resurrect the 'hedonic regression' approach to the measurement of quality change in the Stigler committee staff report (Griliches 1961b). This paper was quite influential, and a whole literature developed in its wake, influencing the measurement of real-estate prices, wage equations, environmental amenities and other aspects of 'qualitative differences'. I myself wrote a number of additional papers (Griliches 1964a; Ohta and Griliches 1976; 1986), supervised several dissertations in this area and edited a book of essays on this range of topics (Griliches 1971a). The introduction to this book provided a review of this literature as of the end of the subsequent decade, and when I had it reprinted in Griliches (1988a) I added a postscript in which I commented briefly on the highlights of this strand of work as it continued to expand in the next two decades. I did not stay in the center of this field for long. But it was gratifying to observe that the methods outlined in this paper have recently received, with a lag of 28 years or so, their official 'approval'. The newly revised US national income accounts incorporate a new index of computer prices based on such 'hedonic' methods (see the January 1986 issue of the *Survey of Current Business*).

This work connected also to my more general interest in the measurement of capital in the context of the measurement of productivity change. Griliches (1963c), produced for the Yehuda Grunfeld memorial volume, represents an early and rather incomplete statement of my position on this matter, which was later to be refined in the joint work with Jorgenson. The difficulty with the available capital measures then, and to a great extent still now, was, in my view, the fact that they were being over-deflated and over-depreciated, that items with different expected lives were being added together in a wrong way, and that no allowance was being made for changes in the utilization of such capital. The over-deflation issue was already alluded to in the discussion of my work on price deflators; it was fed by the strong suspicion that the various available machinery and durable equipment price indexes did not take quality change into account adequately, if at all. This issue connects also to the 'embodied' technical change idea (Solow 1960) and the literature that flowed from it. My view on over-depreciation remains controversial (see Miller 1983). I myself turned early to the evidence of used-machinery markets to point out that the official depreciation numbers were too high, that they were leading to an underestimate of actual capital accumulation, but I also argued that the observed depreciation rates in second-hand markets contain a large obsolescence component, induced by the rising quality of new machines. This depreciation is a valid subtraction from the present value of a machine in current prices, but it is not the right concept to be used in the construction of a constant quality notion of the flow of services from the existing capital stock in 'constant prices'. The fact that new machines are better does not imply that the 'real' flow of services available from the old machines has declined, either potentially or actually. In several places I tried also to explore some of these issues econometrically (see especially Griliches and Pakes 1984) but the available data on types of machinery in place and their actual age structure have been rather sparse, and there has been less progress in this direction than I might have hoped at that time.

A further problem with R&D is that if one is to treat technological change as endogenous, as something that is being 'produced' by the economic system and the actors in it and not like some manna from heaven, one needs to look for its sources, for the activities that cause it, directly or indirectly.

Organized R&D activity is clearly one such source, perhaps the major one, though clearly not the sole one. One way of showing this is to compute the social returns from such investments and show that they are positive and sizeable. Another way is to try to extend the national growth accounts to incorporate R&D as another investment activity and reinterpret them in this light. My R&D papers explore both of these approaches.

Griliches (1958b) presents the first detailed calculation of social returns from a public research program. It was a by-product of my thesis research on hybrid corn diffusion. As part of that research I had also collected information on hybrid corn research expenditures in agricultural experiment stations and private seed companies. I used these data, together with an estimate of the value of the additional corn yielded by hybrids, to construct an estimate of social returns from this activity and compare them to the social cost incurred in generating them.

The ratio of returns to costs turned out, perhaps unsurprisingly so, to be very high, and the resulting number, '743 per cent', was used rather widely in subsequent research funding debates. This number is a benefit-cost ratio. The comparable internal rate of return was estimated at 40 per cent per annum, still a rather high number. The paper also presents similar computations for agricultural research as a whole and a projection of social returns from hybrid sorghum research, which was then only in the beginning of its diffusion phase. The methodology of this kind of calculation was taken over, extended and improved by others. A number of similar calculations were made for other agricultural research programs (a summary of some of these can be found in Evenson *et al.* 1979). A related approach to the computation of private and social returns for a number of manufacturing innovations was developed by Mansfield and his co-workers (Mansfield *et al.* 1977). In general, most efforts to trace the results of individual public and private research endeavors have found rather high social returns to them.

Such individual invention or innovation cost and returns calculations are very data- and time-expensive, and are always subject to attack for not being representative, since they tend to concentrate on the prominent and the successful, and for attributing all the results to the particular research program examined without ever being able to trace back all of the other possible contributors to its success. This is why in later work I turned away from individual event studies to direct econometric estimation of the contribution of R&D to productivity using one or another version of the production function approach to this problem. This approach abandons much of the interesting specific detail about individual innovations, concentrating instead on estimating the relationship between total output or productivity and various measures of current and past R&D expenditures (and other variables). All productivity growth (to the extent that it is measured correctly) is related to all expenditures on R&D, and an attempt is made to estimate statistically the part of productivity growth that might be attributed to R&D (and/or to its various components). The difficulties associated with this approach are surveyed in my *Bell Journal* paper (Griliches 1979a). Examples of this type of analysis can be found in the two agricultural production function papers (Griliches 1963b; 1964b), and will be discussed in somewhat more detail below.

The issues that arise in trying to extend this type of analysis out of the agricultural sector and onto the national scene are discussed in my 'Research expenditures and growth accounting' (Griliches 1973), which was written for an International Economics Association conference in St Anton in 1971. It provides a brief review of the literature as it had evolved up to that time, estimates the social rate of return to R&D in manufacturing at about 30 per cent per annum, using Census of Manufactures data on 85 industries during 1958–63, and discusses how such results could be incorporated into an amended national accounting framework. Besides the usual econometric problems involved in estimating production functions, it raised a number of issues which have continued to worry me over the years to come: (1) difficulties in the measurement of R&D output in the public sector which is its largest 'consumer' (defense, space and health research); (2) difficulties in measuring the output of, and quality improvements in, technologically complex commodities such as computers and communication equipment; (3) accounting problems arising from the fact that R&D labor and capital expenditures are already included once in the conventional labor and capital figures (see Schankerman 1981); and (4) the problem of externalities and 'spillovers', the contribution of research in other laboratories, firms, industries and countries to the success of a particular research project.

In spite of these difficulties I have kept working on this range of problems to this day because I believe in the importance of science and organized research activity to economic growth in this country and the world at large, and in the necessity to comprehend it. In the late 1960s I initiated a large collaborative project with the Bureau of the Census to match the R&D data they had collected for the NSF at the firm level with other economic data on these same firms. The results of this work on R&D returns at the firm level were published in Griliches (1980a). A subsequent round of replication and extension of this work to a later period occupied me for a good part of the 1970s and is summarized in Griliches (1986a). That paper also addresses the issue whether the role of R&D has declined in recent years (concluding in the negative) and emphasizes the contribution of basic research to productivity growth in the 1970s. Recently I have been engaged in a large-scale study trying to use patent data to measure some aspects of R&D 'output', and to understand the invention-innovation process better. For a summary of the results from this range of studies, see Griliches (1984b; 1990).

The role of R&D, if any, in the pervasive productivity growth slowdown in the 1970s and 1980s was the topic of concern in a number of my other papers. I have come to a negative conclusion on this topic (see Griliches and Lichtenberg 1984 and Griliches 1986a) but not because of the unimportance of R&D. It is my belief that one cannot see the impact of R&D on the production possibilities frontier of the economy in periods when the economy is not on this frontier or close to it. When the economy is not operating at full capacity it is hard to tell what is happening to its potential for production and growth. It may indeed be the case that the cessation of growth in real R&D expenditures in the 1960s did contribute to our problems in the 1970s and 1980s. Or so I thought in 1971 when I wrote: 'This [contribution of R&D to growth in 1970] is about two-thirds of the comparable number for 1966 and reflects the rather significant slowdown in the rate of growth of R&D expenditures. Given the lags involved, this reduction may not show up, however, until the mid seventies' (Griliches 1973; p. 73). But one cannot decide that on the basis of the currently available data. The energy price shock-induced worldwide recessions of 1974–5 and 1979–80 make it difficult to find traces of the R&D growth slowdown in the aggregate data; especially since much of the direct effect of such expenditures is not captured in these kind of data in the first place.

8.6   EDUCATION AND GROWTH

I also developed an interest in education, its contribution to economic growth, its impact on economic inequality and the issues involved in trying to assess the quantitative magnitude of such effects. It grew out of my work on adjusting productivity measures for the changing quality of the labor force, especially its level of schooling, and my association at Chicago with Theodore Schultz, Jacob Mincer and Gary Becker who were developing the human capital idea at that time. The labor quality adjustments described in Jorgenson and Griliches (1967) and Griliches (1970) use observed earnings differences by level of schooling to weight different workers. Such computations assume that: (a) differences in earnings correspond to differences in contributions (marginal products) to national or sectoral output; (b) that they are in fact due to schooling and not to other factors such as native ability or family background which happen to be correlated with schooling; and (c) that the production function can be, in fact, written in such a way that the various types of labor can be aggregated into one total quality-adjusted labor input index. These assumptions were obviously controversial and were challenged from many directions. I was uneasy myself with 'adjustments' for which there was no direct evidence. I embarked, therefore, on a series of econometric studies whose basic purpose was to investigate the validity of such estimates of the contribution of education to productivity and economic growth.

'Notes on the role of education' (Griliches 1970) discusses almost all of the issues raised by such computations. The first issue to be tackled is whether differences in schooling do indeed have productivity consequences. The only way I saw of testing it, rather than just assuming that wage differences are proportional to differences in marginal products, was to include an education-based measure of labor quality separately when estimating a production function, and check on its statistical significance and economic importance. If one defines a multiplicative quality index and uses a Cobb-Douglas production function framework, one has the additional implication that the coefficient of such a 'quality' variable should be approximately equal to the coefficient of the labor quantity variable. This is the rationale behind a series of empirical studies of productivity differences in agriculture and manufacturing summarized in the first section of this paper. Besides reviewing the work on regional differences in agricultural productivity it also summarizes my later work on state-industry productivity differences in manufacturing (Griliches 1967b; 1968). In general it supports the use of schooling-per-worker indexes as a productivity-relevant quality dimension of labor input. The inclusion of such variables in production functions results in coefficients that are statistically 'significant' and have the right order of magnitude. This work also anticipates and responds, in a way, to a new strand of criticism which was to arise later in the literature under the label of 'signalling' (Spence 1974). It provides direct evidence on the 'productivity' of education without using the *a priori* theoretical assertion that wage differences reflect marginal product differences. (A survey of similar later work can be found in Jamison and Lau 1982.)

The most direct challenge to the original estimates of the contribution of schooling to economic growth was the issue of 'ability'. To what extent did observed income differentials exaggerate the contribution of schooling because of a positive correlation between native ability and the levels of schooling achieved by different parts of the population? There were rather conflicting views on this at that time (early to mid-1960s). Denison (1964), for example, claimed at first (on the basis of very little data) that as much as 40 per cent of the observed income differentials could be due to the correlation of schooling with ability (though his later estimates do not use this type of adjustment). This seemed rather high to me, and I embarked on a search for data that would throw some light on this topic. I have still to emerge from this search.

The first and most obvious thing to do is to find data on both schooling and ability, and to hold ability constant in calculating the appropriate returns to schooling. The few scattered bits of evidence that were available on this topic at that time led me to the conclusion that 'ability bias' could not be as high as asserted by Denison. I kept looking, however, for more representative and convincing data. The first large dataset I analyzed (in Griliches and Mason 1972) was based on the NORC-CPS 1964 match of US Army veterans with data on earnings, schooling before and after service in the armed forces, family and other demographic background data, and AFQT (Armed Forces Qualification Test) scores. Using AFQT as the 'ability' measure resulted in the conclusion that the bias in the estimated returns to schooling from this source was smaller than had been expected: on the order of 10–15 per cent or about one percentage point of the estimated rate of return of about 6 per cent. This conclusion was later supported by Gary Chamberlain's (1977) reanalysis of these same data using more advanced statistical techniques, and my own work using IQ scores and data on siblings from the National Longitudinal Survey of Young Men (see Griliches 1976; 1977; 1978; 1979b; 1980b; c; and Bound, Griliches and Hall 1986, and the discussion in the postscript on education and economic growth in Griliches 1988a, pp. 220–3).

During the mid-1960s, when much of this work was initiated, I was writing against the background of a rapidly expanding educational system. Very few large industries were growing at anywhere near the same rate. I began to worry, therefore, whether this increase in the number of highly educated workers would not drive down their market price and the associated rate of return to higher education. The superficial signs were all positive, however. The observed relative constancy of skill and educational wage differentials during the 1950s and 1960s could be interpreted as implying that the demand for skilled workers is highly elastic, allowing one to hope that since past expansions in the educated labor force had not reduced them, neither would the current and future expansions.

But I had not noticed that the big demographic swing and the associated accelerator-like expansion in the demand for teachers had greatly distorted the observed data and made the persistence of such trends into the future quite unlikely. Neither did I realize that the big government-financed space-defence-R&D boom was something that might not last forever, or appreciate the fact that much of the impact of the growth in higher education on the labor force was delayed because of the large expansion in graduate education. It was not until 1968 that 'net' production of BAs (those entering the labor market rather than continuing on to graduate school) began rising above its 1952 levels. By the early 1970s an annual wave of about an additional million highly educated workers began arriving at the doors of the full-time labor force and the rate of return to schooling did decline significantly (Freeman 1976).

One of the possible explanations offered for the then-perceived constancy of educational wage differentials and a source of optimism for the future was the 'capital–skill complementarity' hypothesis. This is the idea that skilled labor is complementary to, rather than a substitute for, various advanced forms of machinery and that therefore a rapid rate of capital accumulation (and innovation) will increase the demand for such labor and prevent the fall in its relative price. This argument is already outlined in my 'Notes on the role of education' paper (Griliches 1970), and a more serious attempt at testing it is attempted in my 'Capital–skill complementarity' note (Griliches 1969) which uses data for US manufacturing industries in 1954 and 1963, and shows that skilled labor is more complementary with physical capital than unskilled labor. Further work along these lines has been done by Dougherty (1972), Weiss (1974), Welch (1970), Fallon and Layard (1975), Welch *et al.* (1985) and Morrison and Berndt (1981).

A major recent strand of criticism of human capital work is that schooling does little more than sort individuals according to ability, and that the resulting private returns to schooling overestimate significantly the rather meagre social returns from such an activity (Spence 1974 and Arrow 1973). There are two versions of this argument:

1   Schools do little but sorting. No additional 'real' human capital is embodied (augmented) during the schooling process itself.
2   Sorting itself is not particularly socially productive, it only exacerbates income inequality, and leads people to over-invest in activities such as schooling which are supposed to certify (signal) their potential abilities to ignorant employers.

There is a major important, though not all that novel, theoretical point contained in these criticisms. In a world of uncertainty in which information and the appearance of information has value, the private returns from the production and dissemination of information can easily exceed the social returns from the same activity. But the empirical import of such criticisms appears to me to be quite exaggerated.

Screening and signalling, like ability and motivation, are generalized concepts with few observable empirical counterparts that one could get one's teeth (or computers) into. If the returns to schooling were largely due to the informational content of the certificate and not to the process of schooling itself, one would expect that: (1) cheaper ways of testing and certifying would be developed by employers and employees; (2) the returns to schooling would be lower among the self-employed versus wage and salary workers since, presumably, the self-employed would not pay themselves (or be able to collect) for a false signal (cf. Wolpin 1977); and (3) the returns to schooling should decline with age as more experience is accumulated by employers about the 'true' worth of their employees and as the initial signal provided by schooling fades away into insignificance. None of these effects is observed in the data, leading one to question the empirical import of the 'schooling as a signal' hypothesis.

The issue of who gets schooling was not adequately considered in the earlier literature, and the radical critics have rightfully, I think, focused their attention on the exaggerated hopes for egalitarianism that were implicit in some of the more extreme 'schooling is good for everything' positions. First, it is relatively easy to see that a general expansion in schooling need not result in any reduction in inequality. Second, the large public investments in schooling, like much of other governmental investment, were not as progressive as advertised. Much of the benefit of such subsidies redounded to the children of the middle classes, and was dissipated in the induced rise of teacher salaries. Nevertheless, the critics seem to underestimate the amount of social mobility that did occur in the past and the opportunity provided by the schooling system for class turnover (see Blau and Duncan 1967; Hauser and Featherman 1977; and Jencks *et al.* 1979 on schooling as a source of social mobility in the US), and the use of this route for social mobility by specifically disadvantaged ethnic groups such as Jews in the earlier part of this century and Blacks more recently (cf. Freeman 1973 and Smith and Welch 1986). Nor do they give enough credit to schooling for the rise in the *average* standard of living in the economy as a whole, and the concomitant driving-up of the price of human time, the one resource distributed relatively equally throughout our economic system.

Finally, there is the strand of criticism that takes the position that none of this can matter much, since little of the total observed inequality of incomes (say the variance in the logarithm of income or wages) can be accounted for by differences in schooling (Jencks 1972). At the individual level, detailed regression equations (income-generating functions) explain only between 30 and 50 per cent of the observed inequalities, and the partial role of schooling differences in such an accounting is much smaller (on the order of 10–15 per cent). There are a number of responses to be made to such criticisms. First, some of the more prominent studies claiming to have shown the importance of 'luck' and the negligible impact of schooling are marred by not taking adequate account of the rather large transitory variations in income at the individual level and by ignoring age, life-cycle effects and on-the-job training differences as a source of *ex-post* but not *ex-ante* inequality. Second, in my Lewis volume paper (Griliches 1976), I show that, while schooling by itself does not account for a great deal of the observed variance in wages or income, additional schooling could be and has been used in the US in the 1960s to overcome social class handicaps and to compensate for and eliminate some of the *systematic* sources of observed income inequality. The estimated model implies that two youngsters who are one standard deviation apart on each of a list of family background variables *and* IQ would find themselves, other things equal, about 0.75 and 0.4 of a standard deviation apart on schooling and wages, respectively, implying a rather strong regression toward the mean. But if the youngster with the lower family background and IQ managed somehow to acquire an extra 4 years of schooling (e.g. went on to and completed college), which would be equal to an additional 1.5 standard deviation units of schooling, this would essentially wipe out his original handicap. If, in fact, he had an equal IQ to start out with, he would need only about 2 more years of schooling to compensate him for his lower social class start.

While these various interpretations and intellectual positions were being debated inside the profession, the world outside was changing, and with it the economic fortunes of the educational system. The slowdown in population growth and in economic growth may bring to an end a 200-year-long era of rising importance of, and rewards in, education. The era was initiated by the 'enlightenment' period, fed by the rapid rise in population which started in the West in the eighteenth century and by the great burst in economic growth and technical change that ran through the nineteenth and twentieth centuries. With both population and economic growth slowing down, and with the educational industry seriously over-extended, it may be in for hard times, at least for a while.

There are other changes that may be also impinging on the scarcity value of knowledge. The technology revolution in communication and copying has reduced significantly the transmission costs of knowledge, and made it even harder to appropriate. It has also increased significantly the flow of information (both relevant and irrelevant) that inundates employers, consumers and public officials. Whether or not this will lower or raise the price of knowledge 'handlers', if not of knowledge 'possessors', is still an open question. It is also quite likely that part of the economic value of education arises out of its interaction with technical change. That is, better-educated entrepreneurs and managers use new technology quicker and current technology better, in the sense of allocating the available resources more optimally. This line of thought (due to Nelson and Phelps 1966 and Welch 1970) would imply that much of the returns to schooling would evaporate if there were no new information to process. Up to now these ideas have been tested only on agricultural data (Huffman 1974; 1977). If they are correct, and if we are entering a period of recovery in the rate of economic growth and technical change, this may also explain the recent rise in the scarcity value of education. In spite of some scattered signs to the contrary I see no deceleration in the rate of technical change in the economy in the immediate future, and hence I remain optimistic about the demand for, and the value of, education in our economy. Indeed, as I argued in my Econometric Society presidential address (Griliches 1977), which surveys the whole field (as of that time), if anything, the returns to education have been under, rather than over, estimated. This conclusion has largely stood the test of time (see the recent work and surveys by Angrist and Krueger 1991; Card 1995; Ashenfelter and Krueger 1992; and others).

8.7   GROWTH ACCOUNTING

I also wrote several papers that try to bring all these strands of work together in some kind of a more complete accounting of the sources of economic growth. Probably the best known of these is 'The explanation of productivity change' (Griliches and Jorgenson 1967), and it may be worthwhile to review some of the issues raised there. In a sense, though, my papers on the explanation of productivity growth in agriculture (Griliches 1963b; 1964b), come closer to representing my own point of view on this topic, then and now.

The Jorgenson and Griliches paper argued that a 'correct' index number framework and the 'right' measurement of inputs would reduce greatly the role of the 'residual' ('advances in knowledge', total factor productivity, disembodied technical change and/or other such terms) in accounting for the observed growth in output. It brought together Jorgenson's work on Divisia indexes, on the correct measurement of cost of capital, and on the right aggregation procedures for it, with my own earlier work on the measurement of capital prices and quality change and the contribution of education to productivity growth. It produced the startling conclusion, already foreshadowed in my agricultural papers, that an adjustment of conventional inputs for measurement and aggregation error may eliminate much of the mystery that was associated with the original findings of large unexplained components in the growth of national and sectoral outputs. It did this with a 'Look Ma! No hands!' attitude, neither using additional outside variables such as R&D, nor allowing for economies of scale or other disequilibria (e.g. differences in rates of return to different private and public investments). This did indeed attract attention and also criticism. The most penetrating criticism came from Denison (1969), and led to an exchange between us in the *Survey of Current Business* (Denison 1972; Griliches and Jorgenson

1972).

Denison found a number of minor errors and one major one in our computations. By trying to adjust for changing utilization rates we used data on energy consumption of electric motors in manufacturing, a direct measure of capital equipment utilization in manufacturing, but extrapolated it also to non-equipment components of capital in manufacturing and to all capital outside of manufacturing, including residential structures. There was also the uneasy issue of integrating a utilization adjustment within what was otherwise a pure equilibrium story. Once we conceded most of the utilization adjustment, our 'explanation' of productivity growth shrank from 94 to 43 per cent, and with it also our claim to 'do it all' (without mirrors).

I still believe, however, that we were right in our basic idea that productivity growth should be 'explained' rather than just measured, and that errors of measurement and concept have a major role in this. But we did not go far enough in that direction. We offered improved index number formulae, a better reweighting of capital input components, a major adjustment of the employment data for improvements in the quality of labor, revisions in investment price indexes and estimates of changes in capital utilization. The potential orders of magnitude of the adjustments based on the first two contributions, index number formulae and the reweighting of capital components, are not large enough to account for a major part of the observed 'residual'. The labor quality adjustment was not really controversial, but the capital price indexes and utilization adjustments deserve a bit more discussion. We argued for the idea that technical change could be thought of, in a sense, as being 'embodied' in factor inputs, in new machines and human capital, and that a better measurement of these inputs via the non-tautological route of hedonic index numbers for both capital and labor, could account for most of what was being interpreted as a 'residual'. It became clear, however, that without extending our framework further to allow for increasing returns to scale, R&D, sectoral disequilibria and other externalities we were unlikely to approach a full 'explanation' of productivity change (see Griliches and Jorgenson 1972). Such a wider, less equilibrium-based approach, was already pursued in my earlier agricultural productivity papers. Before I turn, however, to a discussion of these papers, there is still some more to be said about the price indexes and utilization adjustments.

It may appear that adjusting a particular input for mismeasured quality change would not have much of an effect on productivity growth measurement, since one would need also to adjust the output figures for the corresponding industry. But as long as the share of this industry in final output is less than the elasticity of output with respect to this input, the two adjustments will not cancel themselves out. Since the share of investment in output is significantly lower than reasonable estimates of the share of capital in total factors costs, adjusting capital for mismeasurement of its prices does lead to a net reduction in the computed residual. Empirically it is clear that, even without considering any of the potential externalities associated with new capital, there are enough questions about the official price indexes in these areas to make further work on this topic a high priority (see the evidence presented in Griliches 1960b; 1961b; 1971b, and in the subsequent literature discussed in the relevant postscript in Griliches 1988a, pp. 119–22).

The utilization adjustments fit uneasily within the rather strict competitive equilibrium framework of the Jorgenson-Griliches paper. The analogy was made to labor hours, calling for the parallel concept of machine hours as the relevant notion of capital services. We also had in mind the model of a continuous process plant where output is more or less proportional to hours of operation. Since we were interested primarily in 'productivity' change as a measure of 'technical' change, a change that is due to changes in techniques of production, fluctuations in 'utilization', whether a plant worked one shift or two, 10 months or 12, were not really relevant for this purpose. But while labor unemployment was happening off-stage as far as business productivity accounts were concerned, capital 'underemployment' was difficult to reconcile with the maximizing behavior with perfect foresight implicit in our framework.

There are two somewhat separate 'utilization' issues. Productivity as measured is strongly pro-cyclical. Measured inputs, especially capital and labor services, fluctuate less than reported output. The resulting fluctuations in 'productivity' do not make sense if we want to interpret them as a measure of the growth in the level of technology or the state of economically valuable knowledge of an economy. The US economy did not 'forget' 4 per cent of its technology between 1974 and 1975. Nor was there a similar deterioration in the skill of its labor force. (National welfare did go down as the result of OPEC-induced world-wide rise in energy prices, but that is a separate story.)

What is wrong with the productivity numbers in this case is that we do not measure accurately the actual amount of labor or machine hours used rather than just paid for. Since both capital and labor are bought or hired in anticipation of a certain level of activity, and on long-term contracts, actual factor payments do not reflect their respective marginal products except in the case of perfect foresight and only in the long run. Underutilization of factors of production is the result of unanticipated shifts in demand and various rigidities built into the economic system due to longer-term explicit and implicit contracts (and other market imperfections) between worker and employer and seller and buyer. If our interest is primarily in the 'technological' interpretation of productivity measures, we must either ignore such shorter-run fluctuations or somehow adjust for them. This was the rationale behind our original use of energy consumed by electric motors (per installed horsepower) as a utilization adjustment.

We used energy consumption as a proxy for the unobserved variation in machine hours, and not on its own behalf as an important intermediate input. Used in the latter fashion it is a produced input which would cancel out at the aggregate level (as was pointed out by Denison 1969). Alternatively, one could adjust the weight (share) of capital services in one's total input index, to reflect the fact that underutilization of this existing stock of resources should reduce significantly the shadow price of using them (this is the approach suggested in Berndt and Fuss 1986). Unfortunately it is difficult to use the observed factor returns for these purposes, both because prices do not fall rapidly enough in the face of unanticipated demand shocks and because of a variety of longer-run contractual factor payments arrangements which break the link between factor rewards and their current productivity.

In a sense this reflects the failure of the assumption of perfect competition on which much of the standard productivity account is based. The actual world we live in is full of short-run rigidities, transaction costs, immalleable capital and immobile resources, resulting in the pervasive presence of quasi-rents and short-term capital gains and losses. While I do not believe that such discrepancies from 'perfect' competition actually imply the presence of significant market power in most industries (as argued, for example, by Hall 1986), they do make productivity accounting even more difficult.

The other aspect of utilization is the longer-run trend in shift-work, length of the work-week, and changes in hours of operation per day by plants, stores and service establishments. Consider, for example, a decline in overtime or night-shift premia due, say, to a decline in union power. This would reduce the price of certain types of capital services and expand their use. If capital is not measured in machine hours we would show a rise in productivity even though there has been no 'technological' change in methods of production. I would prefer not to include such changes in the productivity definition, since I interpret them as movements along (or toward) a stable production possibilities frontier. But there did occur an organizational change which allowed us to get more 'flow', more hours per day or year, from a given stock of equipment or other resources. One can think of this as a mixture of two types of activities: output production which rents machine and labor hours and the supply of capital (and also effective labor hours) from the existing stock of resources. A decline in overtime premia would be similar to a decline in the tariff on a certain kind of imported input. It would lead to an improvement in 'productivity' but not necessarily to a 'technical' change.

It is still my belief that we need to adjust our data for such capacity utilization fluctuations for a better understanding of 'technical' change, the issue that brought us to this in the first place. A consistent framework for such an adjustment will require, however, the introduction of adjustment costs and *ex-post* errors in the productivity measurement framework. (See Morrison 1985 and the literature cited therein.) It is not clear, however, whether one can separate longer-run developments in the utilization of capital from changes in technology and the organization of society. Much of capital is employed outside continuous process manufacturing and there the connection between productivity and its utilization is much looser. The rising cost of human time and the desire for variety and flexibility have led to much investment in what might be called 'standby' capacity with rather low utilization rates. The hi-fi system in my home is operating only at a fraction of its potential capacity. Much inventory is held in many businesses to economize on other aspects of labor activity. Nor is it clear that an extension of store hours with a resulting decline in productivity per square-foot-hour of store space is necessarily a bad thing. Thus it is difficult to see how one could separate long-run trends in utilization from changes in production and consumption technologies. It is, however, a topic worth studying and a potentially important contributor to 'explanations' of apparent swings in measured productivity statistics.

Whether we include or exclude such changes from our 'productivity' concept will affect our ability to 'account' for them. But that is not the important issue. We do want to measure them, because we do want to understand what happened, to 'explain'. The rest is semantics.

Many of the problems discussed here arise because we do not aggregate adequately and do not describe the production process in adequate detail. A model which would distinguish between the use of capital and labor at different times of the day and year, and would not assume that their shadow prices are constant between different 'hours' or over time, would be capable of handling these kind of shifts. We do not have the data to implement such a program, but it underscores the original message: much of what passes for productivity change in conventional data is the result of aggregation errors, the wrong measurement of input quantities and the use of wrong weights to combine them in 'total factor input' indexes.

Something more should be said about the rather vague notions of 'explanation' and 'accounting'. National income accounts and associated index numbers are economic constructs, based on an implicit model of the economy and a variety of more or less persuasive logical and empirical arguments. It is not well adapted to 'hypothesis testing' or debates about causality. In proposing a better measure of, say, labor, we rely on the evidence of market wage differentials in offering up our improved measure. By bringing in more evidence on this topic we are not just reducing the 'residual' tautologically. But the fact that it goes down as the result of such an adjustment does not make it right either. A different kind of evidence is required to provide a more persuasive justification for such adjustments. That is why I turned early on to the use of production functions for econometric testing. Without moving in such a direction one tends to run into various paradoxes. For example, capital growth accelerated in the 1970s in many industries without a comparable increase in the growth of output. In the index number sense of growth accounting, capital 'explained' a larger fraction of the growth of output and we did, indeed, have a smaller residual. But in spite of this 'accounting', the mystery only deepened.

The 'econometric' approach to growth accounting involves one in the estimation of production functions. This allows one to test or validate a particular way of measuring an input or adjusting it for quality change; to estimate and test the role of left-out public good inputs such as R&D and other externality-generating activities; to estimate economies of scale; and to check on the possibility of disequilibria and estimate the deviation of 'true' output elasticities from their respective factor shares. Production function estimation raises many problems of its own, including issues of aggregation, errors of measurement and simultaneity, but it is one of the few ways available to us for checking the validity of the attribution of productivity growth to its various suggested 'sources'.

Two agricultural production function papers represent my most successful attempts to accomplish this. The first (Griliches 1963b) was based on cross-sectional data for 68 regions of the US in 1949. It used the production function framework to show that education of the farm labor force was an important contributor to productivity, validating this particular adjustment to the measurement of labor input; that the estimated role (elasticity) of farm equipment and machinery was higher and that of farm labor was lower than was implied by their respective factor shares; and that there was evidence of significant economies of scale in agricultural production. These estimates were then applied to the aggregate output and input series for US agriculture in 1940 and 1960, adjusting also the official farm capital series for errors in their deflators, with the result that they 'explained' all, and even somewhat more, of the rise in agricultural output between these years. Griliches (1964b) replicated this approach on state-level data for 1949, 1954 and 1959, and added a measure of public investments in agricultural research and extension to the estimation equation. The results were rather similar: 'education' was significant, and so also was the estimated, though somewhat smaller, economies of scale parameter. The major new finding was the rather large and significant contribution of public R&D and extension expenditures with a rather high implied social rate of return to them. When these estimates were used to analyze aggregate agricultural productivity growth between 1949 and 1959 they could essentially account for all of it, with about one-third to one-half of the total 'explanation' coming from the growth in the scale of the average agricultural enterprise, about one-third coming from public investments in research and extension and the rest being divided about equally between adjustments in the measurement of conventional inputs and adjustments in their relative weights.

This work left me with the conviction that education, investment in research, and economies of scale (both at the level of the firm and at the level of the market) were the important sources of productivity growth in the long run. Since in the paper with Jorgenson we had not allowed for the two latter sources of growth, I was not too surprised or disheartened when it turned out that we could not really explain all of aggregate productivity change by formula and labor quality adjustments alone. It was clear, however, that one would need more and better data to make such additional adjustments more reliable and convincing. I turned, therefore, to trying to amass more data and more evidence on these topics. The task proved harder than I had anticipated, the data sparser and more brittle than one might have wished, and hence my sojourn in this purgatory much longer than I had expected. It is not clear whether we have yet the data to do an adequate and convincing accounting of productivity change at the aggregate level (see, for example, the continued and still unsettled debate about the causes of the recent slowdown in productivity growth). Progress has been made, however, in several directions, and we have now a much better understanding of the measurement issues in the various areas, and also a deeper appreciation of the difficulties involved in saying something definitive about them.

I have already discussed my subsequent work on the productivity of education and the measurement of returns to R&D. The latter topic, which I am still pursuing, suffers especially from the difficulty of tackling the externalities question econometrically. It is difficult, if not impossible, to get a measure of the relative contribution of university science to different industries or of knowledge 'leakages' from one industry or firm to another. But that is where most of what passes for exogenous disembodied technical change may be coming from.

I did pursue the issue of economies of scale quite a bit further. In Griliches (1967b; 1968) I analyzed US manufacturing data by state and industry for 1954, 1958 and 1963, and found persistent and significant but relatively small traces of economies of scale (on the order of 1.05). This work was based on per-establishment averages for different states and industries. Since I thought of economies of scale as primarily a micro-phenomenon, occurring at the plant or firm level, I kept looking around for relevant micro-data to pursue this topic further. In the late 1960s I gained access to the micro-data from the Norwegian Census of Manufactures, and together with Vidar Ringstad produced a detailed study of it (Griliches and Ringstad 1971). There too significant but not very large economies of scale (about 1.05) appeared to be present. In spite of the a *priori* conviction in their importance, it was much harder to find significant traces of economies of scale in manufacturing than in agriculture. The main difficulty arises from the fact that different size plants and firms, even in well-defined industries, rarely produce the same type of product or sell it at the same price. And there is, usually, no adequate price or product detail available at the plant level in census-type data. Thus, despite much work, little convincing evidence has been produced on this topic either in the US or elsewhere. The main evidence on the potential importance of economies of scale has come from data on regulated utilities, where the product is much more homogeneous and the data are more plentiful (see Nerlove 1963 and McFadden 1978 for examples of such work, and the various papers in Fuss *et al.* 1978 for a more extensive discussion of some of these issues).

Even though we now have more data, more advanced econometric technology and better computer resources, the overall state of this field has not advanced greatly in the past 20 years. We are really not much closer to an 'explanation' of the observed changes in the various productivity indexes. A tremendous effort was launched by Jorgenson and his co-workers (Christensen, Fraumeni, Gollop, Nishimizu and others) to improve and systematize the relevant data sources, to produce and analyze a consistent set of industry-level total factor productivity accounts, to extend and generalize our original labor quality adjustments and to extend all of this also to international comparisons of productivity. In the process, however, rather than pursuing the possibly hopeless quest for a complete 'explanation' of productivity growth, they chose to focus instead on developing more precise and detailed productivity measures at various levels of aggregation and devising statistical models for their analysis. Denison (1974; 1979), in parallel, was pursuing his quest for a more complete accounting of the sources of growth, putting together as many reasonable scraps of information as were available, but not embedding them in a clear theoretical framework or an econometrically testable setting. The incompleteness of both approaches, and the unsatisfactory state of this field as a whole, was revealed by the sharp and prolonged slowdown in the growth of measured productivity which began in the mid-1970s. Despite the best attempts of these and other researchers it has not been possible to account for this slowdown within the standard growth accounting framework without concluding that the 'residual' had changed, that the growth rate of total factor productivity growth rate fell some time in the late 1960s or early 1970s (see Denison 1984; Griliches 1980d; Kendrick 1983 and many others).

I do not believe, however, that this slowdown can be interpreted as implying that the underlying rate of technical change has slowed down, that we have exhausted our technological frontiers. In my opinion it was caused by misguided macro-policies induced by the oil price shocks and the subsequent inflation and the fears thereof. Without allowing for errors in capital accumulation (which continued initially at a rather high rate, in spite of the sharp declines in aggregate demand) and widespread underutilization of capacity, it is not possible to interpret the conventional productivity statistics. Surely 'knowledge' did not retreat. Moreover, I do not believe that one can use statistics from such periods to infer anything about longer-term technological trends. If we are not close to our production possibilities frontier we cannot tell what is happening to it, and whether the underlying growth rate of an economy's 'potential' has slowed down or not. We need a better-articulated theoretical framework, one that would allow for long-term factor substitution and short-term rigidities and errors, for dynamics and for adjustment costs, before we are able to understand what has happened to us recently. We also need better data, especially on output and input prices and various aspects of labor and capital utilization.

In the long run productivity grows when we either acquire more resources or figure out better ways of using them. Better ways can mean moving available resources into more productive uses and eliminating various obstacles to their full utilization. It also means finding entirely new ways of satisfying human needs and desires through new products, processes, and new organizational arrangements. All such activities are affected by economic forces and will repay economic study.

8.8   OTHER TOPICS

My interest in production functions and my first foray into manufacturing data led to an unpublished Rotterdam working paper (Griliches 1963a). This was followed by Griliches (1967b) which sets up a large agenda, investigating functional form issues and largely accepting the Cobb-Douglas, looking for economies of scale, and discussing labor and capital measurement issues; all topics that continued to haunt me. There was also a sequel paper on the estimation of CES-type functions based on manufacturing data by states (Griliches 1967c).

Another sequel paper, recomputing some of the results on later data, is Griliches (1968). When I gave a version of this paper at the 1965 World Congress of the Econometric Society in Rome, Arne Amundsen of the Central Statistical Bureau of Norway was my discussant. His main question was why didn't I use micro data on firms directly instead of these funny state aggregates? After hearing my explanation about the difficulties in accessing such data in the US, he invited me to come to Norway and work on their micro data. This led, eventually, to a long and fruitful collaboration with

Vidar Ringstad and the *Economies of scale and the form of the production function* (1971) book and the subsequent monograph by Ringstad (1971) alone. More recently I have resumed my collaboration with the Norwegian Statistical Bureau in a series of papers with Tor Jacob Klette (Klette and Griliches 1996; and Klette, Møen and Griliches 1999).

At about the same time I was conducting a siege of the Bureau of the Census in the US, trying to gain access to firm data, especially their R&D data. Eventually, I was successful, resulting in a series of papers on estimating the effects of R&D on productivity (Griliches 1980a; 1986a). These papers, and the later papers using largely firm-level data in the US, France, Israel and Japan are reproduced in Griliches (1998c).

The next paper, written with Tom Abbott and Jerry Hausman (Griliches *et al.* 1998, unpublished but widely cited – see, for example, Basu and Kimball 1997), was a response to Hall's (1988) claim of high markups in manufacturing and an implicit defense of my production function work which had largely assumed that the firms I was observing were operating in competitive markets. We showed, using both industry and plant-level data, that Hall's results could be explained by fluctuations in capital and labor utilization, proxying the first by changes in energy consumption. A more theoretically grounded argument for our approach was published in Griliches and Eden (1993) and has been supported by the more recent work in macro (see Basu and Kimball 1997; Burnside *et al.* 1995, among others). Despite this 'victory', I have become more sensitive to the problem raised for production function estimation by the fact that many, if not most, of our firms are operating in an imperfectly competitive environment. This topic is discussed further in Klette and Griliches (1996) and in Griliches and Mairesse (1998).

Our paper on 'Heterogeneity in panel data' (Griliches and Mairesse 1990) represents a small tip of the iceberg of my twenty-year collaboration with Jacques Mairesse. It takes the potential heterogeneity issue seriously and tries to estimate a separate production function for each of the firms in our sample. It finds much too much heterogeneity in the estimates, much more than could be explained by sampling variability alone and concludes, with a nod to the 30-years earlier Grunfeld-Griliches paper, that the simple model used must be severely misspecified at the micro-micro level. Whether that matters at the more aggregate levels and in what contexts remains an open question. A related discussion, which pushes the topic further into estimation of individual equations with lagged dependent variables, can be found in Pesaran and Smith (1995).

Another joint paper with Jacques Mairesse (Griliches and Mairesse 1998), is both a history and an up-to-date survey of the state of production function estimation at the micro, firm or plant level. It discusses the 'search for identification' in such models and the continuous trend to estimate them from smaller slices of the data in an attempt to guard oneself against various sources of simultaneity bias. We show how errors in variables may defeat such attempts and discuss a variety of alternative approaches, including the Generalized Method of Moments and the more complex alternative approach advocated by Olley and Pakes (1996). We also summarize the main results of Klette and Griliches (1996) who show what imperfect competition and the presence of endogenous markups may do to the estimated production function parameters. My other papers with Mairesse deal primarily with R&D-related topics.

Another topic to which I devoted a large fraction of my energies, the measurement of quality change, is represented by two papers written with Makoto Ohta (Ohta and Griliches 1976; 1986). Besides the substantive interest of the results, the first paper introduces the concept of 'economic significance' in hypothesis testing (borrowing from Arrow and Leamer) and suggests a relevant metric for it while the second generalizes the usual hedonic regression by making the parameters of some of the characteristics functions of prices of gasoline, producing thereby relative stability in the estimated coefficients across both OPEC-induced oil price shocks. I have continued to be active in this field, working with a number of coauthors on the measurement of computer and pharmaceutical prices: Berndt and Griliches (1993); Berndt *et al.* (1995; 1996); Fisher and Griliches (1995); Griliches and Cockburn (1994); and serving on the US Senate Finance Committee's Advisory Commission on the CPI (see Boskin *et al.* 1996).

Finally, my 'Data issues' survey paper (Griliches 1986b) and my AEA presidential address (Griliches 1994) come close to summarizing many of my interests: in data quality, in model specification and in the promise of and the disappointment in panel data. They reflect my continued struggle to adapt and extend econometric techniques to say something useful about real economic questions and the repeated realization how primitive are our models, how sparse are our data and how thin is the ice on which we skate with our econometric techniques. But in the end we do the best we can. Our duty is not to give up but to keep on trying to find and develop more relevant data. The final product of all of our techniques cannot be much better, however, than the ingredients that we apply them to.

SELECTED WORKS

(1957a) 'Hybrid corn: an exploration in the economics of technological change', unpublished Ph.D. dissertation, University of Chicago.

(1957b) 'Specification bias in estimates of production functions', *Journal of Farm Economics*, 39 (1), pp. 8–20.*

(1957c) 'Hybrid corn: an exploration in the economics of technological change', *Econometrica*, 25 (4), pp. 501–22.*

(1958a) 'The demand for fertilizer: an econometric interpretation of a technical change', *Journal of Farm Economics*, 40 (3), pp. 591–606.

(1958b) 'Research costs and social returns: hybrid corn and related innovations', *Journal of Political Economy*, 66 (5), pp. 419–31.

(1959) 'Distributed lags, disaggregation and regional demand functions for fertilizer', *Journal of Farm Economics*, 41 (1), pp. 90–102.

(1960a) 'The demand for a durable input: US farm tractors, 1929–1957', in A.C. Harberger (ed.) (1960) *The demand for durable goods*. Chicago: University of Chicago Press, pp. 181–207.

(1960b) 'Measuring inputs in agriculture: a critical survey', *Journal of Farm Economics*, 42 (5), pp. 1411–33.

(1960) (with Y. Grunfeld) 'Is aggregation necessarily bad?', *Review of Economics and Statistics*, 42 (1), pp. 1–13.*

(1961a) 'A note on serial correlation bias in estimates of distributed lags', *Econometrica*, 29 (1), pp. 65–73.*

(1961b) 'Hedonic price indexes for automobiles: an econometric analysis of quality change', in NBER (1961) *The price statistics of the federal government*. New York: NBER, pp. 173–96. Rep. in Z. Griliches (ed.) (1971a) **q.v.**, pp. 55–87.

(1962) 'Profitability versus interaction: another false dichotomy', *Rural Sociology*, 27 (3), pp. 327–30.

(1963a) 'Production functions, technical change and all that', Netherlands School of Economics, Econometric Institute, Report no. 6328.*

(1963b) 'The sources of measured productivity growth: United States agriculture, 1940–1960', *Journal of Political Economy,* 71 (4), pp. 331–46.

(1963c) 'Capital stock in investment functions: some problems of concept and measurement', in C.F. Christ (ed.) **q.v.**, pp. 115–37.

(1964a) 'Notes on the measurement of price and quality changes', in NBER (ed.) (1964) *Models of income determination*. NBER studies in income and wealth, vol. 28. New York: Columbia University Press, pp. 381–418.

(1964b) 'Research expenditures, education and the aggregate agricultural production function', *American Economic Review*, 54 (6), pp. 961–74.

(1965) (with N. Wallace) 'The determinants of investment revisited', *International Economic Review*, 6 (3), pp. 311–29.*

(1967a) 'Distributed lags: a survey', *Econometrica*, 35 (1), pp. 16–49.*

(1967b) 'Production functions in manufacturing: some preliminary results', in M. Brown (ed.) (1967) *The theory and empirical analysis of production*. New York: Columbia University Press, pp. 275–322.*

(1967c) 'More on CES production functions', *Review of Economics and Statistics*, 49 (4), pp. 608–10.*

(1967) (with D.W. Jorgenson) 'The explanation of productivity change', *Review of Economic Studies*, 34 (3), pp. 249–83.

(1968) 'Production functions in manufacturing: some additional results', *Southern Economic Journal*, 35 (2), pp. 151–6.

(1969) 'Capital–skill complementarity', *Review of Economics and Statistics*, 51 (4), pp. 465–8.

(1970) 'Notes on the role of education in production functions and growth accounting', in W.L. Hansen (ed.) (1970) *Education, income and human capital*. New York: Columbia University Press, pp. 71–115.

(1970) (with V. Ringstad) 'Errors in the variables bias in non-linear contexts', *Econometrica*, 38 (2), pp. 368–70.*

(1971a) (Ed.) *Price indexes and quality change: studies in new methods of measurement*. Cambridge, MA: Harvard University Press.

(1971b) 'Introduction: hedonic price indexes revisited', in Z. Griliches (ed.) (1971a) **q.v.**, pp. 3–15.

(1971) (with V. Ringstad) *Economies of scale and the form of the production function*. Amsterdam: North Holland.

(1972) 'Cost allocation in railroad regulation', *Bell Journal of Economics and Management Science*, 3 (1), pp. 26–41.

(1972) (with D.W. Jorgenson) 'Issues in growth accounting: a reply to Edward F. Denison' and 'Final reply', *Survey of Current Business*, 52 (5, pt. II), pp. 65–94, 111.

(1972) (with W.M. Mason) 'Education, income and ability', *Journal of Political Economy*, 80 (3, pt. II), pp. S74–S103.

(1973) 'Research expenditures and growth accounting', in B.R. Williams (ed.) (1973) *Science and technology in economic growth*. London: Macmillan, pp. 59–95

(1974) 'Errors in variables and other unobservables', *Econometrica*, 42 (6), pp. 971–98.*

(1975) (with G. Chamberlain) 'Unobservables with a variance-components structure: ability, schooling and the economic success of brothers', *International Economic Review*, 16 (2), pp. 422–49.*

(1976) 'Wages of very young men', *Journal of Political Economy*, 84 (4, pt. 2), pp. S69–S85, S239–S247.

(1976) (with M. Ohta) 'Automobile prices revisited: extensions of the hedonic hypothesis', in N. Terleckyj (ed.) (1976) *Household production and consumption*. Chicago: University of Chicago Press, pp. 325–80.*

(1977) 'Estimating the returns to schooling: some econometric problems', *Econometrica*, 45 (1), pp. 1–22.*

(1978) 'Earnings of very young men', in Z. Griliches, W. Krelle, H.-J. Krupp and O. Kyn (eds) (1978) *Income distribution and economic inequality*. Frankfurt: Campus Verlag, pp. 209–19.

(1978) (with B.H. Hall and J. Hausman) 'Missing data and self-selection in large panels', *Annales de L'Insee*, 30–31, pp. 137–76.*

(1979a) 'Issues in assessing the contribution of research and development to productivity performance', *Bell Journal of Economics*, 10 (1), pp. 92–116.

(1979b) 'Sibling models and data in economics: beginnings of a survey', *Journal of Political Economy*, 87 (5, pt. II), pp. S37–S64.*

(1980a) 'Returns to research and development expenditures in the private sector', in J.W. Kendrick and B. Vaccara (eds) (1980) *New developments in productivity measurement*. Chicago: University of Chicago Press, pp. 419–54.

(1980b) 'Expectations, realizations and the aging of young men', in R.G. Ehrenberg (ed.) (1980) *Research in labour economics*. Greenwich, CT: JAI Press, vol. 3, pp. 1–21.

(1980c) 'Schooling interruption, work while in school and the returns from schooling', *Scandinavian Journal of Economics*, 82 (2), pp. 291–303.

(1980d) 'R&D and the productivity slowdown', *American Economic Review*, 70 (2), pp. 343–8.

(1984a) (Ed.) *R&D, patents and productivity*. Chicago: University of Chicago Press.

(1984b) 'Introduction', in Z. Griliches (ed.) (1984a) **q.v.**, pp. 1–19.

(1984) (with J.A. Hausman and B.H. Hall) 'Econometric models for count data and with application to the patents-R&D relationship', *Econometrica* 52 (4), pp. 909–38.

(1984) (with F. Lichtenberg) 'R&D and productivity growth at the industry level: is there still a relationship?', in Z. Griliches (ed.) (1984a) **q.v.**, pp. 465–96.

(1984) (with A. Pakes) 'Estimating distributed lags in short panels with an application to the specification of depreciation patterns and capital stock constructs', *Review of Economic Studies*, 51 (2), pp. 243–62.*

(1986a) 'Productivity, R&D, and basic research at the firm level in the 1970s', *American Economic Review*, 76 (1), pp. 141–54.

(1986b) 'Economic data issues', in Z. Griliches and M.D. Intriligator (eds) (1986) *Handbook of econometrics*. Amsterdam: North-Holland, vol. 3, pp. 1465–1514.*

(1986) (with J. Bound and B.H. Hall) 'Wages, schooling and IQ of brothers and sisters: do the family factors differ?', *International Economic Review*, 27 (1), pp. 77–105.*

(1986) (with B.H. Hall and J.A. Hausman), 'Patents and R&D: is there a lag?' *International Economic Review*, 27 (2), pp. 265–83.*

(1986) (with J.A. Hausman) 'Errors in variables in panel data', *Journal of Econometrics*, 31 (1), pp. 93–118.*

(1986) (with M. Ohta) 'Automobile prices and quality: did the gasoline price increase change consumer tastes in the US?', *Journal of Business and Economic Statistics*, 4 (2), pp. 187–98.*

(1987) (with A. Pakes and B.H. Hall) 'The value of patents as indicators of inventive activity', in P. Dasgupta and P. Stoneman (eds) (1987) *Economic policy and technological performance*. Cambridge: Cambridge University Press, pp. 97–124.

(1988a) *Technology, education and productivity: early papers with notes to subsequent literature*. Oxford: Basil Blackwell.

(1988b) 'Introduction', in Z. Griliches (1988a) **q.v.**, pp. 1–24.

(1990) 'Patent statistics as economic indicators: a survey', *Journal of Economic Literature*, 28 (4), pp. 1661–1707

(1990) (with J. Mairesse) 'Heterogeneity in panel data: are there stable production functions', in P. Champsaur *et al.* (eds) (1990) *Essays in honor of Edmond Malinvaud. Vol. 3: Empirical economics*. Cambridge, MA: MIT Press, pp. 192–231.*

(1993) (with E.R. Berndt) 'Price indexes for microcomputers: an exploratory study', in M.F. Foss, M.E. Manser and A.H. Young (eds) (1993) *Price measurements and their uses*. Chicago: University of Chicago Press, pp. 63–93.

(1993) (with B. Eden) 'Productivity, market power and capacity utilization when spot markets are complete', *American Economic Review*, 83 (2, Papers and Proceedings), pp. 219–23.

(1994) 'Productivity, R&D and the data constraint', *American Economic Review* 84 (1), 1–23.

(1994) (with I.M. Cockburn) 'Generics and new goods in pharmaceutical price indexes', *American Economic Review*, 84 (5), pp. 1213–32.

(1995) (with E.R. Berndt and N. Rappaport) 'Econometric estimates of price indexes for personal computers in the 1990s', *Journal of Econometrics*, 68 (1), pp. 243–68.

(1995) (with F. Fisher) 'Aggregate price indices, new goods and generics', *Quarterly*

Journal of Economics, 110 (1), pp. 229–44.
(1996) (with E.R. Berndt and I.M. Cockburn) 'Pharmaceutical innovations and market dynamics: tracking effects on price indexes for antidepressant drugs', *Brookings Papers on Economic Activity: Microeconomics*, pp. 133–88.
(1996) (with M. Boskin, E. Dulberger, R.J. Gordon and D. Jorgenson) *Final report of the Advisory Commission to Study the Consumer Price Index*. Washington, DC: US Government Printing Office.
(1996) (with T. Klette) 'The inconsistency of common scale estimators when output prices are unobserved and endogenous', *Journal of Applied Econometrics* 11 (4), pp. 343–61.
(1998a) *Practicing econometrics: essays in method and application*. Cheltenham: Edward Elgar.
(1998b) 'Introduction', in Z. Griliches (1998a) **q.v.**, pp. ix–xix.
(1998c) *R&D and productivity: the econometric evidence*. Chicago: University of Chicago Press.
(1998) (with T. Abbott and J. Hausman) 'Short run movements in productivity: market power versus capacity utilization', in Z. Griliches (1998a) **q.v.**, pp. 330–42.*
(1998) (with J. Mairesse) 'Production functions: the search for identification', in Z. Griliches (1998a) **q.v.**, pp. 383–411* and S. Strøm (ed.) (1998) *Econometrics and economic theory in the 20th century: the Ragnar Frisch centennial symposium*. Cambridge: Cambridge University Press, pp. 169–203.
(1999) (with T. Klette and J. Møen) 'Do subsidies to commercial R&D reduce market failures?: microeconomic evaluation studies', University of Oslo memorandum no. 13/99.

BIBLIOGRAPHY

Aigner, D. and Goldfeld, S. (1974) 'Estimation and prediction from aggregate data when aggregates are measured more accurately than their components', *Econometrica* 42 (1), pp. 113–34.
Almon, S. (1965) 'The distributed lag between capital appropriations and expenditures', *Econometrica*, 33 (1), pp. 178–96.
Angrist, J. and Krueger, A.B. (1991) 'Does compulsory school attendance affect schooling and earnings?', *Quarterly Journal of Economics*, 106 (4), pp. 979–1014.
Arrow, K. (1973) 'Higher education as a filter', *Journal of Public Economics*, 2 (1), pp. 193–216.
Ashenfelter, O.C. and Krueger, A.B. (1992) 'Estimates of the economic return to schooling from a new sample of twins', NBER Working Paper no. 4143.
Atkinson, A.B. and Stiglitz, J.E. (1969) 'A new view of technological change', *Economic Journal*, 79 (3), pp. 573–78.
Barker, T. and Pesaran, M. H. (1990) 'Disaggregation in econometric modelling: an introduction', in T. Barker and M. H. Pesaran (eds) (1990) *Disaggregation in econometric modelling*. London: Routledge, pp. 1–14.
Basu, S. and Kimball, M. (1997) 'Cyclical productivity with unobserved input variation', NBER Working Paper no. 5915.

Berndt, E.R. and Fuss, M. (1986) 'Productivity measurement with adjustments for variations in capacity utilization and other forms of temporary equilibrium', *Journal of Econometrics*, 33 (1/2), pp. 7–29.

Biorn, E. (1996) 'Panel data with measurement errors', in L. Matyas and P. Sevestre (eds) (1996) *The econometrics of panel data: a handbook of the theory with applications*, 2nd edn. Dordrecht: Kluwer, pp. 236–79.

Blau, P.M. and Duncan, O.D. (1967) *The American occupational structure*. New York: John Wiley.

Brandner, L. and Strauss, M.A. (1959) 'Congruence versus profitability in the diffusion of hybrid sorghum', *Rural Sociology*, 24 (4), pp. 381–3.

Burnside, C., Eichenbaum, M. and Rebelo, S. (1995) 'Capital utilization and returns to scale', in B.S. Bernanke and J. Rotemberg (eds) (1995) *NBER macroeconomics annual*. Cambridge: NBER, vol. 10, pp. 67–109.

Cagan, P. (1956) 'The monetary dynamics of hyperinflations', in M. Friedman (ed.) (1956) *Studies in the quantity theory of money*. Chicago: University of Chicago Press, pp. 25–117.

Card, D. (1995) 'Earnings, schooling, and ability revisited', *Research In Labor Economics*, 14 (1), pp. 23–48.

Chamberlain, G. (1977) 'Education, income and ability revisited', *Journal of Econometrics*, 5 (2), pp. 241–57.

Christ, C.F. (ed.) (1963) *Measurement in economics: studies in mathematical economics and econometrics in memory of Yehuda Grunfeld*. Stanford, CA: Stanford University Press.

Cummins, C. (1989) 'Efficient estimation of regression coefficients with missing data', unpublished Ph.D. dissertation, Harvard University.

David, P.A. (1969) 'A contribution to the theory of diffusion', Stanford University Research Centre for Economic Growth memorandum no. 71, June.

Denison, E.F. (1964) 'Measuring the contribution of education', in OECD (ed.) (1964) *The residual factor and economic growth*. Paris: OECD, pp. 13–55.

Denison, E.F. (1969) 'Some major issues in productivity analysis: an examination of estimates by Jorgenson and Griliches', *Survey of Current Business*, 49 (5, pt. II), pp. 1–27.

Denison, E.F. (1972) 'Final comments', *Survey of Current Business*, 52 (5, pt. II), pp. 95–110.

Denison, E.F. (1974) *Accounting for United States economic growth, 1929–1969*. Washington, DC: Brookings Institution.

Denison, E.F. (1979) *Accounting for slower economic growth*. Washington, DC: Brookings Institution.

Denison, E.F. (1984) 'Accounting for slower economic growth: an update', in J.W. Kendrick (ed.) (1984) *International comparisons of productivity and the causes of the slowdown*. Cambridge, MA: Ballinger, pp. 1–46.

Denison, E.F. (1985) *Trends in American economic growth, 1929–82*. Washington, DC: Brookings Institution.

Dougherty, C.R.S. (1972) 'Estimates of labor aggregation functions', *Journal of Political Economy*, 80 (6), pp. 1101–19.

Edwards, J.B. and Orcutt, G.H. (1969) 'Should aggregation prior to estimation be the rule?', *Review of Economics and Statistics* 51 (4), pp. 409–20.

Evenson, R.F., Waggoner, P.F. and Ruttan, V.W. (1979) 'Economic benefits from research: an example from agriculture', *Science*, 205 (14 September), pp. 1101–7.

Ezekiel, M. (1941) *Methods of correlation analysis*, 2nd ed. New York: Wiley.

Fallon, P.R. and Layard, P.R.G. (1975) 'Capital-skill complementarity, income distribution and output accounting', *Journal of Political Economy*, 83 (2), pp. 279–302.

Freeman, R.B. (1973) 'Changes in the labor market for black Americans, 1948–72', *Brookings Papers in Economic Activity*, 1, pp. 67–132.

Freeman, R.B. (1976) *The overeducated American*. New York: Academic Press.

Friedman, M. (1957) *The theory of the consumption function*. Princeton, NJ: Princeton University Press.

Fuss, M.A. and McFadden, D. (eds) (1978) *Production economics: a dual approach to theory and application*, 2 vols. Amsterdam: North-Holland.

Fuss, M.A., McFadden, D. and Mundlack, Y. (1978) 'A survey of functional forms in the economic analysis of production', in M.A. Fuss and D. McFadden (eds) (1978) **q.v.**, vol. I, pp. 219–68.

Grunfeld, Y. (1960) 'The determinants of corporate investment', in A.C. Harberger (ed.) (1960) *The demand for durable goods*. Chicago: University of Chicago Press, pp. 211–66.

Hall, R.E. (1986) 'Market structure and macroeconomic fluctuations', *Brookings Papers on Economic Activity*, 2, pp. 285–322.

Hall, R.E. (1988) 'The relation between price and marginal cost in US industry', *Journal of Political Economy*, 96 (5), pp. 91–147.

Hauser, R.M. and Featherman, D.L. (1977) *The process of stratification: trends and analysis*. New York: Academic Press.

Havens, A.E. and Rogers, E.M. (1961) 'Adoption of hybrid corn: profitability and the interaction effect', *Rural Sociology*, 26 (4), pp. 409–14.

Heckman, J.J. (1979) 'Sample selection as a specification error', *Econometrica*, 47 (1), pp. 153–161.

Huffman, W.E. (1974) 'Decision making: the role of education', *American Journal of Agricultural Economics*, 56 (1), pp. 85–97.

Huffman, W.E. (1977) 'Allocative efficiency: the role of human capital', *Quarterly Journal of Economics*, 91 (1), pp. 59–79.

Jamison, D.T. and Lau, L.J. (1982) *Farm education and farm efficiency*. Baltimore: Johns Hopkins University Press.

Jencks, C. (1972) *Inequality*. New York: Basic Books.

Jencks, C. *et al.* (1972) *Who gets ahead?: the determinants of economic success in America*. New York: Basic Books.

Jorgenson, D. (1966) 'Rational distributed lag functions', *Econometrica*, 34 (1), pp. 135–49.

Kendrick, J.W. (1983) 'International comparisons of recent productivity trends', in S.H. Shurr (ed.) (1983) *Energy, productivity and economic growth*. Cambridge, MA: Oelgeschlager, pp. 71–120.

Klette, T. and Willassen, W. (1993) 'Errors in variables and parameter bounds: an application to the estimation of production relationships', mimeo, Oslo: Central Bureau of Statistics of Norway.

Koyck, L.M. (1954) *Distributed lags and investment analysis*. Amsterdam: North Holland.

Little, R. and Rubin, D. (1987) *Statistical analysis with missing data*. New York: Wiley.

Mansfield, E., Rappaport, J., Romeo, A., Wagner, S. and Beardsley, O. (1977) 'Social and private rates of return from industrial innovations', *Quarterly Journal of Economics*, 91 (2), pp. 221–40.

McFadden, D. (1978) 'Estimation techniques for elasticity of substitution and other production parameters', in M.A. Fuss and D. McFadden (eds) (1978) **q.v.**, vol. II, pp. 73–124.

Miller, E.M. (1983) 'Capital aggregation in the presence of obsolescence-inducing technical change', *Review of Income and Wealth*, 29 (2), pp. 283–96.

Morrison, C.J. (1985) 'On the economic interpretation and measurement of optimal capacity utilization with anticipatory expectations', *Review of Economic Studies*, 52 (2), pp. 295–310.

Morrison, C.J. and Berndt, E.R. (1981) 'Short-run labor productivity in a dynamic model', *Journal of Econometrics*, 16 (3), pp. 339–66.

Nelson, R.R. and Phelps, E.S. (1966) 'Investment in humans, technological diffusion and economic growth', *American Economic Review*, 56 (2, Papers & Proceedings), pp. 69–75.

Nerlove, M. (1956) 'Estimates of the elasticities of supply of selected agricultural commodities', *Journal of Farm Economics*, 38 (2), pp. 496–509.

Nerlove, M. (1958) *The dynamics of supply: estimation of farmers' response to price.* Baltimore, MD: Johns Hopkins Press.

Nerlove, M. (1963) 'Returns to scale in electricity supply', in C.F. Christ (ed.) (1963) **q.v.**, pp. 167–200.

Olley, S. and Pakes, A. (1996) 'The dynamics of productivity in the telecommunications equipment industry', *Econometrica*, 64 (6), pp. 1263–97.

Pesaran, H. and Smith, R. (1995) 'Estimating long run relationships from dynamic heterogeneous panels', *Journal of Econometrics*, 65(1), pp. 79–113.

Ringstad, V. (1971) *Estimating production functions and technical change from micro data.* Economic Studies no. 21, Oslo: Bureau of Statistics.

Schankerman, M. (1981) 'The effects of double-counting and expensing on the measured returns to R&D', *Review of Economics and Statistics*, 63 (2), pp. 275–82.

Smith, J. and Welch, F. (1986) 'Technical change and the aggregate production function', Rand Corporation, R-3330-POL.

Solow, R.M. (1960) 'Investment and technical progress', in K. Arrow, S. Karlin and P. Suppes (eds) (1960) *Mathematical methods in the social sciences.* Stanford, CA: Stanford University Press, pp. 89–104.

Spence, M. (1974) *Market signalling.* Cambridge, MA: Harvard University Press.

Weiss, R. (1974) 'Sources of change in the occupational structure of American manufacturing industries, 1950 to 1960: an application of production function analysis', unpublished Ph.D. dissertation, Harvard University.

Welch, F. (1970) 'Education in production', *Journal of Political Economy*, 78 (1), pp. 35–59.

Welch, F., Murphy, K. and Plant, M. (1985) 'Cohort size and earnings', unpublished paper.

Wolpin, K. (1977) 'Education and screening', *American Economic Review*, 67 (5), pp. 949–58.

Woolridge, J. (1990) 'Distribution-free estimation of some nonlinear panel data models', unpublished paper, Massachusetts Institute of Technology.

9. Richard E. Quandt (b. 1930)[1]

9.1   EARLY LIFE

I was nine years old when Germany started World War II with its attack on Poland and many of my childhood memories are war-related. We lived in Budapest and at first nothing seemed to change, but even as a child I became aware of rationing and the steady deterioration of the quality of food at the boarding school in the country to which I had been sent at age ten. The best part of those unsettled times was that fuel had become scarce by 1942 and, in the winters that followed, school was closed from late November until February.

Hungarian is a beautiful and expressive language but, as my parents frequently observed, of limited usefulness. For this reason they brought me up to be bilingual in Hungarian and German, which turned out to be of great help to me later. At my boarding school Italian was emphasized; I remember that we had ten or twelve classes of Italian every week, so that by age 15 I

---

[1]   Quandt (1992b), as revised by the editors. I have two volumes of selected writings in this series (Quandt 1992a): the first covering microeconomic theory and general econometrics; and the second, my writings in disequilibrium econometrics, planned economies and miscellaneous fields. I have been honored by a festschrift in the form of a special issue of the *Rand Journal of Economics* (Bresnahan and Porter 1997).

was quite fluent in that language as well. As World War II was ending, I decided that English would be a useful language to know. English was not taught formally at the school, but I was determined to learn it and with the help of a teacher succeeded in making rapid progress. I rapidly concluded that English was unrivalled in its clarity as well as its subtlety.

My parents had a substantial library and I read extensively, primarily fiction, by the age of 11. But it was not until I was about 14 that a book on economics fell into my hands. It was about the history of economic thought, and I remember learning from it about the mercantilists and physiocrats, about Adam Smith, David Ricardo, Bentham and List. I cannot imagine that I understood a great deal of what I read, but the subject piqued my curiosity, perhaps because my father was a central banker and dinner table conversations often revolved around problems of the economy.

My father's prominent position and his opposition to the German war effort caused him to be arrested and deported in late 1944. The end of the war found him in a German camp, and when he was freed, he decided to delay his return to Hungary until its political future became clearer. Alas, what became clear was that Hungary had had imposed on it a system of government that my parents objected to as much as they had objected to Nazism, and so, in 1947, my mother, sister and I left Hungary to join my father. By 1948 I had enrolled in a Swiss school near Lucerne where I hoped to complete my high school education. However, it was not to be, because my father had a chance at a good position in New York, where we arrived in March 1949. To be in America was exciting beyond imagination, but I was also panicked because I did not have a high-school diploma and feared that I would have trouble getting into a university.

9.2   PRINCETON, 1949–52

I have to admit that until then I had heard of only two American universities, namely Harvard and Yale. Upon mentioning this to a friend of my father's, he sternly intoned, 'Nonsense, my boy, you will go to Princeton!' I dutifully, but with much trepidation, presented myself to the Admissions Director at Princeton and to my immense surprise found myself admitted to undergraduate studies as a Sophomore (second-year student). Thus began the most exciting intellectual exploration of my life. I enrolled in courses on philosophy, political science, history, mathematics and, of course, economics. The contrast between my Hungarian and Swiss secondary education and that at Princeton could not have been greater. I had not been used to questioning everything or to play with ideas in the American manner that I quickly learned to adopt, and the lectures and classes of Walter Kaufman in Philosophy and Alpheus T. Mason in political science were sheer pleasure.

Economics was an enormous revelation because for the first time in my life I began to understand what economics was about and what the distinction was between its various parts, such as microeconomics and macroeconomics. The first introductory courses in these subjects were enough to convince me that I wanted to specialize in economics. Accordingly, at the end of my Sophomore year, I decided to major in economics. The following year I was lucky enough to attend the classes of William J. Baumol who became my mentor and influenced me in more beneficial ways than I can possibly recount. To begin with, he convinced me early in my career that mathematics was essential for the successful pursuit of most branches of economics and I promptly enrolled in several Mathematics courses. In that subject I was fortunate to have Albert Tucker as my teacher from whom I learned the basics of mathematical programming just around the time that the justly famous paper by Kuhn and Tucker (1951), containing the Kuhn-Tucker Theorem, saw the light of day (Kuhn was subsequently to become my colleague in the Economics Department at Princeton). In my last year I also succeeded in having Baumol as my adviser for my senior thesis on the Ricardo effect. Baumol also advised me to try to enrol in Jacob Viner's graduate course on the history of economic thought, a suggestion that I accepted with alacrity and that greatly broadened my outlook. Viner was an august figure with a fearsome reputation; he could screw up his eyes and glare at a hapless student groping for an answer in a way that reduced the strongest to quivering wrecks. I was terrified throughout most of the term that I sat in his class and it was only much later, when we were colleagues at Princeton and served together on the examination committees, that I found out that he was really very soft-hearted.

In my last year at Princeton I applied for admission to the Ph.D. programme in economics at Harvard, Yale, MIT, Chicago, Johns Hopkins and Princeton. I was fortunate to be admitted by every one of these distinguished institutions with the exception of Princeton, where my professors, who were much wiser than I, decided that I would benefit from a change of intellectual scenery. So, in the autumn of 1952 I began my graduate studies at Harvard.

9.3   HARVARD, 1952–6

I think all of us who arrived there were immediately awed by the amount of new material we had to cope with, by the immense reputations of our professors, and by the excellence of our fellow students. Among the professors I met or studied with in my first two years at Harvard were, first and foremost, my second mentor, Wassily Leontief, as well as Gottfried Haberler, Guy Orcutt, Carl Kaysen, James Duesenberry, John Chipman, Alvin Hansen, Edward Chamberlin and Alexander Gerschenkron. It became clear to me during those first two years that the areas that interested me most were micro theory and econometrics, possibly an unusual combination but one that I found irresistible. Under Leontief's influence I had a special predilection for input-output analysis and by my third year had begun to investigate the properties of input-output systems in which the coefficients were not known with certainty. It seemed obvious to me that in any concrete empirical case the Leontief coefficients were necessarily estimates rather than 'true' values and that the distribution of these would induce a distribution on the solution to the Leontief system. This led me to an investigation of the distribution of the Leontief inverse and to my first encounter with Monte Carlo experiments and large digital computers. It is ironic to reflect that the MARK IV computer that was the most advanced machine at Harvard at the time was a physical giant with the brain of a pea compared to today's entry-level personal computers. I did not at that time do the necessary programming myself but relied on the kind assistance of a graduate student colleague in applied science, Fred Brooks, who later played an important part in designing System 360 for IBM – but more of that later.

While I was in graduate school, two other interesting topics occurred to me. First, I was puzzled by how appropriate the theory of the consumer, as well as the theory of the producer, could be without explicitly taking account of uncertainty. In particular, it seemed to me that it would be useful to characterize commodities in terms of their characteristics and to define the utility function on bundles of characteristics, an idea that was subsequently developed in detail in the important work of Kelvin Lancaster. I further thought that consumers scanned the characteristics of commodities imperfectly and evaluated particular commodities at different times on the basis of different subsets of characteristics. It is then straightforward that apparent nontransitivities can arise in observed choices.

The other topic that came to my attention did so in a most unusual fashion. I had been taking a course from John Chipman on econometric theory and we were working our way through the justly famous Cowles commission monograph by Hood and Koopmans (1953). I happened to be the only student registered in the course for 'credit', which gave Chipman and me a great deal of flexibility as to when to schedule the final examination. We agreed on a particular date and I appeared at the appointed place at the proper time, but John Chipman did not. I was in a panic that I may have misunderstood and that this misunderstanding would cost me dearly. But later in that day, John Chipman telephoned me from Vermont and sheepishly admitted that he had forgotten the examination date we had made. I asked him what we should do about it at this point, and he suggested that I should set my own examination questions and then proceed to answer my own questions.

The optimal course of action was not obvious. The obvious moral hazard was to ask very easy questions, but this might have been self-defeating in that, if I had been in his place, I would have penalized a student who asked himself trivialities. On the other hand, asking very difficult questions might have been equally bad, because I might not have been able to answer any of my own questions. So I decided to ask myself a question that had puzzled me for some weeks; that is, how one would estimate the coefficients of a time series regression equation if one suspected that the regression coefficients underwent a discontinuous change at some unknown point in time. This 'examination question' led to a series of investigations of switching regressions that occupied me for a number of years off and on (Quandt 1958; 1960; 1972; Goldfeld and Quandt 1973a; b) (I should mention that I passed the examination).

The third important thing that happened during those years in graduate school was that conversations with my fellow student James Henderson convinced us that there was no reasonably systematic and mathematically accessible book on microtheory, one that was somewhat easier for the average student of those days than Samuelson's *Foundations of economic analysis* (1947). We decided to remedy this lack and in my last year at Harvard we started to write *Microeconomic theory: a mathematical approach* (Quandt and Henderson 1958), a decision that led to a long and fruitful collaboration and a total of three editions of the book over a span of 23 years.

9.4 RETURN TO PRINCETON, 1956

In my last year at Harvard I got married and, as the academic year reached its midpoint, I decided that I actually needed to earn a living. My Ph.D. dissertation was going to be finished by June and there was no reason why I should not take a regular, full-time job for September 1956. Finding an academic job was more informal in those days than is the case today. The chairman of my Department told me that he had decided that I should take a job at a particular midwestern university; while I had nothing against that institution, it nevertheless irritated me to be told where I had to go. Accordingly, I got on the train and went to Princeton, where I walked into the office of the chairman, Lester Chandler, and asked him for a job. To my enormous surprise, a few weeks later I was appointed Assistant Professor at Princeton.

Balancing the conflicting demands of teaching and research was not easy at first but Princeton encouraged excellence in both, which minimized the feeling that one had to rob Peter to pay Paul. Princeton had no programmes during the summer and was an extremely sleepy little town in July and August. I found good occasions to be away during the early summers. In 1957 I spent some time at a Stanford workshop on linear programming where I worked with Robert Dorfman, from whom I learned more than I can acknowledge, and met Lionel McKenzie who became a good friend. Another summer I spent some time at Amherst College's Merrill Center on Long Island where I met Nicholas (later Lord) Kaldor and worked with Willard Thorp, with whom I wrote a small book on inflation (Quandt and Thorp 1959). At Princeton, I taught both graduate and undergraduate students; graduate econometrics was particularly enjoyable because of the constant new discoveries in estimating the parameters of systems of simultaneous equations. Two-stage least squares and related methods were being discussed all the time; I found the subject intrinsically fascinating but was beginning to be somewhat frustrated that the full information maximum likelihood method was in practice not implementable because the computations were too arduous. I had had a second experience with computers when in 1957–8 I was working on testing the hypothesis that a discontinuous switch occurred in the parameters of a linear regression model at an unknown point in time, but again I had to rely on assistance, this time from Herman Karreman, a kind and older research associate in the Department who gave freely of his time. I had resolved that I could not rely on others to do my computer programming in the future.

In the 1958–9 academic year I was on leave from Princeton and spent some six months at the London School of Economics where I met a number of remarkable people; many of the friendships I made have lasted until the present. I was lucky to be able to participate in Lord Robbins' famous weekly seminar, which was attended by Harold Kuhn (who became my colleague at Princeton that year), Kelvin Lancaster, Chris Archibald, Maurice (now Lord) Peston, and many others. I also met Alan Stuart and James Durbin who gave me good advice on statistical matters for decades thereafter. Returning from London, I learned that the Institute for Defense Analysis, right next to the University, had acquired a Control Data Corporation 1604 computer on which the University had a daily shift of eight hours. With substantial assistance from friends in the engineering school I learnt programming in assembler language, and Harold Kuhn and I started to work on some computations with a view towards examining the performance of the simplex method in linear programming. This was a quite remarkable machine for its day: it had a memory of 32,768 8-bit words and other advanced features to go along with it. An operating system was, to all intents and purposes, nonexistent; when a person was using the computer, he had it all to himself and was sitting at the console pushing buttons. But it was a fast machine and we could solve linear programming problems with 25 variables and 25 constraints in four to six seconds.

The 1960s turned out to be the decade in which I happened to be interested in more topics than I can describe here. I worked on mathematical programming problems, on existence and stability questions in oligopoly models, on various general econometric problems and on transportation, especially estimating the demand for transportation. My work on econometrics received a tremendous boost from Stephen Goldfeld who joined the Department in 1963 and became a lifelong friend and collaborator. Our first joint paper (Goldfeld and Quandt 1965), dealing with heteroscedasticity, led to what is known as the Goldfeld-Quandt test. Equally importantly, we started to think more and more about full information maximum likelihood, particularly in the context of nonlinear structural equations, and resolved that we had to do something about the computability of estimates in nonlinear models. We rapidly discovered that programming Newton's method itself was useful only in limited circumstances, because many functions one may wish to maximize turn out not to be globally concave. This led to the development (with Hale Trotter of the Mathematics Department) of an algorithm we called GRADX which, with various modifications, is still one of the more effective optimizers of general functions. As our need for optimizing functions grew, we realized that it was not sensible to rely on a single algorithm, but that one should have a 'package' of algorithms programmed in such a fashion that the user could easily choose one or the other of the available algorithms. With some assistance from a graduate student, James Ertel, the first version of GQOPT was born: it incorporated at that time GRADX, the Davidon-Fletcher-Powell (DFP) algorithm, the Powell conjugate gradient algorithm of 1964, the Hooke and Jeeves pattern search algorithm, and the Nelder and Mead simplex algorithm (not to be confused with the simplex method of linear programming). Since those days GQOPT has had many new features incorporated in it; the current seventh release has regression and simultaneous equation estimation, contour plotting, new algorithms for optimization such as the Oren-Lunenberg variable metric self-scaling algorithm, constrained optimization, numerical integration in up to four dimensions, and many other features.

I can thank William Baumol for my interest in transportation problems since he persuaded me to join Mathematica, Inc., a consulting firm in Princeton, on a part-time basis. One of the first projects I was affiliated with (jointly with Baumol) was sponsored by the US Department of Commerce, which was interested in estimates of the demand for transportation in the Northeast Corridor. It occurred to us that transportation was one of those commodities where it was almost literally the case that the consumer did not care about what a particular mode of transportation was or what it was called; all the consumer cared about was the attributes of the mode, i.e., its cost, speed, the frequency of its departures, and perhaps its safety and comfort. If one could characterize transportation modes entirely by their attributes, as I had in general suggested in 1956, one might be able to derive demand functions which had only transport attributes and demographic variables as independent variables on the right-hand side of a regression equation. Accordingly, we combined in a regression context a modified gravity model with an attribute characterization of transport modes and hence estimated demand functions for passenger transportation between pairs of nodes in the Northeast Corridor.

While the resulting coefficient estimates were quite sensible and the predictions of demand on existing transport modes for varying attribute configurations reasonable, we had not realized at first that we had run afoul of what became known as the 'blue-bus red-bus paradox'. Imagine that the original transport mode 'buses' suddenly becomes two modes, because half the buses are painted one colour and the other half another colour. Since none of the attributes of the transport mode included in the model had changed, the model would predict the same transport demand for each of the two (new) modes, i.e., an overall increase in demand for bus travel. This was a flaw which a regression model with total passenger traffic as the dependent variable could not easily get around.

The remedy lay in going back to the utility function of the consumer and assuming that the arguments of the utility function were the attributes of the various transport modes. Much influenced in this by the excellent work of Tony Blackburn, I devised a stochastic utility function approach which allowed one to estimate the parameters of the utility function and the probability that this or that mode would be selected from the observed choices of consumers (Quandt 1968). This was my first encounter with numerical integration and the particular model I had devised was rather complicated and difficult to estimate. But it did start a line of investigation that culminated in the now definitive work of McFadden and others, namely the conditional logit model.

The late 1960s and early 1970s saw another interesting development, namely disequilibrium modelling. The seminal work in this area was an article by Fair and Jaffee (1972) in which they posited that markets do not necessarily clear. It was obvious that the ordinary simultaneous equations estimating techniques were no longer relevant in this case. In *Nonlinear methods of econometrics* (Goldfeld and Quandt 1971), we attempted one approach to this estimation problem; it turned out that while we had found a perfectly sensible solution to the switching regressions problem, we had not solved the disequilibrium estimation problem. That was first achieved in general by Maddala and Nelson (1974) after which disequilibrium modelling and estimation became more straightforward, if not much easier in practice, because many types of models required numerical optimization for obtaining the estimates.

An appreciable part of my research efforts in the 1970s and part of the 1980s was spent on disequilibrium modelling in which I investigated theoretical, computational and empirical problems. One of the most interesting and enduring investigations in the last category was my work with my colleague, Harvey S. Rosen. We were interested in modelling the US labour market as a model in which wages do not adjust to clear markets, but are moved by the existence of excess demand. This provoked a certain amount of controversy, partly because some investigators preferred to model this type of phenomenon as a partial adjustment model rather than a disequilibrium model, and partly because our initial excess demand (supply) forecasts could not replicate the Great Depression (Rosen and Quandt 1978). While that turned out to be a minor problem of the specification of the model and was corrected by David Romer (1981), it seemed desirable to introduce further refinements into the model and subsequent versions had separate price and wage adjustment equations while the latest version succeeded in treating output as endogenous (Quandt and Rosen 1989). But it is true that American macroeconomists tended to dislike non-market-clearing models (at the same time that microtheorists were devising increasingly clever models to show why wages might not clear markets), whereas European macroeconomists on the whole accepted the non-market-clearing paradigm with alacrity. In the late 1970s I had written a paper on how one might test the hypothesis that a set of data was generated by an equilibrium rather than a disequilibrium model (Quandt 1978). I would give this paper in various seminars and I remember that in the US my introduction to the paper was usually greeted with a remark such as, 'What you are doing is silly, because everybody knows that prices clear markets, and hence there is nothing to test.' Giving the same paper in Europe, I would usually be greeted with the remark, 'Everybody knows that prices never clear markets, hence there is nothing to test.'

While it seemed perfectly legitimate in the free market context to question the assumption of price and wage rigidities, or at least require that the disequilibrium econometrician provide some justification for why he thought that such rigidities played a significant role, one might have thought that the need for such justification was much diminished in the case of the centrally planned economies. I was most fortunate to spend some six months in London at the beginning of 1981 at Birkbeck College and at the London School of Economics. At Birkbeck, my gracious host, Richard Portes, and I had many conversations about modelling planned economies, particularly because he and David Winter had recently published an article (Portes and Winter 1980) in which they estimated simple disequilibrium models for aggregate consumption in Czechoslovakia, Hungary, Poland and the German Democratic Republic. I was already much interested in the subject, because Wojciech Charemza (then at the University of Gdansk and now at the University of Leicester) and I had begun to work on some econometric formulations for centrally planned economies. Portes and I had resolved that, together with David Winter and Stephen Yeo, we would devise and estimate a more ambitious aggregate consumption model for Poland in which central plans were endogenous. This was accomplished and we were pleased by the performance of the model, particularly by its confirmation that central planners acted so as to diminish the extent of the disequilibria (Portes *et al.* 1987; 1988). However, the model also predicted that, in the aggregate, excess supply had occurred in Poland in some years, a finding that Janos Kornai (1980; 1982) and some others found unpalatable. I never understood why this conclusion was deemed to be so unacceptable. Kornai's theory of shortage rests on the idea of the soft budget constraint and applies to enterprises which, as a result of the soft budget constraint, develop an excessive demand for inputs. The theory does not argue that consumers face a soft budget constraint, and while it is true that queues for some consumer goods have been observable in some centrally planned economies, it is also argued that inventories of unwanted goods accumulate at times. It is thus not surprising that, in the aggregate, excess supply is shown to exist at some times, a finding confirmed by a more disaggregated methodology than the standard disequilibrium analysis (Burkett 1988).

In London I also met Wladyslaw Welfe of the University of Lodz (Poland) and he invited Portes and me to a conference in Łódź at the end of 1983, just after the end of Martial Law. We presented our results at this conference, which was also useful because Charemza, Miroslaw Gronicki and I made final plans to design and estimate a model of the automobile market in Poland. This was an interesting and challenging task, partly because the required data were essentially unavailable and had to be generated by ourselves, and partly because the automobile market consisted of three parallel markets: an official state market in which new automobiles were sold for zlotys and in which we posited the existence of chronic excess demand; a private second market run by the state in which cars were sold for hard currencies, and a second-hand market. In the latter two markets, prices could be safely assumed to perform the clearing function (Charemza *et al.* 1988).

Around 1985 I had come to the conclusion that the amount of econometric methodology that had been devised to cope with disequilibrium models had grown to such an impressive size that it was well worth recording. Accordingly, I set to work and published a book in 1988 that was intended to cover the most important methods and review some of the more interesting applications of disequilibrium econometrics (Quandt 1988).

As I was finishing that book, I found myself increasingly interested in providing a formal microeconomic treatment of some of Kornai's important conjectures concerning the operations of the firm under central planning. As discussed above, one of the cornerstones of Kornai's view is the soft budget constraint. In essence, this means that enterprises are not disciplined by the market when they have negative profits. In market economies negative profits may be borne temporarily, but in the long run they are not compatible with survival (except in the case of the famous bailouts that have occurred and are still occurring in the US economy). In planned economies the state cannot, for a variety of reasons, afford to let enterprises become bankrupt and go out of business; therefore the state routinely hands out subsidies or bailouts to such firms. Kornai had conjectured that this would have the consequence of making the manager demand very large quantities of inputs, substantially larger than without such a bailout mechanism. If this were the case, it would intensify any shortage that might exist. A second reason that would tend to intensify shortages is the expectation of rationing. If managers expect their inputs to be rationed in the future, they will rationally try to build up hoards of the inputs in earlier periods (when perhaps the rationing might have been less intensive for one reason or another). Under these circumstances there will again be an intensification of shortages. Interestingly, these conjectures appeared not to have been formalized before. Stephen Goldfeld and I set ourselves the task of exploring a variety of models in which these phenomena could be analysed (Goldfeld and Quandt 1988; 1990a; b; c).

A final area that has occupied my attention from time to time is the economics of racetrack betting. My attention was directed to this topic by my colleague, Burton Malkiel, and a former student and friend, Peter Asch. It took little effort on their part to convince me that there were very interesting questions about racetrack betting that needed to be answered. In parimutuel betting winners share, in proportion to the size of their bets, the total amount bet in the race minus the amount retained by the racetrack to cover expenses and profit. On average, therefore, racetrack bettors must lose, but it is an interesting question whether there are any strategies that might yield positive profits. This is particularly interesting because racetrack betting appears to have the property of market efficiency in the sense that horses that are objectively more likely to win correspondingly have more money bet on them, so that the average payoff to the winner is smaller. The three of us addressed ourselves to solving a number of interesting puzzles and theoretical and empirical conundrums, which was made all the more pleasant in that we periodically found it desirable to do 'field research' at some not too distant racetracks. It turns out that there are some betting strategies that can improve returns and turn them into mildly positive ones. Asch and I published a book on the subject (Asch and Quandt 1986) and were in the middle of some additional research when he died in 1990.

The last few years have seen major changes in Eastern Europe and I was fortunate enough to be asked by The Andrew W. Mellon Foundation to advise it on a newly established programme in Eastern Europe. The Foundation had decided to concentrate its activities in two directions: in supporting educational and training programmes in economics, business and management and in supporting universities and other institutions of higher learning. It is clear that economics and management expertise is badly needed in the East European countries that are trying to remake their economies, practically from scratch. It is also the case that educational institutions were badly neglected during the past 45 years in Eastern Europe and that their infrastructure is in great need of revitalization and modernization. The Foundation has attacked these problems in Czechoslovakia, Hungary and Poland with vigour and I have been most pleased to be able to participate in making educational improvements in the region where I had my origin. In addition, of course, the economic problems facing the East European countries are both interesting and important, and at least some of my research in the future will focus on this area.

SELECTED WORKS

(1958) 'The estimation of the parameters of a linear regression system obeying two separate regimes', *Journal of the American Statistical Association*, 53 (4), pp. 873–80.*

(1958) (with J. Henderson) *Microeconomic theory: a mathematical approach*. New York: McGraw-Hill.

(1959) (with W.L. Thorp) *The new inflation*. New York: McGraw-Hill.

(1960) 'Tests of the hypothesis that a linear regression system obeys two different regimes', *Journal of the American Statistical Association*, 55 (2), pp. 324–30.*

(1965) (with S.M. Goldfeld) 'Some tests for homoscedasticity', *Journal of the American Statistical Association*, 60 (2), pp. 539–47.*

(1968) 'The estimation of modal splits', *Transportation Research*, 2 (1), pp. 41–50.*

(1971) (with S.M. Goldfeld) *Nonlinear methods of econometrics*. Amsterdam: North Holland.

(1972) 'A new approach to estimating switching regressions', *Journal of the American Statistical Association*, 67 (2), pp. 306–10.*

(1973a) (with S.M. Goldfeld) 'A Markov model for switching regressions', *Journal of Econometrics*, 1 (1), pp. 3–17.*

(1973b) (with S.M. Goldfeld) 'The estimation of structural shifts by switching regressions', *Annals of Economic and Social Measurement*, 2 (4), pp. 475–85.

(1975) (with S.M. Goldfeld) 'Estimation in a disequilibrium model and the value of information', *Journal of Econometrics*, 3 (3), pp. 325–48.

(1978) 'Tests of the equilibrium vs. disequilibrium hypotheses', *International Economic Review*, 19 (2), pp. 435–52.*

(1978) (with H.S. Rosen) 'Estimation of a disequilibrium aggregate labor market', *Review of Economics and Statistics*, 60 (3), pp. 371–9.*

(1980) (with R. Portes and D. Winter) 'Disequilibrium estimates for consumption goods markets in centrally planned economies', *Review of Economic Studies*, 47 (1), pp. 137–59.

(1986) (with P. Asch) *Racetrack betting: the professors' guide to strategies*. Dover, MA: Auburn House Publishing.

(1987) (with R. Portes, D. Winter and S. Yeo) 'Macroeconomic planning and disequilibrium: estimates for Poland, 1955–1980', *Econometrica*, 55 (1), pp. 19–41.*

(1988) *The econometrics of disequilibrium*. Oxford: Basil Blackwell.

(1988) (with W. Charemza and M. Gronicki) 'Modelling parallel markets in centrally planned economies: the case of the automobile market in Poland', *European Economic Review*, 32 (4), pp. 861–83.*

(1988) (with S.M. Goldfeld) 'Budget constraints, bailouts and the firm under central planning', *Journal of Comparative Economics*, 12 (4), pp. 502–20.*

(1988) (with R. Portes and S. Yeo) 'Tests of the chronic shortage hypothesis: the case of Poland', *Review of Economics and Statistics*, 70 (2), pp. 288–95.*

(1989) (with H.S. Rosen) 'Endogenous output in an aggregate model of the labor market', *Review of Economics and Statistics*, 71 (3), pp. 394–400.*

(1990a) (with S.M. Goldfeld) 'Input rationing and bailouts in socialist economies', *Jahrbuch der Wirtschaft Osteuropas*, 14 (1), pp. 17–37.*

(1990b) (with S.M. Goldfeld) 'Output targets, the soft budget constraint and the firm under central planning', *Journal of Economic Behavior and Organization*, 14 (2), pp. 205–22.*

(1990c) (with S.M. Goldfeld) 'Rationing, defective inputs and Bayesian updates under central planning', *Economics of Planning*, 23 (3), pp. 161–73.*

(1992a) *Collected essays*, 2 vols. Aldershot: Edward Elgar.

(1992b) 'Introduction', in R.E. Quandt (1992a) **q.v.**, vol. I, pp. xiii–xxvii.

BIBLIOGRAPHY

Bresnahan, T.F. and Porter, R.H. (1997) 'Articles in honor of Richard E. Quandt', *Rand Journal of Economics*, 28 (0), pp. S1–S189.

Burkett, J.P. (1988) 'Slack, shortage and discouraged consumers in eastern Europe: estimates based on smoothing by aggregation', *Review of Economic Studies*, 55 (3), pp. 493–506.

Fair, R.C. and Jaffe, D.M. (1972) 'Methods of estimation for markets in disequilibrium', *Econometrica*, 40 (3), pp. 497–514.

Hood, W.C. and Koopmans, T.C. (eds) (1953) *Studies in econometric method.* Cowles commission monograph no. 14. New York: John Wiley.

Kornai, J. (1980) *Economics of shortage*, 2 vols. Amsterdam: North-Holland.

Kornai, J. (1982) *Growth, shortage and efficiency: a macrodynamic model of the socialist economy.* Oxford: Basil Blackwell.

Kuhn, H.W. and Tucker, A.W. (1951) 'Nonlinear programming', in J. Neyman (ed.) (1951) *Proceedings of the second Berkeley symposium on mathematical statistics and probability.* Berkeley and Los Angeles, CA: University of California Press, pp. 481–92.

Maddala, G.S. and Nelson, F.D. (1974) 'Maximum likelihood methods for models of markets in disequilibrium', *Econometrica*, 42 (6), pp. 1013–30.

Romer, D. (1981) 'Rosen and Quandt's disequilibrium model of the labor market: a revision', *Review of Economics and Statistics*, 62 (1), pp. 145–6.

Samuelson, P.A. (1947) *Foundations of economic analysis.* Cambridge, MA: Harvard University Press.

10. Yoram Barzel (b. 1931)[1]

10.1   ISRAEL, 1931–57

I was born in Jerusalem in 1931 and reached my teens during the Second World War. Political issues occupied much of my own and my friends' thinking through the waning years of the British Mandate over Palestine. I avidly read the economic section of the newspaper and was excited by the left-wing political discourse of the youth movement. After a brief and painless army service and a stay of a few months on a kibbutz, I started to think about college. With parental financial support, this sounded like more fun than going to work. There were then just two institutions of higher learning in Israel: the Technion (now the Israeli Institute of Technology) in Haifa, and the Hebrew University in Jerusalem. Attending the Technion was out of the question as that would have meant staying in my home town, so in 1950 I enrolled in the Hebrew University.

A friend told me that his sister was studying 'political economy' at the Sorbonne. The idea appealed to me and I decided to follow suit. But 'political economy' was not offered at the Hebrew University, so I reluctantly settled

---

[1]   Barzel (1995b), as revised by the editors. I have one volume of selected writings in this series (Barzel 1995a).

on majoring in plain economics.

My most important freshman course was a year-long introduction to economics taught by Don Patinkin. I very quickly discovered that I loved the subject even though it bore no relation to economic issues as they appeared in the daily newspapers, which is what I thought 'political economy' was about. I devoted most of the little time I spent on studying to this course. However, since my English was rudimentary, for the first few months I spent more time with the dictionary than with the required text.

I can't say that the course gave me a solid grasp of either the principles or the foundations of economics. I found it hard to see the whole for the parts, a problem that continued to plague me for a long time. In spite of this, I managed to make some sense of bits and pieces of what I encountered in my studies. I still operate in this fashion, and not only when it comes to economics.

Patinkin was a wonderful teacher, a gifted expositor who instilled great enthusiasm for the subjects he was teaching. On him rested practically the whole analytical programme in economics. He did not teach intermediate price theory but, by the time I had completed my MA, I had taken his courses in advanced price theory, macro, business cycles and international trade.

During that period Patinkin was completing his *magnum opus, Money, interest and prices* (1956). He exposed his students to the material he was developing, thus creating an atmosphere of intense excitement in the macro course. He also wrote articles, participated in a number of government commissions and ran the Economics Department. He placed his most advanced students in graduate programmes abroad and later recruited some of these and others to the economics faculty at the Hebrew University. How he managed to do all this is hard to fathom, but he accomplished it without sacrificing personal contact with his students.

I took the course in intermediate price theory in my sophomore year. The instructor had studied with George Stigler at Columbia University. He was neither a very good teacher nor a great economist, but in this year-long course the substantial readings provided the opportunity for a thorough study of the subject. These consisted of four books: Alfred Marshall's *Principles* (1890), George Stigler's *The theory of price* (1952), and intermediate texts by Boulding and Bain. I was alternately excited and exasperated by Marshall, I suppose it depended on my mood. Stigler's conciseness made his book difficult to comprehend; a great deal of discipline, which I did not have, was required to study it, but what I did understand filled me with satisfaction. It took longest to understand his jokes. My fellow students and I quickly dismissed the other two texts as shallow; there was no sense of a great mind behind either of them.

I had made only a half-hearted effort in most of my courses thus far, but towards the end of the year I found myself engrossed in price theory material. For a week's time, preparing for the final exam, I worked harder than I ever had in my life. At the end of that week I started to get a feel for economics – the capacity to address systematically real-world problems – that has stayed with me to this day.

I took another course in price theory, this one taught by Abba Lerner. Lerner had come from the US to Israel as a consultant to the government. He was thought to have accepted the job because it gave him a golden opportunity to implement his socialist ideas, since the government was then dominated by socialists (the Mappai party). He was keen on equating marginal costs to marginal valuations everywhere. Not surprisingly, however, the 'socialist' government had little use for Pareto efficiency and preferred to subsidize its supporters and penalize the rest. Lerner displayed 'disloyalty' when he publicly denounced these policies. Apparently he was greatly disheartened by that experience. It seems, however, that he enjoyed living in Israel. He knew Hebrew very well and nobody minded his nonconformity – in fact, with his sandals and long hair, this is how a biblical prophet might have looked. He chose to stay in Israel for a couple of years which gave him plenty of time to teach.

In terms of preparation, Lerner was probably the laziest teacher I ever had, perhaps equating his marginal cost to his marginal revenue. There was a single text for the course: his *The economics of control* (1944). He assigned one chapter for each class meeting and one student to discuss it. Each chapter seemed simply to reiterate the principle of equating on the margins. I was invariably bored by the hapless student who had been given the responsibility of describing it. Before long, however, Lerner would start to ask questions, prodding us to discuss the material critically. He was most effective in getting us thoroughly involved in the discussion. He would gently make us realize the power and applicability of the principle of equating on the margin to conventional and unconventional problems of allocation. Lerner was at his best when he summarized the period's discourse. His exposition was crystal clear and the economic reasoning brilliant. The central issues were separated from the subsidiary ones, and every one of our numerous mistakes was weeded out in the process. Lerner's brilliance more than compensated for his slipshod preparation.

Of everything I read while studying for the MA, two articles made an especially strong impression on me: 'International trade and the equalisation of factor prices' by Paul Samuelson (1948) and 'The case for flexible exchange rates' by Milton Friedman (1953). I was not surprised by the wonderful piece by Samuelson since he had written the elementary text I was raised on (at the time I failed to realize that not all elementary texts were written by the best economists). The flexible exchange rate paper, however, was my first encounter with Friedman and I was flabbergasted. Not only was I greatly impressed by the substance of the argument and by its incisive presentation but, having already developed a 'bias' for the market, I was gratified to see such a convincing additional case for it.

Towards the end of my sophomore year I began to work part time at the Energy Department of the Israeli government, mostly as a compiler of statistical data. When it was time to write my master's thesis, I chose a topic I could pursue there: the efficiency of the gasoline tax. My training equipped me with a solid base for the economic aspect of such a study, but left me totally unprepared when it came to empirical methods. Although I had taken several courses in statistics, the only worthwhile one in the programme was that on probability. Taught by Dvoretsky, who was often dazzling, its material was not useful for empirical work. The instructors in economics were not much help in empirical method either, so I had to improvise as well as I could.

My main focus in the thesis was on the substitution between gasoline and diesel. Gasoline was then taxed at a much higher rate than diesel. I collected some data on the cost of operating gasoline and diesel trucks of different sizes and then estimated their costs under equal tax rates. I concluded that the differential tax rate did not induce much substitution, and that on that score the tax distortion was modest. Though I had never heard of Harberger, my thesis seemed to presage that he would become my mentor.

In spite of my rudimentary methods, this project gave me a taste for empirical research that would shape my work for years to come. When I decided to continue studying towards a Ph.D., I was thinking primarily in terms of a programme that dealt with real data. Here, too, the guidance by the economics faculty in Jerusalem proved inadequate; nor was my own search terribly effective. For a while I wanted to specialize in location theory or industrial economics because I thought that only in these fields did one do empirical work, but I did not know where to find such programmes. I relaxed my criteria and decided to try my luck in the US.

During this period I made and lost one of the closest friends of my life, a fellow student named Yehuda Grunfeld. Yehuda had a profound influence on me. He was smart, very imaginative and charismatic without being conceited. Sadly, this friendship lasted only a short time. He died in a drowning accident when just 31 years old.

I first got to know Yehuda well in an army reserve unit to which we both belonged. He was ahead of me in his studies, so we did not share many courses, but we spent a great deal of time together, discussing economic problems and his pet idea of a world government. A short time later I joined him in the Energy Department where he was writing his master's thesis on the economics of blending oil-refinery output. I was in fact witnessing the independent invention of linear programming. His version was apparently fairly primitive, but quite effective. Soon after getting his MA he went to the University of Chicago to study for a Ph.D.; when I arrived at Chicago, he had just been appointed assistant professor. During the next two summers he ran two projects at the Transportation Center of Northwestern University where I acted as one of his assistants. I had great fun with the empirical research and was paid handsomely. I thoroughly enjoyed Yehuda's company, but it was to be for the last time. He passed away the following summer. He had a rich personal life, magically touching his numerous close friends, and was at the beginning of a brilliant career. He remains the only person of my acquaintance to whom I feel the title of 'leader' truly applied.

10.2   CHICAGO, 1957–61

When concluding my search for a graduate programme, Chicago was not at the top of my list. This was due partly to financial considerations and partly to lack of information, for Chicago was in fact foremost in empirical work in economics. However, after I arrived in the States I visited Yehuda and realized that the empirical emphasis for which I was searching was then almost unique to Chicago. When Chicago offered to 'sweeten the pot', my decision was made.

The intellectual atmosphere at Chicago was electrifying; the economics faculty was free of deadwood and did virtually no consulting. Small talk occurred, of course, but it occupied only a small fraction of our time, the rest of which was relentlessly overtaken by economics. Already then, in Chicago, 'economics' meant nearly everything. Although Gary Becker was no doubt a major contributor to that view, he was not in Chicago then. Indeed, during my first year, neither were Friedman or Stigler. The atmosphere of total involvement was contagious. You couldn't spend two minutes in the company of most graduate students without hearing about the marginal cost of something. I became avidly involved in these discussions in and out of the classroom. In Israel, I had seldom taken part in course discussions, but I became quite aggressive in the classroom immediately after arriving at Chicago, an unplanned, but quick, adjustment to the Chicago style.

At Chicago, of course, the market was king. On my second day there I had lunch with several advanced graduate students. One of them asked what I thought of the US. Since I had never seen freeways before, I said that I was amazed at the sight of the West Side Highway in New York. I added that I was surprised no tolls were charged during rush-hour to reduce the traffic jams. Two members of the group looked at each other and burst out laughing.

I was not sure what was funny. One of them explained: 'If you know that already, what more is there for you to learn at Chicago?'. I didn't fully grasp the significance of that remark then. I thought that everybody knew that tolls reduce congestion. Only after I left did I discover that Chicago differs slightly from the rest of the world.

During the early 1950s the Cowles commission resided at the University of Chicago, with Chicago at the forefront of econometrics and, to a lesser degree, mathematical economics. However, by 1957 when I arrived, the Cowles commission had transferred to Yale. The search for replacements went slowly. During my entire stay at Chicago there were neither theoretical econometricians nor high-powered mathematical economists on the staff. The sole exception was Trygve Haavelmo who visited Chicago during my first year. I took his course in econometrics and found it very stimulating, but most of the material, unfortunately, was over my head. None of the courses in my programme was 'formal', not even Haavelmo's. Indeed, the graduate sequence in statistics, taught in the business school by Harry Roberts, was one of the most informal courses I took. It was partly based on Allen Wallis's notes, which provided a peculiar but powerful feel for statistics. Although little time was spent on theorems, heavy emphasis was placed on rigour in the application phase.

In my first quarter I took a course in price theory from Harberger who was quite a casual instructor. The age difference between us is not large and, since I already had my MA, I initially assumed that I was as good an economist as he was. A few weeks later I was willing to acknowledge that he did perhaps have an edge since I had yet to demonstrate my superiority. Eventually, I also realized that Harberger had (and probably still has) the knack of winning an argument without making the loser feel like a fool. By the end of the quarter I decided that I wanted both to become a member of his workshop and for him to be my dissertation adviser. I was delighted to have both wishes granted.

I spent four years at Chicago. By my reckoning, Harberger was there a total of 21 months during that period! Yet he provided all the help I needed, which was quite a bit. Having him as an adviser also gave me a sense of how to get involved in others' research, which I continue to enjoy.

The workshop system was a great innovation for writing dissertations, its main advantage being the 'socializing' of the writing process. One could see how others were going about it and take part in their progress; one also had a forum for presenting one's own ideas and the benefit of hearing the unadorned reactions of others. Moreover, the discussions often spilled over into hallways and offices. We all took part in each other's work. Writing a dissertation under these conditions was not all that desolate a process.

Chicago was full of impressive individuals. The most prominent among them were Friedman and Stigler. Neither was at Chicago during my first year when I was engaged in all the required course work, so I only audited Friedman's course on price theory and Stigler's on industrial organization. I also attended Friedman's workshop for one term. I did not, however, attend Stigler's industrial organization workshop, a fact which is quite amazing. The significance of both Aaron Director and Ronald Coase, who attended that workshop, completely eluded me. Perhaps this was because the workshop was held in the Law School; Director and Coase were both on the Law School faculty and not in economics, and I was not (and still am not) interested in law. Not many economics departments, not to speak of law schools, can boast that they had at any one time a pair of economists who could match Director and Coase. Twenty years later my work was to belong within the scope of that workshop and Director was to become one of my best friends.

Towards the end of my second year I started to look for a dissertation topic. Several of the doctoral students who preceded me had worked on the estimation of demand functions, concentrating mainly on durable goods. I decided instead to study something related to supply and narrowed my choice to factors that might shift the curve. It took me several months to find an industry that was subject to significant shifts and for which adequate data were available. I settled on the electric power industry which, according to John Kendrick, had experienced a huge increase in productivity during the previous three decades. Moreover, this being a regulated industry, a great deal of data on it were available. Chicago hated regulations but loved the data they generated.

My objective was to determine what accounted for the change in output per unit of input – Kendrick's measure of productivity. I considered this productivity measure a 'residual' and tried to shrink it as much as I could. I hypothesized that, even under constant technology, output per unit of input could increase by a shift to larger plants and by a more intense use of existing plant. I estimated the coefficients for these variables from a cross-section and applied the results to the period covered by Kendrick. I concluded that the bulk of the productivity increase was the result of exploiting existing scale economies and of the more intensive use of available plants, induced by demand increase and by a change in its pattern. Not much remained for 'technical advance'. My work was received well by all except Stigler, who was one of my committee members. He said it was 'fine' but added, without elaborating, that he was not interested in this kind of work. It took me several years to realize that he was looking for the testing of hypotheses rather than 'estimation', by which time I had adopted that view as well.

10.3   SEATTLE, 1961–

In the autumn of 1961 my job search brought me to Seattle, where I still am today. Few people were neutral to Chicago and its graduates then. Some schools would not consider Chicago graduates, while others were eager to have them. The University of Washington belonged in the latter category. Indeed, I found the Economics Department most congenial. Don Gordon was its dominant intellectual figure and I greatly enjoyed, and benefited from, his company. As sometimes happens, much of his creativity got embedded in the writing of others, including my own.

My arrival in Seattle came at a time of phenomenal expansion in the Economics Department which grew from about twenty the year before I arrived to about thirty the year after. This growth was accompanied by substantial turnover. Among this large and fluid crowd it was not hard to find plenty of both professionally and personally compatible individuals. For some reason, however, the Department was always quite contentious and seldom ran peacefully. Within a decade, with the exception of Doug North, those to whom I was closest had left. Don Gordon and Walter Oi went to the University of Rochester, while Al Hynes and John Floyd chose the University of Toronto. However, Doug North, who became chairman after the first two had gone, hired Steve Cheung which proved momentous to the whole Department, and especially to me, in the 1970s and 1980s.

My main research interest during the 1960s was in the supply side of microeconomics. I first extended my empirical work on electricity production and had fun switching from a mechanical calculator to a (mainframe) computer. One problem I dealt with in my dissertation was the construction of a quantity series, which required a quantity index. In the process of publishing the main dissertation results (Barzel 1963b), I also managed to have accepted 'Some observations on the index number problem' in *Econometrica* (1963a), probably one of the least technical papers ever published in that journal. This study empirically exploits the revealed preference principle to bracket the true change in quantity; it is the only time, I believe, that revealed preference has been applied in this way.

My research branched off into two areas: the measurement of productivity change, and innovations. The former led to one paper – 'Productivity and the price of medical services' – in which I used medical insurance coverage as a proxy for a constant quality service (Barzel 1969). After completing this, I decided to move into other research areas. Regarding innovations, I first attempted to do empirical work on patents, using data from Israel. Given the uniqueness of patents, simply counting them seemed unsatisfactory. I decided to give more weight to important than to unimportant patents, and concluded that 'importance' should be measured as the net value of each. That led me to the startling conclusion that all patents should be weighed at zero. The reason was quite simple: under competition among potential inventors, the net expected profit from every invention should be zero, hence the weights. One logical implication of this result was to abandon the project. I felt impelled, however, to ponder the returns from innovation, which ultimately led to my best-known paper – 'Optimal timing of innovations' (Barzel 1968).

In my attempt to deal with this issue, I confronted the notion of the 'public domain' for the first time in my own research and only then began to think seriously about it. Given that the knowledge underlying innovations lies in the public domain, I concluded that the zero-profit condition was the result of competition but was not a condition for efficiency, and that it produced the non-optimal result of premature innovations. When I attempted to publish the paper containing this result, the *JPE* rejected it specifically on the grounds that this argument was wrong. In 1971, however, the *JPE* published my paper 'Investment, scale and growth' that relied on the same idea (Barzel 1971). Subsequently, Dasgupta and Stiglitz published a series of articles based on the timing of innovation results.

During the late 1960s and early 1970s I continued to work on the timing of innovations and other activities subject to decreasing cost, on problems of public goods and on a host of diverse issues. My most eccentric paper, which is also shortest on economic content, is on the Indianapolis 500 (Barzel 1972). Only its concern with speed may explain why it is in the *Journal of Economic Theory* set. Another isolated paper is on monopolistic competition.

My dissatisfaction with conventional textbook treatment triggered two studies on labour. In one I argue that the assumption of a linear budget constraint – which implies that the (per-hour) productivity of a worker is invariant whether he works one, eight or 24 hours a day – is unreasonable. Relaxing that assumption led to the conclusion, among others, that what we usually call 'the wage rate' is actually the average wage in a take-it-or-leave-it wage-hours package, and is not the appropriate rate for marginal decisions (Barzel 1973). The other textbook problem is in drawing the individual labour supply as sloping downward only after initially sloping upward. When the wage rate is very low, however, a person whose entire income comes from work must spend the maximum possible amount of time working just to survive. As the wage rate rises, such a person obviously cannot work more, and may work less. Dick McDonald helped me to formalize the results; in the process we expanded the model to account for non-labour income, determining the conditions under which the textbook result may hold (Barzel and McDonald 1973).

Late in 1971, towards the end of a year-long visit to England, I read an article on 'Discrimination by waiting time in merit goods' by Nichols,

Smolinsky and Tideman (1971). I was greatly intrigued by the subject, but found some of their results unsatisfactory and thus worth reworking. I started to look into this problem after returning to Seattle. This research marks the beginning of a remarkable relationship with Steve Cheung.

Steve came to Seattle in 1969 and it took us much of the first year to size each other up. By the time I had returned from the next year's sabbatical in England, Al Hynes and John Floyd, two of my closest colleagues, had left the University. Steve had a keen interest in the rationing-by-waiting problem which I had started to work on, and it was natural for us to try to collaborate. Steve had come from Chicago, where he had spent the previous three years as an assistant professor, much of the time with Coase. At UCLA he had taken some graduate price theory from Armen Alchian and had written his dissertation on sharecropping under him. On arrival in Seattle he was, in my current view, the top transaction-cost property-rights economist in the profession. I perceived right away that his was a protean force and also that his line of thinking provided the organizing framework I was lacking.

I was not the only one to appreciate Steve's talents. John McGee was probably the first to recognize his extraordinary abilities, and Doug North, who was then chairman, did not take long to see his potential. Doug provided Steve, and the kind of programme he advocated, full support, which included hiring Levis Kochin, a move Steve strongly recommended. Kochin's knowledge of fact, organized by economic reasoning, is probably unequalled in the profession, and for years now he has been my closest colleague. He is not renowned, however, for his orderliness or for timekeeping. Thus Doug took it on himself to support (in addition to Steve) one more unconventional character.

Until the late 1960s, the Department was considered good in applied economics and very good in economic history. By the end of the 1970s economic history was strengthened further, to a substantial degree because of its interaction with the transaction cost group, the latter coming very close to the top of the profession in its speciality. Unfortunately, by the early 1980s, the whole edifice had disintegrated. North and Cheung were allowed to slip away, with an almost audible sigh of relief from those seeking a conventional, or perhaps a staid, Department. The price was paid in mediocrity. The Nobel Prize was eventually awarded to a 'former' University of Washington faculty member, Doug North, in 1993.

During the 1970s Steve and I spent something like half our time at work together and numerous hours at home talking to each other on the telephone. In this intense interaction, I provided a set of tools and problem-solving skills which was almost ideally suited to analyse the kinds of issues that interested us. While I was concerned with the rationing-by-waiting problem, Steve was working on the closely related topic of price controls, part of his project on rent control in Hong Kong. We encountered numerous common puzzles and attacked them from all angles with great zest. On my part, at least, the gain in understanding was exhilarating. The main ingredient common to rationing-by-waiting and to price control is that allocation is not random; on the contrary, people will compete for any commodity that the government either provides free of charge or sells at a below-market price under a price control. The outcome of this competition depends on the criterion by which the good is allocated among demanders. Those with a comparative advantage in meeting the criterion will be the ones to acquire it, making the outcome determinate. The net gain to a marginal person would be zero; the aggregate net gain to participants is necessarily less than the total value of what is given away or placed under a price control.

It took me a long time to realize that the same analysis was fully applicable to private markets where, because of the prohibitive cost of delineating all attributes, some of them are provided at no marginal charge. The other side of the coin is that various apparent 'inefficiencies', such as queues, are present in private, competitive markets. One cannot infer that inefficiency exists simply as a result of observing phenomena such as queues that result from government action.

The rationing-by-waiting paper marked the beginning of my almost exclusive research interest in transaction cost issues during the last two decades. There was one exception, however – my obsession with the law of demand, which began around 1968. Two colleagues, Lowell Bassett and Tom Borcherding, were at that time trying to determine whether factors of production can become Giffen goods. I participated in demonstrating that no Giffen good could emerge in a competitive industry. Even if the production function does accommodate such a good, the Giffen good may emerge only if produced in the inefficient part of its domain. This is inconsistent with cost minimization and can be avoided by altering the scale of operations of the firm (and the number of firms).

Reflecting on this result, I became convinced that an analogous relationship must apply to individuals. I reasoned that the 'scale' (or income) of individuals is determined endogenously, by gambling for instance, and, consequently, that individuals too are able to avoid the Giffen good trap. Intermittently for many years I tried to figure out whether I was right. I was successful in demonstrating for a special case that an individual who is prone to the Giffen good problem will increase his utility by holding an asset portfolio containing more than the commensurate amount of the inferior good. For such a person the income and the substitution effects are in the same direction, so the demand curve must be negatively sloped.

For years, I posed to technically better-skilled colleagues the challenge of proving the proposition for the general case. Only in the early 1990s was this challenge met. Wing Suen, a former student of mine, was able to prove that individuals will gain by taking steps ahead of time to avoid the trap, and that no Giffen good can then emerge. The result (Barzel 1992) was published after a 'gestation' period of almost a quarter of a century!

While wrestling with the Giffen good problem, I arrived at a related demand analysis result. I realized that, under a wide set of conditions, individuals are expected to arrange their endowments so as to reach their consumption point before any price change. This is the case regarding a change in rent when one lives in one's own house, and also regarding the change in any price when one's wage is tied to the cost-of-living index. The income effect is simply absent under such price changes. For this reason, using the conventional method of adjusting income in the estimation of demand is plainly wrong. These ideas were published under the title 'The testability of the law of demand' in the memorial volume for Paul Cootner (Barzel 1982b).

My rationing-by-waiting paper was followed by one on taxation. The idea for the paper came to me almost unconsciously. I sensed that there was an argument regarding taxation that was analogous to that on rationing-by-waiting: first, it should be possible partially to avoid the tax and, second, competition for the avoided tax would be of the same nature as competition for the free good. It took me a long time to articulate the idea, not only to others, but also to myself. I remember spending an aeroplane trip, returning from an annual AEA meeting, trying to explain the idea to Gene Silberberg. All I got in response was a look in his eyes which said, 'What does this crazed man want from me?' When finally able to make sense of the idea, I found it extremely valuable because it underlies the notion that free attributes are everywhere, and that their allocation is a dominant transaction cost problem.

In the per-unit tax case, what corresponds to the free attribute is the ability to pack more 'substance' into each taxed unit, thereby reducing the tax burden. I hypothesized that, as measured, the price of a taxed commodity could rise by more than the tax. Applying the notion to cigarettes, the hypothesis was not rejected (Barzel 1976). An amusing example can be cited from the 1920s when the tax on cigarettes was first imposed. The tax was set on a per-cigarette basis. A cigarette producer then introduced very long cigarettes. After paying the 'unit' tax, the user divided each cigarette into several shorter ones. To ease this job, the producer perforated the cigarettes at convenient division points. Eventually, the Treasury added a maximum length specification to the definition of cigarettes.

In 1977, I published a book jointly with Chris Hall who was then a graduate student. In *The political economy of the oil import quota*, we pursued the idea that, because the quota was valuable, people spent resources to affect it and to qualify for it. Since, for instance, small refiners earned higher proportional quotas, we predicted that refiners would take steps to become 'small'. I had received a grant to work on the quota problem and hired Chris as an assistant, but he very quickly and decisively earned promotion to co-author. One of the best economists I have met, from the beginning of his graduate studies Chris demonstrated a profound understanding of economics. I am constantly impressed by his beautiful empirical work which, unfortunately, transcribes awkwardly to the printed page. Our friendship continues to this day and (though we are half a globe apart) I enjoy talking economics with him more than with anybody else.

I next set out to write the paper 'An economic analysis of slavery' (Barzel 1977a) which had its origin in the teaching of price theory. Friedman's brief analysis in his price theory text about the effect of the prohibition of slavery, such as on the return to investment in human capital, intrigued me. Every time I taught price theory I spent a little more time on the subject. Around 1970, Bob Fogel came to Seattle to give a seminar. I was away that day, but on returning I was told about his remarkable finding that slaves got more calories per day than poor whites did. To my way of thinking, it would have been remarkable had they *not* received more calories. After all, owners could not extract a high level of output on a continuing basis unless they supplied the commensurate amount of calories. In any case, I decided right then that I would like to work on slavery.

I started doing so in earnest after *Time on the cross* by Fogel and Engerman (1974) was published. I did more reading on slavery than on any other problem I have encountered. In this regard, it is my most empirical work. It was also a bit frustrating. I would form new hypotheses on why this or that practice was observed, usually while reading a monograph or an article on slavery, then seek new data to test the new hypothesis. But with each new data source, typically from another society and era, there existed other differences that required a reformulation of the problem and still newer data for a valid test. Even though I think well of the paper that emerged, I was never able to overcome this sense of inability to resolve satisfactorily the problem.

I worked on the slavery problem mostly in 1974–5, during a year-long visit to the Hoover Institute at Stanford. The best thing that happened to me during that visit was meeting Aaron Director. In spite of a full generation gap, he became one of my closest friends. We had endless conversations on the slavery problem. Indirection was his method. He would bring up an observation, such as some debate on a slavery issue in the British parliament and try to deduce the motive for the action taken. As a rule, I could not explain the action, and Aaron seldom offered reasons of his own. Nevertheless, after several conversations I realized I was gaining a better understanding of issues that I thought I had already fully grasped.

Aaron was very critical of the use of unnecessary or overly complex terminology, often stating that 'property rights' was one of these superfluous terms. When I asked what was wrong with it, he said that in the cases he had come across, demand-supply analysis would have been entirely adequate. He was persuaded neither by my claim that what he saw was a biased sample, nor by my attempt to provide better examples. Convinced of my case, I decided to set my idea down in writing. The paper that emerged was titled, somewhat whimsically, 'Transaction costs: are they just costs?' (Barzel 1985). I was greatly relieved when Aaron accepted my argument that the existing framework was inadequate and also that competition does not necessarily bring about Pareto conditions. I was elated when he referred to the paper as written 'for me'.

I never wrote a joint paper with Steve Cheung, but we came close to it once. Around 1975 Zvi Griliches visited us to give a seminar. During lunch, in the course of a conversation on radicals in the Economics Department at Harvard, Zvi described some of the early 'market signalling' results by Michael Spence. I was immediately convinced they were wrong, but needed some time to demonstrate to myself why. The next day I told Steve about Spence's results, and he elucidated the problem so quickly as to make me a bit envious. We decided then that we would collaborate on exploring that issue. To get the ball rolling, I wrote a few pages and gave them to Steve, and subsequently handed him longer and longer manuscripts. Steve never responded. I do not know why. So I completed the paper on my own.

The title of the paper, 'Some fallacies in the interpretation of information costs' (Barzel 1977b) alluded to Frank Knight's (1924) celebrated article on social cost. It was my first methodological paper in the transaction cost area. Its main point is that, under the assumptions of Spence's model, people can always find profitable arrangements that shun information whose net social value is negative. Another result is that when transaction costs are positive, people may suppress potentially wasteful activities. I suggested that this result may explain the restrictions De Beers places on its approved traders in inspecting the diamonds it proffers, and the 'block booking' of films offered to movie theatres.

My paper 'Measurement cost and the organization of markets' (Barzel 1982a) is the most crucial to my understanding of the methodological problems associated with the costs of transacting. For a long time I was trying to get a toehold on these issues by studying insurance practices. My thinking proved to be very messy and my advancement slow until I hit on the magic word 'measurement'. Once pronounced, the thing started to fall into place. What may explain the transformation is that, with measurement, one's attention is immediately focused on marginal costs and benefits, and one no longer has to operate on an all-or-nothing basis, which is natural in the context of insurance.

To exchange, the buyer must know what he receives from the seller. The cost of measurement of a commodity or service increases as it is made more complete, more accurate and more widely available. Transactors wish to economize on this cost but, when they do, one or both can be exploited by the other. This problem does not disappear even where numbers are large. In the paper I analyse these problems and form hypotheses regarding the methods and institutions employed to resolve them. Among other things, this paper may be the first to argue that the violation of marginal principles is not inconsistent with competition. It also reiterates Cheung's claim in his rent control paper that such discrepancies do not imply waste.

In 1981, the Department at the University of Washington decided to add a course on property rights to the undergraduate curriculum. Cheung taught it first, and then promptly moved away. North taught it next, and likewise moved away. In the process of preparing for the course when my turn came, I realized that I had developed a great deal of new material. I decided then to write a book on the subject (Barzel 1989), the unifying theme being that, in every exchange, some attributes of the transaction are not constant and are too costly to price. Failure to price these attributes amounts to placing them in the public domain. Transactors attempt to maximize the value of their exchange in the face of that difficulty. The free attributes that remain unpriced and unconstrained will be consumed to the point where their marginal value is zero. In other cases, transactors will restrict their own actions in various ways. These include, among others, quantity constraints, operating on a wage rather than piece-rate contract, making commitments not to change prices, making guarantees and consenting not to exercise rights (which may appear as the attenuation of rights). Although the book is not empirical, it contains numerous refutable implications that can test the model.

In the 1980s, I, like many other economists, started to dabble in 'political economy' problems. Although this was what I had thought of studying when first at college, I quickly lost sight of it, coming back only with the general awakening to the subject by economists. I made a minor foray into the topic of voting (Barzel and Silberberg 1973) in the early 1970s, but that was an isolated effort. My interest in voting was renewed in the mid-1980s. The problems that I thought were worth studying seemed at first intractable. It occurred to me that since voting is also practised in the business world, the study of business voting could be a good introduction to the study of voting in general. The next big leap was the realization that voting and other procedures within firms are introduced into their constitution by entrepreneurs. All of a sudden I had the seed of a profit-maximizing theory of the constitution.

These ideas led to a paper (with Tim Sass) on voting. In it we construct and test a model of voting as applied to condominiums. The main hypothesis, supported by the data, is that the developers of condominium projects formulate voting and other procedures to minimize the opportunities for wealth-transfer among owners (Barzel and Sass 1990).

With these results in hand, I began to wonder whether the rationale for voting in the political sphere was the same. One candidate for the role of entrepreneur is a dictator. He is able to implement voting and related procedures, and can reap the benefits of associated gains. The model I started with, however, was seriously deficient as it could not cope with the fact that most dictators are in no hurry to take advantage of the opportunities apparently available to them. Eventually I concluded that the personal security of the dictator could be the main restraining factor, and with that I decided to try to apply the idea.

I am doing much of this work by myself, but some of it jointly with Edgar Kiser, a sociologist here with similar interests. This body of work, however, is difficult to 'sell', and thus far only one paper has been published (Kiser and Barzel 1991).

The dictator faces a fundamental trade-off between security and material wealth. He is safer keeping subjects under his yoke, and supervising their inputs allows tight control. The tighter the control, however, the smaller their output and the smaller the amount the dictator can extract. The more freedom he allows, the more they become residual claimants of their actions and the larger the amount he can extract. But subjects granted freedom and the opportunity to accumulate wealth are also better able to depose their ruler. The granting of freedoms, then, is expected to be accompanied by safeguards for the ruler as well as his subjects. As a final point here, subjects that accumulate wealth and power are attractive partners for various projects, especially for war. Large-scale projects with many partners require decisions to be made by voting. My hypothesis is that voting institutions and other constitutional provisions do not necessarily reflect a striving towards democracy, but rather the attempt by the ruler and his most prominent subjects to bolster further their wealth, while at the same time protecting it from confiscation.

This model is being applied in several projects that are at different stages of completion. In one of the joint studies with Kiser we determine that, in broad terms, the model is supported by the steady constitutional progress that occurred in medieval England, and by its initial progress and subsequent decline in medieval France. Other studies include a comparison between medieval England and France regarding the relationship of voting rights to tax payment; the emergence of the state from 'primitive' conditions; the cause of a certain type of revolt; the city-state, and the evolution of the

English parliament. For the time being this subject is, and probably will continue to be, my main research interest.

SELECTED WORKS

(1963a) 'Some observations on the index number problem', *Econometrica*, 31 (3), pp. 391–9.*

(1963b) 'Productivity in the electric power industry, 1929–1955', *Review of Economics and Statistics*, 45 (4), pp. 395–408.*

(1968) 'Optimal timing of innovations', *Review of Economics and Statistics*, 50 (3), pp. 348–55.*

(1969) 'Productivity and the price of medical services', *Journal of Political Economy*, 77 (5), pp. 1014–27.*

(1971) 'Investment, scale and growth', *Journal of Political Economy*, 79 (2), pp. 214–31.*

(1972) 'The rate of technical progress: the "Indianapolis 500"', *Journal of Economic Theory*, 4 (1), pp. 72–81.*

(1973) 'The determination of daily hours and wages', *Quarterly Journal of Economics*, 87 (2), pp. 220–38.*

(1973) (with R.J. McDonald) 'Assets, subsistence and the supply curve of labor', *American Economic Review*, 63 (4), pp. 621–33.*

(1973) (with G. Silberberg) 'Is the act of voting rational?', *Public Choice*, 16, pp. 51–8.*

(1976) 'An alternative approach to the analysis of taxation', *Journal of Political Economy*, 84 (6), pp. 1177–97.*

(1977a) 'An economic analysis of slavery', *Journal of Law and Economics*, 20 (1), pp. 87–110.*

(1977b) 'Some fallacies in the interpretation of information costs', *Journal of Law and Economics*, 20 (2), pp. 291–307.*

(1977) (with C. Hall) *The political economy of the oil import quota.* Stanford, CA: Stanford University Press.

(1982a) 'Measurement cost and the organization of markets', *Journal of Law and Economics*, 25 (1), pp. 27–48.*

(1982b) 'The testability of the law of demand', in W.F. Sharpe and C.M. Cootner (eds) (1982) *Financial economics: essays in honor of Paul Cootner.* New York: Prentice-Hall, pp. 233–45.*

(1985) 'Transaction costs: are they just costs?', *Journal of Institutional and Theoretical Economics*, 141 (1), pp. 4–16.*

(1989) *Economic analysis of property rights.* Cambridge: Cambridge University Press.

(1990) (with T.R. Sass) 'The allocation of resources by voting', *Quarterly Journal of Economics*, 105 (3), pp. 745–71.*

(1991) (with E. Kiser) 'The origins of democracy in England', *Rationality and Society*, 3 (4), pp. 396–422.*

(1992) (with W. Suen) 'The demand curves for Giffen goods are downward sloping', *Economic Journal*, 102 (4), pp. 896–905.*

(1995a) *Productivity change, public goods and transaction costs: essays at the boundaries of microeconomics*. Aldershot: Edward Elgar.
(1995b) 'Introduction', in Y. Barzel (1995a) **q.v.**, pp. xi–xxiii.

BIBLIOGRAPHY

Fogel, R.W. and Engerman, S.L. (1974) *Time on the cross: the economics of American negro slavery*, 2 vols. New York: Little, Brown.
Friedman, M. (1953) 'The case for flexible exchange rates', in M. Friedman (1953) *Essays in positive economics*. Chicago: University of Chicago Press, pp. 157–203.
Knight, F.H. (1924) 'Fallacies in the interpretation of social cost', *Quarterly Journal of Economics*, 38 (4), pp. 582–606. Rep. in F.H. Knight (1935) *The ethics of competition and other essays*. London: George Allen & Unwin, pp. 217–36.
Nichols, D., Smolensky, E. and Tideman, T.D. (1971) 'Discrimination by waiting time in merit goods', *American Economic Review*, 61 (3), pp. 312–23.
Samuelson, P.A. (1948) 'International trade and the equalisation of factor prices', *Economic Journal*, 58 (2), pp. 163–84.
Stigler, G.J. (1952) *The theory of price*, rev. edn. London: Macmillan.

11. Ryuzo Sato (b. 1931)[1]

11.1   HITOTSUBASHI UNIVERSITY, 1950–4

In 1950, just five years after Japan's defeat in World War II, I entered Hitotsubashi University. My first semester there coincided with the beginning of Japan's new university system. Even the school's name was new: it had formerly been called the Tokyo University of Commerce.

Akita Prefecture, where I was born, is at the northernmost tip of Honshu, the main island of Japan, in what is known as the Tohoku region. Perhaps because of the remoteness of the place and the newness of my high school, Yuzawa Prefectural High, no one from there had ever before been accepted by a first-rate Tokyo-based national university directly upon graduation. The only other person from my school to go to Hitotsubashi University before myself was Zosei Ito (now president of Japan Life Co.), who was a year ahead of me.

At first I had considered taking the entrance examination for the University of Tokyo with the intention of specializing in mathematics, but

---

[1]   Sato (1996b; 1999b), as revised by the editors. I have two volumes in the series: the first reprinting selected essays in growth theory and technical change (Sato 1996a) and the second my essays on production, stability and dynamic symmetry (Sato 1999a).

my father promptly vetoed that idea. 'What do you plan to do?' he yelled, 'Teach arithmetic in elementary school? Economics is the subject of the future.' Because I had no confidence in my ability to pay my own way through school, I switched my sights to the Economics Department. My father, who had to deal with MacArthur's land reforms, had a particularly keen interest in economic issues. He instinctively realized that economics would be the key to Japan's postwar reconstruction. When I think about the way I got my start in a field that later came to fascinate me, I can't help being grateful to my father.

It was my father's decision that I take the entrance examination for Hitotsubashi University, because, in those days, Marxist economics was in fashion at the University of Tokyo. Since both the University of Tokyo and Hitotsubashi belonged in the first group of national universities, which meant that their entrance examinations were held on the same day, it was impossible to take the examinations for both Universities.

Hitotsubashi University had its own special teaching system known as the 'seminar'. All students, when they reached their third year, would study in small groups under a single professor. Naturally enough, popular professors were swamped with applicants. The screening process consisted of an interview rather than an examination. The seminar I entered was that of Professor Ichiro Nakayama. Professor Nakayama was not only the president of the university but also the chairman of the Japanese government's Central Labour Relations Committee and in that capacity was then resolutely tackling some of the major issues facing postwar Japan. Reflecting the activities of Professor Nakayama, the seminar was extremely lively. In my year, 15 third-year students entered Professor Nakayama's seminar; my compatriot Zosei Ito had entered the previous year. Professor Nakayama was a major figure in politics, whose name was well known throughout Japan. He had the ability and influence to act as an adviser to prime ministers, though he steadfastly refused to accept a cabinet post. He was also a scholar of great distinction who related the still embryonic trends in economic theory within Japanese academic circles to what was going on in the rest of the world.

In Professor Nakayama's seminar we read Alvin Hansen's *A guide to Keynes* (1953), J. R. Hicks's *A contribution to the theory of the trade cycle* (1950) and *Value and capital* (1939), Roy Harrod's *Towards a dynamic economics* (1948) and Joan Robinson's *The rate of interest and other essays* (1952). I also read Keynes's *General theory* (1936), but found it too difficult; to tell the truth, I couldn't make head nor tail of it. *The economics of J.M. Keynes* (1948) by Dudley Dillard and *The Keynesian revolution* (1947) by Lawrence Klein gave me a sense that I understood something of what Keynes was all about. Students in the Nakayama seminar in those days generally tended to do research on Keynes, post-Keynesian economics or Schumpeter for their graduation thesis. At Professor Nakayama's suggestion, I wrote my thesis on *The economics of control* (1944) by Abba P. Lerner. This gave me my first opportunity to look at the problem of how capitalist principles of competition can be introduced into a socialist economic system. Lerner's name was almost totally unknown in Japan at that time. When I later had the chance to meet Professor and Mrs Lerner personally and heard from his own lips how he came to write that famous book, I felt a strange affinity. Compared with the writings of Keynes, Professor Lerner's English style was much easier for me to read back then.

When I was at Hitotsubashi, not much emphasis was given to microeconomic theory. However, I realize now that Professor Nakayama's book *Junsui Keizaigaku* ('Theory of pure economics'; Nakayama 1933) might well be called the Japanese version of the combined ideas of Walras and Cournot. This work was my introduction to mathematical economics and microeconomics. As I mentioned earlier, at one time I had considered majoring in mathematics, and my interest in the subject remained so great that, in addition to the guidance I received in the Nakayama seminar, I took courses in mathematical economics with Masao Hisatake and Kin'ichi Yamada. It was in these courses that I first came into contact with Paul Samuelson's *Foundations of economic analysis* (1947), a book I was subsequently to translate into Japanese (Sato 1967c). I will discuss my long friendship with Paul later on (see also Samuelson 1998).

In retrospect, I realize that basic education was given short shrift under the Japanese college system, which has the disadvantage of forcing students to specialize in a narrow field of concentration at an early period. Nevertheless, this was the period of confusion after the end of the war, when knowledge of modern economics was surging into Japan, and both Japanese society and the academic world were brimming with energy. With no clearly defined models to pigeonhole me, I spent a fruitful four years at Hitotsubashi absorbing that energy in my own way.

11.2   ASPIRING TO GRADUATE EDUCATION, 1954–9

After graduation in 1954, I entered the Mitsui Trust and Banking Co. I was assigned to the Securities Department, but for the most part my work each day consisted of writing drafts of newspaper articles for the manager. There had been some doubt in my mind whether I would go to work for a bank or stay at the university and continue my studies. Japanese universities in those days did not have a well-developed system of graduate education and provided only an uneasy amalgam of an apprentice system and a self-directed learning process. What is more, in the year that I graduated, the boom brought about by the Korean War had ended and the Japanese economy was in a period of recession. Graduates who couldn't find good jobs would stay in school in the hope of finding better ones the following year. In such circumstances, anyone with a bit of confidence aspired to enter a first-rate company. This was the route I chose. I did not give up scholarship, however, or abandon the hope of continuing my study of theoretical economics. While working at Mitsui Trust, I was groping for some practical way to pursue my research and go to the United States to study. It was during this time that I wrote an article in Japanese entitled 'On growth theory' for *The Economic Studies Quarterly*, the official publication of the Japanese Economic Association (Sato 1956). As I recall, the point of view expressed there was well received. When I later applied for a Fulbright Scholarship, I was able to include this work in my curriculum vitae. I now realize that the basic ideas for the Ph.D. dissertation I submitted to Johns Hopkins (Sato 1962) are contained in this essay.

11.3   JOHNS HOPKINS, 1959–62

When I first went to Michigan as a Fulbright Scholar, I expected to return to Japan in a year and go back to work for the Mitsui Trust and Banking Co. However, I was so impressed by the high quality of graduate school education in the United States that once I had got a glimpse of a world of scholarship unimaginable in Japan, especially in the area of theoretical economics, I was determined to remain in America and go on for my Ph.D. degree. In June 1959, I came to an amicable agreement with Mitsui Trust and left the company. That autumn I headed once again to America, this time with my new bride, Kishie Hayashi. The Ise Bay typhoon, which struck while we were on board ship, made a vivid impression on me. With no guarantees for the future, I had burned my bridges; there was no turning back.

My years at Johns Hopkins posed no major problems as far as my studies were concerned. However, life as a graduate student was hard, both because my wife was unused to living in a foreign country and because, to get around the Bank of Japan's currency restrictions then in effect, I had to supplement my meagre scholarship by exchanging yen for dollars with Americans going to Japan. (This was back when the official exchange rate was 360 yen to the dollar, but the going rate on the black market was 400 yen.) To complicate matters further, our son was born.

Because I had kept up with my studies during the five years since my graduation from Hitotsubashi, my background in mathematical economics was not inferior to that of American specialists in this field. On the other hand, the atmosphere at Johns Hopkins in those days was not favourable to the application of mathematics to economics; Professor Fritz Machlup, for example, had the attitude that anything that could be expressed by mathematics ought to be able to be put into words. He would appear at his lectures carrying a compass and a long ruler, carefully draw a graph, and call this a 'theoretical explanation'. In those days it was customary for speakers at the weekly department seminar to begin a theoretical presentation with an apology for using mathematics. That attitude is poles apart from today when economists apologize if they cannot provide neat mathematical proofs for their work.

As part of my Ph.D. programme I took classes with Kuznets and Ed Mills, but the person who made the greatest impression on me was Richard Musgrave. Although not a mathematical economist himself, Musgrave had a deep appreciation of mathematical methods. I became a statistical research assistant for a project of his on tax-shifting that he later published as *The shifting of the corporation income tax* (Krzyzaniak and Musgrave 1963) and kindly mentioned my contribution in its preface. Every morning I would input all the data by hand and use an electronic data-processing machine to estimate least-square-regressions. From today's perspective, when computer software is available to provide the answers instantaneously, it seems like a completely different world.

As a result of this association, I decided to write my doctoral dissertation under Professor Musgrave – or to be more accurate, such a course of events seemed natural to us both. His book *The theory of public finance* (1959) had just come out, and every day I combed through it in search of a topic to treat in my thesis which hadn't been included.

My interest in growth theory, which had taken shape during my days at Hitotsubashi and which could be glimpsed in my first scholarly work (Sato 1956) became more firmly established at Johns Hopkins. I avidly read Solow (1956) and Swan (1956) which formed the basis for neoclassical growth theory at that time, and I knew their contents so well that I could take the arguments apart and then put them back together again.

The essence of the neoclassical growth model is this: the long-run equilibrium growth rate is determined by the population (labour force) growth rate and by the rate of technical progress, but is not dependent on the savings rate. One day, however, Musgrave said to me: 'If fiscal policy boosts the total savings rate, even in the neoclassical growth model, the growth rate ought to go up.' 'The condition needed for that to happen, I suppose, would be a slow adjustment time for long-run equilibrium', I replied. This conversation of ours led to the writing of my very first article as a graduate student. As soon as I got home that day, I set to work trying to demonstrate the proposition. I completed the calculations in about a week and showed the results to Musgrave. 'So', he said with a satisfied look, 'fiscal policy is relevant even in the neoclassical growth model.' He urged me to write up my findings. The resulting article was the first one I had ever written in English. I showed a draft of it to Musgrave, who complained that he couldn't understand what I was trying to say. He pointed out problems with my English sentences and right in front of me helpfully rewrote parts of the introduction.

Professor Musgrave, who had been born in Germany and received his Ph.D. from Harvard, was particularly careful in his use of the English language. He gave useful advice to someone like me who had been born in Japan and was trying to earn a Ph.D. in America. My first English language paper (Sato 1963) appeared in the *Review of Economic Studies* in 1963, but it had all been completed in 1960. It also became a chapter in my Ph.D. dissertation, which I submitted in 1962. Those are the circumstances under which my article came to be written. In retrospect, I realize the large role played by Professor Musgrave's incomparable scholarly instincts. The controversy over adjustment time continues to this very day in works by Atkinson, King and Rebelo, among others. This theme is also related to the problem of convergence in economic growth as treated, for example, by Barro, Mankiw and Sala-i-Martin.

The actual numerical simulations which I worked out as examples at the time I was writing my 1963 *Review of Economic Studies* paper were published in the *Economic Journal* (Sato 1964a). The conclusion I reached more than 35 years ago of a long adjustment time in the neoclassical model has been tested and modified but remains unchanged. However, should we regard the fact that Japan has caught up to America in a matter of 50 years as slow or fast? That depends, I suppose, on the criteria used.

There are two points about my years at Johns Hopkins to which I would like to draw special attention. The first is the presence of a professor who gave me an interest in history to complement my deep fascination with mathematics. Although Mark Perlman was not my Ph.D. adviser, my fellow students and I all respected him as a good teacher and a kind human being to whom we could talk about even private matters. He was a great asset to Johns Hopkins.

The second point is the freedom I had to pursue my own interest. I imagine that nowadays the Ph.D. programme at Johns Hopkins, as elsewhere, is structured and systematized, but at the time I was there it was extremely flexible. To cite an extreme example, once you took the comprehensive exam, you were then free to do whatever you wanted. After I finished my first article and while my Ph.D. thesis was beginning to take shape, I used the rest of my time at Johns Hopkins to take courses in advanced mathematics. I studied differential geometry and Lie group theory and became very good friends with Hiroshi Gunji (now a professor of mathematics at the University of Wisconsin), who was then a Ph.D. student in the Maths Department. The training I received at that time was very useful and would serve as the mathematical basis for the book I would later publish, *Theory of technical change and economic invariance: application of Lie groups* (Sato 1981; 1999c). In those days, however, I had no intention whatsoever of applying mathematics to economics, but studied it in only a general way because I found the subject interesting. It was only later, under the influence of Professors Paul A. Samuelson and Takayuki Nôno, that I came to realize that differential geometry and Lie groups could be applied to economics.

11.4   EARLY CAREER, 1961–5

My first job was as an assistant professor at the University of Washington in Seattle. Although I had received better offers from other universities, I went to Seattle because at the time the East Coast offered almost nothing in the way of Japanese food or Japanese culture, and my wife, who was homesick, was eager to move to the West Coast where she could be a little bit closer to Japan. The following year I went to the University of Hawaii and was also affiliated with the East-West Center. As a Fulbright Scholar, I had entered the United States on an exchange visa, but I would need a permanent visa if I was to continue teaching in the US. To get it would require going through special formalities with the American immigration authorities. We moved to Hawaii on the condition that the University of Hawaii would prepare the necessary petition to present to immigration on my behalf. Hawaii had the additional advantage of providing Japanese language education for my son, who was then two years old.

My meeting with Professor John Kendrick, who was then a visiting professor at the University of Hawaii, was to bring about a major change in my subsequent career. Professor Kendrick and I were kindred spirits as far as both our personal and academic interests were concerned. He taught me how to combine an empirical perspective with the theoretical grounding I had already gained. The fruits of our joint research during this period were published in the *American Economic Review* (Kendrick and Sato 1963).

Although many of my friends had their doubts as to whether any serious scholarly work could be done in a tropical paradise like Hawaii, the years we spent there, I believe, enabled us to lay the groundwork for our life in both the United States and Japan. Because Hawaii is close to Japan, it was possible for our two children to be enrolled in Japanese schools during the long summer vacations and receive their compulsory education in Japan.

It was also during this early stage of my career that I became interested in production function theory. Whilst at Hawaii I was in charge of an intermediate level course on microeconomics. While I was drawing a graph of a total productivity curve, I thought about expressing the Chicago School's often-used Knight-Stigler curve as a simple function. I naturally assumed that someone had already done so, but when I searched through the literature, I wasn't able to find any mathematical expression for this curve. It suddenly occurred to me that a variety of total productivity curves could be described by using the formula in a paper I had presented at the Econometric Society meetings in 1963. I realized that if certain coefficients are set at specific values, the marginal product of one factor input starts rising, then begins to decrease when the input continues to increase. This was precisely the classic total productivity curve that Frank Knight had envisioned. It could be deduced as a hybrid of a constant elasticity of substitution (CES) productivity function and the well-known Cobb-Douglas type. This is what I set out to do in a one-page exchange of views with several economists in the *American Economic Review* in Sato (1964b). The production function derived in this way has come to be known in work by Fritz Peter Helms (1995), for example, as the 'Sato function'.

Research is a completely unpredictable process. You can put your heart and soul into a line of inquiry, and all your hard work will have hardly any impact whatsoever; at other times you come up with surprising results quite by accident. As a result of this one-page essay in response to an external stimulus, my own eyes were opened to the area of production functions.

11.5   BROWN UNIVERSITY, 1965–85

I went to Brown University as a visitor in 1965, became a full professor there in 1967, and stayed for nearly 20 years. At Brown, I was fortunate to have such good colleagues as Martin Beckmann and Karl Ryder and to participate with them and others in the Harvard-MIT mathematical economics seminar. When the three of us received our first research grant from the National Science Foundation, the direction of my research moved into a new field. In a joint study (Sato and Beckmann 1968a; b) we were the first to deduce a factor-augmenting type of technical change from the concept of neutrality and establish its theoretical legitimacy. Technical change of this type was independently verified by Hugh Rose (1968), a year after our article first appeared. This kind of technical change later became known as the 'Sato-Beckmann neutrality' (Sato and Beckmann 1975), although properly speaking it should be called the 'Sato-Beckmann-Rose type'.

The article I consider a turning point in my thinking was the one that first tested the estimation of the factor-augmenting (Sato-Beckmann-Rose) type of technical change (Sato 1970b). Although the article in the *American Economic Review* (Sato and Beckmann 1969) came out first, the latter had been completed in 1965. At a more theoretical level, Sato and Beckmann (1970) analyses whether balanced growth is possible in a model that posits the existence of the factor-augmenting type of technical change. A more general problem is treated in the article in Sato (1967b).

I subsequently received a Ford Fellowship and a Guggenheim Fellowship and went to Cambridge University and Bonn University to teach and do research. This gave me the opportunity to visit Sir John Hicks. He was interested in difference equations, which he had discussed in his book on *The trade cycle* (1950). I was aware of Kakeya's theorem and, as a result of my discussions with Hicks, I was able to write the article that appeared in the *Journal of Economic Theory* (Sato 1970a).

The 1960s was a time when growth theory developed rapidly through the application of optimal control theory. The article I wrote with Eric Davis, my first Ph.D. student at Brown, was the first to solve the problem of the golden rule of capital accumulation when labour grows endogenously (Sato and Davis 1971). It showed that the 'standard golden rule' had to be modified.

My research then turned to the issues of endogenous growth and endogenous technical change. The joint article on 'endogenous factor augmenting' and the survey paper that I did with Ramachandran, a brilliant student of mine and now my closest colleague, were extremely useful to my future work (Sato and Ramachandran 1980; 1987). My joint paper in the area of the theory of economic development (Sato and Niho 1971), as well as the one I did with Tsutsui (Sato and Tsutsui 1984) that created a model of Schumpeter's hypothesis, are important guideposts to the direction my subsequent research would take.

Two aspects of my life during my years at Brown are worth a special mention. The first was the establishment of a lifestyle that saw us spend four to six months each year in Japan so that my two children could receive a Japanese education. They were thus able to complete their elementary and middle school education simultaneously in both the United States and Japan. During this time, I taught at Japanese universities and did joint research with Japanese scholars. I was also able to keep up my contacts with influential people in Japanese corporations and other sectors of Japanese society. When I later moved to New York University to head the Center for Japan-US Business and Economic Studies, these contacts were to form the basis of a vital pipeline for the Center. The fact that I had not spent my scholarly life exclusively in the United States and had not lost touch with Japan would prove invaluable to my subsequent career.

The second point was that during that twenty-year period I was fortunate to meet many of the most famous and influential economists and mathematicians in the world. In particular, my close personal and scholarly relationship with Professor Paul A. Samuelson continues to this very day. I formed a close personal friendship of a different kind with Professor Takayuki Nôno, who came to Brown University as a visiting professor in the Department of Mathematics. My association with him was crucial in my continuing my research into Lie groups. The training in mathematics I received at Johns Hopkins was a valuable tool for this work.

While I was at Hawaii, I published a Japanese translation of Samuelson's *Foundations* (Sato 1967c). Later, at the Harvard-MIT mathematical economics seminar, I was privileged to have the opportunity to hold many friendly discussions with him and we published one paper together (Samuelson and Sato 1984). In the mid 1970s, by chance I came across an article on conservation laws that Samuelson (1970) had published in a non-economics journal. This prompted me to analyse conservation laws and technical progress through the full-scale application of Lie groups; the result was an article on holotheticity that was published in the *Review of Economic Studies* (Sato 1980) and is also in my book *Theory of technical change* (1981; 1999c). Among the many joint studies I have done with Professor Nôno, I highlight Sato and Nôno (1982) which solves the difficult problem of optimal endogenous technical change using differential-integral equations.

Meanwhile, I also continued my work in production function theory. After deriving what became known as the Sato function the next area I turned to were cases in which the elasticity of substitution is not constant. The accepted opinion of most prominent economists at the time was that CES production functions were sufficient for both theoretical and empirical analyses. Unconvinced by the prevailing view, I set out to solve mathematically the simplest kind of variable elasticity of substitution (VES) production functions, those in which the elasticity of substitution is related to a linear function of the capital-labour ratio. An empirical application of these production functions is Sato and Hoffman (1968).

I first became aware of the existence of non-homothetic CES functions in Sato (1974), a technical article for *The Economic Studies Quarterly* (now *The Japanese Economic Review*). Although in this I show only non-homothetic CES functions of a separable type, I became convinced of the existence of a more general class and later succeeded in discovering the most general class of CES functions. The results of my research were published as Sato (1975), while Sato (1987a) is a comprehensive overview of CES production functions which appeared in *The new Palgrave: a dictionary of economics*. The theory and an empirical analysis of homothetic and non-homothetic CES production functions are found in Sato (1977), while Sato, Beckmann and Schupack (1972) differs from earlier approaches by deriving production functions as the solution to differential equations observable in market behavior.

In a certain sense, production functions and utility functions can be regarded as mirror images of one another. While I was doing research on general non-homothetic CES production functions, it occurred to me that the very same theory could be applied to utility models. The essay on this subject came to see the light of day as the result of the empirical analysis I did with William Barnett and Kenneth Kopecky (Sato *et al.* 1981).

Samuelson and Sato (1984) was a study of whether or not the existing demand theory would hold true when money is introduced into utility functions. By observing the demand function for money and other goods, it was possible to show what conditions are necessary to recover the preference function that lies behind it (i.e. the integrability conditions). If one looks at the present state of Japan (in 1998), it is patently clear that including money in utility functions is not simply a matter of mathematical curiosity, but has practical implications. To be more precise, Japan today has entered a period of ultra-low interest rates, when hoarding and other forms of holding cash enhance the utility of the individual. This has not been seen since seventeenth-century Italy.

Self-dual preferences (Sato 1976) play an important role in both analytical and empirical economics. When preference is known to be self-dual and to be recoverable from demand functions, a direct utility function and an indirect one are immediately identifiable because they have the same mathematical form. This type of preference function does not belong to a limited family; in fact it would be no exaggeration to say that it corresponds to almost all the demand functions that have been used thus far in empirical applications. An example of its application is contained in Sato and Matsushita (1989).

The prevailing theory of stability in general equilibrium analysis was that when commodities are gross substitutes, the system is stable in Hicks's sense. Most goods, however, are actually a mixture of substitutes and complements. Coffee, cream and sugar are complements, for example; coffee and tea, however, are substitutes. An automobile and a train are substitutes for one another, whereas tyres and all the vast number of other car parts are complements of an automobile. The problem I examined in Sato (1972; 1973) is how to deal with the stability of a general equilibrium system, which contains both gross substitutes and complements. The theory worked out in these essays is that this problem can be solved by using the mathematical theory of power-positive matrices. Briefly put, when goods are complements, the matrix contains some negative signs, but by multiplying this matrix several times, i.e., by making a power of it, it is possible to change these negative signs to positive ones. The theory I developed in this way is thought to be useful for analysing a more realistic general equilibrium model of stability. The problem of the stability of oligopoly and the problem of substitutability, complementarity and the theory of derived demand for inputs, as well as my research on the distribution of wealth and intergenerational transfers, are found in Sato and Nagatani (1967), Sato and Koizumi (1970) and Sato and Ionnides (1987). These are areas in which I feel I have made a contribution.

11.6   NEW YORK UNIVERSITY, 1985–

I moved to New York University and the Stern School of Business in 1985 where I was given the C.V. Starr Chair in Economics and became the first director of the Center for Japan-US Business and Economic Studies. In addition, I have continued to hold the teaching position at John F. Kennedy School of Government at Harvard University which I took up towards the end of my stay at Brown.

My responsibilities as director of the Center include organizing research conferences, arranging for monthly panel discussions, and fund-raising. However, these duties have provided me with the quite unexpected incidental benefit of cultivating close personal friendships with an even greater number of distinguished economists in different fields from all over the world than I ever had the opportunity of meeting before. The Center provides a variety of forums in which scholars such as Samuelson, Tobin, Merton Miller, Baumol, Krugman, Gene Grossman, Dixit, Sachs, Zeckhauser and Bhagwati join my NYU colleagues and well-known scholars from Japan to discuss topical issues and ongoing research. The year after I moved to NYU, Samuelson joined the Center as the Long-Term Credit Bank of Japan Visiting Professor.

My enthusiasm for writing scholarly articles suitable for publication in academic journals has been, if anything, stronger than ever. Moreover, because of the nature of my job at the Center, my relationship with Japan has deepened and the length of time I spend there has steadily increased. Japan and the United States are the world's two economic superpowers. My recent work has been a theoretical analysis of the economic problems common to them both; one example of this work is Sato (1988) which uses differential game theory. But, more than anything else, since taking on the position as Chief Editor for *Japan and the World Economy: International Journal of Theory and Policy*, an academic journal published by North Holland, my interests are no longer confined to mathematical economics, but have broadened in scope. In particular, many of my recent papers have been published under the auspices of the technical research symposium which is held by the Center each year to stimulate interest in scholarly research by bringing together experts from Japan and the US.

Although the move to NYU may appear on the surface to have been a career change, in a sense my having spent a part of each year doing research in Japan ever since my days at Brown can be said to have borne fruit at NYU. It is my modest hope that my contributions to the study of theoretical economics and a better understanding between the United States and Japan may continue to be productive in the years to come.

Before I moved to NYU, I had a research project on international competitiveness that Professor Michael Spence, then of Harvard University, and I organized with a grant from the NEC Corporation to Harvard University. At a time when the issue of international competitiveness was not as much talked about as it is today, we brought together some of the most outstanding scholars in the field (for example, Paul Krugman and Lawrence Summers) and did research over a two-year period, before presenting our final reports in Boston and Florida. A book (Spence and Hazard 1988) was the outcome of this symposium, in which I also had a chapter (Sato 1988) on the technology game. I remember that the then-chairman of NEC, the late Dr. Koji Kobayashi, attended the symposium and asked questions that were very astute and to the point. Although my essay, which made use of elementary theory of differential game, is by no means a finished work,[2] it attempts to correct some deficiencies in the existing method of dealing with competition (between technologically advanced countries and technological latecomers), that looks simply at differences in productivity alone. In addition to productivity, how the advanced and the developing countries share the cost of developing basic technology and how the diffusion of basic information is or is not controlled are also important factors that make countries competitive.

My first attempt to apply the option theory of finance was Sato, Ramachandran and Kang (1994). By applying the theory of bank deposit insurance to Japan's city and regional banks, we tried to grapple with the enormous tasks now confronting Japanese financial institutions. This essay was written in the days of Japan's bubble economy when the dream that Japanese banks would one day conquer the world seemed perfectly attainable. No one at the time gave any credence to the unhealthy state of Japan's banks that our research scientifically demonstrated. The bank that was at the very bottom of our list has already gone bankrupt. When I published a summary of this article in the *Nihon Keizai Shimbun* (Sato 1992), I was asked to suppress the names of the banks and refer to them instead by

---

[2] See the note added in Sato (1999a, ch. 16) to the reprinted version.

letters of the alphabet for fear that it would create an uproar. When I look back, hardly any Japanese were aware of the existence of the deposit insurance system nor was it widely known that the upper limit for insurance on bank deposits was ten million yen. The reason I decided to include this essay in my selected essays is not to exacerbate present concerns about Japanese financial institutions; rather, my aim is to show how accurate and powerful a tool scientific analysis can be for understanding current realities. In Japan today, in most cases no steps have been taken even now to move away from amateurish discussions of the economy based on subjective reasoning. Economists overseas believe that Japan will be unable to extricate itself from the present harsh economic climate because of this non-scientific attitude toward managing the economy. In that sense, my aim is to present a different perspective from discussions of the subject normally heard in Japan.

Finally, there is my work on the application of Lie groups to dynamics that have appeared since my book, *Theory of technical change* (1981; 1999c). In Sato (1985) I propose 'income-wealth conservation laws' in their most generalized form, while Sato and Maeda (1990) contains an analysis of economic conservation law in continuous and discrete models. The discrete models, in particular, led to the discovery of conservation laws that had not been previously known. Sato (1987b), another entry for *The new Palgrave*, might be described as an introduction to the application of Lie group theory in the field of economics.

Just as in the case of conservation laws in the natural sciences, economic conservation laws exist in hidden forms. To take an example from biology, hands, feet and eyes on the left- and right-hand sides of the human body are visible symmetries, but many other symmetrical movements are known to exist inside the body that we cannot actually see. In the same way, economic systems too have not only visible symmetries of price and quantity but also many symmetries that react when an external shock is applied. These laws are called hidden symmetries, and their importance is coming to be better known. In Sato, Nôno and Mimura (1984) we analyse several of these problems and demonstrate the usefulness of Noether's theorem. Under certain conditions, for example, the optimal supply price of investment should be constant and invariant (or preserve symmetry) not only in a steady state but in all instances of t (time). This is due to a hidden symmetry, which is discovered in this essay.

Sato and Calem (1983) considers methods of estimating total productivity from the perspective of Lie groups, by exploring once again in greater depth a method proposed in my 1981 book. Two further essays continue my work in this area (Sato *et al.* 1999; Sato and Ramachandran 1999). They set out to prove that by introducing diminishing returns to technical progress functions, an endogenous optimal growth model can achieve stability even when the factor augmentation rate of capital and labour differs (non-Harrodian technical change); moreover, a number of hidden symmetries are proven to exist in these models.

In the research project in which I am currently engaged, I am attempting to test whether or not the actual growth paths in several OECD countries (including the United States and Japan) have maintained their optimal paths. The method used is not the one traditionally employed to test the convergence of actual and simulated growth paths, but rather a method that applies and tests the economic conservation laws discussed here. I expect to publish this work in the near future.

SELECTED WORKS

(1956) 'Growth theory and aggregate supply and demand interactions', *Economic Studies Quarterly*, 6 (3–4), pp. 124–33.

(1962) 'Fiscal policy in a neo-classical growth model', unpublished Ph.D. dissertation, Johns Hopkins University.

(1963) 'Fiscal policy in a neo-classical growth model: an analysis of time required for equilibrating adjustment', *Review of Economic Studies*, 30 (1), pp. 16–23.*

(1963) (with J.W. Kendrick) 'Factor prices, productivity and economic growth', *American Economic Review*, 53 (5), pp. 974–1003.*

(1964a) 'The Harrod-Domar model vs. the neo-classical growth model', *Economic Journal*, 74 (2), pp. 380–7.*

(1964b) 'Diminishing returns and linear homogeneity: comment', *American Economic Review*, 54 (5), pp. 744–5.*

(1967a) 'Linear elasticity of substitution production functions', *Metroeconomica*, 19 (1), pp. 33–41.

(1967b) 'A note on scarcity of specific resources as a limit to output: a correction', *Review of Economic Studies*, 34 (4), pp. 421–6.*

(1967c) Japanese trans. of Samuelson (1947). Tokyo: Keiso-Shobo.

(1967) (with K. Nagatani) 'The stability of oligopoly with conjectural variations', *Review of Economic Studies*, 34 (4), pp. 409–16.*

(1968a) (with M.J. Beckmann) 'Neutral inventions and production functions', *Review of Economic Studies*, 35 (1), pp. 57–66.*

(1968b) (with M.J. Beckmann) 'Neutral inventions and production functions: an addendum', *Review of Economic Studies*, 35 (3), p. 366.*

(1968) (with R.F. Hoffman) 'Production functions with variable elasticity of factor substitution: some analysis and testing', *Review of Economics and Statistics*, 50 (4), pp. 453–60.*

(1969) (with M.J. Beckmann) 'Aggregate production functions and types of technical progress: a statistical analysis', *American Economic Review*, 59 (1), pp. 88–101.*

(1970a) 'A further note on a difference equation recurring in growth theory', *Journal of Economic Theory*, 2 (1), pp. 95–102.*

(1970b) 'The estimation of biased technical progress and the production function', *International Economic Review*, 11 (2), pp. 179–208.*

(1970) (with M.J. Beckmann) 'Shares and growth under factor-augmenting technical change', *International Economic Review*, 11 (3), pp. 387–98.*

(1970) (with T. Koizumi) 'Substitutability, complementarity and the theory of derived demand', *Review of Economic Studies*, 36 (1), pp. 107–18.*

(1971) (with E.G. Davis) 'Optimal savings policy when labor grows endogenously', *Econometrica*, 39 (6), pp. 877–97.*

(1971) (with Y. Niho) 'Population growth and the development of a dual economy', *Oxford Economic Papers*, n.s. 23 (3), pp. 418–36.*

(1972) 'The stability of the competitive system which contains gross complementary goods', *Review of Economic Studies*, 39 (4), pp. 495–9.*

(1972) (with M.J. Beckmann and M. Schupack) 'Alternative approaches to the estimation of production functions and of technical change', *International Economic Review*, 13 (1), pp. 33–52.*

(1973) 'On the stability properties of dynamic economic systems', *International Economic Review*, 14 (3), pp. 753–64.*

(1974) 'On the class of separable non-homothetic CES functions', *Economic Studies Quarterly*, 25 (1), pp. 42–55.*

(1975) 'The most general class of CES functions', *Econometrica*, 43 (5–6), pp. 999–1003.*

(1975) (with M.J. Beckmann) 'A note on economic growth, technical progress and the production function', *Yearbook of Economics and Statistics*, 189 (1/2), pp. 139–42.*

(1976) 'Self-dual preferences', *Econometrica*, 44 (5), pp. 1017–32.*

(1977) 'Homothetic and non-homothetic *CES* production functions', *American Economic Review*, 67 (4), pp. 559–69.*

(1980) 'The impact of technical change on the holotheticity of production functions', *Review of Economic Studies*, 47 (4), pp. 767–76.*

(1980) (with R.V. Ramachandran) 'Measuring the impact of technical progress on the demand for intermediate goods: a survey', *Journal of Economic Literature*, 18 (3), pp. 1003–24.*

(1981) *Theory of technical change and economic invariance: application of Lie groups.* New York: Academic Press.

(1981) (with W.A. Barnett and K.J. Kopecky) 'Estimation of implicit utility models', *European Economic Review*, 15 (3), pp. 247–59.*

(1982) (with T. Nôno) 'A theory of endogenous technical progress: dynamic Böhm-Bawerk effect and optimal R&D policy', *Journal of Economics*, 42 (1), pp. 1–22.*

(1983) (with P.S. Calem) 'Lie group methods and the theory of estimating total productivity' in A. Dogramachi (eds) (1983) *Developments in econometric analyses of productivity measurement and modelling issues.* Dordrecht: Kluwer-Nijhoff, pp. 145–68.*

(1984) (with T. Nôno and F. Mimura) 'Hidden symmetries, Lie groups and economic conservation laws', in H. Hauptmann, W. Krelle and K.C. Mosler (eds) (1984) *Operations research and economic theory: essays in Honor of Martin J. Beckmann.* Heidelberg: Springer-Verlag, pp. 35–54.*

(1984) (with P.A. Samuelson) 'Unattainability of integrability and definiteness conditions in the general case of demand for money and goods', *American Economic Review*, 74 (4), pp. 588–604.*

(1984) (with S. Tsutsui) 'Technical progress, the Schumpeterian hypothesis and market structure', *Journal of Economics*, Suppl. 4, pp. 1–37.*

(1985) 'The invariance principle and income-wealth conservation laws: application of Lie groups and related transformations', *Journal of Econometrics*, 30 (1–2), pp. 365–89.

(1987a) 'CES production functions', in J. Eatwell *et al.* (eds) (1987) **q.v.**, vol. 1, pp. 395–6.*

(1987b) 'Group (Lie group) theory', in J. Eatwell *et al.* (eds) (1987) **q.v.**, vol. 2, pp. 570–1.*

(1987) (with Y.M. Ioannides) 'On the distribution of wealth and intergenerational transfers', *Journal of Labour Economics*, 5 (3), pp. 366–52.*

(1987) (with R.V. Ramachandran) 'Factor price variation and the Hicksian hypothesis: a microeconomic model', *Oxford Economic Papers*, n.s. 39 (2), pp. 343–56.*

(1988) 'The technology game and dynamic comparative advantage: an application to US-Japan competition', in A.M. Spence and H.A. Hazard (eds) (1988) **q.v.**, pp. 373–98.*

(1989) (with M. Matsushita) 'Estimations of self-dual demand functions: an international comparison', in R. Sato and T. Negishi (eds) (1989) *Developments in Japanese economics*. Tokyo: Academic Press, pp. 253–73.

(1990) (with S. Maeda) 'Conservation laws in continuous and discrete models', in R. Sato and R.V. Ramachandran (eds) (1990) *Conservation laws and symmetry: applications to economics and finances*. Boston: Kluwer Academic, pp. 135–74.*

(1992) 'Improving the Japanese deposit insurance system: the ranking of Japanese banks', *Nihon Keizai Shimbun* (Japan Economic Journal). Economics Classroom, 10 June, Tokyo.

(1994) (with R.V. Ramachandran and B. Kang) 'Risk-adjusted deposit insurance for Japanese banks', in R. Sato, R.M. Levich and R.V. Ramachandran (eds) (1994) *Japan, Europe and international financial markets*. Cambridge: Cambridge University Press, pp. 223–39.*

(1996a) *Selected essays*. Vol. I: *Growth theory and technical change*. Cheltenham: Edward Elgar.

(1996b) 'Introduction', in R. Sato (1996a) **q.v.**, pp. ix–xvi.

(1999a) *Selected essays*. Vol. II: *Production, stability and dynamic symmetry*. Cheltenham: Edward Elgar.

(1999b) 'Introduction', in R. Sato (1998a) **q.v.**, pp. ix–xiii.

(1999c) *Theory of technical change and economic invariance: application of Lie groups*, rev. edn. Cheltenham: Edward Elgar.

(1999) (with R.V. Ramachandran) 'Optimal growth with endogenous technical progress: Hicksian bias in a macro model, *The Japanese Economic Review*, forthcoming.

(1999) (with R.V. Ramachandran and C. Lian) 'A model of optimal growth with endogenous bias', *Macroeconomic Dynamics*, forthcoming.

BIBLIOGRAPHY

Dillard, D. (1948) *The economics of J.M. Keynes*. London: Crosby Lockwood.

Eatwell, J., Milgate, M. and Newman, P. (eds) (1987) *The new Palgrave: a dictionary of economics*. London: Macmillan.

Hansen, A.H. (1953) *A guide to Keynes*. New York: McGraw-Hill.

Harrod, R.F. (1948) *Towards a dynamic economics: some recent developments of economic theory and their application to policy*. London: Macmillan.

Helms, F.P. (1995) *Einfuhrung in die Produktionstheorie II*, (Video) Hagen, Germany: Zentrum fur Fernstudienentwicklung, Fem Universitat.

Hicks, J.R. (1939) *Value and capital: an inquiry into some fundamental principles of economic theory*. Oxford: Clarendon Press.

Hicks, J.R. (1950) *A contribution to the theory of the trade cycle*. Oxford: Clarendon Press.

Keynes, J.M. (1936) *The general theory of employment, interest and money*. London: Macmillan.

Klein, L.R. (1947) *The Keynesian revolution*. London: Macmillan.

Krzyzaniak, M. and Musgrave, R.A. (1963) *The shifting of the corporation tax: an empirical study of its short-run effect upon the rate of interest*. Baltimore, MD: Johns Hopkins Press.

Lerner, A.P. (1944) *The economics of control: principles of welfare economics*. London: Macmillan.

Musgrave, R.A. (1959) *The theory of public finance: a study in public economy*. London: McGraw-Hill.

Nakayama, I. (1933) *Junsui Keizaigaku*. Tokyo: Iwanami Shoten.

Robinson, J. (1952) *The rate of interest and other essays*. London: Macmillan.

Rose, H.B. (1968) 'The condition for factor-augmenting technical change', *Economic Journal*, 78 (4), pp. 996–71.

Samuelson, P.A. (1947) *Foundations of economic analysis*. Cambridge, MA: Harvard University Press.

Samuelson, P.A. (1970) 'Laws of conservation of the capital-output ratio', *Proceedings of the National Academy of Science*, 67 (3), pp. 1477–9.

Samuelson, P.A. (1998) 'How *Foundations* came to be', *Journal of Economic Literature*, 36 (3), pp. 1375–86.

Solow, R.M. (1956) 'A contribution to the theory of economic growth', *Quarterly Journal of Economics*, 70 (1), pp. 65–94.

Spence, A.M. and Hazard, H.A. (eds) (1988) *International competitiveness*. Cambridge, MA: Ballinger.

Swan, T.W. (1956) 'Economic growth and capital accumulation', *Economic Record*, 32 (2), pp. 334–43.

12. Peter B. Kenen (b. 1932)[1]

12.1   ON BECOMING AN ECONOMIST, 1950–4

I did not start to think about being an economist until the end of my third year as an undergraduate at Columbia University, and I did not start to consider an academic career until the end of my senior year, when I won a Woodrow Wilson Fellowship for graduate study and had to promise that I would consider it seriously. Before that, I was determined to be an international civil servant. That possibility actually arose much later, but I turned it down to remain an academic.

Like most other children, I had chosen and discarded a number of careers before being old enough to know what they really involved. At one point during the Second World War, I was going to be a naval officer. At another point, I was going to be a surgeon. Both ideas were utterly silly. I could never have met the physical requirements for admission to the US Naval Academy. In fact, I barely passed the swimming test required of Columbia undergraduates. And anyone watching me try to tie a hook to a fishing line

[1]   Kenen (1980b; 1994b), as revised by the editors. I have published two volumes of selected writings: the first (Kenen 1980a) being essays in international economics and the second – that in this series (Kenen 1994a) – being on exchange rates and monetary systems.

would shudder or laugh at my being a surgeon. For a long time, however, I planned to be a biologist, which is why I attended the Bronx High School of Science. It was a remarkable school, not only for the quality of its science courses, but also for its classes in history and the social sciences, where I began to enjoy myself most. I became particularly interested in international politics and, for unusual reasons, the United Nations.

I was born in Cleveland, Ohio, where my father was a journalist. His 'beat' was City Hall, but the talk at our dinner table was about Spain and Munich, aggression, appeasement and isolationism. I can recall very clearly the voices of Adolf Hitler and Franklin Roosevelt coming from the radio in our living room. I can also recall conversations about the plight of Jews in Europe and my father's concern about his own father, who had returned to Poland many years before. We moved to New York in 1943, when my father went to work for the American Jewish Conference, the newly formed alliance of major Jewish organizations concerned to mobilize support for the survivors of the Holocaust and to reopen the doors of Palestine to Jewish immigration. In 1947, he joined the Jewish Agency for Palestine and helped to make its case before the United Nations Special Committee on Palestine. When the State of Israel was established, he became a member of its delegation to the United Nations. He took me to the temporary UN headquarters at Lake Success whenever I had a day off from school.

When I enrolled at Columbia in 1950, I joined the staff of the student radio station and began to broadcast a weekly programme on the United Nations. With help from my father, I obtained my own press card, and would lurk in a corner of the Delegates' Lounge, looking for celebrities to interview. A surprisingly large number of busy people took time to appear on the programme, including Eleanor Roosevelt, who was the American representative on the Human Rights Commission. I learned a great deal about the organization, including its early efforts to promote economic development.

I have never worked harder than I did during my four years at Columbia, and have never been rewarded more richly. In my first and second years, I took the required courses in Western civilization, taught entirely in small classes by some of the University's most distinguished faculty. My great debt to those courses leads me to bridle whenever multiculturalists attack them for being provincial and offensive. I am richer for having taken a full-year course on the civilizations of India, China and Japan, but I would be far poorer if the required courses on Western civilization had not introduced me to the ideas, issues and values that have decisively influenced the social and political institutions of my own country and so many other countries.

Undergraduates at Columbia did not have to major in a single subject, but most of us did that in practice, and I took several courses in political science, including a course on American foreign policy with Paul Seabury and one on Soviet foreign policy with Philip Moseley. I took an introductory course in economics, did not excel, and did not plan to take any more. But Paul Seabury changed my plans by saying what we hear far more frequently today. In the course of a conversation about my own plans, he warned me that I would not be able to understand international politics unless I understood international economics. I took his advice and, therefore, another course in economics.

Unfortunately, the Economics Department at Columbia was different from most others there. It was divided sharply between those who taught graduate courses and those who taught undergraduates. There were exceptions. Harold Barger, who taught money and banking, also gave a graduate course on national-income accounting, and C. Lowell Harriss, who taught public finance, gave a graduate course on state and local taxation. But Columbia's most prominent economists, Ragnar Nurkse, Carl Shoup, Arthur Burns and William Vickrey, to name only a few, did not teach undergraduate courses and did not encourage undergraduates to take their graduate courses. Furthermore, the undergraduate programme did not greatly emphasize economic theory, because some of its members were overtly hostile to it. The senior seminar, conducted by Horace Taylor, was devoted mainly to the works of Thorstein Veblen, John R. Commons and other institutionalists.

I do not know what I would have done if I had known what economics was really like – that theory was vital and that mathematical skills were helpful, although not absolutely essential, as they are today. I might have stuck to my earlier plan and applied to a graduate programme in international studies. I do know that I would not do graduate work in economics if I were starting today. I don't enjoy mathematics sufficiently, and I am not very good at it. I took a course in calculus at Columbia and was lucky to be in a class taught by Samuel Eilenberg, one of the University's leading mathematicians and a fine teacher. But I got through that course with much coaching from the engineering staff at the student radio station. I have learned more mathematics since, and several of my papers make use of mathematical methods. But I would not do well in graduate school today, because mathematics is not my second language.

12.2   POSTGRADUATE EDUCATION, 1954–8

I cannot remember why I applied to Harvard, Columbia and Cornell, and not other graduate programmes in economics. I was accepted by all three and chose Harvard, partly because it had not accepted me as an undergraduate, and it was a good choice for me. The first-year theory course was taught by Edward Chamberlin, who approached the subject historically, devoting much attention to Mill and Marshall and to his own book on monopolist competition, which has since become the basis for the models used most frequently to study trade in differentiated products. Some students skipped Chamberlin's course, going directly into Wassily Leontief's second-year course, which was much more rigorous analytically. But Chamberlin's course filled the gap in my knowledge of theory left by the bias against it I had acquired from my undergraduate teachers at Columbia, and it bought me time to learn more mathematics, so that I could survive Leontief's course in my second year. There was no basic course in macroeconomics, but many first-year students took the monetary course given by Alvin Hansen and John Williams, and I also took Gottfried Haberler's course in international economics.

I was equally interested in both branches of international economics – the trade and monetary sides – and worked on both at Harvard. During my second year, while studying for the general examination, I found a way to extend the geometry developed by Robert Baldwin (1952) to depict equilibrium under free trade and under an optimum tariff, and I used it to derive utility possibility curves for the two regimes. It led to my first publication 'On the geometry of welfare economics' (Kenen 1957) which argues that, as movements along an offer curve redistribute domestic income, they cannot have clear-cut welfare implications: an increase in the foreign demand for a country's exports, improving its terms of trade, will move the country outward on its offer curve, but this outcome by itself does not imply an increase of economic welfare; some citizens will gain and others will lose. To make unambiguous statements about welfare, one must show that the gainers can compensate the losers, and this article supplies the requisite geometry. Borrowing techniques from Baldwin and James Meade, it shows how to derive the situation utility-possibility curve employed by Paul Samuelson to sort out issues in welfare economics and how one can construct an offer curve incorporating compensation. This provided a new way to look at a familiar proposition, as did Kenen (1959) which shows how one must take account of demand conditions before one can say anything about factor scarcities. Product prices determine factor prices, which determine in turn the distribution of income. The income distribution, however, helps to determine the composition of demand, and one must know the composition of demand, as well as the output mix, to be able to construct an offer curve and thus to determine the trade pattern at each set of product prices. In brief, this paper shows how to describe geometrically all of the relationships that lie behind the simple offer curve.

However, I decided to write my thesis on a monetary topic, and looked for one that would give me an excuse to spend a year abroad. At first, I planned to examine the benefits and costs to Britain of being a reserve-currency country. (It did not occur to me or my advisers that the reserve-currency role of the dollar deserved similar study.) But Gottfried Haberler and John Williams urged me to take a different tack – to study the role played by monetary policy in managing the British balance of payments, and the topic served its purpose. It gave me a marvellous year at the London School of Economics.

It was the year in which Lionel Robbins devoted the economics seminar to Don Patinkin's *Money, interest and prices* (1956), and I was allowed to attend, even though my thesis topic classified me as an 'applied' economist. James Meade conducted another seminar, devoted to international economics, and I attended that one too, along with Richard Cooper. Our paths have crossed repeatedly since, to my great benefit. My best days at the LSE, however, were spent with Max Corden, Richard Lipsey and Kelvin Lancaster, who introduced me to the theory of the second best and to Harry Johnson. I was able nonetheless to get on with my thesis, with much help from A.C.L. Day and Richard Sayers at the LSE and from Maurice Allen, the Economic Advisor at the Bank of England, and I brought back a first draft from London. I finished it that summer (Kenen 1958), just before starting to teach at Columbia.

12.3   RETURN TO COLUMBIA, 1958–71

Before leaving for London, I had talked about teaching positions with Seymour Harris at Harvard, for whom I had worked as a research assistant, and with Harold Barger at Columbia. When I wrote to them from London, applying formally, both of them offered me jobs. I knew that I could not expect to stay at either institution. Harvard exported most of its graduate students, and Columbia did not promote instructors in its undergraduate economics programme. My wife and I decided, however, that Harvard was riskier, because Seymour Harris would find more work for me to do, and I accepted Columbia's offer, expecting to stay there briefly.

Weeks after defending my thesis at Harvard, however, Harold Barger asked me to assemble my publications – all three of them at that stage – so that the department might decide whether I should be promoted to Assistant Professor. Soon after my promotion, moreover, Schuyler Wallace, the Dean of the School of International Affairs. invited me to teach a graduate course on US foreign economic policy. (He also told me that my salary would be raised from $5,500 to $6,600, because the new salary had to be divisible by three, in order for the School to pay one-third). Then, in my third year, I was asked to teach the graduate course in international economics, as Ragnar Nurkse would be moving to Princeton, and though the arrangement was meant to be temporary, I taught the course for the next ten years.

In my first year at Columbia, I spent much time revising my thesis for publication. It appeared as *British monetary policy and the balance of payments, 1951–1957* (1960a), and it was reviewed in *Economica* by Dow (1962), who praised my input, but not my output, and commented to the effect – cruelly but rightly – that whilst I had 'left no stone unturned in my search for the truth I had ended up largely recounting what was beneath each stone'.

Two new subjects began to attract my attention as I was revising my thesis. One was the Leontief paradox, the other was the Triffin paradox.

Gary Becker came to Columbia just when I did and had started to develop his ideas on human capital. Donald Keesing arrived soon thereafter and was working on a resolution of the Leontief paradox – the finding that US exports were less capital-intensive than US imports, even though the United States was deemed to be a capital-abundant country. Leontief (1956) had already suggested that the paradox might be resolved by taking account of high labour productivity in the United States and thus treating the United States as a labour-abundant country. He had also noted that US exports use skilled labour intensively, and Keesing (1966) had begun to develop this theme by examining the skill intensities of bilateral trade flows. I took a different tack inspired by the works of Becker and Jacob Mincer on the return to human capital. The United States, I suggested, should still be regarded as a capital-abundant country, but one which invests much of its total capital in the production of skills. I developed a version of the Heckscher-Ohlin model in which countries are endowed by nature with two basic factors of production – land and labour – and they cannot produce commodities until capital is used to improve them. Each economy has therefore to make two sorts of decisions: how to allocate its stock of capital between land and labour, and how to allocate the resulting flows of land and labour services between land-intensive and labour-intensive activities. I also showed that the United States is indeed a capital-abundant country when allowance is made for the human capital embodied in its labour force. My results appeared in 'Nature, capital and trade' (Kenen 1965a), which is still my favourite paper.[2]

A second paper (Kenen 1968) built upon this one using a more general two-country model to draw additional conclusions about the interplay

---

[2] Related work by colleagues and students was published in a volume (Kenen and Lawrence, 1968) collecting research conducted in the International Economics Workshop, which I organized soon after coming to Columbia.

between international trade and investment. Both papers use elaborate apparatus but illustrate a very simple proposition. An economy can be described as having a natural endowment comprising inert stocks of land and labour that must be improved by applying capital. Thereafter, they supply factor-service flows that are the inputs to production – the point of entry into the standard Heckscher-Ohlin model. Investment in the natural endowment is subject to diminishing returns, so that the allocation of the capital stock between land and labour is easily determined once one knows the prices of their factor-service flows. Furthermore, free trade in commodities can equalize factor-service prices, as in the standard Heckscher-Ohlin model, without also equalizing the returns to capital. Accordingly, free trade can coexist with international capital movements. At the end of the first article, I offer an application. When one takes account of human capital (investment in labour) as well as tangible capital (investment in land), one can reverse the Leontief paradox: US exports use more capital per worker, including human capital, than US import-competing production.

Two of my subsequent papers derive from this early work on trade and welfare. One shows that the welfare effects of tariff changes depend on the levels of the tariffs involved and draws some implications for customs-union theory (Kenen 1974c). The other shows how emigration affects the welfare of those left behind in the source country (Kenen 1971). This was, I believe, the first paper to sort out the issues clearly and to deal with them in the context of the Heckscher-Ohlin model. It shows that the welfare effects of international migration derive from its effects on the global output mix and that their distribution between host and source countries depends on the pattern of commodity trade.

My early work on the monetary side was influenced heavily by Robert Triffin's *Gold and the dollar crisis* (1960), in which he argued that the international monetary system was dangerously unstable because of another paradox. The United States would have to run balance-of-payments deficits to provide dollar reserves to other countries, but the corresponding increase of US liabilities would eventually undermine confidence in the dollar as a reserve asset. Triffin proposed the transformation of the International Monetary Fund into a reserve-creating institution. My first paper on the subject (Kenen 1960a) offered a rigorous formulation of the Triffin paradox. To make this point abstractly, I built a model of the gold-exchange standard in which the demand for dollar reserves was assumed to vary directly with the strength of the US reserve position – the ratio of its gold reserves to foreign countries' dollar holdings. I showed that the gold-exchange standard would be stable for as long as that ratio was larger than unity but that the ratio would decline as foreign reserves grew, driving the system into a 'crisis zone' where it would become unstable. We were far from the crisis zone when I wrote the paper, and I wound up on an optimistic note. Furthermore, I made a couple of suggestions that I would reject today. I said, for instance, that the system could be kept out of the crisis zone if new reserve currencies were brought into being – a suggestion that holds much less charm today, as we face the problems of a monetary system having several reserve centres. Nevertheless, the framework I supplied was useful to others; Officer and Willett (1969), for example, used it to examine the behaviour of the system in the crisis zone.

Thereafter, I began empirical work on the reserve-asset preferences of central banks (Kenen 1963a) and, with Elinor Yudin, on the demand for international reserves (Kenen and Yudin 1965). This latter paper was advanced for its day, in that it used a first-order autoregressive process to represent the evolution of a country's balance of payments, then took the standard error of each country's balance-of-payments equation to represent the distribution of exogenous shocks and took the autoregressive coefficient to measure the persistence of those shocks. These were then employed in another regression equation to explain cross-country differences in holdings of reserves. The paper was inspired by dissatisfaction with the measure used most often to gauge the adequacy of reserve supplies – the ratio of reserves to imports – and was the first to use what has since been called the disturbance approach to the demand for reserves. That demand, the paper argues, depends on the need for balance-of-payments financing, not on the levels of payments or receipts, and the need for financing can be approximated by the variability of the balance of payments (of reserve flows themselves). The theory was primitive. So were the estimates. For that very reason, however, the paper led to large amounts of work by others, including attempts to measure the costs of holding reserves and to model the optimization of reserve stocks. As I look back upon this paper and the work that followed it, I wonder if the effort was not misdirected. A full-grown theory of the demand for reserves necessarily subsumes the whole theory of balance-of-payments adjustment and forces it into a narrow stock-optimizing framework. Fritz Machlup (1965), who criticized my work at the time, has argued that reserves are determined residually and influence national policies asymmetrically. Central banks do not try to get rid of large reserves and do not often try to build up their reserves at the expense of other policy objectives. Reserve positions influence national policies only when they are at risk, because of large balance-of-payments deficits – and this brings us back to ordinary balance-of-payments theory. I tend to agree.

12.4 POLICY ADVICE AND LEAVING COLUMBIA

My work on these matters led to my first involvement in the policy-making process. In November 1960, soon after the election of John F. Kennedy, I was appointed to a task force concerned with the US balance-of-payments problem and the international monetary system. It was chaired by George Ball, soon to become Undersecretary of State, and included Robert Triffin and Edward Bernstein, each of whom had a plan of his own to reform the monetary system. Being the youngest member, I was assigned to work with Meyer Rashish on the first draft of the group's report. We worked through the night but sustained ourselves with the belief that we could greatly influence the group's policy recommendations. George Ball rewrote our draft completely, however, and President Kennedy set it aside when he was warned that our recommendations might shake confidence in the dollar. During our work, incidentally, we were asked to draft the statement that the President-elect would make on announcing the appointment of Douglas Dillon as Secretary of the Treasury. Our draft reaffirmed the commitment of the United States to defend the dollar price of gold at $35 per ounce, and all but one of us thought that this was the right course to take. Paul Samuelson was the dissenter; he scribbled a note on his copy of the draft, asking whether Kennedy should 'nail his flag to that mast'. Samuelson has said that he was among the first to wonder whether it might be necessary to devalue the dollar. He was – but I have tried without success to find in my files his copy of the first draft, which would support his claim.

Early in 1961, Walter Heller, the incoming Chairman of the Council of Economic Advisers, asked me to do some more drafting, together with Richard Cooper, who would soon join the Council's staff. We were to prepare a first draft of the President's message on the balance of payments and gold. Once again, late-night sessions and frustrations. Our draft was circulated to other agencies, and they mutilated it. When asked if there was anything left of our draft, I said, 'Yes. The prepositions.'

Actually, one sentence did survive, and it gave me another opportunity to learn about the workings of government. The President's message promised to examine the balance-of-payments effects of US direct investment abroad and to ask if investment was being stimulated by inappropriate tax incentives. Stanley Surrey, Assistant Secretary of the Treasury for Tax Policy, asked me to work with Hal Lary on the implementation of that commitment. We wrote a report recommending the elimination of tax deferral on the reinvested profits of the foreign subsidiaries of US firms. Our recommendation found its way into the first tax bill proposed by the Kennedy administration, but it lost its way in Congress, which adopted provisions limiting the use of foreign tax havens but did not restrict tax deferral *per se.*

My work on the Ball task force had one other consequence. At Robert Triffin's suggestion, I was invited to participate in the first meeting of what came later to be known as the Bellagio group of officials and academics, chaired by Fritz Machlup of Princeton on the academic side and Otmar Emminger of the Bundesbank on the official side. The group met once or twice each year for more than a decade to discuss international monetary issues in an informal setting. The academics included William Fellner, Roy Harrod, Harry Johnson and Robert Mundell; the officials included Andre de Lattre, Kit McMahon, Robert Roosa and Emile van Lennep. It was the most successful endeavour of its kind – I have been involved in several since – and contributed greatly to my own education.

In 1964, at a meeting in Bellagio, a group of economists prepared a report on the international monetary system. It identified three issues: adjustment, liquidity, and confidence. I have addressed all three issues in a number of papers, beginning with Kenen (1963b) which was written in 1962, soon after the negotiation of the first swap agreements and of the General Arrangements to Borrow, supplementing the resources of the International Monetary Fund. Those devices were designed to strengthen confidence in the wake of the gold-price scare of 1960–1 and turbulence in foreign-exchange markets, but the paper argues that the devices did more for liquidity than they did for confidence. It goes on to propose ways of consolidating the new *ad hoc* arrangements, with a view to the development of a reserve system based on overdraft financing rather than holdings of national currencies, and makes a case for giving exchange-rate guarantees on dollars held by foreign official institutions. Like most of those that follow, this paper is dated, but the ideas are not. In a more recent paper on long-run reform, J.J. Polak (1979) has suggested the transformation of IMF quotas into SDR-denominated overdraft facilities, and exchange-rate guarantees are implicit in proposals for creating a 'substitution account' under the aegis of the IMF.

A second paper deals quite explicitly with the links between adjustment and financing (liquidity), and it raises a question that has never been resolved (Kenen 1966). How soon and how fast should adjustment take place, and are there ways of regulating access to financing in order to optimize the process? The paper puts the problem in general terms. It comes up today in three guises: debates about the scope of IMF 'surveillance' and the ways to make it most effective; debates about 'conditionality' of access to IMF resources; and debates about the impact of private capital markets on the quality of the adjustment process.

A third paper was written in 1969, two years before the closing of the gold window and the first devaluation of the dollar (Kenen 1969b). It hints at the need to realign exchange rates but indicates no urgency about the problem. In fact, it rules out unilateral action of the sort taken two years later, arguing that the United States should continue to play a passive *n*th country role in the exchange-rate system. Hence, the paper calls for a multilateral agreement on rules for periodic changes in exchange rates within the framework of the Bretton Woods system. The paper marks the end of my long flirtation with a multiple reserve-currency system and the start of my interest in another theme – the need to consolidate all reserve assets under the auspices of the IMF. The last page of the article offers in a single sentence a plan for a comprehensive substitution account.

My interest in the workings of the monetary system led me away from trade theory and policy. In fact, I wrote only one more paper on trade theory: an analysis of international migration in the context of the Heckscher-Ohlin model, which was published in a volume honouring Charles Kindleberger (Kenen 1971). But I started to look at new issues on the monetary side. My first paper on exchange rate theory was 'Trade, speculation and the forward exchange rate' (Kenen 1965b), written for a volume honouring Gottfried Haberler. Here I used mean-variance analysis to analyse the behaviour of forward exchange rates and thus to reformulate the partial-equilibrium theory of forward exchange handed down from Keynes, by way of S.C. Tsiang and others. In Tsiang's (1959) important paper, the forward foreign-exchange rate is determined by three groups of actors – speculators, hedgers, and arbitrageurs. In my paper, I show that a single, utility-maximizing firm will speculate, hedge and arbitrage at various times and in various ways, and that its attitude toward risk crucially affects the behaviour of the forward rate. I demonstrate, for instance, that covered interest parity holds only under very special circumstances – those one would describe today as meaning risk neutrality. Each optimizing firm, however, will maintain its own 'marginal' interest parity; it will arbitrage among sources of finance, domestic and foreign, with the aim of minimizing borrowing costs. Martin Feldstein (1968) was right to point out that my paper does not treat utility and risk with sufficient rigour. But it was the first to derive conditions for forward-market equilibrium from conditions for portfolio optimization and to work with stocks (wealth holders' positions) rather than with flows.

In a paper for a conference at the University of Chicago (Kenen 1969a), I sought to reformulate the theory of optimum currency areas developed initially by Robert Mundell and Ronald McKinnon. I paid particular attention to the nature of the exogenous shocks affecting individual economies (now described by the distinction between symmetrical and asymmetrical shocks) and to the relevance of fiscal policies for the delineation and functioning of an optimum currency area. This paper has been cited frequently since the revival of interest in European monetary union.

I had to curtail my research, however, when I became chairman of the

Columbia Department in 1967, and subsequent events forced me to suspend it completely. I became deeply involved in dealing with the aftermath of the student demonstrations of 1968, at the same time that I was voicing my own concerns about the Vietnam War by running for election as a delegate to the Democratic National Convention. I won that election, attended the Chicago Convention, and managed to get myself arrested. Radical students at Columbia saw me as an enemy but greeted me warmly when I joined them in a Chicago jail cell. (My children, however, were less enthusiastic about their father's brief criminal career.) In the end I was charged with being a 'pedestrian obstructing traffic' and gladly paid my fine as a small charge for a very satisfying experience.

My next experience was less satisfying. In the fall of 1969, Andrew Cordier, Columbia's Acting President, asked me to become Provost, and I spent the next year doing that. It was very satisfying from one standpoint. Academics cannot learn very much about a large university without venturing out of their own departments. Their colleagues in other disciplines lead lives different from their own, and the problems of the university as a whole are larger than the sum of the problems facing its various schools and departments. I learned a great deal during my year as Provost, but the job was frustrating. I was part of an interim administration in which responsibilities were not clearly allocated, and my time was divided between the demands made by the strident politics of the day and those made by the educational and financial problems of the university. I left the job after a year and left Columbia one year later.

12.5   PRINCETON SINCE 1971

Shortly before becoming Provost at Columbia, I had a call from a colleague at Princeton asking whether I wanted to be considered for the vacancy that would be created by the retirement of Fritz Machlup, who was Walker Professor of Economics and International Finance and Director of the International Finance Section. I said no, because I had just accepted the chairmanship of the Economics Department and felt an obligation to serve out my term. But I called him back three years later to ask whether Princeton might still be interested in me. He said yes, and matters moved quickly thereafter. I joined the faculty at Princeton in the fall of 1971, but took leave right away to spend a year at the Center for Advanced Study in the Behavioral Sciences at Palo Alto, thinking about economics and a new research agenda – which I had not done for three years.

At first, I taught courses similar to those I had taught at Columbia, giving a full-year graduate course in international economics and the lectures in the basic undergraduate course. I also started a research seminar in international economics, in which many colleagues have participated regularly. When Avinash Dixit came to Princeton, however, I ceased to teach the first term of the graduate course, on trade theory and policy. I also ceased to lecture in the basic undergraduate course in order to run a workshop on foreign economic policy for graduate students in the Woodrow Wilson School. The subject of the workshop has changed from year to year, but the organization has not. Each year, we examine intensively a single policy problem and study it by holding mock negotiations. We have worked on increasing IMF quotas and allocating Special Drawing Rights, rescheduling the debts of a hypothetical developing country and working out a stabilization programme with the IMF, and planning the implementation of the Maastricht Treaty.

In my first ten years at Princeton, I worked mainly on the implications of international financial integration for balance-of-payments adjustment and the behaviour of floating exchange rates. In 'Toward a supranational monetary system' (Kenen 1967) I tried to define the institutional requirements for successful monetary integration. Following James Ingram (1962), I stress the need for capital mobility (asset-market integration) to cushion the process of balance-of-payments adjustment, but I also emphasize the importance of a unified fiscal system. I argue, in particular, that the stabilizers built into the fiscal system serve to offset cyclical and structural imbalances in interregional payments, allowing regions to finance or correct imbalances at moderate cost.

In a paper already mentioned, 'The theory of optimum currency areas: an eclectic view' (Kenen 1969a), I bring these same arguments to bear on the problem of delineating currency areas – those within which it is best to peg exchange rates and between which it is best to let them float. I made one additional point there: the degree to which domestic output is diversified may be important for the choice between pegged and floating regimes. Countries (regions) with diversified economies may not have much need to alter their exchange rates. External disturbances may average out, *ex ante*, and when there is need to reallocate resources because of external or internal disturbances, diversification reduces the costs by enhancing domestic mobility. (If making this same point today, I would of course restate it in terms of real exchange rates, as Roland Vaubel does in his work on European monetary integration.) This argument has been cited frequently in the recent debate on the benefits and costs of European monetary union, but I am dissatisfied with my formulation. As a practical matter, the countries that have opted for flexible exchange rates are those that have the largest, most diversified economies. More generally, my paper and most others on the subject are dated by the theory of exchange-rate determination on which they are based. Until recently, we taught that exchange rates are determined in markets dominated by trade and other current-account flows and that current-account balances are affected quickly by exchange-rate changes, producing smooth adjustment to external shocks. That is not what we teach today. But these two papers are precursors of my monograph on monetary integration (Kenen 1976), and they influenced my book with Polly Reynolds Allen (Kenen and Allen 1980), which examines the problems of economic integration and the delineation of currency areas in the context of a multi-country macroeconomic model that takes an asset-market view of exchange-rate determination.

During these years, I also worked on the topic of the coordination of national economic policies, but approached those issues in two ways. First, I worked with two graduate students, Peter Dungan and Dennis Warner, to develop a large model of the US balance of payments and used the model to simulate the effects of fiscal and monetary policies. Our results are summarized in Kenen (1974a); the model itself and more simulations are described in Kenen and Associates (1978). Second, I constructed and analysed small theoretical models designed to identify the main effects of asset-market integration.

I had started this work during my year at the Center for Advanced Study in Palo Alto, taking as my point of departure the important paper by Ronald McKinnon and Wallace Oates (1966), which had amended the Fleming-Mundell model by imposing a portfolio-balance constraint and had thus distinguished clearly between stock and flow equilibria, as well as empirical work by my colleague, William Branson (1968), which pursued the same vital distinction between stocks and flows. My first paper on the subject was published in a volume honouring Jan Tinbergen (Kenen 1974b), but my theoretical model was badly flawed. My next effort was better; it appeared in *Capital mobility and financial integration* (Kenen 1976), a monograph based on a paper that Fritz Machlup had asked me to write for the Budapest Congress of the International Economic Association. But the model in that monograph could not be used to study exchange-rate behaviour, because it contained only one bond, and two bonds are needed to study exchange-rate behaviour in a portfolio-balance framework, one denominated in domestic currency and one denominated in foreign currency. I did not take that next step until I started work with my colleague, Polly Allen, on a project that began quite modestly but grew far larger. The results appeared in our book, *Asset markets, exchange rates and economic integration* (1980).

Although work on portfolio-balance models occupied much of my time in the 1970s, I continued to think about policy problems and the international monetary system. During the deliberations of the Committee of Twenty on the reform of the monetary system,[3] the United States had proposed the use of a reserve indicator to signal the need for balance-of-payments adjustment and the possible need for exchange-rate changes. I was worried about using a stock indicator, the level of reserves, to signal the need for a change in a flow variable, the balance of payments, and raised the issue with a colleague. He said that he could handle it analytically and would get back to me shortly. A few days later, I found a note in my mailbox, saying that the problem was intractable. 'Simulate', it said. I did – and found that the use of a reserve indicator could indeed destabilize the balance of payments (Kenen 1975). Two years later, I published another paper on the role of reserves in the monetary system, written for a conference in memory of J. Marcus Fleming (Kenen 1977), and two more papers on the monetary system, one on the analytics of a substitution account designed to replace dollar reserves with SDR-denominated claims on the IMF (Kenen 1981), and the other on the future of the SDR itself (Kenen 1983).

In the 1980s, I continued to think about policy coordination and the problems facing the IMF, but my work was influenced by new policy issues and analytical innovations. The revival of policy coordination at the 1978 Bonn Summit and the subsequent revival of exchange-rate management under the 1985 Plaza Agreement and 1987 Louvre Accord led many economists to seek ways of modelling policy coordination and to re-examine the effectiveness of official intervention on the foreign-exchange market. The onset of the debt crisis in 1982 led many to look at the nature of sovereign debt, the role of the IMF in managing the crisis, and the case for debt relief. The collapse of the Soviet empire in Eastern Europe and of the Soviet Union itself raised an array of economic issues. The new interest in European monetary union resurrected old questions and posed new ones.

To study the conduct and effects of policy coordination, most economists used the game-theoretic approach introduced earlier by Koichi Hamada (1976). I did, too, but became increasingly sceptical of it. My own use of the approach and my doubts about it appeared initially in a paper drafted in 1983–4, while I was visiting the Reserve Bank of Australia. I developed the paper into a book, *Exchange rates and policy coordination* (Kenen 1988a). I used the game-theoretic approach to contrast the need for policy coordination under pegged and floating exchange rates and came to an odd conclusion – that floating exchange rates could increase the need for policy coordination rather than reduce it. I was bothered by the possibility, however, that this result was due to the strongly symmetrical nature of the economies inhabiting my model, and I built another model to show that some of my findings survive when the economies are not symmetrical. This work is described by

---

[3] Upon which I wrote a number of commentaries (Kenen 1973a; b; 1974b).

two more papers (Kenen 1990a; 1991a): one on the coordination of macroeconomic policies, which summarizes the argument of my book, and one that presents an earlier asymmetrical version of my model. The first of those papers also sets out my objections to the game-theoretic approach; it argues that policy coordination should be viewed as a 'regime preserving' process rather than a 'policy optimizing' process.

The huge swing of real and nominal exchange rates for the dollar in the 1980s strengthened my dissatisfaction with floating exchange rates. I was also impressed with the performance of the European Monetary System in its early years – its apparent success in reconciling short-term stability with medium-term flexibility. Like most economists old enough to recall the defects of the Bretton Woods System, I was doubtful initially about the prospects for the EMS. Unlike many others, however, I was not convinced that its subsequent success could be ascribed to the influence of capital controls in limiting speculative pressures; I attached more importance to the elasticity of the reserve-credit arrangements available for financing intervention and thus warding off those pressures. (The 1992 crisis did not cause me to change my mind, because it occurred after the EMS had become a more rigid regime. That crisis, however, has made me wonder whether pegged-rate regimes may be doomed to become very rigid, on account of the nature of the game played between markets and governments.)

These thoughts and my reflections on the implications of the 1987 Louvre Accord led me to ask whether there can be any viable half-way house between firmly pegged exchange rates and freely floating rates. I raised the question with officials and academics at a meeting of a second Bellagio group, which Richard Cooper and I had organized with the help of Alexander Lamfalussy, the General Manager of the Bank for International Settlements. The question led me to write another book, *Managing exchange rates* (Kenen 1988b), drafted in 1987–8, while I was visiting the Royal Institute of International Affairs in London. It urged the major industrial countries to adopt formal target zones for their currencies and to develop a comprehensive framework for policy coordination. My objections to floating exchange rates were influenced by Paul Krugman's (1989a) lucid lectures in memory of Lionel Robbins; my plan for exchange-rate management bore some resemblance to the 'blueprint' developed by John Williamson and Marcus Miller (1987), although it attached much more weight to official intervention.

My work on the debt crisis is represented by two papers (Kenen 1990b; 1991b). Shortly after the onset of the crisis, I wrote two columns in *The New York Times* suggesting the creation of an International Debt Discount Corporation (IDDC) to buy up the debts of developing countries at a discount and to issue in their place bonds guaranteed indirectly by the developed countries, as sponsors of the IDDC. The proposal was premature analytically and politically. There was as yet little evidence to justify the premise underlying my proposal – that the case-by-case approach to the debt problem would be inadequate, and debt relief would be required. At that early stage, moreover, banks were unwilling to contemplate long-term concessions and debtor countries wanted to prove that they could return quickly to creditworthiness. One banker gave me a left-handed compliment; my proposal, he said, was the most sensible of the many silly plans for solving the debt problem. The finance minister of a debtor country was less courteous. 'Be quiet', he said. 'You are undermining our effort to win credibility.' It took several years for the climate to change, and by the time I published a fully-fledged paper on the subject (Kenen 1990b), the Brady plan had been adopted and the debt burden was being reduced. In the interim, however, I had written a paper on debt buybacks (Kenen 1991b) offering a rationale for debt reduction that does not depend on the assumption made by Krugman (1989b) and others to obtain the so-called Debt Relief Laffer Curve – the assumption that excessive debt depresses domestic investment, reducing the ability of the debtor country to service its debt in the future. My paper develops a model in which partial debt relief is beneficial to debtors and creditors, because it reduces a debtor's incentive to repudiate debt in the future.

My interest in the work of the IMF is represented by two other papers, on IMF surveillance and on the use of IMF credit (Kenen 1987; 1989). My interest in the problems of Central and Eastern Europe is represented by a paper on trade and payments arrangements for that region (Kenen 1991c). It analyses and rejects the case for creating a payments union modelled on the European Payments Union (EPU) of the 1950s.

In 1990–1, I spent the first half of a year's leave from Princeton at the Bank of England and the second half at the IMF. Two papers (Kenen 1992a; 1993) reflect my work at those institutions. At the Bank of England, I was fortunate in being able to follow closely the negotiations that led to the plan for Economic and Monetary Union (EMU) embodied in the Maastricht Treaty; as soon as the Treaty was signed, I began work on a monograph, *EMU after Maastricht* (Kenen 1992b), analysing the provisions of the Treaty and the problems likely to arise during the transition to monetary union. I have since revised and expanded it into a book, *Economic and monetary union in Europe: moving beyond Maastricht* (Kenen 1995). At the IMF, I studied recent trends in the exchange-rate policies of developing countries, contrasting the older case for using exchange rate changes to promote balance-of-payments adjustment with the newer case for pegging the exchange rate to promote price stability. I also examined the challenges posed for exchange-rate and monetary policies by the liberalization of capital markets in developing countries and the resulting capital inflows. That work is summarized in my paper on financial opening (Kenen 1993), prepared for an OECD symposium, and in more recent papers (Kenen and Eichengreen 1994; Kenen 1996a; b).

When I started to study economics, I wanted to work for an international organization, and I had an opportunity to do that in 1979, when Jacques de Larosiere, Managing Director of the IMF, asked me to be Director of the Research Department and Economic Counsellor. I told him that he was asking me to choose between the most attractive jobs I could hope to hold – my Princeton position and the one at the Fund. After long thought, I decided to stay at Princeton, where I could set my own agenda but could still participate in debate about current policies and the future of the monetary system. My Edward Elgar selected essays reflects my agenda in the decade that followed, and I will continue to pursue it, because most of the issues on which I have written are far from being resolved.

SELECTED WORKS

(1957) 'On the geometry of welfare economics', *Quarterly Journal of Economics*, 71 (3), pp. 426–47.

(1958) 'British monetary policy and the balance of payments, 1951–1957', unpublished Ph.D. dissertation, Harvard University.

(1959) 'Distribution, demand and equilibrium in international trade: a diagrammatic analysis', *Kyklos*, 12 (4), pp. 629–38. Rep. in R.E. Caves and H.G. Johnson (eds) (1968) *Readings in international economics.* Homewood, IL: Richard D. Irwin, pp. 90–8.

(1960a) *British monetary policy and the balance of payments, 1951–1957.* Cambridge, MA: Harvard University Press.

(1960b) 'International liquidity and the balance of payments of a reserve-currency country', *Quarterly Journal of Economics*, 74 (4), pp. 572–86.

(1963a) *Reserve-asset preferences of central banks and stability of the gold-exchange standard.* Princeton Studies in International Finance no. 10. Princeton, NJ: International Finance Section, Princeton University.

(1963b) 'International liquidity: the next steps', *American Economic Review*, 53 (2, Papers & proceedings), pp. 130–8.

(1965a) 'Nature, capital and trade', *Journal of Political Economy*, 73 (5), pp. 437–60.

(1965b) 'Trade, speculation and the forward exchange rate', in R.E. Baldwin *et al.* (eds) (1965) *Trade, growth and the balance of payments: essays in honor of Gottfried Haberler.* Chicago: Rand-McNally, pp. 143–69.

(1965) (with E.B. Yudin) 'The demand for international reserves', *Review of Economics and Statistics*, 47 (3), pp. 242–50.*

(1966) 'Financing and adjustment: the carrot and the stick', in W. Fellner, F. Machlup and R. Triffin (eds) (1966) *Maintaining and restoring balance in international payments.* Princeton, NJ: Princeton University Press, pp. 151–5.

(1967) 'Toward a supranational monetary system', in G. Pontecorvo, R.P. Shay and A.G. Hart (eds) (1967) *Issues in banking and monetary analysis*. New York: Holt, Rinehart & Winston, pp. 209–26.

(1968) 'Towards a more general theory of capital and trade', in P.B. Kenen and R. Lawrence (eds) (1968) *The open economy: essays on international trade and finance*. New York: Columbia University Press, pp. 100–23.

(1968) (Eds with R. Lawrence) *The open economy*. New York: Columbia University Press.

(1969a) 'The theory of optimum currency areas: an eclectic view', in R.A. Mundell and A.K. Swoboda (eds) (1969) *Monetary problems of the international economy*. Chicago: University of Chicago Press, pp. 41–60.

(1969b) 'The international position of the dollar in a changing world', *International Organization*, 23 (3), pp. 705–18.

(1971) 'Migration, the terms of trade and economic welfare in the source country', in J.N. Bhagwati *et al.* (eds) (1971) *Trade, balance of payments and growth: papers in international economics in honor of Charles P. Kindleberger*. Amsterdam: North-Holland, pp. 238–60.

(1973a) 'Convertibility and consolidation: a survey of options for reform', *American Economic Review*, 63 (2, Papers & proceedings), pp. 189–98.

(1973b) 'After Nairobi: beware the Rhinopotamus', *Euromoney*, (November), pp. 16, 18, 20.

(1974a) 'The balance of payments and policy mix: simulations based on a US model', *Journal of Finance*, 29 (2), pp. 631–54.*

(1974b) 'Economic policy in a small economy', in W. Sellekaerts (ed.) (1974) *Trade, development and planning: essays in honour of Jan Tinbergen*. London: Macmillan, pp. 73–101.

(1974c) 'A note on tariff changes and world welfare', *Quarterly Journal of Economics*, 88 (4), pp. 692–7.

(1974d) 'Reforming the monetary system – you can't get there from here', *Euromoney*, (October), pp. 19, 21, 22, 23.

(1975) 'Floats, glides, and indicators: a comparison of methods for changing exchange rates', *Journal of International Economics*, 5 (2), pp. 101–51.

(1976) *Capital mobility and financial integration: a survey*. Princeton Studies in International Finance no. 39. Princeton NJ: International Finance Section, Princeton University.

(1977) 'Techniques to control international reserves', in R.A. Mundell and J.J. Polak (eds) (1977) *The new international monetary system*. New York: Columbia University Press, pp. 202–22.

(1978) (in association with D.P. Dungan and D.L. Warner) *A model of the US balance of payments*. Lexington, MA: Lexington Books.

(1980a) *Essays in international economics*. Princeton, NJ: Princeton University Press.

(1980b) 'Preface', in P.B. Kenen (1980a) **q.v.**, pp. vii–xv.

(1980) (with P.R. Allen) *Asset markets, exchange rates and economic integration*. Cambridge: Cambridge University Press.

(1981) 'The analytics of a substitution account', *Banca Nazionale del Lavoro Quarterly Review*, 34 (3), pp. 403–26.*

(1983) 'Use of the SDR to supplement or substitute for other means of finance', in G.M. von Furstenberg (ed.) (1983) *International money and credit: the policy roles*. Washington, DC: IMF, pp. 327–60.*

(1987) 'What role for IMF surveillance?', *World Development*, 15 (12), pp. 1445–

56.*

(1988a) *Exchange rates and policy coordination*. Ann Arbor, MI: University of Michigan Press.

(1988b) *Managing exchange rates*. London: Royal Institute of International Affairs.

(1989) 'The use of IMF credit', in C. Gwin and R.E. Feinberg (eds) (1989) *The International Monetary Fund in a multipolar world: pulling together*. New Brunswick, NJ: Transaction Books, pp. 69–91.*

(1990a) 'The coordination of macroeconomic policies', in W.H. Branson, J.A. Frenkel and M. Goldstein (eds) (1990) *International policy coordination and exchange rate fluctuations*. Chicago: University of Chicago Press, pp. 63–102.*

(1990b) 'Organizing debt relief: the need for a new institution', *Journal of Economic Perspectives*, 4 (1), pp. 7–18.*

(1991a) 'Exchange rates and policy coordination in an asymmetric model', in C. Carraro *et al.* (eds) (1991) *International economic policy co-ordination*. Oxford: Basil Blackwell, pp. 83–107.*

(1991b) 'Debt buybacks and forgiveness in a model with voluntary repudiation', *International Economic Journal*, 5 (1), pp. 1–13.*

(1991c) 'Transitional arrangements for trade and payments among the CMEA countries', *IMF Staff Papers*, 38 (2), pp. 235–67.*

(1992a) 'The European central bank and monetary policy in stage three of EMU', *International Affairs*, 68 (3), pp. 457–74.*

(1992b) *EMU after Maastricht*. Washington, DC: Group of Thirty.

(1993) 'Financial opening and the exchange rate regime', in H. Reisen and B. Fischer (eds) (1993) *Financial opening: policy issues and experiences in developing countries*. Paris: OECD, pp. 237–62.*

(1994a) *Exchange rates and the monetary system: selected essays*. Aldershot: Edward Elgar.

(1994b) 'Introduction', in P.B. Kenen (1994a) **q.v.**, pp. ix–xix.

(1994c) (Ed.) *Managing the world economy: fifty years after Bretton Woods*. Washington, DC: Institute for International Economics.

(1994) (with B.J. Eichengreen) 'Managing the world economy under the Bretton Woods system: an overview', in P.B. Kenen (ed.) (1994c) **q.v.**, pp. 3–57.

(1995) *Economic and monetary union in Europe: moving beyond Maastricht*. Cambridge: Cambridge University Press.

(1996a) 'The feasibility of taxing foreign exchange transactions', in M. ul Haq, I. Kaul and I. Grunberg (eds) (1996) *The Tobin tax: coping with financial volatility*. Oxford: Oxford University Press, pp. 109–28.

(1996b) 'Analyzing and managing exchange rate crises', *Open Economies Review*, 7 (Supplement 1), pp. 469–92.

BIBLIOGRAPHY

Baldwin. R.E. (1952) 'The new welfare economies and the gains in international trade', *Quarterly Journal of Economics*, 66 (1), pp. 91–101.

Branson, W.H. (1968). *Financial capital flows in the US balance of payments*. Amsterdam: North-Holland.

Dow, J.C.R. (1962) Review of Kenen (1960), *Economica*, n.s. 29 (3), pp. 302–4.

Feldstein, M. (1968) 'Uncertainty and forward exchange speculation', *Review of Economics and Statistics*, 50 (2), pp. 189–92.

Hamada, K. (1976) 'A strategic analysis of monetary interdependence', *Journal of Political Economy*, 84 (4, pt I), pp. 677–700.

Ingram, J.C. (1962) 'A proposal for financial integration of the Atlantic community', in Joint Economic Committee of the US Congress (1962) *Factors affecting the United States balance of payments: compilation of studies prepared for the Subcommittee on international exchange and payments*. Washington, DC: Government Printing Office.

Keesing, D.B. (1966) 'Labor skills and comparative advantage', *American Economic Review*, 56 (2, Papers & Proceedings), pp. 249–58.

Krugman, P.R. (1989a) *Exchange-rate instability*. Cambridge MA: MIT Press.

Krugman. P.R. (1989b) 'Market-based debt-reduction schemes', in J.A. Frenkel, M.P. Dooley, and P. Wickham (eds) (1989) *Analytical issues in debt*. Washington, DC: IMF, pp. 258–78.

Leontief, W.W. (1956) 'Factor proportions and the structure of American trade: further theoretical and empirical analysis', *Review of Economics and Statistics*, 38 (4), pp. 386–407.

Machlup, F. (1965) 'The cloakroom rule of international reserves: reserve creation and resource transfer', *Quarterly Journal of Economics*, 79 (2), pp. 337–55.

McKinnon, R. and Oates, W. (1966) *The implications of international economic integration for monetary, fiscal and exchange rate policy*. Princeton Studies in International Finance no. 16. Princeton, NJ: International Finance Section, Princeton University.

Officer, L. and Willett, T.D. (1969) 'Reserve asset preferences and the confidence problem in the crisis zone', *Quarterly Journal of Economics*, 83 (4), pp. 688–95.

Patinkin, D. (1956) *Money, interest and prices: an integration of monetary and value theory*. New York: Harper & Row.

Polak, J.J. (1979) *Thoughts on an International Monetary Fund based fully on the SDR*. Washington, DC: IMF.

Triffin, R. (1960) *Gold and the dollar crisis: the future of convertibility*. New Haven, CT: Yale University Press.

Tsiang, S.C. (1959) 'The theory of forward exchange and the effects of government intervention on the forward exchange market', *IMF Staff Papers*, 7 (1), pp. 75–106.

Williamson, J. and Miller, M.H. (1987) *Targets and indicators: a blueprint for the international coordination of economic policies*. Policy Analyses in International Economics no. 22. Washington, DC: Institute for International Economics.

13. G. S. Maddala
(1933–99)[1]

13.1   BEGINNINGS

I was born on 21 May 1933, the fifth of my parents' six children. My eldest brother died before I was born. My father was a school teacher and very unstable. He moved to a new place every two years. My mother was worried about our future but he would say: 'Don't worry. Once the British leave India and we get independence, the government will take care of all of us.' My mother was very religious. Though she had only elementary school education, she studied Sanskrit all by herself and even read the philosophical works of the great Indian philosopher Sankara. In high school, my ambition was to become a Sanskrit scholar. I graduated from high school in 1947 but lost in the competition for a scholarship to study Sanskrit in college. I did join a college but dropped out after six months because of poor health.

---

[1]   Maddala (1994b), as revised by the author. I have published two volumes of selected writings in the series (Maddala 1994a): the first covering production functions and productivity, distributed lag models, panel data, pseudo data, simultaneous equation models, income distribution and tests for rationality; and the second, qualitative variable models, limited dependent variable models, self-selection models, disequilibrium models and money and finance. I have been honoured by a festschrift (Hsiao *et al.* 1999); see also the *ET* interview by Lahiri (1999).

The partition of India took its toll on our family. My older brother was lost (we never heard of him again). My mother was distressed by the loss of her son, and by my dropping out of college. She became ill and died in 1949. Although I recovered from my illness after my mother's death, going back to college was out of the question. I did not have the money or even the interest. I started helping my father in his tutoring classes on Hindi, and was earning some money to support our family. While I was doing this I read books on Indian history and philosophy. I read the works of Swami Vivekananda and Tolstoy's stories and essays. One piece that had great influence on me was Tolstoy's short story, 'What men live by'. Another book I liked was Mazzini's *Duties of man.*

In late 1952, a friend of mine (by name 'Prasad') suggested that the Board of Education in Ajmer allowed students to take the AA (two year college degree) examination without attending college, and that with an AA degree and a diploma in Hindi, one could get a teacher's job in a middle school. I thought it was a good idea and we started studying for the examination. Unfortunately his father died before we left for Ajmer and I had to go alone. It was over 1,000 miles from where we lived. I prepared for history (my favourite subject) and political science and mathematics.

In India 1953 was the year of the railway centenary. They had a third class railway pass for 30 rupees (about $6 then) that allowed unlimited travel for one month. From our town (Kakinada) I had to go to Bezwada (about 200 miles) and change trains. I had to catch the Grand Trunk Express going to Delhi. In Bezwada, the train arrived on the platform but I could not get in. It was jam-packed with people blocking the doors and windows. I knew I would miss my examination if I did not get in, but that did not worry me much. I was more worried that I would not be able to see the Railway Exhibition in Delhi, and that my ticket would be wasted.

Finally, when the train started, a porter came and asked me for a half a rupee (about a dime) to put me on the train. I agreed and he lifted me and my bag (about 105 pounds – I had a small bag with only clothes and no books (my life was very simple then) and threw me inside through a window that was unblocked. Those inside the compartment were angry but they could not do anything. The important thing was that I got on the train. I took the AA examination, and went to see the Railway Exhibition in Delhi. I also saw one of my (maternal) uncles whom I had never met before. He had only a high-school education and rose to the position of a chief accountant at Burmah-Shell. I realized I had hope for myself. He kindly gave me 100 rupees ($20). With that I felt very rich and I went to Agra to see the Taj Mahal. I also visited Jaipur and other tourist attractions.

The results of the AA examination were to be announced in a newspaper published in Delhi. Since the paper was also available in Bombay, my sister in Bombay offered to look it up. Finally after two months the results were announced. Besides giving the identification numbers of the candidates that passed, the newspaper also gave the names of the top ten candidates. My sister was delighted to find my name at the top of the list and sent me a telegram.

I decided to continue my studies for a B.A. and joined the local college (in Kakinada) majoring in mathematics (I was told only the poorest students went into history). But my admission was conditional. The principal of the college said he had never heard of Ajmer, and that there was something suspicious about my AA degree that I got without attending a college. My certificate was sent to the registrar's office at the Andhra University for investigation.

Six months passed but there was no word. I was told that they were still checking and couldn't find the Ajmer Board. Meanwhile, I was doing well and the principal of my college decided not to pursue the matter. I passed the B.A. examination in 1955 standing first in the University. My professor of mathematics had a friend, Dr K.S. Rao, teaching statistics in Bombay University. He sent me there to do my Master's in statistics. I took my M.A. in statistics in 1957, passing in first class.

I applied for the Ph.D. programme in statistics at the University of California at Berkeley. I was offered an assistantship but I had no money to travel to the USA. I asked them for a loan from my assistantship, but the request was denied. I went back to Andhra University and taught statistics for one year. But I missed Bombay and returned to Bombay in 1958 as a research statistician at the Bombay School of Economics.

13.2   AMERICA SINCE 1960

In 1960 I heard that the Fulbright Fellowships also provided for travel to the USA. I applied for their competitive examination. When I was selected, I was ready to go to Berkeley to do my Ph.D. in statistics. Then the director of the Bombay School of Economics suggested that I should do my Master's in economics. He argued that India had too many theoretical statisticians and that a Ph.D. in statistics would assure me of only a lecturer's job (assistant professorship), whereas a Master's in economics (along with my background in statistics) would offer me a job as a reader (associate professor) in econometrics. He suggested that I should go to the University of Chicago and obtain a Master's in economics.

I went to the University of Chicago in 1960, but found that they did not have a Master's programme. All students enrolled in the Ph.D. programme and took the same qualifying examinations. The Master's degree was more a consolation degree. One of my friends, Raj Krishna, who was finishing his Ph.D. told me that I did not have to study at all, and that passing the qualifying examinations at the Master's level was a cake-walk. So I did not study for the tests. I took them all in 1961. The questions were all very general. In those days all you needed was a little bit of knowledge of mathematics and statistics and some common sense. Moreover, I had to pass the examinations only at the Master's level.

I passed all the examinations in 1961 at the Ph.D. level. Since I was told that all I had to do was write an 'acceptable' thesis, I saw no point in returning to India with a Master's degree. Because of my background in statistics, I was told to see Robert Basmann for a thesis topic. He suggested that I should write a thesis on the non-existence of moments for GCL estimators. I asked him how long it would take me to obtain a Ph.D. He replied that the problem was very complicated and that it would take quite a number of years. I decided that I did not want to wait that long, and moreover I did not see any relevance of that topic for whatever I would be doing in India. Also, I wanted to go back to India at least by 1963. I decided to work under Zvi Griliches and wrote a thesis on 'Productivity in the bituminous coal industry'. It was an acceptable thesis, but the econometrics merely consisted of estimation by OLS of a couple of Cobb-Douglas production functions. I obtained my Ph.D. in 1963 from the University of Chicago (Maddala 1963).

In 1963, I was given a job at Stanford as an assistant professor. Everyone said it would be stupid for me to return to India without getting some experience in the USA. Since I had an exchange visa, I knew I had to go back in 1964 anyway.

Before I went to Stanford, I went back to India for a couple of months, and wanted to bring back the books on Indian philosophy that my mother had read. When I went to pick up the wooden box in which I had left them (when I left for the USA), I found it empty. The white ants had eaten all the books.

Soon after joining Stanford in 1963, I met Paul Baran (the Marxist economist). He called me into his office and said, 'Don't talk to this fellow Nerlove. He will ask you to work on spectral analysis. A young man like you should work on important problems of India's economic development, and not waste your energies on spectral analysis.' When he asked me to read his book, *The political economy of growth* (1957), I told him that I had read it already. He then told me that he had some ideas on what I should be working on. I thought it was a good idea to arrange an appointment with him. When I went to see him again, I found out that he had died of a heart attack the previous day.

I thus gave up Indian philosophy and Indian economic development and decided to call myself an econometrician. Though I did not know much econometrics, that was the closest approximation I could think of.

In 1963, while having a drink at the 'Top of the Mark' in San Francisco, I wondered what my mother would have thought about her son going to 'America'. When she died she was sure that I was a college drop-out. I also wondered what my life would have been if the porter had not thrown me on to the Grand Trunk Express in 1953 for half a rupee.

All through my life I have been a bit schizophrenic about econometrics. I often hated the elaborate mathematical apparatus. I even find quite a few papers on econometrics Greek and Latin to me. I see 'more art and less matter' in them. Anyway, I call myself an econometrician, and it is too late to complain about it.

Over the years I have worked in several areas of econometrics: production functions and productivity; distributed lag models; simultaneous equation models; panel data models; pseudo data; limited dependent and qualitative variables; disequilibrium models; bootstrap methods; Bayesian inference; unit roots and cointegration. In my work, I have tried to follow Thoreau's advice: 'Simplicity, simplicity, let your thoughts be as simple as two and three.' I almost always swam against the major currents (fads) in econometrics when I felt they were wrong and this has affected my career. There is a tendency for most econometricians to grab the latest technique fast and get on the bandwagon. I have criticized these in my writings but the bandwagons keep moving. There are several examples. A couple are frontier production functions and panel data unit root tests.

Three econometricians had a major influence on me: Zvi Griliches, who was my thesis supervisor and for whom I worked as a research assistant at Chicago; Marc Nerlove, whom I met at Stanford and with whom I have been in touch all my life; and Art Goldberger with whom I had professional contacts throughout my life. They were all people who emphasized basic concepts in econometrics and did not get carried away by technique. I also had the good luck of coming into contact with C.R. Rao (one of the top five statisticians in the world of all time) with whom I edited three volumes of the *Handbook of statistics* (Maddala *et al.* 1993; Maddala and Rao 1996; 1997).

In my book *Econometrics* (1977) I started a new style of writing econometrics, which others have copied (and made a lot of money and left me behind). This was also the fate of my *Introduction to econometrics* (1998). My 1977 book was the first to use empirical examples throughout after each technique, giving references to them. Previous books on econometrics were all full of algebra, derivations and proofs. I relegated these to the appendices.

Over the years I have supervised fifty dissertations (at Stanford, Rochester, University of Florida and Ohio State University). These covered several areas of applied and theoretical econometrics. I have served on the thesis committees of several others. I had three good students at Rochester: Kajal Lahiri, Lung-Fei Lee and Forrest Nelson. Lahiri and Lee, together with Hsiao and H.M. Pesaran, have edited my festschrift (Hsiaro *et al.* 1999), and Zvi Griliches (1999) kindly wrote a foreword to the volume. I have learnt a lot from all my students and I am thankful to them.

SELECTED WORKS

(1963) 'Technical change in the bituminous coal industry, 1919–54', unpublished Ph.D. dissertation, University of Chicago.

(1977) *Econometrics*. New York: McGraw-Hill.

(1988) *Introduction to econometrics*. New York: Macmillan.

(1993) (Eds with C.R. Rao and H.D. Vinod) *Handbook of statistics*. Vol. 11: *Econometrics*. Amsterdam: North-Holland.

(1994a) *Econometric methods and applications*, 2 vols. Aldershot: Edward Elgar.

(1994b) 'How I became an econometrician', in G.S. Maddala (1994a) **q.v.**, vol. I, pp. xv–xviii.

(1996) (Eds with C.R. Rao) *Handbook of statistics*. Vol. 14: *Statistical methods in finance*. Amsterdam: Elsevier.

(1997) (Eds with C.R. Rao) *Handbook of statistics*. Vol. 15: *Robust inference*. Amsterdam: Elsevier.

BIBLIOGRAPHY

Baran, P.A. (1957) *The political economy of growth*. New York: Monthly Review Press.

Griliches, Z. (1999) 'Foreword', in C. Hsiao *et al.* (eds) (1999) **q.v.**, pp. ix–x.

Hsiao, C., Lahiri, K., Lee, L.-F. and Pesaran, H.M. (eds) (1999) *Analysis of panels and limited dependent variable models*. Cambridge: Cambridge University Press.

Lahiri, K. (1999) 'ET interview: Professor G.S. Maddala', *Econometric Theory*, 15 (5), pp. 753–76.

14. Dan Usher
(b. 1934)[1]

14.1   INTRODUCTION

Academics strike a strange bargain with the rest of society. Doctorate in hand and subject to a favourable tenure decision, they are provided with an adequate salary for life and expected to go discover something. They are also expected to teach and to take part in the administration of the university, but about half their time is earmarked for research to be conducted in whatever manner and on whatever subjects they think best. Salary depends in part on the quantity and quality of the research as assessed by one's peers, but a reasonable standard of living is provided regardless. The assumption behind this bargain would seem to be that society needs a certain number of almost completely independent researchers – untied to any business, department of government or pressure group – to generate types of information that no organization would have an interest in generating or that no centrally-directed research would be likely to discover. A multitude of self-directed researchers scours corners of the world that a great organization might

[1]   Usher (1994b), as revised by the author. I have two volumes of selected essays in the series: the first on national accounts and theory (Usher 1994a) and the second on welfare economics and public finance (Usher 1994c).

overlook. The rationale of society's bargain with its academics is not an implicit condemnation of organized research. It is a presumption that there is a place within the university for something else besides.

In introducing my research the most useful service I can perform for the reader is to say as best I can how the mandate to go discover something was discharged. Certainly, as a graduate student, what I most wanted to know about the old folks in the profession was how they came to choose their subjects of research and from whence came the basic ideas out of which their discoveries evolved. I am still curious on that score about my fellow economists and I am vain enough to suppose that others may be curious about me.

14.2 MONTREAL, CHICAGO AND BANGKOK, 1950–61

I became an economist by accident. In 1950, as a teenager, I took a job as junior counsellor at a Summer Camp for poor children of the Jewish community of Montreal. It turned out, unknown, I would imagine, to the respectable gentlemen who administered the Jewish charities at that time, that the director of the camp was a communist or fellow traveller, a term now almost forgotten referring to someone who follows the party line but is not actually a card-carrying member of the party. For a young man from a proper, middle-class, utterly non-political family, the encounter with the extreme 'left' was an electrifying experience. I learned about workers of the world with nothing to lose but their chains, the starving and the downtrodden, capitalist exploitation, heroic trade unions, Joe Hill murdered by the copper bosses, the Soviet Union as the motherland of the working people, the Communist party as the vanguard of the proletariat, the stringing out of all political issues on a scale from left to right, *The Peoples' songbook* and the guitar as (so it seemed, for I had never heard folk music before) the natural musical instrument of the proletariat.

Intrigued as I was with the world of the left as I encountered it, I reserved judgement about the virtues and vices of the society in which I was brought up and I resolved, on entering McGill University the following year, to learn something about political science and psychology. At that time, I was primarily interested in science and I had imagined I might become an engineer, but, after my experiences at camp, I decided to take a few courses in social science. When registering, I encountered Professor Jack Weldon who quickly persuaded me that psychology would not provide the answers to my questions about the organization of society and that I should study something called economics as well as political science, perhaps because

McGill was then one of the last universities to teach economics and political science in the same department. By the second year at McGill, I was a student in the department of economics and political science, and I opted in the end to specialize in economics because microeconomics, as taught by Jack Weldon, was as technical as I imagined engineering to be and had some of the quality of Euclidian geometry which was, by far, my favourite course in high school.

After graduating from McGill in 1955, I did a year of mathematics at the University of Chicago where I encountered great mathematicians among my professors and fellow students and where I learned that I was not cut out to be a mathematician. I transferred to the economics department which was then dominated by the personality and scholarship of Milton Friedman whose justly famous course in microeconomics conveyed, not the theorems (for I had already learned most of what was necessary for the course at McGill), but a sense of the importance of economics as the great key to unlock the secrets of the world. It is hard to describe the Chicago department at that time without a touch of satire, but it was a fine education and a wonderful experience for the graduate students who were being transformed into professional economists. Friedman's own style of teaching was Socratic. He would conduct dialogues with his students in which he would pose questions of the form, 'Does not such-and-such a phenomenon constitute a violation of the laws of economics?' 'How does that square with the basic assumption of universal, rational self-interested behaviour?' The theory – there was only one true theory, or so it seemed to me at the time – was placed in jeopardy, only to be vindicated in the end as its subtle implications were finally appreciated. The Ph.D. comprehensive exams were of the same form. If you really understood, as a fellow student put it at the time, that 'it is all true', you could be expected to do reasonably well in the exams. Yet, we graduate students were not 'yes-men'. You did not become an economist like the parrot in the old joke that is taught to say 'supply and demand' over and over again. One really did have to understand.

The economics department of the University of Chicago was a place where things were really happening, where the frontiers of knowledge were being pushed back in a big way. Close links with the Business School and the Law School were about to give birth to the modern science of finance and to the discipline of 'law and economics'. Friedman was taking on Keynes. The world's consensus about the genesis and control of business cycles was about to be dissolved. The forces of monetarism were about to defeat the wisdom of the central banks. It was a heady time to be a student of economics. You can often judge the tone of a place by its afternoon tea time or coffee hour. At Chicago in those days, the faculty and graduate students assembled every day in the faculty lounge to discuss, to analyse and to argue. There was, as I remember, no respite and little gossip. Economics was too important. As a professor, I would like to teach as Milton did and to generate the enthusiasm of Chicago at that time. Of course, I cannot, and must make do with presenting material clearly. The sense that big things are happening is a gift that descends upon an institution mysteriously and then just as mysteriously disappears. I have since been at other universities where excellent research was under way, but I have never again seen the vigour and dedication of the University of Chicago at that time.

My doctorate was on the debt-equity ratio (Usher 1960). About nine months elapsed between the completion of my course work and the finding of a topic. I tried one thing after another, but nothing seemed quite right until I chanced upon Modigliani and Miller's discussion paper showing that, under certain reasonable conditions, the debt-equity ratio could have no effect upon the market value of the firm as a whole. Their paper appeared subsequently in the *American Economic Review* and helped to win them a Nobel prize (Modigliani and Miller 1958). This was a beautiful problem for a dissertation, and many, many dissertations have been spawned by it. The Modigliani-Miller result was correct on its assumptions. The assumptions appeared to be part and parcel of the basic structure of economic theory and, so it seemed at first, could not be jettisoned without at the same time jettisoning a great deal of what we knew to be true of other parts of the economy. Yet the principal implication of the Modigliani-Miller theorem is that a great deal of the behaviour of firms in financial markets is foolish, wasteful and irrational, something that no properly-indoctrinated Chicago student could ever accept. Irrationality, Friedman said on more than one occasion, is the last resort of a bad theorist. It seemed to me that the solution to the problem might lie in differences among investor's evaluations of financial instruments. In particular, investors in stocks and bonds may differ in their degree of aversion to risk, in their expectations about the prospects of a firm, in their relative burdens of taxation on stocks and on bonds, and in their preferences for assets denominated in money terms as against assets that increase or decrease in value with the rate of inflation. The dissertation showed how each of the first two of these considerations could generate a unique optimum debt-equity ratio dependent on the characteristics of the firm. I can still remember the exciting moment when I worked out the first of the little models in which the debt-equity ratio became determinate, proving to myself, if no one else, that I could theorize. These moments of creativity that come to every scientist or social scientist who is any good at all in his trade are among the great pleasures of the academic life. I never published my dissertation as a book or as articles; the only published trace is an abstract (Usher 1961).

Dissertation in hand and reasonably confident that I could find an academic job eventually (it was a time when academic jobs were plentiful and holders of doctorates were scarce), but suffering from what might have been a postpartum depression from my dissertation, I resolved that my first job would give me some experience outside the comfortable little world of the universities that I had known over the preceding decade. The ideal job at that time had two characteristics: It must be located far away from Montreal where I grew up and far away from Chicago. I made my situation known to acquaintances all over the world. When informed of a job in a place called Bangkok, I looked up Bangkok in an atlas, discovered it was satisfactorily far away, applied for the job, and soon found myself in Bangkok as a junior economist with the United Nations Economic Commission for Asia and the Far East (ECAFE).

Working in ECAFE and living in Thailand was the ideal vantage point from which to see that everything I had been taught at the University of Chicago was true, specifically, that markets worked and governments did not. It is often said that the assumptions of microeconomics are appropriate for the rich countries in which those assumptions evolved but altogether inappropriate for poor countries, underdeveloped nations, developing nations, the Third World or whatever the appropriate term is today. Actually, the situation is, in my opinion, almost exactly the reverse. Thailand in the early 1960s seemed a good deal closer than the United States or Canada to the world of Adam Smith where agriculture was predominant, private firms were small and efficient unless monopoly was fostered by the state, and governments were self-interested and untrustworthy. ECAFE, on the other hand, was a bureaucracy that might have been invented by Charles Dickens. It was a bureaucracy which, quite simply, had nothing to do and had to make work for itself to keep the administrators busy. Since there were United Nations Commissions for Europe and Latin America, there had to be one for Asia too; and it would be an affront to somebody's dignity to pay professionals at ECAFE less than the going wage elsewhere in the United Nations, a wage set equal to that for comparable skills in the United States. The organization was a shell with no funds to undertake real development projects and not quite enough verve, spirit or creativity among the professionals to develop a serious line of research that might have been of use to the region. There were annual reports on economic development in Asia, a project for an Asian highway (when the project was initiated, one could actually drive from Constantinople to Saigon, but, as time passed, the route was cut in place after place as countries in the ECAFE region had less and less peaceful contact with their immediate neighbours), a project to design an Asian ship, conferences on all sorts of topics and 'field trips' (mine was to Cambodia, which impressed me as the most peaceful, tranquil and happy place I had ever seen) with no apparent purpose. Economists from all over Asia, many of whom were imbued with the ideals of the United Nations and would have dearly liked to do their bit for economic development, were drawn to ECAFE and trapped there by salaries ten times what they could earn in more useful work at home.

14.3 THE NATIONAL INCOME OF THAILAND, 1960–7

While at ECAFE, I fell upon a line of research that was to occupy me for the next fifteen years. It began with the simple observation that the ordinary people of Thailand, while not rich by American standards, were significantly better off than one would infer from the statistics by which real incomes of different countries were then commonly compared. National income is measured in the first instance in the local currency and can only be compared among countries by conversion into a common currency such as US dollars. As the widely-accepted figure for Thailand was about US $100 per head, the impression was conveyed that the Thai were desperately if not impossibly poor. One could not survive in the United States on $100 per year, yet even the poorest people in Thailand, who earned very much less than the national income per head, did somehow manage to survive and appeared not to be in danger of starvation. There had to be something wrong with the method by which the national incomes of different countries were being converted to US dollars. The point is not that seemingly poor people were not really poor, but that the numbers used to measure the poverty of nations were absurd.

The standard method for converting national incomes of many countries into US dollars was to deflate national income in the local currency by the foreign exchange rate. From studies in Europe, it was known that conversion through the foreign exchange rate provides a significantly different measure of a country's national income in US dollars than conversion by revaluing quantities consumed or invested, one by one, at American prices or by deflating national income in the local currency with an index of the ratio of local prices to American prices for a suitable bundle of goods. It was also known that the discrepancy between conversion by the foreign exchange rate and conversion by the repricing of quantities is very much larger in poor countries than in rich countries. Missing was an explanation of why conversion by the foreign exchange rate, which should have provided the right answer, did not. My problem was to supply a mechanism, consistent with the principles of international trade, to explain the observed phenomenon.

Anomalies in statistics of real income among countries might be attributed to some or all of five considerations:

1. The imputation to the measure of national income for non-market activity might be less complete in some countries than in others;
2. Local prices, converted by the foreign exchange rate into US dollars, might conform to American prices for traded goods but not for untraded goods, so that differences among countries in the relative price of traded and non-traded goods would appear in the national accounts as differences in real income.
3. International transport cost as a percentage of the value of exports might be larger for some countries than for others. A country with exports that are relatively expensive to transport would, in equilibrium, have a relatively low price level.
4. Price levels in the countryside or in places far from ports or airports may be low because domestic transport cost of goods sold by the country to the city is greater than that of goods sold by the city to the country.
5. Tariffs and export taxes create a further discrepancy between local prices and world prices.

In principle, these considerations need not bias down incomes of poor countries as compared with incomes of rich countries, but, in practice, they usually do because poor countries tend to export food, raw materials and semi-processed goods that are expensive per unit of value to transport, while rich countries tend to export manufactured goods that are relatively cheap to transport, and because poor countries tend to have a comparative advantage in non-traded goods (such as housing, hair cuts and car repair) as compared with traded goods (such as aeroplanes and computers). In fact, when I looked closely at the Thai national accounts, it seemed that the first of these considerations, missing imputations, was not of great quantitative importance. Models incorporating the second and third considerations are presented in 'The transport bias in comparisons of national income' (Usher 1963). The fourth consideration is analysed in 'Equalizing differences in income and the interpretation of national income statistics' (Usher 1965a) for a disc-shaped country with a city in the middle. The fifth consideration is discussed in 'The Thai rice trade' (Usher 1968).

After a year at ECAFE, I was awarded a research fellowship at the University of Manchester, which was extended for a second year and followed by a three-year research fellowship at Nuffield College in Oxford. In the middle year of the Nuffield fellowship, I returned to Thailand to collect data on local prices and the national accounts: to confirm that the Thai national income was biased down because Thai prices, when converted to a common currency by the foreign exchange rate, were lower than prices elsewhere; and to test the hypothesis that Thai prices were low because Thai agricultural products were heavy, bulky and costly to transport per unit of value and because middlemen took a large cut of the retail or export price. It seemed natural to look at the middleman's cut because everybody in Thailand seemed to know that the middleman was gouging the farmers.

I focused upon the price of rice which was the major Thai export at that time. There was really only one way to test my conjectures, and that was to follow the entire chain of prices from the Thai farmer to the consumer of rice in some more prosperous country. England was chosen for no better reason than that I was living there at the time. My intention was to learn enough about the pattern of costs and prices to account for the entire difference between the Thai farm price and the English retail price. I had to observe the price of paddy on the farm, milling cost, prices of different grades of rice at the mill, local transport cost by water, rail and truck, traders' profit, bribes, export tax in Thailand, international shipping cost, import tax in England and distribution cost in England, with due account for variations in costs and prices from place to place. Published statistics were not designed to answer my questions and did not do so. I had to collect the data myself and pull it all together as best I could. The better part of nine months was spent wandering about in a jeep with an interpreter asking questions of anybody who might supply useful information, an unorthodox, but in the circumstances necessary and most agreeable method of data collection.

As it turned out, my conjectures were largely wrong. Local transport was cheap, not dear. The Thai could use trucks as efficiently as anybody else, and transport by water was even less expensive than transport by land. Also, so far as I could tell, rice milling and rice trading were highly competitive industries that absorbed a smaller percentage of the price of rice in the city than comparable services in most rich countries. Even extortion by the police, much talked about in Thailand at the time, took up a very small percentage of the price; officials can become quite rich on a tiny margin. What really mattered were trade taxes. Thailand imposed a 100% tax on the export of rice (that is, 50% of the world price f.o.b. Bangkok) and substantial import duties on manufactures to protect local, mostly urban, industries. The combined effect of these taxes was to impose a massive transfer of income from the countryside to the cities. Formally untaxed, Thai agriculture bore a heavier incidence of taxation than other sectors of the economy. Cities alone were taxed directly, but in such a way that the burden of the tax was largely shifted to the farmers. Measured income on the farm was biased down in comparison with income in the cities, and the income per head in Thailand, assessed through the foreign exchange rate in US dollars, was biased downward accordingly. The impact of trade taxes on the distribution of income in Thailand is discussed in an appendix to Usher (1968). My work in the 1960s on the theory and practice of income comparison among countries was brought together in *The price mechanism and the meaning of national income statistics* (Usher 1969).

14.4   ECONOMIC GROWTH

I returned to Canada in 1967 to take up a post at Queen's University where I remain today. Back home with a wife and young family, and less inclined than I had been to travel about the world, my interest shifted from the comparison of income among countries to the comparison of income over time. It seemed reasonable to suppose that the mismeasurement of income which caused people in poor countries to appear worse off than they really were might also cause people in poor times to appear worse off as well, and might generate an upward bias in rates of economic growth. I began to study the measurement of economic growth, with special reference to Canada. The purpose of the study was to determine what we really mean by economic growth and how best to marshal primary data into statistics of real national income to reflect that meaning. It seemed to me that there is no unique, universally-correct measure of real income because real income has a family of meanings, each corresponding to a particular use of income statistics and each requiring a somewhat different statistical design. The emphasis in my research was primarily on real income as a measure of welfare rather than productivity. With this emphasis, the purpose of a time series of real income per head is to answer questions of the form, 'How large an income would I need today to be as well off as my grandfather fifty years ago?' or, more generally, 'What proportion of the income of the typical Canadian today would one need to be as well off as the typical Canadian fifty years ago?'

Posed in that way, the question leads naturally to the consideration of longevity. Part of the reason I am better off than my grandfather was at my age is that my expectation of life now is greater than his was then. Incorporation of changes in longevity into a measure of real income per head gives rise to a number of messy theoretical problems. It might be argued that, since life expectancy increases less rapidly over time than quantities of ordinary goods and services, the incorporation of longevity into a measure of real income should reduce the estimated rate of economic growth. I argued the opposite. I argued that careful attention to the meaning of economic growth and to the translation of that meaning into statistical procedures, yields a method of incorporating longevity such that the measured rate of economic growth increases when there is any increase in life expectancy at all. This proposition is discussed in 'An imputation to the measure of economic growth for changes in life expectancy' (Usher 1973). Many of the same analytical problems arise in placing values on lives saved – in medical technology, in safety devices on aeroplanes or in road improvements – for cost-benefit analysis where the saving of lives is among the benefits of public expenditure. Measurement of the 'value of life' in this context is discussed in 'Problems in the valuation of life for decision-making in the public sector' (Usher 1985).

Since 'value' equals 'price' times 'quantity', and since real income is essentially an indicator of quantity, one might suppose that a time-series of real income could equally well be constructed directly by weighting observed quantities each year with an invariant set of prices, or indirectly by deflating the value of income each year by a price index. The choice of method should make no difference to the measurement of economic growth. In practice, it makes a great deal of difference, not just because statistics of value, price and quantity are typically constructed from different bodies of data, but because time series of 'quantity' and time series of 'value divided by price' provide different kinds of information. The official statistics of real national income are constructed by deflating money income by prices or price indices. The principal advantage of deflation is that it can incorporate quality change into statistics of real income. The corresponding disadvantage is that the user of the statistics cannot connect the overall measure of economic growth with any specific set of improvements in people's lives. The great advantage in constructing real income directly from quantity data is that the measures of real income and economic growth are automatically grounded upon the specifics of how people are becoming better off over time. Ideally, a time-series of real income per head would occupy the final and summary column of a very long table (with one row for each year) in which every other column shows the amount consumed each year of an ordinary good and service – pounds of meat, pounds of vegetables, floor space of housing, motor cars per person (properly adjusted for quality) and so on – or an imputation for some unpurchased aspect of welfare such as leisure and life-expectancy. Total income in the final column would be a weighting the numbers in each of the preceding columns by prices for a given base year. Though there are good reasons why income is measured as it is in the official national accounts, there is extra information to be gained from an alternative measure constructed directly from quantity data. A comparison of time series for Canada and a general discussion of the theoretical issues are presented in 'Measuring real consumption from quantity data' (Usher 1976a).

A different set of problems arises over the distinction between income and consumption. Though the appropriately-measured money values of 'saving' and 'investment' are the same, their real values are not, and there is no single, unambiguously right way to measure the contribution this year to consumption in the future. The common money value of saving and investment might be deflated first by a price index of consumption goods, for a measure of real saving (real consumption forgone in the process of investment), or secondly, by a price index of investment goods, for a measure of real investment, or thirdly, by a price index reflecting the present value of the future marginal products of investments today, for a measure of future consumption acquired. More generally, real income may be looked upon as an indicator of potential consumption in the current year, of the location of the production possibility frontier for the economy as a whole or of the amount of present and future consumption that is produced today. These matters are discussed in 'The measurement of real income' (Usher 1976b).

As a user of index numbers, I became embroiled in the old controversy over the properties of the Divisia index. Too much, in my opinion, has been claimed for the Divisia index. It is sometimes put forward as the unique ideal index for the measurement of economic aggregates. So it is on certain assumptions, but if these assumptions are not reflected in the data, as they frequently are not, then the Divisia index can be seriously misleading. The matter is discussed in Usher (1974).

During the years I was working on the comparison of national income, I was also interested in a number of theoretical problems with little or no connection to the accounts. These studies did not originate, as I remember, in observations of market phenomena, but from reading economic literature and noticing weaknesses in arguments or alternative assumptions that might be explored. 'The welfare economics of invention' (Usher 1964) is a simple exposition of a well-known argument for patents: that the right to patent one's invention provides an incentive to undertake research leading to the discovery of new products, and that the social benefit from the availability of new products is always greater than the social cost of the monopoly power that patents convey. This is demonstrated by a simple comparison of areas under the demand curve for a new product.

'The derivation of demand curves from indifference curves' (Usher 1965a) generalized a body of literature on the interpretation of demand curves. It is customary to interpret the demand curve as a relation between price and quantity when income is held constant. That is not the only possible interpretation and is not the 'natural' interpretation in many contexts where the demand curve is used in economic argument. The demand curve is always a relation between quantity and price (as a rate of substitution in use), but the constancy of income may be replaced in the relation by the constancy of utility, conformity to the production possibility frontier, or other general constraints that emerge in the problem at hand. In particular, the constancy of income is inappropriate when the demand curve is employed in measuring the social cost of the monopoly conveyed by patents on inventions.

'Traditional capital theory' (Usher 1965b) is about how to represent technology in a simple intertemporal model of the economy. The paper is a throwback to the debates in the 1930s between the proponents of real capital and the proponents of the period of production as the basis of an explanation of the rate of interest. In fact, both views are internally consistent, and the dominance of the real capital paradigm in economic analysis over the last half century is a consequence of its conformity to concepts in the national accounts and its convenience in models of the growth over time in the economy as a whole. 'The price of capital and the real rate of interest' (Usher 1971) makes the simple point that rates of interest, as relative prices of money or goods due at different times, must depend on taste as well as technology. The common identification of the rate of interest with the marginal product of capital, which would convert the rate of interest into a strictly technological parameter at any moment of time, is invalid except on the special assumption that the supply curve of new capital goods is flat. The rate of interest depends on technology alone in the same circumstances that any other price depends on technology alone.

In the early 1970s, the national accounts gave out for me as a subject of research. I had a sense that I had solved all the interesting problems, and enough self-knowledge to realize that when you feel that way about a topic you are almost certainly wrong and you had better start thinking about something else. I completed work in progress but that was all. My studies of economic growth were brought together in *The measurement of economic growth* (Usher 1980a). A brief return to the subject later on yielded 'Income and the Hamiltonian' (Usher 1994e), a critique and rejection of the common view that the single correct interpretation of real income is the amount of consumption per year that could be sustained forever, and that this interpretation of real income is automatically reflected in the Hamiltonian of the appropriately-chosen model of the economy.

14.5   GIVING, TAKING AND VOTING

I then turned to two new subjects which, on the face of it, had nothing in common. I started to read elementary game theory and I began to study a Canadian programme of subsidization of investment by worthy firms in poor regions of the country. It was from my reading of game theory that I was first made aware of the exploitation problem in majority rule voting, a problem that has bothered me and guided much of my research ever since. Imagine a group of people who must allocate a sum of money among themselves and who must determine each person's share by voting. In particular, imagine that the allocation of the entire national income is to be determined in a legislature or parliament with no prior constraint on who is entitled to what. It is evident what happens. When voters are self-interested, as economists assume people to be, a bare majority of voters forms a coalition to appropriate the entire sum for themselves, leaving nothing for the minority at all. If this is the natural consequence of majority rule voting, it is hard to understand why anybody would be prepared to tolerate majority-rule voting for decision-making in the public sector. Government by majority rule voting would seem destined to self-destruct. Dissolution into dictatorship or monarchy would seem to be inevitable unless majority coalitions are somehow constrained by principles of equity or generally-accepted rules.

The problem has been recognized for centuries; avoidance of exploitation of minorities by majorities is a long-standing preoccupation of democratic thought. Foremost among the constraints is a system of private property guaranteeing that one's income is to a significant extent dependent on what one owns, including of course one's labour, rather than on one's success as a voter or one's influence with the government of the day. This consideration supplies a powerful justification for private property, but it also points to circumstances where property rights might reasonably be modified or curtailed. The political argument, that private ownership of the means of production is a requirement for democratic government, is consistent with and complementary to the economic argument that an economy based on private property is likely to be more efficient and more prosperous than an economy where the means of production are owned by the state.

These themes were first developed in 'The problem of equity' (Usher 1975a) and then expounded more fully in *The economic prerequisites to democracy* (1981) where it is argued that public policy should be assessed under three headings, efficiency, equality and equity. Efficiency and equality are the standard criteria in public finance. As a criterion for economic policy, equity refers to the apportionment among people of benefits and costs in accordance with universal and well-defined rules. Policy would be found wanting on this criterion in so far as it required arbitrary determinations on the part of the government, provoking in a minor way the scramble for advantage that occurs when people vote over the allocation among themselves of the entire national income.

'The significance of the probabilistic voting function' (Usher 1994d) is a defence of the old-fashioned pessimistic view of government by majority-rule voting against arguments in some recent literature that there is a voting equilibrium after all, and that the equilibrium in voting is likely to be every bit as efficient as the equilibrium in a competitive market. Though these propositions are true on certain assumptions, they offer cold comfort about the prospects for democratic government because the assumptions under which they are derived are exceedingly artificial and because the propositions are not robust to changes in the assumptions.

The connection between the exploitation problem in majority rule voting and the firm-specific subsidization of investment is that property rights are no defence of democracy if government can take property from whomsoever it pleases. Since giving must be financed by taxation, the government's unrestricted authority to give property through firm-specific investment grants is for all practical purposes the unrestricted authority to take. Giving and taking are at bottom the same. Giving and taking by the public sector are a weakening of property rights. They are precisely that allocation of the national income by the government which a democratic society cannot undertake to any significant extent without destroying itself. Firm-specific subsidization of investment is the equivalent on the expenditure side of the public accounts of *ad hominem* taxation. It is the extreme antithesis of horizontal equity. It is the direct allocation – by the government in the first instance and ultimately by the voters – of a portion of the national income to worthy recipients. To be sure, democratic societies are resilient enough to withstand a certain amount of gift-giving by the government, but all gift-giving is somewhat corruptive, and there is a limit to how much can be tolerated.

The unfortunate political consequences of firm-specific investment grants might be avoided if there were an unambiguous, socially-desirable *quid pro quo* on the part of the recipient firms, if these grants were really purchases by the government of behaviour by the recipient firms that would not otherwise be profitable. This is almost never so, for it is typically all but impossible to tell *ex post* whether the alleged objective of a grant was attained. The subsidized investment might have taken place regardless, or it might bump other equally-desirable investment which would have been undertaken instead. Programmes of firm-specific investment grants may be counterproductive or simply corrupt. At the same time, the political rhetoric of firm-specific investment grants is often singularly misleading and, to my taste, singularly offensive. Governments speak of 'creating jobs' through investment grants, counting all jobs in subsidized projects as created, ignoring the possibility that some or all grants are redundant, overlooking the connection between employment in a single firm and economy-wide macro-variables such as the money supply, and placing themselves in the role of public benefactors as though the grants were the personal charitable donations of the grantors. I began to look upon firm-specific investment grants as the enemy to be tracked down and exposed whenever possible, though I had to recognize that grants may be socially-advantageous in some circumstances. I discuss these matters with special reference to Canada in 'Some questions about the Regional Development Incentives Act' (Usher 1975b) and 'The benefits and costs of firm-specific investment grants' (Usher

1983), and with special reference to Malaysia in 'The economics of tax incentives to encourage investment in Less Developed Countries' (Usher 1977a).

Another aspect of giving and taking is examined in 'Victimization, rent-seeking and just compensation' (Usher 1995a). Even governments that respect property rights in general must take property rights from time to time: houses in the path of a new road, mining concessions on land designated for a national park, buildings demolished by the fire brigade in the path of a fire, the abolition in response to changing economic conditions of the hitherto unrestricted rights to use streams as depositories for waste or to develop land as one pleases. A general, though by no means universal, rule in such cases is that the government may take private property for public use without the consent of its owners, but that the owners must be compensated 'fairly'. The rationale for the rule is to prevent property owners from 'holding up' the government for more than the value of the property in its original use to capture the social surplus in public use. The rule has come under attack from two opposite quarters. It is said to promote inefficiency because the assurance of compensation removes the incentive upon property-owners to curtail investment on property that might be expropriated. It is also said that the rule is too narrowly applied. Authors have professed to see a constitutional injunction against taking which, appropriately interpreted, would block all redistribution of income as a taking of the property of the rich for the benefit of the poor. I argue that both objections are unwarranted. The first objection is unwarranted because the failure to supply compensation for taking would provoke a great rent-seeking contest among potential victims, a contest likely to be far more wasteful of resources than any excess incentive to invest might ever be. The second objection is unwarranted because the systematic redistribution of income is exempt from most of the cost of rent seeking when the government is free to take pieces of property without compensation. Though it is difficult to identify a clear line between government actions warranting compensation to the losers and government actions where no such compensation is warranted, one can reject the extreme positions according to which all compensation is inefficient or all redistribution of income is constitutionally blocked as taking without compensation.

14.6   PUBLIC FINANCE

Also during the 1970s, a long-standing interest in cost-benefit analysis evolved into the study of public finance. Like a good many others at that time, I began to suspect that the existing rules of cost-benefit analysis were biased in favour of expanding the role of the state beyond what could be justified in the interest of the typical citizen. The culprit is shadow-pricing. If, for example, a public project uses imported inputs which are expensive because they are subject to a large tariff, it would be deemed appropriate to value those imported inputs at the lower pre-tariff price. That is not wrong *per se*, in my opinion, but there is something amiss in not recognizing that the import duties and other taxes are what they are because tax revenue is required to finance just such projects as the one being considered. Without the project, the taxes could be somewhat lower and the corresponding deadweight loss from taxation – inclusive of the wastage of resources and social cost of tax avoidance and tax evasion – somewhat less. That consideration ought to be factored into the assessment of costs and benefits. The way to do so is to recognize the presence of a marginal cost of public funds; each additional dollar of public expenditure would be seen as imposing a cost of, for instance, two dollars upon the taxpaying public.

A number of economists had constructed measures of the marginal cost of public funds, emphasizing the effect of taxation upon the labour-leisure choice. My principal contribution was to demonstrate a connection with tax evasion. As the rate of any tax is increased, the taxpayer acquires an extra incentive to reduce his tax base, not only by diverting time and resources from taxed to untaxed activity (for instance, from taxed work to untaxed leisure), but by concealing income from the tax collector. Both types of evasive action carry social costs which need to be taken into account in the decision to engage in any additional item of public expenditure. The connection between deadweight loss and tax evasion is examined in 'Tax evasion and the marginal cost of public funds' (Usher 1986b). 'An instructive derivation of the expression for the marginal cost of public funds' (Usher 1984) is exactly as specified in the title: a derivation that is cumbersome but useful for showing why the benefit of a public project should be significantly greater than the cost as measured in the public accounts if the project is to be worthwhile. The marginal cost of public funds is examined in a broader perspective in 'The hidden cost of public expenditure' (Usher 1991a).

My 'Public property and the effects of migration upon other residents of the migrants' countries of origin and destination' (Usher 1977c) was written against a background of concern about the brain drain in Canada and the exodus of educated people from poor countries. The paper makes the simple point that, as the immigrant acquires a share of the publicly-owned capital in the country to which he goes and gives up a share of the publicly-owned capital in the country from which he comes, he must by the act of migrating impose a cost on the former country and confer a benefit on the latter. Publicly-owned capital in this context includes roads, bridges, schools, and public lands as well as the public's share of all labour and property income acquired through the tax system. Of course the public's gain from the immigrant's share of the cost of pure public goods, from his responsibility for a share of the national debt and from his (positive or negative) net contribution to the redistribution of income through the tax system must be considered in a final assessment of the costs and benefits of migration to the citizens of the countries from which the migrant comes and to which he goes.

'The welfare economics of the socialization of commodities' (Usher 1977b) is an attempt to explain why some commodities are provided by the government in equal amounts to all citizens, while other commodities are acquired within the private sector in accordance with what each person chooses to buy. What exactly is it about health and education that they are often supplied by the public sector, while food and clothing are not? The problem was to explain why a majority of citizens might choose to socialize some commodities rather than others. There are many reasons, but the decision to socialize is seen in this paper as a balance in the assessment of the median voter between his gain from the implicit redistribution of income in the provision of the socialized commodity and his loss of the option of consuming more (or less) of the socialized commodity than is provided by the state. With proportional income taxation, the expenditure per head on a programme of socialization exceeds the tax price of the programme for every member of some majority coalition because the skewness of the typical income distribution ensures that the tax price to a voter with the median income is less than the average tax price in the population as a whole. But, the financial benefit of socialization must be sufficient to compensate each person in the majority coalition for the constraint on consumption. Since everybody receives the same amount of the socialized commodity and since people differ in their taste for the socialized commodity, there is hardly anybody who would not acquire a different amount than is provided by the government if the commodity were not socialized and was for sale in the market instead. The more similar are people's tastes for a given commodity, the less important is the latter consideration to the typical voter and the more likely is the commodity in question to be socialized.

'Rawls, rules and objectives' (Usher 1997a) is an attempt to disassociate the 'veil of ignorance' test for identifying the common good from the maximization of the income of the worst-off person in society. All discourse about public policy must be with reference to some notion of the common good, some notion of what is best for society as a whole. In the evaluation of public policy, economists are accustomed to postulate social welfare function for weighing benefits and costs to different people on a common scale. The veil of ignorance test links social welfare to self-interest. Consider the choice between two policies: public vs. private medical care, a change in the tax system vs. the status quo, or any other pair of options. Imagine yourself behind a veil of ignorance where you know a good deal about how society works and about the consequences for society of each policy, but all you know about your place in society is that you will have an equal chance of replicating the circumstances of each and every person when the veil is finally lifted. The test, though not the name, was proposed by the economist John Harsanyi as a justification of the doctrine of utilitarianism. The test was taken up by John Rawls in *A theory of justice* (1972) as justification for a two-part rule for choosing among policies: to provide equal liberty for everyone and to maximize the income of the worst off person in society. Later on, in *Political liberalism* (1993), Rawls advocated his two-part rule as the only basis for the preservation of what most people see as the good society. The argument has had a good deal of influence on the economics profession. I claimed that the argument is simply wrong. A person behind the veil of ignorance would not choose among policies to maximize the income of the worst off person. More importantly, Rawls' exclusive emphasis on the criterion for public policy and on abstract rules of justice presumed to be self-evidently binding on people of good will diverts attention from the technology of social action and from the study of the full consequences of alternative economic arrangements.

14.7   THE CANADIAN CONSTITUTION

Like every Canadian with an interest in public finance, I had to have my say about the Canadian constitution. My papers on the Canadian constitution are the outcome of my concern that a common English Canadian interest is not adequately represented by the Federal government or by the governments of the English Canadian provinces. It is often said that Canada is a compromise between French and English, where French and English are to be understood in the distinctly Canadian sense of referring not to the language of one's ancestors, but to one's preferred language for communication in public with one's fellow Canadians. Compromise implies an underlying conflict of interest. The conflict of interest is in the first instance over language.

Canada could not have been established as a unified country and could not be preserved today without recognition of French and English as official languages and without effective use of both languages in the Federal government. The conflict over language is about the extent of bilingualism. With English as the international language, French Canadians must fear the loss of their native tongue but must at the same time learn English well to play any role outside the narrow confines of Quebec. By contrast, except in

Quebec itself, English Canadians can live their lives without French and they learn French (if at all and rarely well) for no other reason than to participate in Federal institutions. Conflict over the extent of bilingualism becomes conflict over jobs, public expenditure, Federal-provincial transfers and office.

There is a derivative conflict of interest over provincial authority and jurisdiction. French Canadians in Quebec have a strong common interest in expanding the scope of provincial jurisdiction, especially in matters of language, for fear of being outvoted by the English in the national Parliament. English Canada has a strong common interest in expanding the scope of Federal jurisdiction, especially over programmes with a substantial sharing or redistribution of income, for such ethnic, linguistic, economic and religious differences as exist within English Canada are not for the most part on provincial lines. For the French, the problem is compounded by the preference of the vast majority of immigrants for English over French. For the English, the problem is compounded by the absence of any government representing the common interest of English Canadians exclusively and in its entirety, not the Federal government which is, as it should be, a balancing of the concerns of the English and the French, not the nine provincial governments within English Canada which, like provincial governments everywhere, seek to enhance their powers and authority at the expense of the Federal government.

'How should the redistributive powers of the state be divided between federal and provincial governments' (Usher 1980b) develops the proposition that redistribution among people should be conducted at the national rather than at the regional level so as to avoid welfare-induced migration of the poor to the more generous regions of the country and of the rich to the less generous regions. The conflict of interest between French and English is discussed more generally in 'The interests of English Canada' (Usher 1995b).

Another, perhaps more serious, concern is that English Canada is at present unprepared to reorganize itself in the event that Quebec secedes. There is a more than negligible risk that Quebec will secede. One of the two major parties in Quebec is dedicated to separation. There seems to be an understanding within Canada that Quebec will not be prevented from seceding by force. Yet there is no consensus within English Canada about a form of government for the rest of Canada in the event that Quebec does go. I am one of a very small number of Canadians who have not respected the taboo against discussion of this matter. 'The English response to the prospect of the separation of Quebec' (Usher 1978) was written at a time when risk of the secession of Quebec seemed considerable, while 'The design of a government for an English Canadian country' (Usher 1991b) was written in the wake of the failure of the Meech Lake Accord. It is argued in the latter paper, that, although a Canada that includes Quebec must be a federation, a

Canada without Quebec – an English-speaking country of some twenty million people – would be better off as a unitary state like France and Holland, with no constitutionally-recognized provinces at all.

Several long-standing interests came together in *The uneasy case for equalization payments* (1996). Mandated by Section 36(2) of the Canadian Constitution, equalization payments are transfers from the Federal government to the governments of the have-not provinces 'to ensure that provincial governments have sufficient revenues to provide reasonably comparable levels of services at reasonably comparable levels of taxation.' The Canadian programme of equalization payments is examined under the headings of equality, efficiency and equity. It might be supposed that a programme called 'equalization payments' would promote equality, but that need not be so. Equalization of revenues among provinces does not necessarily imply equalization of incomes among people. It may do so but it need not, and the trail to the ultimate effects of the programme is so hard to follow. Equalization payments are from the Federal government to the have-not provinces in the first instance, then from rich provinces to poor provinces, and finally from some people to other people, where not all the ultimate recipients are poor and not all the ultimate donors are rich. The losers are poor people as well as rich people in the rich provinces. The winners are rich people as well as poor people in the poor provinces. Nor can one be certain about the efficiency of the programme because there are forces pushing every which way. Efficiency can be identified in this context with the maximization of the national income for Canada as a whole. The programme forestalls migration from poor provinces to rich provinces, which may or may not be efficient depending on whether migration would or would not have equalized wages in the absence of the programme. If so, the programme could be efficient. If not, if comparably-skilled people are significantly worse off in poor provinces with or without the programme, then the programme is likely to have been inefficient. There is another dimension to efficiency. Like any tax or expenditure, equalization payments generate incentives on the part of the recipients. Recipient governments are induced to tax and spend in ways that augment entitlement to equalization payments but may at the same time lower the national income of Canada as a whole. An extensive literature on these questions is summarized in the book, and the outcome is profoundly inconclusive. The effects of the programme under the heading of equity are equally mixed and uncertain. The constitutional mandate for the programme would seem to warrant clear rules about who is entitled to what. In practice, the rules are not strictly applied and there is reason to believe that the frequent changes in the rules are in response to political winds that blow the programme this way or that. The formula determining each province's entitlement under the programme does not correspond to the constitutional mandate and is vague enough to accommodate pressures to favour one province or another.

14.8   ANARCHY, DESPOTISM AND THE LIBERAL SOCIETY

In the early 1980s, I became preoccupied with theft as a pattern of departures from efficiency in the public and private sectors of the economy. Economists are accustomed to subsume a wide variety of departures from efficiency under the general heading of 'externalities'. To characterize departures from efficiency as externalities is to treat them as the innocent by-products of ordinary production of goods and services, rather than as the outcome of a serious effort to get the better of one's neighbour. I find this, not so much wrong as unsatisfactory. The concept of the externality seems too effete, too passive and too obscure a notion to bear the weight of the entire range of departures from efficiency. The concept fails to capture the multiplicity and variety of the ways self-interested behaviour may fail to promote the common good, even in the limited sense that no change in the composition and distribution of output could make everybody better off. Appropriately interpreted, theft seems to be at worst a supplement and at best a distinct improvement. To treat theft as the quintessential departure from efficiency is to differentiate between making and taking, between the deployment of one's resources to build stuff for use or sale and the deployment of one's resources to appropriate stuff from other people.

On the analogy with theft, departures from efficiency can be classified under four headings according to the types of social cost they impose: waste of the labour of the thief, waste of the labour of the victim in protecting himself, destruction of product, and deadweight loss in diverting resources from the production of goods that are easily appropriated by others to the production of goods, such as leisure, that are difficult or impossible to appropriate. The first two categories are exemplified by rent seeking and overuse of common property when people employ resources in competition for shares of a fixed pie. The third category is exemplified by manoeuvres to acquire or maintain control of a corporation in so far as these manoeuvres tend to lower the market value of the corporation. Classical externalities fit the fourth category exactly. A model of production and appropriation is presented in 'Theft as a paradigm for departures from efficiency' (Usher 1987). In the model, people choose to be farmers or thieves so that incomes are equalized in the two occupations.

The model is of some interest in its own right, and it proved amenable to developments I had not at first anticipated. A police force was introduced in 'Police, punishment and public goods' (Usher 1986a). The role of the police is to reduce the incidence of theft by lowering the productivity of thieves. When policemen's wages are set to equalize incomes of farmers and policemen, the optimal size of the police force can be determined to maximize income per head. Though an indispensable function of government, policing is not appropriately characterized as a 'public good' in the ordinary sense of the term in the literature of economics, for policing is neither an argument in the utility function nor a factor of production. 'Education as a deterrent to crime' (Usher 1997b) contains a formal model of the common view that education inculcates a willingness on the part of the student to respect the law. Education was introduced into the farmers and thieves model as reducing the utility of a life of crime as compared with a life of honest toil.

The obvious next step was to model policemen as predators. The thieves become bandits because theft is a legal category and I wanted to be able to talk about a society without law or government. The police become a ruling class that exploits the ordinary citizen as a shepherd exploits a flock of sheep and hunts bandits to preserve its revenue. I postulated two extreme types of nasty societies: anarchy where bandits confront farmers in the absence of police protection, and despotism where predatory rulers, who tax farmers and hunt bandits, are constrained in their choice of tax rates by the farmer's option to become a bandit instead. Having gone that far, it seemed natural to suppose that encounters among farmers, bandits and rulers are violent as well as costly, and that violence entails a risk of loss of life. From my work on the value of life as an imputation to the national accounts, I incorporated survival rates as arguments in the utility functions of all social classes.

An interesting feature of these models was the displacement of marginal productivity by actual or potential violence as the principal determinant of the distribution of income. Under some rather strong assumptions, a complete distribution of income for every rank in a hierarchical and entirely predatory ruling class is derived in 'The distribution of income in a despotic society' (Usher and Engineer 1987). Occupants of each rank in the hierarchy are supplied with just enough income that it is not in their interest to rebel, where rebellion entails a risk of loss of life for the rebels and for the personnel of the government against whom they rebel. A curious, but perhaps realistic, feature of this model is that population growth simultaneously lowers incomes of the farmers at the bottom of the hierarchy (for the usual Malthusian reasons) and increases incomes of the rulers at the top.

While working on predatory behaviour, I learned that the distinction between anarchy and despotism, as the polar opposites of the nasty societies from which the liberal democracies had emerged and into which they may yet deteriorate, was actually commonplace in the nineteenth century and that, in so far as I was advancing beyond what was known then, I was to some extent treading in the footsteps of the Virginia School. My model of anarchy had a good deal in common with a model developed by Winston Bush (1972) some years before, though my interpretation and usage of the model was not the same. Gordon Tullock (1987) had already investigated the economics of despotism, though his analysis was rather informal and differed significantly from mine in the constraints upon predation by the ruling class. In Geoffrey Brennan and James Buchanan's (1980) 'Leviathan', a despotic society with a revenue-maximizing ruling class is constrained by a constitution that specifies which types of taxes are permitted and which are not.

'The dynastic cycle and the stationary state' (Usher 1989) is an attempt to supply a formal model of an ancient theory in Chinese historiography connecting the rise and fall of dynasties with periods of prosperity and want, population growth and population decline. The dynastic cycle had captured my imagination ever since my days with the United Nations in Bangkok, and I happened to be reading the wonderful ancient Chinese novel about the rise and fall of dynasties, *The romance of the three kingdoms* (my candidate for non-Western literature to make the university syllabus politically correct), while I was working on predatory behaviour. It seemed reasonable to attribute the downswing of the dynastic cycle to the shrinkage of the surplus to the ruling class brought about by population growth, the corresponding decline in output per head and the rise in the incidence of banditry. Eventually, the ruling class disintegrates because it can no longer exact enough revenue through taxation to ensure that the welfare of its members exceeds the common welfare of farmers and bandits. Disintegration of the ruling class precipitates a time of chaos when the old dynasty has 'lost the mandate of heaven'. The life of the ordinary citizen becomes especially precarious, and the population declines precipitously, setting the stage for successful bandits to establish themselves as the new ruling class.

Anarchy and despotism are paradigms, or ideal types, of predatory tendencies in all societies and of the nasty societies into which more attractive societies may deteriorate when things go wrong. As such, anarchy and despotism may be contrasted with a third ideal type incorporating essential features of what most people see as a good society. My latest book, *The welfare economics of markets, voting and predation* (Usher 1994f), contrasts anarchy and despotism with the 'liberal society' characterized by majority rule voting and by a significant degree of private ownership of the means of production. Few readers would question the inclusion of majority rule voting. I include private property because it is a requirement for prosperity and because, as discussed in 'The problem of equity' (Usher 1975a), I believe property and voting to be mutually-dependent institutions. I exclude civil rights, not because I consider civil rights to be of secondary importance, but because the narrower definition is sufficient for the purpose at hand and because I see property and voting as technical requirements for civil rights and other qualities of a good society. Oddly enough, there seems to be no commonly accepted name for a society where people are doubly entitled as property-owners and as voters. The word democracy is too vague, too exclusively political and too suggestive of every conceivable public virtue. In the nineteenth century, the word liberal carried the appropriate reference to the government and to the economy, and was precise enough in its meaning that liberalism could actually be opposed. The word has since acquired other, somewhat different, connotations, but there remains enough of the older meaning for the word to serve as the alternative to anarchy and despotism.

Economic policy is all-too-often analysed and evaluated as though policy were to be implemented by a public-spirited government devoted exclusively to the advancement of the common good as represented by a social welfare function. Reasonable and appropriate in some contexts, this stance toward government and the economy places too much emphasis on 'market failure' and too little upon the social cost of government. It promotes the excessive expansion of government because the balance of cost and benefit is more likely to favour public action when government is entirely benevolent than when government is in some degree predatory. It diverts attention from the political consequences of economic policy and from the possibility that ill-chosen policy may undermine the foundations of the liberal society. It inculcates a state of mind among the occupants of a liberal society, or some real-world approximation thereto, in which the virtues of the liberal society are seen as permanent and indestructible. It fosters the illusion that anarchy and despotism throughout the world are reserved for others less virtuous than ourselves. In focusing upon the extremes of predatory behaviour in markets and government, the study of anarchy and despotism – as predatory tendencies in the liberal society and as nasty societies into which the liberal society may disintegrate – is ultimately directed to learning how the liberal society might be protected and preserved.

SELECTED WORKS

(1960) 'The debt-equity ratio', unpublished Ph.D. dissertation, University of Chicago.
(1961) 'The debt-equity ratio', *Journal of Finance*, 16 (1), pp. 103–4.*
(1963) 'The transport bias in comparisons of national income', *Economica*, n.s. 30 (2), pp. 140–58.*
(1964) 'The welfare economics of invention', *Economica*, n.s. 31 (3), pp. 279–87.*

(1965a) 'The derivation of demand curves from indifference curves', *Oxford Economic Papers*, n.s. 17 (1), pp. 24–46.*

(1965b) 'Traditional capital theory', *Review of Economic Studies*, 32 (2), pp. 169–86.*

(1965c) 'The Thai national income at United Kingdom prices', *Bulletin of the Oxford Institute of Statistics*, 25 (3), pp. 199–214.*

(1968) 'The Thai rice trade', in T. Silcock (ed.) (1968) *Thailand: social and economic studies*. Canberra: Australian National University Press, pp. 206–30.

(1969) *The price mechanism and the meaning of national income statistics*. Oxford: Clarendon Press.

(1971) 'The price of capital and the real rate of interest', *Oxford Economic Papers*, n.s. 23 (1), pp. 1–18.*

(1973) 'An imputation to the measure of economic growth for changes in life expectancy', in M. Moss (ed.) (1973) *The measurement of economic and social performance*. NBER studies in income and wealth, vol. 38. New York: Columbia University Press, pp. 193–232.*

(1974) 'The suitability of the Divisia index for the measurement of economic aggregates', *Review of Income and Wealth*, 20 (3), pp. 273–88.*

(1975a) 'The problem of equity', Queen's University Economics Department Discussion Paper no. 181.*

(1975b) 'Some questions about the Regional Development Incentives Act', *Canadian Public Policy*, 1 (4), pp. 557–75.*

(1976a) 'Measuring real consumption from quantity data: Canada, 1935–1968', in N.E. Terleckyj (ed.) (1976) *Household production and consumption*. NBER studies in income and wealth, vol. 40. New York: Columbia University Press, pp. 585–642.*

(1976b) 'The measurement of real income', *Review of Income and Wealth*, 22 (4), pp. 305–29.*

(1977a) 'The economics of tax incentives to encourage investment in less developed countries', *Journal of Development Economics*, 4 (2), pp. 119–48.*

(1977b) 'The welfare economics of the socialization of commodities', *Journal of Public Economics*, 8 (2), pp. 151–68.*

(1977c) 'Public property and the effects of migration upon other residents of the migrants' countries of origin and destination', *Journal of Political Economy*, 85 (5), pp. 1001–20.*

(1978) 'The English response to the prospect of the separation of Quebec', *Canadian Public Policy*, 4 (1), pp. 57–70.*

(1980a) *The measurement of economic growth*. Oxford: Basil Blackwell.

(1980b) 'How should the redistributive power of the state be divided between federal and provincial governments?', *Canadian Public Policy*, 7 (1), pp. 16–29.*

(1981) *The economic prerequisites to democracy*. Oxford: Basil Blackwell.

(1983) 'The benefits and costs of firm-specific investment grants: a study of five federal programs', Queen's University Economics Department Discussion Paper no. 511.*

(1984) 'An instructive derivation of the expression for the marginal cost of public funds', *Public Finance*, 39 (3), pp. 406–10.*

(1985) 'Problems in the valuation of life for decision-making in the public sector', *Social Philosophy and Policy*, 2 (2), pp. 168–191.*

(1986a) 'Police, punishment and public goods', *Public Finance*, 41 (1), pp. 96–114.*

(1986b) 'Tax evasion and the marginal cost of public funds', *Economic Inquiry*, 24 (4), pp. 563–86.*

(1987) 'Theft as a paradigm for departures from efficiency', *Oxford Economic Papers*, n.s. 39 (2), pp. 235–52.*

(1987) (with M. Engineer) 'The distribution of income in a despotic society', *Public Choice*, 54 (3), pp. 261–76.*

(1989) 'The dynastic cycle and the stationary state', *American Economic Review*, 79 (5), pp. 1031–44.*

(1991a) 'The hidden costs of public expenditure', in R.M. Bird (ed.) (1991) *More taxing than taxes?: the taxlike effects of nontax policies in LDCs*. San Francisco, CA: ICS Press, pp. 11–65.*

(1991b) 'The design of a government for an English Canadian country', R.W. Broadway, T.J. Courchene and D.D. Purvis (eds) (1991) *Economic dimensions of constitutional change*. Kingston, Ontario: Eighth John Deutsch round table on economic policy, vol. I, pp. 91–116.*

(1994a) *Collected essays*. Vol. I: *National accounting and economic theory*. Aldershot: Edward Elgar.

(1994b) 'Introduction', in D. Usher (1994a) **q.v.**, pp. ix–xxv.

(1994c) *Collected essays*. Vol. II: *Welfare economics and public finance*. Aldershot: Edward Elgar.

(1994d) 'The significance of the probabilistic voting function', *Canadian Journal of Economics*, 27 (2), pp. 433–45.

(1994e) 'Income and the Hamiltonian', *Review of Income and Wealth*, 40 (2), pp. 123–41.

(1994f) *The welfare economics of markets, voting and predation*. Manchester: Manchester University Press.

(1995a) 'Victimization, rent-seeking and just compensation', *Public Choice*, 83 (1/2), pp. 1–20.

(1995b) 'The interests of English Canada', *Canadian Public Policy*, 21 (1), pp. 72–84.

(1996) *The uneasy case for equalization payments*. Vancouver: Fraser Institute.

(1997a) 'Rawls, rules and objectives: a critique of the two principles of justice', *Constitutional Political Economy*, 7 (2), pp. 103–26.

(1997b) 'Education as a deterrent to crime', *Canadian Journal of Economics*, 30 (2), pp. 367–84.

(1998) 'The Coase theorem is tautological, incoherent or wrong', *Economic Letters*, 61 (1), pp. 3–11.

BIBLIOGRAPHY

Brennan, G. and Buchanan, J.M. (1980) *The power to tax: analytical foundations of a fiscal constitution*. Cambridge: Cambridge University Press.

Bush, W. (1972) 'Individual welfare in anarchy', in G. Tullock (ed.) (1972) *Explorations in the theory of anarchy*. Blacksburg, VA: Center for the Study of Public Choice, pp. 5–18.

Modigliani, F. and Miller, M.H. (1958) 'The cost of capital, corporation finance and the theory of investment', *American Economic Review*, 48 (3), pp. 261–97.

Rawls, J.A. (1972) *A theory of justice*. Oxford: Clarendon Press.
Rawls, J.A. (1993) *Political liberalism*. New York: Columbia University Press.
Tullock, G. (1987) *Autocracy*. Dordrecht: Kluwer Academic.

15. Takeshi Amemiya (b. 1935)[1]

15.1   EARLY LIFE

On 26 April 1941 I sailed from Yokohama on the N.Y.K. liner *Asama-maru* for Lima, Peru, with my mother and sister, to join my father, who was already in Lima working for the N.Y.K. office there. I had just turned six. (Many of the details of the subsequent account of the trip to and from Peru are based on the diary of my late sister Hiroko who was twenty years old at the time.) We had a suite on the C deck, and everything was luxurious on the ship: food, games, a swimming pool, and parties. The first Wrigley's chewing-gum I tasted on the ship had a strong impression on me. After stopping over in Honolulu one day, the ship arrived in San Francisco in the early morning of 10 May. I still vividly remember looking up at the Golden Gate Bridge from a cabin window as the ship sailed under it. The bridge was only four years old then. No one could have guessed at that time that I would sail again under the bridge seventeen years later as a student and drive over it numerous times as an adult. We stayed in Yamato Hotel on California St. for five nights. The hotel is no longer there. I remember seeing in a street near

---

[1]   Amemiya (1994b), as revised by the author. I have one volume of selected writings in econometric theory in the series (Amemiya 1994a).

the hotel a spot which still showed remnants of the damage caused by the 1906 earthquake. One day we crossed the Bay Bridge (then five years old) to visit the University of California at Berkeley. Unfortunately, we did not visit Stanford University. On 15 May we boarded the N.Y.K. freighter *Ginyo-maru*. After stopping over at Los Angeles, Manzanillo, Acapulco, Balboa and Buenaventura for freight loading and unloading, the *Ginyo-maru* arrived in Callao, the port of Lima, on June 13.

Our life in Lima was comfortable and pleasant until that fateful day, 7 December 1941. We lived in a spacious two-storey house in a central residential area of Lima called Miraflores. I attended the first grade of a Japanese school. In spite of its name, all the subjects except the Japanese language were taught in Spanish. As a result, my grades were all B's (generous ones) except A's in music and mathematics, which did not require so much knowledge of Spanish. (Nor of Japanese, I should say, for I got a B in Japanese as well.) I remember with nostalgia the trips to and from school every day with several neighbourhood kids squeezed in a small old car driven by a school chauffeur, the unforgettable smell of the corner bakery and candy store, the four-day carnival in February during which one could hit anybody of the opposite sex with balloons filled with water, and pedlars who came to sell all sorts of food with melodious calls.

On 7 December 1941 the Pacific war broke out. Late that evening I was awakened by an unusual noise coming from downstairs, and I found my family huddled around a huge old-fashioned radio we had in the saloon, listening intensely to a short-wave broadcast from Japan announcing the outbreak of war in the Pacific. I can still recall the atmosphere of tension and anxiety that filled the room. After that day our life remained at least superficially normal for a while, even though my parents and my sister, who was old enough to understand, must have been quite concerned about our future. The matter became more urgent on 24 January 1942, when Peru suddenly severed its diplomatic relations with Japan. It was the first country in South America to do so. Immediately the Peruvian government started rounding up influential Japanese, diplomats and senior employees of major Japanese firms as well as immigrants who held important positions, for interrogation. My father was taken away to a barrack in Callao the next day and was detained there until 28 March. Although this was obviously a period of great anxiety, we did not suffer any harassment or feel any animosity from the Peruvians we met in our ordinary lives. In the meantime an agreement was reached between Japan and Peru that all the Japanese nationals were to be sent home.

On 14 April we embarked on a long travel home aboard a passenger ship called the *Acadia*. It was a relatively small ship (9,000 tons) and on its side the word DIPLOMATIC was painted in huge white letters. The ship was extremely crowded with diplomats and businessmen of Japanese, German and Italian nationality. The diplomats occupied the better quarters; my father slept on a hammock in a crowded cabin with many other men, and my mother, my sister and I were quartered in a windowless muggy cabin of approximately 12 by 12 feet. The food was reasonable, and the crew was efficient and kind. The *Acadia* stopped at Guayaquil, Ecuador and Buenaventura, Colombia to pick up more diplomats, and passing through Panama Canal and crossing the Gulf of Mexico, arrived in the port of New Orleans on April 24.

The next morning only the diplomats were allowed to leave the ship, and the rest of us had to wait aboard until after dinner without knowing where we would be taken from there. Finally, at about nine in the evening we started disembarking, and by looking at the luggage tags someone had put on our trunks we found that Seagoville, Texas was to be our next destination. Seagoville is a small town, about ten miles southeast of Dallas; we were to stay in a relocation camp transformed from a prison for women. Our train left the New Orleans station at about 10 p.m. and arrived in Dallas on the morning of the second day. The train was comfortable and the meals in the dining car were much better than on the *Acadia*. The waiter gave me a second helping of shrimp potage for lunch. At the Dallas station we got on two Greyhound buses and arrived at the camp in about forty minutes.

The camp impressed me as a bright, comfortable place, with many two-storey buildings scattered on spacious grounds. Around each building there were well-maintained lawns, flower beds and walking paths paved with bricks. The building we lived in looked like a college dorm. My father and my sister each had their own room, and my mother and I occupied another room. Each room was small, with the minimum necessities, but comfortable. I have mostly good memories of life in Seagoville: oatmeal at breakfast, many friends to play with all day long, big delicious oranges as many as we could eat, colourful lollipops we could buy at the canteen, and the beautiful sunset in the big Texas sky. The only bad experience I had was when I was confined in a hospital room with a cold and had to keep shouting 'yo quiero agua' until finally a nurse who understood Spanish came by. Most of the Americans who worked on the premises, all of whom were women because of the former nature of the place, were nice to us. From what I later found out, our experience in Seagoville was far better than that of the Japanese Americans in their internment camps. Even a worse fortune awaited the Japanese Peruvians who were arrested by representatives of the United States government on false charges such as spying, sent to the United States and taken away their Peruvian passports on the ridiculous charge of entering the United States illegally, and, after having been interned in various locations, were sent back to Japan. Many of those Japanese Peruvians still live in Japan.

After many years of grievances, they have finally won an apology and a small remuneration from the United States government this year.

A major source of anxiety for the adults during our stay in Seagoville was, however, that for a long while we were uninformed about when and how we would get to Japan. Only in early June did we start hearing about the plan for 'exchange ships', which would carry the Japanese from the United States and the Americans from Japan and exchange them at Lourenço Marques (now called Maputo) in Mozambique (then a colony of Portugal, which was a neutral country during W.W.II).

The day of departure finally came on 9 June, after forty-three days of waiting. We went back to Dallas on a bus and in the evening got on a train for New York. After spending two nights on the train, we arrived at Pennsylvania Station in New York City at around noon. The only thing I remember of this train ride is the long tunnel under the Hudson River right before the train arrived in New York City. From the station we were escorted by many policemen to the Pennsylvania Hotel (now called New York Penta) across 7th Avenue. After having lunch in a restaurant on the top floor of the 18-storey hotel, my family was taken to a luxurious suite on the fourth floor. Even to this day that is the most luxurious hotel room I have ever stayed in. The only fly in the ointment was that every match box in the room bore the inscription 'Remember Pearl Harbor'. During our one week stay in the hotel, we were not allowed to go outside, except once when we were taken to the rooftop, from which I remember seeing the Empire State Building very close by. Although we could not go shopping ourselves, we were able to ask hotel employees to buy a few things for us. In that way we bought a few boxes of Hershey's Kisses, which we took back to Japan. They became a family treasure back home during the war.

Suddenly on the morning of 18 June, the officers announced that we were to board the ship that day. A bus took us to Jersey City across the Hudson River, where we boarded the *Gripsholm*, a Swedish ship weighing 17,000 tons. At 11.25 pm. on 18 June 1942, the *Gripsholm* departed from Jersey City carrying 1,500 Japanese diplomats and businessmen and their families. On the ship were a few notable people, some of whom I got to know well after I became an adult. They included an internationally acclaimed xylophonist Yoichi Hiraoka, for whom my sister played piano accompaniments in many concerts on the ship; Shigeto Tsuru, a classmate of Paul Samuelson's at Harvard who later became my colleague at Hitotsubashi University in Tokyo, and Mrs. Tsuru; Ms. Kiyoko Cho and Ms. Tane Takahashi, who later became a professor of history of thought, and the head librarian, respectively, at the International Christian University, where I obtained my B.A. degree; Shizuo Kakutani, a leading Japanese mathematician famous among economists by his fixed-point theorem; Kazuko and her brother Shunsuke Tsurumi, noted essayists.

The *Gripsholm* arrived in Rio de Janeiro on 3 July, took in more repatriates, and departed the next day. On 20 July she reached her final destination, Lourenço Marques. The next day we went shopping in the city, stepping on the earth for the first time in a little over a month. The only thing I remember about Lourenço Marques is that my mother bought me the best lollipops I have ever tasted. On 22 July the *Asama-maru* and the Italian ship *Conte Verde* arrived from Japan carrying the repatriates going back to the United States and other Allied countries. It was most exciting for the Japanese aboard the *Gripsholm*, especially for us because we sailed on the *Asama-maru* a year ago, to discover the *Asama-maru* from afar and watch her familiar figure loom larger and larger as she approached us. So many passengers gathered on one side of our ship to watch and greet the *Asama-maru* that stewards came to warn us that the ship had started to lean toward one side and urged some of the people to move to the other side.

The day of the exchange was 23 July. A long row of freight cars was placed on the railroad tracks alongside the pier, and the Americans were to walk on one side of the cars, and the Japanese on the other side. I have later heard that despite such a precaution some people crossed the tracks between cars and greeted their old friends, who were now on the opposing sides of the conflict. The Japanese from North America boarded the *Asama-maru*, and those from Middle and South America boarded the *Conte Verde*. The day after we boarded the *Conte Verde* we went shopping in the city again; in a store we came across a few friendly Americans, who had come out to the city from the *Gripsholm*, and we exchanged our US dollars with their Japanese yen.

The two East-bound ships departed from Lourenço Marques on 26 July and sailed alongside of each other toward home. I enjoyed my life on the *Conte Verde*. Our cabin was comfortable and the meals were quite good. Except for a two-hour study period, we had a lot of fun running around on the decks and up and down the stairs over the several levels of the big ship as if going through a maze. In addition, there were movies, concerts and even an athletic meet on the deck. After stopping over two nights in Singapore, we came back to Yokohama on 20 August. I cried, not wanting to leave the ship.

15.2   UNDERGRADUATE STUDIES, 1954–8

The foregoing journey, although consciously remembered mostly by Wrigley's chewing-gum, Hershey's Kisses and lollipops, must have registered a much deeper impact on the subconscious. A desire to go to the

United States gradually strengthened in my mind during my adolescence. I chose the International Christian University (ICU) partly for the purpose of satisfying this desire.

A plan to found an international university based on Christian beliefs had been formulated many years before the war, but it gained momentum after the war through a joint effort of Japanese and American Protestant Christians. One of the leaders of this project was Hachiro Yuasa, who became the first president of ICU. ICU, patterned after a small liberal arts college in the United States, admitted its first class in 1953 and I entered it in the following year.

There were several international (mostly American) faculty members, and lectures were given both in Japanese and English. Students were expected to become bilingual; in the first year the Japanese students studied almost solely English, and the foreign students, Japanese. By the time I graduated from high school, I was able to read most difficult English books, but my hearing and speaking were extremely deficient. By the end of my first year at ICU, I could truly say I was fluent in English. I majored in economics, not because I wanted to study the subject seriously but because in Japan that was the subject customarily chosen by a student who did not have a clear idea of what field he or she wanted to specialize in. Indeed, I did not study economics seriously and spent more time reading American literature.

15.3   AMERICA AND POSTGRADUATE EDUCATION, 1958–64

Even though my desire to go to America was intense, I did not start contemplating any concrete plan to accomplish this goal until the deadline for applying to graduate schools approached. When I sought advice, Professor Alan Gleason, who to this day has remained my revered teacher and friend, looking at my less-than-B-average grades, rightly advised against my going to graduate school right after graduating from ICU. Following his advice, I applied and was admitted to Guilford College, a small Quaker college in North Carolina, as a nonmatriculate special student. I was recommended to Guilford by Professor Iwao Ayusawa, a Quaker and an internationally known scholar of labour relations.

On 3 August 1958 I sailed from Yokohama aboard the N.Y.K. freighter *Shiga-maru*. I was somewhat apprehensive about my uncertain future because I still did not have a concrete idea about what to do after one year in Guilford. I entertained a vague possibility of coming back after one year and working for an English language newspaper in Japan. At any rate I did not want to think too far ahead. I would take one year at a time.

The life on a freighter was very pleasant. The ship carried only twelve passengers, and there was a friendly, family-like atmosphere. It was a long voyage, stopping at San Francisco and Los Angeles, going through the Panama Canal, all the way to New York City, arriving there on 30 August. It was for me a nostalgic return to San Francisco and New York City. I enjoyed sight-seeing in New York for eleven days and in Washington, D.C. for two days, each time staying in the home of my parents' friends. On 11 September I got on a Southern Railway night train heading for Greensboro, North Carolina, and became all alone for the first time. The train arrived in Greensboro early the next morning, where I was met by someone who took me to Guilford College only a few minutes away. The first two days I stayed with Professor and Mrs. Algie Newlin, friends of the Ayusawas, and then moved to a dormitory.

My year at Guilford was an enjoyable one. I owe much of this to the warm hospitality of the Newlins on my frequent visits to their home and to my friendship with my roommate Jeff Hartsell. I was also fortunate to meet my English teacher Dr. Chauncey Ives and his wife. My and later my family's friendship with the Ives continued until Dr. Ives' death in 1992. (Mrs. Ives had died a few years earlier.) Dr. Ives was a man of exceptional intelligence and courage. He had a law degree from Yale and a Ph.D. in English literature from Harvard. His first teaching job was at the University of North Carolina, from which he was fired because he failed several football players. Then he moved to Guilford College, from which he was fired again soon after I left Guilford because of his passionate crusade to end segregation there. Afterwards he taught at a small women's college in New Jersey until his retirement.

The year I was in Guilford, the equal-rights movement for the blacks under the leadership of Dr. Martin Luther King, Jr. was just gaining momentum. I was in the midst of a radical change in the American South. In 1958 most of the schools in the South including Guilford were segregated; so were buses, restaurants and public rest rooms. All this quickly changed soon after I left Guilford, beginning with the famous sit-in strike at a Greensboro diner.

It is important to recognize that there is much more to the difference between the North and the South than in their attributed attitudes toward race. Sometimes I detect in the mind of the elite of the Eastern establishment irrational contempt and aversion toward the South. The Japanese students who study in an Eastern university and go home without experiencing the other cultures within the United States tend to be influenced by this attitude. I am glad I went to the South first, to become free of this bias. When I went to Guilford, it was only 13 years after the end of W.W.II, and I was a little bit anxious about how Americans felt about the Japanese. There was no reason to worry because the Southerners remembered the 'War Between the States' more vividly than W.W.II! One student said, half jokingly and half seriously, 'I hope you will be on our side when we rise again.'

I was fortunate to have Dr. E. Kidd Lockard as my teacher of economics at Guilford. I took his courses on Money and Banking and Public Finance, and these subjects aroused so much interest in me that toward the end of the year at Guilford I decided to apply for graduate schools. My plan at that time was to obtain an M.A. in economics and then go home and work for a newspaper company. I was accepted by the American University in Washington, D.C. with a small scholarship ($350 a year as I remember), so I went there in the fall of 1959. All the graduate courses in the American University were offered in the evening starting at 7 p.m. to benefit those who worked in the daytime in US government or international agencies. I was able to sustain myself for two years by working in the school library in the daytime, with the help of the scholarship and the savings from a job as a camp counsellor during the two consecutive summers.

While attending the American University, I lived in the home of Mr. and Mrs. Raymond Wilson, friends of both the Ayusawas and the Newlins. Living with the Wilsons was a far better education than attending any university. Mr. Wilson was a founder and Executive Secretary of the Friends Committee on National Legislation, a Quaker lobbyist group, and was a man truly dedicated to world peace. The fact that Mr. Wilson never received a Nobel Peace Prize has made me regard that prize in very low esteem. Mr. Wilson took me to Congress and to conferences on peace. In one of these conferences I heard a speech by Professor Kenneth Boulding, a noted economist and a pacifist, and was greatly impressed by it. I also learned a great deal from his graduate textbook *Economic analysis* (1941). In 1991 I had the honour of meeting him in person at the University of Colorado. Mrs. Wilson was an extremely charming person whom everybody loved. She was like a second mother to me.

The two years in Washington were fruitful academically, as well. I was exposed to rigorous economic theory for the first time in the course on Soviet economy taught by a young professor named Dr. Bowles. His stimulating lectures had a great deal to do with my eventual decision to go on toward a Ph.D. At the same time I gave up the idea of going into journalism and started contemplating a teaching position after obtaining a Ph.D. In my second year at the American University, I applied to several graduate schools. My main interest in economics in those days was in the areas of Soviet economy and socialist economics; therefore, my first choice was Stanford University, where Paul Baran taught. But, ironically, I was rejected by Stanford and so went to Johns Hopkins University, which offered me a fellowship. One never knows what is one's fortune and misfortune. Paul Baran lived only for one more year and I went to Stanford as an assistant professor in three years; most of the students who were admitted to Stanford in the same year I was rejected were still there.

After obtaining a Master's degree from the American University, I went back to Japan for the first time in three years. I took a train from Washington, D.C. to Los Angeles and sailed from there on a freighter. It was a most exciting moment when Japanese land gradually came into view. You do not get the same feeling if you go by air. After a three-months vacation in Japan, I sailed again from Yokohama to San Francisco and then took a train to Baltimore. This was the third and last time I crossed the Pacific by ship, for soon afterward the N.Y.K. discontinued the service of carrying passengers on its freighters.

I am glad I went to Johns Hopkins. One gets a truly first-class education there because of the small size of the department and the very close tie among the faculty and students. One of its attractive features was that all the faculty members and all the graduate students attended a weekly seminar. At first, seminars were frightening because the participants seemed to take special pleasure in using jargon I had never heard before, such as multicollinearity and heteroscedasticity. As time went by, however, they turned out to be an excellent educational process. Taking Richard Musgrave's course on public finance was another excellent educational process. I learned more economics from his well-known textbook on public finance (Musgrave 1959) than from any other book. Another attractive feature of Johns Hopkins was that professors were easily accessible to graduate students. Most notably, Professor Edwin Mills always kept his office door open and welcomed me whenever I wanted to speak to him.

After completing the preliminary exams in the first year, I became a research assistant to Professor Mills in his project on the water resources development in the State of Maryland because of my interest in economic planning and policy. But later I found out that in order to do serious research in this area you have to be familiar with the chemistry of water, and after attending the geology library continuously for about one month I became quite bored by hydrology and my morale was weakened. So at the end of the second year Professor Mills kindly relieved me of my duty in his project, and at about the same time, following a suggestion of Professor Carl Christ, applied for a Ford Foundation dissertation fellowship in the area of econometric theory. At around this time I was beginning to be somewhat disillusioned by economic theory in general, and I felt that by studying statistics I could do useful things for a wider range of problems.

Having received the Ford Foundation fellowship, I started my dissertation research in econometric theory in my third year at Hopkins, with Professor

Christ as the main advisor. The other members of the thesis committee were
Professors Mills and Geoffrey Watson of the Statistics Department. At first it
seemed unlikely that I would be able to complete the thesis in one year.
When I learned in the middle of the year that my father was perhaps
terminally ill, I decided to try to complete it in time for the June graduation
so that I could go home with a diploma while my father was still alive. I did
in the end accomplish this objective (Amemiya 1964), but it would never
have been possible without the kind help of Professor Christ. I imposed on
him to read a draft of my thesis and comment on it in a far shorter time than a
professor is normally required to do. Now that I have advised many thesis
students myself, I have realized how much sacrifice he had to make to meet
the deadline I forced upon him. My father remained conscious and alert for
one week after I came home and died a week later.

A memorable occasion during my last year at Hopkins was the annual
economists' meetings held that year in Boston. I was interviewed by more
than twenty professors representing ten universities. (I believe this was about
an average for a graduate student in the job market.) I have never
experienced such hectic three days in my life. For Stanford I was interviewed
by Marc Nerlove, who later phoned me from Stanford and offered me a
position.

15.4   STANFORD-HITOTSUBASHI-STANFORD, 1964 TO PRESENT

In the summer of 1964, I spent three months in Tokyo attending to my
father's funeral and other related businesses and joined the Stanford faculty
in September. During my second year at Stanford I received an offer of a
lecturer's position from Hitotsubashi University in Tokyo thanks to the help
of Professor Tsuru. I accepted the offer because a position in a major
university in Japan becomes available only infrequently. In the fall of 1966, I
resigned from Stanford and went to Hitotsubashi. For various reasons,
however, I went back to Stanford in the fall of 1968 as an associate professor
with tenure. During the two years in Japan, I met Yoshiko Miyaki, a Japanese
literature major at Ferris Women's College in Yokohama. We got married in
May 1969 and she joined me in Stanford. Our daughter Naoko was born in
1970 and our son Kenta in 1973.

In 1968, the year I went back to Stanford, Ted Anderson left Columbia
and joined Stanford as professor of statistics and economics. He kindly
suggested we should apply for a research grant from the National Science
Foundation together, and from that time on we shared NSF research grants

for many years. It was a very beneficial collaboration for me; on numerous occasions Ted offered me invaluable advice on statistical theory. During the first several years of my research career, I worked mainly on the statistical problems of time series. One day in 1972 my colleague Michael Boskin came to my office and asked me about statistical problems arising in the model James Tobin proposed in his 1958 *Econometrica* article. I was fascinated by the problems and this became a turning point of my career; since then my research interests have shifted away from time series toward limited and qualitative dependent variables models.

Over the last several years I have developed another interest – Ancient Greek culture and society. It started when I spent a total of six months in Germany as a Humboldt fellow in 1988 and 1990. My interest in the history of Germany took me all the way back to the invasion of the Indo-Europeans into Europe and into Greece in particular. I was also influenced by the writings of a German poet Hölderlin and a French philosopher Simone Weil, both of whom are noted Hellenists. Once I started studying the Ancient Greek culture and society, however, what sustained and sharpened my interest was a great similarity between the Ancient Greek culture and the Japanese culture. For example, their religions are similar and their attitudes toward families and ancestors are similar. Earlier this year I published a Japanese translation of *Aristotle's ethics* by J.O. Urmson, a noted Oxford philosopher. This was a most enjoyable experience not only because Professor Urmson is a cherished friend but also because it provided me an opportunity to compare three languages, English, Japanese, and Classical Greek. Some of my current research interests are, besides the comparison of the Japanese and Greek cultures, a study of the Athenian economy and a clarification of the anti-utilitarian stance of Plato and Aristotle.

SELECTED WORKS

(1964) 'Specification analysis in econometrics', unpublished Ph.D. dissertation, Johns Hopkins University.
(1994a) *Studies in econometric theory: collected essays.* Aldershot: Edward Elgar.
(1994b) 'Introduction', in T. Amemiya (1994a) **q.v.**, pp. xiii–xx.

BIBLIOGRAPHY

Boulding, K.E. (1941) *Economic analysis.* New York: Harper & Row.

Musgrave, R.A. (1959) *The theory of public finance: a study in public economy.*
    London: McGraw-Hill.
Tobin, J. (1958) 'Estimation of relationships for limited dependent variables',
    Econometrica, 26 (1), pp. 24–36.

16. David Laidler (b. 1938)[1]

16.1 LIFE BEFORE ECONOMICS

I was born on Tyneside in 1938. I was an only child. The depression had caused my parents to delay the start of a family and the war deterred them from continuing with the enterprise. Those two catastrophes therefore very much formed me and they also dominate my early memories, the war directly, and the depression at second hand through the overheard and only partly understood conversations of adults. The bombing we experienced in Whitley Bay was negligible in comparison to that visited on many of my contemporaries, but it came often enough and close enough to kill a few neighbours, children as well as adults, injure others, and damage our house more than once – with me inside it, because we had no garden in which a shelter could be dug and air-raids were therefore spent under a steel-topped kitchen table. I doubt that the war had much direct effect on my later attitude to economics, but it left me with an abiding belief that there is a large arbitrary element to life's outcomes. That is probably why I am irredeemably

[1] Laidler (1997b), as revised by the editors. I have one volume of selected essays, on money and macroeconomics, in the series (1997a). Further details of my career and writings can be found in the 1995 interview I gave to Christof Rühl (Rühl and Laidler 1998).

'wet' when it comes to judging the merits of those redistributive arrangements that go under the label 'Welfare State'. The depression was more directly influential in a completely conventional way: even at second hand, its memory prompted the usual questions: why? what could have been done? could it happen again? etc. etc; and I have little patience for economics not motivated by socially important questions.

My father was self-employed, a fishmonger by day and a fish-fryer in the evening. Neither of my parents had more than a pre-First World War primary school education, and they were acutely insecure about their position in that appalling pecking order known as the British class structure. To be a self-employed shop-keeper put one in the lower-middle classes, but to be a fish-fryer, and on Tyneside at that, ensured that the emphasis was heavily on 'lower'. Education was the way-up of choice in such families. My father was a little too old for the army in 1939, and in any case he had been gassed in France in late 1917. Thus the shops were open during and immediately after the war, and the fish trade being rather profitable in those years, I was duly sent to a private day school, Tynemouth School, where, it was hoped, I would acquire not only the knowledge but also the accent and manners that might enable me to succeed – as an accountant, say, or even a solicitor.

From my early teens onwards, I worked with my father during school holidays, and sometimes on Saturdays too. The day started at 7.30 am with a buying trip to North Shields fish quay, and ended at about 11 p.m. after the last few stragglers from the pubs had bought their suppers and gone home. This too was meant to be part of my education, inculcating first-hand knowledge of what the future had in store if I did not pay attention to my studies. The experience certainly had that effect, but I am afraid that I never quite picked up the manners and accent that my parents had intended for me. After all, at the school they had chosen, boys were regularly reprimanded if they were seen eating fish and chips on the street. That, and more generally the repulsive snobbery it represented, strained my loyalty to the institution, and I quite self-consciously resisted much of the social influence that the place was supposed to exert.

Academically Tynemouth School was a curate's egg: the science side was mediocre, and I took only mathematics, and then only to GCE O level. On the other hand, History, English Literature and French, my three A level subjects, were superbly taught. History, and Economic History in particular, fascinated me. Although the syllabus for the latter stopped somewhere in the late nineteenth century, its relevance to my immediate surroundings – the coal industry, railways, engineering and all that – was both readily apparent and extremely appealing. Since the alternative was two years' military service, I had no difficulty in deciding to try for university, although, much to my headmaster's anger, I refused to apply to Oxford or Cambridge. In the firm belief that economics would be just like economic history, I entered the London School of Economics (LSE) in 1956.

16.2   THE LSE, 1956–9

I had been well enough taught at Tynemouth School to win a State Scholarship which provided a pretty good living in those days, even in London. Since that was a merit award, and not a grant, I can, and do, take pride in having been self-supporting through scholarships and work since the age of eighteen. After a miserable period boarding in suburban Kingsbury with distant family friends who had moved South to find work in the 1930s, I moved to Bayswater and began to take advantage of the city.

I had consumed music, but particularly opera, second hand at home, largely thanks to the BBC, and in the face of a certain amount of disapproval from my parents, who did not think that this was an interest that would be useful to a future accountant or solicitor (perhaps even an Urban District Councillor!). In London opera was there to be explored at first hand, and at very reasonable prices. A gallery seat at Covent Garden, for example, was 5 shillings (7/6 for Maria Callas I think), which was not much more than it cost to feed the gas-meter to heat a bed-sitter on a winter evening, and I spent a great deal of time there and at Sadlers Wells. I picked up a lifelong habit which it has cost me a small fortune, and a prodigious amount of time, to feed. How many extra papers might have been written had I spent fewer evenings in opera houses is hard to imagine but, given the list of my writings, it is quite clear that, on the margin, even more time given over to Mozart, Verdi, Janacek, Britten *et al.* would have been time well reallocated.

There was also politics. I had actually been a member of the Young Conservatives before university, but the summer and autumn of 1956, which coincided with my move to the LSE, saw the Suez Crisis. I joined the extreme left-wing Socialist (note, not Labour) Society, and took up the chorus of 'Eden must go!' I still think I was on the right side there, but I am decidedly less sure now about my support for unilateral nuclear disarmament! My conversion to Socialism was not based on any hard analysis. It was mainly a matter of renouncing residual aspirations to the Urban District Council, but I took the Socialist Society seriously, serving as its secretary for a while. I attended meetings, listened and argued, and I read. I learned at least something of what Marxian Socialism was about, and if I eventually came to find the doctrine unconvincing, I was surely none the worse for knowing why.

By now the reader must be wondering if I had any time left to pursue the studies which had brought me to London in the first place. At that time, the first examinations LSE students encountered, Part I of the BSc (Econ.), occurred at the end of the second year. There was plenty of time to get into trouble in the interim, and I did, not least because, to my great confusion, economics turned out to have very little to do with A level economic history. But there was more to it. The plain fact is that it was much further, socially, culturally, and intellectually from Tyneside to London in 1956 than it is nowadays, and the transition left me bewildered. At the time, I thought of myself as making a big splash, but other observers, not least my later self, would find floundering around out of my depth a more accurate metaphor. My Part I results were unimpressive, and, as the LSE Careers Adviser cheerfully informed me at about this time, thinking that he was giving me good news, I seemed to be firmly on track for lower second class honours, followed by military service and a return ticket to Tyneside, perhaps as a secondary modern school teacher.

What saved me was the particular age structure of the LSE Economics Department at that time. To the outsider the place was dominated by such luminaries as Roy Allen, James Meade, Frank Paish, Henry Phelps Brown, Arnold Plant, Lionel Robbins, Richard Sayers, *et al.* Robbins held an informal Friday afternoon seminar for third year specialists, which often took the form of a dialogue between him and my classmate Sam Hollander, whose intelligence and erudition were even then completely awe-inspiring. I do, therefore, count Robbins among my teachers. As to the others, however, undergraduates like me only saw them, if at all, from a distance in large lecture theatres. Serious teaching was done in small groups (there were only about a dozen specialists in Economics Analytic and Descriptive in my year) by those known as 'the younger members of the staff': Chris Archibald, Bernard Corry, Bob Gould, Kurt Klappholz, Kelvin Lancaster, Dick Lipsey, Maurice Peston, not to mention Ed Mishan, Bill Phillips and Jack Wiseman, who belonged to this group in intellectual spirit if not quite in years. And further instruction was on offer in the Three Tuns (the School pub) at lunch time and in the early evening, particularly from Archibald, Corry and Lipsey. For this group, economics was a way of life, and an enjoyable one too, rather than merely an academic subject, and to someone like me, who was looking for just that, the example they set was irresistible. The fact that I was also beginning to see how economics might offer some answers to those conventional questions about the depression was an added bonus. In my third year, with Bernard Corry as my tutor, I got interested in my studies.

The LSE's third year syllabus in Economics Analytic and Descriptive led to examinations in economic theory, applied economics, the history of economic thought, and two options; here I chose the 'Essay' paper – answer one question from a menu that covered the whole syllabus – and (I think) public finance. The emphasis was, in fact, on 'Economics Analytic' and we learned how to do economic analysis at what was then a pretty high level. Stigler's *The theory of price* (1952) was a Part I book, as was Hansen's *A guide to Keynes* (1953), and in the third year, in preparation for Part II, we read selections from the once ubiquitous American Economic Association (AEA) series of *Readings* in various topics, one or two monographs – for example Lerner's *The economics of control* (1944), and Patinkin's *Money, interest and prices* (1956), with important supplementary material from Archibald and Lipsey (1958) and some up-to-date journal articles as well – notably by Phillips (for example, 1954) on stabilisation issues. We also read every page (well, Sam Hollander did!) of *The Wealth of Nations* (1776), and of Ricardo's (1817) and Marshall's *Principles* (1890), and some of us read Thornton's *Paper credit* (1802) as well.

The 'descriptive' part of the syllabus did not get much attention, and I do not recall that the format of examinations in applied economics or public finance required it. An examinee was probably well advised, other things equal, to find out which British industries were in public ownership, but on balance it was better to learn a little more about the virtues and limitations of the application of marginal cost pricing rules in the public sector – Jack Wiseman was disconcertingly persuasive, even to someone like me, who still held socialist views, on those limitations. Extra points were also to be earned by those able to paraphrase the Lipsey-Lancaster (1956) 'Second best' theorem. And, on the macro side an appreciation of the implications of time lags for the feasibility of stabilisation policies was a lot more prized than knowledge of the size and growth rate of the British national income, its composition, or any other set of mere facts.

All this was enormously appealing, and I acquired the knack of manipulating simple economic models. I also began to suspect that economics was one of those subjects in which a little knowledge of the basic analytic tools would take one a long way. I was right; indeed it took me a lot further than I had expected. In the summer of 1959, to my utter astonishment, and to the amazement of a lot of other people too, no doubt, I graduated with first class honours – evidently, not all of life's arbitrary shocks are adverse. My old friends Archibald, Corry and Lipsey have often told me since, usually after a few beers, that my first was the most marginal ever awarded in the history of the LSE, and for all I know they have been telling the truth. It did not matter though, because in those days, a first was a first. My escape from Tyneside and the lower-middle classes was now permanent if that was what I wanted, and I did. I went to America.

16.3   GRADUATE SCHOOL IN AMERICA, 1959–63

My applications to American graduate schools had been sent off long before I took final exams. My teachers had told me that proper postgraduate training was only available in America, true enough at that time before taught Masters programmes were introduced in Britain; American schools would also give firm acceptances before degree results were out, which meant that, even with the forecast lower second, I might get one more year of deferment from military service; and besides, I had an American girlfriend. But it was not quite straightforward after all. My mediocre performance at Part I had presumably been noted in letters of reference, and of the half dozen or so schools to which I applied, only the University of Syracuse would take a chance on me.

My continued membership of the Socialist Society perhaps had something to do with the trouble I encountered in getting a visa. Past membership of the Young Conservatives turned out to have its uses after all, and Dame Irene Ward MP wrote on my behalf to the Embassy, presumably assuring them that I was unlikely to use either force or violence to overthrow the Government of the United States if I was allowed into the country for a year or so. I got the visa, but I was turned down for a Fulbright travel grant. The LSE loaned me the money for the fare, however, and off I went, on an elderly ship, named the *New York*, registered in Greece. Sam Hollander, whose first had been predicted, went to Princeton, crossing on the *Queen Mary*: I was a little jealous.

Syracuse is one of those middle rank American universities which Europeans always undervalue. It is more famous for its football team than its Economics department, but there was no nonsense about the MA programme that I followed. Its theory component repeated quite a lot of what I had done the year before, as it would have done at even the most prestigious schools, and I was finally forced to learn basic calculus, linear algebra and some statistics. All of this came too late to make me anything other than a very mediocre technician, but that was a good deal better than nothing. I could now at least read a lot more of the literature, and in due course teach it too. I also got used to the American routine of examinations two or three times a term rather than once or twice in a lifetime! Syracuse was close enough to New York City that I was twice able to visit the old Metropolitan Opera House. But the most exciting music of the year was at the university, a student performance of excerpts from *Susannah*, with, if I am not mistaken, Floyd Carlisle himself providing the piano accompaniment. Europeans, as I have said, undervalue universities like Syracuse.

But by now I had my first, and with compulsory military service abolished in Britain in the nick of time, I tried again for a place in one of the top American departments. The response was very different this time, except from Yale which refused me admission – another of life's arbitrary shocks, and one that perhaps explains why I am not a Keynesian – and I chose Chicago. At LSE I had attended Karl Popper's lectures on methodology, and the optional paper in Logic and Scientific Method had produced one of the few bright spots in my Part I results. I was completely convinced of the importance of testing economic theories against empirical evidence, as were most of my third year teachers who were then in the middle of a brief but fruitful flirtation with Popper's ideas. At Chicago too, as I knew from Milton Friedman's writings, they were interested in testing theories; and besides, Harry Johnson, whom I had never met but whom the younger LSE faculty who had taught me revered, was now there as well, having left Manchester a year or so earlier. And Chicago had then, as it still does, a most distinguished opera company.

My American girl friend and I got married in the summer of 1960, and set off for Chicago in my recently acquired second-hand Citroen 2cv. The marriage was not a good idea; it fell apart almost as quickly as did the car. Whatever each of us was trying to accomplish by marrying the other could certainly have been achieved by less self-destructive means, but we had to learn this and a number of other lessons the hard way; let us leave it at that. Fortunately, when we parted three years later, there were no children to worry about.

I was only physically present in Chicago for two years, because I took a year out of my studies in 1961–2 as a temporary assistant lecturer at LSE, but Chicago's impact on me was enormous. To begin with, the sheer quality of my fellow students restored some of the intellectual humility that getting a first had temporarily undermined. Eitan Berglas, Glen Cain, Martin Carnoy, Ed Feige, John Floyd, Giora Hanoch, Jim Holmes, Allan Hynes, Bob Lucas, G.S. Madalla, Sam Peltzman, Maurice Perlman, Sherwin Rosen and Neil Wallace, were among my contemporaries, and that is a list of names I am very proud to be able to drop! At Chicago, economics was treated as a relevant and socially useful discipline, not a compendium of intellectual games to be played for the fun of it; but as such, as Al Harberger in particular managed to convey in his teaching, it could still be immensely enjoyable. Friedman taught me price theory (giving me the only B of my graduate career in the first term – I took more care in the second!). His style was to assume that we had already read his mimeoed lecture notes, soon to be published as *Price theory: a provisional text* (1962) and to lecture rather discursively, sometimes reading out a quotation from *Time* or the *New York Times* as a prelude to suggesting 'Let's analyse this'. Once, probably because the core exams were approaching, I asked him when we were going to cover the Slutsky equation, to which the friendly but pointed reply was, as I recall, 'When you've learned to read newspapers intelligently will be time enough.'

Monetary economics at Chicago for me was mainly a matter of Harry Johnson. He taught the Ph.D. level course in 1960–1, and in 1962–3 he ran the workshop, because Friedman was on Sabbatical. Al Marty taught the course that year. Harry was a self-effacing teacher who insisted that his students should get to know 'the literature' and not just those bits of it that were being locally produced. Chicago then, and now, was said to inculcate narrow-mindedness in its students, 'brainwash' was the verb sometimes used, but seldom can a reputation have been less deserved than in the years I was there. Sceptics are referred to Johnson's (1962) *American Economic Review* survey of monetary economics: that is what we were taught in the formal course. And although Friedman and Meiselman presented their work on the relative stability of velocity and the multiplier at the money workshop (see Friedman and Meiselman 1963) a guest called Allan Meltzer impressed upon us the importance of the rate of interest as a systematic influence on velocity (see Meltzer 1963) while a little later another, Grant Reuber, suggested that we think about the Phillips curve as a policy constraint subject to which a quantifiable social utility function could be maximised (see Reuber 1964). Joan Robinson's first visit to the United States was in 1961, and at Chicago, unlike anywhere else, she was granted classroom time to expound her views on capital theory to the graduate students. And it is worth mentioning that I, still a self-proclaimed socialist (although weakening fast) was supported in my final year (1962–3) by a fellowship in the personal gift of Friedman.

I absorbed one other important lesson in those years. I learned to take data seriously, from Margaret Reid, who was on my thesis committee, and from Anna Schwartz for whom I worked during the summer of 1961 as a research assistant on the *Monetary history of the United States* (Friedman and Schwartz 1963). They showed me that data were not merely items to be looked up in tables, should one ever stop talking about testing a theory and actually get down to doing so. I learned that data had to be created by somebody; that how that might be done was not independent of the purpose to which they were going to be put, and that anyone using data to test a theory would be well advised to spend a little time enquiring where they had come from in order to ensure their relevance to the problem at hand, and perhaps checking them for accuracy against their primary source, too. Finally, I learned that people who deal with data are just as thoughtful, intelligent and useful as are theorists. I am still appalled by the average academic economist's lack of respect for those who do the archival research and field work upon which the empirical basis of our discipline depends.

My year at LSE in 1961–2 was a welcome break from studies. I had finished my Chicago course requirements, passed the core and a field exam in money, all in the previous year, and I was ready for a change of pace, My teaching duties in London were light, consisting mainly of giving back-up tutorials to Dick Lipsey's first year lecture course, from which his *Positive economics* (1963) would soon emerge. Unfortunately the pay, £860 per annum, was well matched to the arduousness of the work, and the Laidlers were very poor. So was nearly everyone else, however, so it did not matter much.

The 'younger members of the staff' were still a very cohesive group, and had been joined by John Grant, Miles Kennedy, Max Steuer and Jim Thomas, while Bertie Hines and Vicky Chick, then both graduate students, were very much part of the circle. The M2T (methodology measurement and testing) seminar, the main outcome of the economists' flirtation with Popper's ideas, was still flourishing, with Frank Brechling and Dick Lipsey on trade credit (see Brechling and Lipsey 1963) and Chris Archibald on the predictive powers of maximising models (see, for example, Archibald 1965) prominently on the programme. I remember going to lots of parties, and I remember leaving some of them – drink was very much part of the LSE economist's way of life in those days. But I did do some work, notably to prepare, with considerable help from Bernard Corry, for my remaining Chicago field examination in the History of Economic Thought which I took in absentia, and passed, in the early summer of 1962.

By the time I got back to Chicago in September all that remained was to write a thesis. My topic was 'Income tax incentives for owner-occupied housing'. Al Harberger was my committee chairman, and given that I also participated in the money workshop, then under Harry Johnson's temporary supervision, I discovered that drink could be very much part of the Chicago economist's way of life too. Indeed, I was a good year into my first appointment at Berkeley before I realised that economists' parties were not, in fact, always intended to be events at which everyone got a bit drunk, as a preliminary to offering frank criticism of everyone else's work: I am not sure what my Californian colleagues made of me, and I should prefer not to guess.

My thesis, which involved an empirical investigation of the positive and normative consequences of the United States failure to tax the imputed rental income yielded by owner occupied housing, did get finished, however (Laidler 1964; revised and published as Laidler 1969d). It may seem odd that someone destined to specialise in monetary economics, and who had already made a major intellectual investment in that field, should write a thesis in public finance, but it was not quite so strange then. Both LSE and Chicago, or at least the faculty with whom I had the privilege of working in those places, still encouraged their students to think of themselves as economists first, and specialists second; and the standard analysis of the demand for a durable good whose services-in-kind were subject to taxation or subsidy, on which my thesis was based, a few years later turned out to be applicable with virtually no modification to the analysis of inflation. So the thesis was not a detour after all.

16.4 BERKELEY, 1963–6

The early 1960s saw a huge expansion of higher education, and those of us who had gone into graduate school in the expectation of living ever after in genteel poverty received a wonderful surprise when we came to look for jobs. They were there in abundance, and at high and rising salaries too, particularly in the United States. I had acquired a Green Card during the year back at LSE, and hence was a fully qualified participant in a very hot labour market. Partly at my wife's urging – we were by then separated, but on better terms than before as we planned our eventual divorce – I accepted an offer from Berkeley and we drove out there together in my new Corvair convertible, not a much better choice than the Citroen, as it turned out, but I had not heard of Ralph Nader then. I am not sure why Berkeley hired me. The department was very much a part of the East-Coast sphere of influence (a salt-water as opposed to fresh-water school as people would now put it) and people from Chicago were not usually invited in; but I am glad I was: permit me to drop a few more names, this time of my fellow assistant professors: Peter Diamond, Dan McFadden, Bernie Saffran, Oliver Williamson and Sidney Winter.

In the monetary economics field, things were not so good. Howard Ellis was about to go to Brazil on a State Department mission, and Hyman Minsky would soon leave for Washington University in St. Louis, although not before I had learned a lot from him about the nature of a monetary economy that helped me begin to make sense of some of the things Victoria Chick had been on about in London, but which would not find their way into my own work until much later. Tom Mayer was there, however, as a visitor for a while, but even when teaching at Davis he lived in Berkeley, and I saw a good deal of him. In due course I met Karl Brunner down at University of California at Los Angeles (UCLA), and he was usually to be found on the other end of the telephone if one called for advice, as I sometimes did. And Dale Jorgenson's expertise in applied econometrics was at the disposal of anyone who was interested. There were visitors too, among them at various times Dick Lipsey, Bob Gould and Bernard Corry. I was hardly isolated, then, and there were advantages in the thinness with which my own field was staffed. I became more quickly involved with graduate teaching than I otherwise would, and when Minsky left I also inherited the workshop (or continuing seminar as we called it) which he had set up and raised some funds for at about the time of my arrival. It met in the evening (Thursday, I think), and a willingness to visit a bar after the paper was the main prerequisite for membership.

Friedman's (1959) 'The demand for money: some theoretical and empirical results' had caused quite a stir. At a time when conventional wisdom took the liquidity trap doctrine for granted, it appeared to show that velocity might be essential independent of interest rates. Like anyone else teaching monetary economics, I needed to come to grips with this paper. I found two potential flaws in it. First, Friedman seemed to have some details of what he called the 'shock absorber' approach to the demand for money wrong; second, he seemed to have overlooked the possibility of there being a secular relationship between interest rates and velocity when he had designed the test which appeared to show that there were no cyclical interest rate effects at work. With the help of a National Science Foundation (NSF) grant, I got to work on what became my first two published papers (Laidler 1966a; b). I did not get the individual-market experiment distinction quite straight when dealing with shock absorber effects and, perhaps as a result, I did not return to those matters for nearly ten years, but I did better with the second issue. It was also at Berkeley that I began to investigate the dynamics implicit in the lagged dependent variables that empirical work suggested were so badly needed in some key structural equations. As a student of Popper, I had learned that the results of empirical work should be used to modify theories, with a view to generating further predictions, so this seemed a natural thing to do (Laidler 1968). I also wrote a short paper on the Phillips curve with Bernard Corry (Corry and Laidler 1967).

While all this was going on, I found time to remarry, this time more wisely. Antje was recently arrived from Germany and a trainee buyer in her uncle and aunt's fashion store. We lived on Telegraph Avenue and were early evening regulars at the Pic (Café [sic] Medditerraneum, formerly Piccolo Espresso) and later evening regulars at either the Steppenwolf or the Albatross where something a little stronger was on sale. This was Berkeley on the eve of the university's first round of troubles, before the Bay area drug scene got nasty, and before anyone had heard the word 'counterculture'. For a year or two we were part of a social circle whose willingness to live and let live may have been naive, but is still a joy to recall – even if one or two people did express a little surprise that Antje and I had made the effort to get married, while one or two others found our opera-going habits a bit exotic.

An unpleasant example of life's arbitrariness brought this existence to an abrupt end in the summer of 1966. By then the University of California had managed to radicalise its student body by attempting to prevent campus facilities being used for the organisation of civil rights demonstrations in Oakland – some of these students had risked their lives in Mississippi, and they were not about to stand for petty nonsense from university administrators. The Vietnam War was expanding rapidly enough to attract attention too. On the personal front, a preliminary review of my academic progress had convinced the majority of my senior colleagues that my work 'lacked seriousness' – their phrase – and one of them had laughed out loud when I confessed that I was writing a paper on Thomas Tooke's views on Peel's 1844 Bank Act. It was probably time to leave, but I was not permitted the luxury of making up my own mind about that. Along with the acquisition of my Green Card in 1962 had gone the obligation to register for military service, which had not seemed to matter at the time. Student and faculty deferments were automatic and, besides, I would be over-age by 1963; but that was before the Vietnam War became serious. Early in 1966, my deferment was cancelled, and in July I was summoned to a pre-induction medical, which I passed with flying colours. No one in authority at the university seemed to want to know about these problems and, something I still find hard to excuse, I had the distinct impression that there was a reluctance to testify to the 'essential' nature of my work lest that testimony be used in a future tenure case.

Rather than risk induction, which usually followed the medical by a couple of weeks, I resigned my position at Berkeley at once. I spent a few nights on the telephone to friends in Canada and Britain. The academic market was still very much on the sellers' side, and within a few days Chris Archibald had offered me a lectureship (with tenure!) at Essex where he and Lipsey were in the process of building a brand new department. Antje's uncle and aunt, who knew a few things about hasty emigration decisions, having left Germany in 1933 and France in the early 1940s, gave us much support and help; we needed it, for, even in California, Vietnam was not, in 1966, the widely unpopular cause it was to become, and my departure had to be as quiet as it was quick. I made a brief visit to my parents, who were delighted to have me back in Britain, and then went to Wivenhoe to find housing (and to buy some Covent Garden tickets for October) before the autumn term began. Antje tidied up our affairs in California and, somewhat to the surprise of some of our Telegraph Avenue friends, who never took such things for granted, joined me just before term began.

16.5   ESSEX, 1966–9

No one could ever convict members of the Berkeley Economics department of not being completely dedicated to their discipline, but to my way of thinking the prevailing attitude there, particularly at the senior levels, had been excessively earnest. What had attracted me to economics at the LSE, and had continued to do so at Chicago, were working atmospheres in which people not only thought that what they were doing was important, but in which they were evidently enjoying themselves as well. The Essex department in the late 1960s was another such place, not surprisingly perhaps, since it was the creation of Chris Archibald and Dick Lipsey, with some help from Frank Brechling.

The university as a whole had been set up to encourage easy informal interaction among faculty and students, and in the Economics department, where the faculty were young, that worked. Even though the university as a whole quickly acquired a well-deserved reputation for student radicalism and activism, excitement in the Economics department continued to be found, not at the barricades, but in the classroom, at workshops, and in various pubs, not least the Buck's Horns in Colchester, where department members attained standards in table football that were at least as high as those they reached in economics. There was lots of money for visitors, who came for a year or a term rather than a week or a day. Again, a little name dropping is in order. In the three years I spent at Essex, in addition to my permanent colleagues, who for various periods included, in addition to Archibald and Lipsey, Bob Clower, Gene Savin and Joe Ostroy, the following were long-term visitors: Carl Christ, Ed Feige, Art Goldberger, Herschel Grossman, Murray Kemp, Al Marty, Michio Morishima and Colin Simkin.

Most important as far as my own work was concerned, it was at Essex that Michael Parkin and I first became colleagues. Although we produced no joint work at that time, our interaction was continuous and enormously fruitful. I taught him the monetary economics that I had learned at Chicago and he taught me what I would have learned had I gone to Yale. He had begun to master the latter material while working in the relative isolation of Sheffield and Leicester, and he made it sound a good deal more sensible that anything I had heard from the newly minted Yale Ph.D.s who had passed through Berkeley from time to time on job market tours.

Essex was as unstable as it was exciting. New universities had not been expected to challenge the intellectual standards prevailing at the old, but, in economics at least, Essex had, and that was not altogether welcome among the British academic establishment. I was too junior to know just who was taking which decisions, and why, but by 1968–9 even I noticed that the funding needed to consolidate what had been achieved was beginning to dry up, and that Archibald and Lipsey might leave in frustration, as, in fact, they eventually did; so when, in quick succession, I was interviewed at Manchester for a Chair, and advised by Harry Johnson (who had by then replaced Lionel Robbins at the LSE) to accept it if offered, accept it I did. We moved to Manchester in September 1969. For the next six years, regular visits to the Free Trade Hall to hear the Hallé orchestra ensured that our musical tastes continued to expand, and English and Welsh National Opera touring productions ensured that we were not entirely deprived of opera either.

16.6   MANCHESTER, 1969–75

Work had gone well at Essex. I had finished everything that I had started while in California (including my paper on Thomas Tooke, Laidler 1972a), I had written the first edition of my little book, *The demand for money* (1969a), which was probably to do more for my reputation than any other single publication, and I had also written two papers (Laidler 1969b; c) that grew out of the Pesek and Saving (1967) controversy, one of the many attempts at that time to bring some further badly needed theoretical coherence to monetary economics in the wake of Patinkin's pioneering efforts in that regard. It was here that expertise in stock-flow analysis and some of its welfare applications, acquired during my Ph.D. work on the demand for housing, came in handy. I write all this a little defensively. Although my CV as it stood in 1969 would probably be worth a tenured position in many respectable Economics departments even today, younger readers of this memoir will probably wonder what kind of standards, if any, were adhered to in making appointments to provincial chairs in Britain in the late 1960s. The problem, of course, from the point of view of those making the appointments, was that it was still very much a seller's market. Universities that were not willing to take chances on appointments that would have been regarded as premature in normal times simply did not fill their vacancies.

Not that I was welcomed with open arms at Manchester: Alan Prest, the Jevons Professor and Head of the Department of Economics, made it quite clear, with that consummate rudeness masked as courtesy which only graduates of the older British universities seem to be able to command, that I was not welcome in his department and a number of my new junior (in rank but not in years) colleagues shared his views. I could not believe my luck when he announced that he was leaving for the LSE a few months after my arrival (and I hope because of it), not least because that created a vacancy which Michael Parkin might fill. Although some of the old guard in the Manchester Economics department were genuinely welcoming – Dennis Coppock, John Knapp and Richard Harrington in particular – I badly needed some support in an environment that was a lot more hostile than I had expected, and I had not entered it with my eyes closed.

The fundamental problem at Manchester was that it had three separate departments, Economics, Econometrics, and Agricultural Economics, the majority of whose members could barely talk intelligibly to one another. A single department would have been a great deal better. I knew all that before accepting my appointment, but I thought I had secured the support of the Professors of Econometrics (Jack Johnston) and Agricultural Economics (Wat Thomas) to move towards an eventual merger of the departments. I suppose 'eventual' is a vague term, but, in 1969 I had something a little earlier in mind than 1995 (when in fact such a merger finally took place). What had made my appointment at Manchester possible, and would make Michael Parkin's possible too, was that filling a chair there was a matter for a Senate Committee with relatively minor departmental representation. Michael and I were never fully accepted in the Department of Economics, and we created our own research environment through the 'Manchester Inflation Workshop'. This was a broadly based research programme on the 'Causes, consequences and cures of inflation' which, at the beginning of the 1970s, was becoming a pressing policy issue. Members of all three Economics departments, not to mention Accounting, could, and some did, participate; and since it was funded by a Social Science Research Council (SSRC) grant, we were able to support a few junior people of our own choosing as full-time researchers too.

The early 1970s saw a strong surge of interest in monetary economics in general, and in what came to be called 'monetarism' in particular, in both Britain, and Western Europe. Alan Walters and his Birmingham colleagues Richard Barrett, Noel Kavanagh and David Sheppard had started to apply Chicago-style models to British monetary data in the mid-1960s (see Walters 1970 for a survey and relevant references) at about the same time that Harry Johnson had gone to the LSE and I had gone to Essex, but it took a few years for any of this to have a noticeable impact. In Britain, the Money Study Group (MSG) played a crucial role. It was founded immediately after the 1969 Hove Conference which Johnson had organised to celebrate the tenth anniversary of the Radcliffe Report, and its executive committee consisted of Johnson, Bob Nobay, Michael Parkin and myself. With a little help from David Worswick and Cathy Cunningham, the MSG soon obtained modest but invaluable SSRC funding. It ran workshops in London once or twice a term, to which academics, working in what were even then rather isolated provincial departments, could get their travel expenses paid, and it also organised occasional conferences that eventually evolved into annual affairs held at Oxford. The MSG was the prototype for similar organisations in other branches of economics.

On the continent, conferences organised by Emil Claassen and Pascal Salin at Paris-Dauphine, and, quite crucially, Karl Brunner's annual Konstanz seminar, which began in 1970 and is still going strong, provided the main organisational infrastructure through which intellectual contacts were made and ideas were transmitted. Michael Parkin and I did a lot of travelling in the early 1970s both to keep in touch with what others were up to, and also to present the results of our own ongoing work at Manchester. I will leave it to others to sort out just who contributed what to the spread of monetarism in Britain, and indeed Europe, and when they did it. One thing I will insist on, however: although monetarism was originally an import from America, the local product nevertheless quickly became distinct. We did add considerable content to the doctrine, not least, I still like to think, at Manchester, and some of that content was re-exported. No one did better work on assembling the evidence on the ineffectiveness of incomes policies than Michael Parkin and Michael Sumner (see Parkin and Sumner 1972) and although Harry Johnson and Alexander Swoboda with their London-Geneva group obviously had a lot to do with establishing monetarism's relevance to the international economy, so did Michael, this time working in particular with George Zis (see Parkin and Zis 1976).

While still in Berkeley, I had worked out some implications for the properties of the IS-LM model of what were learning empirically about the demand for money function, and I had sent a copy of my paper (Laidler 1968) to Friedman. He was kind about the paper, but pointed out that it dealt with a fixed price level system. The real challenge, he suggested, was to get the interaction of output and inflation into such a model. He was, of course, drawing my attention to what later came to be called the 'missing equation' problem, and it became the central focus of my own contribution to the Manchester Inflation Workshop. I was then, and I still am, unable to understand why Friedman himself did not explore the potential of his own (1968) work on the expectations augmented Phillips curve in this role, but he did not. I did, and after a false start (Laidler 1973a), I followed the advice of Michael Parkin (offered, I distinctly remembered, as we walked down the stairs to the cab-rank in Euston station) to forget about the full employment/unemployment dichotomy, and concentrate on variations in output *per se*. I soon succeeded in combining a Phillips curve with a simple quantity equation to produce what must have been one of the first versions of the now commonplace IS-LM plus expectations-augmented-Phillips-curve-macro-models (Laidler 1972c).

The LM curve of my model was vertical, which made the system very simple to analyse, but it also put many people off because that made it too monetarist for their taste. However, empirical work which I carried out during a brief visit to the St. Louis Fed. in early 1973 (made in the course of a longer stay at Brown) showed that the model held up remarkably well against US data. But the St. Louis Fed. people did not like the work either, because, as I felt I could tell, a Phillips curve, even one incorporating expectations with an *estimated* long-run coefficient of unity, was too 'Keynesian' a device for their taste. Having invited me to write up my work for the *Review*, they declined to publish it. The resulting paper ended up in the *Manchester School* (Laidler 1973b) with a spin-off in the *American Economic Review* (Laidler 1974b).

This little story is typical of the reception given at the time to my contribution to 'Manchester monetarism'. It was too close to American monetarism in its emphasis on the money supply, or domestic credit as the main source of output and price level fluctuations to be acceptable among then orthodox Keynesians, particularly British Keynesians; but American monetarists disliked its emphasis on the Phillips curve as representing some sort of disequilibrium phenomenon. 'Equilibrium modelling' was even then becoming the new fashion in those circles. Still a Popperian of sorts, I thought of myself as trying to build small macro-models whose validity should be judged by their empirical content rather than their conformity to anyone's theoretical preconceptions, but I had quite a few uncomfortable workshop presentations during that period, particularly in the US in the first half of 1973, as a result of sticking to that agenda. An analytic paper analysing an open-economy system (see Laidler 1972c for its origins) was also coolly received and, having been rejected by the *Journal of Money, Credit and Banking*, which sat on it for about eighteen months before doing so, appeared for the first time in my own contribution to the Manchester Inflation Workshop's series of volumes *Essays on money and inflation* (Laidler 1975a).

I would highlight three of my essays from that collection. The first of these (Laidler 1971) was on the expectations-augmented Phillips curve and its policy implications, while the second (Laidler 1972b) was an informal exposition of the framework in terms of which I was then coming to think about inflation, delivered as the Lister Lecture to the British Association for the Advancement of Science (BAAS) in 1972. Quite how I came to be honoured with that lectureship is a mystery to me. It certainly had nothing to do with Joan Robinson, that year's President of Section F. Indeed, I suspect that I was smuggled on to her programme by a BAAS committee, which included Harry Johnson, with the express purpose of irritating her. If that was its intention, the committee certainly succeeded. In introducing me to the journalists, schoolchildren and interested lay people who made up my audience, she noted, first, that the Lister Lecture was supposed to be given by someone under thirty-five years of age who had made a distinguished contribution to the social sciences, and second, that I was indeed under thirty-five, and hence satisfied the first criterion. She then sat down!

The third of the above-mentioned papers (Laidler 1974a) marked a major turning-point in my work. In 1973, I was invited to a conference in Lund sponsored by the Arne Ryde Foundation, and my contribution was written in the summer of that year, immediately after the visit to the US during which my work had received such a rough ride, not least at St. Louis. The topic was loosely specified by the conference organisers – they wanted something on the economics of information – but the paper's content was the result of a self-conscious effort to answer the criticism that my version of monetarism was *ad hoc* and lacking in proper theoretical foundations. That effort took me in exactly the wrong direction as far as my critics were concerned: this paper marks the first appearance in my writings of what has, ever since, been a constant theme: namely, that money is a social institution which is a substitute for, and not a complement to, the Walrasian market, so that conventional general equilibrium theory and monetary economics do not mix: shades of much earlier discussions with Vicky Chick and Hy Minsky, I now suspect, but I was not conscious of this at the time. I was, however, aware of the influence of Brunner and Meltzer (1971) and Axel Leijonhufvud, while Charles Goodhart was also thinking along similar lines (see Goodhart 1975).

The paper from my time in Manchester that attracted the most attention was none of these. Rather it was the 'Inflation: a survey' (Laidler and Parkin 1975) which Michael Parkin and I prepared for the *Economic Journal*. It says something about the insularity of the Royal Economic Society in those years that, when Dick Lipsey suggested that Michael be asked to write such a survey, and when he in turn asked that I be invited to become a co-author, they did not have the faintest idea of what kind of a paper they were likely to get. This paper seems very middle-of-the-road now, but in 1975 in Britain it was a different matter. In that time and place, the doctrine of the 'new inflation' was at its most influential: that doctrine held that whatever may have been true in the past, the current inflation was not a monetary but a socio-political phenomenon, requiring a considerable extension of the corporate state to rein it in. Our survey claimed, to the contrary, that the evidence showed inflation still to be an economic phenomenon, and primarily a monetary one at that. Brian Reddaway, the editor of the *Economic Journal*, acted with great integrity: dislike our product though he did, he nevertheless published it. I am told, however, that the most he would say for it, if directly asked, was that it had not turned out to be quite as bad as he had, at one stage, feared!

By the time our inflation survey appeared, Michael Parkin and I were both in Canada. It had become clear that there was no room for further progress at Manchester; no-one but us wanted to merge its three departments of economics; funding for our work was getting tighter and tighter, and there was no prospect of keeping together anything but a skeleton of the team with which we had worked. My salary had never been high – after five years it was still well below the professorial average – and it was falling fast in real terms as a result of inflation. The red ink on the bank statement was becoming more prominent by the month, sometimes, indeed, there was no black to be seen. And on top of that, my heavily mortgaged house, bought new in 1969, had serious problems with its foundations which were not covered by the Housebuilders' Association guarantee, and I was involved in expensive litigation with the builder. So when Grant Reuber, whom I had met all those years earlier at the Chicago workshop, approached me about moving to the University of Western Ontario, and Harry Johnson encouraged me to take the bait, I did. I also drew attention to Michael's availability.

It was a hard decision to uproot myself from Britain. I had made a big investment, not just in Manchester but in the British profession at large. I had helped found, and was a member of the executive of the Money Study Group, and I was also on the Association of University Teachers of Economics (AUTE) executive. I had served on the SSRC and Council on National Academic Awards (CNAA) subject committees at a time when those bodies were helping to promote a new level of professionalism in economic research and teaching in universities, but also in polytechnics (now the new universities). I had acted as an editorial advisor to Philip Allan as he began to build up a list that significantly raised the quality of economics textbooks available to British readers, and I had done a great deal of external examining, both at universities and polytechnics.

I had also achieved a certain amount of visibility beyond the academic community as an exponent of the monetarist approach to the analysis of inflation in particular, and of macro-policy in general. Indeed, I had begun to attract the attention of politicians after my evidence to the House of Commons Expenditure Committee in 1974 (Laidler 1975b) – 'Britain in "Economic Soup" says Professor' was one headline.[2] Robert Carr invited me to lunch at the House of Commons, and I had two or three private talks with Keith Joseph. I even received a letter from Margaret Thatcher. But although I had strong views on macroeconomic policy, which can be summarised by saying that the quantity theory of money was a much greater threat to the Heath government than was the National Union of Mineworkers, I did not want to get too close to any of these. Academic economists who get too closely involved with political parties or particular politicians always seem to end up defending the indefensible on behalf of their friends, and in the process they damage not only their own credibility, but that of the discipline too.

Be that as it may, much as I enjoyed living in Manchester, my base at the university was becoming untenable, and red ink on the bank statements was

---

2 *Financial Times*, 27 June 1974.

pushing me into doing more in the way of paid outside work – a talk or broadcast here, a newspaper column there – than I knew would be good for me in the longer run. So I had to write off my investment in Britain in order to continue to function as an academic economist. With the law-suit against the builder settled (more or less in my favour) just in time, we left for Canada in July 1975. My parents had taken my remaining in Britain pretty much for granted, and they had gained much satisfaction from seeing my name in the newspapers or hearing me on the radio from time to time. They never quite understood my decision to emigrate. What was there to go to in Canada, when I was already a professor in Britain? And the move caused them considerable personal distress too, because it would deprive them of regular contact with our daughter, their only grandchild. Emigration, however, seemed the only way of ensuring that I could continue to be a full-time and productive academic economist, and that was, when all was said and done, the way of life I had chosen.

16.7   WESTERN ONTARIO SINCE 1975

The Western Ontario Department was already strong when Michael Parkin and I arrived in the summer of 1975, although it had not yet attained the level of visibility it deserved. Grant Reuber was by then moving up through the university administration and would soon leave to begin a distinguished career in banking and public service, and Ron Bodkin, whose work on the inflation-unemployment trade-off had attracted a good deal of attention, left just as Michael and I arrived – there was no causative relationship here, I hasten to add. But in macroeconomics, Tom Courchene and Joel Fried were there, while Ron Wonnacott and Jim Melvin had already established Western as an important place in international trade. A number of the younger people who were to do so much to raise the department's reputation over the next decade were also already there in 1975: Russ Boyer in International Finance who pioneered the analysis of currency substitution, Jim Markusen, an important contributor to the integration of monopolistic competition and trade theory, and Peter Howitt, who for twenty years was to be my most valued colleague (see Howitt 1990 to see why) were all untenured assistant professors in 1975. John Whalley, Knick Harley, Ron Wintrobe and Glenn MacDonald, among others, were recruited shortly thereafter.

Don Patinkin was a regular short-term visitor to the department in the 1970s. He was then deeply involved in his studies of the origins of the Keynesian revolution, and for those of us who were interested in this topic, Fried, Howitt and myself, he was the best colleague imaginable. It was Don, more than anyone else, who encouraged me to pursue my interest in the history of economic thought with more energy, and it was from him that I learned the importance of reading literature in the context of what its authors and their contemporaries knew, rather than of what we know nowadays. It is a hard trick, and no-one masters it completely, but it is surely one of the keys to good work in the area. Our professional interaction grew into a friendship that easily outlasted the end of his visiting arrangement at Western.

Western, like all Ontario universities, was well funded in the 1970s, and research support was readily available. Teaching loads were relatively light, and in any case the exceptional quality of the students in the graduate and honours BA programmes made those loads a pleasure to bear. I had emigrated because I very much wanted to combine being a full-time academic with providing a reasonable standard of living for my wife and daughter. Western made that possible, as it would not have been had I remained in Britain. Once in Canada, moreover, my wife was also able to do what she had always really wanted to do – go to art school and pursue a career in drawing and printmaking – and from London Ontario, it is only a 240-mile round trip to the opera in Toronto. I was approached discreetly about returning to the UK when the Thatcher Government was elected, but I had no difficulty in deciding to stay put.

Not that everything was now to be plain sailing in my academic life: the fact is that, from the mid-1970s onwards, things were pretty rough for those who, like myself, did not recant the views which had led the profession at large to pin the 'Monetarist' label on them. The attacks came from two sides. First of all, stability of the demand for money function had been the keystone of monetarist doctrine, and new empirical results were beginning to cast doubt upon it. Second, but more fundamentally, new-classical economics, based on explicit Walrasian micro-foundations, and incorporating the rational expectations hypothesis, was on the rise, and its exponents found my style of monetarism unacceptably *ad hoc.*

The first of these lines of attack was, to a degree, unfair, but only to a degree. The money demand function that first began to break down in the early 1970s was Steven Goldfeld's (1973) well-known quarterly United States function, based on Gregory Chow's (1966) partial adjustment model. It was very much a short-run relationship, of the kind that had to be stable if monetary policy was to be used for fine-tuning; but monetarism had never been about fine-tuning. If out of steady-state adjustment mechanisms were not stable, that presented an interesting phenomenon to be investigated, but it did not matter very much for monetarist policy prescriptions. Unpredictable shifts in the underlying long-run relationship were much more serious, however, because if they were occurring, then that undermined the case for reducing policy to a suitably chosen rule for the money growth rate. I worked on both sets of issues in the later 1970s, and presented my main results in a long paper at a Carnegie-Rochester conference (Laidler 1980). Both kinds of problem seemed, in fact, to be at work, and so it became necessary to abandon advocacy of the money growth rule (see, for example, Laidler 1981a). To that extent, my monetarism had to be toned down a bit in the face of empirical evidence around 1980.

Friends have sometimes commented that my viewpoint not just on monetary rules but on economics in general seemed to shift to the 'left' during my first ten years or so in Canada. That, I think, is largely an illusion created by two facts: I was never particularly right wing on many microeconomic policy matters to begin with (see Laidler 1985 for the evidence); and in macroeconomics, under the influence of new-classical economics, a large number of other people were in fact shifting to the 'right' at that time, while I, apart from the matter of the money growth rule, was standing my ground as best I could.

I have already mentioned that, once I had begun to think about the matter (in around 1973), I came to the conclusion that Walrasian general equilibrium theory and money ought not to be mixed; but new-classical economics did just that, in a way that claimed to produce an altogether deeper theoretical case against policy activism than more traditional monetarist doctrine had ever developed. Erstwhile monetarists who joined the new-classical camp often seemed to believe that they were doing nothing more than putting the old monetarist superstructure on technically more secure microeconomic foundations. Michael Parkin was one of this group, and our intellectual differences now made it impossible to work as closely together as we had in the past. This is not the place to refight old battles. Let me just reiterate my long-held view that new-classical economics was indeed a radical new doctrine, not merely a mathematically tighter reformulation of monetarism, and that it was also a doctrine whose empirical content was decidedly suspect from the very outset (see Laidler 1981a; 1983). At Western, I went on developing the ideas on which I had been working when I left Manchester.

Shortly after I had published Laidler (1974a) I had met Peter Jonson, who was on leave from the Reserve Bank of Australia to complete a Ph.D. at the LSE under Harry Johnson's supervision. He was interested in a style of macroeconometric model in which expenditure flows in goods, labour and asset markets responded to discrepancies between desired and actual stocks of assets, financial assets and money in particular. The econometric techniques needed to work along these lines had been developed by Rex Bergstrom and Clifford Wymer, both New Zealanders, although Bergstrom was at Essex and Wymer at the LSE. Their nationality was not quite irrelevant, however, because what they were doing was carrying forward the research programme on macro-stabilisation issues which Bill Phillips had initiated, and to which I had been introduced as an undergraduate by his lectures (see Bergstrom and Wymer 1974).

Peter was already thinking about what kind of theoretical underpinnings would go with such applied work, and, upon reading my paper, he saw that our minds were moving in very much the same direction. His nowadays sadly neglected (1976) paper, published in *Kredit und Kapital*, bears witness to this. Peter also recognised that the empirical paper I had written at St. Louis in 1973 (Laidler 1973b) was not as compatible with those theoretical underpinnings as was the empirical work that he had in progress. He quickly convinced me of this – not a difficult task, given the relationship between those underpinnings and the Archibald-Lipsey (1958) extension of Patinkin's analysis which I had first encountered as an undergraduate – and also that the econometric tools that Wymer had developed were well suited to my own ambitions of building really small-scale macroeconometric models that had serious empirical content while remaining simple enough in their structure to be taken into the undergraduate classroom. Between 1975 and 1981 I put a good deal of time into working on such models, not least during the long and fruitful (northern hemisphere) summer vacation of 1977 spent at the Reserve Bank of Australia. Patrick O'Shea, my research assistant there, had access to dress rehearsals at the Sydney Opera House, so our collaboration was doubly enjoyable. We produced a small econometric model of the UK (Laidler and O'Shea 1980), and later, working with various research assistants, I would also build little models of the Canadian (Laidler *et al.* 1983) and United States (Laidler and Bentley 1983) economies along similar lines.

This work did not catch on widely. Partly, perhaps mainly, that was because models in this style ran very much contrary to new-classical principles in their lack of explicit microeconomic foundations; they were easy to criticise, therefore in a knee-jerk sort of way, particularly for those who were more interested in scoring points than in understanding how the economy functions; it was hard to improve on those models' empirical performance, however, without moving to much more elaborate systems. Crucially, they predicted that 'unanticipated money' would affect real variables directly through real balance effects, rather than through the price fluctuations required by the new-classical framework, and which, as the data showed (and as Lucas (1996, p. 679) has now acknowledged), simply did not occur. There was, nevertheless, a straightforward empirical reason why I abandoned this line of work: the productivity growth slowdown that hit all Western economies in the mid-1970s played havoc with any empirical model, mine included, in which capacity output was represented by a simple time trend, and I did not have the faintest idea how to cope with this problem. If I was doing this kind of work nowadays, I would, I suppose, use some kind of explicit stochastic growth model to anchor the economy's supply side, and then try to superimpose monetary shocks upon it with their consequences for real variables amplified by a little price stickiness. As the currently fashionable real-business-cycle research programme expands to accommodate the investigation of monetary policy questions, it may well end up doing something of this sort.

Small econometric models were not my only effort to keep my own version of the monetarist research agenda going. My 1981 book *Monetarist perspectives* (Laidler 1981b) tackled theoretical issues, and its second chapter filled two important gaps in that agenda. First, it reconciled some important stylised facts about the role of lagged dependent variables in the demand for money function with the mechanics of the monetary transmission mechanism which I was embodying in my small models; and second, in relating the presence of those lagged dependent variables to the whole transmission mechanism of monetary policy, it provided good reasons not to worry about the fact that their coefficients often proved econometrically unstable. My 1983 Harry Johnson Lecture (Laidler 1984) carried these arguments further, putting them in a broader context, and in 1988 my Presidential Address to the Canadian Economics Association (CEA) (Laidler 1988a) tried to relate all this to the non-Walrasian vision of a monetary economy that I had first adopted in 1973.

In 1981 I agreed to take my turn as Department Chairman at Western. The fact that, in 1984, I ended a seven-year appointment after three years demonstrates that this venture into administration was not a success. The immediate reason for my early departure was straightforward: a student appealed a mark, and the mark went down on a colleague's re-reading; the student appealed to the Dean who proposed to restore the original mark without further assessment; I protested, and secured the Dean's assent to have the paper read by an examiner external to the university; but when the external examiner awarded a grade consistent with the department's reread, the Dean restored the original mark anyway, informing me only after he had informed the student. Someone had to go, and modern universities being what they are, it was the chairman. I stayed on for a year as a 'lame duck' so that my successor, Michael Parkin as it turned out, could be selected in an orderly fashion. The year 1983–4 was the most miserable one of my career.

I was not altogether sorry to be forced into resignation, however, for in the early 1980s I began to find myself increasingly at odds with some of my colleagues about appointments and tenure decisions. Western is a big department (close to fifty positions at that time) in a rather small country, and it seemed to me, as it still does, that it needed to accommodate considerable diversity of viewpoint and approach if it was to do its job properly; more, certainly, than any American department needs to, for any department there is 'small' relative to the size of the economics profession as a whole, which can and does provide for diversity among, rather than within, individual departments. However, my view that academic heaven was unlikely to be found in, shall we say, a department just like that at Rochester but three times the size, was not widely shared at Western and, inevitably, it was the majority who carried the day. At Berkeley I had been a bit discomfited by the way in which academic seriousness sometimes turned into a humourless earnestness; now at Western, particularly among some of the younger people whom I myself had helped hire and promote, that same seriousness bred self-righteous intolerance. In the view of some of them, anyone who doubted the verities of new-classical economics was not merely misguided, but professionally incompetent. I am told that, at about the time I gave up the chairmanship, I caused considerable offence to some of my colleagues by referring to them as the 'Thought Police'. I had not deliberately set out to offend them, but, all the same, and after due reflection, it was the least they deserved.

Western was by no means the only Economics department to suffer such stresses in the 1980s. Young academics are always inclined to take themselves a bit too seriously, as I am sure some of my older Manchester colleagues, even the friendly ones, must have remarked about me. But in the 1980s, demographic facts ensured that a large number of young people were entering an academic market that had turned against the seller at last. Their sheer numbers, and the extraordinarily competitive nature of the environment they encountered, were bound to make them aggressive and hard to get along with. This is a problem, I think, that the simple passage of time will take care of and, although it made life difficult for some of us for a few years, I doubt that it will turn out to have done any lasting damage to the discipline. It did do harm to the department at Western, however, because a number of talented people who simply could not be bothered with the constant sniping of some of their colleagues left for more congenial appointments elsewhere.

Another trend of the 1980s also did much to undermine the attractiveness of Western's academic environment, at least in my eyes; namely, the growing 'professionalization' of the university's administration, again a local manifestation of a widespread phenomenon. By the early 1990s, the university's President and Vice-Presidents – who at that time were multiplying like Cantillon's 'mice in a barn' – were straight-facedly referring to themselves as 'senior management', and to students as 'clients', while academic staff had become a sub-set of the institution's 'human resources' whose task it was to 'service' the above-mentioned 'clients'. Indeed, for a year or two the whole university was urged to dedicate itself to the provision of 'Total Quality Service', and 'Service Improvement Co-ordinators' – nouns always seemed to travel in trios at that time – were appointed here, there and everywhere to ensure that principles which allegedly had done wonders for Japanese manufacturing in the 1960s, were observed with suitable reverence.

All of this was comical, but I also found the attitude that underlay it, namely that a university's faculty, who actually do the job of creating, preserving and disseminating knowledge, are less important than its administrators, to be profoundly demoralising. I am still waiting for a note of congratulations from senior management on having been elected President of the Canadian Economics Association for the academic year 1987–8; I still get angry when I pass the new buildings they had erected without making budgetary provision for such matters as heating, lighting and cleaning; and I get even angrier when I have to waste time typing and filing my own correspondence, emptying my own waste bin, and so on as a consequence of the economies that the university subsequently, and quite foreseeably, was forced to make as a consequence of their decisions. More fundamentally, although I suppose that 'servicing clients' whose main aim in life is to become accountants or solicitors is one function of the tertiary education sector, that is not exactly what my generation of academics thought a university was for.

A few bright spots remain at Western, though. Our department still maintains a separate undergraduate honours programme, which offers a real education in economics to serious students who are willing to make the effort to acquire it; and despite the best efforts of the Thought Police, whose ranks are now considerably depleted, the department still attracts a few independently minded graduate students and junior faculty who, like the best of the honours students, seem to want to make economics their own way of life just as much as I did.

In the last ten years, my interests have become less directed towards monetary theory *per se*, and more towards its history. Even as I wrote my CEA presidential address (Laidler 1988a), I was conscious of using it more to sum up past work than to break new ground. I have taken the history of economic thought seriously from my undergraduate days onwards, but this is a field in which a great deal has to be read before anything of significance can be written, and the simple passage of time helps a great deal here. Also, I acquired mathematical technique far too late for it ever to have become a natural part of my way of thinking, and I long ago found that there is no fun to be had from learning new technical tricks solely for the purpose of being better able to teach economic models that I do not believe to be socially useful anyway. It is, therefore, mainly a matter of comparative advantage that I now work less on monetary theory and more on its history. Others can judge whether this move should really be called a 'retreat', as I am told by Al Marty some have done, or simply a natural consequence of getting older; and in any event, I try to ensure that my work is as accessible to monetary economists as it is to historians (see Laidler 1991b). The shift into history has added a nice touch of symmetry to my career, however, because Sam Hollander, my fellow undergraduate from the 1950s, and a member of the Department of Economics at the University of Toronto since 1964 has once again played an important part in my academic life, this time as the co-organiser, with Margaret Schabas, of the York University–University of Toronto History of Economic Thought Workshop which I try to attend regularly.

I also spend a good deal of time these days working on economic policy issues. Again, this is not a new activity, but like the history of economic thought, policy discussion gets relatively easier as one gets older, and in my case this effect is amplified by the fact that, although monetarist-style models are no longer academically fashionable, they remain very useful as tools for policy analysis (see Laidler 1988b; 1992; 1993). Much of my policy-related work in the last six or seven years has been carried out under the auspices of the Toronto located C.D. Howe Institute, and in collaboration with Bill Robson – it is a small world, for Bill is the son of John Robson, whose John Stuart Mill project had much to do with first attracting Sam Hollander to the University of Toronto in 1964. Toronto is a pleasant city (with good and still improving opera!) so I do not mind spending a good bit of time there. I must confess, though, with some regret, that one reason I do so is that I am intellectually isolated at Western these days. Over the years, the efforts of the Thought Police and senior managers did take quite a toll on the quality of my working environment.

I have not yet retired. Indeed, 1998–9 has been one of the busiest years of my career, spent in the newly-created 'Special Advisor' position at the Bank of Canada. The excuse for this essay is that I am unlikely to do any further serious work in monetary economics *per se* and not that I have given up economics. I hope that this is an acceptable reason for not concluding it with a long list of 'lessons that I have learned from life'. The fact is that I stumbled into academic economics almost by accident, not so much as a career, but as a way of life that appeared much preferable to the alternatives available in the late 1950s. I am not sure how I would have fared as a solicitor, accountant or secondary modern school teacher on Tyneside, but I cannot imagine that I would have had nearly as much satisfaction, not to mention fun, from such work as I have had from economics, rough patches and all. So far, the balance of the arbitrary shocks to my life seems to have been comfortably positive.

SELECTED WORKS

(1964) 'Income tax incentives for owner-occupied housing', unpublished Ph.D. dissertation, University of Chicago.

(1966a) 'Some evidence on the demand for money', *Journal of Political Economy*, 74 (1), pp. 55–68.

(1966b) 'The rate of interest and the demand for money: some empirical evidence', *Journal of Political Economy*, 74 (6), pp. 543–55.*

(1967) (with B.A. Corry) 'The Phillips relation: a theoretical explanation', *Economica*, n.s. 34 (2), pp. 189–97.

(1968) 'The permanent-income concept in a macro-economic model', *Oxford Economic Papers*, n.s. 20 (1), pp. 11–23.*

(1969a) *The demand for money: theories and evidence.* Scranton, PA: International Textbook Co.

(1969b) 'The definition of money: theoretical and empirical problems', *Journal of Money, Credit and Banking*, 1 (3), pp. 508–25.

(1969c) 'Money, wealth and time preference in a stationary economy', *Canadian Journal of Economics*, 2 (4), pp. 526–35.*

(1969d) 'Income tax incentives for owner-occupied housing', in A.C Harberger and M.J. Bailey (eds) (1969) *The taxation of income from capital.* Washington, DC: Brookings Institution, pp. 50–76.

(1971) 'The Phillips curve, expectations and incomes policy', in H.G. Johnson and N.R. Nobay (eds) (1971) *The current inflation.* London: Macmillan, pp. 75–98.*

(1972a) 'Thomas Tooke on monetary reform', in M. Peston and B.A. Corry (eds) (1972) *Essays in honour of Lord Robbins.* London: Weidenfeld & Nicolson, pp. 168–85.

(1972b) 'The current inflation: explanations and policies', *National Westminster Bank Quarterly Review*, November, pp. 6–21.*

(1972c) 'Monetarist models of inflation in closed and open economies', unpublished.*

(1973a) 'Simultaneous fluctuations in prices and output: a business cycle approach', *Economica*, n.s. 40 (1), pp. 60–72.

(1973b) 'The influence of money on real income and inflation: a simple model with some empirical tests for the United States, 1953–1972', *Manchester School*, 41 (4), pp. 367–95.

(1974a) 'Information, money and the macroeconomics of inflation', *Swedish Journal of Economics*, 76 (1), pp. 26–41.*

(1974b) 'The 1974 report of the President's Council of Economic Advisors: the control of inflation and the future of the international monetary system', *American Economic Review*, 64 (4), pp. 535–43.

(1975a) *Essays on money and inflation.* Manchester: Manchester University Press.

(1975b) 'A brief note on fiscal policy, inflation and the balance of payments', and Transcript of Oral Evidence, in HMSO (1975) *Ninth report from the Expenditure Committee: public expenditure, inflation and the balance of payments*, HC 328 (1974), pp. 48–63.

(1975) (with J.M. Parkin) 'Inflation: a survey', *Economic Journal*, 85 (4), pp. 741–809.

(1980) 'The demand for money in the United States yet again', in K. Brunner and A.H. Meltzer (eds) (1980) *The state of macroeconomics.* Carnegie-Rochester conference series, vol. 12. Amsterdam: North-Holland, pp. 219–72.

(1980) (with P. O'Shea) 'An empirical macro-model of an open economy under fixed exchange rates: the United Kingdom, 1954–1970', *Economica*, n.s. 47 (2), pp. 141–58.

(1981a) 'Monetarism: an interpretation and an assessment', *Economic Journal*, 91 (1), pp. 1–28.*

(1981b) *Monetarist perspectives*. Oxford: Philip Allan.

(1983) 'Did macroeconomics need the rational expectations revolution?', in G. Mason (ed.) (1983) *Macroeconomics: theory, policy and evidence*. Winnipeg: Institute for Social and Economics Research, University of Manitoba, pp. 1–17.*

(1983) (with B. Bentley) 'A small macro model of the post-war United States', *Manchester School*, 51 (4), pp. 317–40.*

(1983) (with B. Bentley, D. Johnson and S.T. Johnson) 'A small macroeconomic model of an open economy: the case of Canada', in E. Claassen and P. Salin (eds) (1982) *Recent issues in the theory of flexible exchange rates*. Amsterdam: North Holland, pp. 149–71.

(1984) 'The "buffer stock" notion in monetary economics', *Economic Journal*, 94 (1), pp. 17–34.*

(1985) 'Economic ideas and social issues', in D.E.W. Laidler (eds) (1985) *Approaches to economic well-being*. Royal commission on the economic union and development prospects for Canada (Macdonald commission), research studies, vol. 26. Toronto: University of Toronto Press, pp. 1–47.

(1988a) 'Taking money seriously', *Canadian Journal of Economics*, 21 (4), pp. 687–713.*

(1988b) 'What remains of the case for flexible exchange rates?', *Pakistan Development Review*, 27 (4), pp. 425–50.*

(1991a) *The golden age of the quantity theory: the development of neoclassical monetary economics, 1870–1914*. Hemel Hempstead: Harvester Wheatsheaf.

(1991b) 'The quantity theory is always and everywhere controversial – why?', *Economic Record*, 67 (4), pp. 289–306.*

(1992) 'Monetarism: the unfinished business', *Cyprus Journal of Economics*, 5 (2), pp. 60–74.*

(1993) 'Price stability and the monetary order', in K. Shigehara (ed.) (1993) *Price stabilization in the 1990s*. London: Macmillan, pp. 331–56.*

(1997a) *Money and macroeconomics: selected essays*. Cheltenham: Edward Elgar.

(1997b) 'Economics as a way of life: a personal memoir', in D.E.W. Laidler (1997a) **q.v.**, pp. ix–xxxi.

(1997c) 'Notes on the microfoundations of monetary economics', *Economic Journal*, 107 (5), pp. 1213–23.

(1999) *Fabricating the Keynesian revolution: studies of the interwar literature on money, the cycle and unemployment*. Cambridge: Cambridge University Press.

BIBLIOGRAPHY

Archibald, G.C. (1965) 'The qualitative content of maximizing models', *Journal of Political Economy*, 73 (1), pp. 27–36.

Archibald, G.C. and Lipsey, R.G. (1958) 'Monetary and value theory: a critique of Lange and Patinkin', *Review of Economic Studies*, 26 (1), pp. 1–22.

Bergstrom, A.R. and Wymer, C.R. (1974) 'A model of disequilibrium neoclassical growth and its application to the UK', unpublished paper, LSE.

Brechling, F.P.R. and Lipsey, R.G. (1963) 'Trade credit and monetary Policy', *Economic Journal*, 73 (4), pp. 618–41.

Brunner, K. and Meltzer, A.H. (1971) 'The uses of money: money in the theory of an exchange economy', *American Economic Review*, 61 (5), pp. 784–805.

Chow, G. (1966) 'On the long-run and short-run demand for money', *Journal of Political Economy*, 74 (2), pp. 111–31.

Friedman, M. (1959) 'The demand for money: some theoretical and empirical results', *Journal of Political Economy*, 67 (4), pp. 327–51.

Friedman, M. (1962) *Price theory: a provisional text*. Chicago: Aldine.

Friedman, M. (1968) 'The role of monetary policy', *American Economic Review*, 58 (1), pp. 1–17.

Friedman, M. and Meiselman, D. (1963) 'The relative stability of monetary velocity and the investment multiplier in the United States, 1897–1958', in E.C. Brown *et al.* (1963) *Stabilization policies: research studies prepared for the commission on money and credit*. Englewood Cliffs, NJ: Prentice-Hall, pp. 165–268.

Friedman, M. and Schwartz, A.J. (1963) *A monetary history of the United States, 1867–1960*. Princeton NJ: Princeton University Press.

Goldfeld, S.M. (1973) 'The demand for money revisited', *Brookings Paper on Economic Activity*, 3, pp. 577–638.

Goodhart, C.A.E. (1975) *Money, information and uncertainty*. London: Macmillan.

Hansen, A.H. (1953) *A guide to Keynes*. New York: McGraw-Hill.

Howitt, P.W. (1990) *The Keynesian recovery and other essays*. Hemel Hempstead: Philip Allan.

Johnson, H.G. (1962) 'Monetary theory and policy', *American Economic Review*, 52 (3), pp. 335–84.

Jonson, P.D. (1976) 'Money, prices and output: an integrative essay', *Kredit und Kapital*, 4 (2), pp. 499–518.

Lerner, A.P. (1944) *The economics of control: principles of welfare economics*. London: Macmillan.

Lipsey, R.G. (1963) *An introduction to positive economics*. London: Weidenfeld & Nicholson.

Lipsey, R.G. and Lancaster, K. (1956) 'The general theory of the second best', *Review of Economic Studies*, 24 (1), pp. 11–32.

Lucas, R.E. (1996), 'Monetary neutrality', *Journal of Political Economy*, 104 (4), pp. 661–82.

Marshall, A. (1890) *Principles of economics*, 8th edn (1920), London: Macmillan.

Meltzer, A.H. (1963) 'The demand for money: the evidence from the time series', *Journal of Political Economy*, 71 (3), pp. 219–46.

Parkin, J.M. and Sumner, M.T. (eds) (1972) *Incomes policy and inflation*. Manchester: Manchester University Press.

Parkin, J.M. and Zis, G. (eds) (1976) *Inflation in the world economy*. Manchester: Manchester University Press.

Patinkin, D. (1956) *Money, interest and prices: an integration of monetary and value theory*. New York: Harper & Row.

Pesek, B. and Saving, T. (1967) *Money, wealth and economic theory*. New York: Macmillan.

Phillips, A.W.H. (1954) 'Stabilization in a closed economy', *Economic Journal*, 64 (2), pp. 290–323.

Reuber, G.L. (1964) 'The objectives of Canadian monetary policy: empirical "trade-offs" and the reaction function of the authorities', *Journal of Political Economy*, 72 (2), pp. 109–32.

Ricardo, D. (1817) *On the principles of political economy and taxation*. Works and correspondence of David Ricardo, Vol. I, ed. P. Sraffa (1951). Cambridge: Cambridge University Press.

Rühl, C. and Laidler, D.E.W. (1998) 'Perspectives on modern macroeconomic theory and its history: an interview with David Laidler', *Review of Political Economy*, 10 (1), pp. 27–56.

Smith, A. (1776) *An inquiry into the nature and causes of the wealth of nations*, ed. E. Cannan (1937). New York: Modern Library.

Stigler, G.J. (1952) *The theory of price*, rev. edn. London: Macmillan.

Thornton, H. (1802) *An inquiry into the nature and effects of the paper credit of Great Britain*, ed. F.A. von Hayek (1939). London: George Allen & Unwin.

Walters, A.A. (1970) 'The Radcliffe Report – ten years after: a survey of empirical evidence', in D.R. Croome and H.G. Johnson (eds) (1970) *Money in Britain, 1959–1969*. Oxford: Oxford University Press, pp. 39–68.

17. Dennis C. Mueller (b. 1940)[1]

17.1 BEGINNINGS

In reflecting upon the major developments of my intellectual life. I have been
struck by the important role chance events played at several instances, as I
shall make clear below. Here, perhaps, is a lesson worth learning. My
background is decidedly middle-class. My father did not graduate from high
school, and worked for more than a quarter of a century as a cab driver. My
mother did graduate from high school, and completed a short course at a
business professional school that qualified her as a bookkeeper. She worked
as a bookkeeper both before my parents were married, and again after they
were divorced in 1945.

From 1945 until 1957, when my parents remarried, I lived with my
grandmother and my mother in the same house on the north side of
Milwaukee in which my mother grew up. It was in what used to be a typical,
ethnic Milwaukee neighbourhood. The same German and Italian families
lived on either side of us when I grew up as when my mother was a child. I

---

[1] Mueller (1986c; 1993b), as revised by the editors. I have published two volumes of selected
essays: the first, my papers on industrial organization (Mueller 1986b); and the second,
which is in the series, my papers on public choice (Mueller 1993a).

went to the same elementary school as she did and had many of the same teachers. Thus, despite my parents' divorce, my elementary and high school years were characterized by a degree of home environment stability that is far rarer today.

My mother was one of seven children and most of my family contacts were with my aunts, uncles, and cousins on her side. Only one of the six brothers and sisters completed college. Although the atmosphere at home was not unintellectual, there was little pressure on me to perform well in school and certainly little pressure to think about going to college as I progressed in the Milwaukee public school system.

Although I was more interested in sports than in studies during my high school years, my grades tended to be mostly As. Thus, it seemed 'natural' that I would go to college upon graduation from high school. Neither of my parents, nor any of my other relatives, gave me much advice, however, as to which college to attend or what to study. Since I was doing well in mathematics and science, engineering seemed the obvious choice for a college major. I had little idea, however, as to what it meant to be an engineer, and was certainly not enthralled by the idea of following this profession. I thus decided to apply to several liberal arts colleges that offered 3–2 engineering programmes. Although I did not much like the idea of having to spend five years to get a four-year degree, or even two four-year degrees, my lack of commitment to engineering as a profession led me to favour the flexibility of a 3–2 programme. Thus, when the time to apply to colleges came around, my applications were directed towards those schools offering the 3–2 programme.

At this juncture, important chance event number one arose. During the autumn of my senior year in high school an interviewer from a prestigious men's liberal arts college visited my high school. Following my interview with him, and on the basis of the advice of the high school counsellor for college studies, I had made up my mind to attend this college should I be awarded a scholarship. The college held an interview weekend in the spring, at which time prospective entrants for the autumn semester visited the college. Interviews with faculty members took place and it was on the basis of these interviews that scholarships were awarded. On the Saturday night of that weekend, a reception was held for the prospective students at the college. I met a couple of members of the college who had formerly been students at my high school. I and a couple of other recruits went off with them to their fraternity house after the reception. We sat around drinking beer and watching 'skin flicks' into the small hours. I am not now and was certainly not at that time prudish. Nevertheless, the thought of spending my weekends sitting around drinking beer and watching 'skin flicks' at an all-boys college near a small town in the middle of nowhere I found extremely unappealing.

Upon returning to Milwaukee from the college, I decided I must go somewhere else.

My best friend throughout my youth was my cousin, Tom Dornbach. He was attending Colorado State College in Greeley at the time. He had been through Colorado Springs and was impressed by the town and had heard that the school there was 'pretty good'. On the basis of this sound advice, I placed an application with Colorado College. I was lucky enough to be awarded a scholarship in chemistry on the basis of my expressed interest in chemical engineering as part of the college's 3–2 engineering programme. The terms of its scholarship award were significantly less attractive than those of the prestigious men's college. Nevertheless, I decided to go to Colorado College, because of its coeducational status, and what seemed to someone who had never been further west than Madison, Wisconsin, its exotic location at the foot of the Rocky Mountains.

17.2   UNDERGRADUATE EDUCATION, 1958–62

My first two years at Colorado College were arduous. My preparation in high school was probably somewhat weaker than those of my classmates, but most importantly being in the pre-engineering programme required that I take extra courses so that I could get in all of the liberal arts and engineering related courses I would need in the three years I was there. In addition, since my scholarship did not cover any of my living costs, I worked in the cafeteria as a waiter's assistant to pay for my meals. During my first two years, therefore, I had little time to pursue intellectual topics beyond those assigned in my science and mathematics-dominated engineering programme, and also little time to pursue anything else, including, ironically, the coeds at the college.

In retrospect, perhaps the most important event which occurred during my first two years at Colorado College was my exposure to one Professor Egbert Miles. Professor Miles had, like several professors at Colorado College at that time, retired from an eastern university, in his case Yale, to live in Colorado Springs and teach one or two courses at the college. Miles was my teacher for calculus over my first two years at Colorado College. He used a quasi-text written by himself. It started with the basic five Peano postulates and proved all of the major theorems in calculus from these postulates upward. Miles was an extraordinarily gifted teacher even then, when he must have been at least seventy-five (his first position after his retirement from Yale had been at Wesleyan). Yet his enthusiasm for the subject matter was contagious. The first, subconscious inclination to become a teacher was undoubtedly born in Miles's class.

The third year in Colorado College's 3–2 engineering programme was spent catching up on the liberal arts part of the programme. I took psychology, philosophy and economics in that year. What different pictures of man and his behaviour were presented in these courses! For perhaps the first time in my life, I became totally absorbed in my studies. I found each course fascinating and could easily have been convinced to stay on at Colorado College and major in any one of the three, had I not been so far advanced in my study plan. But by the time thoughts such as these began to occur to me, I had already interviewed a representative from Columbia University.

Columbia had a nuclear engineering programme. Although my original plan was to specialize in chemical engineering, I had found physics more interesting than chemistry and was thus attracted to Columbia's nuclear engineering programme (this was but a few years after Sputnik, and nuclear physics seemed very much the thing). The representative from Columbia thought I would have no trouble getting financial aid and so I applied to that school. It was the only one to which I did apply.

As the spring wore on, I continued to enjoy my chosen electives. The dates for hearing whether I had been awarded financial aid from Columbia passed. I heard nothing. One of my best friends at Colorado College had decided not to go on to an engineering school after his third year, but to stay on and finish a bachelor's degree. He was talking to one of the economics professors about doing graduate work in economics after leaving the college. I made an appointment to see my professor in principles of economics, Kenneth Curran, to discuss the same option. Kenneth Curran was the second, truly great teacher I had encountered at Colorado College, a school with many fine teachers. He had returned in mid-life to Princeton to get a Ph.D., and after a short stint as an assistant professor at Princeton had gone straight into the chairmanship of Colorado College's economics department. Curran thought I would not have difficulty getting into a good graduate programme in economics. During the second semester of principles of economics with Kenneth Curran, I decided to go to graduate school in economics and become a teacher. I never wrote to Columbia to find out definitely whether I had been admitted and received financial aid. The next year, the same representative from Columbia came to the Colorado College campus. He was surprised to find me there. I had been awarded a scholarship the year before. Notification of the award had for some reason not reached me. Had I been notified of the award at the proper time, I would have accepted it, and would have been off to Columbia to study nuclear engineering. What I would be doing today is anyone's guess.

As it was, I was finishing up a major in mathematics at Colorado College (the only subject for which my pre-engineering programme had provided me enough credits to graduate in four years) and thinking about going to graduate school. I approached three of the department's members for advice on which university to attend. Curran recommended Princeton. Al Johnson had studied at Stanford and recommended that school. Ray Werner had a Ph.D. from Nebraska, but had spent a summer at the University of Chicago, and was clearly, I can say today, influenced by the Chicago way of thinking. He recommended Chicago. I applied to these three schools and added MIT on my own initiative. I was applying for an NSF fellowship and thought the National Science Foundation would be more impressed by my application if I stated that I wanted to study at a science-engineering school. Also, I had studied principles from Samuelson's text and thought that a school good enough to have someone who could write such a fine textbook must be pretty good. Such is the sophistication of even a fairly intelligent college senior's thought process in choosing a graduate school.

I received the NSF, but by the time it was awarded my admiration and respect for Curran had grown still further. Moreover, I was taking public finance in the spring, from yet another excellent teacher, Ray Werner, and had decided I wanted to specialize in public finance: from this course choice began my career in public choice. Werner touted Richard Musgrave as the profession's leading authority in public finance, and Musgrave had just joined the Princeton faculty. Thus, Curran and I agreed that I should try to get the NSF fellowship transferred to Princeton. I succeeded and have never regretted the decision. But, a few years later when I became aware of the importance of departmental rankings, I realized that with more neutral advice I could easily have gone off to MIT.

17.3   GRADUATE EDUCATION, 1962–5

During my first year at Princeton the faculty engaged in the kind of soul searching that all departments with graduate programmes periodically undertake to determine how it could speed up the average graduate student's progress. Princeton's graduate programme had the usual format. The first year was devoted to theory and econometrics, the second to courses in fields of specialization. In the third year one was supposed to start on the dissertation. But often this year was devoted to 'thinking about the dissertation', with the start delayed until the fourth year, completion thus being pushed back to the fifth, the sixth or the nth. The faculty decided to try to accelerate this process by requiring that each student submit a dissertation proposal during the spring of his/her second year. No student was to be allowed to take part in the General Examinations at the end of that year unless this requirement had been met.

Submitting a proposal during the second semester essentially meant that it had to be based on one's course work through the first semester of the second year. Unfortunately for my career in public finance, Richard Musgrave was on leave during the first semester of my second year. I thus had to try to come up with a dissertation topic that would appeal to both me and a man whom I had then barely even met. I tried, but could not identify one.

At that time students in economics at Princeton were required to offer four speciality fields in addition to micro and macro theory when they took the General Examinations. Industrial organization was one of the four fields which I had chosen, having taken the industrial organization course in the fall. The study of technological change and research and development was a new hot topic at that time. I did have some ideas for a thesis on R&D, and thus drafted a proposal on that topic. At first, I wanted to remain in the public finance area and formulated my thesis proposal as a cost-benefit study of R&D. It became obvious that this topic was unmanageable and so the cost-benefit part of the proposal was dropped. The thesis evolved as a study of the determinants of R&D, and set me off into the industrial organization field. In my case the innovation introduced by the Princeton faculty in my second year worked exactly as intended. I was off and running on my dissertation as soon as I passed the General Examinations in May, and had a completed draft of the dissertation by the end of the summer of my third year (Mueller 1966). A possible unintended consequence was that I had been forced to switch fields to meet the proposal requirement.

I was extremely fortunate that both Markham and Musgrave were at Princeton while I was there (both left for Harvard shortly after my graduate work was completed). I took the second semester of the public finance sequence from Musgrave. This semester dealt with the expenditure side of public finance. I was exposed to the classic works by Wicksell, Samuelson, Arrow and Buchanan, as well as the charismatic Musgrave himself. Ideas were implanted during this semester which would subsequently take root in several pieces of research.

The Ford Foundation had made a large grant to study technological change to a group of economists, which included my thesis advisor, Jesse Markham. Markham helped me tap into those funds and with them I financed my own R&D questionnaire, patterned after the NSF questionnaire. With the data I gathered from this questionnaire, I was able to write my thesis and produce several articles, including what became Grabowski and Mueller (1972).

F.M. Scherer was also at Princeton when I was there. Many an afternoon was spent in discussion in his office, despite his not being officially on my dissertation committee and despite the pressures on his time that an assistant professor's appointment carries. Our paths have crossed many times since, to my continual benefit.

I was impatient to cease being a student and went into the job market in my third year. My thesis turned out to be based around empirical tests of two models. Only preliminary results on the first model were available when I 'went on the road' for my job interviews in December and January. My audiences were obviously unimpressed and no offers appeared during the usual time interval. Determined to be done with studenthood, I applied to places as far away as Edinburgh and accepted an offer to teach in Vancouver, Canada, at a school that had not yet opened, from a man I had never seen, Parzival Copes, then in England. My Wanderlust had once again surfaced.

17.4   SIMON FRASER-BROOKINGS, 1965–8

My first year as a professor was also my employer's first year as a university. Everyone including myself was excited about the prospects for Simon Fraser University in its inaugural year, but everyone who was at SFU during that first year, including myself, was also terribly busy helping to get the university started. I was one of five that made up the department of business and economics at Simon Fraser during its first year. We were expanding by fourteen and recruitment was a major preoccupation. Since both the department and the university were spanking new, constitutions had to be drafted for everything. I was on the department graduate curriculum committee, its representative to the university's graduate curriculum committee, and on, and on. When an offer from the Brookings Institution arrived in March 1966, I was wondering whether I would ever find time to do research at Simon Fraser. I decided to return to the East and do full-time research. Shortly after I accepted Brookings' offer, the rain clouds began to lift in Vancouver and I discovered the magnificent city and environment in which I was living. By the time I left for Washington in August of 1966, it was with great reluctance.

My dissertation had acquainted me with the work of Schumpeter and, like so many others, I was captivated by Schumpeter's description of capitalist development. During my first year at Brookings, I decided to study the growth of corporations, using a sort of Schumpeterian framework in which I analysed growth by technological innovation, growth by marketing innovation, and growth by organizational innovation. The study was to consist of theoretical discussion illustrated by case studies. As an example of growth through innovation, I chose Xerox. Several trips to Rochester were made and I was fortunate in being able to interview Chester Carlson, Xerography's inventor, Joseph Wilson, the president of Xerox (then Haloid) when it decided to take up the invention, John Dessauer, the vice president in charge of R&D, who first brought the invention to Wilson's attention, and several other key executives. For my marketing innovation, I chose the discount department store, 'invented' by Eugene Ferkauf, the founder of E. J. Korvette's. As an organizational innovation, I decided to look at mergers. Since there were many *different* patterns to growth through merger, I had selected several companies to illustrate this form of growth.

It was through these case studies that the idea of the corporate life cycle impressed itself upon me. Xerox appeared to be going through such a cycle and was still in a fairly early phase of it when I was studying it (1967). Korvette had rocketed through its life cycle and had already been rescued from its creditors in 1966 through an acquisition by Spartan Industries, only eighteen years after Ferkauf opened his first discount store. Many of the companies, which chose to grow by acquisition, seemed to do so because they lacked any other avenue for growth, that is, they were in a mature phase of their corporate life cycle, when internal growth through technological and marketing innovations seemed blocked. This life cycle view of corporate development, gained during my research at Brookings, has influenced the way I look at corporate development ever since. It is apparent in Mueller and Tilton (1969), Mueller (1970; 1972; 1987), Grabowski and Mueller (1975) and Mueller and Yun (1998).

As I began to examine more closely each of the companies I had chosen to illustrate growth by merger, I discovered that it was typically not possible to claim that this growth strategy had been successful in the sense of increasing profitability. In some cases, growth-through-mergers had been clearly at the expense of profits and had nearly destroyed the firm. I looked around for a company which would clearly illustrate the positive side of the growth-through-merger strategy. I selected Litton Industries, a company frequently featured in the business press at that time (mid-1967) as the archetype, new-breed corporation that grew through acquisition.

As I was pulling together the various parts of the book, my showpiece example of growth-through-merger, Litton, began to disintegrate. The first articles on its myriad merger troubles began to appear. Litton began to look like the other growth-through-merger companies, successful at growing but not necessarily at generating profits.

It was at this time that I began to marry the idea that managers would pursue growth to satisfy their own interests and the life cycle idea. I had been greatly impressed by Marris (1964) on managerial capitalism and carried along his managers-maximize-growth hypothesis as one to be examined with my case studies. The growth performance of Xerox up through the late 1960s had been extraordinary and its management certainly talked as if that was their primary goal. But Xerox's profit and common share performance had been equally spectacular and it was difficult to see any conflict between managerial and shareholder interests here.

The same could have been said of E. J. Korvette's until around 1960. But starting then its share price ceased to rise, and instead bobbed erratically around roughly the same mean value. Ferkauf had announced a policy of not paying dividends and ploughing back all of the earnings to finance the expansion of the firm. He owned enough shares so that takeover attempts could be warded off, and they were until 1966. Litton had the same policy of not paying cash dividends and Litton's managers also owned a substantial fraction of the outstanding shares. E. J. Korvette and Litton seemed to embody the kind of behaviour Marris described. Marris's model of managerial capitalism seemed to fit these and other mature corporations. I revised the book manuscript to include this theme.

Shortly after arriving in Ithaca in the autumn of 1968, the manuscript was finished. I sent it to Joe Pechman, then director of the economics section at Brookings. Pechman read the manuscript and said Brookings would not publish it. It was not the kind of thing Brookings published: case studies of corporations illustrating various arguments in the theory of the firm. I originally intended to submit the book to another publisher, but never did. John Tilton had been working on his book on transistors when I was there and we had written a paper that incorporated some of the insights he had gained from his work on transistors and I on xerography (Mueller and Tilton 1969). The *Quarterly Journal of Economics* accepted the theoretical introduction to the mergers' case studies (Mueller 1969) and I had begun a major empirical study with Henry Grabowski. Although it seemed a waste not to publish all of the case study material I had written, particularly that based on the interviews with the key personnel at Xerox, the two years at Brookings turned out to have had a major impact on my future research. I had gained insights into corporate behaviour and the modern capitalist process that influenced my work for the next two decades.

I had been hired by Brookings to work with William Capron in the industrial organization area. Such are the luxuries of a research institute, however, that I had time not only to continue my research in industrial organization, but also to read and think about topics outside of IO and even outside of the academic industrial organization field. The war in Vietnam was heating up at that time and I had joined a local peace group. Its president was Martin Carnoy, who was also a colleague of mine at Brookings. We joined forces on a short article on the war issue that was published in the *New Republic*; this in turn led to my first appearance in the *Congressional Record*, on radio and on television.

What would prove to be a more important diversion occurred when I happened to read an article by James Coleman in the *American Economic Review*. Coleman (1966) had put forward the intriguing argument that the implicit trading of votes via logrolling in Congress achieved the same kind of revelation of intensities as the trading of goods does in markets, thereby bringing about Pareto optimality in public goods provision and largely avoiding 'the Arrow problem'. Although I believed (and still believe) that the idea of improving the performance of voting mechanisms by inducing them to reveal intensity differences is extremely important, I also believed that the sort of implicit and partial trading that goes on in Congress would not achieve all of the possible advantages Coleman claimed for it or all that it could potentially achieve. It was necessary literally to trade votes in vote markets to achieve Pareto optimal allocations of public goods. These thoughts became a comment on Coleman's paper – my first contribution to the public choice literature (Mueller 1967) – and thereby rekindled my interest in public expenditure issues. Unfortunately, my plate of IO topics to research was full and so I did not dabble in public choice again while I was at the Brookings Institution.

17.5   CORNELL WITH INTERLUDES, 1968–74

I arrived at Cornell just as Alfred Kahn was leaving the economics department to become Dean of the Arts College. I was sorry to learn of this at the time and my disappointment grew as I came to realize just how brilliant a mind Kahn has. But even as Dean, Kahn took the time to read some of my papers and offered many truly insightful comments. I sometimes wonder how much more research I might have done had Kahn been just another colleague down the hall.

As it was, my main collaborator while I was at Cornell turned out to be someone at Yale. Henry Grabowski and I had been graduate students together at Princeton and had both done dissertations on the determinants of R&D using an overlapping data set. We first decided to follow up our dissertation work, which involved cash flow models of R&D, by recasting the simultaneous equations model I had employed in my dissertation in such a way so that we could test a managerial version of the model against a neoclassical one (Grabowski and Mueller 1972). This paper led to several others (e.g. Grabowski and Mueller 1975). Certainly one of the luckier things that has happened to me down through the years is to have had Henry as collaborator and friend.

A year or so after I arrived in Ithaca, my colleague Jaroslav Vanek approached me about a student of his who was looking for a dissertation topic. Jaroslav was completing his *magnum opus* on labour management at that time and was interested in different democratic procedures (Vanek 1970). We had discussed the idea of establishing Walrasian markets for votes as a way of revealing intensities on public goods, and were interested in finding out if it really would work. Jaroslav's student, Geoffrey Philpotts, had not studied public choice (few had in 1970), but was good at computer programming. The idea of simulating a system of Walrasian markets in votes on public goods led to Mueller *et al.* (1972) and also to a very cogent dissertation by Geoffrey Philpotts.

George von Furstenburg had been a graduate student at Princeton in the class one year behind mine and was then an assistant professor at Cornell. He became animated by Harold Hochman and James Rodgers's (1969) seminal piece on Pareto optimal redistribution, and we began to kick around a follow-up piece. Another opportunity to dabble in public choice issues having thus presented itself, the outcome became von Furstenberg and Mueller (1971).

About that time Thomas Willett and Robert Tollison joined the Cornell School of Business and Public Administration. They had both received their graduate education at the University of Virginia during the 1960s, an era which time would reveal as being one of tremendous intellectual activity and innovation in Virginia's Economics Department. They were infected by a love for ideas and hard work and proceeded to write what seemed like an article every week. Tollison had been a student of James Buchanan's and was working on a variety of public choice questions. Willett was willing to tackle any and every economic question one could think of. My flirtation with public choice began to develop into a romance, with Mueller, Tollison and Willett (1972; 1974a; b; 1975) being the result.

The political tumult that hit many campuses during the Vietnam War arrived at Cornell in the spring of 1969. It quickly trickled down to the Economics Department, which split down the middle. For completely unrelated reasons my marriage was coming apart during the winter and spring of 1972, making a change of scenery seem in order. James Buchanan and Gordon Tullock had both left the University of Virginia by then and been reunited at the Virginia Polytechnic Institute and State University in Blacksburg. The Center for the Study of Public Choice had been established there, and they had initiated a postdoctoral fellowship as part of their programme. After Bob Tollison intervened on my behalf, I was off to Blacksburg for the 1972–3 academic year as a somewhat aged (I already was a tenured associate professor at Cornell) postdoc.

Blacksburg (Virginia) is not a place with which all visitors fall in love, but I had a fantastic year there. This was my first personal contact with both James Buchanan and Gordon Tullock. Buchanan is as impressive in person as he is on paper, one of the truly great intellects of the profession. Tullock dazzles with a stream of facts and questions. Accordingly, the intellectual atmosphere at the Center was terrific. In addition to Buchanan and Tullock, there was a very good younger group that included Thomas Borcherding, Winston Bush, Charles Goetz and Robert Mackay. Despite Blacksburg's out-of-the-way location, a steady stream of top-notch visitors passed through; James Meade and his wife spent the spring there.

The Center itself was housed in a century-old mansion that used to be the President of the University's house. It was both centrally located and yet isolated, being perched on a good-sized hill in the middle of campus, a few minutes walk from the nearest other building. My office was a former upstairs bedroom. Coffee was in constant supply in the kitchen. A trip to get coffee would often develop into a discussion with Winston Bush about anarchy, a confrontation with Gordon Tullock in which I would be falsely accused of favouring a minimum wage or some such liberal policy – *and then challenged to defend it* – or other similar event. I had research in industrial organization under way but, given the atmosphere at the Center, I naturally found myself spending a lot of time on public choice questions. Mueller (1974a; b) got written as a result.

The 1973–4 academic year found me back in Ithaca, with Tollison, Willett and myself finishing our joint research. We would soon all depart in different directions, however, in my case to the International Institute of Management in Berlin (IIM). In December of 1973 I presented a paper at the AEA meetings in New York, at a session which included papers by John Rawls and James Buchanan. I came across a former Cornell colleague, Paul Hohenberg, in one of the hotel corridors, and we began to exchange greetings. As so often happens in the chaos of an AEA convention, someone else came by, who knew Paul, and I began chatting with the person with whom Paul had originally been talking. It turned out he had the same last name, 'aber mit Umlaut'. Jürgen Müller had studied at Stanford with Paul, and was now at the IIM in Berlin. Although the Institute was only three years old, I had heard of it because Mike Scherer had gone there. But Mike was leaving, I then learned, and they were looking for someone in industrial organization. My Wanderlust was again stirred, and come September of 1974 I was in Berlin. The Institute was housed in a villa that once belonged to a tobacco baron who fled Berlin in the 1930s. I again had an upstairs bedroom as my office, a fantastic wood-panelled room with a balcony overlooking a large garden. The Germans knew how a scholar likes to be treated!

The IIM's research programme was organized around projects. To make sure that what I was doing would be acceptable to the institute's directors, I had proposed, prior to accepting an offer, to conduct an international comparison of merger activity. I had published one paper on mergers

(Mueller 1969), but beyond that had done nothing on the topic. Nor had anyone else done much on the 1960s' merger wave at that time, especially in Europe. An international comparison fitted in well with the character of the Institute. The idea was to collect data and test a common set of hypotheses across as many countries as possible. The first year was largely spent using the Institute's ample travel budget travelling Europe to find willing and able participants for the project, and working up the set of hypotheses to be tested. I was lucky to find scholars meeting these criteria in six different countries.

To my knowledge, no study exists in economics of precisely the same kind as 'the merger project': seven studies conducted by seven sets of scholars for seven different countries, each testing a common set of hypotheses for nearly the same time periods using a common methodology. Having spent six years acting as entrepreneur, manager, cheerleader, and final product editor, I now know why. But the merger study was in many ways a most rewarding experience. Its main findings were published as Mueller (1980).

The history and reputation of Berlin are such that many wish to see it. We had no trouble attracting outstanding visitors. Oliver Williamson visited and presented a quasi-critique of Stephen Marglin's 'What do bosses do?' (1974). About the same time, Michael Jensen came through and presented his paper with William Meckling on agency costs (Jensen and Meckling 1976). My colleague Felix FitzRoy and I found ourselves in partial disagreement with both papers. The seeds were sown for what would eventually become FitzRoy and Mueller (1984).

Another visitor was Keith Cowling, who stayed the summer of 1975. I had initiated a brown bag seminar in IO shortly after my arrival at the institute. Since our numbers were small, we often discussed work emanating from outside. One such session, while Keith was visiting, was on Comanor and Smiley's (1975) *QJE* article on the costs of monopoly. The paper got us thinking about the original social cost of monopoly question Harberger had posed, and eventually to the paper, which appeared as Cowling and Mueller (1978). Indirectly, it also led to Mueller (1977).

In writing our paper on the social costs of monopoly, Cowling and I had to wrestle with the conceptual issue as to how a world, which was perfectly competitive in all markets, really would look. The answer we gave, although breaking with tradition in some respects, was, like the literature preceding it, a static representation. But, this exercise led me to begin to try and envisage how a world, which was perfectly competitive over time, would look. I can recall quite vividly, barging into John Cable's office one morning to try out on him the methodological ideas that were to underlie Mueller (1977).

17.6   PUBLIC CHOICE: A SURVEY

I had no teaching responsibilities at the IIM and almost no bureaucratic duties. Consequently, I was able to proceed with the IO work that I had been hired to do and still have plenty of time left over to pursue my evolving interests in public choice. I am not sure whether Mark Perlman, who was editor of the *Journal of Economic Literature* at that time, approached James Buchanan and asked him to write a survey of the public choice literature, or merely asked Buchanan for suggestions for an author. I do know that Buchanan gave Perlman my name, and that he pursued the suggestion.

I had agreed to write the survey (Mueller 1976) while still in Ithaca, but it was essentially written in Berlin. It was fortunate that I was asked to do this at a time when I had no teaching responsibilities. I was able to devote a lot of time to it – more time per page, I am sure, than for anything I had written up to that point. My first draft was 110 double-spaced pages, almost twice the maximum length Perlman allowed. Eventually I was able to chop it down to the page limits required by the *Journal of Economic Literature* and in June of 1976 it appeared.

The public choice field was beginning to attract a lot of interest by the mid-1970s, with many people in the profession curious about its content. My survey appeared at a most opportune time, making my name known to people who had never read any of my work in industrial organization or public choice. At about the time the survey came out, Colin Day introduced himself to me at an IO conference in England. He was the economics editor for Cambridge University Press at that time. CUP planned to start a series of monographs in cooperation with the *JEL* that would consist of extended versions of some of the *JEL* surveys. Day wanted to know what I thought the demand would be for a book-length survey of public choice; if it seemed likely to be great enough, would I be willing to expand my survey to the required scale? As I recall, I expressed some uncertainty about the likely demand. There were few, if any, courses that I knew of in public choice (remember that I was still based in Europe at that time), and while I expected that some professors would want to assign a survey of public choice to their public finance students, the article in the *Journal of Economic Literature* would probably suffice for that purpose. On the other hand, it would almost certainly capture most of whatever demand there was, since in the mid-1970s the number of books surveying public choice was nil, and no full-blown textbooks existed either. So we went ahead (Mueller 1979). The book sold far more copies than I, and I'm sure Day, ever expected.

For the second time, I greatly underestimated the time it would take to write the survey. I had thought that I could just go back to my 110-page draft, expand this and that topic a little and be done. But the task of trying to state what other people had written, in such a way that would be both true to the original author's intent and informative in a condensed form to the reader, again proved to be very time consuming.

One of the additions to the book from the survey was a comparison of the simple majority rule and the unanimity rule. While I was working on that chapter I found myself puzzling again, as I and so many others had before, over why one could not simply use the unanimity rule to decide public goods quantities and tax shares, since in principle all could be made better off from the provision of a public good. As I mulled this question over and gazed out of my office window on the huge garden behind the Institute, the thought came to me that the problem with the unanimity rule was that every member of the committee effectively had an infinite number of vetoes to cast. One needed to limit each committee member to a single veto. This idea would develop into 'voting by veto' (Mueller 1978; 1984).

Some ten years later, as I reworked the chapter contrasting the unanimity and majority rules for the revision of *Public choice* (Mueller 1989c), I again found myself puzzling over the same question of why one cannot simply use the unanimity rule to make public goods decisions. Once again I concluded that some sort of voting rule that included a random process to encourage consensus was a possible answer. The result of these deliberations is Mueller (1989b).

17.7   MARYLAND AND INTERLUDES, 1977–94

One of the visitors during my stay at the IIM in 1974–7 had been Robin Marris. Robin had taken over the chairmanship at the University of Maryland in the autumn of 1976, and came to Berlin to give a seminar that year. Discussions began on what was to become a move back to America, to the city of College Park. Thus, in August of 1977 ended three of the happiest and most productive years of my life. I had arrived in Berlin carrying the scars of a recent divorce. I left with a wife and a new-born son. Such is the attraction of Berlin, and of these memories, that I have returned several times since.

Although Robin Marris's presence at Maryland was one of the attractions in going there, his chairmanship duties kept us from having much intellectual contact during the first couple of years. An invitation to Robin from Mark Perlman, to write an essay on corporate capitalism for the *Journal of Economic Literature* led to lunch to discuss what might go into such a survey. My work on the social costs of monopoly had led me into the rent-seeking and nonprice competition literatures and I thought that that was a dimension of capitalist competition that was underemphasized. Robin agreed, and what became Marris and Mueller (1980) was under way.

A few months after my arrival at Maryland, I was asked to give a seminar at the Federal Trade Commission (FTC). I was interested in following up my paper on the persistence of profits with a larger study to explain why one observed persistent differences in profits across firms. I had learned that the FTC had collected market share data for 1972 as a follow-up to their 1950 survey. I wished to test for the impact of market share on profitability and inquired about the availability of the 1972 data. Dave Qualls was head of the Industry Analysis section at the time. It turned out that he had recently completed a paper on the profit-stability question, and was interested in the persistence issue. Thus began a research project that was to last too long, and a friendship that was to end too quickly. One meets but a few people in one's life for whom the adjective good can be applied to describe every aspect of their personality and character. Dave Qualls was one of these rare individuals. The persistence of profits project proved to be as ambitious and exhausting as the merger project. But after five years, an FTC report did finally emerge in 1983, with a fuller treatment of the issue contained in Mueller (1986d).

Upon arriving at the University of Maryland in the autumn of 1977, I discovered that the Department offered no graduate courses in public choice and of course no field in this area. With Mancur Olson's presence in the department and my interests in the subject, this seemed a pity. Moreover, Maryland's Government Department had just hired Joe Oppenheimer, who was also working in public choice. We thus decided to create a field in public choice for Maryland Economics students. Enrolments from economics were small at the beginning; in fact, the first couple of years the course was combined with the Government Department's formal theory course, with Joe Oppenheimer and I jointly teaching it. Joe is a great teacher with much enthusiasm, and I enjoyed and learned much from that experience. Unfortunately, when I went on leave, the two courses got separated and were never reunited. I think the students have been the worse for this.

By 1981, when I was again ready for a break from teaching, the opportunity presented itself in the form of an invitation to return to the IIM in Berlin. I was again hired to work in the industrial organization area and chose to develop my work on persistent differences in profits. Thus, during my second sustained stay at the IIM between 1981 and 1983, I once again found myself contacting scholars from different countries to investigate whether systematic differences in profitability exist across firms in other countries. This research eventually led to the set of studies published in Mueller (1990b). Again, however, I found time to pursue public choice questions. My colleague from Maryland, Peter Murrell, spent the 1982–3 academic year there also, and we began working on what would eventually become Mueller and Murrell (1986) and Mueller, Coughlin and Murrell (1990).

As a result of my year in Blacksburg, I became one of the many alumni of the Public Choice Center who reassemble at meetings of the Southern Economic Association, Public Choice Society and similar such occasions. I have formed many friendships within this group and always look forward to these reunions. I was therefore particularly flattered in 1985 to be asked to inaugurate the series of annual 'Virginia School' lectures. Having accepted the invitation, I found the task of writing the lecture far more difficult than I had anticipated. The page output per hour of input for this essay (Mueller 1985) is much lower than one is likely to guess upon reading it.

The *JEL* survey and the first edition of *Public choice* were written before I had ever taught a course in public choice. Once I did, I found some glaring lacunae in my original treatment of the public choice literature. Ronald Coase and the 'Coase theorem' were nowhere mentioned, while empirical questions like the causes of the growth of government were only touched upon. I had not intended that *Public choice* serve as a textbook, but when I began to teach in the area I found myself assigning it along with other readings. Although this decision might be dismissed as an obviously non-random event, I began to discover that other more objective instructors were doing the same. Thus, when I eventually decided to revise the book, I attempted to make it of greater pedagogic value to both the student and the teacher of public choice, while maintaining more or less the survey format. Accomplishing this objective and updating *Public choice* as a survey proved, as with its two predecessors, a far bigger task than I had anticipated. Indeed, the second edition so little resembled the first that I entertained giving it a different title – like *Collective choice*. But one of the most often quoted items in the survey article and first edition was my definition of public choice, and thus it seemed 'public choice' would have to be part of the title in some form. I decided to place a *II* behind *Public choice* to try to suggest that the book was an offspring of *Public choice*, but possibly one which was not a close sequel.

I took the occasion of my sabbatical year to tackle the rewriting of *Public choice*. The first half of that year (summer/autumn of 1986) was spent at Monash University in the suburbs of Melbourne (Australia). We had an extremely convenient apartment on campus, 100 metres from a fenced-in area operated by the University that contained kangaroos and wallabies. This proved to be a great attraction for my children and helped to remind me each day as I walked to my office of where I was. Our impression was that the Australians were an extremely friendly, open and helpful people. This was certainly true of Michael Porter, Richard Snape, Yew-Kwang Ng and others at Monash who were in a sense our immediate hosts.

Our next stop on my sabbatical year was Istanbul, where we lived for eight months. I had a Fulbright Fellowship to teach at Marmara University. Fortunately, the Dean of the Economics Faculty, Ahmet Serpil, allowed me to concentrate my teaching on a single day, and so I was able to make good progress on *Public choice II*. This good fortune increased in late February when a metre and a half of snow fell upon Istanbul. Such an event is unusual in most parts of the world – in Istanbul it is unusual to the point of being a near catastrophe. We were living in a charming apartment in an old house on a steep hill overlooking the Bosporus which, in good weather, we could reach by an invigorating 10-minute walk. (Uphill it was a 15-minute walk that took one past the point of being invigorated.) After the metre and a half of snow had fallen, we found ourselves in a location that would be completely inaccessible to any motorized vehicle for two weeks. During this period we in turn lost our telephone, water, electricity and eventually heat (the oil trucks could not even plough through). After the oil ran out, all members of the family were essentially confined to one room, which we were able to keep moderately warm with a propane space heater, a room which became at once our living room, dining room, playroom and my study. We learned that prolonged close physical proximity does not have an unambiguously positive impact on the strength of family bonds. My good fortune came from the fact that the two trunks full of books and articles I had brought with me were all in the apartment. Curiously, I made more progress on *Public choice II* then than in any other two-week interval during my sabbatical year.

In retrospect it is a wonder that I accomplished as much on *Public choice II* as I did during the eight months we were in Turkey. What a fascinating country it is to visit! The people we met, almost without exception, were wonderful to us. Anyone who has not visited Turkey should – for as long as they possibly can. Despite the many pleasant distractions of the orient, *Public choice II* was essentially finished by the time I got back to College Park in September of 1987. Unfortunately, Colin Day left Cambridge University Press for the University of Michigan Press at the end of that year, and the book's production suffered in consequence. Two full years elapsed before the somewhat less than up-to-date survey became available.

I had delayed my sabbatical by one year after being elected President of the Public Choice Society in 1984. Unlike the bigger professional associations to which economists belong (like the Southern or American Economic Associations), the Public Choice Society has no permanent staff or administrative officers. The person elected President automatically also becomes its Secretary, its Treasurer and all-round ambassador of goodwill. With the honour of being President comes the pleasure of organizing each of the two meetings of the society that occur under one's 'reign'. To have tried to organize one of these meetings from Australia or Turkey would have been folly of unbounded proportions.

I had chosen to have the 1986 meetings of the Society in Baltimore which is a great city in the upper tail of the distribution of cities in the US that are worth visiting. Unfortunately this fact does not appear to be well known to most members of the Public Choice Society and attendance was somewhat down that year. The weather was unusually chilly for Baltimore, however, and so when I gave my Presidential address, the room was filled to capacity. I chose the occasion to criticize the strong form of rationality often assumed in economics and public choice research. I reasoned that if I was going to preach to the profession, the Presidential podium was the best location from which to do it. I had fun and I gather at least some of the audience did. This address appears as Mueller (1986a). I have returned to this theme in my presidential address to both the European Association for Research in Industrial Economics (EARIE) and the International Joseph Schumpeter Society (Mueller 1992; forthcoming).

When Robert Tollison, Thomas Willett and I were together at Cornell, we discussed writing a quasi-normative book in which we would develop and extend the ideas about different voting rules that were contained in our jointly authored papers. Our simultaneous departures scuttled this project. The thought that such a book was needed has stayed with me over the 20 years since then. So much of public choice seems concerned with the failures of democratic government, with the impossibility of achieving this or that normative goal. But without denying the importance of these sorts of findings, I have been equally impressed with the cheerier results that public choice has produced. Some voting methods do work better than others; some even have quite attractive normative properties. While a perfect system of government may be unobtainable, we can do considerably better than at present in some democratic countries – and public choice can shed light on how such improvements could be brought about. This was, at any rate, the presumption upon which I began working on *Constitutional democracy* (1996). This book took an extremely long time to complete, in part because I had to sift through vast literatures of which I knew very little so as to bring as much accumulated knowledge as exists to bear on the question. Offshoots of this research also appeared as Mueller (1989a; 1991a; b; 1997).

During the summer of 1992 I made my first visit to East Asia, lecturing in Taiwan, Korea and Japan. On one occasion I presented 'Constitutional Rights' at a kind of miniconference graciously organized by Hirofume Shibata in Osaka that also included papers by Peggy and Richard Musgrave. As luck would have it, the three papers complemented one another quite nicely. Richard Musgrave's (1939) paper was on Knut Wicksell and the nature of government. As I listened to him speak, I recalled my first exposure to Wicksell's classic essay on government as a student in Musgrave's public finance course at Princeton. After 30 years, Musgrave had lost none of his enthusiasm for the ideas of Wicksell and for the subject of public economics. Nor had he lost the capacity to instil in his listeners that same enthusiasm. Anyone who reads my survey article of the public choice literature, its later book-length version, *Constitutional democracy*, or almost any of my other works in public choice will recognize that my thinking about government has also been greatly influenced by Wicksell's essay. It was Musgrave who first exposed me to Wicksell's ideas and made me aware of their importance.

Probably the only other modern economist to have been influenced as much by Knut Wicksell as Musgrave is James Buchanan. This is quite remarkable and a further tribute to the power of Wicksell's ideas since Musgrave and Buchanan are in many ways total opposites. Richard Musgrave is a liberal Democrat-type whom one would not have been surprised to find working in the Kennedy Administration. In terms of government, Richard Musgrave would almost certainly think first of the good it can do. James Buchanan is a libertarian conservative-type who on principle would undoubtedly refuse to be part of any administration. If he had worked in government he would probably have been most comfortable in a Reagan Administration. When James Buchanan considers Washington, he almost certainly thinks first of the evil that government can do.

Yet both men are indirectly students of Knut Wicksell. James Buchanan's first article was on the relevance of Wicksell's work to public finance (Buchanan 1949); Musgrave's (1939) first article was also on the 'voluntary exchange approach to government' introduced by Wicksell (although it dealt more directly with the work of Wicksell's student, Eric Lindahl). Wicksell's influence on Musgrave is most apparent in his division of the work of government into allocation and distribution branches (along with a third stabilization branch) in *The theory of public finance* (Musgrave 1959). Wicksell's influence on Buchanan is equally conspicuous in his separation of the work of government into two stages in *The calculus of consent* (Buchanan and Tullock 1962) and many of his other writings. Both men have had a profound influence on my thinking and on my appreciation of the importance of the ideas of Wicksell; indeed, of the importance of ideas in general. For perhaps the most significant characteristic that these two opposites have in common is the intensity of their regard for ideas, their belief in the power and importance of what we know.

I have never been asked to write specifically about Richard Musgrave and so my longest discussion of him is in this essay. However, I have been asked to consider the work of James Buchanan on several occasions (Mueller 1985; 1990a; 1998).

17.8   VIENNA SINCE 1994

Chance would again be an important factor in my next professional move. At one of the annual EARIE meetings in the early 1990s, I bumped into Jörg Finsinger, a former colleague of mine at the IIM in Berlin. He had recently taken up a professorship in the new business programme at the University of Vienna. Three chairs in economics had been created in conjunction with the initiation of this programme, and he asked me whether I knew any young economists in industrial organization that might be interested in a position in Vienna. My immediate response was to inquire how young one had to be to apply. Jörg Finsinger's mere mentioning of the possibility of a position in Europe had rekindled my Wanderlust. When I mentioned the possibility of returning to Europe to my wife, she too immediately responded positively. After some subsequent hesitation and delay, we found ourselves back in Europe, not as short-run visitors with a job and a home to return to, as we had been on previous occasions, however, but as immigrants who had permanently left their homeland.

When I announced my decision to leave Maryland, my long-time good friend and colleague, Mancur Olson, attempted to persuade me to stay, as he had successfully done in 1983, when I came very close to remaining in Berlin as the director of the IIM. One of the arguments Mancur used was that a move to Europe at my age might be interpreted as a decision 'to retire' from active professional life. I have never been especially concerned about 'my image' in the profession, and thus was not persuaded this time by Mancur's arguments. Upon arriving in Vienna, I became involved in several research projects – including yet another large international comparison study, this time of corporate governance systems. Add to this the additional teaching and administrative work that accompanies being a professor in Austria and, ironically, life in Vienna turned out to be if anything busier than at Maryland. Retirement will have to wait a few more years.

17.9   CONCLUSION

I am often asked why it is that I have chosen to work in such seemingly different fields as public choice and industrial organization. This question probably stems from the suspicion that I suffer from a rather bizarre form of schizophrenia, or perhaps that some fundamental, but hidden, similarities exist between the two fields. In fact I think there are important similarities between public choice and at least that part of industrial organization – firms and corporations – in which I have done most of my research. I view firms in

Coasian-Williamsonian terms as teams of factor owners brought together to achieve gains from cooperation in production. The peculiar form of organization that we identify as a firm – a hierarchy of individuals joined by rather vague and implicit contracts – arises to economize on the transaction and decision-making costs of markets, as well as on more market-like production arrangements that involve formal explicit contracts. Government, in turn, is an organization for economizing on decision-making costs in joint consumption activities.

Although the similarities between firms and governments seem obvious and fundamental to me now, I must confess that they only became apparent gradually in the course of my career studying both corporate and governmental institutions. The similarities were not evident to me from the outset, and my presence in both fields I attribute entirely to chance.

I conclude with the observation that chance events have played an important role in the course of my intellectual professional life. The gone astray notification of a fellowship in nuclear engineering at Columbia brought me to Princeton to study economics. Musgrave's one-semester leave when I first took public finance led me to write a dissertation in industrial organization instead of in public finance, and a long teaching and research career in this field. Robert Tollison's decision to take his first job at Cornell led indirectly to my spending a year at the Public Choice Center in Blacksburg, my meeting James Buchanan and Gordon Tullock, and a long teaching and research career in public choice. Chance encounters with old friends at the AEA and EARIE meetings on two separate occasions led to appointments in Berlin and Vienna. Whether chance holds more surprises and adventures for me, I of course cannot predict, but up until now, I would have to say that she has been fairly kind.

SELECTED WORKS

(1966) 'Determinants and effects of research and development', unpublished Ph.D. dissertation, Princeton University.

(1967) 'The possibility of a social welfare function: comment', *American Economic Review*, 57 (5), pp. 1304–11.

(1969) 'A theory of conglomerate mergers', *Quarterly Journal of Economics*, 83 (4), pp. 643–59.

(1969) (with J.E. Tilton) 'Research and development costs as a barrier to entry', *Canadian Journal of Economics*, 2 (4), pp. 570–9.

(1970) 'A theory of conglomerate mergers: reply', *Quarterly Journal of Economics*, 84 (4), pp. 674–9.

(1971) (with G.M. von Furstenberg) 'The Pareto optimal approach to income redistribution: a fiscal application', *American Economic Review*, 61 (4), pp. 628–37.*

(1972) 'A life cycle theory of the firm', *Journal of Industrial Economics*, 20 (3), pp. 199–219.

(1972) (with H.G. Grabowski) 'Managerial and stockholder welfare models of firm expenditures', *Review of Economics and Statistics*, 54 (1), pp. 9–24.

(1972) (with G.C. Philpotts and J. Vanek) 'The social gains from exchanging votes: a simulation approach', *Public Choice*, 13, 55–79.*

(1972) (with R.D. Tollison and T.D. Willett) 'Representative democracy via random selection', *Public Choice*, 12, pp. 57–68.*

(1974a) 'Achieving the just polity', *American Economic Review*, 64 (2, Papers & Proceedings), pp. 147–52.*

(1974b) 'Intergenerational justice and the social discount rate', *Theory and Decision*, 5 (3), pp. 263–73.*

(1974a) (with R.D. Tollison and T.D. Willett) 'The utilitarian contract: a generalization of Rawls' theory of justice', *Theory and Decision*, 4 (4), pp. 345–67.*

(1974b) (with R.D. Tollison and T.D. Willett) 'On equalizing the distribution of political income', *Journal of Political Economy*, 82 (2), pp. 414–22.* Rep. in J.M. Buchanan and R.D. Tollison (eds) (1984) **q.v.**, pp. 413–21.

(1975) (with H.G. Grabowski) 'Life-cycle effects on corporate returns on retentions', *Review of Economics and Statistics*, 57 (4), pp. 400–9.

(1975) (with R.D. Tollison and T.D. Willett) 'Solving the intensity problem in representative democracy', in R. Amacher, R.D. Tollison and T.D. Willett (eds) (1975) *Political economy and public policy: readings in the relevance of economics as a guide for social policy*. Ithaca: Cornell University Press, pp. 54–94.*

(1976) 'Public choice: a survey', *Journal of Economic Literature*, 14 (2), pp. 395–433.* Rep. in J.M. Buchanan and R.D. Tollison (eds) (1984) **q.v.**, pp. 23–37.

(1977) 'The persistence of profits above the norm', *Economica*, n.s. 44 (4), pp. 369–80.

(1978) 'Voting by veto', *Journal of Public Economics*, 10 (1), pp. 57–75.* Rep. in J.J. Laffont (eds) (1979) *Aggregation and the relevance of preferences*. Amsterdam: North-Holland, pp. 225–41 and (with corrections) in J.M. Buchanan and R.D. Tollison (eds) (1984) **q.v.**, pp. 23–67.

(1978) (with K. Cowling) 'The social costs of monopoly power', *Economic Journal*, 88 (4), pp. 727–48.

(1979) *Public choice*. Cambridge: Cambridge University Press.

(1980) (Ed.) *The determinants and effects of mergers: an international comparison*. Cambridge, MA: Oelgeschlager, Gunn and Hain.

(1980) (with R.L. Marris) 'The corporation, competition and the invisible hand', *Journal of Economic Literature*, 18 (1), pp. 32–63. Rep. (abridged version) in E. Mansfield (ed.) (1985) *Microeconomics: selected readings*, 5th edn. New York: W.W. Norton, pp. 91–104.

(1984) 'Voting by veto and majority rule', in H. Hanusch (ed.) (1984) *Public finance and the quest for efficiency*. Detroit: Wayne State University Press, pp. 69–85.*

(1984) (with F.R. FitzRoy) 'Cooperation and conflict in contractual organizations', *Quarterly Review of Economics and Business*, 24 (4), pp. 24–49.

(1985) 'The "Virginia school" and public choice'. Lectures on Virginia Political Economy, Centre for Study of Public Choice, George Mason University, April.*

(1986a) 'Rational egoism versus adaptive egoism as fundamental postulate for a descriptive theory of human behavior', *Public Choice*, 51 (1), pp. 3–23.*

(1986b) *The modern corporation: profits, power, growth and performance*. Brighton: Wheatsheaf Books.

(1986c) 'An autobiographical essay', in D.C. Mueller (1986b) **q.v.**, pp. ix–xx.

(1986d) *Profits in the long run*. Cambridge: Cambridge University Press.

(1986) (with P. Murrell) 'Interest groups and the size of government', *Public Choice*, 48 (2), pp. 125–45.*

(1987) *The corporation: growth, diversification and mergers*. London: Harwood Academic.

(1989a) 'Individualism, contractarianism and morality', *Social Justice Research*, 3 (1), pp. 1–19.*

(1989b) 'Probabilistic majority rule', *Kyklos*, 42 (2), pp. 151–69.*

(1989c) *Public choice II: a revised edition of Public choice*. Cambridge: Cambridge University Press.

(1990a) 'James M. Buchanan: economist cum contractarian', *Constitutional Political Economy*, 1 (2), pp. 169–96.*

(1990b) (Ed.) *The dynamics of company profits*. Cambridge: Cambridge University Press.

(1990) (with P.J. Coughlin and P. Murrell) 'Electoral politics, interest groups and the size of government', *Economic Inquiry*, 28 (4), pp. 682–705.*

(1991a) 'Choosing a constitution in east Europe: lessons from public choice', *Journal of Comparative Economics*, 15 (2), pp. 325–48.*

(1991b) 'Constitutional rights', *Journal of Law, Economics and Organization*, 7 (2), pp. 313–33.*

(1993a) *The public choice approach to politics*. Aldershot: Edward Elgar.

(1993b) 'Introduction', in D.C. Mueller (1993a) **q.v.**, pp. xii–xxii.

(1993c) 'The future of public choice', *Public Choice*, 77 (1), pp. 145–50.*

(1997) 'Federalism and the European Union: a constitutional perspective', *Public Choice*, 90 (1–4), pp. 255–80. Rep. in C.K. Rowley (ed.) (1997) *Constitutional political economy in a public choice perspective*. Dordrecht: Kluwer, pp. 255–80.

(1998) 'Buchanan, James McGill', in P. Newman (ed.) (1998) *The new Palgrave dictionary of economics and the law*. London: Macmillan, vol. 1, pp. 179–85.

(1998) (with S.L. Yun) 'Rates of return over the firm's lifecycle', *Industrial and Corporate Change*, 7 (2), pp. 347–68.

(forthcoming) 'Capitalism, democracy and rational individual behavior', *Journal of Evolutionary Economics*.

BIBLIOGRAPHY

Buchanan, J.M. (1949) 'The pure theory of government finance: a suggested approach', *Journal of Political Economy*, 57 (6), pp. 496–505.

Buchanan, J.M. and Tollison, R.D. (eds) (1984) *The theory of public choice II*. Ann Arbor, MI: University of Michigan Press.

Buchanan, J.M. and Tullock, G. (1962) *The calculus of consent: logical foundations of constitutional democracy*. Ann Arbor, MI: University of Michigan Press.

Coleman, J. (1966) 'The possibility of a social welfare function', *American Economic Review*, 56 (5), pp. 1105–22.

Comanor, W.S. and Smiley, R.H. (1975) 'Monopoly and the distribution of wealth', *Quarterly Journal of Economics*, 89 (2), pp. 177–94.

Hochman, H.M. and Rodgers, J.D. (1969) 'Pareto optimal redistribution', *American Economic Review*, 59 (4), pp. 542–57.

Jensen, M.C. and Meckling, W.H. (1976) 'Theory of the firm: managerial behavior, agency costs and ownership structure', *Journal of Financial Economics*, 3 (2), pp. 305–60.

Marglin, S.A. (1974) 'What do bosses do?: the origins and functions of hierarchy in capitalist production', *Review of Radical Political Economy*, 6 (2), pp. 33–60.

Marris, R.L. (1964) *The economic theory of 'managerial' capitalism*. London: Macmillan.

Musgrave, R.A. (1939) 'The voluntary exchange theory of public economy', *Quarterly Journal of Economics*, 53 (2), pp. 213–37.

Musgrave, R.A. (1959) *The theory of public finance: a study in public economy*. London: McGraw-Hill.

Vanek, J. (1970) *The general theory of labour-managed market economies*. Ithaca, NY: Cornell University Press.

18. Orley Ashenfelter (b. 1942)[1]

Photograph by Denise Applewhite
Princeton University

Did you grow up in an environment that might have led you to become interested in economics?

Yes. The main thing that made me interested in economics was unemployment. In the area where I lived in California there was always a very noticeable boom and bust business cycle. Many people moved into and out of unemployment from time to time and I was always struck by the presence of unemployment and interested in it. Although only unemployed once or twice, my own father worried about his job prospects all of his adult life.

Were there people in your family or others early in your childhood who influenced your decision to choose economics?

No, not at all. No one in my family even went to college, so the idea of being a professor wasn't a very common one in my family. It was definitely uncommon. My interest in academic economics was stimulated by Orme

---

[1] Hallock and Ashenfelter (1997), an interview of the former by the latter, as revised by the authors. I have three volumes of collected writings in the series: the first assembles my papers on employment, labor unions and wages (Ashenfelter 1997a); the second, those on education, training and discrimination (Ashenfelter 1997b); and the third, those on economic institutions and the demand and supply of labor.

Phelps, a labor economist in the college I attended, who convinced me and several other people to study and specialize in labor economics in graduate school.

Did you go into college knowing you wanted to study economics?

No, I didn't. I primarily studied economics, but I did it mainly because the small college – Claremont McKenna College in 1964 – I went to had a very substantial economics program. The college was built around, in part, economics, so there were probably more economics courses to take than would normally be available in a small college. I also found that I liked the subject of economics because it seemed like such a natural way to think about important problems.

When did you decide that you were going to go to graduate school and become an academic?

The professor I mentioned earlier, Orme Phelps, convinced me to give it a try. And, to some extent I was lured to graduate school by economic incentives; that is, a pretty good fellowship.

Were there places other than Princeton you applied?

Oh sure. Especially in California; Berkeley, in particular.

What made you decide to come so far to Princeton?

If you lived in California when I did, Ivy League schools had a certain magic sound to them. In addition, I knew I wanted to study labor economics from the beginning, so I tried to learn which were the good places to go. At that time Fred Harbison, Dick Lester, and Bill Bowen were all active at Princeton and it seemed like a good place.

When you were a student at Princeton what was it like? Were there other students you are still in contact with?

It was a very lively place with quite a few very good people who were attracted to the subject, people that I wrote a lot of papers with: Jim Heckman, who's at The University of Chicago, John Pencavel who's at Stanford University. There were also many visitors around, like George Johnson of the University of Michigan, and a string of others.

Who were your advisors?

I'm not sure who my final advisors were. I started with Bill Bowen, but he went on to be an administrator. I'm sure he wasn't on my committee. I think probably Dick Quandt and Steve Goldfeld were on it, and I think Al Rees at the end. Al had just moved to Princeton from the University of Chicago while I was a student.

I'm sort of curious about how you transformed from being a student to a faculty member at Princeton. Your thesis is dated 1970 but you joined the faculty in 1968 and went to Washington for a bit (which we'll get to in a minute) but then became Director of the Industrial Relations Section only a few years later in 1973. How did all this happen?

Well, I started teaching in 1968. I didn't have my dissertation finished so the actual date of the dissertation was 1970. I had published quite a few articles by then but I had never been happy that I had enough material to make a dissertation on the topic I had chosen, which was the economics of discrimination. I felt I needed to get enough material in order to have a dissertation on that one topic. I felt very strongly about the importance of the subject, but it took a while to get three papers that were substantial enough to really make up a Ph.D. thesis. In fact one of the three essays was never actually published.[2] I never was entirely happy with it.

I became Director of the Industrial Relations Section at a very tender age primarily because of the shortage of labor economists in the Princeton Department. The senior people had all taken other positions, mainly as administrators. Dick Lester had become Dean of the Faculty, Bill Bowen had become Provost (and subsequently President) of the University, and Fred Harbison became heavily involved in development economics and had his main appointment in the Woodrow Wilson School (of Public and International Affairs at Princeton). Al Rees often served as Chair of the Department, and also spent a number of years in Washington and as Provost of the University also. So there really weren't that many people available for the job. In fact, I was the only senior faculty member in labor economics who was active here for a number of years.

Going back to the thesis. It seems today that students can write a thesis on three or four entirely separate topics. Do you think the movement from more of a book style thesis to a group of not necessarily related topics is a bad one?

---

2   'The inter-industry structure of the relative wages of negro workers'. The other two papers are Ashenfelter (1970; 1972).

I think it is probably a good thing, but at the time I wrote my dissertation it was unusual to even have a series of essays. Normally the dissertation was supposed to be a book, and certainly if you had a series of essays they ought to be on the same topic! Today no one seems to think that's important and I think that's a better system really.

Between when you joined the faculty and became Director of the Industrial Relations Section you went to Washington to become Director of the Office of Evaluation in the Department of Labor. Aside from that year in the Department of Labor and testifying before Congress a few times you've not really been in Washington too much. Do you feel that economists should try to influence government policy or was this a personal preference?

Well it depends on the opportunities you get. I had an unusual opportunity to go to Washington in a position that actually involved trying to generate information about government programs and their effectiveness in the labor market. That's a little different from trying to influence policy directly. I was more interested in trying to find out what the policies did, if anything. My position in Washington was unusual because it was very helpful with my research and it got me interested in topics that are both interesting as economic analysis and very important for public policy.

But the business of being an advisor, a policy advisor, is really a different thing and I think it depends a little on your age. I don't think it makes a lot of sense for someone who's a very inexperienced economist to become a policy advisor because they don't really know how to participate in the politics that goes with policy making. I was never too terribly interested in being an advisor to governments because I wasn't sure I knew what advice to give them. (laughter)

How have you seen the evolution of labor economics in the past 30 years? Are there questions that labor economists had in 1965 that have now been solved? Are there things that still need lots of work or you feel haven't really been explored at all? What about the switch away from Industrial Relations?

Well there are some things, I think, that are known. Sometimes people think that there's no progress, but there's definitely progress in knowledge. I think most of the real progress has been in our ability to measure things that we didn't have data on a long time ago. For example a big issue of controversy that I wrote about in my own dissertation was the impact of trade unions on black workers. Now at the time that I worked on that subject we didn't actually know what the racial composition of trade union membership was in the US because there was no survey question that people answered about whether they were in unions. I found out in some early tabulations that, in fact, black workers were just about as likely to belong to trade unions as white workers and I actually wrote a paper in which I anticipated that they would become more likely to belong to unions than white workers, a prediction which was correct. The idea that blacks were excluded from trade unions was probably false from around 1940 onward and I think most people now may actually know that is the case. So in a way it seems like an elementary point, but it was an extremely major political dispute at one time and it's essentially a dead one now. I think the issue was resolved, in part, by new research which correctly concluded that trade unions probably are not harmful to black workers and certainly haven't been in the postwar period.

On the other hand, on most of the biggest questions I don't think we have made as much progress as we would like. For example, probably the most important question in labor economics is the role of incentives in people's behavior, but the magnitude of incentive effects on people's behavior is still a pretty much open question. So with respect to some of the most important questions I don't think there's been all that much progress, although there's been some.

Do you think the computer has changed empirical labor economics?

I don't actually think the computer has changed labor economics all that much because the subject has always been very empirical, and the measurement of how the labor market works has always been a major part of the labor economics job description. It is true that the use of the computer has made some important questions easier to study, but I don't think the use of computers in our research has been the major force causing changes.

What would you say are your most important papers or contributions if you had to select a few?

No one ever likes to say which are their most important papers because they like to think everything is very important. I'm no different than anybody else in that regard!

Which ones maybe had the biggest impact?

Well I think actually the papers that are the best papers in some ways haven't had as big an impact as I would have hoped. A paper that's had a fairly big impact is the paper I wrote on training programs and evaluating their effectiveness (Ashenfelter 1978a) – that spawned a whole literature, and justifiably so. It was an area that was an important subject for government policy and developing methods to study the question of whether training programs pay off was an important question. I think my interest in that topic probably stimulated other people to be interested in it too. In fact, generally speaking, you could say the research I've done on evaluating the effect of government behavior on institutions in the labor market is my most important work.

On the other hand, my paper on the determinants of participation in income maintenance programs (Ashenfelter 1983) makes the simple point that people with low incomes are more likely to be in those programs, regardless of the incentive effects of the programs. I think this is a paper with a very important set of ideas, but it has never really had much impact on the study of poverty programmes. Hardly anybody appears to understand it. So I don't think the quality of the paper really tells you what the influence is going to be.

Judging by citations, a very influential paper is the piece George Johnson and I wrote on bargaining and strike activity (Ashenfelter and Johnson 1969). In a way it sets out a formal model of what most people in the field of industrial relations thought was a sensible way to think about strikes. From the view point of many economists this model is not logically pure. And I tend to agree that there are some aspects of the problem that are not fully worked out in that paper. On the other hand, the paper seems to have had a big influence because it captures some aspects of the actual behavior of trade unions. But it's not clear that it should have such a big influence. (laughter)

All of the papers concerning unions that are included in the Edward Elgar volumes are from the 1970s. What do you think about the decline of unionism in the United States and what does this mean for economic research on unionism and for those papers?

I think it's an interesting fact that unions have declined in scale in the United States, although in other countries they haven't declined in the same way. I think that something has been lost by US workers as a result of the decline of trade unions. In particular, trade unions have always served as agents for workers and they tended to be cost-effective agents. Most workers would like to have an agent to negotiate for them with their employer, but generally speaking the cost of an agent is too great relative to the salary of an ordinary worker to make this affordable. I believe that trade unions have often served as cost-effective agents. It's no accident that unions have always found it easier to organize into large establishments and into industries where large establishments prevailed because these are the places where they are most cost-effective. The difficulty with most trade unions is that the standardization that you need in order to get cost-effective representation as an agent doesn't seem to fit with the modern way that firms are evolving where growth is heavily involved in smaller firms rather than larger firms and more flexibility in the work environment is a major order of the day. As a result I think the thing that unions did well, which was to serve as cost-effective agents, is something that they are finding it difficult to do now. Workers are probably going to have to find some other mechanism if they are going to be able to afford agents in the same way as they have in the past. I think that is the disadvantage of declining unionization in the US.

On the other hand, there is an advantage to workers in the decline in trade unions. The advantage is that there were always some trade unions, not all, maybe even a minority, that took advantage of the fact that they were agents and sometimes violated the interests of the principal that they were supposed to be representing. This is a classic problem. Extreme cases, as in the United Mine Workers, resulted in widespread corruption, even murder. In addition, trade unions may sometimes have adversely influenced resource allocation and harmed the efficiency of the economy.

On the whole I think the demise of trade unions in the US has probably had a deleterious effect on workers. Still, I don't see how trade unions in a capitalist economy like the US could have kept going the way they did unless some new institution evolved. In practice the trade union movement is really not a major force in the US and probably never will be again.

You mentioned earlier that you became interested in economics because of the high unemployment you saw growing up. What do you think about full employment and recent unemployment and what do you think we have learned about unemployment in the last 30 years?

I think the unemployment issue is still a major puzzle. I wrote one paper with the simple title, 'What is involuntary unemployment?' (Ashenfelter 1978b) and I wrote several other papers that addressed the same question (for example, Ashenfelter 1980). They were all inspired by the same idea, which is that unemployment is behavior off a person's supply curve – in that sense it's involuntary. Unfortunately, even though I think that's correct, having said that, I don't think it leads automatically to a clear-cut discussion of what kinds of public policy we should engage in. Unemployment is a problem in the US, but frankly it's a much bigger problem in other countries and many other countries look to the US now to see how we have set up our institutions to try to reduce unemployment. I don't think it's clear what exactly it is about our institutions that makes unemployment lower. The unemployment question is one of the most difficult in economics and I think some things that have been said about it are useful. I think, for example, the fact that people are off their supply curves some of the time is what unemployment means and I think the evidence that they are off their supply curves is pretty substantial. Unfortunately, constructing a model of the labor market where people are off their supply curves that actually has testable and empirical implications is difficult to do. I don't think it's been successfully done yet.

What are your thoughts on dispute resolution, both legal and otherwise, and do you think what economists have studied in regards to dispute resolution could help change things?

I think the discussion of dispute resolution by economists including papers, some of which I co-authored with Henry Farber (Ashenfelter *et al.* 1992) and David Bloom (for example, Ashenfelter and Bloom 1984) but also in work that Bloom and Farber, and Harry Katz (see Farber and Katz 1979; Bloom 1986) have done should be more broadly understood by people who study dispute resolution problems and, in particular, by anybody who studies the operation of the legal system. The approach that economists have taken to study arbitration, I think, is the correct model for understanding litigation and the American legal system. Unfortunately very few people in the law and economics field are aware of this material. In fact, to some extent, I think this material will have to be introduced into the law and economics literature before it makes any progress.

A simple statement of the main point in this literature is in my paper 'Arbitration and the negotiation process: arbitrator behavior' (Ashenfelter 1987); empirical evidence is presented in 'Models of arbitrator behavior: theory and evidence' (Ashenfelter and Bloom 1984) and in 'An experimental comparison of dispute rates in alternative arbitration systems' (Ashenfelter *et al.* 1992). All of those papers outline the dispute resolution process as one where a third party arbitrator (or judge or jury) is characterized as having an element of randomness in his or her decision. I've come to believe that that's the crucial characteristic of most dispute resolution systems, including the Anglo-American legal system. I don't think this is widely understood by very many people. The reason that the third party's decision must be random is because if it is not, the two parties can predict what the outcome will be, and so they will not agree to use the third party. Thus, there has to be a component of the process which is unpredictable in order to get the acceptance of the two parties to the dispute to accept the decision of a third party.

This is the secret, for example, to the jury system. Juries are unpredictable and the fact that they are unpredictable is what allows the system to be acceptable to the parties. This basic point is not very well understood and its implications are not very well understood by lawyers or by anybody else. It implies, for example, that there's inevitably going to be *ex-post* horizontal inequity because different juries, in the same factual situations, are going to make different decisions. I think a great deal of misunderstanding about all dispute resolution systems results from the failure to recognize this simple point and its implications. This is an area where a great deal more work will have to be done before it's ever going to have the impact that it should have. That's a shame.

How would you assess the current debate over the minimum wage?

The minimum wage is an important subject primarily because it's a crucial public policy test of the notion that firms are operating on downward sloping labor demand curves. I think the argument over the minimum wage in public policy discussions is blown out of all proportion to its actual impact on the economy. But, it's politically controversial because it focuses in one very specific way on what economists say about demand curves. I have always been suspicious that the impact of the minimum wage on the economy is much smaller than people – economists in particular – have claimed. I originally thought that because of some work which I did with Bob Smith called 'Compliance with the minimum wage law' (Ashenfelter and Smith 1979), where we discovered when I worked in the Labor department that there was no penalty for the failure to comply with the minimum wage law. Ignorance of the law is actually a defense in the courts. We discovered that the typical penalty for non-compliance with the minimum wage was that you pay what you would have paid if you had been paying the minimum wage in the first place. So I always suspected that if the minimum wage law had a dramatic effect on the economy, then we'd see lots of non-compliance. You do see some non-compliance, there's no doubt about that, but I don't think it's on a massive scale.

More recently, of course, David Card and Alan Krueger have been studying the effect of the minimum wage on employment directly (Card and Krueger 1995). One paper, written with David Card over ten years ago (Ashenfelter and Card 1981), was an attempt by the two of us to test for the effects of the minimum wage on employment. It's a very straightforward kind of test, but we never published it because we were not entirely happy with our implementation of it. The idea behind the test is that, according to the conventional theory, many workers who are earning less than the minimum wage ought to lose their jobs if it's really the case that their output is worth less than what they are paid. For the empirical analysis we studied what happened to people who were earning below the new minimum wage in the year before the minimum was raised in 1973. In fact, we didn't find any evidence that people who were paid below the minimum were less likely to be employed in the year after the minimum wage increase than those who were paid above. So we did not find much evidence of the effect of the minimum wage on employment in what I thought was a pretty convincing study. In general it has always been difficult to find convincing empirical evidence of the effect of the minimum wage on employment. Most recently there have been some studies that seem to show a positive effect of the minimum wage on employment. That may not be the correct answer either, but I do think the power of economists' empirical work in finding minimum wage effects has always been overstated.

Can you describe how your thesis fits into the discrimination literature and what do you perceive as the major differences in issues in the economics of discrimination today as compared with what they were when you first began studying discrimination?

Actually two of the essays in the Edward Elgar volumes were in my Ph.D. dissertation (Ashenfelter 1970; 1972). A follow-on paper (Ashenfelter and Godwin 1971) is very closely related to that same work. I think most of the issues are very similar today to what they were then. There's never been a completely satisfactory theory of the economics of discrimination. The best statement we can make is that discrimination wouldn't be rational if people, employers and employees, were strict cost minimizers. I think that discrimination is best characterized the way Gary Becker (1957) characterized it as a taste or a preference which somehow the forces of the market do not discipline sufficiently to keep from appearing in the form of wage differences or employment differences as between blacks and whites or males and females or between other groups. I think the question of why the market doesn't discipline these preferences enough is still an important puzzle that is not fully resolved. So I don't think there has been great progress on the theory beyond what existed thirty years ago.

On the other hand, I think that the actual measurement of the extent of discrimination has progressed quite dramatically because there is so much more data available to study this question than there was 30 years ago. When I studied the effect of trade unions on racial discrimination 30 years ago, it was the first time that there were actually micro data available on blacks and whites and their wages and whether they belonged to trade unions. The existence of data like that has allowed us to make some progress.

Probably the main area that hasn't really been touched on by economists is the question of discrimination based on age. Age discrimination is not a subject which is heavily studied by economists and it's not clear what model one would use. The possible existence of age discrimination in employment pops up constantly in popular discussions and certainly in court cases, but economists have not, on the whole, addressed this issue. Since everybody inevitably ages, the discussion of this subject necessarily involves some analysis of life-cycle decision making that is not a characteristic of most of the other studies of discrimination.

One of the big issues in labor economics is that of labor supply. How would you sum up what we have learned about labor supply in the last 30 years and do we still have a lot to learn?

Well, I agree with you that the incentive question is the most important question, not just in labor economics, but probably in economics generally. What we've learned is that it's very difficult to measure the incentives in people's labor supply decisions. I think that this might be the one area where there's been more research and less genuine progress than almost any other area where I have worked. I don't know why that's true. I don't really know how to tackle the question of measuring incentives in a way that's different from what I've done and I don't think that the work that has been done has been very successful at isolating incentives.

To some extent I think that the work that was done with the negative income tax experiments represents an example where we missed the boat because those experiments really should have had a better data collection mechanism than they had. Data collection wasn't done through administrative records, but instead was done through ordinary surveys. As a result there was a lot of attrition from those surveys, and much of the data from those experiences was really squandered. I didn't actually realize the extent of the problem until we wrote Ashenfelter and Plant (1990). It is possible that we may not make any really dramatic progress in the study of labor supply until we have the chance to engage in field experiments again. Although I still think that bright people tackling the question might be able to make some further progress. The result of what research we have is that it's hard to make credible claims about the strength of labor supply incentives. Most of the evidence is consistent with possibly weak incentive effects in male labor supply, and somewhat stronger effects in female labor supply, but I think even that is open to some question.

What would you say are the ingredients of a good paper?

For me a really good paper addresses an important question, lays out a model of behavior that's being explored, and then provides a really convincing empirical test of the question involved. That's a really classic and excellent paper and I should add that there aren't very many of them.

It seems that many authors have trademarks in their papers. Is there such a thing as an Ashenfelter paper and what are the characteristics?

The only thing I can think of that's in common amongst these papers is that I have tried to write them so they are clear – so that you can actually understand the English that's in the paper, and so the exposition is good enough so that someone can follow it without great difficulty. Other than that, I don't think there's any particular trademark.

If you could resolve one issue in labor economics what would it be?

Oh, I would like to know what the incentive effects are in the labor supply behavior. I'd like to know how to produce a model that would allow me to predict with real confidence the effects of taxation or legislative changes on various aspects of a person's budget constraint and how that would affect their labor supply.

Some of your current work studies auctions and other market and non-market institutions. Would you like to summarize some of this work?

Well auctions are fascinating and I got into them because I was trying to learn about a market where it is easiest to buy the product at an auction: older wines. It was fascinating because as I went to the auctions and collected data on them, I came to see that some of the things that happened in the auction are not what I'd expected as an economist. So in a way I was led to study auctions because of the anomalies I saw. But I really use auctions for two purposes. One is to collect data on prices in the market place. I think that the auction system provides an extraordinarily good indicator of value in the market place – much better, for example, than posted prices because you never know when a person posts a price whether or not the thing sold for that price. So the auction system has this great advantage that people buy things, you know that a transaction took place, the price is recorded, and in a typical auction system the protocol is that you're supposed to report the price so the public will know what it was. The primary value of auctions to economists is that you get to see prices for actual transactions. You don't have to worry about whether a transaction took place. That's the main reason I find auctions interesting.

Of course, the other reason auctions are interesting is that economists have a clear idea about how market prices should behave in an auction. For example in a paper I wrote, called 'How auctions work for wine and art' (Ashenfelter 1989), I learned that a lot of people write about auctions without understanding how they actually work. But I also learned that, for example, if two identical lots of wine are sold, it's more likely that the price will go down for the second lot than that it will go up, although what is most likely is that it will sell at the same price. I call this the declining price anomaly, and I found that it was also true in a paper that I did about real estate auctions

(Ashenfelter and Genesove 1992). Auctions are interesting institutions in themselves, but they are especially interesting because they generate very useful information about what the market is doing.

You have many recent papers focusing on the returns to education. How do you perceive the current debate over the return to education?

I think that most economists now think that we have underestimated the economic returns to schooling. In part this is because the return to schooling is at a historical relative high in the United States. In addition, I think it's likely that some economists have underestimated the economic returns to schooling for econometric reasons. This all suggests that schooling may have an even bigger redistributional impact on earnings than we once thought.

At Princeton you teach an undergraduate course in econometrics and you also teach in the graduate labor economics sequence. Do you like to teach and how do you perceive your relationship with your students?

I do like teaching, although I like to teach subjects where either I'm actively involved in research or where I have some missionary zeal. I teach econometrics to undergraduates and I have some missionary zeal there even though I'm typically teaching material that is very well known. In labor economics, we have a set-up at Princeton where several of us teach together in a year-long graduate course. By having several of us teach in the course it makes it possible to teach the material that you are more comfortable with either because you are actively researching it at the time or because you have a little missionary zeal you can use in talking about it.

Could you tell me a little about your current and recent research including papers with David Bloom, Alan Krueger, and David Zimmerman?

Yes. One part of my current research involves the economic returns to schooling. Two of those papers are an attempt to grapple with the issue of whether the observed correlations between schooling and income are really due to the schooling or due to some ability factors that haven't been measured. One is a study of fathers and sons and brothers (Ashenfelter and Zimmerman 1997) and the other is a study of twins (Ashenfelter and Krueger 1994). Both studies indicate that it's really the schooling and not the ability that's causing the income of the better educated person to be higher. I think that's an important subject. I think there's an increasing consensus that the burden of proof strongly suggests that schooling has a very substantial economic payoff, although it's still not definitive.

The other paper is an extremely controversial paper on lawyers. In it I show how the legal system may be set up such that the costs and benefits associated with legal representation give incentives very much like the prisoners' dilemma. It's a controversial paper, in my opinion, because no one really wants to hear, certainly lawyers don't want to hear, that what they're doing may not really be productive but is instead an artificial reaction to a set of incentives which are derived from the Anglo-American legal set-up (Ashenfelter and Bloom 1993). Others have written papers about this topic, but this particular paper is empirical and provides some evidence that the incentives in the legal system are like the prisoners' dilemma. It's an interesting subject.

I also wanted to ask about what is known as natural experiments. What really is the debate and how do you see this?

Well, it's about credibility. It's *an* important subject. What it's really about is establishing causation in a credible way when experimentation is not possible. For example, when we measure the effect of schooling on income we'd like to believe that the differences in schooling we use are really exogenous differences that cause income differences. So this is really a debate about credibility. A good natural experiment inevitably falls slightly short of what would be even better, a real experiment where the investigator has genuine control over the variable he or she is trying to measure the effect of. So, for example, in a real experiment with schooling we'd randomize some people into different schooling levels and observe the differences in incomes that come out of that process. There are cases where we can actually use randomized trials, but it's often difficult to do in economics. When it's difficult to do experimentation you have to worry about the credibility of your results. A natural experiment is just a way of explaining that you think that you are studying the effect of something that is really exogenous.

You have become increasingly popular in some quarters and decreasingly popular in others as a result of your recent interest in wine. Would you like to describe what it's all about?

Well it's an interesting subject which is becoming more and more mysterious to me. What I discovered was that there was a very good empirical or statistical relationship between the weather and the quality of grapes and thus between the weather and the quality of the wine made from the grapes. In particular, the price of older French wines is very closely related to the weather that created the vintage. What's interesting about this finding is that it implies that once the weather is complete you can say quite a bit about what the wines will be like without even having to make the wines, let alone taste them.

The controversy results from the fact that much of the wine trade doesn't like to have this information available, since they're usually in a position where they are trying to sell the wines at prices that are unrelated to their long-term quality. So I get in trouble because it's possible for me to tell people whether or not the wines are really going to be any good and to give them advice about whether they ought to buy them or not quite independently of what the so-called expert tasters say.

The increasing mystery to me is that the whole procedure is so logical, and yet it has no effect on the market. It's no more than saying that good weather makes good grapes and good grapes make good wine, and all this can be measured. Most economists and statisticians find the connection between the weather data and the prices extremely convincing. What's getting to be more mysterious is that it doesn't have any influence on the market. People simply do not use the readily available information on the weather, which is fairly easy to come by, in making decisions about buying. Otherwise the prices would adjust in the short run to make the price of the wine reflect the weather. But generally speaking the prices reflect the weather only when the wines are quite old. This seems to be an example of a very inefficient market, one that can't use really elementary information. This is what makes it so interesting for economic analysis.

It seems that of your co-authored papers, many are written with former students. Why is that?

It's because I've always thought that collaborative research was a good idea and one of the ways to collaborate is with students. Also, I've had many good students, and so I've always wanted to work with them. Working with students is one way to engage in the educational process that makes it a two-way street. Lots of my co-authors, even though students, taught me things that I wouldn't have known if they hadn't taught it to me!

You started as a student at Princeton in 1966 and have stayed here ever since. Surely you have been asked by other universities to join them. Why have you stayed at Princeton?

Well, the main reason is that for me Princeton has always been a very good place to work. There are extremely good resources in the labor economics field at Princeton and there has been an evolving commitment from the University to be sure that we have the best people and access to resources for research. Although I have been tempted to leave, and may even eventually do so, there is a long tradition of labor economists having an easy life at Princeton.

SELECTED WORKS

(1969) (with G.E. Johnson) 'Bargaining theory, trade unions and industrial strike activity', *American Economic Review*, 59 (1), 35–49.

(1970) 'Changes in labor market discrimination over time', *Journal of Human Resources*, 5 (4), pp. 403–30.

(1971) (with L.I. Godwin) 'Some evidence on the effect of unionism on the average wage of black workers relative to white workers, 1900–1967', in G.G. Somers (ed.) *Proceedings of the 24th annual winter meeting of the Industrial Relations Association*, December, pp. 217–24.

(1972) 'Racial discrimination and trade unionism', *Journal of Political Economy*, 80 (3), pp. 435–64.

(1978a) 'Estimating the effect of training programs on earnings', *Review of Economics and Statistics*, 60 (1), pp. 47–57.

(1978b) 'What is involuntary unemployment?', *Proceedings of the American Philosophical Society*, 122 (3), pp. 135–8.

(1979) (with R.S. Smith) 'Compliance with the minimum wage law', *Journal of Political Economy*, 87 (2), pp. 333–50.

(1980) 'Unemployment as disequilibrium in a model of aggregate labor supply', *Econometrica*, 48 (3), pp. 547–64.

(1981) (with D. Card) 'Using longitudinal data to estimate the effects of the minimum wage', unpublished paper.

(1983) 'Determining participation in income-tested social programs', *Journal of the American Statistical Association*, 78 (383), pp. 517–25.

(1984) (with D.E. Bloom) 'Models of arbitrator behavior: theory and evidence', *American Economic Review*, 74 (1), pp. 111–24.

(1985) (with D. Card) 'Using the longitudinal structure of earnings to estimate the effect of training programs', *Review-of-Economics-and-Statistics*, 67 (4), pp. 648–60.

(1987) 'Arbitration and the negotiation process: arbitrator behavior', *American Economic Review*, 77 (2, Papers & Proceedings), pp. 342–6.

(1989) 'How auctions work for wine and art', *Journal of Economic Perspectives*, 3 (3), pp. 23–36.

(1990) (with M.W. Plant) 'Non-parametric estimates of the labor-supply effects of negative income tax programs', *Journal of Labor Economics*, 8 (1, pt. 2), pp. S396–S415.

(1992) (with J. Currie, H.S. Farber and M. Spiegel) 'An experimental comparison of dispute rates in alternative arbitrations systems', *Econometrica*, 60 (6), pp. 1407–33.*

(1992) (with D. Genesove) 'Testing for price anomalies in real estate auctions', *American Economic Review*, 82 (2, Papers & Proceedings), pp. 501–5.

(1993) (with D. Bloom) 'Lawyers as agents of the devil in a prisoner's dilemma game', NBER Working Paper no 4447.

(1994) (with A.B. Krueger) 'Estimates of the economic return to schooling from a new sample of twins', *American Economic Review*, 84 (5), pp. 1157–73.

(1997a) *Collected essays*, ed. K. Hallock. Vol. I: *Employment, labor unions and wages*. Cheltenham: Edward Elgar.

(1997b) *Collected essays*, ed. K. Hallock. Vol. II: *Education, training and discrimination*. Cheltenham: Edward Elgar.

(1997c) *Collected essays*, ed. K. Hallock. Vol. III: *Economic institutions and the demand and supply of labor*. Cheltenham: Edward Elgar.

(1997) (with K.F. Hallock) 'Introduction', in O.C. Ashenfelter (1997a) **q.v.**, pp. ix–xxii.

(1997) (with D. Zimmerman) 'Estimates of the return to schooling from sibling data: fathers, sons and brothers', *Review of Economics and Statistics*, 79 (1), pp. 1–9.

BIBLIOGRAPHY

Becker, G. (1957) *The economics of discrimination*. Chicago: University of Chicago Press.

Bloom, D. (1986) 'Empirical models of arbitrator behavior under conventional arbitration', *Review of Economics and Statistics*, 68 (4), pp. 578–85.

Card, D. and Krueger, A.B. (1995) *Myth and measurement: the new economics of the minimum wage*. Princeton, NJ: Princeton University Press.

Farber, H.S. and Katz, H.C. (1979) 'Interest arbitration, outcomes and the incentive to bargain', *Industrial and Labor Relations Review*, 33 (1), pp. 55–63.

19. Michael P. Todaro (b. 1942)[1]

19.1　SOME AUTOBIOGRAPHICAL INFORMATION

The past quarter century has been a period in which I was fortunate enough to participate in an exciting intellectual venture with substantial social relevance. The study of economic development in what has come to be known as the Third World presented both a unique opportunity and a daunting challenge for a young economist. It was an opportunity to be part of an emerging new field of analysis, one in which many of the conventional theories of 'advanced' industrial economies had to be modified and, in some cases, overturned to fit the socioeconomic, cultural and historical realities of the emerging nations of Africa, Asia and Latin America. At the same time it was a challenge to see the world, as best one could, through the eyes of diverse groups of poor, uneducated and largely illiterate populations where simple survival strategies often dominated the individual and group economic calculus. Markets were primitive, behaviour was often prescribed by convention, and the broad set of assumptions and equilibrium adjustment mechanisms that guide Western economic analysis simply did not apply. To

---

[1]　Todaro (1995b), as revised by the editors. I have one volume of collected essays in the series (Todaro 1995a).

be a good and effective development economist required not only an openness to new methods of analysis and new ways of perceiving economic behaviour, but perhaps more importantly it required a willingness to delve into the complex array of 'non-economic' variables that assume such significance in the economic life of developing nations.

When I graduated from Haverford College in 1964 it was a period of intense interest in the politics and economics of newly emerging nations, no doubt spurred on by the Cold War rivalries between the communist and capitalist worlds. Thousands of idealistic young people were participating in President Kennedy's Peace Corps, working in far-flung corners of the globe. A new generation of students who would later be known as the 'baby boomers' was beginning to exert its enormous influence on social and economic relations both at home and abroad. I wanted to be part of this process. So when an unexpected opportunity arose for me to spend a year teaching and writing in Africa, at the then famous Makerere University College in Kampala, Uganda, I deferred my graduate studies at Yale in order to join my Haverford professor and mentor, Philip W. Bell, in East Africa. I had been Phil Bell's student at Haverford where, as a sophomore in the spring of 1962, I had the great good fortune to participate in a small but amazing seminar run by Phil. It featured weekly guest visits and lectures by an extraordinary group of eminent economists, many of whom would later receive Nobel prizes in economics. In addition to benefiting from their lectures, I was often the campus host which enabled me to spend long hours listening to them talk about economic issues and policies. The list is truly amazing: Jan Tinbergen, Kenneth Arrow, James Tobin, Milton Friedman, Lawrence Klein, Sir Roy Harrod, Leonid Hurwicz and Robert Solow. Then when I went to Uganda in 1964, I was part of a group of leading intellectuals who would later emerge as key figures in the field of development studies: Paul Clark, Richard Jolly, Charles Frank, Dharam Ghai, Brian van Arkadie, Henry Bienen, Colin Leys and Ali Mazrui among others. By participating in their seminars, joining them in research projects as well as teaching three courses (including economic development) and co-authoring a unique new text on economic theory for developing countries (Bell and Todaro 1969) and a book on development planning (Todaro 1971a), I can say without hesitation that my education as a development economist was well along before I entered graduate school at Yale University in 1965.

The intense intellectual and visual experience of my year in Africa enabled me to study economic development at Yale (then by far the best US graduate development programme with its influential Economic Growth Center) with the advantage of being able to connect theory with reality and abstract models with concrete experiences. Guided by leading scholars such as Gus Ranis, Lloyd Reynolds, Charles Frank, Howard Pack and a young Joseph

Stiglitz, I was able to finish my Ph.D. in the relatively short span of two years. It was during this period of writing my thesis on a theoretical model of internal migration that I was able to combine my graduate training in the prevailing development paradigm of the Lewis-Ranis-Fei model with my experience in Uganda studying urban unemployment. I simply could not reconcile the theory with my experience, particularly the market-clearing assumptions of traditional labour migration theory. Specifically, how could one explain the rising numbers of migrants to the cities of Africa, Asia and Latin America in the face of growing urban unemployment? If urban wages were not adjusting to equate supply and demand as in the traditional equilibrium model, then surely we must be dealing with a disequilibrium process – one in which wages were sticky, expected incomes rather than nominal wage differentials were guiding rural migration, and the urban unemployment *rate* was in fact acting as the equilibrating mechanism between rural and urban expected incomes. However, if this were true, it would mean that urban unemployment would not slow down migration until it became high enough to offset the rising urban-rural wage gap. Eventually migration, in theory, would cease. But at what social and economic cost?

While this theory of migration, later to become widely known as the 'Todaro theory' and the 'Harris-Todaro model' (Todaro 1969a; 1976a; Todaro and Harris 1970) represented a break with the traditional, neoclassical equilibrium model of labour markets and a demonstration of how conventional Western theory needed to be adjusted to fit the realities of developing nations, it was more important, to my mind, in what it said about development policy. Until then, almost all of development theory focused on promoting industrialization and, by implication, urbanization. Whether it was the Lewis-Ranis-Fei model or the 'Big Push' theory of Rosenstein-Rodan or a variant of the Rostow/Harrod-Domar growth model, the message was basically the same: invest in modern industry and let the traditional surplus labour, rural agricultural economy serve as the base for providing costless labour, cheap food and forced savings (through terms of trade manipulation) to the growing urban, modern economy. Bias investments towards the urban, modern industrial economy and, eventually, the needed structural transformation will be realized.

What my model demonstrated and later experience confirmed was that by neglecting the rural sector, prospects for an orderly and efficient transformation of the urban economy would be greatly diminished. More importantly, attempts to solve the growing urban unemployment problem by creating more urban jobs (e.g. through Keynesian deficit spending) was likely to *worsen* the problem as more and more rural migrants would leave their impoverished environment and head for the cities in search of the elusive, but highly paid, urban job. This is the so-called 'Todaro paradox', that an urban solution to the urban unemployment problem might only worsen it. Only by greater emphasis on rural development (e.g. through higher farm prices, better infrastructure, small town industrial investment, administrative decentralization, etc.) will urban development and ultimately overall economic development be realized. Thus, the model was one of the first to call into question the prevailing development paradigm of the 1950s and 1960s.

As the reader can see from my published work, my interest in development issues and problems goes well beyond my most well-known and widely recognized work on internal migration theory. I have done research and written about a wider range of topics including population, education, technology, the environment and ethics. Again, I can trace my interest in these topics to my early non-academic experience working for the Rockefeller Foundation in Africa (1968–70), New York (1970–4) and again in Africa (1974–6), as well as my ongoing part-time association with the Population Council in New York (1977 to the present) as a Senior Associate in what was formerly known as the Center for Policy Studies and now is called the Research Division. This latter affiliation has coincided with my full time academic appointment as Professor of Economics at New York University.

My work with the Rockefeller Foundation in particular enabled me to travel throughout the developing world. In my capacity as an Associate Director of Social Sciences I was responsible for overseeing Foundation support for universities in Africa, Asia and Latin America. Working with colleagues in the other social sciences and in particular with Dr Kenneth W. Thompson, then Vice President of the Foundation, and now Professor of Government and Director of The Miller Center of Public Affairs at the University of Virginia, I was exposed to a broad range of ideas and viewpoints about the development process. My primary area of programmatic responsibility entailed the training of a core group of Third World economists who received fellowship support to study at US and British universities under Rockefeller Foundation auspices. They would then return to their local universities to staff a newly formed (in the case of Africa) or expanded (in the case of Latin America and Asia) economics faculty. The Foundation had ongoing programmes at the Universities of Ibadan in Nigeria and Nairobi in Kenya, at the newly formed University of Bahia in Brazil and the relatively advanced Universidad del Valle in Colombia, and at the University of the Philippines and Thammassat University in Thailand. I was fortunate enough to be able to spend a considerable amount of time at each of these universities where I would meet with local economists, give lectures and seminars, and discuss economic policy with government planners and decision-makers. This experience enabled me to obtain a first-hand and in-depth understanding of the economies of Asia and Latin America, which along with my five years living and working in Africa, provided me with a unique comparative perspective on development problems in a wide range of structurally different societies. I discovered, for example, that although the growth rate of cities varied from region to region, there were common elements leading to an inexorable flow of new migrants into crowded urban slums despite high levels of unemployment. My travels also provided an opportunity to collect data and discuss conceptual issues with both academic and government economists and statisticians. Many of my writings were undoubtedly influenced by this very special assignment.

While at the Rockefeller Foundation, I was also given responsibilities for coordinating and operating the social science components of the Foundation's programmes in the environment and agricultural development. In the case of the environment, which at that time was largely a domestic United States programme, I studied the emerging new literature on environmental economics and met with the most well-known environmental economists to discuss how public policy might be designed to counter some of the deleterious resource-depleting effects of economic progress. This knowledge was to serve me well a decade later when development economists first became concerned with the problem of environmental degradation and the need to promote more 'sustainable' patterns of economic progress in Third World countries. My essay on the environment and development (Todaro 1994, pp. 325–58) reflects some of that experience.

With regard to the Rockefeller Foundation's famous programme in agricultural development, where it pioneered the creation of new varieties of wheat and rice that led to what has come to be known as the 'Green Revolution', I had the opportunity to spend large blocks of time working with agronomists, plant pathologists and other specialists in farm technology who were intimately involved in the ongoing research. I visited the two major agricultural research centres in Mexico (CIMMYT) and the Philippines (IRRI) where new varieties of wheat and rice were respectively being developed. As a social scientist, I tried to explore some of the potential economic and employment consequences of the new technology – particularly its impact on small farmers and landless labourers. I spent time both at the research stations and in the field. It became clear to me that although food production was likely to rise, the Green Revolution was also destined to have some rather large negative social and economic consequences that the agricultural scientists could not anticipate. And so I learned much about Third World farming systems, problems of agricultural mechanization, issues of integrated rural development and linkages between new agricultural technologies and the emergence of a growing class of landless labourers and potential rural-urban migrants.

It was this experience working and travelling for the Rockefeller Foundation which permitted me to avoid being captured by some of the more restrictive academic theories of development and allowed me to widen my intellectual horizons. I felt free to place my economic analysis in a broader political, cultural and social context. I think that this is reflected in many of my essays and especially in my very popular and widely adopted text, *Economic development* (7th edn, 2000) which has now been translated into ten languages. Had I gone directly from an undergraduate degree to graduate studies and then to a single disciplinary-based academic appointment, I believe that I could not have accomplished all that I have nor benefited from the intellectual guidance of so many eminent social scientists.

19.2   A BRIEF OUTLINE OF MY SELECTED ESSAYS

In selecting my essays for the Edward Elgar collection I divided my work into four parts. Part I explores the analytical, quantitative and policy-related issues of urbanization, rural-urban migration and urban unemployment. In part II we examine various aspects of the relationship between education and development and the role of technology. The essays in part III then scrutinize the many ways in which population growth influences and is in turn influenced by the development process and how growing environmental concerns can be reconciled with economic progress. Finally, in part IV we take a broader perspective on the development process, first by analysing and evaluating some of the leading theories and strategies of development, and then by discussing the important role of ethical issues and value choices in the formulation of development theory and policy.

The first part begins with an examination of the urbanization dilemma in developing countries (Todaro 1980c). This sets forth some of the key issues and provides relevant data on trends and prospects for urban population growth for the final two decades of the twentieth century. In it I try to make a case for the historical and economic uniqueness of Third World urban growth and why many development policies have greatly exacerbated the problem of urban unemployment and underemployment.

The rest of part I forms the core of this volume's essays as it focuses on the key articles for which I am most recognized – i.e. my theoretical writings on 'internal' (rural-urban) and international migration. As mentioned previously, my concern with the problem of growing urban unemployment and accelerating rural-urban migration grew out of observations and research notes that I collected while teaching in Uganda in 1964–5. This culminated in my 1967 Yale Ph.D. thesis (Todaro 1968), the essence of which became my widely recognized model of labour migration and urban unemployment in less developed countries (Todaro 1969a). While this paper stimulated a great deal of discussion and controversy, it was a follow-up paper with Professor John Harris which extended the basic Todaro model in a number of new directions that probably had the greatest and longest lasting impact on the profession (Todaro and Harris 1970). The 'Harris-Todaro model' had a rather major impact not only on the theoretical, empirical and policy-oriented debate about urban unemployment and development policy, but also and almost of equal importance, on much of the international trade literature. It spawned many Ph.D. theses during the 1970s and 1980s and, along with my basic 1969 model, became both the received and the most controversial theory of internal migration in developing countries. Many of my papers that followed these two seminal essays were designed to enhance, extend and empirically verify the two basic Todaro migration models.

Six of the most significant of these articles were selected for inclusion in the section on internal migration. They include Todaro (1971b) which focused specifically on income expectations, rural-urban migration and employment in Africa. There followed a third key theoretical paper published as a lead article in the September 1976 issue of the *Journal of Development Economics* (Todaro 1976a) that expanded the basic Todaro model by setting forth the conditions under which the 'Todaro paradox' of more urban job creation leading to even higher levels and rates of urban unemployment would be observed. This article spurred a new round of theoretical and empirical research by scholars in both the developing and developed world.

It seemed an appropriate time now to prepare an initial survey paper examining the migration literature of the first half of the 1970s. This became Todaro (1976b). A follow-up but more detailed and comprehensive survey paper appeared as Todaro (1980a) which provided a more definitive confirmation of the empirical validity of my basic theory in a wide range of Third World nations. At the same time, a more issues-oriented piece appeared as a lead article in the *Journal of Economic Development* (Todaro 1980b).

The final migration paper selected for this volume is an essay that I prepared jointly with Dr Veena Thadani that looked specifically at the growing phenomenon of female migration in developing countries. In Todaro and Thadani (1984) we tried to recast the basic Todaro model to account for a number of unique factors and constraints affecting women's migration decision-making and then document the relevance of this approach by drawing on a wide range of emerging new feminist literature.

The second section of part I deals with the phenomenon of international labour migration, both legal and illegal. Two theoretical papers have been selected for inclusion in this volume. The first (Todaro and Maruszko 1987a) explores the growing incidence of undocumented illegal migration into the United States. It was co-authored with Lydia Maruszko both as a theoretical contribution to the international migration literature and as an analytical examination of the then proposed and controversial United States Immigration Reform and Control Act (IRCA). The essay set out to accomplish two tasks. First, it was designed as a theoretical model of illegal migration which built on the basic Todaro model to include two key new variables unique to illegal migration: the probability and risk of capture at clandestine border crossings and what I called an 'illegality tax' which reflected the discriminatory, below-market wages paid to illegal workers by US employers. The second objective was to evaluate through a computer simulation exercise based on the model the likelihood that the proposed immigration law would succeed in its design to stem the flow of illegal migration. Our research clearly showed that this would not happen and events over the past seven years have amply confirmed our findings. Border migration has, if anything, accelerated. The second theoretical paper develops a three-sector model in which individual decisions about both internal and international migration in the context of high domestic unemployment are jointly determined (Todaro and Maruszko 1987b). The analytical findings of this essay are particularly relevant for understanding the growing phenomenon of short-term international migration within the developing world.

The five essays in part II focus on the issues relating education to development and the impact of imported technology on labour absorption during the process of industrialization. With regard to the relationship between education and development, I have included two co-authored papers (Todaro and Edwards 1973; 1974), both of which were originally written for a Bellagio conference attended by the heads of all major international donor agencies. The first essay, 'Educational demand and supply in the context of growing unemployment in less developed countries', takes the then very unconventional view that the rapid expansion of educational investment in the absence of significant job creation could easily lead to a growing class of frustrated and highly politicized educated unemployed youth. Events over the past two decades have borne out this early warning. The second paper takes a broader perspective on the relationship between education, society and the economy and is more prescriptive and policy-oriented than the first. It was designed with international assistance agencies in mind and, therefore, it tries to identify how foreign assistance can help to make education more supportive of economic and social development.

My papers on technology and development were written early in my career. These begin with a theoretical article (Todaro 1969b) which tried to set forth the conditions under which successive vintages of imported capital-intensive technology could make domestic labour an 'inferior' factor of production. This is followed by a broader conceptual piece (Pack and Todaro 1969) with the focus once again on the impact of technological dependency and the potential benefits of generating a domestic capital goods industry. Finally, I included a somewhat eclectic essay on technology transfer (Todaro 1970) that was first published in the *Eastern Africa Economic Review* in June 1970 while I was a Visiting Rockefeller Foundation Professor at the University of Nairobi.

Part III contains six of my most significant papers exploring various aspects of the relationship between population growth and economic development as well as a very early and very recent essay on environmental and resource depletion problems. My essay, 'Population growth and economic development: causes, consequences, and controversies' is drawn from the fifth edition of my text *Economic development* (Todaro 1994, pp. 178–216). Unlike other texts in fields such as microeconomics, macroeconomics, monetary economics or international trade – where there is a standard format, a generally received theory, comparable quality data and little variation in presentation – my text in development economics represented an entirely new way of approaching what was then (Todaro 1977a) and still is a highly contentious field of analysis with no received theory, poor quality data and no standard format. My approach was to focus on key development problems and to present the subject in what amounted to a series of original essays – one for each topic such as poverty, population, education, rural development, private investment, foreign aid, etc. – that focused on the major issues, relevant theories, available data and alternative policy options. My essay on population therefore represents not only a survey of issues and controversies but, more importantly, an analysis of how population growth affects and is affected by economic development and what both Third World governments and international assistance agencies can do to alleviate the negative consequences of rapid population growth.

My 'Development policy and population growth: a framework for planners' (Todaro 1977b) represented an attempt to incorporate population growth into economic development planning and policy. Economists had typically treated population growth as an exogenous variable unrelated to the pattern and style of economic growth. In this essay I argue that, on the contrary, population change is strongly influenced by the nature of economic growth, specifically who benefits and who participates. I formulate two analytical models of induced fertility change and attempt to link these demographic outcomes to measures of social welfare and the evaluation of alternative development policies. This theoretical analysis was extended to deal with induced demographic change over time in Todaro (1984). This was prepared for a *Festschrift* volume of original papers honouring Professor

Lloyd Reynolds of Yale University. The purpose of my essay was to develop a set of measurable criteria for judging the success or failure of development policies in terms of their direct and indirect effects on population growth over time and to demonstrate how these demographic consequences could alter the social cost/benefit rankings of alternative investment projects. The final population essay chosen is a paper that I prepared jointly with Professor Eleanor Fapohunda entitled, 'Family structure, implicit contracts and the demand for children in Southern Nigeria' (1988). Its most distinctive contribution was its analytical and empirical demonstration that the standard 'household model' of fertility behaviour originally formulated by Professor Gary Becker was not applicable to societies like those in West Africa whose culture, traditions and economic structure were so very different from those of the typical nuclear household of North America or Western Europe. Specifically, the assumption of a common utility function, pooled household resources and monogamous nuclear family decision-making does not hold in a world of extended families, spouse-specific budgetary and spending patterns, and the availability through polygyny of multiple marriages. We argue that instead of a common household utility function, a bargaining or 'transactions' framework better expresses the dynamics of fertility choice in Southern Nigeria and proceed to use data collected from our field survey to demonstrate these conflicting choices.

Part III concludes with two essays on the environment and development: one written in 1973 when environmental issues were at the bottom of the development agenda and the other in 1993 when they were near the top. The earlier paper (Todaro 1973) focuses on how rapid urbanization and rising unemployment were contributing to an emerging environmental crisis in Third World cities. The more recent and extensive essay attempts to document and analyse the many direct and indirect interrelationships between economic development and general environmental change (Todaro 1994, pp. 325–58). The paper is drawn once again from the 5th edition of my *Economic development* book and begins by demonstrating how population and poverty are critical elements in both the destruction of Third World environmental resources and in the determination of who is most adversely affected by environmental degradation. The essay then proceeds to analyse both domestic and global environmental issues, the relevance of economic theory for understanding the causes of environmental decline, and the range of policy options that Third World governments might pursue in order to promote environmentally 'sustainable' economic development.

Part IV contains two broad-based essays, one dealing with the general state of development economics and the other looking at the role of ethics and values in both the study and evaluation of development performance. Todaro (1979) reviewed and commented on the changing nature of development economics, the vigorous ongoing debate between advocates of the neoclassical and the institutional/structuralist paradigms of development, the conflict over competing development strategies, the importance of population and demographic change, and the intellectual challenge of the 'New International Economic Order' (NIEO). Much of the debate contained in this 1970s paper is still relevant today.

Finally, I selected Todaro (1985) for two reasons. First, I believe that in the field of economic development, more so perhaps than in any other field of economics, ethical issues and subjective value judgements about fundamental issues such as the most desirable development path and the most appropriate development strategy play a central and critical role. Second, I believe that development economics is a unique and still emerging field of research in which universal 'laws', fundamental 'principles' and received 'Western' theories of growth and distribution need to be viewed with a certain degree of scepticism. *'Homo economicus'* is difficult to locate in economically advanced Western societies; he or she is often largely non-existent in many Third World nations. We need, therefore, to be modest in our claims to universality and catholic in our approach to analysing the dynamics (as well as the 'statics') of the emerging economic systems of developing nations.

19.3   SOME CLOSING COMMENTS

In choosing the most representative and most important of my papers for the Edward Elgar collection I should state, however, in closing that although those essays, particularly the ones on rural-urban migration, represent the work for which I am most widely recognized in the scholarly community, it is my economic development text of which I am most proud. Every year for the past twenty years many thousands of students throughout both the developed and developing world have been exposed to my ideas and hopefully challenged by my analysis. They seem to enjoy reading the book and I am gratified by the hundreds of letters I have received expressing their enthusiasm. It is an economic development textbook writer's dream that somewhere in Africa, Asia and Latin America former students who once studied my book are now in positions of great influence. Perhaps they will even translate some of my ideas into the kinds of policies that will help to alleviate the widespread poverty and suffering that still afflicts so many inhabitants of the less developed world. For, in the final analysis, this is what development economics is all about.

SELECTED WORKS

(1968) 'An analysis of industrialization, employment and unemployment in less developed countries', *Yale Economic Essays*, 8 (2), pp. 329–402.

(1969a) 'A model of labor migration and urban unemployment in less developed countries', *American Economic Review*, 59 (1), pp. 138–48.*

(1969b) 'A theoretical note on labour as an "inferior" factor in less developed economies', *Journal of Development Studies*, 5 (4), pp. 252–61.*

(1969) (with P.W. Bell) *Economic theory*. Nairobi: Oxford University Press.

(1969) (with H. Pack) 'Technological transfer, labour absorption and economic development', *Oxford Economic Papers*, n.s. 21 (3), pp. 395–403.*

(1970) 'Some thoughts on the transfer of technology from developed to less developed nations', *East African Economic Review*, 2 (1), pp. 53–64.*

(1970) (with J.R. Harris) 'Migration, unemployment and development: a two-sector analysis', *American Economic Review*, 60 (1), pp. 126–42.*

(1971a) *Development planning: models and methods*. Nairobi: Oxford University Press.

(1971b) 'Income expectations, rural-urban migration and employment in Africa', *International Labour Review*, 104 (5), pp. 387–413.*

(1973) 'Industrialization, unemployment and the urban environment', in K. Wohlmuth (ed.) (1973) *Employment creation in developing societies*. New York: Praeger, pp. 41–60.*

(1973) (with E.O. Edwards) 'Educational demand and supply in the context of growing unemployment in less developed countries', *World Development*, 1 (3/4), pp. 107–17.*

(1974) (with E.O. Edwards) 'Education, society and development: some main themes and suggested strategies for international assistance', *World Development*, 2 (1), pp. 2530.*

(1976a) 'Urban job expansion, induced migration and rising unemployment: a formulation and simplified empirical tests for LDCs', *Journal of Development Economics*, 3 (3), pp. 211–25.*

(1976b) 'Rural-urban migration, unemployment and job probabilities: recent theoretical and empirical research', in A.J. Coale (ed.) (1976) *Economic factors in population growth*. London: Macmillan, pp. 367–85.*

(1977a) *Economic development in the Third World: an introduction to problems and policies in a global context*. London: Longman.

(1977b) 'Development policy and population growth: a framework for planners', *Population and Development Review*, 3 (1/2), pp. 23–43.*

(1979) 'Current issues in economic development', in M.B. Mallabon (ed.) (1979) *Economic perspectives: an annual survey of economics*. New York: Harwood Academic, vol. I, pp. 221–52.*

(1980a) 'Internal migration in developing countries: a survey', in R.A. Easterlin (ed.) (1980) *Population and economic change in developing countries*. Chicago: University of Chicago Press, pp. 361–402.*

(1980b) 'Internal migration, urban population growth and unemployment in developing nations: issues and controversies', *Journal of Economic Development*, 5 (1), pp. 7–23.*

(1980c) 'Urbanization in developing nations: trends, prospects and policies', *Journal of Geography*, 79 (5), pp. 164–74.*

(1984) 'Intergenerational income-fertility linkages in developing countries: a conceptual framework', in G. Ranis *et al.* (eds) (1984) *Comparative development perspectives: essays in honor of Lloyd G. Reynolds.* Boulder, CO: Westview Press, pp. 42–62.*

(1984) (with V.N. Thadani) 'Female migration: a conceptual framework', in J.T. Fawcett *et al.* (eds) (1984) *Women in the cities of Asia: migration and urban adaptation.* Boulder, CO: Westview Press, pp. 36–59.*

(1985) 'Ethics, values and economic development', in K.W. Thompson (ed.) (1985) *Ethics and international relations: ethics in foreign policy.* New Jersey: Transaction Books, vol. 2, pp. 75–97.*

(1987a) (with L. Maruszko) 'Illegal migration and US immigration reform: a conceptual framework', *Population and Development Review*, 13 (1), pp. 101–14.*

(1987b) (with L. Maruszko) 'Internal migration', in J. Eatwell, M. Milgate and P. Newman (eds) (1987) *The new Palgrave: a dictionary of economics.* London: Macmillan, vol. 2, pp. 912–17.*

(1988) (with E.R. Fapohunda) 'Family structure, implicit contracts and the demand for children in southern Nigeria', *Population and Development Review*, 14 (4), pp. 571–94.*

(1994) *Economic development*, 5th edn. London: Longman.

(1995a) *Reflections on economic development.* Aldershot: Edward Elgar.

(1995b) 'Introduction', in M.P. Todaro (1995a) **q.v.**, pp. xiii–xxii.

(2000) *Economic development*, 7th edn. London: Addison Wesley Longman.

20. William H. Lazonick (b. 1945)[1]

20.1   THE MAKING OF A CRITICAL ECONOMIST

Since inclusion in this volume marks me as an 'exemplary' economist, it is perhaps proper that, at the outset, I state my views on the ideological and methodological shortcomings of the discipline of economics as currently practised. The central flaw of conventional economics is its failure to comprehend the role of business enterprise in the development of the economy. With its idealization of an economy that gives free vent to individualistic behavior, the discipline has no way of comprehending why, in a so-called market economy, a business organization that brings together thousands or tens of thousands – indeed sometimes even hundreds of thousands – of people could be anything but a burdensome market imperfection, much less an institution that is central to the process of economic development. More generally, the discipline's methodological obsession with equilibrium conditions – an orientation that in the 1920s and 1930s became a standard methodology precisely because it enabled market-oriented economists to avoid the analysis of the growth of the firm (Lazonick

---

[1]   Lazonick (1992b), as revised by the author. I have one volume of collected essays in the series (Lazonick 1992a) and another autobiographical essay (Lazonick 1991b).

1991a, ch.5) – has meant that today's well-trained economists normally lack the ability to analyze the microeconomics of innovative enterprise. As a result they have great difficulty comprehending how the strategies and structures of business organizations might be critical determinants of the process of economic development.

When, in recent years, conventional economists have sought to comprehend the role of the business enterprise in the modern economy, they have started with the proposition that, to quote the foremost proponent of transaction-cost economics, 'in the beginning there were markets' (Williamson 1985, p. 87). That is indeed what I was led to believe in the many economic theory courses that I took as an undergraduate student in 'Commerce and Finance' at the University of Toronto in the mid-1960s. In microeconomics courses I learned about the theory of the optimizing firm, a productive unit that achieves success by equating marginal revenues and marginal costs subject to externally imposed technological and market constraints. The firm thus depicted is a passive entity (one hesitates to use the word 'actor') in an economy in which labor, capital and product markets aggregate the autonomous production, saving and consumption decisions of millions of households to determine economic outcomes. Within such a market economy, 'technology' is an infinitely malleable combination of factors of production ('labor' and 'capital'), with the relative prices of these factors determining the actual combinations of labor and capital that firms choose.

At the same time, in macroeconomics courses I learned that government economic policies had roles to play in eliminating instability and rectifying inequity. Fiscal and monetary policies could smooth out what was, in a full employment economy, left of the business cycle. Tax and subsidy policies could redistribute income to offset the inequitable impacts of market failures. In all cases, the desired policies were those that would not give the government a permanent role in the allocation of resources and would not distort the workings of the market mechanisms in the microeconomy. American liberalism was then in its heyday, and, imported from Canada's 'neighbor to the south', the main economic perspective to which I was exposed was Paul Samuelson's grand neo-classical synthesis that sought to rationalize government intervention within the theory of the market economy.

Yet, even as I was absorbing this theoretical synthesis that assumed away all questions of political power and national institutions, there was a growing debate in Canada – fuelled in part by a growing revulsion toward the 'ugly American' throughout the world – concerning American domination of the Canadian economy. A required course on Canadian economic history helped me to start thinking about the relation between the textbook theory of the market economy and the historical process of national economic development. [2]

A year doing a master's degree in economics at the London School of Economics in 1968–9 provided me with the in-depth understanding of neo-classical economic theory that would subsequently enable me to address this issue in a serious manner. At the LSE the neo-classical guru was Harry Johnson, the Canadian-born economist who brought the Chicago school to Britain. At the time of his death in 1977, Johnson was reputed to be the most published economist in history. Be that as it may, there was certainly no history in his economics. Johnson preached the static theory of the market economy. But Johnson and his followers really believed in the efficacy of market coordination. Hence they made clear their substantive assumptions of how the world works rather than, as was becoming increasingly the trend among American liberal economists, hiding their ideological orientation behind the scientific façade of mathematical formulae. The fundamental assumptions of the system of economic thought that they taught at the LSE could be easily grasped, and hence, if one had the inclination, easily questioned. The proponents of Chicago-style neo-classical orthodoxy were not necessarily ready and eager for debate, but their candour and consistency in espousing their view of the world made it possible to discern the key issues that a critical perspective had to address.

As a critic of neo-classical economic orthodoxy, I was made, not born. When I came to the LSE in the fall of 1968, I basically believed that perfectly competitive markets represented an ideal mode of economic organization. Although questions about national economic development had been raised in my mind as an undergraduate at the University of Toronto, I had not been exposed to any other type of economic theory. Moreover my life experience through my undergraduate years can only be described as petty bourgeois. The theory that a modern economy could operate on the basis of autonomous household decisions to produce, save and consume was consistent with what I knew of the world. My presumption was that, if the real world of the economy did not conform to the idealized theory of a market economy, then it was the reality, not the theory, that needed to be changed.

Yet, by the summer of 1969, I knew that the neo-classical story was fundamentally flawed. Throughout the 1968–9 academic year, the LSE had been a focal point for political confrontations around issues of imperialism, and, as a result, a cauldron of debate about economics, politics and much else besides. As I was getting a superb education in neo-classical economics, I was also becoming aware that it was an economic theory with a flawed

---

2 Taught by Abraham Rotstein, the contents of this course reflected the influence on Canadian economic history of the work of Harold Innis.

conception of social reality. I particularly remember that, after a stirring debate at the LSE between Joan Robinson and Harry Johnson on income distribution, I began telling anyone who would listen that the price system had to be studied as a set of social relationships. As a heretic among economists, I was on my way.

I also deviated from the intense and narrow academic curriculum at the LSE to read John Kenneth Galbraith's *The new industrial state* (1967). This book attacked economic orthodoxy for its neglect of the planning system – a system that, Galbraith argued, characterized the modern corporate economy. Galbraith's book provided a compelling snapshot of the US economy dominated by the large corporation in the 1950s and 1960s. But it provided little in the way of historical perspective about how these corporations arose, why they persisted, and the conditions under which they might decline. At the time I was unaware of Alfred Chandler's *Strategy and structure* (1962), and reading Galbraith (who to my knowledge has never made reference to any of Chandler's work) did nothing to alert me to this organizational approach to understanding American business history.[3]

In the LSE library, I also stumbled across another book that has become a classic on the business enterprise. In Edith Penrose's *The theory of the growth of the firm* (1959) I got my first exposure to a theory that characterized the enterprise as a dynamic social organization. But, given my scant knowledge of the subject of the modern industrial enterprise, Penrose's arguments were too abstract to provide me with compelling answers concerning the social foundations of a modern economy. In effect, the book contains a theoretical treatment of an historical subject without making explicit the historical foundations on the basis of which one could evaluate the relevance of the theory. It would be many years before, through what I now call 'the integration of theory and history',[4] I would develop a sufficient understanding of the historical dynamics of American business enterprise to appreciate fully the power of Penrose's profound theoretical arguments.

When I left LSE in the summer of 1969, I was confident that, firstly, I understood conventional economic theory, and that, secondly, it could not provide a guide to exploring the realities of economic activity as I perceived them. But I had also become aware that I knew very little about how an advanced economy actually worked. I had also rejected the notion that the problem was to reshape reality according to the theory of the market

---

3 Perhaps fittingly enough I first became aware of Chandler (1962) as a Harvard graduate student in the early 1970s through the work of Stephen Hymer, a Canadian who, after completing his MIT Ph.D. dissertation on the international operation of national firms, became a leading radical economist: see Hymer (1972). On the work of Hymer, who died prematurely in 1974, see Cohen *et al.* (1979).

4 See my discussion of Penrose's work in Lazonick (1999a).

economy. Rather I began to perceive that theory itself had to be the product of our understanding of history, so that theory could provide an intellectual basis for exploring, rather than ignoring, reality.

So what does a young person, thirsting for knowledge about the real world, do? I went to Switzerland to study at the Institut Universitaire de Hautes Etudes Internationales in Geneva. In terms of my personal economics, it was a good deal. This was a time when one US dollar bought four and a half Swiss francs (and when the Canadian dollar was worth more than the US dollar), when a good meal could be had in a Geneva café for less than 10 francs, and when (through some fortuitous contacts that only a student can make) I got a quarter-share in an apartment in the center of Geneva and a half-share in a country residence by Lac Léman for a total monthly rent of US$45. What's more, I had managed to get a scholarship from the Swiss government without even applying for one (that I had been Harry Johnson's student at LSE had more than something to do with it). If I was searching for the real world of economics, I had surely found it!

Naturally, I spent most of the winter months and part of the spring skiing in the Swiss Alps – taking full advantage of the physical education program of the University of Geneva. In between trips to places such as St. Moritz, Zermatt and Grindelwald, I could be found reading, debating and drinking in the very same café in Geneva that V.I. Lenin had frequented before his return to Russia in 1917. But, lest I be accused of having been totally self-indulgent at a time when I should have been focused first and foremost on the pursuit of a career, I should point out that, when skiing, I always took a book with me to read on the mountain trains, cable cars, gondolas and chair lifts. One book that I read on my way up and around the mountains in the winter of 1970 was Jean-Jacques Servan-Schreiber's, *Le Défi Americain* (1967), published a couple of years before. Servan-Schreiber's main point was that Europe had to build the scale and scope of its business organizations if it hoped to avoid becoming an economic, and perhaps cultural, colony of the United States. As a Canadian, the arguments about the dangers of American corporate dominance had a certain resonance. This book, more than any other, convinced me that, once I had my fill of the Swiss Alps, I should continue to study economics at the heart of the global economic beast – in the United States of America.

For if, as Servan-Schreiber argued, the American model of economic organization revealed the future to the rest of the world, then it was the American model that had to be studied. And needless to say, the US corporations that Servan-Schreiber saw challenging Europe hardly fit the model of the passive and powerless business firms portrayed in the many courses in microeconomics that I had taken. Rather they seemed to have much more in common with the types of corporations that characterized the planning system about which I had read in Galbraith's *The new industrial state*.

On one brilliantly sunny day during that winter of 1970, as the mountain train from Zermatt passed through the shadow of the Matterhorn, a woman spotted me reading Galbraith's *American capitalism* (1951) – the book that introduced the term 'countervailing power' into the discourse of American political economy. She told me that she had met Galbraith while skiing at Gstaad, the fashionable Swiss resort where the famous professor had a mountain home. Indeed, Galbraith had invited her to dinner.

Now, for a student of economics in 1970, Galbraith was, along with Milton Friedman and Paul Samuelson, one of America's (and hence the world's) three most famous living economists. And of the three, Galbraith was the only one who was not neo-classical. His *New industrial state* was quickly becoming what I would suppose is the most widely read book written by a twentieth-century economist. So I wrote a letter to Galbraith in which I recounted the conversation engendered by my mountainside reading of *American capitalism*. I informed Galbraith that I too happened to be in Switzerland, and that it would be no trouble whatsoever for me to come meet him in Gstaad. I did not request a dinner invitation, but I did divulge that I was in the midst of applying to the Harvard Ph.D. program in economics. A few days later, at my city residence in Geneva, I received a polite note from Professor Galbraith in which he stated that he reserved his time at Gstaad for 'writing and requisite physical exercise', but that perhaps he would see me at Harvard the following year.

20.2   IN SEARCH OF A THEORY OF DEVELOPMENT

I do not know whether my communication with Galbraith helped me to gain admission to Harvard. Although Galbraith would shortly thereafter be elected president of the American Economic Association, he wasn't taken at all seriously by the mainstream of the economics profession, including a growing number of his Harvard colleagues. Fortunately, when I came to Harvard in the fall of 1970, I found that, quite apart from the iconoclast Galbraith, there were some 15 to 20 students and four faculty members in the Harvard Economics Department who, in opposition to neo-classical orthodoxy, had styled themselves as 'radical economists'. Indeed, in 1970, compared with what came later, the tenured faculty of the Harvard

Economics Department was a heterodox bunch.[5] Even Kenneth Arrow, the doyen of neo-classical mathematical economics, was incredibly open-minded; some five years later he would indeed be largely responsible for my position as assistant professor in the Harvard Economics Department.

Yet a narrow-minded, and somewhat cynical, neo-classicism was already asserting its domination over the graduate curriculum and new faculty appointments. At the LSE, those who taught neo-classical theory appeared to really believe that individualism exercised through impersonal markets leads to optimal economic outcomes. At Harvard, however, the neo-classical professors did not really seem to believe the free-market story, and substituted mathematics for substance in what they taught. One such professor, who served as my first-year advisor at Harvard, quickly informed me that my training in economic theory at the LSE had been virtually worthless for its lack of mathematical sophistication. I did not think so then, and I do not think so now. At the LSE, I had received a rigorous education in the neo-classical view of the economic world that would prove invaluable for exploring how and why that worldview went wrong. With the important exception of the microeconomics course taught by Stephen Marglin (a tenured prodigy turned 'radical'), the offerings in economic theory at Harvard in the early 1970s were exercises in obfuscation of not only the real world economy but also the foundations of neo-classical economic thought.

At the same time, largely as a result of the anti-war movement on American campuses, a concerted effort was being made by some, mostly younger, economists to bring real-world relevance to the economics discipline. Toward this end, they had formed the Union for Radical Political Economics (URPE). Like the participants in the social protest movements of the 1960s, the ideological and political orientations of radical economists were diverse and partially formed. Intellectually, we knew too little and had read too much to be dogmatic about how the world worked. What we did know was that the economic theory that we were being taught did not provide the answers to the questions we were asking. Binding together the radical economics movement was a critique of neo-classical economics as epitomized by the teachings of both the conservative Milton Friedman and the liberal Paul Samuelson.

At Harvard, most of the radical economists of the early 1970s assumed that the Marxian tradition in political economy was relevant to our search for a theoretical alternative. But none of us had had a prior exposure to Marxian

---

5 They included not only Galbraith, but also Hollis Chenery, James Duesenberry, John Dunlop, Alexander Gerschenkron, Albert Hirschman, John Kain, Simon Kuznets (about to retire), Harvey Liebenstein, Wassily Leontief, Stephen Marglin, John Meyer, Richard Musgrave, Dwight Perkins, Henry Rosovsky and Thomas Schelling.

economics in any serious way. If there was an intellectual tradition in which the most useful work by the Harvard radical economists of the early 1970s could be cast, it was that of American institutionalism, with a heavy emphasis on the development of, and social divisions within, the labor force (see Bowles and Gintis 1976; Edwards 1978; and Gordon *et al.* 1982). The Marxian influence on this work was in terms of not so much specific economic theory but rather a methodological concern with the dynamic interaction between the relations and forces of production – between organization and technology – in the process of historical evolution. This focus found particular emphasis in the provocative contribution of Stephen Marglin, 'What do bosses do?: the origins and functions of hierarchy in capitalist production.'[6] Marglin's argument was that the mainstream economist's notion of efficiency ignores the structures of social power that characterize labor-management relations, and the ways in which structures of social power influence the level of productivity and shape the direction of technological change. The issues raised by Marglin's work had an important impact on my own decision to undertake a detailed examination of the dynamic interaction of organization and technology in the evolution of the British cotton textile industry.

20.3 EXPLAINING BRITISH ECONOMIC DECLINE

At the outset, I had no intention of becoming an 'economic historian', much less an authority on cotton spinning in Britain, and indeed it was not until I was an associate professor at Harvard that I began to make serious contact with economic historians. But, in line with Joseph Schumpeter's (1954, pp. 12–13) statement that 'most of the fundamental errors currently committed in economic analysis are due to the lack of historical experience more often than to any other shortcoming of the economist's equipment', I wanted to develop my capability to use historical analysis to generate economic theory, and then use that economic theory as a guide to the further analysis of history. In the attempt to integrate history and theory in this way, the problem is that the further analysis of history also has to test the assumptions of the very theory that is guiding the historical research. To do so requires that the verified strengths and the potential weaknesses of the theory always be kept in view. One has to guard against theory taking on a life of its own – against imposing one's preconceptions on historical reality – rather than studying

---

6 Written around 1970, the paper circulated widely as a working paper, and was even published in French, before it was published in English as Marglin (1974).

that reality in a way that can enhance the relevance of the theory being employed.

In the history of economics, the one economist who explicitly sought to bring history and theory into a symbiotic relation with each other was Karl Marx. Joseph Schumpeter viewed Marx's contribution in this regard as of 'fundamental importance to the methodology of economics'. As Schumpeter (1942, p. 44) put it:

> Economists always have either themselves done work in economic history or else used the historical work of others. But the facts of economic history were assigned to a separate compartment. They entered theory, if at all, merely in the role of illustrations, or possibly of verifications of results. They mixed with it only mechanically. Now Marx's mixture is a chemical one; that is to say, he introduced them into the very argument that produces the results. He was the first economist of top rank to see and to teach systematically how economic theory may be turned into historical analysis and how the historical narrative may be turned into *histoire raisonnée*.

From this perspective, the validity and utility of a body of theory must be judged in terms of its ability to capture the essence of the historical record that it is trying to explain. In Marx's case, the relevant history was the rise to international industrial leadership of Britain in the nineteenth century. While I employed the Marxian theory of the labor process in generating surplus value as a framework for my empirical research, my extended case study of the British cotton textile industry showed that Marx had not correctly understood the evolution of employment relations in particular and business organization more generally in nineteenth-century Britain. This conclusion was reaffirmed by case studies of other British industries that revealed similar patterns of organizational fragmentation on the part of employers and the exercise of considerable control over conditions of work and pay by key groups of craft workers. Marx had vastly overestimated the extent to which British capitalists wielded power over British workers. He did not recognize the extent to which, even in the presence of mechanization, capitalists remained reliant on the skills and efforts of particular groups of operatives, in large part because key categories of operatives performed what we would today consider to be managerial roles on the shop floor. Nor did he recognize the extent to which fragmented competition among British capitalists often gave the much more cohesive organizations of workers the upper hand in determining the conditions of work and pay.

When the institutional evolution of nineteenth-century British capitalism is properly understood, moreover, it is impossible to accept Marx's well-known argument that 'the country that is more developed industrially only shows, to the less developed, the image of its own future' (Marx 1977, p. 91). However effective the British model of capitalist development was for securing economic leadership in the last half of the nineteenth century, it is simply not a model that enables one to comprehend the rise to industrial power of Germany, the United States and Japan in the twentieth century. Compared with the institutions of market-coordinated capitalism that enabled the British economy to assume a position of international dominance in the late nineteenth century, managerial coordination of economic activity, particularly at the level of the business organization, characterized the institutions that enabled the economies of Germany, the United States and Japan to become international economic powers in the twentieth century.

In the first part of my book, *Competitive advantage on the shop floor* (Lazonick 1990a), I wrote in detail about the strengths and weaknesses of the Marxian analysis of nineteenth-century capitalist development. After drawing out the implications of my case study of the British cotton textile industry, I provided a comparative analysis of shop-floor labor in the development of the British, US and Japanese economies during the twentieth century. The basic framework for the analysis argued that the relation between labor and management in the determination of levels of effort and pay was an important institutional determinant of technological change and productivity, with managerial investments in shop-floor skills as the critical intervening variable (Lazonick 1990a, app.).

I did this work on the rise and decline of the British economy, and its implications for a theory of economic development while an assistant professor (1975–80) and then associate professor (1980–84) in the Harvard Economics Department. At the outset, this research had been a continuation of work that I had done as my Ph.D. thesis that, in search of an alternative to neo-classical economic theory, sought to relate the history of British capitalism in the nineteenth century to Marx's theory that was purportedly based on that history. By the early 1980s, however, my detailed research on the interaction of organization and technology in the British cotton textile industry led me into debates with 'neo-classical' economic historians – that is, historians trained as conventional economists whose methodology for doing economic history is to apply neo-classical economic theory and methodology to historical data.

In our edited volume, *The decline of the British economy* (Elbaum and Lazonick 1986), Bernard Elbaum and I argued that Britain was impeded from making a successful transition to mass production and corporate organization in the twentieth century by an inflexible nineteenth-century institutional legacy of atomistic economic organization. Fragmented as a group by horizontal competition and vertical specialization, British industrialists failed to confront and transform the market relations that limited their abilities to develop and utilize mass-production technologies (Elbaum and Lazonick

1984). In showing that, whatever its competitive advantages in the nineteenth century, market coordination of the British economy could not meet the global competitive challenges of the twentieth century, we confronted the neo-classical belief in the efficacy of the highly individualistic market-coordinated economy. In the debate on the timing, measures, and sources of Britain's relative economic decline from the late nineteenth century, neo-classical economic historians such as Donald (now Deirdre) McCloskey and Lars Sandberg treated the choice of technology as a constrained optimization problem, and asked whether the managers of British cotton spinning factories acted as cost-minimizers in the technological choices that they actually made (Sandberg 1969; 1974; 1984; McCloskey and Sandberg 1971). If they could show that such had been the case, then, they argued, one would have to reject the hypothesis of British 'entrepreneurial failure', as put forward by traditional economic historians.

From my perspective, the main problem with the 'entrepreneurial failure' argument as an explanation for British decline was that it did not explain why British entrepreneurs could have been so successful up to the late nineteenth century and so lacking in entrepreneurial abilities and motivations after that time. The hypothesis posited a cultural change on the part of those who managed British enterprises without analyzing how the changing social organization of enterprises and industries in international competition may have been responsible for how British top managers were able and willing to pursue strategies to develop and utilize new technologies. At the same time, my view was that the neo-classical economic historians had so narrowed the notion of what constitutes a 'good' manager so as to trivialize the debate over British decline. For me, the critical issue was not whether British managers optimized subject to constraints but whether the constraints that they faced in the British environment discouraged them from developing and utilizing advanced technology. The task of the economic historian was then to identify the constraints on technological change, and to ask why, as economic actors, British industrialists would not or could not overcome these constraints (Lazonick 1981a).

The constrained-optimization technique is a useful analytical device. It enables the researcher to identify the industrial, organizational, and institutional conditions that are constraining the development and utilization of productive resources at a point in time as a prelude to asking why such constraints existed in one time and place but not in another time and place. The researcher can then explore what social forces had to be put in place to transform the critical constraints.[7] Used in this way, constrained optimization

---

7 Recently, I have been working on an articulation of what I now call the 'historical-transformation' methodology (Lazonick 1999b).

becomes a mere analytical tool rather than an all-encompassing methodology for analyzing the economy. In my work on the dynamic interaction of organization and technology in the cotton textile industry, I showed that during the last half of the nineteenth century, when the British cotton textile industry was virtually unchallenged in international competition, the organization of the industry became increasingly vertically specialized and horizontally fragmented. Market relations coordinated the activities of thousands of firms engaged in cotton brokerage, spinning, weaving, and marketing. I went on to show how, when challenged by international competition based on textile technologies capable of achieving much higher levels of throughput than the traditional technologies used in Britain, the market-coordinated British industry had great difficulty in reorganizing itself through horizontal concentration and vertical integration to permit the adoption of high-throughput technologies. The industry's market coordinated structure prevented an innovative competitive response.

These arguments generated an appreciable amount of debate among economic historians, often focusing on apparently esoteric issues of spinning technology – whether mule spinning machines designed to spin warp yarns could be converted to spinning weft yarns, and whether the paper tubes that could be used on the spindles of ring spinning machines performed the same function as the paper tubes that could be used on the spindles of mules (Mass and Lazonick 1990). Larger issues were, however, at stake. In my initial debate with McCloskey and Sandberg, the larger issue was the adequacy of the constrained-optimization technique for analyzing changes in technological and economic leadership (Lazonick 1981a; b; c). In my subsequent debate with Gary Saxonhouse and Gavin Wright (1984; 1987), the larger issue concerned the determinants of global competitive advantage (Lazonick 1984; 1987).

My argument concerning the organizational determinants of British relative decline in cotton textiles had taken the US cotton textile industry as the relevant model of technological success. Yet, as Saxonhouse and Wright noted, the US cotton textile industry had only limited success in capturing foreign markets, and indeed had a protected home market. The competitive problem, as my collaborator on the textile research, William Mass, and I argued, was that, despite having by far the highest productivity of any cotton textile industry, US cotton textiles was a relatively labor-intensive and low value-added industry that had to compete for labor in a high-wage economy driven by more capital-intensive and high value-added industries such as steel, automobiles, and heavy machinery. Given the wage levels that more labor-intensive industries had to pay in the United States, technological success in these industries did not translate into competitive success (Lazonick and Mass 1984).

The national industry that beat out British cotton textiles during the interwar period was that of Japan. According to Saxonhouse and Wright (1984), the Japanese industry was even more vertically specialized than the British industry. The source of Japanese competitive advantage, they asserted, was not the use of managerial coordination to introduce high-throughput technologies as Mass and I had argued, but simply cheap labor. In a paper, 'The British cotton industry and international competitive advantage: the state of the debates' (Lazonick and Mass 1990) we confronted the cheap labor argument. Of critical importance to the rise to global leadership in cotton textiles from the 1910s into the 1930s were both the organization of its industry, from the purchasing of cotton to the marketing of cloth, and the development of an indigenous technological capability. From an early stage, the Japanese cotton textile industry had a very highly concentrated spinning sector that integrated forward into weaving, in part by developing (rather than importing) high-throughput technologies engineered to be used with blended cotton and unskilled labor. Access to relatively cheap labor did not hurt Japan's competitiveness on global markets. But cheap labor cannot explain why, by the 1930s, the Japanese cotton textile industry was dominating world markets – not only in cotton textiles but also in cotton textile machinery – whereas the Indian cotton textile industry had developed no indigenous technological capability and could only survive behind tariff barriers.

We also argued that in developing the indigenous capabilities that brought the Japanese cotton textile industry to world dominance by the 1930s, Japan laid some of the organizational and technological foundations for its remarkable economic growth from the 1950s (Lazonick and Mass 1995; see also Mass and Robertson 1996). This comparative analysis became part of a broader project on business organization and technological change in the comparative and historical development of the Japanese economy.[8] The Japanese challenge to the United States came, not in industries in which the United States was weak, but in the mass-production consumer-durable industries and related capital-goods industries in which US manufacturers had been world leaders. Again, as in the earlier case of the cotton textile industry, low wages and long working hours alone cannot explain Japan's sustained success in the post-World War II decades. By the 1980s, US manufacturers had come to recognize the organizational foundations of the

8 This research was funded by grants for US-Japanese collaborative research from the US National Science Foundation, the Japan Society for the Promotion of Science, and the Center for Global Partnership of the Japan Foundation. Our principal Japanese collaborators have been Takeshi Abe of Osaka University and Kazuo Wada of Tokyo University.

so-called Japanese 'miracle', and were adopting a whole array of Japanese management practices, most of which integrated managerial learning with learning on the shop floor (Lazonick 1998a).

20.4   THE MYTH OF THE MARKET ECONOMY

By the mid-1980s, my work became heavily influenced by my involvement with Alfred Chandler and the Business History Group at the Harvard Business School (HBS).[9] By the early 1980s I was well acquainted with Chandler and his work. But, despite the fact that I had been in the Harvard Economics Department since 1970, I had had little contact with HBS on 'the other side of the river'. A close relation developed, however, after one of my cotton textile articles that was published in *Business History Review* won the prize for best article in 1983 (Lazonick 1983). Following this unexpected accolade, I was awarded the Harvard-Newcomen Fellowship in Business History at HBS in 1984–5, and, in the transition from being an untenured associate professor at Harvard to a tenured professor at Columbia University, spent an additional year as a research fellow at HBS in 1985–6.

Indeed, for the next three years, even when I was teaching in New York, I remained a central participant in the HBS Business History Seminar, to which I presented a number of the papers that would eventually appear as chapters in *Business organization and the myth of the market economy* (Lazonick 1991a). The HBS seminar proved to be a stimulating intellectual environment in which to develop my approach to the integration of business history with economic theory in explaining national economic development and shifts in international competitive advantage.[10] So too were the meetings of the Business History Conference (BHC), the main professional organization of business historians in the United States. Reflecting the deep interest among many BHC members in elaborating an historically relevant theory of the business enterprise, in 1990–1 I served as BHC president (see Lazonick 1991b, my presidential address).

Business organization and the myth of the market economy (Lazonick 1991a) provided a cross-national comparative perspective on the development of collective capabilities within major business enterprises in

---

9 See the photograph of the Business History Group at Harvard Business School in 1985, which appears in McCraw (1988), as well as on the back cover of *Business History Review*, 71 (Summer 1997).

10 For a review of my work to the early 1990s that focuses on Lazonick (1991a), see Carstensen (1996). For a more sceptical evaluation, see Robertson (1993). See also Galambos (1993).

Britain, United States and Japan. I argued that over the course of the twentieth century, the development and utilization of these collective – or organizational – capabilities had become of increasing importance for gaining and sustaining international competitive advantage. Hence 'the myth of the market economy' – the orthodox economist's notion that market rather than organizational coordination of economic activity was responsible for superior economic performance. For me, as for Chandler, Galbraith and Penrose, the locus of this organizational coordination has been business much more than government (but see Ferleger and Lazonick 1993). From this perspective, the role of the modern business corporation in the development of the economy manifests organizational success, not market failure. The book outlines the rudiments of a theory of innovative enterprise in which, in Schumpeterian fashion, enterprises, through their investment strategies and organizational structures, shape their cost structures rather than take the technologies and factor markets underlying these cost structures as given. From this perspective, economies of scale and scope are an outcome, not an explanation, of the success of such innovative investment strategies.

The result of this approach is to turn the standard textbook theory of the firm on its head. As a managerial practice, constrained optimization becomes the enemy of innovative enterprise and economic development. In *Business organization and the myth of the market economy*, I summarized the theoretical and historical perspectives that can provide intellectual foundations for a theory of economic development that is both rigorous and relevant (see also Lazonick 1991d). The construction of the theory requires rigorous comparative-historical research on the process of economic development to derive the fundamental assumptions and functional relationships that constitute the central economic model. The resultant theory is relevant because the central economic model is not only derived from comparative-historical research but also provides a basis for focused empirical research that can test the hypotheses that the theory generates. In the book, I employed this approach to show, first, what was lost when Marshallian economics was transformed from a theory of economic development into a theory of the optimizing firm; second, how and why transaction-cost economics (à la Oliver Williamson) cannot comprehend either the innovative enterprise or the development of the economy, and third, how many economists working in the developmental traditions of Marx, Schumpeter and Marshall have made contributions to our understanding of economic development as a dynamic social process.

20.5   THE SOCIAL FOUNDATIONS OF DEVELOPMENT

In a highly productive year at the Institute for Advanced Study in Princeton in 1989–90, I completed *Competitive advantage on the shop floor* (Lazonick 1990a) and *Business organization and the myth of the market economy* (Lazonick 1991a). I then elaborated upon these themes in a book of my collected essays, *Organization and technology in capitalist development* (Lazonick 1992a). A much-prized (and quite unexpected) reward for these efforts was an honorary doctorate from Uppsala University in 1991 for my work on economic development.

My association with Uppsala University began in the early 1980s when I was doing research at Harvard into the so-called 'Horndal effect' – a phenomenon that became well-known among economists in the 1960s as an explanation of sustained productivity growth without technical change (see Lazonick and Brush 1985). The phenomenon was based on the productivity experience of a Swedish iron works in the town of Horndal from the mid-1930s to the mid-1950s. An application to the Svenksa Handelsbanken Foundation for Social Science Research for a modest amount of funds to translate some Swedish-language materials at Harvard resulted in a request from the Foundation that I apply for a much larger grant that would permit me to enter into serious collaboration with Bo Gustafsson and his research group at Uppsala's Department of Economic History. From 1984 I became a frequent visitor to Uppsala and, after it was founded in 1986, the Swedish Collegium for Advanced Study in the Social Sciences (Gustafsson was a co-director of SCASSS for the first ten years of its existence).

One result of this collaboration was an in-depth study, based on the archival materials of the Horndal iron works, that revealed that a complex set of organizational and institutional factors lay behind the 'Horndal effect' (Genberg 1992) – factors that were not even hinted at by economists such as Kenneth Arrow (1962) and Harvey Leibenstein (1966), both of whom had used a third-hand account of the 'Horndal effect' as prime anecdotal evidence to motivate seminal theoretical contributions to economics. This project also resulted in what has been my most data-intensive single piece of research – an effort that was, in part, a response to some work by Paul David (1972), who claimed to have found a case of the Horndal effect in a textile mill in Lowell, Massachusetts from the 1830s to the 1860s. Following the lead of Arrow, David attributed the sustained productivity growth in the Lowell mill to 'learning-by-doing'. In view of a number of potentially significant changes in the character of the labor force and labor-management relations in Massachusetts over the period in question, my co-author, Thomas Brush and I put forth the 'production-relations hypothesis' as an alternative, or at least additional, explanation for the observed productivity changes in the textile mill. Brush and I collected monthly data on, among other things, productivity, work experience, work conditions, and ethnicity of every worker who had worked in the weave rooms of Lawrence Mill No. 2 in Lowell over a period of some twenty years. Our analysis of this data set (made up of in excess of 13,000 observations) provided support for both the learning-by-doing and the production-relations hypotheses as determinants of the textile mill's productivity growth.

We cautioned, however, that, despite the extreme microeconomic character of our analysis, our results were sensitive to how one interpreted the underlying phenomena measured by several key variables. The case study should, therefore, give pause to those who would draw conclusions from even more aggregated quantitative data without questioning whether the quantitative measures actually merited the qualitative meanings that were being attached to them. More data can be useful, but they do not in and of themselves provide explanations. For understanding the phenomena in question, one needs an economic theory of the business enterprise as a social organization that is in turn embedded in a theory of the social organization in its institutional environment.

Through the mid-1980s, my efforts to build such a theory of the economy approached the issue from the side of labor, observing the business organization from the shop floor. This bottom-up perspective fit well with Alfred Chandler's top-down approach that stressed the importance of 'economies of speed' in the managerial organization (Lazonick 1990a, ch. 7). The common focus was on the utilization of productive resources rather than their development. But it is the development of productive resources that provides the foundation for the growth of an enterprise and that commits the enterprise to high fixed-cost investments, thus creating an imperative for their high-speed utilization. Essential to what I came to call a 'theory of innovative enterprise' were issues of development finance and organizational learning in different institutional environments.

I began working on these issues while at Columbia University, where my main professorial appointment was in the very congenial Barnard Economics Department, chaired by the critical monetary economist, Duncan Foley. Besides teaching the graduate course in economic history in the Columbia Economics Department (a course that was attended by students from a wide range of disciplines throughout the university), I ran a seminar with Richard Nelson in the School of Public and International Affairs on innovation and national institutions. By the late 1980s and early 1990s, I was producing a number of papers on the roles of 'financial commitment' and 'organizational integration' in the process of industrial development (Lazonick 1988; 1990b; c; 1991c; e; 1993; 1994).

In 1993, I decided to move from Columbia University to the University of Massachusetts Lowell. Located about a half hour drive from Cambridge (where I had also maintained my intellectual base during my years at Columbia), UMass Lowell is a technology university with long historic roots in a region that was the birthplace of the American industrial revolution and that is now part of the 'Route 128' electronics district. For me, the main attraction of UMass Lowell was the commitment that the Chancellor, William Hogan, and the Vice-Chancellor of Development, Frederick Sperounis, had made to integrate the work of the university with regional economic development. They understood the need to integrate across disciplines within the university as a basis for effective interaction between the university and the region to address economic and social needs. As I well knew from my years at Harvard and Columbia, such functional integration is an incredibly difficult endeavor in the modern university, driven as it is by the 'expert' knowledge of academics whom a handful of other academics designate as the world's foremost authorities of a sub-discipline of some sub-discipline. At UMass Lowell, I have pursued this program of integration and outreach as a director of a research center, as co-chair of the university-wide collaborative effort to promote the economic development mission, and as an initiator and member of an innovative and interdisciplinary graduate department for the economic and social development of regions.

My own subsequent research efforts have focused on comparative industrial development, international competition and national economic performance. Soon after my move to UMass Lowell, I began collaborative work on these issues with Mary O'Sullivan. When I met her, she was in the business economics program at Harvard University, and had started working with Stephen Marglin, my own former thesis adviser and long-time colleague at Harvard. Together, O'Sullivan and I wrote a number of comparative-historical papers on the institutions of industrial finance and skill formation that set the stage for our still ongoing collaborative project on corporate governance, innovation, and economic performance (Lazonick and O'Sullivan 1996a; b; c; 1997a; b; c; d).[11]

Our objective in this research is to bring the history of comparative industrial development up to date so that an understanding of the social foundations and dynamics of the development process can be used to inform public debates on how to generate stable and equitable economic growth (Lazonick and O'Sullivan forthcoming). By 1996 this project had become

---

11 One of our papers (Lazonick and O'Sullivan 1996c) was a contribution to the *International Encyclopedia of Business and Management (IEBM)*, edited by Malcolm Warner. I have since become editor of the *IEBM Handbook on Economics* and economics editor for the second edition of IEBM, scheduled for publication in 2001.

truly international not only in terms of research but also location, as we began pursuing this work through affiliations with research institutions and collaborations with scholars in the United States, Japan and Europe.

In the United States, we developed the project in collaboration with several of my colleagues at UMass Lowell and with support from the Jerome Levy Economics Institute.[12] A key motivation for this research is to explore the relation between, on the one side, the worsening of the distribution of income and wealth in the United States since the 1970s, and, on the other side, the rise to dominance of the objective of 'maximizing shareholder value' as a principle of US corporate governance. Hence the research seeks to explain the relation between modes of corporate resource allocation and the creation of employment opportunities that can enable a larger proportion of the population to become increasingly productive over a sustained period of time. The central focus of the research that seeks to identify this link is the 'skill-base hypothesis' – the argument that different social environments, characterized in particular by different employment and financial institutions, encourage (or bias) business enterprises operating in those environments to invest in different types of skill bases that integrate the skills and efforts of people with different functional capabilities and hierarchical re-sponsibilities.[13] To test the skill-base hypothesis requires comparative case studies of corporate investment strategies in the same industries across nations.

Over the past decade much of my own empirical research has focused on the institutional conditions that have supported corporate investments in different types of skill bases in the United States and Japan throughout the twentieth century. From the late nineteenth century both nations experienced a 'managerial revolution' characterized by integrated skill bases of administrative and technical personnel within major corporations that could effectively develop and utilize technology. In the post-World War II period, however, by building integrated skill bases that also included shop-floor workers and subsidiary suppliers, Japanese corporations were able to challenge their US competitors in a range of mechanical and electronic industries in which US corporations had been the world's foremost mass producers (Lazonick 1998a).

Growing out of my collaborative research on Japanese industrialization

---

12 For the Levy Institute working papers and policy briefs that were the products of this project, see <http://www.levy.org>.

13 For an application of the hypothesis to the comparative development of the US and Japan, see Lazonick (1998a); on alternative theories of corporate governance and the implications for understanding the comparative economic development of, and current economic challenges, for the US and Germany, see O'Sullivan (2000).

with Professor Kazuo Wada of Tokyo University,[14] in 1996–7 I had the opportunity to spend the better part of a year in Japan teaching and researching comparative industrial development and international competition in the Faculty of Economics of Tokyo University. Although the appointment was, for all intents and purposes, as a visiting professor for a term of one year, it turned out that my actual status was as a tenured professor at Tokyo University and hence a 'lifetime' employee of the Ministry of Education. When I 'resigned' from this position at the end of March 1997, therefore, I officially became a retired Japanese civil servant! During my stay at Todai, I did extensive research on the development of the Japanese financial system that resulted in papers on the history of Japanese industrial finance well as on the current problems of the Japanese economy and the implications for corporate governance reform (Lazonick and O'Sullivan 1997c; Lazonick 1998b; forthcoming). This work has subsequently resulted in the launching of a long-term project in collaboration with Kazuo Wada on the evolution of share ownership and managerial control from the Meiji era to the present.

In the late 1990s, arguments for the efficacy of maximizing shareholder value, imported from the United States, have made corporate governance a hotly debated topic in Europe. Such was not the case when, beginning in 1994, O'Sullivan and I began developing the European focus of our project on corporate governance, innovation and economic performance as research associates of the STEP (Studies in Technology, Innovation and Economic Policy) Group, a research organization in Oslo, Norway. Keith Smith, STEP Group's director, had the foresight, a few years before corporate governance was to emerge as a hot political issue in Europe, to see the importance of linking corporate governance to the European debates on national systems of innovation.[15] Our work on corporate governance with the STEP Group led to our involvement in a project on 'Innovation systems and European integration' directed by Charles Edquist with funding from the Targeted Socio-Economic Research (TSER) Programme of the European Commission (Directorate-General XII).

Following my stay in Japan, I began to split my time between the University of Massachusetts Lowell, where I am University Professor in the interdisciplinary Department of Regional Economic and Social Development that I helped to found, and the European Institute of Business Administration (INSEAD) in Fontainebleau, France, where my role is to develop my research projects on comparative industrial development and where Mary O'Sullivan is a faculty member. From INSEAD, starting in 1999, O'Sullivan

14 See note 8 above.
15 For the work of STEP Group, see <http://www.step.no>.

and I secured TSER funding for our own three-year project, 'Corporate governance, innovation, and economic performance in the EU'.[16] Defining a system of corporate governance as the institutions that influence the ways in which business corporations allocate resources and returns, the objectives of this project are:

- to analyze how corporate governance systems in EU nations, the United States, and Japan influence the investment strategies and the distribution of corporate revenues of industrial corporations based in those nations;
- to compare the influence of corporate governance on corporate investment strategy and revenue distribution among EU nations and with the United States and Japan;
- to determine the extent to which international competition and intergenerational dependence are creating pressures on national systems of corporate governance that will affect the incentives and abilities of corporations to invest in innovation and contribute to an equitable distribution of income; and
- to elaborate the policy implications of the analysis of comparative corporate governance for economic growth, employment opportunities, and income distribution in the European Union, the United States, and Japan.

There remains plenty of work to be done.

SELECTED WORKS

(1981a) 'Factor costs and the diffusion of ring spinning in Britain prior to World War I', *Quarterly Journal of Economics*, 96 (1), pp. 89–109.*

(1981b) 'Competition, specialization and industrial decline', *Journal of Economic History*, 41 (1), pp. 31–8.

(1981c) 'Production relations, labor productivity and choice of technique: British and US cotton spinning', *Journal of Economic History*, 41 (3), pp. 491–516.

(1983) 'Industrial organization and technological change: the decline of the British cotton industry', *Business History Review*, 57 (2), pp. 195–236.*

(1984) 'Rings and mules in Britain: a reply', *Quarterly Journal of Economics*, 99 (2), pp. 393–8.

(1984) (with B. Elbaum) 'The decline of the British economy: an institutional perspective', *Journal of Economic History*, 44 (2), pp. 567–83.* Rep. in B. Elbaum and W.H. Lazonick (eds) (1986) **q.v.**, pp. 1–17.

(1984) (with W. Mass) 'The performance of the British cotton industry, 1870–1913', *Research in Economic History*, 9, pp. 1–44.

(1985) (with T. Brush) 'The "Horndal effect" in early US manufacturing', *Explorations in Economic History*, 22 (1), pp. 53–96.*

16 See the CGEP project website, <http://www.insead.fr/cgep/>.

(1986) (Eds with B. Elbaum) *The decline of the British economy*. Oxford: Clarendon Press.

(1987) 'Stubborn mules: some comments', *Economic History Review*, 2nd ser., 40 (1), pp. 80–6.

(1988) 'Financial commitment and economic performance: ownership and control in the American industrial corporation', *Business and Economic History*, 2nd ser., 17, pp. 115–28.

(1990a) *Competitive advantage on the shop floor*. Cambridge, MA: Harvard University Press.

(1990b) 'Organizational capabilities in American industry: the rise and decline of managerial capitalism', *Business and Economic History*, 2nd ser., 19 (1), pp. 35–54.*

(1990c) 'Organizational integration in three industrial revolutions,' in A. Heertje and M. Perlman (eds) (1990) *Evolving technology and market structure: studies in Schumpeterian economics*. Ann Arbor, MI: University of Michigan Press, pp. 77–97.

(1990) (with W. Mass) 'The British cotton industry and international competitive advantage: the state of the debates', *Business History*, 32 (4), pp. 9–65.*

(1991a) *Business organization and the myth of the market economy*. Cambridge: Cambridge University Press.

(1991b) 'Business history and economics', *Business and Economic History*, 2nd ser., 20 (1), pp. 1–13.

(1991c) 'Organizational capabilities in American industry: the rise and decline of managerial capitalism', in H.F. Gospel (ed.) (1991) *Industrial training and technological innovation: a comparative and historical study*. London: Routledge, pp. 213–34.

(1991d) 'What happened to the theory of economic development?', in P. Higgonet, D.S. Landes and H. Rosovsky (eds) (1991) *Favorites of fortune: technology, growth and economic development since the industrial revolution*. Cambridge, MA: Harvard University Press, pp. 267–96.

(1991e) 'Business organization and competitive advantage: capitalist transformations in the twentieth century', in G. Dosi, R. Giannetti and P.A. Toninelli (eds) (1991) *Technology and enterprise in a historical perspective*. Oxford: Oxford University Press, pp. 119–63. Transl. into Italian in R. Giannetti and P.A. Toninelli (eds) (1991) *Innovazione Impresa e Sviluppo Economico*. Bologna: Il Mulino, pp. 141–93.

(1992a) *Organization and technology in capitalist development*. Aldershot: Edward Elgar.

(1992b) 'Introduction: placing history at the service of economics', in W.H. Lazonick (1992a) **q.v.**, pp. vii–xvii.

(1993) 'Industry clusters and global webs: organizational capabilities in the US economy', *Industrial and Corporate Change*, 2 (1), pp. 1–24.

(1993) (Eds with W. Mass) *Organizational capabilities and competitive advantage*. Aldershot: Edward Elgar.

(1993) (with L. Ferleger) 'The managerial revolution and the developmental state: the case of US agriculture', *Business and Economic History*, 2nd ser., 22 (2), pp. 67–98.

(1994) 'Social organization and technological leadership', in W.J. Baumol, R.R. Nelson and E.N. Wolff (eds) (1994) *Convergence of productivity: cross-national studies and historical evidence*. Oxford: Oxford University Press, pp. 164–93.

(1995) (with W. Mass) 'Indigenous innovation and industrialization: foundations of Japanese development and advantage', in Association for Japanese Business Studies (1995) *Best Papers 1995*. Ann Arbor, MI: AJBS, pp. 1–24.

(1996a) (with M. O'Sullivan) 'Organization, finance and international competition', *Industrial and Corporate Change*, 5 (1), pp. 1–49.

(1996b) (with M. O'Sullivan) 'Formazione delle competenze e sviluppo economico' ['Skill formation and economic development'], in R. Giannetti (ed.) (1996) *Nel Mito di Prometeo*. Firenze: Ponte Alle Grazie, pp. 207–35.

(1996c) (with M. O'Sullivan) 'Big business and corporate control', in M. Warner (ed.) (1996) *International Encyclopedia of Business and Management*. London: Routledge, pp. 365–85.

(1997a) (with M. O'Sullivan) 'Investment in innovation, corporate governance and corporate employment', Jerome Levy Economics Institute Policy Brief no. 37.

(1997b) (with M. O'Sullivan) 'Finance and industrial development, part I: the United States and the United Kingdom', *Financial History Review*, 4 (1), pp. 7–29.

(1997c) (with M. O'Sullivan) 'Financial and industrial development, part II: Japan and Germany', *Financial History Review*, 4 (2), pp. 113–34.

(1997d) (with M. O'Sullivan) 'Big business and skill formation in the wealthiest nations: the organizational revolution in the twentieth century', in A.D. Chandler, F. Amatori and T. Hikino (eds) (1997) *Big business and the wealth of nations*. Cambridge: Cambridge University Press, pp. 497–521.

(1998a) 'Organizational learning and international competition', in J. Michie and J.G. Smith (eds) (1998) *Globalization, growth and governance*. Oxford: Oxford University Press, pp. 204–38.

(1998b) 'Japanese corporate governance and strategy: adapting to financial pressures for change', Jerome Levy Economics Institute Policy Brief no. 48.

(1999a) 'Innovative enterprise in theory and history', University of Massachusetts Lowell and INSEAD working paper, February.

(1999b) 'Innovative enterprise in a national economy: the theory and method of historical transformation', University of Massachusetts Lowell and INSEAD working paper, May.

(forthcoming), 'The Japanese economy and corporate reform: what path to sustainable prosperity?', *Industrial and Corporate Change*.

(forthcoming) (Eds with M. O'Sullivan) *Corporate governance and sustainable prosperity*. London: Macmillan, forthcoming.

BIBLIOGRAPHY

Arrow, K.J. (1962) 'The economic implications of learning by doing', *Review of Economic Studies*, 29 (2), pp. 155–73.

Bowles, S. and Gintis, H. (1976) *Schooling in capitalist America: educational reform and the contradictions of economic life*. New York: Basic Books.

Carstensen, F. (1996) 'William Lazonick' in W.J. Samuels (ed.) (1996) *American economists of the late twentieth century*. Cheltenham: Edward Elgar, pp. 159–73.

Chandler, A.D. (1962) *Strategy and structure: chapters in the history of the industrial enterprise*. Cambridge, MA: MIT Press.

Cohen, R.B., Felton, N., Nkosi, M. and van Liere, J. (eds) (1979) *The multinational corporation: a radical approach.* Cambridge: Cambridge University Press.

David, P.A. (1972) 'The "Horndal effect" in Lowell, 1834–1856: a short-run learning curve for integrated cotton textile mills', *Explorations in Economic History*, 10 (2), pp. 131–50.

Edwards, R. (1978) *Contested terrain: the transformation of the workplace in the twentieth century.* New York: Basic Books.

Galambos, L. (1993) 'The innovative organization: viewed from the shoulders of Schumpeter, Chandler, Lazonick, *et al.*', *Business and Economic History*, 2nd ser., 22 (1), pp. 79–91.

Galbraith, J.K. (1951) *American capitalism: the concept of countervailing power.* Boston, MA: Houghton Mifflin.

Galbraith, J.K. (1967) *The new industrial state.* Boston, MA: Houghton Mifflin.

Genberg, M. (1992) 'The Horndal effect: productivity growth without capital investment in Horndalsverken between 1927 and 1952', unpublished Ph.D. dissertation, Uppsala University.

Gordon, D.M., Edwards, R. and Reich, M. (1982) *Segmented work, divided workers: the historical transformation of labor in the United States.* Cambridge: Cambridge University Press.

Hymer, S.H. (1972) 'The multinational corporation and the law of uneven development,' in J.N. Bhagwati (ed.) (1972) *Economics and world order from the 1970s to the 1990s.* New York: Macmillan, pp. 113–40.

Leibenstein, H. (1966) 'Allocative efficiency vs. "X-efficiency"', *American Economic Review*, 56 (3), pp. 392–415.

Marglin, S.A. (1974) 'What do bosses do?: the origins and functions of hierarchy in capitalist production', *Review of Radical Political Economics*, 6 (2), pp. 33–60.

Marx, K. (1977) *Capital.* Volume 1. New York: International Publishers.

Mass, W. and Robertson, A. (1996), 'From textiles to automobiles: mechanical and organizational innovation in the Toyoda Enterprises, 1895-1933', *Business and Economic History*, 2nd ser., 25 (2), pp. 1–37.

McCloskey, D.N. and Sandberg, L.G. (1971) 'From damnation to redemption: judgements on the late Victorian entrepreneur', *Explorations in Economic History*, 9 (1), pp. 89–108. Rep. in D.N. McCloskey (1981) *Enterprise and trade in Victorian Britain: essays in historical economics.* London: George Allen & Unwin, pp. 55–72.

McCraw, T.K. (ed.) (1988) *The essential Alfred Chandler.* Cambridge, MA: Harvard Business School Press.

O'Sullivan, M. (2000) *Contests for corporate control: corporate governance and economic performance in the United States and Germany.* Oxford: Oxford University Press.

Penrose, E. (1959) *The theory of the growth of the firm.* Oxford: Basil Blackwell.

Robertson, P.L. (1993) 'Innovation, corporate organisation and policy: William Lazonick on the firm and economic growth', *Prometheus*, 11 (2), pp. 271–87.

Sandberg, L.G. (1969) 'American rings and English mules: the role of economic rationality', *Quarterly Journal of Economics*, 83 (1), pp. 25–43.

Sandberg, L.G. (1974) *Lancashire in decline: a study in entrepreneurship, technology and international trade.* Columbus, OH: Ohio State University Press.

Sandberg, L.G. (1984) 'The remembrance of things past: rings and mules revisited', *Quarterly Journal of Economics*, 99 (2), pp. 387–92.

Saxonhouse, G.R. and Wright, G. (1984) 'New evidence on the stubborn English mule and the cotton industry, 1878–1920', *Economic History Review*, 2nd ser., 37

(4), pp. 507–19.

Saxonhouse, G.R. and Wright, G. (1987) 'Stubborn mules and vertical integration: the disappearing constraint?', *Economic History Review*, 2nd ser., 40 (1), pp. 87–94.

Schumpeter, J.A. (1942) *Capitalism, socialism and democracy*. New York: Harper.

Schumpeter, J.A. (1954) *History of economic analysis*. Oxford: Oxford University Press.

Servan-Schreiber, J.-J. (1967) *Le défi américain*. Paris: Denoël.

Williamson, O.E. (1985) *The economic institutions of capitalism: firms, markets, relational contracting*. New York: Free Press.

Appendix: Economists of the Twentieth Century

Monetarism and Macroeconomic
Policy
Thomas Mayer

Studies in Fiscal Federalism
Wallace E. Oates

The World Economy in Perspective
Essays in International Trade and European
Integration
Herbert Giersch

Towards a New Economics
Critical Essays on Ecology, Distribution and
Other Themes
Kenneth E. Boulding

Studies in Positive and Normative
Economics
Martin J. Bailey

The Collected Essays of Richard E.
Quandt (2 volumes)
Richard E. Quandt

International Trade Theory and Policy
Selected Essays of W. Max Corden
W. Max Corden

Organization and Technology in
Capitalist Development
William Lazonick

Studies in Human Capital
Collected Essays of Jacob Mincer,
Volume 1
Jacob Mincer

Studies in Labor Supply
Collected Essays of Jacob Mincer,
Volume 2
Jacob Mincer

Macroeconomics and Economic Policy
The Selected Essays of Assar Lindbeck
Volume I
Assar Lindbeck

The Welfare State
The Selected Essays of Assar Lindbeck
Volume II
Assar Lindbeck

Classical Economics, Public
Expenditure and Growth
Walter Eltis

Money, Interest Rates and Inflation
Frederic S. Mishkin

The Public Choice Approach to Politics
Dennis C. Mueller

The Liberal Economic Order
Volume I Essays on International
Economics
Volume II Money, Cycles and Related
Themes
Gottfried Haberler

Edited by Anthony Y.C. Koo
Economic Growth and Business Cycles
Prices and the Process of Cyclical
Development
Paolo Sylos Labini

International Adjustment, Money and
Trade
Theory and Measurement for Economic
Policy Volume I
Herbert G. Grubel

International Capital and Service Flows
Theory and Measurement for Economic
Policy Volume II
Herbert G. Grubel

Unintended Effects of Government
Policies
Theory and Measurement for Economic
Policy Volume III
Herbert G. Grubel

The Economics of Competitive
Enterprise
Selected Essays of P.W.S. Andrews
*Edited by Frederic S. Lee and Peter E.
Earl*

The Repressed Economy
Causes, Consequences, Reform
Deepak Lal

Economic Theory and Market
Socialism
Selected Essays of Oskar Lange
Edited by Tadeusz Kowalik

Trade, Development and Political
Economy
Selected Essays of Ronald Findlay
Ronald Findlay

General Equilibrium Theory
The Collected Essays of Takashi Negishi
Volume I
Takashi Negishi

The History of Economics
The Collected Essays of Takashi Negishi
Volume II
Takashi Negishi

Studies in Econometric Theory
The Collected Essays of Takeshi Amemiya
Takeshi Amemiya

Exchange Rates and the Monetary
System
Selected Essays of Peter B. Kenen
Peter B. Kenen

Econometric Methods and Applications
(2 volumes)

G.S. Maddala

National Accounting and Economic
Theory
The Collected Papers of Dan Usher, Volume
I
Dan Usher

Welfare Economics and Public Finance
The Collected Papers of Dan Usher, Volume
II
Dan Usher

Economic Theory and Capitalist
Society
The Selected Essays of Shigeto Tsuru,
Volume I
Shigeto Tsuru

Methodology, Money and the Firm
The Collected Essays of D.P. O'Brien
(2 volumes)
D.P. O'Brien

Economic Theory and Financial Policy
The Selected Essays of Jacques J. Polak
(2 volumes)
Jacques J. Polak

Sturdy Econometrics
Edward E. Leamer

The Emergence of Economic Ideas
Essays in the History of Economics
Nathan Rosenberg

Productivity Change, Public Goods and
Transaction Costs
Essays at the Boundaries of
Microeconomics
Yoram Barzel

Reflections on Economic Development
The Selected Essays of Michael P. Todaro
Michael P. Todaro

The Economic Development of Modern
Japan
The Selected Essays of Shigeto Tsuru
Volume II
Shigeto Tsuru

Money, Credit and Policy
Allan H. Meltzer

Macroeconomics and Monetary Theory
The Selected Essays of Meghnad Desai
Volume I
Meghnad Desai

Poverty, Famine and Economic Development
The Selected Essays of Meghnad Desai
Volume II
Meghnad Desai

Explaining the Economic Performance of Nations
Essays in Time and Space
Angus Maddison

Economic Doctrine and Method
Selected Papers of R.W. Clower
Robert W. Clower

Economic Theory and Reality
Selected Essays on their Disparities and Reconciliation
Tibor Scitovsky

Doing Economic Research
Essays on the Applied Methodology of Economics
Thomas Mayer

Institutions and Development Strategies
The Selected Essays of Irma Adelman
Volume I
Irma Adelman

Dynamics and Income Distribution
The Selected Essays of Irma Adelman
Volume II
Irma Adelman

The Economics of Growth and Development
Selected Essays of A.P. Thirlwall
A.P. Thirlwall

Theoretical and Applied Econometrics
The Selected Papers of Phoebus J. Dhrymes
Phoebus J. Dhrymes

Innovation, Technology and the Economy
The Selected Essays of Edwin Mansfield
(2 volumes)
Edwin Mansfield

Economic Theory and Policy in Context
The Selected Essays of R.D. Collison Black
R.D. Collison Black

Location Economics
Theoretical Underpinnings and Applications
Melvin L. Greenhut

Spatial Microeconomics
Theoretical Underpinnings and Applications
Melvin L. Greenhut

Capitalism, Socialism and Post-Keynesianism
Selected Essays of G.C. Harcourt
G.C. Harcourt

Time Series Analysis and Macroeconometric Modelling
The Collected Papers of Kenneth F. Wallis
Kenneth F. Wallis

Foundations of Modern Econometrics
The Selected Essays of Ragnar Frisch
(2 volumes)
Edited by Olav Bjerkholt

Growth, the Environment and the Distribution of Incomes
Essays by a Sceptical Optimist
Wilfred Beckerman

The Economics of Environmental Regulation
Wallace E. Oates

Econometrics, Macroeconomics and Economic Policy
Selected Papers of Carl F. Christ
Carl F. Christ

Strategic Approaches to the International Economy
Selected Essays of Koichi Hamada
Koichi Hamada

Economic Analysis and Political Ideology
The Selected Essays of Karl Brunner
Volume One
Edited by Thomas Lys

Growth Theory and Technical Change
The Selected Essays of Ryuzo Sato
Volume One
Ryuzo Sato

Industrialization, Inequality and Economic Growth
Jeffrey G. Williamson

Economic Theory and Public Decisions
Selected Essays of Robert Dorfman
Robert Dorfman

The Logic of Action One
Method, Money, and the Austrian School
Murray N. Rothbard

The Logic of Action Two
Applications and Criticism from the Austrian School
Murray N. Rothbard

Bayesian Analysis in Econometrics and Statistics
The Zellner View and Papers
Arnold Zellner

On the Foundations of Monopolistic Competition and Economic Geography
The Selected Essays of B. Curtis Eaton and Richard G. Lipsey
B. Curtis Eaton and Richard G. Lipsey

Microeconomics, Growth and Political Economy
The Selected Essays of Richard G. Lipsey
Volume One
Richard G. Lipsey

Macroeconomic Theory and Policy
The Selected Essays of Richard G. Lipsey
Volume Two
Richard G. Lipsey

Employment, Labor Unions and Wages
The Collected Essays of Orley Ashenfelter
Volume One
Edited by Kevin F. Hallock

Education, Training and Discrimination
The Collected Essays of Orley Ashenfelter
Volume Two
Edited by Kevin F. Hallock

Economic Institutions and the Demand and Supply of Labour
The Collected Essays of Orley Ashenfelter
Volume Three
Edited by Kevin F. Hallock

Monetary Theory and Monetary Policy
The Selected Essays of Karl Brunner
Volume Two
Edited by Thomas Lys

Macroeconomic Issues from a Keynesian Perspective
Selected Essays of A.P. Thirlwall
Volume Two
A.P. Thirlwall

Money and Macroeconomics
The Selected Essays of David Laidler
David Laidler

The Economics and Politics of Money
The Selected Essays of Alan Walters
Edited by Kent Matthews

Economics and Social Justice
Essays on Power, Labor and Institutional Change
David M. Gordon
Edited by Thomas E. Weisskopf and Samuel Bowles

Practicing Econometrics
Essays in Method and Application
Zvi Griliches

Economics Against the Grain
Volume One
Microeconomics, Industrial Organization and Related Themes
Julian L. Simon

Economics Against the Grain
Volume Two
Population Economics, Natural Resources
and Related Themes
Julian L. Simon

Advances in Econometric Theory
The Selected Works of Halbert White
Halbert White

The Economics of Imperfect
Knowledge
Collected Papers of G.B. Richardson
G.B. Richardson

Economic Performance and the Theory
of the Firm
The Selected Papers of David J. Teece
Volume One
David J. Teece

Strategy, Technology and Public Policy
The Selected Papers of David J. Teece
Volume Two
David J. Teece

The Keynesian Revolution, Then and
Now
The Selected Essays of Robert Eisner
Volume One
Robert Eisner

Investment, National Income and
Economic Policy
The Selected Essays of Robert Eisner
Volume Two
Robert Eisner

International Trade Opening and the
Formation of the Global Economy
Selected Essays of P. J. Lloyd
P. J. Lloyd

Production, Stability and Dynamic
Symmetry
The Selected Essays of Ryuzo Sato
Volume Two
Ryuzo Sato

Variants in Economic Theory
Selected Works of Hal R. Varian
Hal R. Varian

Political Economy, Oligopoly and
Experimental Games
The Selected Essays of Martin Shubik
Volume One
Martin Shubik

Money and Financial Institutions
A GAME THEORETIC APPROACH
The Selected Essays of Martin Shubik
Volume Two
Martin Shubik

Index